Ford Sierra Owners Workshop Manual

A K Legg T Eng MIMI

Models covered

All Ford Sierra Hatchback, Saloon (Sapphire) and Estate models, including special/limited editions, Ghia, fuel injection models, and Economy & E-Max versions.
1294 cc, 1593 cc, 1597 cc, 1796 cc & 1993 cc four-cylinder petrol engines

Does not cover V6, 1.8 litre CVH or Diesel engines, four-wheel-drive models or RS Cosworth. Partially covers P100 pick-up

ISBN 1 85010 441 7

© Haynes Publishing Group 1983, 1984, 1985, 1987, 1988
All rights reserved. No part of this book may be reproduced or transmitted in any form or by any means, electronic or mechanical, including photocopying, recording or by any information storage or retrieval system, without permission in writing from the copyright holder.

Printed in England *(903-2P4)*

ABCDE

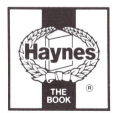

THE BOOK ®

Haynes Publishing Group
Sparkford Nr Yeovil
Somerset BA22 7JJ England

Haynes Publications, Inc
861 Lawrence Drive
Newbury Park
California 91320 USA

British Library Cataloguing in Publication Data
Legg, A. K. (Andrew K.), *1942–*
Ford Sierra owners workshop manual.
1. Cars. Maintenance & repair – Amateurs' manuals
I. Title   II. Series
629.28'722
ISBN 1-85010-441-7

Acknowledgements

Special thanks are due to the Ford Motor Company for the supply of technical information and certain illustrations. Duckhams Oils provided lubrication data, and the Champion Sparking Plug Company supplied the illustrations showing the various spark plug conditions.

Sykes-Pickavant provided some of the workshop tools. Thanks are also due to all those people at Sparkford who helped in the production of this manual.

About this manual

Its aim

The aim of this manual is to help you get the best value from your vehicle. It can do so in several ways. It can help you decide what work must be done (even should you choose to get it done by a garage), provide information on routine maintenance and servicing, and give a logical course of action and diagnosis when random faults occur. However, it is hoped that you will use the manual by tackling the work yourself. On simpler jobs it may even be quicker than booking the car into a garage and going there twice, to leave and collect it. Perhaps most important, a lot of money can be saved by avoiding the costs a garage must charge to cover its labour and overheads.

The manual has drawings and descriptions to show the function of the various components so that their layout can be understood. Then the tasks are described and photographed in a step-by-step sequence so that even a novice can do the work.

Its arrangement

The manual is divided into thirteen Chapters, each covering a logical sub-division of the vehicle. The Chapters are each divided into Sections, numbered with single figures, eg 5; and the Sections into paragraphs (or sub-sections), with decimal numbers following on from the Section they are in, eg 5.1, 5.2, 5.3 etc.

It is freely illustrated, especially in those parts where there is a detailed sequence of operations to be carried out. There are two forms of illustration: figures and photographs. The figures are numbered in sequence with decimal numbers, according to their position in the Chapter – eg Fig. 6.4 is the fourth drawing/illustration in Chapter 6. Photographs carry the same number (either individually or in related groups) as the Section or sub-section to which they relate.

There is an alphabetical index at the back of the manual as well as a contents list at the front. Each Chapter is also preceded by its own individual contents list.

References to the 'left' or 'right' of the vehicle are in the sense of a person in the driver's seat facing forwards.

Unless otherwise stated, nuts and bolts are removed by turning anti-clockwise, and tightened by turning clockwise.

Vehicle manufacturers continually make changes to specifications and recommendations, and these, when notified, are incorporated into our manuals at the earliest opportunity.

Whilst every care is taken to ensure that the information in this manual is correct, no liability can be accepted by the authors or publishers for loss, damage or injury caused by any errors in, or omissions from, the information given.

Introduction to the Ford Sierra

The Ford Sierra was first introduced in late 1982 with the option of seven different engines and four different trim levels. The manual covers the four-cylinder in-line overhead camshaft petrol engines, but other models in the range are fitted with V6 or diesel engines.

The Ford Motor Company, having brought the long production run of the Cortina to an end, introduced the Sierra in a new era of the aeroback body style designed to reduce the air drag coefficient to a minimum in the interests of fuel economy. Mechanically the Sierra is similar to the Cortina with the exception of a five speed gearbox and independent suspension all round, however low weight materials have been utilized in a number of areas.

For the home mechanic, the Sierra is an ideal car to maintain and repair since design features have been incorporated to reduce the actual cost of ownership to a minimum, with the result that components requiring relatively frequent attention (eg the exhaust system) are easily removed.

Contents

	Page
Acknowledgements	2
About this manual	2
Introduction to the Ford Sierra	2
General dimensions, weights and capacities	6
Buying spare parts and vehicle identification numbers	7
Tools and working facilities	8
Jacking and towing	10
Recommended lubricants and fluids	12
Safety first!	13
Routine maintenance	14
Fault diagnosis	19
Chapter 1 Engine	23
Chapter 2 Cooling system	53
Chapter 3 Fuel and exhaust systems	63
Chapter 4 Ignition system	82
Chapter 5 Clutch	92
Chapter 6 Manual gearbox and automatic transmission	97
Chapter 7 Propeller shaft	126
Chapter 8 Final drive and driveshafts	130
Chapter 9 Braking system	137
Chapter 10 Electrical system	151
Chapter 11 Suspension and steering	207
Chapter 12 Bodywork and fittings	224
Chapter 13 Supplement: Revisions and information on later models	244
General repair procedures	351
Conversion factors	352
Index	353

Ford Sierra GL

Ford Sierra Ghia

Ford Sierra L Estate

General dimensions, weights and capacities

For modifications, and information applicable to later models, see Supplement at end of manual

Dimensions in (mm)	Hatchback	Estate
Overall length (nominal)	173.5 (4407)	176.0 (44.70)
Overall width	67.7 (1720)	68.1 (1730)
Overall height (unladen)	55.9 (1420)	57.4 (14.58)
Wheelbase	102.7 (2609)	102.7 (2609)
Track:		
Front	57.2 (1453)	57.3 (1453)
Rear	57.8 (1468)	57.4 (1458)
Turning circle ft (m)	32.8 (10.0)	32.8 (10.0)

Weights lb (kg)		
Kerb weight:		
1.3/1.6 litre	2180 (989)	2291 (1039)
2.0 litre	2258 (1024)	2346 (1064)
Maximum roof rack load	165 (75)	165 (75)

Capacities	
Engine oil:	
With filter	6.6 pt (3.75 litre)
Without filter	5.7 pt (3.25 litre)
Cooling system (including heater)	14.1 pt (8.0 litre)
Fuel tank	13.2 gal (60.0 litre)
Manual gearbox:	
Type A (4 speed)	1.7 pt (0.98 litre)
Type B (4 speed)	2.6 pt (1.46 litre)
Type C (4 speed)	2.2 pt (1.25 litre)
Type N (5 speed)	3.3 pt (1.9 litre)
Automatic transmission	11.08 pt (6.3 litre)
Final drive:	
6.5 in type	1.4 pt (0.8 litre)
7.0 in type	1.6 pt (0.9 litre)
Power-steering	1.3 pt (0.75 litre)

Buying spare parts and vehicle identification numbers

Buying spare parts

Spare parts are available from many sources, for example: Ford Garages, other garages and accessory shops, and motor factors. Our advice regarding spare parts sources is as follows:

Officially appointed Ford garages – This is the best source for parts which are peculiar to your car and are not generally available (eg complete cylinder heads, internal gearbox components, badges, interior trim etc). It is also the only place at which you should buy parts if your vehicle is still under warranty – non-Ford components may invalidate the warranty. To be sure of obtaining the correct parts it will always be necessary to give the storeman your car's vehicle identification number, and if possible, to take the 'old' part along for positive identification. Remember that many parts are available on a factory exchange scheme – any parts returned should always be clean! It obviously makes good sense to go straight to the specialists on your car for this type of part for they are best equipped to supply you

Other garages and accessory shops – These are often very good places to buy materials and components needed for the maintenance of your car (eg oil filters, spark plugs, bulbs, drivebelts, oils and greases, touch-up paint, filler paste, etc). They also sell general accessories, usually have convenient opening hours, charge lower prices and can often be found not far from home.

Motor factors – Good factors will stock all of the more important components which wear out relatively quickly (eg clutch components, pistons, valves, exhaust systems, brake cylinders/pipes/hoses/seals/shoes and pads etc). Motor factors will often provide new or reconditioned components on a part exchange basis – this can save a considerable amount of money.

Vehicle identification numbers

Modifications are a continuing and unpublicised process in vehicle manufacture quite apart from major model changes. Spare parts manuals and lists are compiled upon a numerical basis, the individual vehicle numbers being essential to correct identification of the component required.

When ordering spare parts, always give as much information as possible. Quote the car model, year of manufacture, body and engine numbers as appropriate.

The vehicle identification plate is mounted on the right-hand side of the front body panel and may be seen once the bonnet is open (photo).

The engine number is located on the right-hand side of the cylinder block in front of the engine mounting arm (photo).

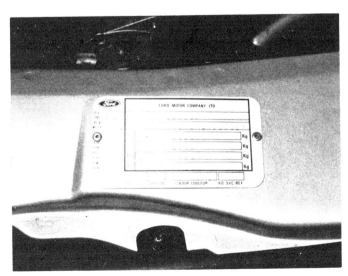

Vehicle identification number (VIN) plate

Engine number location

Tools and working facilities

Introduction

A selection of good tools is a fundamental requirement for anyone contemplating the maintenance and repair of a motor vehicle. For the owner who does not possess any, their purchase will prove a considerable expense, offsetting some of the savings made by doing-it-yourself. However, provided that the tools purchased are of good quality, they will last for many years and prove an extremely worthwhile investment.

To help the average owner to decide which tools are needed to carry out the various tasks detailed in this manual, we have compiled three lists of tools under the following headings: *Maintenance and minor repair, Repair and overhaul,* and *Special.* The newcomer to practical mechanics should start off with the *Maintenance and minor repair* tool kit and confine himself to the simpler jobs around the vehicle. Then, as his confidence and experience grow, he can undertake more difficult tasks, buying extra tools as, and when, they are needed. In this way, a *Maintenance and minor repair* tool kit can be built-up into a *Repair and overhaul* tool kit over a considerable period of time without any major cash outlays. The experienced do-it-yourselfer will have a tool kit good enough for most repair and overhaul procedures and will add tools from the *Special* category when he feels the expense is justified by the amount of use to which these tools will be put.

It is obviously not possible to cover the subject of tools fully here. For those who wish to learn more about tools and their use there is a book entitled *How to Choose and Use Car Tools* available from the publishers of this manual.

Maintenance and minor repair tool kit

The tools given in this list should be considered as a minimum requirement if routine maintenance, servicing and minor repair operations are to be undertaken. We recommend the purchase of combination spanners (ring one end, open-ended the other); although more expensive than open-ended ones, they do give the advantages of both types of spanner.

Combination spanners - 10, 11, 12, 13, 14 & 17 mm
Adjustable spanner - 9 inch
Gearbox/rear axle drain plug key
Spark plug spanner (with rubber insert)
Spark plug gap adjustment tool
Set of feeler gauges
Brake bleed nipple spanner
Screwdriver - 4 in long x $\frac{1}{4}$ in dia (flat blade)
Screwdriver - 4 in long x $\frac{1}{4}$ in dia (cross blade)
Combination pliers - 6 inch
Hacksaw (junior)

Tyre pump
Tyre pressure gauge
Oil can
Fine emery cloth (1 sheet)
Wire brush (small)
Funnel (medium size)

Repair and overhaul tool kit

These tools are virtually essential for anyone undertaking any major repairs to a motor vehicle, and are additional to those given in the *Maintenance and minor repair* list. Included in this list is a comprehensive set of sockets. Although these are expensive they will be found invaluable as they are so versatile - particularly if various drives are included in the set. We recommend the $\frac{1}{2}$ in square-drive type, as this can be used with most proprietary torque wrenches. If you cannot afford a socket set, even bought piecemeal, then inexpensive tubular box spanners are a useful alternative.

The tools in this list will occasionally need to be supplemented by tools from the *Special* list.

Sockets (or box spanners) to cover range in previous list
Reversible ratchet drive (for use with sockets)
Extension piece, 10 inch (for use with sockets)
Universal joint (for use with sockets)
Torque wrench (for use with sockets)
'Mole' wrench - 8 inch
Ball pein hammer
Soft-faced hammer, plastic or rubber
Screwdriver - 6 in long x $\frac{5}{16}$ in dia (flat blade)
Screwdriver - 2 in long x $\frac{5}{16}$ in square (flat blade)
Screwdriver - 1$\frac{1}{2}$ in long x $\frac{1}{4}$ in dia (cross blade)
Screwdriver - 3 in long x $\frac{1}{8}$ in dia (electricians)
Pliers - electricians side cutters
Pliers - needle nosed
Pliers - circlip (internal and external)
Cold chisel - $\frac{1}{2}$ inch
Scriber
Scraper
Centre punch
Pin punch
Hacksaw
Valve grinding tool
Steel rule/straight-edge
Allen keys
Selection of files
Wire brush (large)
Axle-stands
Jack (strong scissor or hydraulic type)

Special tools

The tools in this list are those which are not used regularly, are expensive to buy, or which need to be used in accordance with their manufacturers' instructions. Unless relatively difficult mechanical jobs are undertaken frequently, it will not be economic to buy many of these tools. Where this is the case, you could consider clubbing together with friends (or joining a motorists' club) to make a joint purchase, or borrowing the tools against a deposit from a local garage or tool hire specialist.

The following list contains only those tools and instruments freely available to the public, and not those special tools produced by the vehicle manufacturer specifically for its dealer network. You will find occasional references to these manufacturers' special tools in the text of this manual. Generally, an alternative method of doing the job without the vehicle manufacturers' special tool is given. However, sometimes, there is no alternative to using them. Where this is the case and the relevant tool cannot be bought or borrowed, you will have to entrust the work to a franchised garage.

> Valve spring compressor (where applicable)
> Piston ring compressor
> Balljoint separator
> Universal hub/bearing puller
> Impact screwdriver
> Micrometer and/or vernier gauge
> Dial gauge
> Stroboscopic timing light
> Dwell angle meter/tachometer
> Universal electrical multi-meter
> Cylinder compression gauge
> Lifting tackle
> Trolley jack
> Light with extension lead
> Splined sockets (see Chapter 1)

Buying tools

For practically all tools, a tool factor is the best source since he will have a very comprehensive range compared with the average garage or accessory shop. Having said that, accessory shops often offer excellent quality tools at discount prices, so it pays to shop around.

Remember, you don't have to buy the most expensive items on the shelf, but it is always advisable to steer clear of the very cheap tools. There are plenty of good tools around at reasonable prices, so ask the proprietor or manager of the shop for advice before making a purchase.

Care and maintenance of tools

Having purchased a reasonable tool kit, it is necessary to keep the tools in a clean serviceable condition. After use, always wipe off any dirt, grease and metal particles using a clean, dry cloth, before putting the tools away. Never leave them lying around after they have been used. A simple tool rack on the garage or workshop wall, for items such as screwdrivers and pliers is a good idea. Store all normal wrenches and sockets in a metal box. Any measuring instruments, gauges, meters, etc, must be carefully stored where they cannot be damaged or become rusty.

Take a little care when tools are used. Hammer heads inevitably become marked and screwdrivers lose the keen edge on their blades from time to time. A little timely attention with emery cloth or a file will soon restore items like this to a good serviceable finish.

Working facilities

Not to be forgotten when discussing tools, is the workshop itself. If anything more than routine maintenance is to be carried out, some form of suitable working area becomes essential.

It is appreciated that many an owner mechanic is forced by circumstances to remove an engine or similar item, without the benefit of a garage or workshop. Having done this, any repairs should always be done under the cover of a roof.

Wherever possible, any dismantling should be done on a clean, flat workbench or table at a suitable working height.

Any workbench needs a vice: one with a jaw opening of 4 in (100 mm) is suitable for most jobs. As mentioned previously, some clean dry storage space is also required for tools, as well as for lubricants, cleaning fluids, touch-up paints and so on, which become necessary.

Another item which may be required, and which has a much more general usage, is an electric drill with a chuck capacity of at least $\frac{5}{16}$ in

(8 mm). This, together with a good range of twist drills, is virtually essential for fitting accessories such as mirrors and reversing lights.

Last, but not least, always keep a supply of old newspapers and clean, lint-free rags available, and try to keep any working area as clean as possible.

Spanner jaw gap comparison table

Jaw gap (in)	Spanner size
0.250	$\frac{1}{4}$ in AF
0.276	7 mm
0.313	$\frac{5}{16}$ in AF
0.315	8 mm
0.344	$\frac{11}{32}$ in AF; $\frac{1}{8}$ in Whitworth
0.354	9 mm
0.375	$\frac{3}{8}$ in AF
0.394	10 mm
0.433	11 mm
0.438	$\frac{7}{16}$ in AF
0.445	$\frac{3}{16}$ in Whitworth; $\frac{1}{4}$ in BSF
0.472	12 mm
0.500	$\frac{1}{2}$ in AF
0.512	13 mm
0.525	$\frac{1}{4}$ in Whitworth; $\frac{5}{16}$ in BSF
0.551	14 mm
0.563	$\frac{9}{16}$ in AF
0.591	15 mm
0.600	$\frac{5}{16}$ in Whitworth; $\frac{3}{8}$ in BSF
0.625	$\frac{5}{8}$ in AF
0.630	16 mm
0.669	17 mm
0.686	$\frac{11}{16}$ in AF
0.709	18 mm
0.710	$\frac{3}{8}$ in Whitworth; $\frac{7}{16}$ in BSF
0.748	19 mm
0.750	$\frac{3}{4}$ in AF
0.813	$\frac{13}{16}$ in AF
0.820	$\frac{7}{16}$ in Whitworth; $\frac{1}{2}$ in BSF
0.866	22 mm
0.875	$\frac{7}{8}$ in AF
0.920	$\frac{1}{2}$ in Whitworth; $\frac{9}{16}$ in BSF
0.938	$\frac{15}{16}$ in AF
0.945	24 mm
1.000	1 in AF
1.010	$\frac{9}{16}$ in Whitworth; $\frac{5}{8}$ in BSF
1.024	26 mm
1.063	$1\frac{1}{16}$ in AF; 27 mm
1.100	$\frac{5}{8}$ in Whitworth; $\frac{11}{16}$ in BSF
1.125	$1\frac{1}{8}$ in AF
1.181	30 mm
1.200	$\frac{11}{16}$ in Whitworth; $\frac{3}{4}$ in BSF
1.250	$1\frac{1}{4}$ in AF
1.260	32 mm
1.300	$\frac{3}{4}$ in Whitworth; $\frac{7}{8}$ in BSF
1.313	$1\frac{5}{16}$ in AF
1.390	$\frac{13}{16}$ in Whitworth; $\frac{15}{16}$ in BSF
1.417	36 mm
1.438	$1\frac{7}{16}$ in AF
1.480	$\frac{7}{8}$ in Whitworth; 1 in BSF
1.500	$1\frac{1}{2}$ in AF
1.575	40 mm; $\frac{15}{16}$ in Whitworth
1.614	41 mm
1.625	$1\frac{5}{8}$ in AF
1.670	1 in Whitworth; $1\frac{1}{8}$ in BSF
1.688	$1\frac{11}{16}$ in AF
1.811	46 mm
1.813	$1\frac{13}{16}$ in AF
1.860	$1\frac{1}{8}$ in Whitworth; $1\frac{1}{4}$ in BSF
1.875	$1\frac{7}{8}$ in AF
1.969	50 mm
2.000	2 in AF
2.050	$1\frac{1}{4}$ in Whitworth; $1\frac{3}{8}$ in BSF
2.165	55 mm
2.362	60 mm

Jacking and towing

The jack supplied with the car tool kit should only be used for changing roadwheels (photo). When using a trolley jack position the jack under the front suspension crossmember or rear final drive casing, and always supplement the jack with axle stands positioned under the bodyframe members.

Towing eyes are provided at the front and rear of the car (photos). When being towed the ignition switch should be in position II so that the steering lock is released and the direction indicators, horn and stop lights are operational. On automatic transmission models the selector lever must be in neutral (N), the towing speed must not exceed 25 mph, and the towing distance must not exceed 12 miles (20 km). For longer distances the propeller shaft should be removed or the rear of the car lifted clear of the ground.

Push or tow starting is not possible on cars fitted with automatic transmission.

Remove the cover in the luggage compartment ...

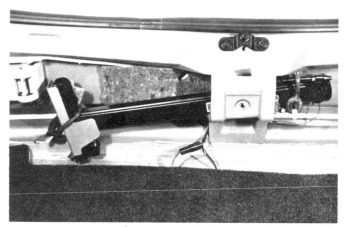

... for access to the jack

Spare wheel located in the luggage compartment

Using the wheel brace end to remove the wheel cap

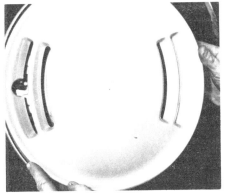

Showing cut-out in wheel cap for tyre valve

Rear jacking point

Jack location by front wheel

Using an axle stand

Front towing eye

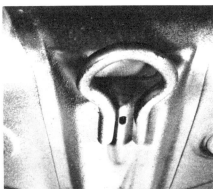

Rear towing eye

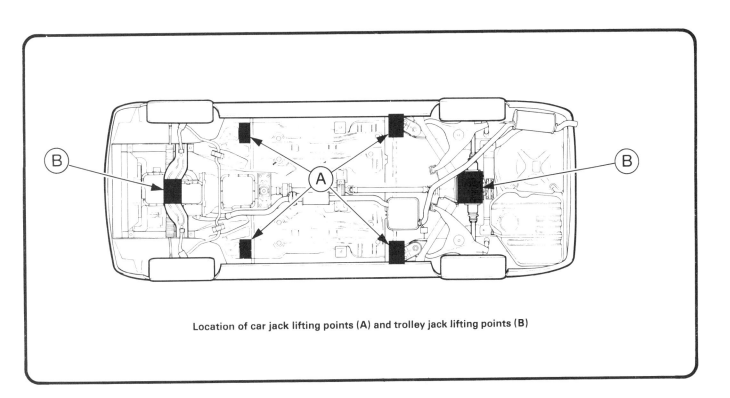

Location of car jack lifting points (A) and trolley jack lifting points (B)

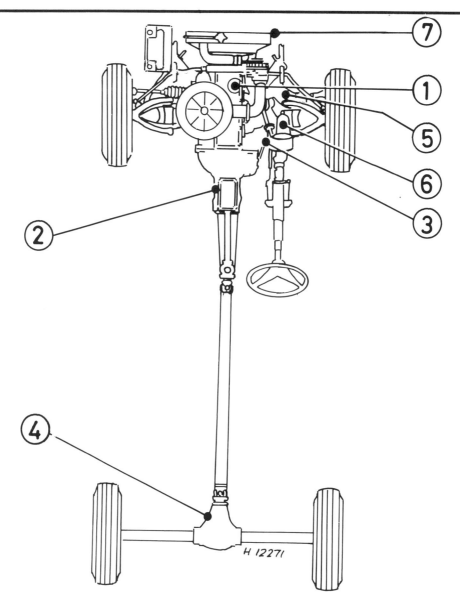

H 12271

Recommended lubricants and fluids

Component or system	Lubricant type/specification	Duckhams recommendation
1 Engine	Multigrade engine oil, viscosity range SAE 10W/30 to 20W/50, to API SF/CC or better	Duckhams QXR, Hypergrade, or 10W/40 Motor Oil
2 Manual gearbox		
4-speed	Gear oil, viscosity SAE 80 EP, to Ford spec SQM-2C 9008-A	Duckhams Hypoid 80
5-speed	Gear oil, viscosity SAE 80 EP, to Ford spec ESD-M2C 175-A	Duckhams Hypoid 75W/90S
3 Automatic transmission	ATF to Ford spec SQM-2C 9010-A	Duckhams D-Matic
4 Final drive	Hypoid gear oil, viscosity SAE 90 EP to Ford spec SQM-2C 9002-AA or 9003-AA	Duckhams Hypoid 90S
5 Power-assisted steering	ATF to Ford spec SQM-2C 9010-A	Duckhams D-Matic
6 Brake hydraulic system	Brake fluid to Ford spec Amber SAM-6C 9103-A	Duckhams Universal Brake and Clutch Fluid
7 Cooling system	Soft water and antifreeze to Ford spec SSM-97B 9103-A	Duckhams Universal Antifreeze and Summer Coolant

Safety first!

Professional motor mechanics are trained in safe working procedures. However enthusiastic you may be about getting on with the job in hand, do take the time to ensure that your safety is not put at risk. A moment's lack of attention can result in an accident, as can failure to observe certain elementary precautions.

There will always be new ways of having accidents, and the following points do not pretend to be a comprehensive list of all dangers; they are intended rather to make you aware of the risks and to encourage a safety-conscious approach to all work you carry out on your vehicle.

Essential DOs and DON'Ts

DON'T rely on a single jack when working underneath the vehicle. Always use reliable additional means of support, such as axle stands, securely placed under a part of the vehicle that you know will not give way.

DON'T attempt to loosen or tighten high-torque nuts (e.g. wheel hub nuts) while the vehicle is on a jack; it may be pulled off.

DON'T start the engine without first ascertaining that the transmission is in neutral (or 'Park' where applicable) and the parking brake applied.

DON'T suddenly remove the filler cap from a hot cooling system – cover it with a cloth and release the pressure gradually first, or you may get scalded by escaping coolant.

DON'T attempt to drain oil until you are sure it has cooled sufficiently to avoid scalding you.

DON'T grasp any part of the engine, exhaust or catalytic converter without ascertaining that it is sufficiently cool to avoid burning you.

DON'T allow brake fluid or antifreeze to contact vehicle paintwork.

DON'T syphon toxic liquids such as fuel, brake fluid or antifreeze by mouth, or allow them to remain on your skin.

DON'T inhale dust – it may be injurious to health (see *Asbestos* below).

DON'T allow any spilt oil or grease to remain on the floor – wipe it up straight away, before someone slips on it.

DON'T use ill-fitting spanners or other tools which may slip and cause injury.

DON'T attempt to lift a heavy component which may be beyond your capability – get assistance.

DON'T rush to finish a job, or take unverified short cuts.

DON'T allow children or animals in or around an unattended vehicle.

DO wear eye protection when using power tools such as drill, sander, bench grinder etc, and when working under the vehicle.

DO use a barrier cream on your hands prior to undertaking dirty jobs – it will protect your skin from infection as well as making the dirt easier to remove afterwards; but make sure your hands aren't left slippery. Note that long-term contact with used engine oil can be a health hazard.

DO keep loose clothing (cuffs, tie etc) and long hair well out of the way of moving mechanical parts.

DO remove rings, wristwatch etc, before working on the vehicle – especially the electrical system.

DO ensure that any lifting tackle used has a safe working load rating adequate for the job.

DO keep your work area tidy – it is only too easy to fall over articles left lying around.

DO get someone to check periodically that all is well, when working alone on the vehicle.

DO carry out work in a logical sequence and check that everything is correctly assembled and tightened afterwards.

DO remember that your vehicle's safety affects that of yourself and others. If in doubt on any point, get specialist advice.

IF, in spite of following these precautions, you are unfortunate enough to injure yourself, seek medical attention as soon as possible.

Asbestos

Certain friction, insulating, sealing, and other products – such as brake linings, brake bands, clutch linings, torque converters, gaskets, etc – contain asbestos. *Extreme care must be taken to avoid inhalation of dust from such products since it is hazardous to health.* If in doubt, assume that they *do* contain asbestos.

Fire

Remember at all times that petrol (gasoline) is highly flammable. Never smoke, or have any kind of naked flame around, when working on the vehicle. But the risk does not end there – a spark caused by an electrical short-circuit, by two metal surfaces contacting each other, by careless use of tools, or even by static electricity built up in your body under certain conditions, can ignite petrol vapour, which in a confined space is highly explosive.

Always disconnect the battery earth (ground) terminal before working on any part of the fuel or electrical system, and never risk spilling fuel on to a hot engine or exhaust.

It is recommended that a fire extinguisher of a type suitable for fuel and electrical fires is kept handy in the garage or workplace at all times. Never try to extinguish a fuel or electrical fire with water.

Fumes

Certain fumes are highly toxic and can quickly cause unconsciousness and even death if inhaled to any extent. Petrol (gasoline) vapour comes into this category, as do the vapours from certain solvents such as trichloroethylene. Any draining or pouring of such volatile fluids should be done in a well ventilated area.

When using cleaning fluids and solvents, read the instructions carefully. Never use materials from unmarked containers – they may give off poisonous vapours.

Never run the engine of a motor vehicle in an enclosed space such as a garage. Exhaust fumes contain carbon monoxide which is extremely poisonous; if you need to run the engine, always do so in the open air or at least have the rear of the vehicle outside the workplace.

If you are fortunate enough to have the use of an inspection pit, never drain or pour petrol, and never run the engine, while the vehicle is standing over it; the fumes, being heavier than air, will concentrate in the pit with possibly lethal results.

The battery

Never cause a spark, or allow a naked light, near the vehicle's battery. It will normally be giving off a certain amount of hydrogen gas, which is highly explosive.

Always disconnect the battery earth (ground) terminal before working on the fuel or electrical systems.

If possible, loosen the filler plugs or cover when charging the battery from an external source. Do not charge at an excessive rate or the battery may burst.

Take care when topping up and when carrying the battery. The acid electrolyte, even when diluted, is very corrosive and should not be allowed to contact the eyes or skin.

If you ever need to prepare electrolyte yourself, always add the acid slowly to the water, and never the other way round. Protect against splashes by wearing rubber gloves and goggles.

When jump starting a car using a booster battery, for negative earth (ground) vehicles, connect the jump leads in the following sequence: First connect one jump lead between the positive (+) terminals of the two batteries. Then connect the other jump lead first to the negative (–) terminal of the booster battery, and then to a good earthing (ground) point on the vehicle to be started, at least 18 in (45 cm) from the battery if possible. Ensure that hands and jump leads are clear of any moving parts, and that the two vehicles do not touch. Disconnect the leads in the reverse order.

Mains electricity

When using an electric power tool, inspection light etc, which works from the mains, always ensure that the appliance is correctly connected to its plug and that, where necessary, it is properly earthed (grounded). Do not use such appliances in damp conditions and, again, beware of creating a spark or applying excessive heat in the vicinity of fuel or fuel vapour.

Ignition HT voltage

A severe electric shock can result from touching certain parts of the ignition system, such as the HT leads, when the engine is running or being cranked, particularly if components are damp or the insulation is defective. Where an electronic ignition system is fitted, the HT voltage is much higher and could prove fatal.

Routine maintenance

For modifications, and information applicable to later models, see Supplement at end of manual

Maintenance is essential for ensuring safety and desirable for the purpose of getting the best in terms of performance and economy from your car. Over the years the need for periodic lubrication – oiling, greasing, and so on – has been drastically reduced if not totally eliminated. This has unfortunately tended to lead some owners to think that because no such action is required, components either no longer exist, or will last for ever. This is certainly not the case; it is essential to carry out regular visual examination as comprehensively as possible in order to spot any possible defects at an early stage before they develop into major expensive repairs.

Every 250 miles (400 km) or weekly – whichever comes first

Engine
Check the oil level and top up if necessary (photo).
Check the coolant level and top up if necessary (photo).

Tyres
Check the tyre pressures and adjust if necessary (photo).

Every 6000 miles (10 000 km) – additional

Engine
Clean the oil filler cap in fuel and allow to dry
Check for oil, fuel and water leaks
Check the condition and security of vacuum hoses
Check the condition of drivebelts and adjust tension if necessary (photo)
Change the engine oil and renew the oil filter (photo)
Check the engine slow running adjustment (adjust slow running mixture only at first 6000 miles/10 000 km)

Brakes
Check the hydraulic fluid level in the reservoir and top up if necessary (photo). A slight drop due to wear of the disc pads is acceptable but if regular topping up is required the leak should be located and rectified.
Check hydraulic lines for leakage
Check servo vacuum hose for condition and security
Check disc pads and rear brake shoes for wear

Tyres
Check tyres for condition and wear (photo)
Check wheel nuts for tightness

Bodywork
Check the fluid level in the windscreen washer reservoir and top up if necessary.
Check seat belt webbing for cuts, fraying etc.

Every 12 000 miles (20 000 km) – additional

Engine
Check the exhaust system for leaks
Clean battery terminals, check them for tightness, and apply petroleum jelly
Renew the spark plugs
Check and if necessary adjust the valve clearances

Manual gearbox
Check and if necessary top up the oil level (photos)

Automatic transmission
Lubricate the driveshaft cable and linkage, and shaft lever linkage
Check and if necessary top up the automatic transmission fluid level

Driveshafts and final drive
Check the gaiters for condition and security
Check and if necessary top up the final drive oil level (photos)

Brakes
Check operation of the brake fluid level warning light

Electrical system
Check the operation of all electrical equipment and lights

Suspension and steering
Check all linkages and balljoints for wear and damage

Bodywork
Lubricate all hinges and catches
Check the underbody for corrosion and damage

Every 24 000 miles (40 000 km) – additional

Engine
Renew the crankcase emission vent valve
Renew the air filter element
Lubricate distributor and clean distributor cap and HT leads
Check condition of distributor cap, rotor and HT leads
Check operation of air cleaner temperature control

Automatic transmission
Adjust the front brake band

Every 36 000 miles (60 000 km) or two years whichever occurs first

Engine
Flush the cooling system and fill with new antifreeze/corrosion inhibitor
Check cooling system pressure cap and seal – renew if necessary

---

Every 36 000 miles (60 000 km) or three years whichever occurs first

Engine
Renew timing belt if wished

Brakes
Renew the hydraulic brake fluid and check the condition of the visible rubber components of the brake system

Engine oil level dipstick

Topping up the engine oil level

Topping up the coolant level

Checking the tyre pressure

Checking alternator/water pump drivebelt tension

Engine oil drain plug in sump

Checking tyre tread depth with a special gauge

Topping up the brake fluid level

Manual gearbox filler plug location

Topping up the manual gearbox oil level

Removing the final drive filler plug using 10 mm key

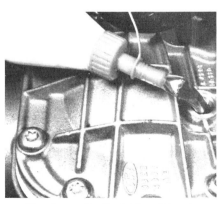

Topping up the final drive oil level

Under-bonnet view (air cleaner removed)

1 Brake hydraulic fluid reservoir
2 Windscreen wiper motor
3 Battery
4 Ignition coil
5 Carburettor
6 Distributor
7 Fuel pressure regulator
8 Coolant pump
9 Radiator top hose
10 Upper fan shroud
11 Alternator
12 Windscreen washer reservoir
13 Oil filler cap
14 Coolant expansion tank

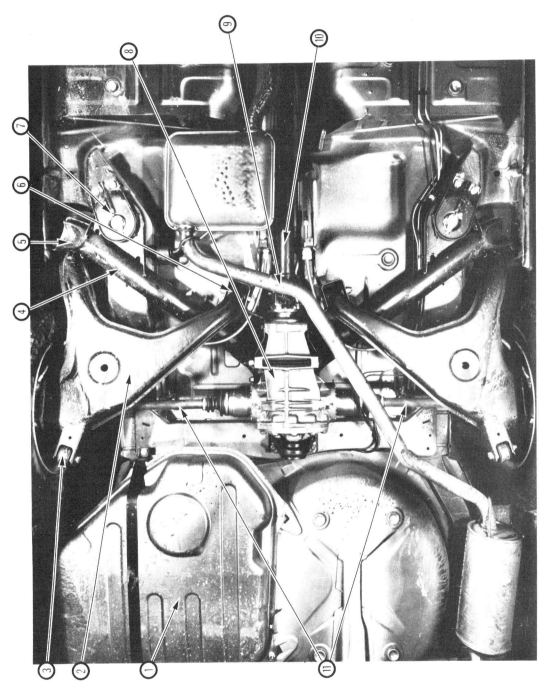

View of rear underside of car

1 Fuel tank
2 Lower suspension arm
3 Lower shock absorber

    mounting
4 Rear axle crossmember
5 Outer rubber bush

6 Inner rubber bush
7 Guide plate and mounting rubber
8 Differential

9 Exhaust system
10 Propeller shaft
11 Driveshafts

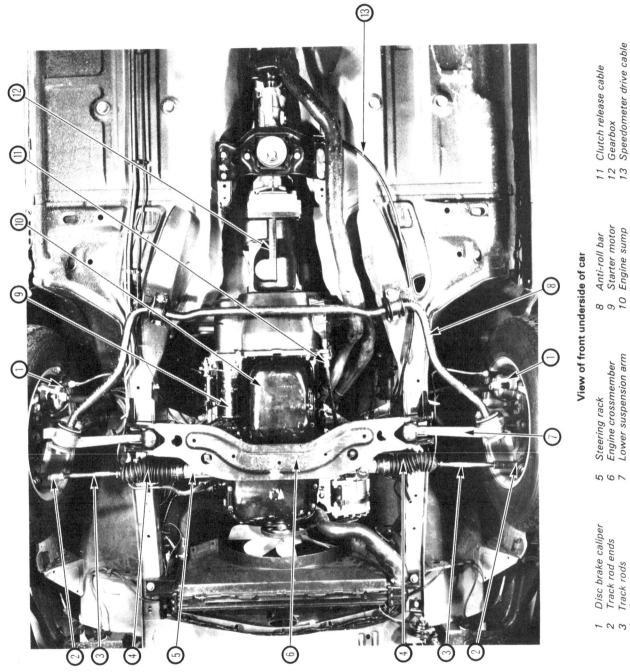

View of front underside of car

1 Disc brake caliper
2 Track rod ends
3 Track rods
4 Bellows

5 Steering rack
6 Engine crossmember
7 Lower suspension arm

8 Anti-roll bar
9 Starter motor
10 Engine sump

11 Clutch release cable
12 Gearbox
13 Speedometer drive cable

Fault diagnosis

Introduction

The vehicle owner who does his or her own maintenance according to the recommended schedules should not have to use this section of the manual very often. Modern component reliability is such that, provided those items subject to wear or deterioration are inspected or renewed at the specified intervals, sudden failure is comparatively rare. Faults do not usually just happen as a result of sudden failure, but develop over a period of time. Major mechanical failures in particular are usually preceded by characteristic symptoms over hundreds or even thousands of miles. Those components which do occasionally fail without warning are often small and easily carried in the vehicle.

With any fault finding, the first step is to decide where to begin investigations. Sometimes this is obvious, but on other occasions a little detective work will be necessary. The owner who makes half a dozen haphazard adjustments or replacements may be successful in curing a fault (or its symptoms), but he will be none the wiser if the fault recurs and he may well have spent more time and money than was necessary. A calm and logical approach will be found to be more satisfactory in the long run. Always take into account any warning signs or abnormalities that may have been noticed in the period preceding the fault – power loss, high or low gauge readings, unusual noises or smells, etc – and remember that failure of components such as fuses or spark plugs may only be pointers to some underlying fault.

The pages which follow here are intended to help in cases of failure to start or breakdown on the road. There is also a Fault Diagnosis Section at the end of each Chapter which should be consulted if the preliminary checks prove unfruitful. Whatever the fault, certain basic principles apply. These are as follows:

Verify the fault. This is simply a matter of being sure that you know what the symptoms are before starting work. This is particularly important if you are investigating a fault for someone else who may not have described it very accurately.

Don't overlook the obvious. For example, if the vehicle won't start, is there petrol in the tank? (Don't take anyone else's word on this particular point, and don't trust the fuel gauge either!) If an electrical fault is indicated, look for loose or broken wires before digging out the test gear.

Cure the disease, not the symptom. Substituting a flat battery with a fully charged one will get you off the hard shoulder, but if the underlying cause is not attended to, the new battery will go the same way. Similarly, changing oil-fouled spark plugs for a new set will get you moving again, but remember that the reason for the fouling (if it wasn't simply an incorrect grade of plug) will have to be established and corrected.

Don't take anything for granted. Particularly, don't forget that a 'new' component may itself be defective (especially if it's been rattling round in the boot for months), and don't leave components out of a fault diagnosis sequence just because they are new or recently fitted. When you do finally diagnose a difficult fault, you'll probably realise that all the evidence was there from the start.

Electrical faults

Electrical faults can be more puzzling than straightforward mechanical failures, but they are no less susceptible to logical analysis if the basic principles of operation are understood. Vehicle electrical wiring exists in extremely unfavourable conditions – heat, vibration and chemical attack – and the first things to look for are loose or corroded connections and broken or chafed wires, especially where the wires pass through holes in the bodywork or are subject to vibration.

All metal-bodied vehicles in current production have one pole of the battery 'earthed', ie connected to the vehicle bodywork, and in nearly all modern vehicles it is the negative (–) terminal. The various electrical components – motors, bulb holders etc – are also connected to earth, either by means of a lead or directly by their mountings. Electric current flows through the component and then back to the battery via the bodywork. If the component mounting is loose or corroded, or if a good path back to the battery is not available, the circuit will be incomplete and malfunction will result. The engine and/or gearbox are also earthed by means of flexible metal straps to the body or subframe; if these straps are loose or missing, starter motor, generator and ignition trouble may result.

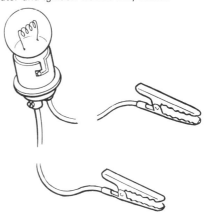

A simple test lamp is useful for tracing electrical faults

Assuming the earth return to be satisfactory, electrical faults will be due either to component malfunction or to defects in the current supply. Individual components are dealt with in Chapter 10. If supply wires are broken or cracked internally this results in an open-circuit, and the easiest way to check for this is to bypass the suspect wire temporarily with a length of wire having a crocodile clip or suitable connector at each end. Alternatively, a 12V test lamp can be used to verify the presence of supply voltage at various points along the wire and the break can be thus isolated.

If a bare portion of a live wire touches the bodywork or other earthed metal part, the electricity will take the low-resistance path thus formed back to the battery: this is known as a short-circuit. Hopefully a short-circuit will blow a fuse, but otherwise it may cause burning of the insulation (and possibly further short-circuits) or even a fire. This is why it is inadvisable to bypass persistently blowing fuses with silver foil or wire.

Spares and tool kit

Most vehicles are supplied only with sufficient tools for wheel changing; the *Maintenance and minor repair* tool kit detailed in *Tools and working facilities,* with the addition of a hammer, is probably sufficient for those repairs that most motorists would consider attempting at the roadside. In addition a few items which can be fitted without too much trouble in the event of a breakdown should be carried. Experience and available space will modify the list below, but the following may save having to call on professional assistance:

Spark plugs, clean and correctly gapped
HT lead and plug cap – long enough to reach the plug furthest from the distributor
Drivebelt(s) – emergency type may suffice
Spare fuses
Set of principal light bulbs
Tin of radiator sealer and hose bandage
Exhaust bandage
Roll of insulating tape
Length of soft iron wire
Length of electrical flex
Torch or inspection lamp (can double as test lamp)
Battery jump leads
Tow-rope
Ignition waterproofing aerosol
Litre of engine oil
Sealed can of hydraulic fluid
Emergency windscreen
'Jubilee' clips
Tube of filler paste

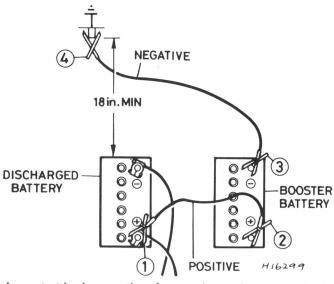

Jump start lead connections for negative earth – connect leads in order shown

If spare fuel is carried, a can designed for the purpose should be used to minimise risks of leakage and collision damage. A first aid kit and a warning triangle, whilst not at present compulsory in the UK, are obviously sensible items to carry in addition to the above.

When touring abroad it may be advisable to carry additional spares which, even if you cannot fit them yourself, could save having to wait while parts are obtained. The items below may be worth considering:

Clutch and throttle cables
Cylinder head gasket
Alternator brushes
Tyre valve core

One of the motoring organisations will be able to advise on availability of fuel etc in foreign countries.

Engine will not start

Engine fails to turn when starter operated

Flat battery (recharge, use jump leads, or push start if possible)

Carrying a few spares can save you a long walk!

Battery terminals loose or corroded
Battery earth to body defective
Engine earth strap loose or broken
Starter motor (or solenoid) wiring loose or broken
Automatic transmission selector in wrong position, or inhibitor switch faulty
Ignition/starter switch faulty
Major mechanical failure (seizure)
Starter or solenoid internal fault (see Chapter 10)

Starter motor turns engine slowly
Partially discharged battery (recharge, use jump leads, or push start if possible)
Battery terminals loose or corroded
Battery earth to body defective
Engine earth strap loose
Starter motor (or solenoid) wiring loose
Starter motor internal fault (see Chapter 10)

Starter motor spins without turning engine
Flat battery
Starter motor pinion sticking on sleeve
Flywheel gear teeth damaged or worn
Starter motor mounting bolts loose

Engine turns normally but fails to start
Damp or dirty HT leads and distributor cap (crank engine and check for spark) (photo)
No fuel in tank (check for delivery at carburettor) (photo)
Excessive choke (hot engine) or insufficient choke (cold engine)
Fouled or incorrectly gapped spark plugs (remove, clean and regap)
Other ignition system fault (see Chapter 4)
Other fuel system fault (see Chapter 3)
Poor compression (see Chapter 1)
Major mechanical failure (eg camshaft drive)

Engine fires but will not run
Insufficient choke (cold engine)
Air leaks at carburettor or inlet manifold
Fuel starvation (see Chapter 3)
Other ignition fault (see Chapter 4)

Engine cuts out and will not restart

Engine cuts out suddenly – ignition fault
Loose or disconnected LT wires
Wet HT leads or distributor cap (after traversing water splash)
Coil failure (check for spark)

Other ignition fault (see Chapter 4)

Engine misfires before cutting out – fuel fault
Fuel tank empty
Fuel pump defective or filter blocked (check for delivery)
Fuel tank filler vent blocked (suction will be evident on releasing cap)
Carburettor needle valve sticking
Carburettor jets blocked (fuel contaminated)
Other fuel system fault (see Chapter 3)

Engine cuts out – other causes
Serious overheating
Major mechanical failure (eg camshaft drive)

Engine overheats

Ignition (no-charge) warning light illuminated
Slack or broken water pump drivebelt – retension or renew (Chapter 2)

Ignition warning light not illuminated
Coolant loss due to internal or external leakage (see Chapter 2)
Thermostat defective
Low oil level
Brakes binding
Radiator clogged externally or internally
Viscous cooling fan not operating correctly
Engine waterways clogged
Ignition timing incorrect or automatic advance malfunctioning
Mixture too weak

Note: *Do not add cold water to an overheated engine or damage may result*

Low engine oil pressure

Gauge reads low or warning light illuminated with engine running
Oil level low or incorrect grade
Defective gauge or sender unit
Wire to sender unit earthed
Engine overheating
Oil filter clogged or bypass valve defective
Oil pressure relief valve defective
Oil pick-up strainer clogged
Oil pump worn or mountings loose
Worn main or big-end bearings

Using a spare spark plug to check for HT spark – do not remove original plug from engine otherwise fuel/air mixture may ignite causing fire

Checking for fuel delivery at pressure regulator

Note: *Low oil pressure in a high-mileage engine at tickover is not necessarily a cause for concern. Sudden pressure loss at speed is far more significant. In any event, check the gauge or warning light sender before condemning the engine.*

Engine noises

Pre-ignition (pinking) on acceleration
Incorrect grade of fuel
Ignition timing incorrect
Distributor faulty or worn
Worn or maladjusted carburettor
Excessive carbon build-up in engine

Whistling or wheezing noises
Leaking vacuum hose

Leaking carburettor or manifold gasket
Blowing head gasket

Tapping or rattling
Incorrect valve clearances
Worn valve gear (cam followers and camshaft)
Broken piston ring (ticking noise)

Knocking or thumping
Unintentional mechanical contact (eg fan blades)
Worn big-end bearings (regular heavy knocking, perhaps less under load)
Worn main bearings (rumbling and knocking, perhaps worsening under load)
Piston slap (most noticeable when cold)

Chapter 1 Engine

For modifications, and information applicable to later models, see Supplement at end of manual

Contents

Ancillary components – refitting	44
Ancillary components – removal	7
Auxiliary shaft – examination and renovation	29
Auxiliary shaft – refitting	39
Auxiliary shaft – removal	12
Camshaft and cam followers – examination and renovation	28
Camshaft – refitting	41
Camshaft – removal	9
Crankcase ventilation system – description and maintenance	22
Crankshaft and bearings – examination and renovation	25
Crankshaft and main bearings – refitting	34
Crankshaft and main bearings – removal	20
Crankshaft front oil seal – renewal	15
Crankshaft rear oil seal – renewal	16
Cylinder block and bores – examination and renovation	26
Cylinder head – decarbonising, valve grinding and renovation	32
Cylinder head – dismantling	10
Cylinder head – reassembly	40
Cylinder head – refitting	42
Cylinder head – removal	8
Engine – adjustment after major overhaul	47
Engine – refitting	45
Engine – removal	5
Examination and renovation – general	23
Engine mountings – renewal	21
Engine dismantling – general	6
Engine reassembly – general	33
Fault diagnosis – engine	48
Flywheel/driveplate – refitting	38
Flywheel/driveplate – removal	13
Flywheel ring gear – examination and renovation	31
General description	1
Major operations only possible after removal of the engine from the car	3
Major operations possible with the engine in the car	2
Method of engine removal	4
Oil filter – renewal	18
Oil pump – examination and renovation	24
Oil pump – refitting	36
Oil pump – removal	17
Pistons and connecting rods – examination and renovation	27
Pistons and connecting rods – refitting	35
Pistons and connecting rods – removal	19
Sump – refitting	37
Sump – removal	14
Timing belt and sprockets – refitting	43
Timing belt and sprockets – removal	11
Timing belt – examination and renovation	30
Valve clearances – adjustment	46

Specifications

Type	Four cylinder in-line, single overhead camshaft
Firing order	1-3-4-2

General

	1.3 HC	1.6 HC Economy	1.6 HC	2.0 HC
Engine code	JCT	LCS	LCT	NET/NES
Bore	79.02 mm (3.111 in)	87.67 mm (3.452 in)	87.67 mm (3.452 in)	90.82 mm (3.576 in)
Stroke	66.00 mm (2.598 in)	66.00 mm (2.598 in)	66.00 mm (2.598 in)	76.95 mm (3.030 in)
Cubic capacity (cc)	1294	1593	1593	1993
Compression ratio	9.0 to 1	9.2 to 1	9.2 to 1	9.2 to 1
Compression pressure at starter speed	11 to 13 bar (160 to 189 lbf/in^2)	11 to 13 bar (160 to 189 lbf/in^2)	11 to 13 bar (160 to 189 lbf/in^2)	11 to 13 bar (160 to 189 lbf/in^2)
Maximum continuous engine rpm	6200	5800	5800	5800
Maximum intermittent engine rpm	6425	6100	6100	6100
Engine power (DIN) kW at rpm	44 at 5700	55 at 5700	55 at 5300	77 at 5200
Engine torque (DIN) Nm at rpm	98 at 3100	120 at 2900	120 at 2900	157 at 4000
Engine weight (lb)	293	293	293	302

Cylinder block

Bore diameter mm (in):	1.3 litre	1.6 litre	2.0 litre
Standard 1	79.000 to 79.010 (3.1102 to 3.1106)	87.650 to 87.660 (3.4508 to 3.4512)	90.800 to 90.810 (3.5748 to 3.5752)
Standard 2	79.010 to 79.020 (3.1106 to 3.1110)	87.660 to 87.670 (3.4512 to 3.4516)	90.810 to 90.820 (3.5752 to 3.5756)
Standard 3	79.020 to 79.030 (3.1110 to 3.1114)	(87.670 to 87.680 (3.4516 to 3.4520)	90.820 to 90.830 (3.5756 to 3.5760)
Standard 4	79.030 to 79.040 (3.1114 to 3.1118)	87.680 to 87.690 (3.4520 to 3.4524)	90.830 to 90.840 (3.5760 to 3.5764)
Oversize A	79.510 to 79.520 (3.1303 to 3.1307)	88.160 to 88.170 (3.4709 to 3.4713)	91.310 to 91.320 (3.5949 to 3.5953)
Oversize B	79.520 to 79.530 (3.1307 to 3.1311)	88.170 to 88.180 (3.4713 to 3.4717)	91.320 to 91.330 (3.5953 to 3.5957)
Oversize C	79.530 to 79.540 (3.1311 to 3.1315)	88.180 to 88.190 (3.4717 to 3.4720)	91.330 to 91.340 (3.5957 to 3.5961)
Standard service size	79.030 to 79.040 (3.1114 to 3.1118)	87.680 to 87.690 (3.4520 to 3.4524)	90.830 to 90.840 (3.5760 to 3.5764)
Oversize 0.5	79.530 to 79.540 (3.1311 to 3.1315)	88.180 to 88.190 (3.4717 to 3.4720)	91.330 to 91.340 (3.5957 to 3.5961)
Oversize 1.0	80.030 to 80.040 (3.1508 to 3.1512)	88.680 to 88.690 (3.4913 to 3.4917)	91.830 to 91.840 (3.6154 to 3.6157)

Crankshaft

Endfloat .... 0.08 to 0.28 mm (0.003 to 0.011 in)
Number of main bearings 5
Main bearing journal diameter:
    Standard .... 56.970 to 56.990 mm (2.2429 to 2.2437 in)
    Undersize 0.25 .... 56.720 to 56.740 mm (2.2331 to 2.2339 in)
    Undersize 0.50 .... 56.470 to 56.490 mm (2.2232 to 2.2240 in)
    Undersize 0.75 .... 56.220 to 56.240 mm (2.2134 to 2.2142 in)
    Undersize 1.00 .... 55.970 to 55.990 mm (2.2035 to 2.2043 in)
Main bearing running clearance .... 0.010 to 0.064 mm (0.0004 to 0.0025 in)
Crankpin journal diameter:
    Standard .... 51.980 to 52.000 mm (2.0465 to 2.0472 in)
    Undersize 0.25 .... 51.730 to 51.750 mm (2.0366 to 2.0374 in)
    Undersize 0.50 .... 51.480 to 51.500 mm (2.0268 to 2.0276 in)
    Undersize 0.75 .... 51.230 to 51.250 mm (2.0169 to 2.0177 in)
    Undersize 1.00 .... 50.980 to 51.000 mm (2.0071 to 2.0079 in)
Big-end bearing running clearance .... 0.006 to 0.060 mm (0.0002 to 0.0024 in)
Main bearing thrust washer thickness:
    Standard .... 2.30 to 2.35 mm (0.0906 to 0.0925 in)
    Oversize .... 2.50 to 2.55 mm (0.0984 to 0.1004 in)

Camshaft

Number of bearings 3
Drive .... Toothed belt
Thrust plate thickness .... 3.98 to 4.01 mm (0.1567 to 0.1579 in)
Bearing journal diameter:
    Front .... 41.987 to 42.013 mm (1.6530 to 1.6541 in)
    Centre .... 44.607 to 44.633 mm (1.7562 to 1.7572 in)
    Rear .... 44.987 to 45.103 mm (1.7711 to 1.7722 in)
Endfloat .... 0.104 to 0.204 mm (0.004 to 0.008 in)

Auxiliary shaft

Endfloat .... 0.050 to 0.204 mm (0.0020 to 0.008 in)

Pistons

Diameter mm (in):	1.3 litre	1.6 litre	2.0 litre
Standard 1	78.965 to 78.975 (3.1089 to 3.1093)	87.615 to 87.625 (3.4494 to 3.4498)	90.765 to 90.775 (3.5734 to 3.5738)
Standard 2	78.975 to 78.985 (3.1093 to 3.1096)	87.625 to 87.635 (3.4498 to 3.4502)	90.775 to 90.785 (3.5738 to 3.5742)
Standard 3	78.985 to 78.995 (3.1096 to 3.1100)	87.635 to 87.645 (3.4502 to 3.4506)	90.785 to 90.795 (3.5742 to 3.5746)
Standard 4	78.995 to 79.005 (3.1100 to 3.1104)	87.645 to 87.655 (3.4506 to 3.4510)	90.975 to 90.805 (3.5746 to 3.5750)
Standard service size	78.990 to 79.015 (3.1098 to 3.1108)	87.640 to 87.665 (3.4504 to 3.4514)	90.780 to 90.805 (3.5740 to 3.5750)
Oversize 0.5	79.490 to 80.515 (3.1295 to 3.1699)	(88.140 to 88.165 (3.4701 to 3.4711)	91.280 to 91.305 (3.5937 to 3.5947)
Oversize 1.0	79.990 to 80.015 (3.1492 to 3.1502)	88.640 to 88.665 (3.4898 to 3.4907)	91.780 to 91.805 (3.6134 to 3.6144)
Clearance in bore (new)	0.015 to 0.050 (0.0006 to 0.0020)	0.015 to 0.050 (0.0006 to 0.0020)	0.025 to 0.060 (0.0010 to 0.0024)

Ring gap (fitted):	1.3 litre	1.6 litre	2.0 litre
Top and centre	0.30 to 0.66 (0.012 to 0.026)	0.30 to 0.66 (0.012 to 0.026)	0.38 to 0.64 (0.015 to 0.025)
Bottom	0.40 to 1.40 (0.016 to 0.055)	0.40 to 1.40 (0.016 to 0.055)	0.40 to 1.40 (0.016 to 0.055)

Gudgeon pin

Length – 1.3	60.0 to 60.8 mm (2.3622 to 2.3937 in)
1.6	68.0 to 68.8 mm (2.6772 to 2.7087 in)
2.0	72.0 to 72.8 mm (2.8346 to 2.8661 in)
Diameter – Red	23.994 to 23.997 mm (0.9446 to 0.9448 in)
Blue	23.997 to 24.000 mm (0.9448 to 0.9449 in)
Yellow	24.000 to 24.003 mm (0.9449 to 0.9450 in)
Clearance in piston	0.008 to 0.014 mm (0.0003 to 0.0006 in)
Interference in connecting rod	0.018 to 0.039 mm (0.0007 to 0.0015 in)

Connecting rod

Big-end parent bore diameter	55.00 to 55.02 mm (2.1654 to 2.1661 in)
Small-end parent bore diameter	23.964 to 23.976 mm (0.9435 to 0.9439 in)

Cylinder head

Cast marking:	
1.3 litre	3
1.6 litre	6
2.0 litre	0
Valve seat angle	44° 30' to 45° 00'
Valve seat width	1.5 to 2.0 mm (0.059 to 0.079 in)
Valve stem bore:	
Standard	8.063 to 8.088 mm (0.3174 to 0.3184 in)
Oversize 0.2	8.263 to 8.288 mm (0.3253 to 0.3263 in)
Oversize 0.4	8.463 to 8.488 mm (0.3332 to 0.3342 in)

Valves

Valve clearance (cold):	
Inlet	0.20 mm (0.008 in)
Exhaust	0.25 mm (0.010 in)

Valve timing

	1.3/1.6 litre	2.0 litre
Inlet opens	22° BTDC	24° BTDC
Inlet closes	54° ABDC	64° ABDC
Exhaust opens	64° BBBC	70° BBDC
Exhaust closes	12° ATDC	18° ATDC

Inlet valve

	1.3 litre	1.6 litre	2.0 litre
Length	112.65 to 113.65 mm (4.435 to 4.474 in)	112.65 to 113.65 mm (4.435 to 4.474 in)	110.65 to 111.65 mm (4.356 to 4.396 in)
Head diameter	38.30 to 38.70 mm (1.508 to 1.524 in)	41.80 to 42.20 mm (1.646 to 1.661 in)	41.80 to 42.20 mm (1.646 to 1.661 in)

Stem diameter:	
Standard	8.025 to 8.043 mm (0.3159 to 0.3167 in)
Oversize 0.2	8.225 to 8.243 mm (0.3238 to 0.3245 in)
Oversize 0.4	8.425 to 8.443 mm (0.3317 to 0.3324 in)
Oversize 0.6	8.625 to 8.643 mm (0.3396 to 0.3403 in)
Oversize 0.8	8.825 to 8.843 mm (0.3474 to 0.3481 in)
Stem to guide clearance	0.020 to 0.063 in (0.0008 to 0.0025 in)
Spring free length	47.0 mm (1.85 in)

Exhaust valve

	1.3 litre	1.6 litre	2.0 litre
Length	112.05 to 113.75 mm (4.4114 to 4.4783 in)	112.05 to 113.75 mm (4.4114 to 4.4783 in)	110.10 to 112.05 mm (4.3346 to 4.4114 in)
Head diameter	29.80 to 30.20 mm (1.173 to 1.189 in)	34.00 to 34.40 mm (1.339 to 1.354 in)	35.80 to 36.20 mm (1.409 to 1.425 in)

Stem diameter:	
Standard	7.999 to 8.017 mm (0.3149 to 0.3156 in)
Oversize 0.2	8.199 to 8.217 mm (0.3228 to 0.3235 in)
Oversize 0.4	8.399 to 8.417 mm (0.3307 to 0.3314 in)
Oversize 0.6	8.599 to 8.617 mm (0.3385 to 0.3393 in)
Oversize 0.8	8.799 to 8.817 mm (0.3464 to 0.3471 in)
Stem to guide clearance	0.046 to 0.089 mm (0.0018 to 0.0035 in)
Spring free length	47.0 mm (1.85 in)

Lubrication system

Type	Bi-rotor pump driven by auxiliary shaft
Oil type/specification	Multigrade engine oil, viscosity range SAE 10W/30 to 20W/50, to API SF/CC or better (Duckhams QXR, Hypergrade, or 10W/40 Motor Oil)
Oil capacity – without filter	3.25 litre; 5.7 pt
with filter	3.75 litre; 6.6 pt
Minimum oil pressure – 750 rpm	1.0 bar (14.5 lbf/in²)
2000 rpm	2.5 bar (36.25 lbf/in²)
Relief valve opens at	4.00 to 4.70 bar (58.0 to 68.2 lbf/in²)
Warning light operates at	0.3 to 0.6 bar (4.4 to 8.7 lbf/in²)
Oil pump clearances:	
Rotor to body	0.150 to 0.301 mm (0.006 to 0.012 in)
Inner rotor to outer rotor	0.05 to 0.20 mm (0.002 to 0.008 in)
Rotor to cover	0.039 to 0.104 mm (0.001 to 0.004 in)

Torque wrench settings

	lbf ft	Nm
Main bearing cap	65 to 75	88 to 102
Big-end bearing cap	30 to 35	40 to 47
Crankshaft pulley bolt (class 8.8)	41 to 44	55 to 60
Camshaft sprocket	33 to 37	45 to 50
Auxiliary shaft sprocket	33 to 37	45 to 50
Flywheel	47 to 52	64 to 70
Oil pump	13 to 15	17 to 21
Oil pump cover	7 to 10	9 to 13
Sump – stage 1	0.7 to 1.5	1 to 2
stage 2	4 to 6	6 to 8
stage 3 (after 20 minutes running)	6 to 8	8 to 10
Sump drain plug	15 to 21	21 to 28
Oil pressure switch	9 to 11	12 to 15
Valve adjustment ball-pins	37 to 41	50 to 55
Cylinder head – stage 1	30 to 41	40 to 55
stage 2	37 to 52	50 to 70
stage 3 (after 20 minutes)	54 to 61	73 to 83
stage 4 (after 15 minutes running)	70 to 85	95 to 115
Valve cover sequence (see Section 42)		
Bolts 1 to 6	4 to 5	5 to 7
Bolts 7 and 8	1.5 to 1.8	2 to 2.5
Bolts 9 and 10	4 to 5	5 to 7
Bolts 7 and 8	4 to 5	5 to 7
Front crankshaft oil seal housing	10 to 13	13 to 17
Timing belt tensioner – bolt	15 to 18	20 to 25
pin	13 to 15	17 to 21

1 General description

The engine is of four cylinder, in-line overhead camshaft type mounted at the front of the car and available in 1.3, 1.6 and 2.0 litre versions.

The crankshaft incorporates five main bearings. Thrust washers are fitted to the centre main bearing in order to control crankshaft endfloat.

The camshaft is driven by a toothed belt and operates the slightly angled valves via cam followers which pivot on ball pins.

The auxiliary shaft which is also driven by the toothed belt, drives the distributor, oil pump and fuel pump.

The cylinder head is of crossflow design with the inlet manifold mounted on the left-hand side and the exhaust manifold mounted on the right-hand side.

Lubrication is by means of a bi-rotor pump which draws oil through a strainer located inside the sump, and forces it through a full-flow filter into the engine oil galleries where it is distributed to the crankshaft, camshaft and auxiliary shaft. The big-end bearings are supplied with oil via internal drillings in the crankshaft. The undersides of the pistons are supplied with oil from drillings in the big-ends. The distributor shaft is intermittently supplied with oil from the drilled auxiliary shaft. The camshaft cam followers are supplied with oil via a drilled spray tube from the centre camshaft bearing.

A semi-closed crankcase ventilation system is employed whereby piston blow-by gases are drawn into the inlet manifold via an oil separator and control valve.

2 Major operations possible with the engine in the car

The following operations can be carried out without having to remove the engine from the car:

(a) Removal and servicing of the cylinder head
(b) Removal of the camshaft after removal of the cylinder head
(c) Removal of the timing belt and sprockets
(d) Removal of the sump
(e) Removal of the oil pump
(f) Removal of the pistons and connecting rods
(g) Removal of the big-end bearings
(h) Removal of the engine mountings
(i) Removal of the clutch and flywheel
(j) Removal of crankshaft front and rear oil seals
(k) Removal of the auxiliary shaft

3 Major operations only possible after removal of the engine from the car

The following operations can only be carried out after removal of the engine from the car:

(a) Renewal of the crankshaft main bearings
(b) Removal of the crankshaft

4 Method of engine removal

The engine may be lifted out either on its own or together with the gearbox. Unless work is also necessary on the gearbox it is recommended that the engine is removed on its own. Where automatic transmission is fitted the engine should be removed on its own owing to the additional weight.

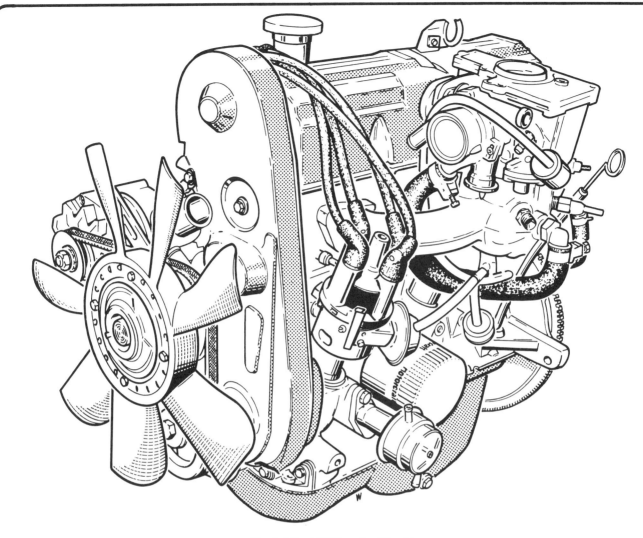

Fig. 1.1 Ford OHC engine (Sec 1)

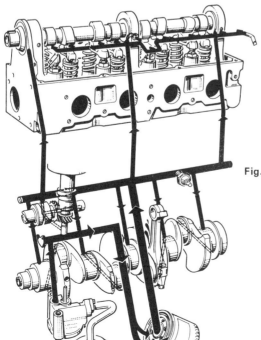

Fig. 1.2 Diagram of the lubrication system (Sec 1)

5   Engine – removal

1   Disconnect the battery negative lead.
2   Remove the bonnet as described in Chapter 12.
3   Remove the radiator as described in Chapter 2.
4   Remove the air cleaner as described in Chapter 3.
5   Disconnect the expansion tank hose from the thermostat housing, and also the heater hoses from the water pump and automatic choke. Unclip the heater hose from the exhaust manifold bracket.
6   Disconnect the wiring from the alternator, distributor, dipstick switch if fitted, temperature sender, oil pressure switch, and starter motor (photo).
7   Disconnect the HT lead from the coil.
8   Disconnect the accelerator cable and remove the bracket where applicable with reference to Chapter 3. Also disconnect the downshift cable where applicable (Chapter 6).
9   On the carburettor disconnect the lead from the anti-dieseling solenoid if fitted.
10   Disconnect the brake servo vacuum hose from the inlet manifold, also disconnect the ignition control vacuum hose.
11   Disconnect and plug the fuel pipes from the carburettor and fuel pump.
12   Remove the viscous fan unit with reference to Chapter 2.
13   Remove the top hose from the thermostat housing and the bottom hose from the water pump.
14   Where applicable detach the power-steering pump and tie it to one side with reference to Chapter 11.
15   Remove the complete exhaust system as described in Chapter 3.
16   Note the location of the earth straps on the top bellhousing bolt and inlet manifold end stud, then unscrew the bolt and nut and remove them.
17   Unscrew and remove the two engine mounting nuts.

Engine without gearbox/automatic transmission

18   Jack up the front of the car and support on axle stands. Unscrew the lower bellhousing bolts and unbolt the engine to gearbox brace.
19   Remove the starter motor as described in Chapter 10.
20   Drain the engine oil.
21   On automatic transmission models unscrew the torque converter to driveplate nuts with reference to Chapter 6.
22   Lower the car to the ground and support the gearbox with a trolley jack.
23   Unscrew the remaining bellhousing bolts.
24   Attach a suitable hoist to the two engine hangers so that the engine is supported horizontally.
25   Raise the engine so that the mounting arms clear the mounting studs then pull the engine forwards from the gearbox and lift it out of the engine compartment (photo). On automatic transmission models keep the torque converter fully engaged with the transmission oil pump with reference to Chapter 6.

Engine with gearbox

26   Remove the propeller shaft as described in Chapter 7.
27   Disconnect and unclip the reversing light switch wiring from the gearbox.
28   Unbolt the anti-roll bar rear mountings and lower the anti-roll bar as far as possible.
29   Disconnect the speedometer cable and clutch cable with reference to Chapter 10 and 5 respectively.
30   Working inside the car remove the gear lever with reference to Chapter 6.
31   Drain the engine oil.
32   Support the gearbox with a trolley jack, then unbolt and remove the gearbox mounting crossmember. Note the location of the speedometer cable heat shield.
33   Attach a suitable hoist to the two engine hangers so that the engine and gearbox will assume a steep angle of approximately 40° to 45° as it is being removed.
34   Raise the engine and gearbox so that the mounting arms clear the mounting studs. Then ease the assembly forwards and at the same time lower the trolley jack. Lift the assembly from the engine compartment being careful not to damage surrounding components (photo). Fit a plastic bag over the rear of the gearbox and retain with an elastic band to prevent oil dripping on the floor.
35   With the engine and gearbox removed temporarily refit the anti-roll bar rear mounting bolts if the car is to be moved.

5.6 Oil pressure switch location

5.25 Removing the engine without the gearbox

5.34 Removing the engine with the gearbox

36 To remove the gearbox from the engine, remove the starter motor (Chapter 10) and bellhousing bolts (refer to Chapter 6).

6 Engine dismantling – general

1 It is best to mount the engine on a dismantling stand, but if this is not available, stand the engine on a strong bench at a comfortable working height. Failing this, it will have to be stripped down on the floor.

2 Cleanliness is most important, and if the engine is dirty, it should be cleaned with paraffin while keeping it in an upright position.

3 Avoid working with the engine directly on a concrete floor, as grit presents a real source of trouble.

4 As parts are removed, clean them in a paraffin bath. However, do not immerse parts with internal oilways in paraffin as it is difficult to remove, usually requiring a high pressure hose. Clean oilways with nylon pipe cleaners.

5 It is advisable to have suitable containers to hold small items according to their use, as this will help when reassembling the engine and also prevent possible losses.

6 Always obtain complete sets of gaskets when the engine is being dismantled, but retain the old gaskets with a view to using them as a pattern to make a replacement if a new one is not available.

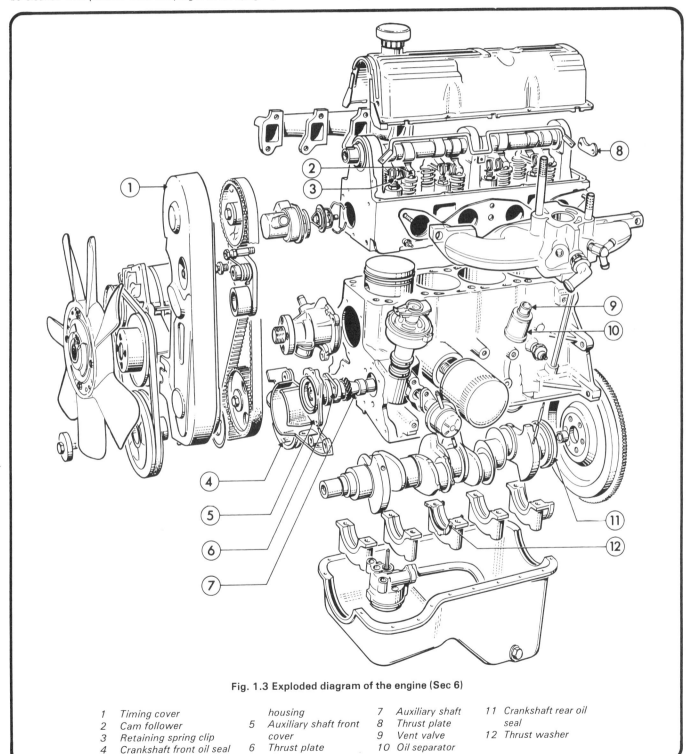

Fig. 1.3 Exploded diagram of the engine (Sec 6)

1 Timing cover	housing	7 Auxiliary shaft	11 Crankshaft rear oil
2 Cam follower	5 Auxiliary shaft front	8 Thrust plate	seal
3 Retaining spring clip	cover	9 Vent valve	12 Thrust washer
4 Crankshaft front oil seal	6 Thrust plate	10 Oil separator	

7   When possible, refit nuts, bolts, and washers in their location after being removed, as this helps protect the threads and will also be helpful when reassembling the engine.

8   Retain unserviceable components in order to compare them with the new parts supplied.

9   Two splined sockets are required when removing the cylinder head, oil pump and timing belt tensioner (photos).

7   Ancillary components – removal

Before dismantling the main engine components, the following externally mounted ancillary components can be removed. The removal sequence need not necessarily follow the order given:

Inlet manifold and carburettor (Chapter 3)
Exhaust manifold (Chapter 3)
Fuel pump and operating rod (Chapter 3)
Alternator (Chapter 10)
Distributor, HT leads and spark plugs (Chapter 4)
Water pump and thermostat (Chapter 2)
Oil pressure switch (photo) and water temperature switch
Oil filter (Section 18 of this Chapter)
Dipstick (photo)
Engine mounting arms (photos)
Crankcase ventilation valve and oil separator

Clutch (Chapter 5)
Alternator mounting bracket (photo)

8   Cylinder head – removal

If the engine is still in the car, first carry out the following operations:

(a)   *Disconnect the battery negative lead*
(b)   *Remove the inlet and exhaust manifolds (Chapter 3)*
(c)   *Disconnect the top hose and expansion tank hose from the thermostat housing*
(d)   *Disconnect the lead from the water temperature sender*
(e)   *Disconnect the HT leads and remove the distributor cap and spark plugs*

1   Unscrew the bolts and withdraw the timing cover (photo). Note the location of the cover in the special bolt.

2   Using a socket on the crankshaft pulley bolt, turn the engine clockwise until the TDC (top dead centre) notch on the pulley is aligned with the pointer on the crankshaft front oil seal housing, and the pointer on the camshaft sprocket is aligned with the indentation on the cylinder head (photo). Note the position of the distributor rotor arm.

3   Loosen the timing belt tensioner bolt and pivot using the special splined socket (photo). Press the tensioner against the spring tension and tighten the bolt to retain it in its released position.

6.9a Splined sockets required for removing cylinder head bolts, oil pump and timing belt tensioner

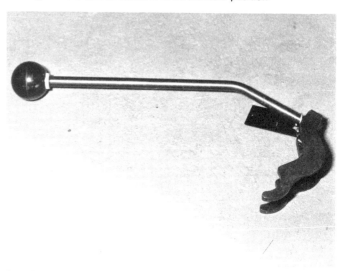

6.9b Special tool which can be used to compress the valve springs (tool number 21-005-A)

7.1 Oil pressure switch

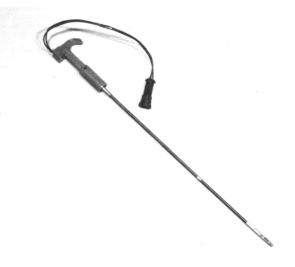

7.2 Oil level dipstick

7.3 Removing the right-hand engine mounting arm

7.4 Removing the left-hand engine mounting arm

7.5 Removing the alternator mounting bracket

8.1 Removing the timing cover

8.2 Camshaft sprocket TDC pointer and indentation

8.3 Loosening the timing belt tensioner pivot

4   Remove the timing belt from the camshaft sprocket and position it to one side without damaging it or bending it.
5   Unscrew the bolts and remove the rocker cover (valve cover) and gasket (photo).
6   Using the special splined socket unscrew the cylinder head bolts half a turn at a time in the reverse order to that shown in Fig. 1.10.
7   With the bolts removed, lift the cylinder head from the block (photo). If it is stuck, tap it free with a wooden mallet. *Do not insert a lever into the gasket joint otherwise the mating surfaces will be damaged.* Place the cylinder head on blocks of wood to prevent damage to the valves.
8   Remove the cylinder head gasket from the block.

8.5 Removing the valve cover

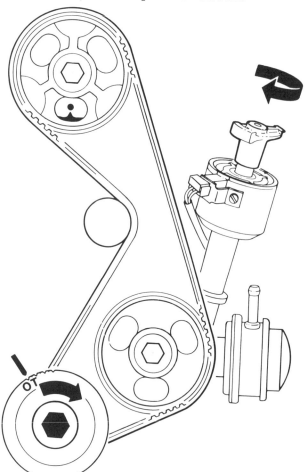

Fig. 1.4 Showing No 1 cylinder TDC (top dead centre) alignment marks on the crankshaft pulley and camshaft sprocket, also distributor rotor rotation (Sec 8)

8.7 Removing the cylinder head

9   Camshaft – removal

1   Remove the cylinder head as described in Section 8.
2   Unscrew the camshaft sprocket bolt while holding the camshaft stationary with a spanner on the camshaft special lug (photo).
3   Remove the camshaft sprocket using a puller if necessary. Remove the backplate (photos).
4   Unscrew the bolts and remove the camshaft oil supply tube (photos).
5   Note how the cam follower retaining spring clips are fitted then unhook them from the cam followers (photo).
6   If the special tool 21-005-A is available compress the valve springs in turn and remove the cam followers keeping them identified for location. Alternatively loosen the locknuts and back off the ball-pins until the cam followers can be removed (photo).
7   Unscrew the bolts and remove the camshaft thrust plate (photos).
8   Carefully withdraw the camshaft from the rear of the cylinder head taking care not to damage the bearings (photos).
9   Prise the oil seal from the front bearing (photo).

9.2 Removing the camshaft sprocket bolt ...

9.3a ... sprocket ...

9.3b ... and backplate

9.4a Unscrew the bolts ...

9.4b ... and remove the camshaft oil supply tube

9.5 Note the location of the retaining spring clips ...

9.6 ... and remove the cam followers

9.7a Unscrew the bolts ...

9.7b ... and remove the camshaft thrust plate

9.8a Removing the camshaft

9.8b View of the camshaft

9.9 Prising out the camshaft front oil seal

10 Cylinder head – dismantling

1   Remove the camshaft as described in Section 9, however if tool 21-005-A is available leave the camshaft in position while the valve springs are being compressed.
2   Using a valve spring compressor, compress each valve spring in turn until the split collets can be removed. Release the compressor and remove the cap and spring keeping them identified for location (photos). If the caps are difficult to release do not continue to tighten the compressor but gently tap the top of the tool with a hammer. Always make sure that the compressor is held firmly over the cap.
3   Remove each valve from the cylinder head keeping them identified for location (photo).
4   Prise the valve stem oil seals from the tops of the valve guides (photo).
5   If necessary unscrew the cam follower ball-pins from the cylinder head keeping them identified for location.
6   If necessary unscrew the bolt and pivot and remove the timing belt tensioner (photo).
7   Remove the thermostat housing with reference to Chapter 2.

10.2a Compressing the valve springs

10.2b Removing the valve springs and caps

10.3 Removing a valve

10.4 Removing a valve stem oil seal

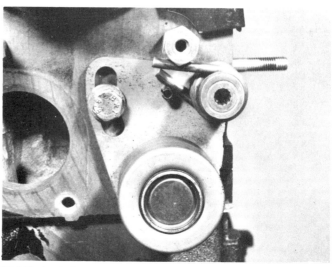

10.6 Timing belt tensioner

11 Timing belt and sprockets – removal

If the engine is still in the car, first carry out the following operations:

(a) *Disconnect the battery negative lead*
(b) *Remove the radiator (Chapter 2) and disconnect the top hose from the thermostat housing*
(c) *Remove the alternator/power-steering pump drivebelt with reference to Chapter 2*

1   Unscrew the bolts and withdraw the timing cover. Note the location of the cover in the special bolt.
2   Using a socket on the crankshaft pulley bolt, turn the engine clockwise until the TDC (top dead centre) notch on the pulley is aligned with the pointer on the crankshaft front oil seal housing, and the pointer on the camshaft sprocket is aligned with the indentation on the cylinder head. Note the position of the distributor rotor arm.
3   Loosen the timing belt tensioner bolt and pivot using the special splined socket. Press the tensioner against the spring tension and tighten the belt to retain it in its released position.
4   Remove the timing belt from the camshaft sprocket.
5   On vehicles with manual transmission, select 4th gear and have an assistant apply the brake pedal hard. On automatic transmission models, remove the starter motor (Chapter 10) and hold the crankshaft against rotation using a lever in the starter ring gear teeth. This method

may be used as an alternative on manual transmission versions.
6   Unscrew the crankshaft pulley bolt and remove the pulley and guide washer (photos).
7   Remove the timing belt from the crankshaft and auxiliary shaft sprockets.
8   Remove the crankshaft sprocket using a puller if necessary (photo).
9   Unscrew the auxiliary shaft sprocket bolt while holding the sprocket stationary with a screwdriver inserted through one of the holes.
10   Remove the auxiliary shaft sprocket using a puller if necessary (photo).
11   Unscrew the camshaft sprocket bolt while holding the sprocket stationary with a screwdriver engaged in one of the grooves. Alternatively remove the valve cover and use a spanner on the camshaft special lug.
12   Remove the camshaft sprocket using a puller if necessary, then remove the backplate. Note that the oil seal can be removed using a special removal tool or by using self-tapping screws and a pair of grips.

12 Auxiliary shaft – removal

1   Remove the timing belt and auxiliary shaft sprocket only as described in Section 11.
2   Remove the distributor as described in Chapter 4.

11.6a Removing the crankshaft pulley ...

11.6b ... and guide washer

11.8 Removing the crankshaft sprocket

11.10 Removing the auxiliary shaft sprocket

3   Remove the fuel pump and operating rod as described in Chapter 3.
4   Unscrew the bolts and remove the auxiliary shaft front cover (photos).
5   Unscrew the cross-head screws using an impact screwdriver if necessary, remove the thrust plate and withdraw the auxiliary shaft from the block (photos).
6   Cut the front cover gasket along the top of the crankshaft front oil seal housing and scrape off the gasket.

---

13 Flywheel/driveplate – removal

If the engine is still in the car remove the clutch as described in Chapter 5 or the automatic transmission as described in Chapter 6.
1   Hold the flywheel/driveplate stationary using the method described in Section 38, then unscrew the bolts and withdraw the unit from the crankshaft.
2   If necessary remove the engine backplate from the dowels (photo).

---

14 Sump – removal

If the engine is still in the car, first carry out the following operations:

(a) Disconnect the battery negative lead
(b) Jack up the front of the car and support with axle stands. Apply the handbrake
(c) Drain the engine oil into a suitable container
(d) Remove the starter motor as described in Chapter 10
(e) Unscrew the engine mounting bolts
(f) Unscrew the bolt retaining the steering intermediate shaft to the column, swivel the plate to one side and remove the shaft from the column
(g) Support the engine with a bar and blocks of wood, and a chain on the engine hangers. The engine may be lifted slightly by using the bar as a lever before resting it on the wooden block *(photos)*
(h) Support the front suspension crossmember with a trolley jack

12.4a Auxiliary shaft front cover and oil seal (engine inverted)

12.4b Removing the auxiliary shaft front cover (engine inverted)

12.5a Auxiliary shaft thrust plate location (engine inverted)

12.5b Removing the auxiliary shaft thrust plate (engine inverted)

12.5c Removing the auxiliary shaft (engine inverted)

13.2 Removing the engine backplate

14.1gA Make up wooden blocks ...

14.1gB ... to fit on the front suspension struts ...

14.1gC ... to take a metal bar ...

14.1gD ... and suspend the engine

14.1h Unscrew the front suspension crossmember bolts ...

14.1iA ... lower the suspension ...

14.1iB ... (showing approximate distance to lower suspension) ...

14.1iC ... unscrew the bolts ...

14.1iD ... and remove the sump

14.1iE Showing engine with sump removed

14.2 Removing the sump

15.3a Removing the crankshaft front oil seal housing

then unscrew the bolts securing it to the underbody (photo)

(i) *Lower the front suspension crossmember sufficiently to remove the sump (photos)*

1   Unscrew the bolts and remove the sump (photo). If it is stuck tap the sump sideways to free it.

2   Remove the gaskets and sealing strips from the block.

15 Crankshaft front oil seal – removal

1   Remove the timing belt and crankshaft sprocket only as described in Section 11.

2   If an oil seal removal tool is available, the oil seal can be removed at this stage. It may also be possible to remove the oil seal by drilling the outer face and using self-tapping screws and a pair of grips.

3   If the oil seal cannot be removed as described in paragraph 2, remove the sump as described in Section 14, then unbolt the oil seal

housing and auxiliary shaft front cover and remove the gasket. The oil seal can then be driven out from the inside (photos).

4   Clean the oil seal seating then drive in a new seal using metal tubing or a suitable socket (photo). Make sure that the sealing lip faces into the engine, and lightly oil the lip.

5   If applicable fit the oil seal housing and auxiliary shaft front cover to the block together with a new gasket and tighten the bolts. Make sure that the bottom face of the housing is aligned with the bottom face of the block (photos). Fit the sump as described in Section 37.

6   Refit the timing belt and crankshaft sprocket as described in Section 43.

16 Crankshaft rear oil seal – renewal

1   Remove the flywheel/driveplate and engine backplate as described in Section 13.

2   Using a special removal tool extract the oil seal. However it may

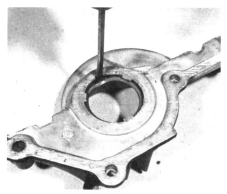

15.3b Driving out the crankshaft front oil seal

15.4 Using a socket to install the new crankshaft front oil seal

15.5a Crankshaft front oil seal housing and auxiliary shaft cover gasket on the front of the cylinder block

15.5b Checking the alignment of the crankshaft front oil seal housing

16.2 Crankshaft rear oil seal location

17.2 Unscrewing the oil pump strainer bracket bolt

17.3 Removing the special oil pump retaining bolts

17.4 Removing the oil pump driveshaft

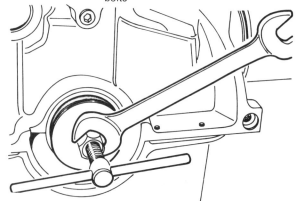

Fig. 1.5 Removing the crankshaft rear oil seal using a special removal tool (Sec 16)

be possible to remove the oil seal by drilling the outer face and using self-tapping screws and a pair of grips (photo).
3   Clean the oil seal seating then drive in a new seal using a suitable metal tube. Make sure that the sealing lip faces into the engine, and lightly oil the lip.
4   Fit the flywheel/driveplate and engine backplate as described in Section 38.

17 Oil pump – removal

1   Remove the sump as described in Section 14.
2   Unscrew the bolt securing the pick-up tube and strainer to the block (photo).
3   Using the special splined socket unscrew the bolts and withdraw the oil pump and strainer (photo).
4   Withdraw the hexagon shaped driveshaft which engages the bottom of the distributor, noting which way round it is fitted (photo).

18 Oil filter – renewal

1   The oil filter should be renewed every 6000 miles (10 000 km). Place a container directly beneath the oil filter, then using a strap wrench, unscrew and remove the filter (photos). If a strap wrench is not available it may be possible to unscrew the filter by driving a screwdriver through the filter canister and using it as a lever.

2   Wipe clean the filter face on the block.

3   Smear a little oil on the new filter seal and screw on the filter until it just contacts the block, then tighten it a further three quarters of a turn.

19 Pistons and connecting rods – removal

1   Remove the sump as described in Section 14, and the cylinder head as described in Section 8.

2   Check the big-end caps for identification marks and if necessary use a centre-punch to identify the caps and connecting rods (photo).

3   Turn the crankshaft so that No 1 crankpin is at its lowest point, then unscrew the nuts and tap off the cap. Keep the bearing shells in the cap and connecting rod.

4   Using the handle of a hammer, push the piston and connecting rod up the bore and withdraw from the top of the cylinder block. Loosely refit the cap to the connecting rod (photo).

5   Repeat the procedure in paragraphs 3 and 4 on No 4 piston and connecting rod, then turn the crankshaft through half a turn and repeat the procedure on Nos 2 and 3 pistons and connecting rods.

20 Crankshaft and main bearings – removal

1   With the engine removed from the car, remove the pistons and connecting rods as described in Section 19, however unless work is required on the pistons or bores it is not necessary to completely remove the pistons from the cylinder block.

2   Remove the timing belt and crankshaft sprocket with reference to Section 11 and remove the flywheel/driveplate as described in Section 13.

3   Unbolt the crankshaft front oil seal housing and auxiliary shaft front cover and remove the gasket.

4   Remove the oil pump and strainer as described in Section 17.

5   Check the main bearing caps for identification marks and if necessary use a centre-punch to identify them (photo).

6   Before removing the crankshaft check that the endfloat is within the specified limits by inserting a feeler blade between the centre crankshaft web and the thrust washers (photo). This will indicate whether new thrust washers are required or not.

7   Unscrew the bolts and tap off the main bearing caps complete with bearing shells (photos). If the thrust washers are to be re-used identify them for location.

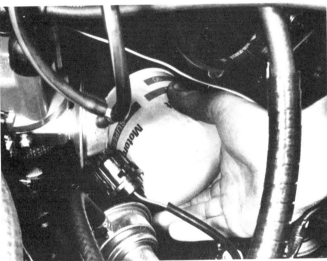

18.1a Removing the oil filter

18.1b Showing the threaded tube onto which the oil filter is located

19.2 Showing big-end cap and connecting rod identification numbers

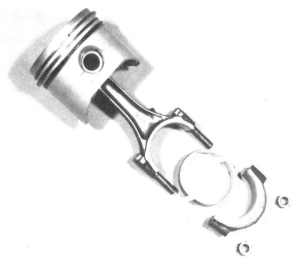

19.4 View of piston, connecting rod, big-end cap and bearing shells

20.5 Showing main bearing cap identification marks — the arrow must face front of engine

20.6 Checking the crankshaft endfloat with a feeler blade

20.7a Removing the centre main bearing cap

20.7b Removing the rear main bearing cap

20.8a Removing the crankshaft

20.8b Removing the thrust washers from the centre main bearing

20.9 Removing the centre main bearing shell

21.2 Removing the engine mounting bolts

21.3a Removing an engine mounting

21.3b Engine mounting platform on the front suspension crossmember

21.3c An engine mounting

8   Lift the crankshaft from the crankcase and remove the rear oil seal. Remove the remaining thrust washers (photos).
9   Extract the bearing shells keeping them identified for location (photo).

21 Engine mountings – renewal

1   The engine mountings incorporate hydraulic dampers and must be renewed if excessive engine movement is evident.
2   Unscrew the central nut and the bolts securing the mounting to the suspension crossmember (photo).
3   Raise the engine using a hoist or trolley jack and remove the mounting from the arm (photos). If necessary unbolt and remove the arm.
4   Fit the new mounting using a reversal of the removal procedure.

22 Crankcase ventilation system – description and maintenance

The crankcase ventilation system consists of the special oil filler cap, containing a steel wool filter, and an oil separator and vent valve on the left-hand side of the engine. This is connected by hose to the inlet manifold. The system operates according to the vacuum in the inlet manifold. Air is drawn through the filler cap, through the crankcase, and then together with piston blow-by gases through the oil separator and vent valve to the inlet manifold. The blow-by gases are then drawn into the engine together with the fuel/air mixture.

Every 24 000 miles (40 000 km) renew the vent valve by pulling it from the oil separator and loosening the hose clip (photos). Fit the new valve, tighten the clip, and insert it into the oil separator grommet.

23 Examination and renovation – general

With the engine completely stripped, clean all the components and examine them for wear. Each part should be checked, and where necessary renewed or renovated as described in the following Sections. Renew main and big-end shell bearings as a matter of course, unless you know that they have had little wear and are in perfect condition.

24 Oil pump – examination and renovation

1   Unscrew the bolts and remove the oil pump cover (photo).
2   Using feeler gauges check that the rotor clearances are within the limits given in Specifications. If not, unbolt the pick-up tube and strainer and obtain a new unit (photos). Fit the pick-up tube and strainer to the new pump using a new gasket, and tighten the bolts.
3   If the oil pump is serviceable refit the cover and tighten the bolts.

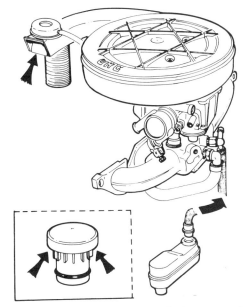

Fig. 1.6 Diagram of the crankcase ventilation system (Sec 22)
Inset shows oil filler cap

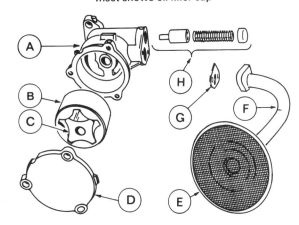

Fig. 1.7 Exploded diagram of the oil pump (Sec 24)

A	Body	D	Cover	G	Gasket
B	Outer rotor	E	Strainer	H	Relief valve
C	Inner rotor	F	Pick-up tube		

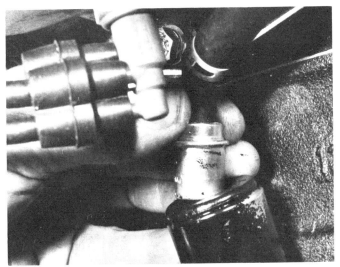

22.1 Removing the vent valve from the oil separator

22.2 Crankcase ventilation vent valve

24.1 Removing the oil pump cover

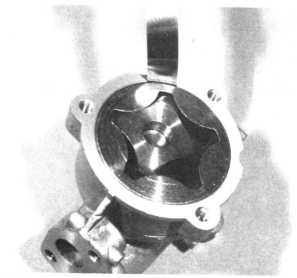

24.2a Checking the oil pump rotor to body clearance

24.2b Checking the oil pump inner to outer rotor clearance

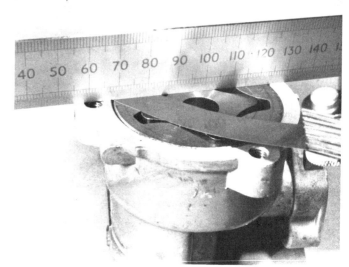

24.2c Checking the oil pump rotor to cover clearance

24.2d Removing the oil pump pick-up tube and strainer

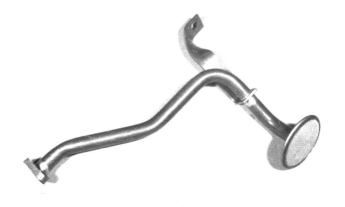

24.2e Oil pump pick-up tube and strainer

25 Crankshaft and bearings – examination and renovation

1 Examine the bearing surfaces of the crankshaft for scratches or scoring and, using a micrometer, check each journal and crankpin for ovality. Where this is found to be in excess of 0.001 in (0.0254 mm) the crankshaft will have to be reground and undersize bearings fitted.
2 Crankshaft regrinding should be carried out by a suitable engineering works, who will normally supply the matching undersize main and big-end shell bearings.
3 If the crankshaft endfloat is more than the maximum specified amount, new thrust washers should be fitted to the centre main bearing, these are usually supplied together with the main and big-end bearings on a reground crankshaft.
4 An accurate method of determining bearing wear is by the use of Plastigage. The crankshaft is located in the main bearings (and big-end bearings if necessary) and the Plastigage filament located across the journal which must be dry. The cap is then fitted and the bolts/nuts tightened to the specified torque. On removal of the cap the width of the filament is checked with a plastic gauge and the running clearance compared with that given in the Specifications (photos).
5 If the spigot bearing in the rear of the crankshaft requires renewal extract it with a suitable puller. Alternatively fill it with heavy grease and use a close fitting metal dowel driven into the centre of the bearing. Drive the new bearing into the crankshaft with a soft metal drift.

25.4a Showing flattened Plastigage filament

25.4b Checking the bearing running clearance with the special gauge

26 Cylinder block and bores – examination and renovation

1 The cylinder bores must be examined for taper, ovality, scoring and scratches. Start by examining the top of the bores; if these are worn, a slight ridge will be found which marks the top of the piston ring travel. If the wear is excessive, the engine will have had a high oil consumption rate accompanied by blue smoke from the exhaust.
2 If available, use an inside dial gauge to measure the bore diameter just below the ridge and compare it with the diameter at the bottom of the bore, which is not subject to wear. If the difference is more than 0.006 in (0.152 mm), the cylinders will normally require reboring with new oversize pistons fitted.
3 Provided the cylinder bore wear does not exceed 0.008 in (0.203 mm), however, special oil control rings and pistons can be fitted to restore compression and stop the engine burning oil.
4 If new pistons are being fitted to old bores, it is essential to roughen the bore walls slightly with fine glasspaper to enable the new pistons rings to bed in properly.
5 Thoroughly examine the crankcase and cylinder block for cracks and damage and use a piece of wire to probe all oilways and waterways to ensure they are unobstructed.

27 Pistons and connecting rods – examination and renovation

1 Examine the pistons for ovality, scoring, and scratches. Check the connecting rods for wear and damage.
2 The gudgeon pins are an interference fit in the connecting rods, and if new pistons are to be fitted to the existing connecting rods the work should be carried out by a Ford garage who will have the necessary tooling. Note that the oil splash hole on the connecting rod must be located on the right-hand side of the piston (the arrow on the piston crown faces forwards).
3 If new rings are to be fitted to the existing pistons, expand the old rings over the top of the pistons. The use of two or three old feeler blades will be helpful in preventing the rings dropping into empty grooves. Note that the oil control ring is in three sections.
4 Before fitting the new rings to the pistons, insert them into the cylinder bore and use a feeler gauge to check that the end gaps are within the specified limits (photos).
5 Fit the oil control ring sections with the spreader ends abutted opposite the front of the piston. The side ring gaps should be 25 mm (1.0 in) either side of the spreader gap. Fit the tapered lower compression ring with the 'TOP' mark towards the top of the piston and the gap 150° from the spreader gap, then fit the upper compression ring with the gap 150° on the other side of the spreader gap. Note that the compression rings are coated with a molybdenum skin which must not be damaged.

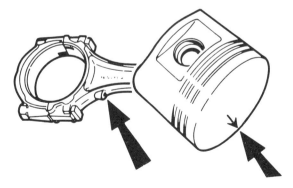

Fig. 1.8 Showing correct relationship of piston and connecting rod (Sec 27)

28 Camshaft and cam followers – examination and renovation

1 Examine the surface of the camshaft journals and lobes, and the cam followers for wear. If excessive, considerable noise would have been noticed from the top of the engine and a new camshaft and followers must be fitted.

27.4a Checking the piston ring gap at the top of the cylinder

27.4b Checking the piston ring gap at the bottom of the cylinder

2   Check the camshaft bearings for wear and if necessary have them renewed by a Ford garage.

3   Check the camshaft lubrication tube for obstructions and make sure that the jet holes are clear.

29 Auxiliary shaft – examination and renovation

1   Examine the auxiliary shaft for wear and damage and renew it if necessary.

2   If the auxiliary shaft endfloat is outside the limits given in the Specifications fit a new thrust plate and renew the shaft if necessary.

30 Timing belt – examination and renovation

Whenever the timing belt is removed it is worthwhile renewing it especially if it has covered a high mileage. This is more important on the 2.0 litre engine where stripped teeth on the timing belt can cause the pistons to foul the valves.

31 Flywheel ring gear – examination and renovation

1   If the ring gear is badly worn or has missing teeth it should be renewed. The old ring can be removed from the flywheel by cutting a notch btween two teeth with a hacksaw and then splitting it with a cold chisel.

2   To fit a new ring gear requires heating the ring to 400°F (204°C). This can be done by polishing four equal spaced sections of the gear, laying it on a suitable heat resistant surface (such as fire bricks) and heating it evenly with a blow lamp or torch until the polished areas turn a light yellow tinge. Do not overheat or the hard wearing properties will be lost. The gear has a chamfered inner edge which should go against the shoulder when put on the flywheel. When hot enough place the gear in position quickly, tapping it home if necessary and let it cool naturally without quenching in any way.

32 Cylinder head – decarbonising, valve grinding and renovation

1   This operation will normally only be required at comparatively high mileages. However, if persistent pinking occurs and performance has deteriorated even though the engine adjustments are correct, de-carbonising and valve grinding may be required.

2   With the cylinder head removed, use a scraper to remove the carbon from the combustion chambers and ports. Remove all traces of gasket from the cylinder head surface, then wash it thoroughly with paraffin.

3   Use a straight edge and feeler blade to check that the cylinder head surface is not distorted. If it is, it must be resurfaced by a suitably

equipped engineering works.

4   If the engine is still in the car, clean the piston crowns and cylinder bore upper edges. but make sure that no carbon drops between the pistons and bores. To do this, locate two of the pistons at the top of their bores and seal off the remaining bores with paper and masking tape. Press a little grease between the two pistons and their bores to collect any carbon dust; this can be wiped away when the piston is lowered. To prevent carbon build-up, polish the piston crown with metal polish, but remove all traces of the polish afterwards.

5   Examine the heads of the valves for pitting and burning, especially the exhaust valve heads. Renew any valve which is badly burnt. Examine the valve seats at the same time. If the pitting is very slight, it can be removed by grinding the valve heads and seats together with coarse, then fine, grinding paste.

6   Where excessive pitting has occurred, the valve seats must be recut or renewed by a suitably equipped engineering works.

7   Valve grinding is carried out as follows. Place the cylinder head upside down on a bench on blocks of wood.

8   Smear a trace of coarse carborundum paste on the seat face and press a suction grinding tool onto the valve head. With a semi-rotary action, grind the vale head to its seat, lifting the valve occasionally to redistribute the grinding paste. When a dull matt even surface is produced on both the valve seat and the valve, wipe off the paste and repeat the process with fine carborundum paste as before. A light spring balanced under the valve head will greatly ease this operation. When a smooth unbroken ring of light grey matt finish is produced on both the valve and seat, the grinding operation is complete.

9   Scrape away all carbon from the valve head and stem, and clean away all traces of grinding compound. Clean the valves and seats with a paraffin soaked rag, then wipe with a clean rag.

10 If the guides are worn they will need reboring for oversize valves or for fitting guide inserts. The valve seats will also need recutting to ensure they are concentric with the stems. This work should be given to your Ford dealer or local engineering works.

11 If the valve springs have been in use for 20 000 miles (32 000 km) or more, renew them. Always renew the valve stem oil seals when the valves are removed.

33 Engine reassembly – general

1   To ensure maximum life with minimum trouble from a rebuilt engine, not only must everything be correctly assembled, but it must also be spotlessly clean. All oilways must be clear, and locking washers and spring washers must be fitted where indicated. Oil all bearings and other working surfaces thoroughly with engine oil during assembly.

2   Before assembly begins, renew any bolts or studs with damaged threads.

3   Gather together a torque wrench, oil can, clean rag, and a set of engine gaskets and oil seals, together with a new oil filter (photo).

33.3 Complete engine gasket set

34.9 Lubricating the crankshaft main bearing shells

34 Crankshaft and main bearings – refitting

1 Wipe the bearing shell locations in the crankcase with a soft, non-fluffy rag.

2 Wipe the crankshaft journals with a soft, non-fluffy rag.

3 If the old main bearing shells are to be renewed (not to do so is a false economy, unless they are virtually new) fit the five upper halves of the main bearing shells to their location in the crankcase.

4 Identify each main bearing cap and place in order. The number is cast on to the cap and on intermediate caps an arrow is also marked which should point towards front of engine.

5 Wipe the cap bearing shell location with a soft non-fluffy rag.

6 Fit the bearing half shell onto each main bearing cap.

7 Apply a little grease to each side of the centre main bearing so as to retain the thrust washer.

8 Fit the upper halves of the thrust washers into their grooves either side of the main bearing. The slots must face outwards.

9 Lubricate the crankshaft journals and the upper and lower main bearing shells with engine oil (photo) and locate the rear oil seal (with lip lubricated) on the rear of the crankshaft.

10 Carefully lower the crankshaft into the crankcase.

11 Lubricate the crankshaft main bearing journals again and then fit No. 1 bearing cap. Fit the two securing bolts but do not tighten yet.

12 Apply a little sealing compound to the crankshaft rear main bearing cap (photo).

13 Fit the rear main bearing cap. Fit the two securing bolts but as before do not tighten yet.

14 Apply a little grease to either side of the centre main bearing cap so as to retain the thrust washers. Fit the thrust washers with the tag located in the groove and the slots facing outwards (photo).

15 Fit the centre main bearing cap and the two securing bolts. Then refit the intermediate main bearing caps. Make sure that the arrows point towards the front of the engine.

16 Lightly tighten all main cap securing bolts and then fully tighten in a progressive manner to the specified torque wrench setting.

17 Check that the crankshaft rotates freely, then check that the endfloat is within the specified limits by inserting a feeler blade between the centre crankshaft web and the thrust washers.

18 Make sure that the rear oil seal is fully entered onto its seating. Coat the rear main bearing cap wedges with sealing compound then press them into position with the rounded red face towards the cap (photo).

19 Refit the oil pump and strainer as described in Section 36.

20 Refit the crankshaft front oil seal housing, and auxiliary shaft front cover, if applicable, together with a new gasket and tighten the bolts. Make sure that the bottom face of the housing is aligned with the bottom face of the block.

21 Refit the flywheel/driveplate (Section 38) and timing belt and crankshaft sprocket (Section 43).

22 Refit the pistons and connecting rods as described in Section 35.

34.12 Applying sealing compound to the rear main bearing cap

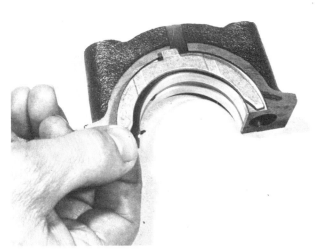

34.14 Locating the thrust washers on the centre main bearing cap

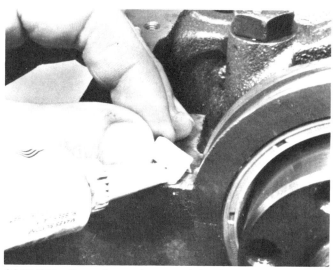

34.18 Fitting the wedges to the rear main bearing cap

35.2a Fitting the bearing shells to the big-end bearing caps

35 Pistons and connecting rods – refitting

1   Clean the backs of the bearing shells and the recesses in the connecting rods and big-end caps.
2   Press the bearing shells into the connecting rods and caps in their correct positions and oil them liberally. Note that the lugs must be adjacent to each other (photos).
3   Lubricate the cylinder bores with engine oil (photo).
4   Fit a ring compressor to No 1 piston then insert the piston and connecting rod into No 1 cylinder. With No 1 crankpin at its lowest point, drive the piston carefully into the cylinder with the wooden handle of a hammer, and at the same time guide the connecting rod onto the crankpin. Make sure that the arrow on the piston crown is facing the front of the engine (photos).
5   Oil the crankpin then fit the big-end bearing cap in its previously noted position, and tighten the nuts to the specified torque (photos).
6   Check that the crankshaft turns freely.
7   Repeat the procedure given in paragraphs 4 to 6 inclusive on the remaining pistons.
8   Refit the cylinder head as described in Section 42 and the sump as described in Section 37.

35.2b Showing the big-end bearing shell lugs adjacent to each other

35.3 Lubricating the cylinder bores

35.4a Fitting a ring compressor to a piston

35.4b Showing the arrow on the piston crown which must face the front of the engine

35.5a Lubricating a crankpin

35.5b Tightening the big-end bearing cap nuts

36 Oil pump – refitting

1   Insert the oil pump driveshaft into the cylinder block in its previously noted position.
2   Prime the oil pump by injecting oil into the pump outlet, then locate the pump on the cylinder block, insert the bolts, and tighten them with the special splined socket (photo).
3   Insert the pick-up tube securing bolt and tighten it.
4   Where applicable refit the crankshaft front oil seal housing together with a new gasket and tighten the bolts. Make sure that the bottom face of the housing is aligned with the bottom face of the block.
5   Refit the sump as described in Section 37.

37 Sump – refitting

1   Apply sealing compound to the corners of the front and rear rubber sealing strip locations then press the strips into the grooves of the rear main bearing cap and crankshaft front oil seal housing (photos).
2   Apply a little sealing compound to the bottom face of the cylinder block. Then fit the sump gaskets in position and locate the end tabs beneath the rubber sealing strips (photo).
3   Locate the sump on the gaskets and insert the bolts loosely.
4   Tighten the bolts to the specified torques in the two stages given in Specifications. Refer to Fig. 1.9 and tighten to the first stage in circular sequence starting at point A, then tighten to the second stage starting at point B. Tighten to the third stage after the engine has been running for twenty minutes.
5   If the engine is in the car reverse the introductory procedure given in Section 14.

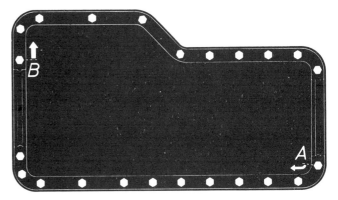

Fig. 1.9 Sump bolt tightening sequence – refer to text (Sec 37)

38 Flywheel/driveplate – refitting

1   If applicable, locate the engine backplate on the dowels on the rear of the cylinder block.
2   Wipe the mating faces then locate the flywheel/driveplate on the rear of the crankshaft (photo).
3   Coat the threads of the bolts with a liquid locking agent then insert them (photo). Note that the manufacturers recommend using new bolts.
4   Using a piece of angle iron (photos) hold the flywheel/driveplate stationary then tighten the bolts evenly to the specified torque in diagonal sequence (photos).
5   If the engine is in the car refit the automatic transmission as described in Chapter 6 or the clutch as described in Chapter 5.

39 Auxiliary shaft – refitting

1   Oil the auxiliary shaft journals then insert the shaft into the cylinder block.
2   Locate the thrust plate in the shaft groove, then insert the cross-head screws and tighten them with an impact screwdriver.
3   Support the front cover on blocks of wood and drive out the old oil seal. Drive in the new seal using a suitable metal tube or socket

36.2 Priming the oil pump with oil

37.1a Apply the sealing compound ...

37.1b ... then fit the rubber sealing strips

37.2 Locate the sump gaskets beneath the sealing strips

38.2 Flywheel located on the crankshaft

38.3 Apply a liquid locking agent to the flywheel bolts

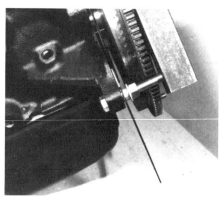

38.4a Method of retaining the flywheel when tightening the bolts

38.4b Tightening the flywheel bolts

39.3a Driving out the auxiliary shaft cover oil seal

39.3b Using a socket to fit the new auxiliary shaft cover oil seal

40.3 Showing ball-pin locations and cam follower retaining spring clips

41.1 Using a socket to fit the camshaft front oil seal

(photo). Make sure that the sealing lip faces toward the engine. Smear a little oil on the lip.

4   If applicable cut the unwanted top half of a new gasket and locate it on the cylinder block, then fit the front cover and tighten the bolts.

5   Refit the fuel pump and operating rod as described in Chapter 3.

6   Refit the distributor as described in Chapter 4.

7   Refit the auxiliary shaft sprocket and timing belt as described in Section 43.

40 Cylinder head – reassembly

1   Refit the thermostat housing with reference to Chapter 2.

2   If applicable, locate the timing belt tensioner on the front of the cylinder head and screw in the bolt and pivot.

3   If applicable, screw the cam follower ball-pins in their correct locations (photo).

4   Oil the valve stems and insert the valves in their correct guides.

5   Wrap some adhesive tape over the collet groove of each valve, then oil the oil seals and slide them over the valves onto the guides. Use a suitable metal tube if necessary to press them onto the guides. Remove the adhesive tape.

6   Working on each valve in turn, fit the valve spring and cap then compress the spring with the compressor and insert the split collets. Release the compressor and remove it. Tap the end of the valve stem with a non-metallic mallet to settle the collets. If tool 21-005-A is being used, first locate the camshaft in its bearings.

7   Refit the camshaft as described in Section 41.

41 Camshaft – refitting

1   Drive the new oil seal into the camshaft front bearing location on the cylinder head using a suitable metal tube or socket (photo). Smear the lip with engine oil.

2   Lubricate the bearings with hypoid SAE 80/90 oil then carefully insert the camshaft (photo).

3   Locate the thrust plate in the camshaft groove then insert and tighten the bolts.

4   Using feeler gauges check that the endfloat is as given in the Specifications.

5   Lubricate the ball-pins with hypoid SAE 80/90 oil, then fit the cam followers in their correct locations and retain with the spring clips. It will be necessary to rotate the camshaft during this operation.

6   Fit the oil supply tube and tighten the bolts.

7   Fit the camshaft sprocket backplate and sprocket. Insert and tighten the bolt while holding the camshaft stationary with a spanner on the special lug (photo).

8   Refit the cylinder head as described in Section 42.

42 Cylinder head – refitting

1   Adjust the valve clearances as described in Section 46. This work is easier to carry out on the bench rather than in the car.

2   Turn the engine so that No 1 piston is approximately 2 cm (0.8 in) before top dead centre. This precaution will prevent any damage to open valves.

3   Make sure that the faces of the cylinder block and cylinder head are perfectly clean. Then locate the new gasket on the block making sure that all the internal holes are aligned (photo). *Do not use jointing compound.*

4   Turn the camshaft so that the TDC pointer is aligned with the indentation on the front of the cylinder head.

5   Lower the cylinder head onto the gasket. The help of an assistant will ensure that the gasket is not dislodged.

6   Lightly oil the complete cylinder head bolts, then insert them.

7   Using the special splined socket tighten the bolts in the order given in Fig. 1.10 to the three stages given in Specifications. Stage four will be completed after the engine has been running for 15 minutes.

8   Fit the valve cover together with new gaskets and tighten the bolts to the specified torque in the order given in Fig. 1.11.

41.2 Lubricating the camshaft bearings

41.7 Fitting the camshaft sprocket backplate

42.3 Fitting the cylinder head gasket

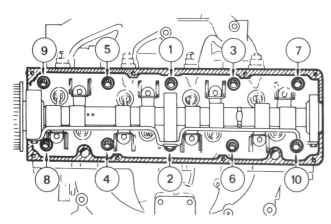

Fig. 1.10 Cylinder head bolt tightening sequence (Sec 42)

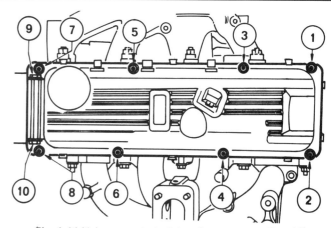

Fig. 1.11 Valve cover bolt tightening sequence (Sec 42)

43 Timing belt and sprockets – refitting

1   If applicable fit the camshaft sprocket backplate and sprocket. Then insert and tighten the bolt while holding the camshaft stationary either with a screwdriver engaged in one of the grooves or with a spanner on the camshaft special lug (photo).

2   Fit the auxiliary shaft sprocket, insert the bolt, and tighten it while holding the sprocket stationary with a screwdriver through one of the holes. Note that the reinforcement ribs on the sprocket must be towards the engine (photo).

3   Fit the crankshaft sprocket to the front of the crankshaft with the chamfered side innermost.

4   Make sure that the TDC pointer on the camshaft sprocket backplate is aligned with the indentation on the front of the cylinder head.

5   Temporarily locate the crankshaft pulley on the crankshaft and turn the crankshaft by the shortest route until the TDC notch in the pulley is aligned with the pointer on the crankshaft front oil seal

housing (photo). Remove the pulley.

6   Fit the distributor (Chapter 4) and then turn the auxiliary shaft sprocket until the contact end of the rotor arm is aligned with No 1 HT segment position in the distributor cap.

7   Press the timing belt tensioner against the spring tension and tighten the bolt to retain it in its released position.

8   Locate the timing belt on the sprockets and around the tensioner then loosen the tensioner bolt and pivot (photo) to tension the belt.

9   Locate the guide washer with its convex side innermost on the crankshaft then fit the pulley.

10   Insert the bolt and tighten it to the specified torque while holding the crankshaft stationary with a lever on the starter ring gear or by engaging 4th gear (manual gearbox only) (photo).

11   Turn the engine clockwise two complete turns and tighten the tensioner bolt followed by the pivot (photo).

12   Fit the timing cover and tighten the bolts.

13   If the engine is in the car, reverse the introductory procedure given in Section 11.

43.1 Tightening the camshaft sprocket bolt

43.2 Tightening the auxiliary shaft sprocket bolt

43.5 Temporarily fitting the crankshaft pulley in order to set the crankshaft at TDC No 1 cylinder

43.8 Fitting the timing belt

43.10 Tightening the crankshaft pulley bolt

43.11 Showing the timing belt fitted to the sprockets

44 Ancillary components – refitting

Refer to Section 7 and refit the listed components with reference to the Chapters indicated. Apply a liquid locking agent to the crankcase ventilation oil separator tube before pressing it into the cylinder block.

45 Engine – refitting

Reverse the removal procedure given in Section 5 but note the following additional points:

(a) Adjust the clutch cable (if applicable) as described in Chapter 5
(b) Fill the engine with oil
(c) Top up the gearbox/automatic transmission with oil/fluid
(d) Adjust the tension of the alternator/power-steering pump drivebelt(s) as described in Chapter 2
(e) Adjust the accelerator cable with reference to Chapter 3
(f) Adjust the downshift cable with reference to Chapter 6
(g) Fill the cooling system as described in Chapter 2

46 Valve clearances – adjustment

1   The valve clearances must be adjusted with the engine cold. First remove the air cleaner as described in Chapter 3.
2   Disconnect the HT leads from the spark plugs and valve cover.
3   Unscrew the bolts and remove the valve cover and gaskets.
4   Turn the engine clockwise with a socket on the crankshaft pulley bolt, until the exhaust valve of No 1 cylinder is fully closed, ie the cam lobe is pointing upwards.
5   Insert a feeler blade of the correct thickness between the cam follower and the heel of the cam lobe. It should be a firm sliding fit (photo). If not, loosen the locknut and adjust the ball-pin position accordingly, then tighten the locknut (photo). Allowance must be made

for tightening the locknut as this tends to decrease the valve clearance gap. Recheck the adjustment.
6   Repeat the procedure given in paragraphs 4 and 5 for the remaining valves. With the carburettor fitted some difficulty may be experienced when adjusting the inlet valve clearances, and a suitable open ended spanner bent to 90° will be found helpful. Numbering from the front (camshaft sprocket) end of the engine, the exhaust valves are 1, 3, 5 and 7, and the inlet valves 2, 4, 6 and 8.
7   Check the valve cover gaskets for damage and renew them if necessary.
8   Refit the valve cover and tighten the bolts in the order given in Fig. 1.11.
9   Refit the HT leads and the air cleaner (Chapter 3).

47 Engine – adjustment after major overhaul

1   With the engine refitted to the car, make a final check to ensure that everything has been reconnected and that no rags or tools have been left in the engine compartment.
2   If new pistons or crankshaft bearings have been fitted, turn the carburettor slow running speed screw in about half a turn to compensate for the initial tightness of the new components.
3   Start the engine. This may take a little longer than usual as the fuel pump and carburettor float chamber may be empty.
4   As soon as the engine starts check that the oil pressure light goes out.
5   Check the oil filter, fuel hoses and water hoses for leaks.
6   Run the engine to normal operating temperature then adjust the slow running as described in Chapter 3.
7   After the engine has been running for 15 minutes, stop it and remove the valve cover. Then tighten the cylinder head bolts to the stage 4 setting in the order given in Fig. 1.10.
8   When the engine has completely cooled check and if necessary adjust the valve clearances as described in Section 46.
9   If new pistons or crankshaft bearings have been fitted, the engine must be run-in for the first 500 miles (800 km).

46.5a Checking the valve clearances

46.5b Loosening a ball-pin locknut

48 Fault diagnosis – engine

Symptom	Reason(s)
Engine fails to start	Discharged battery Loose battery connection Loose or broken ignition leads Moisture on spark plugs, distributor cap or HT leads Incorrect spark plug gap Cracked distributor cap or rotor Dirt or water in carburettor Empty fuel tank Faulty fuel pump Faulty starter motor Low cylinder compression Faulty electronic ignition system
Engine idles erratically	Inlet manifold air leak Leaking cylinder head gasket Worn camshaft lobes Incorrect valve clearances Loose crankcase ventilation hoses Incorrect slow running adjustment Uneven cylinder compressions Incorrect ignition timing
Engine misfires	Incorrect spark plug gap Faulty coil or electronic ignition Dirt or water in carburettor Slow running adjustment incorrect Leaking cylinder head gasket Distributor cap cracked Incorrect valve clearances Uneven cylinder compressions Moisture on spark plugs, distributor cap or HT leads
Engine stalls	Slow running adjustment incorrect Inlet manifold air leak Ignition timing incorrect
Excessive oil consumption	Worn pistons and cylinder bores Valve guides and valve stem seals worn Oil leaking from gasket or oil seal
Engine runs on after switching off	Anti-dieseling valve (if applicable) faulty Excessive carbon build-up in combustion chambers

Chapter 2 Cooling system

For modifications, and information applicable to later models, see Supplement at end of manual

Contents

Antifreeze/corrosion inhibitor mixture – general 5
Cooling system – draining 2
Cooling system – filling 4
Cooling system – flushing 3
Expansion tank and coolant level sensor – removal and refitting 11
Fault diagnosis – cooling system 13
General description 1

Radiator – removal, inspection, cleaning and refitting 6
Temperature gauge transmitter – removal and refitting 12
Thermostat – removal, testing and refitting 7
Thermo-viscous cooling fan – removal and refitting 10
Water pump – removal and refitting 8
Water pump/alternator drivebelt – checking, renewal and adjustment 9

Specifications

System type .... Pressurised, with belt driven pump, crossflow radiator, thermo-viscous fan, thermostat, and expansion (degas) tank

Expansion tank cap pressure .... 12.0 to 15.7 lbf/in² (0.85 to 1.10 bar)

Thermostat
Nominal temperature rating .... 88°C (190°F)
Opening temperature .... 85° to 89°C (185° to 192°F)

Water pump/alternator drivebelt tension .... 10.0 mm (0.4 in) deflection midway between water pump and alternator (or power-steering pump) pulleys under firm thumb pressure

Coolant type/specification .... Soft water and antifreeze to Ford spec SSM-97B 9103-A (Duckhams Universal Antifreeze and Summer Coolant)

System capacity (including heater) .... 8.0 litre; 14.1 pint

Antifreeze/corrosion inhibitor concentration .... 50% antifreeze, 50% water

Antifreeze and water mixture specific gravity 1.077

Torque wrench settings	**lbf ft**	**Nm**
Radiator – upper	15.1 to 18.8	20.5 to 25.5
lower	5.9 to 8.8	8.0 to 12.0
Water pump – M8	12.5 to 15.5	17.0 to 21.0
M10	25.8 to 31.0	35.0 to 42.0
Thermostat outlet	12.2 to 15.1	16.6 to 20.4
Fan shroud	5.9 to 8.1	8.0 to 11.0
Water pump pulley	15.1 to 18.8	20.5 to 25.5
Fan to coupling	5.9 to 7.4	8.0 to 10.0
Alternator link bolt	15.1 to 18.8	20.5 to 25.5

1 General description

The cooling system is of pressurised type and includes a front mounted crossflow radiator, belt driven water pump, temperature conscious thermo-viscous fan, wax type thermostat, and an expansion and degas tank.

The radiator matrix is of copper and brass construction and the end tanks are of plastic. On automatic transmission models the right-hand side end tank incorporates the transmission oil cooler.

The thermostat is located behind the water outlet elbow at the front of the cylinder head, and its purpose is to ensure rapid engine warm-up by restricting the flow of coolant in the engine when cold, and also to assist in regulating the normal operating temperature of the engine.

The expansion tank incorporates a pressure cap which effectively pressurises the cooling system as the coolant temperature rises thereby increasing the boiling point temperature of the coolant. The tank also has a further degas function. Any accumulation of air bubbles in the coolant, in particular in the thermostat housing and the radiator, is returned to the tank and released in the air space thus maintaining the efficiency of the coolant.

The radiator is not provided with a drain plug, however a drain plug is provided on the right-hand side of the cylinder block.

The system functions as follows. Cold water in the bottom of the radiator circulates through the bottom hose to the water pump where the pump impeller pushes the water through the passages within the cylinder block, cylinder head and inlet manifold. After cooling the cylinder bores, combustion surfaces, and valve seats, the water reaches the underside of the thermostat which is initially closed. A small proportion of water passes through the small hose from the thermostat housing to the expansion tank, but because the thermostat is closed the main circulation is through the inlet manifold, automatic choke, and heater matrix, returning to the water pump. When the coolant reaches the predetermined temperature the thermostat opens and hot water passes through the top hose to the top of the radiator. As the water circulates down through the radiator, it is cooled by the passage of air past the radiator when the car is in forward motion, supplemented by the action of the thermo-viscous fan when necessary. Having reached the bottom of the radiator, the water is now cooled and the cycle is repeated. Circulation of water continues through the expansion tank, inlet manifold, automatic choke, and heater at all times, the heater temperature control being by an air flap.

The thermo-viscous fan is controlled by the temperature of air behind the radiator. When the air temperature reaches a predetermined level, a bi-metallic coil commences to open a valve within the unit and silicon fluid is fed through a system of vanes. Half of the vanes are driven directly by the water pump and the remaining half are connected to the fan blades. The vanes are arranged so that drive is transmitted to the fan blades in relation to the drag or viscosity of the fluid, and this in turn depends on ambient temperature and engine speed. The fan is therefore only separated when required, and compared with direct drive type fans represents a considerable improvement in full economy, drivebelt wear and fan noise.

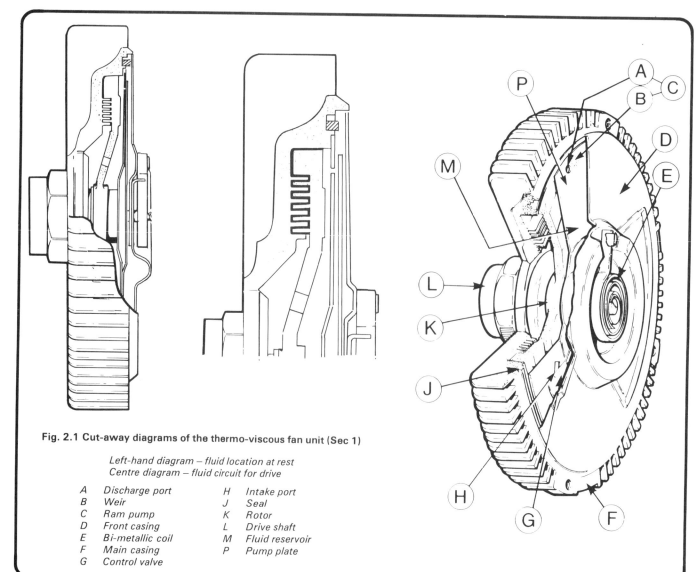

Fig. 2.1 Cut-away diagrams of the thermo-viscous fan unit (Sec 1)

Left-hand diagram – fluid location at rest
Centre diagram – fluid circuit for drive

A	Discharge port	H	Intake port
B	Weir	J	Seal
C	Ram pump	K	Rotor
D	Front casing	L	Drive shaft
E	Bi-metallic coil	M	Fluid reservoir
F	Main casing	P	Pump plate
G	Control valve		

2 Cooling system – draining

1   It is preferable to drain the cooling system with the engine cold. If this is not possible, place a thick cloth over the expansion tank filler cap and turn it slowly 90° in an anti-clockwise direction until the first step is reached, then wait until all the pressure has been released. Be prepared for the emission of very hot steam, as the release of pressure may cause the coolant to boil.
2   Remove the filler cap.
3   Place a suitable container beneath the right-hand side of the radiator.
4   Loosen the clip and ease the bottom hose away from the radiator outlet (photo). Drain the coolant into the container.
5   Place a second container beneath the right-hand side of the cylinder block, unscrew the drain plug and drain the coolant (photo).

3 Cooling system – flushing

1   After some time the radiator and engine waterways may become restricted or even blocked with scale or sediment, which reduces the efficiency of the cooling system. When this occurs, the coolant will appear rusty and dark in colour and the system should then be flushed. Begin by draining the cooling system as just described.
2   Disconnect the top hose from the radiator (photo), then insert a hose and allow water to circulate through the radiator until it runs clear from the outlet.
3   Insert the hose in the expansion tank filler neck and allow water to run out of the cylinder block and bottom hose until clear.
4   Disconnect the inlet hose from the inlet manifold, connect the hose, and allow water to circulate through the manifold, automatic choke, heater and out through the bottom hose until clear.
5   In severe cases of contamination the system should be reverse flushed. To do this, remove the radiator, invert it, and insert a hose in the outlet. Continue flushing until clear water runs from the inlet.
6   The engine should also be reverse flushed. To do this, remove the thermostat and insert the hose into the cylinder head. Continue flushing until clear water runs from the cylinder block drain plug and bottom hose.
7   The use of chemical cleaners should only be necessary as a last resort, and the regular renewal of the antifreeze/corrosion inhibitor solution should prevent the contamination of the system.

4 Cooling system – filling

1   Refit the radiator and thermostat.
2   Reconnect the hose(s) then refit and tighten the cylinder block drain plug.
3   Pour coolant into the expansion tank filler neck until it reaches the maximum level mark, then refit the cap.
4   Run the engine at a fast idling speed for several minutes, then stop the engine and check the level in the expansion tank. Top up the level as necessary, being careful to release pressure from the system before removing the filler cap.

5 Antifreeze/corrosion inhibitor mixture – general

Note: *The antifreeze/corrosion inhibitor mixture is toxic and must not be allowed to contact the skin. Precautions must also be taken to prevent the mixture contacting the bodywork and clothing.*
1   The antifreeze/corrosion inhibitor should be renewed every two years or 36 000 miles (60 000 km) whichever comes first. This is necessary not only to maintain the antifreeze properties (although the antifreeze content does not deteriorate), but mostly to prevent corrosion which would otherwise occur as the properties of the inhibitors become progressively less effective.
2   Always use the antifreeze recommended in the Specifications as this has been tested by the manufacturers.
3   Before adding the mixture, the cooling system should be completely drained and flushed, and all hose connections checked for tightness.
4   The mixture consists of 50% antifreeze and 50% water. Mix the required quantity in a clean container then fill the cooling system with reference to Section 4.

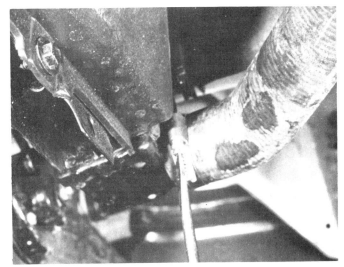
2.4 Disconnecting the bottom hose

2.5 Cylinder block drain plug location

3.2 Radiator top hose

5   After filling, a label should be attached to the radiator stating the
type of antifreeze and the date installed. Any subsequent topping up
should be made with the same type and concentration of antifreeze.

6   Radiator – removal, inspection, cleaning and refitting

1   Disconnect the battery negative lead.
2   Drain the cooling system as described in Section 2.
3   Disconnect the top hose and expansion tank hose from the
radiator (photo).
4   On automatic transmission models place a suitable container
beneath the oil cooler pipe connections to the radiator. Unscrew the
union and plug the upper pipe then unscrew the union and plug the
lower pipe.
5   Apply the handbrake. Jack up the front of the car and support it on
axle stands.
6   Unscrew and remove the mounting nuts and bolts, and lower the
radiator, tilting it as necessary to clear the fan blades (photos). For
better access first remove the shroud from the radiator and bring it
over the fan blades, however it is not essential to do this.

6.3 Disconnecting the expansion tank hose from the radiator

6.6a Unscrewing radiator top mounting nut

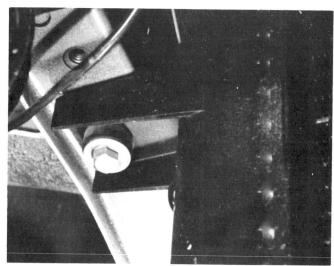

6.6b Radiator bottom mounting bolt

6.6c Removing the radiator

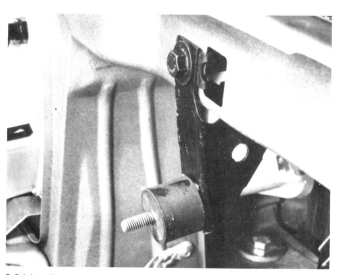

6.6d A radiator top mounting

7   Radiator repair is best left to a specialist, however minor repairs may be made using a proprietary repair kit or coolant additive. As the end tanks are of plastic the use of a soldering iron on the matrix requires extra care.

8   Clear the matrix of flies and small leaves with a soft brush or by hosing. Reverse flush the radiator as described in Section 3. Examine the hoses and clips and renew them if they are damaged or deteriorated. Also check the lower mounting rubbers.

9   Refitting is a reversal of removal, but fill the cooling system as described in Section 4. On automatic transmission models tighten the oil cooler unions to the torque setting given in Chapter 6.

the water and check that it is fully closed when cold.

7   Renew the thermostat if the opening temperature is not as given in the Specifications or if the unit does not fully close when cold.

8   Clean the housing and the mating face of the cylinder head. Check the thermostat sealing ring for condition and renew it if necessary.

9   Refitting is a reversal of removal, but use a new gasket. Note that the thermostat wax capsule must face into the cylinder head with the flow direction arrow facing forward (photo). Refill the cooling system as described in Section 4.

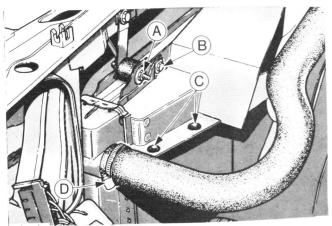

Fig. 2.2 Radiator upper mounting and shroud (Sec 6)

A   Mounting nut   C   Shroud securing clips
B   Shroud securing bolt D   Top hose clip

Fig. 2.3 Thermostat and sealing ring (Sec 7). Note the flow direction arrow

7   Thermostat – removal, testing and refitting

1   Disconnect the battery negative lead.

2   Drain the cooling system as described in Section 2. As it is not necessary to completely drain the radiator, the bottom hose can be disconnected from the water pump.

3   Disconnect the expansion tank and top hoses from the thermostat housing at the front of the cylinder head (photos).

4   Unscrew the bolts and remove the housing and gasket (photo).

5   Using a screwdriver prise the retaining clip from the housing, and extract the thermostat and sealing ring (photos).

6   To test the thermostat suspend it with a piece of string in a container of water. Gradually heat the water and note the temperature at which the thermostat starts to open. Remove the thermostat from

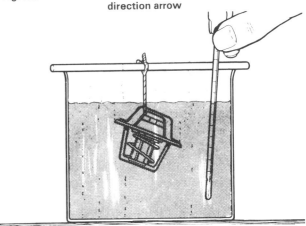

Fig. 2.4 Method of checking the thermostat opening temperature (Sec 7)

7.3a Disconnecting the expansion tank hose from the thermostat housing

7.3b Top hose location on the thermostat housing

7.4 Removing the thermostat housing

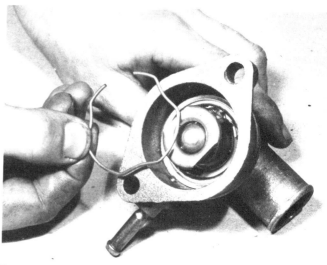

7.5a Prise out the retaining clip ...

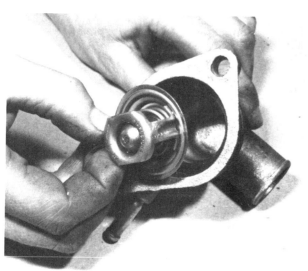

7.5b ... and extract the thermostat ...

7.5c ... and sealing ring

7.9 Showing thermostat flow direction arrow

8 Water pump – removal and refitting

1   Disconnect the battery negative lead.
2   Drain the cooling system as described in Section 2. As it is not necessary to completely drain the radiator, the bottom hose can be disconnected at the water pump (photo).
3   Disconnect the heater return hose from the water pump.
4   Remove the thermo-viscous fan and the water pump pulley as described in Section 10.
5   Unbolt and remove the timing cover (refer to Chapter 1 if necessary).
6   Unscrew the retaining bolts and remove the water pump and gasket from the front of the cylinder block. Note on certain models that the alternator adjusting link is located on the right-hand retaining bolt (photos).
7   If the water pump is faulty renew it, as it is not possible to obtain individual components.
8   Clean the mating faces of the water pump and cylinder block.
9   Refitting is a reversal of removal, but use a new gasket and tighten the retaining bolts to the specified torque (photo). Refer to Section 10 when refitting the thermo-viscous fan and water pump pulley, and refill the cooling system as described in Section 4.

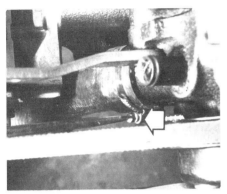

8.2 Disconnecting the bottom hose from the water pump

8.6a Removing the water pump bolts

8.6b Note the location of the alternator adjusting link on the right-hand retaining bolt

8.6c Water pump

8.9 Locating a new gasket on the water pump

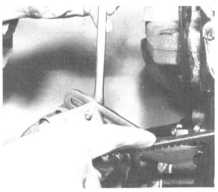

9.5 Adjusting the tension of the water pump/alternator drivebelt

9 Water pump/alternator drivebelt – checking, renewal and adjustment

1   The drivebelt(s) should be checked and if necessary re-tensioned every 12 000 miles (20 000 km). Check the full length of the drivebelt(s) for cracks and deterioration. It will be necessary to turn the engine in order to check the position of the drivebelt(s) in contact with the pulleys. If the drivebelt is unserviceable renew it as follows. Note that two drivebelts are fitted to models equipped with power-assisted steering, and both should be renewed if either one is unserviceable.

2   Disconnect the battery negative lead.

3   Loosen the alternator mounting and adjustment nuts and bolts, and swivel the alternator in towards the cylinder block.

4   Slip the drivebelt(s) from the alternator, water pump, crankshaft and where applicable the power-steering pump pulleys and ease it (them) over the fan blades.

5   Fit the new drivebelt(s) over the pulleys, then lever the alternator away from the cylinder block until the specified tension is achieved (photo). Lever the alternator on the drive end bracket to prevent straining the brackets. It is helpful to semi tighten the adjustment link bolt before tensioning the drivebelt.

6   Tighten the alternator mounting and adjustment nuts and bolts in the order shown in Fig. 2.6.

7   Reconnect the battery negative lead.

8   The drivebelt(s) tension should be rechecked and if necessary adjusted after the engine has run for a minimum of ten minutes.

Fig. 2.5 Drivebelt tension checking point (Sec 9)

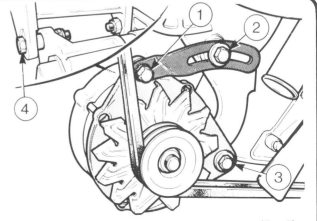

Fig. 2.6 Alternator mounting tightening sequence (Sec 9). Note twin belt type shown as fitted to models with power-steering

10 Thermo-viscous cooling fan – removal and refitting

1   Disconnect the battery negative lead.

2   Remove the upper fan shroud by releasing the clips and removing the screws (photos).

3   Using a 32 mm (1.25 in AF) spanner with a jaw thickness of 5 mm (0.2 in) or less, (modified as shown in Fig. 2.7) unscrew the fan hub nut from the water pump drive flange (photo). Note that the nut has a left-hand thread. Hold the water pump pulley stationary while loosening the nut, and if necessary tap the end of the spanner with a mallet to release the nut.

4   If a spanner of the correct thickness is not available, first remove the drivebelt(s) as described in Section 9 then unscrew and remove the water pump pulley retaining bolts. The fan unit can then be removed from the water pump drive flange using a spanner of normal thickness.

5   Unscrew the four bolts and separate the fan blades from the thermo-viscous clutch hub (photo).

6   Refitting is a reversal of removal, but when assembling the fan blades to the clutch hub take care not to tighten the bolts in excess of the specified torque otherwise thread damage may require the unit to be renewed. Refer to Section 9, where applicable, when tensioning the drivebelt(s). Note that the special torque cover support bolt must be located in the water pump bottom hole *before* fitting the pulley (photos).

11 Expansion tank and coolant level sensor – removal and refitting

1   With the engine cold turn the expansion tank filler cap 90° in an anti-clockwise direction and release any remaining pressure from the cooling system. Remove the filler cap.

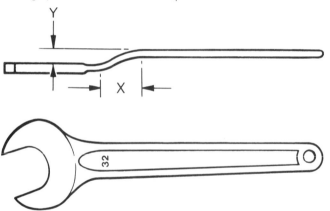

Fig. 2.7 Modified spanner required for removing the thermo-viscous coupling fan (Sec 10)

X   = 25 mm (1.0 in)   Y   = 12 mm (0.5 in)

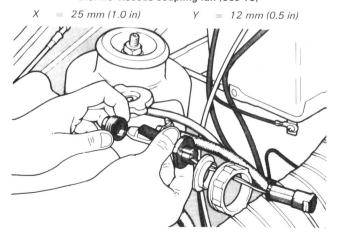

Fig. 2.8 Removing the coolant level sensor from the expansion tank (Sec 11)

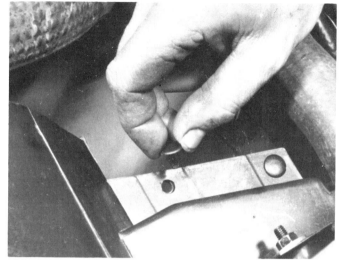

10.2a Release the clips ...

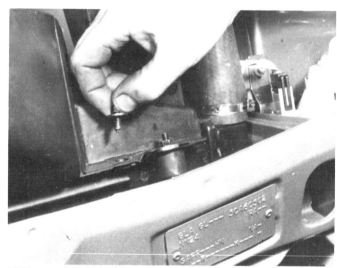

10.2b ... remove the screws ...

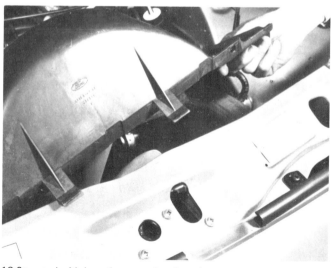

10.2c ... and withdraw the upper fan shroud

10.3 Removing the thermo-viscous fan hub

10.5 Removing the thermo-viscous fan blades

10.6a Locate the timing cover support bolt (arrowed) in the water pump hole ...

10.6b ... before fitting the pulley

2   Place a suitable container beneath the expansion tank.

3   Disconnect and plug the upper hose.

4   Disconnect the coolant level sensor wiring (where applicable).

5   Unscrew the expansion tank retaining bolts and tilt the tank so that the coolant is at the sealed end.

6   Disconnect and plug the lower hose.

7   Drain the expansion tank and remove it.

8   Unscrew the collar from the coolant level sensor and withdraw the spacer, sensor and seal. Note that the sensor can only be fitted in one position.

9   Refitting is a reversal of removal. Top up the coolant level to the maximum mark using the recommended antifreeze/corrosion inhibitor mixture. Refit the cap then run the engine at a fast idling speed for several minutes and check the expansion tank for leaks. Stop the engine and top up the coolant level if necessary.

12 Temperature gauge transmitter – removal and refitting

1   The temperature gauge transmitter is located on the front left-hand side of the cylinder head, just in front of the inlet manifold. To remove it, first make sure that the engine is cold.

2   Turn the expansion tank filler cap 90° in an anti-clockwise direction to release any remaining pressure from the cooling system, then refit the cap.

3   Disconnect the wire from the terminal on the transmitter (photo).

12.3 Disconnect the lead ...

4   Unscrew and remove the transmitter from the cylinder block and temporarily plug the aperture with a suitable rubber or cork bung (photo).

5   Smear a little sealing compound on the transmitter threads and refit it using a reversal of the removal procedure. Top up the cooling system if necessary.

12.4 ... and unscrew the temperature gauge transmitter

13.1 Core plug location behind the alternator mounting bracket

13 Fault diagnosis – cooling system

Symptom	Reason(s)
Overheating	Low coolant level
	Faulty expansion tank pressure cap
	Thermostat sticking shut
	Drivebelt(s) slipping
	Clogged radiator matrix
	Faulty thermo-viscous fan unit
	Retarded ignition timing
Slow warm up	Thermostat sticking open
	Faulty thermo-viscous fan unit
Coolant loss	Damaged or deteriorated hose
	Leaking water pump or thermostat housing gasket
	Blown cylinder head gasket
	Leaking radiator
	Cracked cylinder head
	Leaking core plug (photo)

Chapter 3 Fuel and exhaust systems

For modifications, and information applicable to later models, see Supplement at end of manual

Contents

Accelerator cable 8
Accelerator pedal – removal and refitting 9
Air cleaner and element – removal and refitting 2
Air cleaner temperature control – testing 3
Carburettor – removal and refitting 10
Carburettor – slow running adjustment 11
Exhaust manifold – removal and refitting 18
Exhaust system – checking, removal and refitting 19
Fault diagnosis – fuel and exhaust systems 20
Ford variable venturi (VV) carburettor – general description 12
Ford variable venturi (VV) carburettor – overhaul 13

Fuel gauge sender unit – removal and refitting 7
Fuel pressure regulator – removal and refitting 5
Fuel pump – testing, removal, servicing and refitting 4
Fuel tank – removal, servicing and refitting 6
General description 1
Inlet manifold – removal and refitting 17
Weber twin venturi (2V) carburettor – general description 14
Weber twin venturi (2V) carburettor – overhaul 15
Weber twin venturi (2V) carburettor automatic choke – overhaul
and adjustment 16

Specifications

Air cleaner
Type .... Automatic air temperature control, with renewable paper element
Heat sensor temperature rating:
    1.3 and 1.6 litre .... 20°C (68°F)
    2.0 litre .... 28°C (82°F)

Fuel pump
Type .... Mechanical, diaphragm, operated by pushrod and eccentric on auxiliary shaft
Delivery pressure .... 3.5 to 5.5 lbf/in^2 (0.24 to 0.38 bar)

Fuel tank
Capacity .... 60 litre (13.1 gallon)

Ported vacuum switch (PVS)
operating temperature .... 52° to 55°C (125° to 131°F)

Fuel octane rating .... 97 RON

Carburettor
Application and type:
    1.3 and 1.6 litre .... Downdraught, Ford variable venturi (VV)
    2.0 litre .... Downdraught, Weber twin venturi (2V)

Ford VV carburettor
Idle speed .... 800 ± 25 rpm
Idle CO% .... 1.5 ± 0.5

Weber 2V carburettor
Note: *Oblique line indicates Primary stage/Secondary stage*
Idle speed .... 800 ± 25 rpm
Idle CO% .... 1.5 ± 0.2
Fast idle speed (see text, Section 16) .... 2900 ± 100 rpm
Float level setting (without gasket) .... 41.0 mm (1.61 in) brass float, 35.3 mm (1.39 in) plastic
Choke vacuum pull-down .... 6.5 ± 0.25 mm (0.26 ± 0.01 in)
Choke phasing dimension .... 1.5 ± 0.25 mm (0.06 ± 0.01 in)
Automatic choke setting .... Centre index
Throttle barrel diameter 32/36
Venturi diameter 26/27
Idle jet 45/45
Main jet:
    Manual gearbox 130/130
    Automatic transmission 130/132
Air jet:
    Manual gearbox 165/120
    Automatic transmission 170/120
Emulsion tube:
    Manual gearbox F66/F66
    Automatic transmission F50/F66

Torque wrench settings

	lbf ft	Nm
Inlet manifold	13 to 15	17 to 21
Exhaust manifold	15 to 18	21 to 25
Fuel pump	10 to 13	14 to 18
Exhaust manifold/downpipe flange	26 to 30	35 to 40
Exhaust U-bolt clamp	28 to 33	38 to 45
Exhaust central flange	26 to 30	35 to 40

1   General description

The fuel system consists of a rear mounted fuel tank, pushrod operated fuel pump incorporating a nylon mesh filter, downdraught carburettor, and a thermostatically controlled air cleaner.

The exhaust system is in three sections, namely the front downpipe, centre pipe with resonator and silencer, and the tailpipe with silencer.

Before working on the fuel system read the precautions given in 'Safety First' at the front of this manual.

2   Air cleaner and element – removal and refitting

1   Unscrew the air cleaner retaining bolts and screw from the top of the air cleaner (photo).
2   Release the spring clips where applicable then prise off the cover (photos).
3   Withdraw the element from the air cleaner body (photo). The element should be renewed every 24 000 miles (40 000 km) and the interior surfaces of the air cleaner wiped clean with a fuel-moistened cloth.

2.1 Removing the air cleaner cover retaining screw

2.2a Release the clips ...

2.2b ... and lift off the air cleaner cover

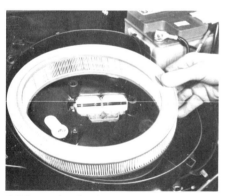

2.3 Removing the air cleaner element

2.4 Disconnecting the ducting from the air cleaner

2.5a Disconnecting the temperature control vacuum pipe from the inlet manifold

2.5b Air cleaner hot air ducting

2.6a Showing air cleaner with cover and element removed

2.6b Disconnecting the air cleaner inlet ducting from the front body panel

4   To remove the air cleaner body first unclip the ducting from the inlet tube (photo).
5   Disconnect the vacuum pipe from the inlet manifold and the hot air ducting from the inlet tube (photos).
6   Withdraw the air cleaner body from the carburettor. If necessary remove the ducting from the exhaust manifold shroud and front body panel (photos).
7   Refitting is a reversal of removal.

3   Air cleaner temperature control – testing

1   With the engine cold disconnect the ducting from the air cleaner inlet tube.
2   Look into the inlet tube and check that the control flap is fully shut onto the warm air port.
3   Start the engine and allow it to idle. Check that the flap is now fully open to admit warm air from the exhaust manifold shroud. If the flap does not fully open check the diaphragm unit and heat sensor as follows.
4   Disconnect the diaphragm vacuum pipe at the heat sensor and using a vacuum pump apply a vacuum of 100 mm (4.0 in) Kg. If the flap now opens, the heat sensor or vacuum line must be faulty. If the flap remains shut, the diaphragm unit or control flap is faulty (photos).
5   After completing the test reconnect the ducting.

4   Fuel pump – testing, removal, servicing and refitting

1   The fuel pump is located on the left-hand side of the engine next to the oil filter. To test its operation disconnect the outlet hose and hold a wad of rag near the pump (photo). Disconnect the low tension negative wire from the ignition coil.
2   Have an assistant spin the engine on the starter and check that well defined spurts of fuel are ejected from the fuel pump outlet.
3   If a pressure gauge is available the fuel pump can be checked more accurately. Twist connect it to the pump outlet. Do not disconnect the coil low tension wire. Start the engine and allow it to idle, then check that the delivery pressure is as given in the Specifications. Note that for the engine to run there must be sufficient fuel in the carburettor.
4   To remove the fuel pump disconnect and plug the inlet and outlet hoses.
5   Unscrew the two bolts and withdraw the pump from the cylinder block. Remove the gasket. If necessary extract the pushrod (photos).
6   Clean the exterior of the pump in paraffin and wipe dry. Clean all traces of gasket from the cylinder block and pump flange.
7   If the fuel pump has a removable cover, remove the screw and withdraw the cover and nylon mesh filter with seal (photos). Clean the filter, cover and pump in fuel. Locate the filter in the cover and fit the cover to the pump so that the pip and indentation are aligned. Tighten the screw.

3.4a Bottom view of air cleaner heat sensor

3.4b Top view of air cleaner heat sensor

3.4c Air cleaner temperature control diaphragm unit

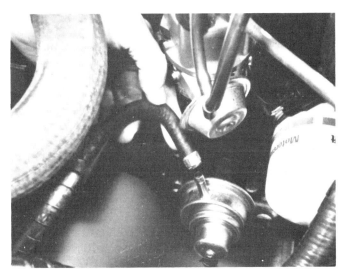

4.1 Disconnecting the fuel pump outlet hose

4.5a Removing the fuel pump ...

4.5b ... and pushrod

4.7a Removing the fuel pump cover, showing alignment indentations

4.7b Fuel pump cover with filter fitted

4.7c Fuel pump cover with filter removed

5.1 Fuel pressure regulator location

6.2 Removing the fuel tank filler cap

6.5 A fuel tank mounting bolt

6.6 Fuel tank retaining strap bolt

8   Refitting is a reversal of removal, but fit a new gasket and tighten the bolts to the specified torque. If necessary discard the crimped type hose clips and fit screw type clips.

5   Fuel pressure regulator – removal and refitting

1   The fuel pressure regulator is located on the left-hand side of the engine compartment (photo). Identify the three hoses then disconnect them from the regulator.
2   Remove the cross-head screws and withdraw the regulator from the engine compartment.
3   Refitting is a reversal of removal, but if necessary discard the crimped type hose clips and fit screw type clips.

6   Fuel tank – removal, servicing and refitting

Note: For safety the fuel tank must always be removed in a well ventilated area, never over a pit.

1   Disconnect the battery negative lead.
2   Remove the tank filler cap then syphon or pump out all the fuel (there is no drain plug) (photo).
3   From inside the filler cap recess remove the filler neck retaining screws.
4   Chock the front wheels then jack up the rear of the car and support on axle stands.
5   Unscrew the two mounting bolts from the left-hand side tank flange (photo).
6   Support the tank then remove the bolt from the retaining strap (photo). Unhook the strap from the underbody.
7   Lower the tank sufficiently to disconnect the wiring plugs from the sender unit.
8   Identify then disconnect and plug the fuel lines from the sender unit.
9   Withdraw the fuel tank from under the car.
10   Remove the sender unit with reference to Section 7.
11   Loosen the clips where necessary and remove the filler and ventilation pipes (photos). Remove the seal.
12   If the tank is contaminated with sediment or water, swill it out

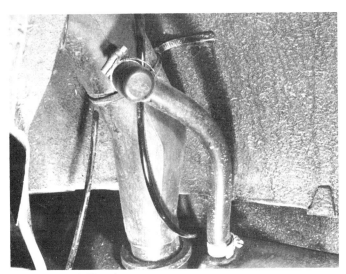

6.11a Fuel tank filler pipe

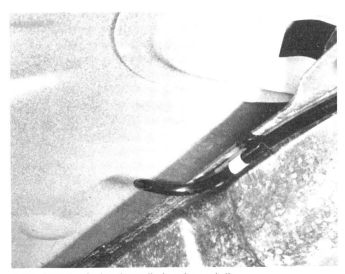

6.11b Showing fuel tank ventilation pipe and clip

with clean fuel. If the tank leaks or is damaged, it should be repaired by specialists or alternatively renewed. *Do not under any circumstances solder or weld a fuel tank.*

13 Refitting is a reversal of removal, but locate the ventilation pipe in the groove provided in the top of the tank. If necessary discard the crimped type hose clips and fit screw type clips.

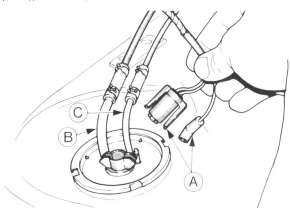

Fig. 3.1 Disconnecting the fuel tank sender unit wiring (A), outlet pipe (B) and inlet pipe (C) (Sec 6)

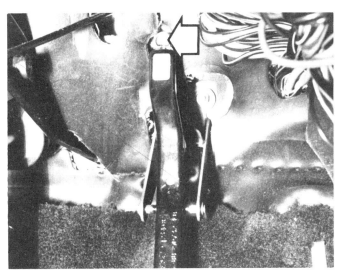

8.3 Accelerator pedal and cable location

7 Fuel gauge sender unit – removal and refitting

1 Remove the fuel tank as described in Section 6.
2 Using two crossed screwdrivers, turn the sender unit anti-clockwise and withdraw it from the tank.
3 Refitting is a reversal of removal, but always fit a new seal as the existing seal will have been distorted on removal. Refer to Section 6 when refitting the fuel tank.

8 Accelerator cable – removal, refitting and adjustment

1 Disconnect the battery negative lead.
2 Remove the panel from beneath the facia inside the car on the right-hand side.
3 Prise off the clip retaining the cable to the accelerator pedal, and unhook the cable (photo).
4 Working in the engine compartment release the cable from the bulkhead and pull it through.
5 Remove the air cleaner as described in Section 2.
6 Rotate the throttle lever segment to open the throttle then disconnect the inner cable from the segment or disconnect the inner cable as applicable (photo).

8.6 Disconnecting the inner cable from the throttle linkage (Weber 2V carburettor)

7   Prise the spring clip from the cable bracket using a screwdriver.

8   Depress the four plastic legs and withdraw the cable from the bracket (photo). If difficulty is experienced make up a tool as shown in Fig. 3.2 and push it onto the plastic fitting to depress the legs.

9   Refitting is a reversal of removal, but before refitting the air cleaner adjust the cable as follows. Using a broom or length of wood fully depress the accelerator pedal and retain it in this position. On automatic transmission models make sure that the downshift cable does not restrict the accelerator pedal movement. Unscrew the cable ferrule at the carburettor end until the throttle lever segment is fully open. Release the accelerator pedal then fully depress it again and check that the throttle lever segment is fully open.

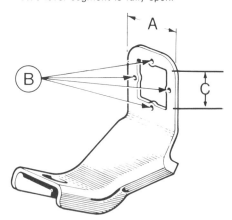

Fig. 3.2 Tool for removing the accelerator cable (Sec 8)

*A   25.4 mm (1.0 in)   B   Centre punch holes   C   16.0 mm ($^5/_8$ in)
                                                     square hole*

9   Accelerator pedal – removal and refitting

1   Disconnect the battery negative lead.

2   Remove the lower facia panel on the right-hand side.

3   Prise off the clip retaining the cable to the accelerator pedal, and unhook the cable.

4   Unscrew the retaining nuts, one inside the car and one inside the engine compartment, and withdraw the accelerator pedal.

5   Refitting is a reversal of removal, but adjust the accelerator cable as described in Section 8.

10   Carburettor – removal and refitting

1   Disconnect the battery negative lead.

2   Remove the air cleaner as described in Section 2.

3   Remove the filler cap from the cooling system expansion tank. If the engine is warm refer to Chapter 2 for safety precautions. After releasing the pressure refit the cap.

4   Identify the hoses for position then loosen the clips and disconnect the hoses from the automatic choke. Either plug the hoses or secure them with their ends facing upwards to prevent loss of coolant.

5   Disconnect the wire from the anti-dieselling valve on the VV carburettor only.

6   Disconnect the vacuum and fuel pipes (photo).

7   Disconnect the throttle linkage or cable as applicable (photo).

8   Unscrew the nuts and withdraw the carburettor from the inlet manifold (photos). Remove the gasket.

9   Refitting is a reversal of removal, but make sure that the mating faces are clean and always fit a new gasket. On the Weber carburettor make sure that the heat shield is correctly fitted. If necessary discard the crimped type hose clips and fit screw type clips, but make sure that they do not obstruct any surrounding component. Finally check and adjust the idling speed and mixture as described in Section 11.

11   Carburettor – slow running adjustment

1   Run the engine to normal operating temperature then stop it.

2   Connect a tachometer and, if available, an exhaust gas analyser to the engine.

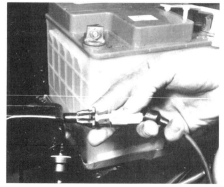

8.8 Disconnecting the accelerator outer cable from the bracket

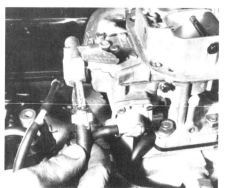

10.6 Disconnecting the fuel pipe

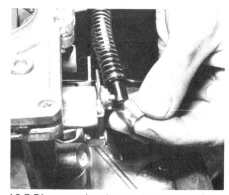

10.7 Disconnecting the accelerator cable (Ford VV carburettor)

10.8a Remove the retaining nuts (Ford VV carburettor) ...

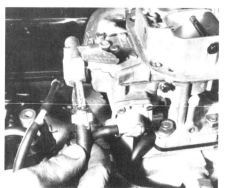

10.8b ... and withdraw the carburettor

10.8c Removing the carburettor (Weber 2V) – note the position of the heat shield

3 Run the engine at 3000 rpm for 30 seconds, then allow it to idle and note the idle speed and CO content.

4 Adjust the idle speed screw to give the specified idle speed.

5 Adjustment of the CO content (mixture) is not normally required during routine maintenance, but if the reading noted in paragraph 3 is not as given in the Specifications first remove the tamperproof plug. On the VV carburettor use a thin screwdriver, but on the Weber carburettor remove the air cleaner and use a tamperproof plug removal tool to extract the plug. Refit the air cleaner on the Weber carburettor.

6 Run the engine at 3000 rpm for 30 seconds then allow it to idle. Adjust the mixture screw within 10 to 30 seconds. If more time is required run the engine at 3000 rpm again for 30 seconds.

7 Adjust the idle speed if necessary and recheck the CO content.

8 Fit new tamperproof plugs. Note that it is not possible to adjust the idling mixture accurately without an exhaust gas analyser.

12 Ford variable venturi (VV) carburettor – general description

The Ford variable venturi carburettor is theoretically more efficient than fixed jet types due mainly to the improved fuel atomisation especially at low engine speeds and loads. The carburettor operates as follows.

Fuel is supplied to the carburettor via a needle valve which is actuated by the float. When the fuel level is low in the float chamber in the carburettor, the float drops and opens the needle valve. When the correct fuel level is reached the float will close the valve and shut off the fuel supply.

The float level on this type of carburettor is not adjustable since minor variations in the fuel level do not affect the performance of the carburettor. The valve needle is prevented from vibrating by means of a ball and light spring and to further ensure that the needle seals correctly it is coated in a rubber-like coating of Viton.

The float chamber is vented internally via the main jet body and carburettor air inlet, thus avoiding the possibility of petrol vapour escaping into the atmosphere.

The air/fuel mixture intake is controlled by the air valve which is opened or closed according to the operating demands of the engine. The valve is actuated by a diaphragm which opens or closes according to the vacuum supplied through the venturi between the air valve and the throttle butterfly. As the air valve and diaphragm are connected they open or close correspondingly.

When the engine is idling the air intake requirement is low and therefore the valve is closed, causing a high air speed over the main jet exit. However as the throttle plate is opened, the control vacuum (depression within the venturi) increases and is channelled to the diaphragm which then opens the air valve to balance the control spring and control vacuum.

When the throttle is opened further this equality of balance is maintained as the air valve is progressively opened to equalise the control spring and control vacuum forces throughout the speed range.

Fuel from the float chamber is drawn up the pick-up tube and then regulated through two jets and the tapered needle and into the engine. The vacuum within the venturi draws the fuel. This is shown in Fig. 3.6. At low engine speeds the needle taper enters the main jet to restrict the fuel demand. On acceleration and at high engine speeds the needle is withdrawn through the main jet by the action of the air valve to which it is attached. As the needle is tapered, the amount by which it is moved regulates the amount of fuel passing through the main jet.

The sonic idle system as used on other Ford fixed jet carburettors is also employed in the VV type, with 70% of the idle fuel mixture supplied via the sonic idle system and 30% from the main system. When idling, fuel is drawn through the main pick-up tube (Fig. 3.7), passes through the idle jet and then mixes with the air stream being supplied from the air bleed in the main jet body. The air/fuel mixture then passes on through the inner galleries at the mixture control screw which regulates the fuel supply at idle. This mixture then mixes with

Fig. 3.3 Idle speed (A) and mixture (B) adjusting screw locations on the Ford VV carburettor (Sec 11)

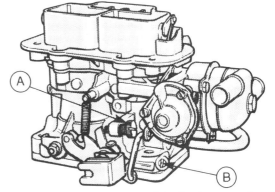

Fig. 3.4 Idle speed (A) and mixture (B) adjusting screw locations on the Weber 2V carburettor (Sec 11)

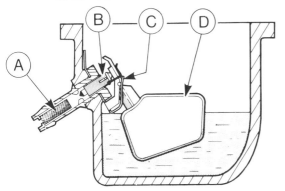

Fig. 3.5 Cross section of the float chamber on the Ford VV carburettor (Sec 12)

A	Filter	C	Pivot
B	Needle valve	D	Float

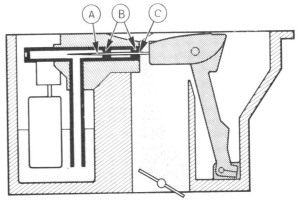

Fig. 3.6 Main jet system on the Ford VV carburettor (Sec 12)

A   Tapered metering rod
B   Main and secondary jets
C   Main fuel outlets

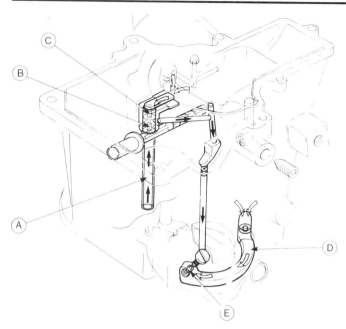

Fig. 3.7 Sonic idle system on the Ford VV carburettor (Sec 12)

A	Main pick up tube	D	By-pass gallery
B	Idle fuel jet	E	Sonic discharge tube
C	Idle air jet		

the air from the by-pass idle channel and finally enters the inlet manifold via the sonic discharge tube at an accelerated rate of flow.

Throttle actuation is via a progressive linkage which has a cam and roller mechanism. The advantage of this system is that a large initial throttle movement allows only a small throttle plate opening. As the throttle is opened up and approaches its maximum travel the throttle plate movement accelerates accordingly. This system aids economy, gives a good engine response through the range on smaller engines, and enables the same size of carburettor to be employed on other models in the range.

To counterbalance the drop in vacuum when initially accelerating, a restrictor is fitted into the air passage located between the control vacuum areas and the control diaphragm. This restrictor causes the valve to open slowly when an increase in air flow is made which in turn causes a higher vacuum for a brief moment in the main jet, caused by the increase in air velocity. This increase in vacuum causes the fuel flow to increase thus preventing a 'flat spot'. The large amounts of fuel required under heavy acceleration are supplied by the accelerator pump.

The accelerator pump injects fuel into the venturi direct when acceleration causes a drop in manifold vacuum. This richening of the mixture prevents engine hesitation under heavy acceleration. The accelerator pump is a diaphragm type and is actuated from vacuum obtained from under the throttle plate. During acceleration the vacuum under the throttle plate drops, the diaphragm return spring pushes the

diaphragm and the fuel in the pump is fed via the inner galleries through the one-way valve and into the venturi. The system incorporates a back bleeder and vacuum break air hole. Briefly explained, the back bleed allows any excess fuel vapour to return to the float chamber when prolonged idling causes the carburettor temperature to rise and the fuel in the accelerator pump reservoir to become overheated. The vacuum break air hole allows air into the pump outlet pipe to reduce the vacuum at the accelerator pump jet at high speed. Fuel would otherwise be drawn out of the accelerator pump system.

A fully automatic choke system is fitted incorporating a coolant operated bi-metallic spring. According to the temperature of the coolant, the spring in the unit opens or closes. This in turn actuates the choke mechanism, which consists of a variable needle jet and a variable supply of air. Fuel to the choke jet is fed from the main pick-up tube via the internal galleries within the main jet body. When the bi-metal spring is contracted (engine cold), it pulls the tapered needle from the jet to increase the fuel delivery rate. The spring expands as the engine warms up and the needle reduces the fuel supply as it re-enters the jet. The choke air supply is supplied via the venturi just above the throttle plate. The fuel mixes with the air in the choke air valve and is then delivered to the engine.

A choke pull-down system is employed whereby if the engine is under choke but is only cruising, ie not under heavy loading, the choke is released. This is operated by the vacuum piston which is connected to the choke spindle by levers.

Last but not least, an anti-dieselling valve is fitted on the outside of the body of the carburettor. This valve shuts off the fuel supply to the idle system when the engine is turned off and so prevents the engine running on or 'dieselling'. The solenoid valve is actuated electrically. When the ignition is turned off, it allows a plunger to enter and block the sonic discharge tube to stop the supply of fuel into the idle system. When the ignition is switched on the solenoid is actuated and the plunger is withdrawn from the tube.

13 Ford variable venturi (VV) carburettor – overhaul

Note: *Before attempting to overhaul a well worn carburettor, ensure that spares are available and reasonably priced. It may be both quicker and cheaper to obtain a complete carburettor on an exchange basis.*

1　Before dismantling the carburettor clean it off externally and prepare a suitable work space on the bench to lay out the respective components in order of appearance.
2　Unscrew and remove the seven carburettor cover retaining screws. Carefully lift the cover clear trying not to break the gasket. Remove the gasket (photo).
3　Drain any remaining fuel from the float chamber.
4　If the variable choke metering rod (or needle) is to be removed, prise the tamperproof plug from the body and insert a suitable screwdriver through the hole. Unscrew the metering rod and withdraw it. However note that the manufacturers do not recommend removing the rod. If the rod is damaged, the carburettor should be renewed.
5　To remove the main jet body, unscrew the four retaining screws (photo), and carefully lift the body clear, noting gasket. If the metering rod is still in position, retract it as far as possible from the jet, press the float down and carefully pull the jet body clear of the metering rod (photo). Great care must be taken here not to bend or distort the rod in any way.

13.2 Removing the carburettor cover (Ford VV carburettor)

13.5a Main jet body retaining screw locations (Ford VV carburettor)

13.5b Removing the main jet body (Ford VV carburettor)

Fig. 3.8 Exploded view of the Ford VV carburettor (Sec 13)

A	Throttle spindle	H	Air valve
B	Mixture screw	J	Choke assembly
C	By-pass leak adjuster	K	Bi-metal coil
D	Float	L	Vacuum diaphragm
E	Needle valve	M	Accelerator pump
F	Main jet body		diaphragm
G	Metering rod		

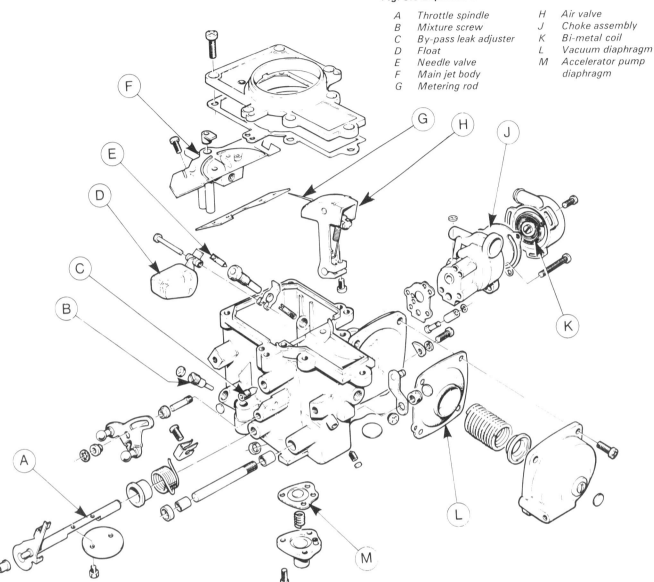

6   The accelerator pump outlet one-way valve ball and weight can now be extracted by inverting the carburettor body.

7   Withdraw the float pivot pin followed by the float and needle valve (photo).

8   Unscrew and remove the four screws retaining the control diaphragm housing. Carefully detach the housing, spring, and seat, taking care not to split or distort the diaphragm. Fold back the diaphragm rubber from the flange. Using a small screwdriver, prise free the retaining clip to release the diaphragm. Put the clip in a safe place to prevent it getting lost before reassembly (photos).

13.7 Float and needle valve (Ford VV carburettor)

13.8a Remove the circlip (Ford VV carburettor) ...

13.8b ... and detach the diaphragm

9 Now remove the accelerator pump by unscrewing the three retaining screws. Remove the housing, spring and diaphragm.

10 To remove the choke housing, note its positional markings, unscrew the retaining screws and carefully withdraw the housing (photos). Unscrew the solenoid unit.

11 The carburettor is now dismantled and the various components can be cleaned and inspected.

12 Check the body and components for signs of excessive wear and/or defects and renew as necessary. In particular inspect the main jet in the body. Excessive wear is present if the body is oval. Also pay particular attention to the air valve and linkage, the throttle plate (butterfly), its spindle and the throttle linkages for wear. The diaphragm rubber must be in good condition and not split or perished. Check also that the metering rod spring is correctly fitted to the air valve (Fig. 3.9). Renew all gaskets and seals during assembly and ensure that the mating surfaces are perfectly clean.

13 Commence assembly by refitting the accelerator pump. Locate the gasket face of the diaphragm towards the pump cover and when in position it must not be distorted at all. Fit the spring and cover and tighten the screws evenly.

14 Reconnect the diaphragm to the control linkage and retain by fitting the circlip., This is fiddly and requires a steady hand and a little patience. Check that the clip is fully engaged when in position. As the diaphragm is fitted ensure that the double holes on one corner align with the corresponding holes in the carburettor body (photo). With the diaphragm in position, relocate the housing and spring and insert the retaining screws to secure. Take care not to distort the diaphragm as the housing is tightened.

15 If removed, refit the mixture adjustment screw, but don't relocate the tamperproof plug yet as the mixture must be adjusted when the engine is restarted. Do not overtighten the screw! Back off the screw three full turns.

16 Insert the float needle, the float and the pivot pin. When installing the needle valve the spring-loaded ball must face towards the float.

17 Locate the accelerator pump ball and weight into the discharge gallery, fit a new gasket into position and then refit the main jet body. If the metering rod is already in position, retract and raise it to re-engage the main jet housing over the rod and then lower it into position. Do not force or bend the rod in any way during this operation. Tighten the jet body retaining screws. If the metering rod is still to be fitted, do not fully tighten the jet body retaining screws until after the jet is fitted and known to be centralised. If still to be fitted, slide the metering rod into position and screw it in until the rod shoulder aligns with the main body vertical face. Do not overtighten the rod. Should it bend during assembly, try re-centralising the main jet body, then tighten the retaining screws. Using a straight edge check that the main jet body alignment flanges are flush with the top face of the carburettor. Where applicable fit the plug to the metering rod extraction hole in the carburettor body.

18 Position the new top cover gasket in position and refit the top cover. Tighten the retaining screws progressively and evenly (photo).

19 The auto choke housing can be refitted to complete assembly. Ensure that the body alignment marks correspond and as it is fitted engage the bi-metal coil with the middle choke lever slot (photo). Use a new gasket. Refit the three retaining screws and before tightening check that the body alignment markings correspond.

13.10a Note the alignment marks (Ford VV carburettor) ...

13.10b ... then remove the automatic choke housing

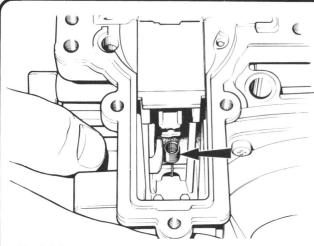

Fig. 3.9 Correct position of the metering rod spring (Sec 13)

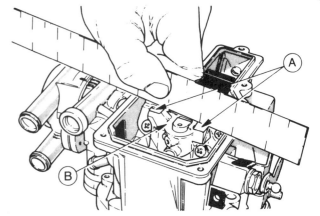

Fig. 3.10 Using a straight edge to check the alignment of the main jet body (Sec 13)

A   Alignment flanges   B   Main jet body

13.14 Align the diaphragm holes correctly (Ford VV carburettor)

13.18 Fit a new gasket before installing the main jet body (Ford VV carburettor)

13.19 Engage the automatic choke coil with the middle slot of the lever (Ford VV carburettor)

14 Weber twin venturi (2V) carburettor – general description

The Weber twin venturi carburettor is, of fixed jet, progressive choke type. The primary throttle valve operates alone up to three-quarter opening, from then on both throttle valves operate until at full throttle both are fully open. This arrangement ensures good economy during light acceleration and cruising, but also gives maximum power at full throttle. The primary throttle barrel and venturi diameters are smaller than their secondary counterparts.

The carburettor body comprises two castings which form the upper and lower bodies. The upper incorporates the float chamber cover, float pivot brackets, fuel inlet and return unions, gauze filter, spring-loaded needle valve, twin air intakes, choke plates and the section of the power valve controlled by vacuum. Incorporated in the lower body is the float chamber, accelerator pump, two throttle barrels and integral main venturis, throttle plates, spindles, levers, jets and the automatic choke. The accelerator pump discharges only into the primary barrel.

The automatic choke is operated by a bi-metallic coil which responds to the engine coolant temperature. At normal operating temperature the choke valves are fully open.

The carburettor incorporates idling, progression and main fuel supply circuits. The accelerator pump is of diaphragm type.

To stabilise idling when the engine is cold, the carburettor incorporates a low vacuum enrichment system which senses low

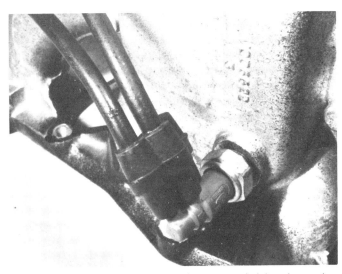

14.1a Low vacuum enrichment ported vacuum switch location on the inlet manifold (Weber 2V carburettor)

14.1b Low vacuum enrichment vacuum hose locations (Weber 2V carburettor)

vacuum fluctuations caused by temporary stalling and enriches the mixture to compensate. A ported vacuum switch (PVS), operated by engine coolant temperature, shuts the vacuum line when the engine reaches normal operating temperature (photos).

15 Weber twin venturi (2V) carburettor – overhaul

Note: *Before attempting to overhaul a well worn carburettor, ensure that spares are available and reasonably priced. It may be both quicker and cheaper to obtain a complete carburettor on an exchange basis. Refer to Section 16 for automatic choke overhaul.*

1   Before dismantling the carburettor clean it off externally and prepare a suitable work space on the bench to lay out the respective components in order of appearance.
2   Carefully prise out the U-clip with a screwdriver and disconnect the choke plate operating link (photo).
3   Remove the six screws and detach the carburettor upper body (photo).
4   Unscrew the brass nut located at the fuel intake and detach the fuel filter.
5   Tap out the float retaining pin, and detach the float and needle valve.
6   Remove the three screws and detach the power valve diaphragm assembly.
7   Unscrew the needle valve housing.
8   Unscrew the jets and jet plugs from the carburettor body, noting the positions in which they are fitted (photo).
9   Invert the carburettor body and, with the air correction jets removed, extract the emulsion tubes.
10 Remove four screws and detach the accelerator pump diaphragm, taking care that the spring is not lost (photo).
11 Remove the four screws and detach the low vacuum enrichment cover, spring and diaphragm (photo).
12 If necessary remove the mixture screw and spring noting the number of turns necessary to remove it. However it will first be necessary to remove the tamperproof plug using a special removal tool.
13 Clean the jets and passageways using clean, dry compressed air. Check the float assembly for signs of damage or leaking. Inspect the power valve and pump diaphragms and gaskets for splits or deterioration. Examine the mixture screw, needle valve seat and throttle spindle for signs of wear. Renew parts as necessary. Make sure that the carburettor body is serviceable.
14 Refit the accelerator pump spring, diaphragm, gasket and cover, and tighten the screws in diagonal sequence. Make sure that the diaphragm is not kinked.
15 Insert the emulsion tubes and refit all the jets and jet plugs.
16 Refit the low vacuum enrichment diaphragm, spring and cover and tighten the screws in diagonal sequence. Make sure that the diaphragm is not kinked.
17 Refit the mixture screw and spring in its original setting.
18 Refit the power valve diaphragm assembly, but before tightening the screws compress the return spring so that the diaphragm is not kinked. Check that the diaphragm is correctly seated by compressing the spring then blocking the air bleed with a finger. When the diaphragm is released it should stay down.
19 Refit the needle valve housing, needle valve and float, and tap in the retaining pin.

Float level adjustment

20 Hold the upper body vertically so that the needle valve is closed by the float, then measure the dimension from the face of the upper body to the base of the float (photo). Adjust to the specified figure by bending the tag.
21 Refit the fuel inlet filter and brass nut.
22 Position a new gasket and refit the carburettor upper body to the main body. Ensure that the choke link locates correctly through the upper body. Tighten the screws in diagonal sequence.
23 Reconnect the choke link and refit the U-circlip.

15.2 Removing the circlip from the choke link (Weber 2V carburettor)

15.3 Lower view of the upper body (Weber 2V carburettor)

15.8 View of the main body with upper body removed (Weber 2V carburettor)

15.10 Accelerator pump location (Weber 2V carburettor)

15.11 Low vacuum enrichment cover location (Weber 2V carburettor)

15.20 Checking the float level adjustment (Weber 2V carburettor)

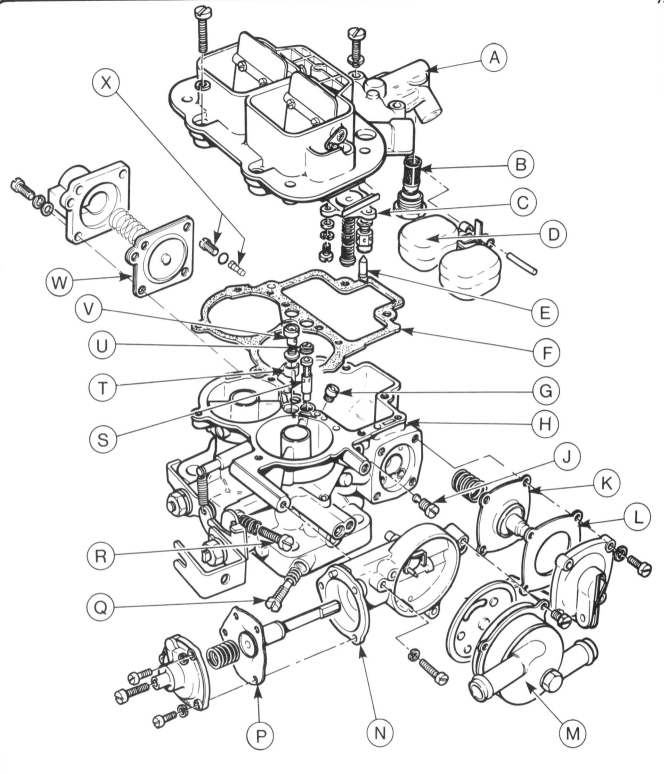

Fig. 3.11 Exploded view of the Weber 2V carburettor (Sec 15)

A	Top cover assembly	J	Primary idle jet assembly	N	Automatic choke assembly	U	Air correction jet
B	Fuel filter			P	Pull down diaphragm assembly	V	Accelerator pump outlet check ball valve assembly
C	Power valve assembly	K	Accelerator pump diaphragm	Q	Mixture screw	W	Low vacuum enrichment diaphragm
D	Float	L	Accelerator pump gasket	R	Idle speed screw		
E	Needle valve	M	Automatic choke bi-metal housing assembly	S	Emulsion tube	X	Secondary idle jet and holder
F	Gasket			T	Accelerator pump jet		
G	Main jet						
H	Main body assembly						

16 Weber twin venturi (2V) carburettor automatic choke – overhaul and adjustment

1 Disconnect the battery earth lead.
2 Remove the air cleaner, as described in Section 2.
3 Remove the filler cap from the cooling system expansion tank. If the engine is warm refer to Chapter 2 for safety precautions. After releasing the pressure refit the cap.
4 Loosen the clips and disconnect the hoses from the automatic choke. Either plug the hoses or secure them with their ends facing upwards to prevent loss of coolant.
5 Unscrew the centre bolt and remove the cover (photo).
6 Remove the three screws and withdraw the clamp ring, bi-metal coil bearing, and heat shield.
7 Remove the single U-circlip and disconnect the choke plate operating link.
8 Remove the three screws, disconnect the choke link at the operating lever and detach the choke assembly.
9 Remove the three screws and detach the vacuum pull-down diaphragm cover, spring and diaphragm assembly (photo).
10 Dismantle the remaining components if necessary with reference to Fig. 3.12.
11 Clean all the components and examine them for wear and damage. Check the diaphragm for splits. Do not use any lubricants during the reassembly procedure.

12 Reassemble the components to the main body as applicable.
13 Refit the vacuum pull-down diaphragm, spring and cover, but position the rod so that the diaphragm is not kinked before tightening the screws.
14 Check that the O-ring is located correctly on the body then locate the assembly on the carburettor with the link located through the upper body.
15 Locate the link on the choke lever and refit the circlip.

Vacuum pull-down

16 Fit an elastic band to the choke plate lever and position it so that the choke plates are held closed. Open, then release, the throttle to ensure that the choke plates close fully. Using a screwdriver inside the choke housing push the diaphragm rod against the spring tension onto its stop. Push the rod on its sleeve. The choke vacuum pull-down can now be measured using a twist drill between the bottom edge of the choke plate and the intake wall. If the dimension is not as given in the Specifications, remove the end plug from the diaphragm cover and use a thin screwdriver to reposition the adjusting screw. Refit the end plug and remove the elastic band on completion.

Choke phasing

17 Hold the throttle partly open and position the fast idle cam so that the fast idle adjusting screw locates on the upper section of the cam. Release the throttle to hold the cam in this position, then push the

16.5 Automatic choke cover and housing (Weber 2V carburettor)

16.9 Automatic choke vacuum pull-down cover (Weber 2V carburettor)

16.17a For the choke phasing adjustment (Weber 2V carburettor) position the fast idle screw on the cam high section ...

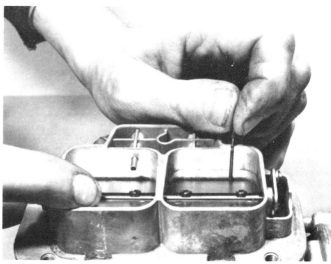

16.17b ... and check the gap with a twist drill

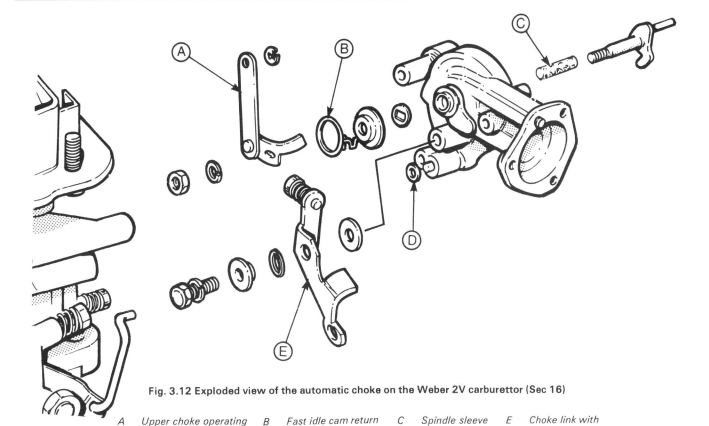

Fig. 3.12 Exploded view of the automatic choke on the Weber 2V carburettor (Sec 16)

A   Upper choke operating   B   Fast idle cam return   C   Spindle sleeve   E   Choke link with
      link   spring   D   Sealing ring   adjusting screw

Fig. 3.13 Choke phasing adjustment on the Weber 2V carburettor
(Sec 16)

A   Twist drill   B   Adjustment tag

choke plates down until the stop on the cam jams against the adjusting screw. Measure the clearance between the bottom edge of the choke plate and the intake wall using a twist drill (photos). If the dimension is not as given in the Specifications, bend the tag as necessary (Fig. 3.13).

18 Refit the internal heat shield ensuring that the hole in the cover locates correctly onto the peg cast in the housing.

19 Connect the bi-metal spring to the choke lever, position the choke housing and clamp ring and loosely fit the three retaining screws. Align the housing mark with the centre index then tighten the clamp screws.

20 Refit the choke cover together with a new gasket, then insert and tighten the centre bolt.

21 Reconnect the coolant hoses and tighten the clips.

22 Check and if necessary top up the cooling system with reference to Chapter 2.

23 Reconnect the battery earth lead.

Fast idle speed adjustment

24 Run the engine to normal operating temperature then switch off and connect a tachometer. Open the throttle partially, hold the choke plates fully closed then release the throttle so that the choke mechanism is held in the high cam/fast idle position. Release the choke plates, checking that they remain fully open (if they are not open, the assembly is faulty or the engine is not at operating temperature). Without touching the accelerator pedal, start the engine and adjust the fast idle screw as necessary to obtain the correct fast idle rpm.

25 Refit the air cleaner as described in Section 2.

17 Inlet manifold – removal and refitting

1   Disconnect the battery negative lead.

2   Drain the cooling system as described in Chapter 2.

3   Remove the air cleaner as described in Section 2.

4   Loosen the clips and disconnect the coolant hoses from the automatic choke cover and inlet manifold.

5   Note their position then disconnect the vacuum and fuel pipes from the carburettor and inlet manifold as necessary.

6   Disconnect the throttle linkage at the carburettor.

7   Disconnect the crankcase ventilation and brake servo vacuum pipes from the inlet manifold. Note that the brake servo pipe is attached with a union nut (photos).

8   Disconnect the accelerator cable with reference to Section 8 then unbolt the throttle lever mechanism from the inlet manifold as applicable (photo).

9   Disconnect the wire from the anti-dieselling valve on the VV carburettor only.

17.7a Disconnecting the crankcase ventilation hose from the inlet manifold

17.7b Disconnecting the brake servo pipe from the inlet manifold

17.8 Unbolting the throttle lever mechanism (Weber 2V carburettor)

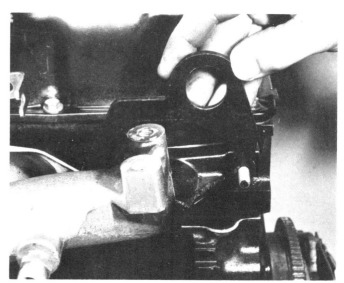

17.10 Rear engine hanger location

17.11a Removing the inlet manifold with carburettor ...

17.11b ... and the gasket

10 Unscrew the retaining nuts and bolts noting the location of the rear engine hanger (photo).

11 Withdraw the inlet manifold from the cylinder head and remove the gasket (photos).

12 Unscrew the nuts and withdraw the carburettor from the inlet manifold. Remove the gasket (photo).

13 Refitting is a reversal of removal, but first make sure that all mating faces are perfectly clean. Fit new gaskets and apply sealing compound either side of the water aperture. Fill the cooling system as described in Chapter 2 and refit the air cleaner as described in Section 2. Adjust the accelerator cable as described in Section 8. Adjust the slow running as described in Section 11.

18 Exhaust manifold – removal and refitting

1 Remove the air cleaner as described in Section 2.

2 Unscrew the nuts securing the downpipe to the manifold then lower the downpipe onto an axle stand and remove the gasket (photo).

3 Unbolt the hot air shroud from the exhaust manifold noting that the heater hose bracket is located on the front bolt (photos).

4 Disconnect the HT leads from the spark plugs.

5 Unscrew the retaining nuts noting the location of the front engine hanger (photos).

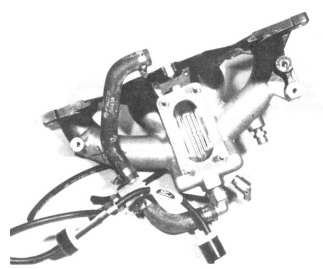

17.12 Inlet manifold with Weber 2V carburettor removed

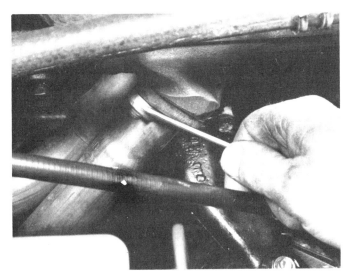

18.2 Removing the exhaust downpipe to manifold nuts

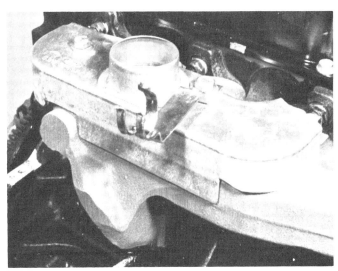

18.3a Exhaust manifold and hot air shroud

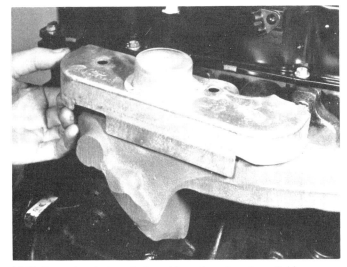

18.3b Removing the hot air shroud from the exhaust manifold

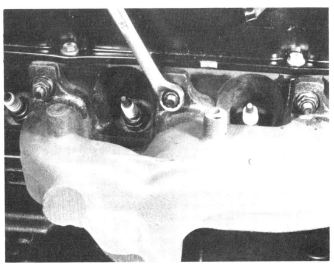

18.5a Removing the exhaust manifold nuts

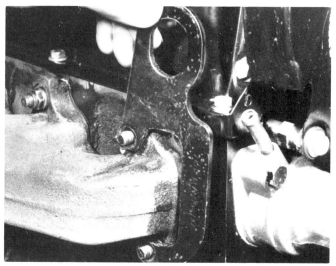

18.5b Front engine hanger location

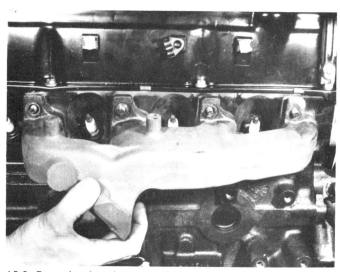

18.6a Removing the exhaust manifold ...

18.6b ... and gaskets

19.3a Lower view of exhaust downpipe to manifold nuts

19.3b Exhaust downpipe and flange gasket

6   Withdraw the exhaust manifold from the cylinder head and remove the gaskets (photos).

7   Refitting is a reversal of removal, but first make sure that all mating faces are perfectly clean. Fit new gaskets and tighten the nuts to the specified torque.

19 Exhaust system – checking, removal and refitting

1   The exhaust system should be examined for leaks, damage, and security every 12 000 miles (20 000 km). To do this, apply the handbrake and allow the engine to idle. Lie down on each side of the car in turn and check the full length of the exhaust system for leaks while an assistant temporarily places a wad of cloth over the tailpipe. If a leak is evident, stop the engine and use a proprietary repair kit to seal it. If the leak is excessive or damage is evident, renew the section. Check the rubber mountings for deterioration, and renew them if necessary.

2   To remove the exhaust system jack up the front and rear of the car and support it on axle stands.

3   Unscrew the nuts from the manifold flange, lower the exhaust downpipe and remove the gasket (photos).

4   Disconnect the mounting rubbers and lower the complete system from the car (photos).

19.4a Exhaust centre mounting

19.4b Exhaust rear mounting

19.7 Exhaust central flange joint

5   Refitting is a reversal of removal, but clean the flange mating faces and fit a new gasket. Tighten the flange nuts to the specified torque.
6   To fit a service tailpipe and silencer, use a hacksaw to cut the intermediate pipe at the point shown in Fig. 3.14. Apply exhaust sealer to the new tailpipe, push it onto the intermediate pipe and, after aligning it, fit the U-bolt and tighten the nuts to the specified torque.
7   Assuming that a service tailpipe and silencer have been fitted, the front silencer section can be renewed by removing the bolts from the central flanged joint and removing the nuts from the rear U-bolt (photo). Tap around the rear joint to release it. Refit in reverse order, but apply exhaust sealer to the joints. Tighten the nuts to the specified torque.
8   It is important that no part of the exhaust system is less than 25 mm (1.0 in) away from the underbody.

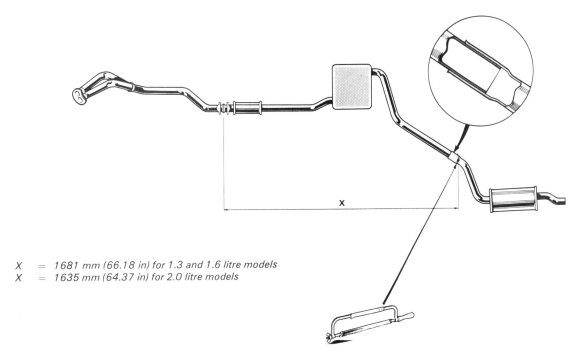

X = 1681 mm (66.18 in) for 1.3 and 1.6 litre models
X = 1635 mm (64.37 in) for 2.0 litre models

Fig. 3.14 Cutting point dimension when fitting a service tailpipe or front silencer section (Sec 19)

20 Fault diagnosis – fuel and exhaust systems

Symptom	Reason(s)
Excessive fuel consumption	Air cleaner element choked
	Leaks in carburettor, fuel tank or fuel lines
	Float level incorrect
	Mixture adjustment incorrect
	Excessively worn carburettor
Insufficient fuel supply or weak mixture	Faulty fuel pump
	Mixture adjustment incorrect
	Leaking inlet manifold or carburettor gasket
	Leaking fuel line
Difficulty starting	Faulty automatic choke or out of adjustment

Chapter 4 Ignition system

For modifications, and information applicable to later models, see Supplement at end of manual

Contents

Coil – description and testing 5
Distributor – removal, examination and refitting 3
Electronic module – removal and refitting 7
Fault diagnosis – ignition system 9
General description 1

Ignition timing – adjustment 4
Routine maintenance 2
Spark plugs and HT leads – general 6
Vacuum advance sustain valve and fuel trap – removal and
refitting 8

Specifications

| **System type** .... | Electronic, breakerless distributor with remote module and coil |

Coil

Output (minimum) .... 25.0 kilovolt
Primary winding resistance .... 0.72 to 0.88 ohm
Secondary winding resistance .... 4500 to 7000 ohm

Distributor

Rotor rotation .... Clockwise (viewed from above)
Dwell angle .... Automatically controlled by electronic module
Ignition timing advance control – 1.6 litre Economy ...... By electronic module
All models except 1.6 Economy .... Centrifugal weights on distributor shaft, and vacuum unit
Firing order .... 1 – 3 – 4 – 2

Ignition timing

Initial static (idling with vacuum hose(s) disconnected):
   1.3 litre .... 12° BTDC
   1.6 litre Economy .... 10° BTDC
   1.6 litre (except Economy) .... 12° BTDC
   2.0 litre .... 8° BTDC

Additional no-load advance (at 2000 rpm with vacuum hose(s) connected):

	Centrifugal	Vacuum
1.3 litre	4.5° to 11.8°	13.0° tp 19.0°
1.6 litre Economy	23.0° to 29.0°	(total electronic)
1.6 litre (except Economy)	10.5° to 17.2°	9.0° to 15.0°
2.0 litre	11.1° to 17.5°	8.0° to 14.0°

Total no-load advance including initial static (at 2000 rpm with vacuum hose(s) connected):
   1.3 litre .... 29.5° to 42.8°
   1.6 litre Economy .... 33.0° to 39.0°
   1.6 litre (except Economy) .... 31.5° to 44.2°
   2.0 litre .... 27.1° to 39.5°
Note: *Maximum vacuum advance occurs at 2000 rpm and above under no-load conditions*

Vacuum advance (maximum, additional to initial static):
   1.3 litre .... 13.0° to 19.0° at 199 mm (7.8 in) Hg
   1.6 litre Economy .... 8.0° to 13.0° at 200 mm (7.9 in) Hg
   1.6 litre (except Economy) .... 9.0° to 15.0° at 233 mm (9.2 in) Hg
   2.0 litre .... 8.0° to 14.0° at 263 mm (10.4 in) Hg

Spark plugs

Make and type:
   1.3 litre .... Motorcraft BF 22X
   1.6 litre (except Economy) .... Motorcraft BF 22X
   1.6 litre (Economy) .... Motorcraft BRF 22X
   2.0 litre .... Motorcraft BRF 32X
Electrode gap .... 0.75 mm (0.030 in)

HT leads

Maximum resistance per lead .... 30 000 ohm

Distributor magnetic trigger control (Bosch)

Resistance .... 1000 to 1200 ohm

Torque wrench settings

	lbf ft	Nm
Spark plugs	15 to 21	20 to 28

1 General description

An electronic ignition system is fitted, consisting of the battery, coil, distributor, remote module, and spark plugs. The distributor is driven by a skew gear on the auxiliary shaft located on the left-hand side of the engine.

In order that the engine can run correctly it is necessary for an electrical spark to ignite the fuel/air mixture in the combustion chamber at exactly the right moment in relation to engine speed and load. The ignition system is based on feeding low tension voltage from the battery to the coil where it is converted to high tension voltage. The high tension voltage is powerful enough to jump the spark plug gap in the cylinders many times a second under high compression pressures, providing that the system is in good condition. The low tension (or primary) circuit consists of the battery, the lead to the ignition switch, the lead from the ignition switch to the low tension or primary coil windings (terminal +/15) and also to the supply terminal on the electronic module, and the lead from the low tension coil windings (terminal -/1) to the control terminal on the electronic module. The low tension circuit is switched on and off by a magnetic trigger system in the distributor. The high tension (or secondary) circuit consists of the high tension or secondary coil windings, the HT lead from the coil to the distributor cap, the rotor arm, HT leads to the spark plugs, and the spark plugs.

The system functions in the following manner. Current flowing through the low tension coil windings produces a magnetic field around the high tension windings. As the engine rotates, the magnetic trigger system in the distributor produces an electrical impulse which is amplified in the electronic module and used to switch off the low tension circuit. The subsequent collapse of the magnetic field over the high tension windings produces high tension voltage which is then fed to the relevant spark plug via the distributor cap and rotor arm. The low tension circuit is automatically switched on again by the electronic module, to allow the magnetic field to build up again before the firing of the next spark plug. The ignition is advanced and retarded automatically to ensure that the spark occurs at the correct instant in relation to the engine speed and load. On the 1.6 litre Economy engine this function is carried out electronically by the module which is programmed to respond to engine speed and thirty-two different vacuum input signals. On all other engines the ignition advance and retard is controlled by the conventional method using centrifugal bobweights and a vacuum unit in the distributor. The centrifugal mechanism advance rotates the trigger arm or vane clockwise in relation to the pick-up sensor. The vacuum advance system rotates the pick-up sensor anti-clockwise, the effect in both cases being to advance the ignition timing.

Two types of magnetic trigger system are used in the distributor. The 1.6 litre Economy engines are fitted with the Hall effect type where a vane, incorporating four slots, rotates between the permanent

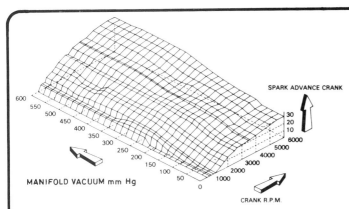

Fig. 4.1 Three dimensional ignition chart for the 1.6 litre Economy engine (Sec 1)

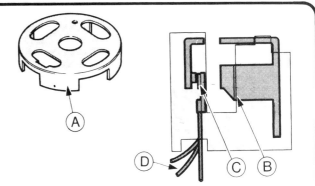

Fig. 4.2 Trigger components in the Lucas Hall Effect distributor (Sec 1)

A   Vane   *C   Sensor*
B   Permanent magnet   *D   Wires*

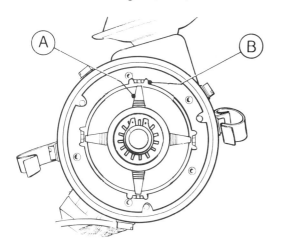

Fig. 4.3 Magnetic reluctance components in the Bosch distributor (Sec 1)

A   Trigger rotor   *B   Stator pick-up post*

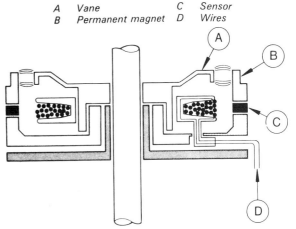

Fig. 4.4 Cross section diagram of the Bosch magnetic reluctance system (Sec 1)

A   Trigger rotor   *C   Permanent magnet*
B   Stator pick-up post *D   Wires*

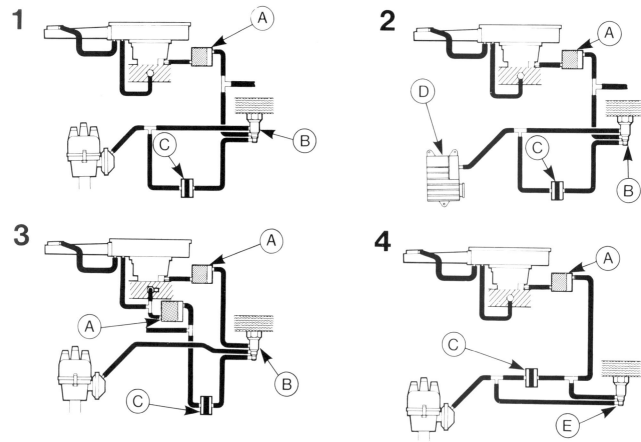

Fig. 4.5 Vacuum sustain valve system (Sec 1)

1	1.3 and 1.6 litre engines with manual gearbox	*engines*	A	Fuel trap
		3 1.6 litre engines with automatic transmission	B	Temperature controlled vacuum switch (3 port)
2	1.6 litre Economy	4 2.0 litre engines	C	Sustain valve

1   1.3 and 1.6 litre
     engines with manual   *engines*   A   Fuel trap   D   Electronic module
     gearbox   3   1.6 litre engines with   B   Temperature controlled   E   Temperature controlled
2   1.6 litre Economy   automatic transmission   vacuum switch (3 port)   vacuum switch (2 port)
                           4   2.0 litre engines   C   Sustain valve

magnet and pick-up sensor. All other engines are fitted with the magnetic reluctance type where a trigger rotor, incorporating four arms, rotates between a stator with four pick-up posts. With both types an electrical impulse is induced when the magnetic field is at a maximum.

On all engines the vacuum advance system incorporates a sustain valve which effectively prolongs the vacuum advance during the engine warm up period by means of a coolant temperature controlled vacuum switch (see Fig. 4.5).

When working on the electronic ignition system remember that the high tension voltage can be considerably higher than on a conventional system and in certain circumstances could prove fatal. Depending on the position of the distributor trigger components it is also possible for a single high tension spark to be generated simply by knocking the distributor with the ignition switched on. It is therefore important to keep the ignition system clean and dry at all times, and to make sure that the ignition switch is off when working on the engine.

2 Routine maintenance

1   Every 12 000 miles (20 000 km) the spark plugs should be renewed and the gaps checked in accordance with the information given in the Specifications.
2   Every 24 000 miles (40 000 km) remove the distributor cap and HT leads and wipe them clean. Also wipe clean the coil tower and make sure that the plastic safety cover is securely fitted where applicable. Remove the rotor arm then visually check the distributor cap, rotor arm, and HT leads for hairline cracks and signs of arcing. Where applicable, apply two or three drops of engine oil to the recess

in the top of the distributor spindle. When refitting the distributor cap, check that the ends of the HT leads are fitted securely to the cap, plugs, and coil. Also make sure that the spring tensioned carbon brush in the centre of the distributor cap moves freely, and that the HT segments are not worn excessively (photo).

2.2 Showing HT segments and spring tensioned carbon brush in the distributor cap

3 Distributor – removal, examination and refitting

Note: *During manufacture the engine ignition timing is set using a microwave process, and sealant applied to the distributor clamp bolt. Removal of the distributor should be avoided except where excessive bearing wear has occurred due to high mileage or during major engine overhaul.*

1 Disconnect the battery negative lead.

2 Disconnect the HT leads from the spark plugs by pulling on the connectors, not the leads. Note that the location of No 1 HT lead is marked on the distributor cap by a small indentation. The remaining HT lead locations are shown in Fig. 4.6.

3 On the Bosch distributor (red cap) prise away the spring clips with a screwdriver and remove the distributor cap (photo).

4 On the Lucas distributor (blue cap) remove the crosshead screws and lift off the distributor cap.

5 Pull the HT lead from the coil, slide the rubber HT lead holder from the valve cover clip, and withdraw the distributor cap (photos).

6 On the Bosch distributor disconnect the vacuum advance pipe (photo).

7 Turn the engine so that the specified BTDC notch on the crankshaft pulley is aligned with the timing pointer on the timing cover. Use a socket on the crankshaft pulley bolt to turn the engine.

8 On the Bosch distributor pull off the rotor arm and remove the dust cover. Then refit the rotor arm and check that it is pointing towards the scribed line on the body rim (photo).

9 On the Lucas distributor check that the oblong cut-out in the vane is aligned with the stator sensor (Fig. 4.8).

10 Disconnect the distributor multi-plug by depressing the spring tensioned plates (photo).

11 Mark the distributor body and cylinder block in relation to each other.

12 Scrape the sealant from the distributor clamp bolt then unscrew and remove the bolt and clamp (photo).

13 Withdraw the distributor from the engine (photo). As it is removed it will be noticed that the rotor arm will turn clockwise due to the skew gear drive. Mark the new position of the rotor arm on the body rim.

14 Check the distributor spindle for excessive side-to-side movement. If evident, the distributor must be renewed as it is not possible to obtain individual components.

15 To refit the distributor, first check that the timing marks on the crankshaft pulley and timing cover are still aligned.

16 On the Bosch distributor turn the rotor arm to the position shown in Fig. 4.9. This position is approximately 40° clockwise from the scribed line on the body rim and should coincide with the mark made in paragraph 13 (photo).

17 On the Lucas distributor align the rotor arm with the mark made in paragraph 13 which should be approximately 40° clockwise from the position where the oblong cut-out in the vane aligns with the stator sensor.

18 Hold the distributor directly over the aperture in the cylinder block with the previously made marks aligned, then lower it into position. As the skew gear drive meshes, the rotor arm will turn anti-clockwise.

19 With the distributor fully entered and the body mark aligned with the mark on the block, check that on the Bosch distributor the rotor arm is pointing towards the scribed line on the body rim. On the Lucas distributor the oblong cut-out in the vane is aligned with the stator sensor.

20 On the Bosch distributor the rotor arm should point away from the engine at 90° to the centre line of the crankshaft. Also with the rotor arm and dust cover removed, the trigger rotor arms should be aligned with the stator pick-up posts when the engine is turned to align the initial static advance timing marks (photo).

21 On the Lucas distributor the multi-plug socket should be towards the inlet manifold at an angle of 45° to the cylinder block.

22 Refit the clamp, then insert and tighten the bolt.

23 Refit the multi-plug and on the Bosch distributor reconnect the vacuum advance pipe and refit the rotor arm and dust cover.

24 Refit the distributor cap and reconnect the HT leads to the spark plugs and coil.

25 Reconnect the battery negative lead.

26 Check and adjust the ignition timing as described in Section 4.

3.3 A distributor cap spring clip (Bosch)

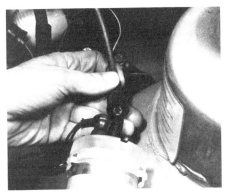

3.5a Removing the main feed HT lead from the coil

3.5b Removing the HT lead rubber holder

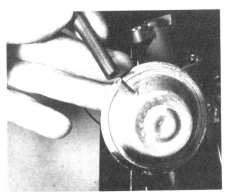

3.6 Disconnecting the vacuum advance pipe

3.8 Rotor arm aligned with the BTDC mark (Bosch)

3.10 Disconnecting the wiring multi-plug

3.12 Unscrewing the distributor clamp bolt

3.13 Removing the distributor

3.16 Upper view of Bosch distributor rotor arm alignment prior to installation

3.20 Trigger rotor arm alignment on the Bosch distributor at initial static advance

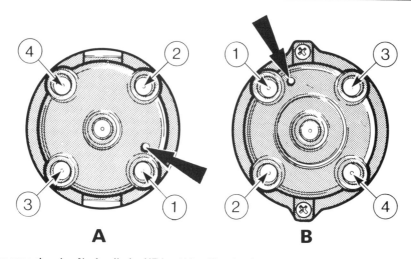

Fig. 4.6 Distributor caps showing No 1 cylinder HT lead identification (arrowed) and remaining HT lead locations (Sec 3)

    A   Bosch distributor cap   B   Lucas distributor cap

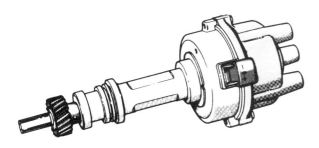

Fig. 4.7 Lucas Hall Effect distributor (Sec 3)

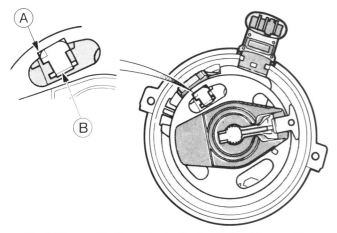

Fig. 4.8 Lucas distributor in the No 1 cylinder firing position (Sec 3)

A   Vane cut-out   B   Stator sensor

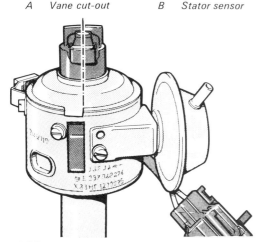

Fig. 4.9 Alignment of the Bosch distributor rotor arm prior to installation (Sec 3)

4   Ignition timing – adjustment

Note: *During manufacture the engine ignition timing is set using a microwave process, and sealant applied to the distributor clamp bolt. Because the electronic components require no maintenance, checking the ignition timing does not constitute part of the routine maintenance and the procedure is therefore only necessary after removal and refitting of the distributor.*

1   Disconnect and plug the vacuum pipe(s) at the distributor or electronic module as applicable.

2   Wipe clean the crankshaft pulley notches and timing cover pointer. If necessary, use white paint or chalk to highlight the marks.

3   Connect a stroboscipic timing light to the engine in accordance with the manufacturer's instructions (usually to No 1 spark plug HT lead).

4   Connect a tachometer to the engine in accordance with the manufacturer's instructions.

5   Start the engine and run it to normal operating temperature, then allow it to idle at the recommended idling speed (see Chapter 3).

6   Point the timing light at the timing marks on the crankshaft pulley and check that the appropriate initial static timing notch is in alignment with the pointer on the timing cover. Note that the first heavy notch indicates TDC (top dead centre) and the remaining heavy notches are at 4° (also 4 mm) intervals (photo).

7   If adjustment is necessary (ie the appropriate notch is not aligned with the pointer) loosen the distributor clamp bolt and turn the distributor body anti-clockwise to advance the timing or clockwise to retard the timing. As a safety precaution the engine should be switched off before adjusting the distributor. Note that the distributor movement will be half of the crankshaft movement (eg adjustment of 5° on the crankshaft will require the distributor to be turned 2.5°). Tighten the clamp bolt when the setting is correct.

8   On engines fitted with the Bosch distributor run the engine at 2000 rpm and check that the *additional* centrifugal advance is within the limits given in Specifications.

9   On *all* engines reconnect the vacuum pipe(s) then run the engine at 2000 rpm and check that the *total* advance is within the limits given in Specifications.

10   If the results obtained from paragraphs 8 and 9 are correct, it can be assumed that the vacuum advance is also correct. If the result of paragraph 8 is correct, but the result of paragraph 9 is below limits, check the vacuum hoses for condition and security. On the Bosch distributor also check the vacuum unit. If a vacuum pump and gauge are available, check that the maximum vacuum advance is within the limits given in Specifications.

11   Switch off the engine and remove the tachometer and timing light.

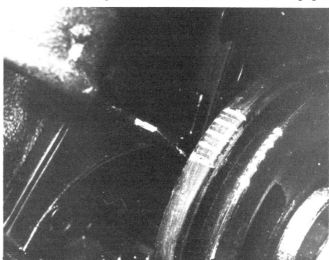

4.6 Showing crankshaft pulley timing marks (at TDC) and timing cover pointer

5   Coil – description and testing

1   The coil is located on the left-hand side of the engine compartment and is retained by a metal strap (photo). It is of high output type and the HT tower should be kept clean at all times to prevent possible arcing. Bosch and Femsa coils are fitted with protective plastic covers and Polmot coils are fitted with an internal fusible link.

2   To ensure the correct HT polarity at the spark plugs, the LT coil leads must always be connected correctly. The black lead must always be connected to the terminal marked +/15, and the green lead to the terminal marked -/1. Incorrect connections can cause bad starting, misfiring, and short spark plug life.

3   To test the coil first disconnect the LT and HT leads. Connect an ohmmeter between both LT terminals and check that the primary winding resistance is as given in the Specifications. Connect the ohmmeter between the HT terminal (terminal 4) and either LT terminal and check that the secondary winding resistance is as given in the Specifications. Reconnect the leads after making the test.

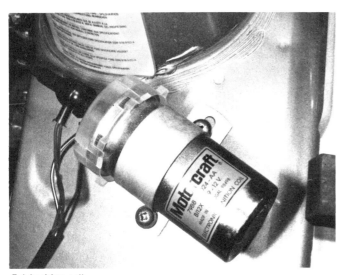

5.1 Ignition coil

6.3a Using a plug spanner ...

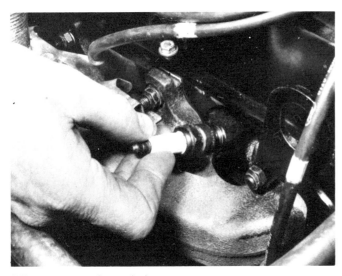

6.3b ... to remove the spark plugs

6 Spark plugs and HT leads – general

1   The correct functioning of the spark plugs is vital for the correct running and efficiency of the engine. The spark plugs should be renewed every 12 000 miles (20 000 km). However, if misfiring or bad starting is experienced in the service period, they must be removed, cleaned, and regapped.

2   To remove the spark plugs, disconnect the HT leads by pulling on the connectors, not the leads. If necessary identify the leads for position (see Fig. 4.6). For better access, remove the air cleaner and or inlet hose with reference to Chapter 3.

3   Clean the area around each spark plug using a small brush, then using a plug spanner (preferably with a rubber insert) unscrew and remove the plugs (photos). Cover the spark plug holes with a clean rag to prevent the ingress of any foreign matter.

4   The condition of the spark plugs will tell much about the overall condition of the engine.

5   If the insulator nose of the spark plug is clean and white, with no deposits, this is indicative of a weak mixture, or too hot a plug. (A hot plug transfers heat away from the electrode slowly – a cold plug transfers it away quickly).

6   If the tip and insulator nose is covered with hard black-looking deposits, then this is indicative that the mixture is too rich. Should the plug be black and oily, then it is likely that the engine is fairly worn, as well as the mixture being too rich.

7   If the insulator nose is covered with light tan to greyish brown deposits, then the mixture is correct and it is likely that the engine is in good condition.

8   If there are any traces of long brown tapering stains on the outside of the white portion of the plug, then the plug will have to be renewed, as this shows that there is a faulty joint between the plug body and the insulator, and compression is being lost.

9   Plugs should be cleaned by a sand blasting machine, which will free them from carbon more thoroughly than cleaning by hand. The machine may also test the condition of the plugs under compression. Any plug that fails to spark at the recommended pressure should be renewed.

10 The spark plug gap is of considerable importance, as, if it is too large or too small, the size of the spark and its efficiency will be seriously impaired. The spark plug gap should be set to the figure given in the Specifications at the beginning of this Chapter. To set it, measure the gap with a feeler gauge, and then bend open, or close the *outer* plug electrode until the correct gap is achieved. The centre electrode should *never* be bent as this may crack the insulation and cause plug failure, if nothing worse.

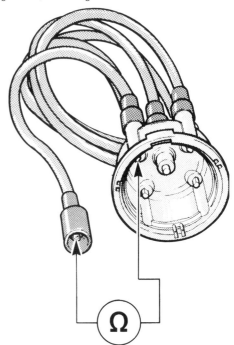

Fig. 4.10 Method of testing an HT lead with an ohmmeter (Sec 6)

Measuring plug gap. A feeler gauge of the correct size (see ignition system specifications) should have a slight 'drag' when slid between the electrodes. Adjust gap if necessary

Adjusting plug gap. The plug gap is adjusted by bending the earth electrode inwards, or outwards, as necessary until the correct clearance is obtained. Note the use of the correct tool

Normal. Grey-brown deposits, lightly coated core nose. Gap increasing by around 0.001 in (0.025 mm) per 1000 miles (1600 km). Plugs ideally suited to engine, and engine in good condition

Carbon fouling. Dry, black, sooty deposits. Will cause weak spark and eventually misfire. Fault: over-rich fuel mixture. Check: carburettor mixture settings, float level and jet sizes; choke operation and cleanliness of air filter. Plugs can be re-used after cleaning

Oil fouling. Wet, oily deposits. Will cause weak spark and eventually misfire. Fault: worn bores/piston rings or valve guides; sometimes occurs (temporarily) during running-in period. Plugs can be re-used after thorough cleaning

Overheating. Electrodes have glazed appearance, core nose very white — few deposits. Fault: plug overheating. Check: plug value, ignition timing, fuel octane rating (too low) and fuel mixture (too weak). Discard plugs and cure fault immediately

Electrode damage. Electrodes burned away; core nose has burned, glazed appearance. Fault: pre-ignition. Check: as for 'Overheating' but may be more severe. Discard plugs and remedy fault before piston or valve damage occurs

Split core nose (may appear initially as a crack). Damage is self-evident, but cracks will only show after cleaning. Fault: pre-ignition or wrong gap-setting technique. Check: ignition timing, cooling system, fuel octane rating (too low) and fuel mixture (too weak). Discard plugs, rectify fault immediately

11 Before fitting the spark plugs check that the threaded connector sleeves are tight and that the plug exterior surfaces are clean. As the plugs incorporate taper seats also make sure that the 18 mm threads and seats are clean.

12 Screw in the spark plugs by hand then tighten them to the specified torque. *Do not exceed the torque figure.*

13 Push the HT leads firmly onto the spark plugs and where applicable refit the air cleaner.

14 The HT leads and distributor cap should be cleaned and checked at the intervals given in Section 2. To test the HT leads remove them together with the distributor cap as described in Section 3 then connect an ohmmeter to each end of the leads and the appropriate terminal within the cap in turn. If the resistance is greater than the maximum given in the Specifications, check that the lead connection in the cap is good before renewing the lead.

---

7 Electronic module – removal and refitting

Note: *Do not run the engine with the module detached from the body panel as the body acts as an effective heat sink and therefore damage may occur through internal overheating.*

1 Disconnect the battery negative lead.

2 Disconnect the multi-plug from the module. Pull on the multi-plug and not on the wiring (photo).

3 On 1.6 litre Economy models disconnect the vacuum pipe.

4 Remove the crosshead screws and withdraw the module. Note on 1.6 litre Economy models that the coil strap is located on top of the module bracket.

4 Refitting is a reversal of removal, but make sure that the underside of the module and the corresponding area of the body panel are clean.

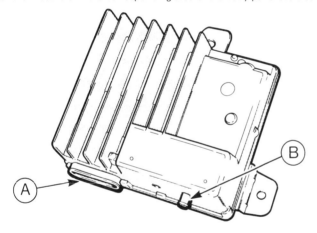

Fig. 4.11 Electronic module fitted to 1.6 litre Economy engines (Sec 7)

| A | Multi-plug socket | B | Inlet manifold vacuum pipe connection |

---

8 Vacuum advance sustain valve and fuel trap – removal and refitting

1 If the fuel trap is to be removed, first remove the air cleaner as described in Chapter 3.

2 Note the fitted position of the unit then disconnect the vacuum pipes and withdraw the unit.

3 Refitting is a reversal of removal. On the fuel trap, the black side (marked CARB) must face the carburettor and the white side (marked DIST) must face the distributor. On the sustain valve the white side (marked VAC) must face the coolant temperature controlled vacuum switch, and the coloured side (marked DIST) must face the distributor. The fuel trap pipe should be routed over the top of the carburettor automatic choke housing.

---

9 Fault diagnosis – ignition system

The electronic ignition fitted is far less likely to cause trouble than the contact breaker type fitted to many cars, largely because the low

7.2 Ignition electronic module location

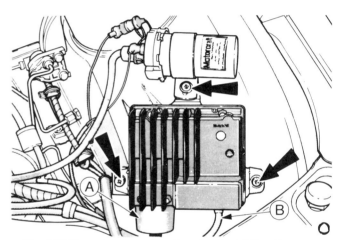

Fig. 4.12 Mounting screw locations for the 1.6 litre Economy engine electronic module (Sec 7)

| A | Multi-plug | B | Vacuum pipe |

tension circuit is electronically controlled. However the high tension circuit remains identical and therefore the associated faults are the same. There are two main symptoms indicating ignition faults. Either the engine will not start or fire, or the engine is difficult to start and misfires. If it is a regular misfire, ie the engine is only running on two or three cylinders, the fault is almost sure to be in the secondary, or high tension circuit. Loss of power and overheating, apart from incorrect carburettor settings, are normally due to incorrect ignition timing.

Engines fails to start

1 If the starter motor fails to turn the engine check the battery and starter motor with reference to Chapter 10.

2 Disconnect an HT lead from any spark plug and hold the end of the cable approximately 5 mm (0.2 in) away from the cylinder head using *well insulated pliers*. While an assistant spins the engine on the starter motor, check that a regular blue spark occurs. If so, remove, clean, and re-gap the spark plugs as described in Section 6.

3 If no spark occurs, disconnect the main feed HT lead from the distributor cap and check for a spark as in paragraph 2. If sparks now occur, check the distributor cap, rotor arm, and HT leads as described in Sections 2 and 6, and renew them as necessary.

4 If no sparks occur check the resistance of the main feed HT lead as described in Section 6 and renew as necessary. Should the lead be serviceable check that all wiring and multi-plugs are secure on the electronic module and distributor.

5 Disconnect the wire to the coil terminal marked +/15 and connect a voltmeter or 12 volt test lamp between the wire and an earth point.

With the ignition switched on (position II), battery voltage should be registered or the testlamp should light. If not, check the ignition switch and wiring with reference to Chapter 10.

6   Disconnect both wiring connectors from the coil LT terminals and connect a 12 volt, 21 watt test bulb between the connectors. Spin the engine on the starter and check that the bulb flashes. If so, the coil is proved faulty and should be renewed.

7   If the bulb does not flash proceed as follows.

Bosch distributor (ie all models except 1.6 litre Economy)

Disconnect the distributor multi-plug and connect an ohmmeter between the two parallel pins. If the resistance is not as given in the Specifications, renew the distributor complete.

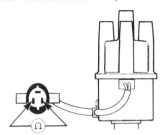

Fig. 4.13 Method of checking the resistance of the Bosch distributor trigger coil (Sec 9)

Lucas distributor (ie 1.6 litre Economy models)

Disconnect the distributor multi-plug and connect it to a substitute distributor. If the bulb flashes when the substitute distributor shaft is rotated clockwise (viewed from the top), renew the existing distributor complete.

8   If the distributor is not proved faulty as a result of the test in paragraph 7, renew the electronic module as described in Section 7,

then spin the engine on the starter and check that the test bulb flashes as in paragraph 6.

9   Remove the test bulb and reconnect the wiring to the coil.

10   The engine will now start.

Engine misfires

11   If the engine misfires regularly, run it at a fast idling speed. Pull off each of the plug HT leads in turn and listen to the note of the engine. *Hold the plug leads with a well insulated pair of pliers as protection against a shock from the HT supply.*

12   No difference in engine running will be noticed when the lead from the defective circuit is removed. Removing the lead from one of the good cylinders will accentuate the misfire.

13   Remove the plug lead from the end of the defective plug and hold it about 5 mm (0.2 in) away from the cylinder head. Restart the engine. If the sparking is fairly strong and regular, the fault must lie in the spark plug.

14   The plug may be loose, the insulation may be cracked, or the points may have burnt away, giving too wide a gap for the spark to jump. Worse still, one of the points may have broken off. Either renew the plug, or clean it, reset the gap, and then test it.

15   If there is no spark at the end of the plug lead, or if it is weak and intermittent check the HT lead from the distributor to the plug. If the insulation is cracked or perished or if its resistance is incorrect, renew the lead. Check the connections at the distributor cap.

16   If there is still no spark, examine the distributor cap carefully for tracking. This can be recognised by a very thin black line running between two or more electrodes, or between an electrode and some other part of the distributor. These lines are paths which now conduct electricity across the cap, thus letting it run to earth. The only answer in this case is a new distributor cap. Tracking will also occur if the inside or outside of the distributor cap is damp. If this is evident use a proprietary water repellent spray or alternatively thoroughly dry out the cap.

Chapter 5 Clutch

For modifications, and information applicable to later models, see Supplement at end of manual

Contents

Fault diagnosis – clutch 8
General description 1
Clutch – inspection 5
Clutch – refitting 7

Clutch – removal 4
Clutch cable – removal and refitting 3
Clutch pedal – removal, overhaul and refitting 2
Clutch release bearing and arm – removal and refitting 6

Specifications

Clutch type .... Single dry plate, diaphragm spring, cable operated

Clutch plate diameter
1.3/1.6 litre .... 190.5 mm (7.5 in)
2.0 litre .... 215.9 mm (8.5 in)

Clutch plate lining thickness (new) .... 3.75 to 3.95 mm (0.148 to 0.156 in)

Torque wrench settings	lbf ft	Nm
Pressure plate	15 to 18	20 to 25

1 General description

The clutch is of single dry plate type with a diaphragm spring pressure plate. The unit is dowelled and bolted to the rear face of the flywheel.

The clutch plate (or disc) is free to slide along the splined first motion shaft and is held in position between the flywheel and the pressure plate by the pressure of the pressure plate spring. Friction lining material is riveted to the clutch plate and it has a spring cushioned hub to absorb transmission shocks and to help ensure a smooth take off.

The circular diaphragm spring is mounted on shoulder pins and held in place in the cover by two fulcrum rings. The spring is also held to the pressure plate by three spring steel clips which are riveted in position.

The clutch is actuated by a cable controlled by the clutch pedal. Wear of the friction linings is compensated for by an automatic pawl and quadrant adjuster on the top of the clutch pedal. The clutch release mechanism consists of a ball bearing which slides on a guide sleeve at the front of the gearbox, and a release arm which pivots inside the clutch bellhousing.

Depressing the clutch pedal actuates the clutch release arm by means of the cable. The release arm pushes the release bearing forwards to bear against the release fingers so moving the centre of the diaphragm spring inwards. The spring is sandwiched between two annular rings which act as fulcrum points. As the centre of the spring is pushed in, the outside of the spring is pushed out, so moving the pressure plate backwards and disengaging the pressure plate from the clutch plate.

When the clutch pedal is released the diaphragm spring forces the pressure plate into contact with the friction linings on the clutch plate and at the same time pushes the clutch plate a fraction of an inch forwards on its splines so engaging the clutch plate with the flywheel. The clutch plate is now firmly sandwiched between the pressure plate and the flywheel so the drive is taken up.

2 Clutch pedal – removal, overhaul and refitting

This procedure applies to LHD vehicles. For RHD vehicles the procedure is similar to that described for the Sapphire (Chapter 13, Section 10).

1   Disconnect the clutch cable from the release arm and clutch pedal as described in Section 3, paragraphs 1 to 7 inclusive.

2   Prise the spring clip from the end of the pedal shaft and remove the spacer washer(s).

3   Withdraw the pedal complete with automatic adjuster from the shaft.

4   Prise the bushes from each side of the pedal and extract the toothed segment. Unhook the spring.

5   Prise one of the clips from the pawl shaft, withdraw the shaft and remove the pawl and spring.

6   Clean all the components and examine them for wear and damage. Renew them as necessary.

7   Lubricate the bores of the pawl and segment with graphite grease.

8   Assemble the pawl, spring and shaft to the pedal with reference to Fig. 5.2, then refit the clip.

9   Attach the spring to the toothed segment, then insert the segment into the pedal and press in the two pivot bushes.

10 Lift the pawl and turn the segment so that the pawl rests on the smooth curved surface at the end of the teeth.

11 Attach the segment spring to the pedal.

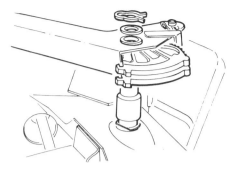

Fig. 5.1 Clutch pedal and shaft components (Sec 2)

Fig. 5.3 Clutch pedal toothed segment at initial setting
(Sec 2)

12 Lubricate the pedal shaft with a molybdenum disulphide based grease, then fit the pedal assembly.
13 Fit the spacer washer(s) and spring clip.
14 Reconnect the clutch cable to the clutch pedal and release arm as described in Section 3.

3 Clutch cable – removal and refitting

1 Jack up the front of the car and support it on axle stands. Apply the handbrake.
2 Working beneath the car squeeze the sides of the rubber boot and release it from the gearbox (photo).
3 Place a wooden block under the clutch pedal to raise it fully which will hold the automatic adjuster pawl clear of the toothed segment.
4 Pull the inner cable from the release arm, remove the rubber

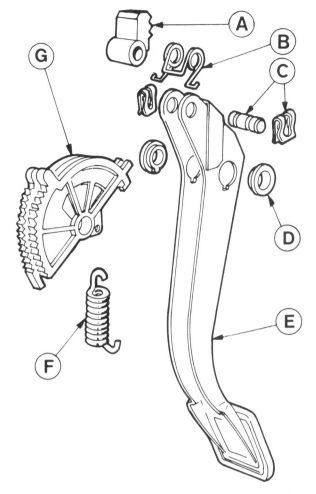

Fig. 5.2 Clutch pedal and automatic adjuster components (Sec 2)

A Pawl	E Clutch pedal
B Spring	F Toothed segment
C Pawl pin and clip	tension spring
D Bush	G Toothed segment

retainer then disconnect the cable by guiding the end nipple through the large hole (photos).
5 Remove the rubber boot from the cable.
6 Remove the lower facia panel.

3.2 Rubber boot on the gearbox covering the clutch cable and release arm

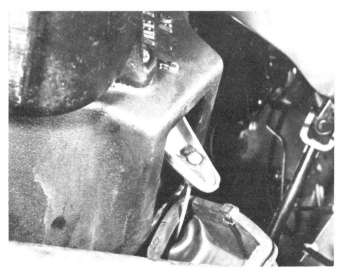

3.4a Showing clutch cable attachment to the release arm

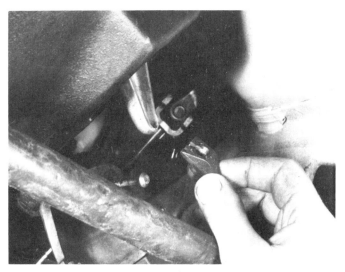

3.4b Removing the clutch cable retainer

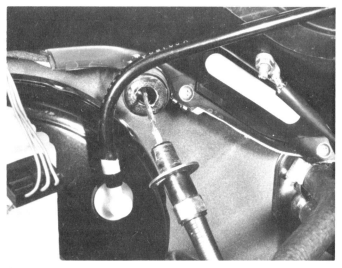

3.8 Removing the clutch cable from the bulkhead

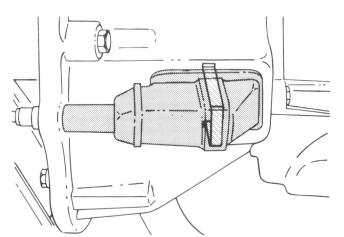

Fig. 5.4 Location of rubber boot and clip over the clutch release arm and cable (Sec 3)

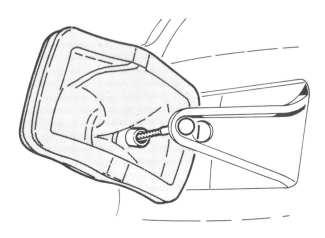

Fig. 5.5 Showing the clutch cable attachment to the release arm (Sec 3)

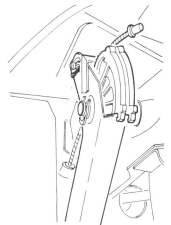

Fig. 5.6 Disconnecting the clutch cable from the toothed segment (Sec 3)

7 Unhook and remove the inner cable from the toothed segment on the pedal.
8 Withdraw the clutch cable through the bulkhead into the engine compartment (photo), and pull the end fitting from the hole in the clutch housing. Remove the rubber insulation bush where applicable.
9 Refitting is a reversal of removal.

4 Clutch – removal

1 The clutch may be removed by two alternative methods. Either remove the engine (Chapter 1) or remove the gearbox (Chapter 6). Unless the engine requires a major overhaul or the crankshaft rear oil seal requires renewal, it is easier and quicker to remove the gearbox.
2 With a file or scriber mark the relative positions of the clutch cover and flywheel which will ensure identical positioning on refitting. This is not necessary if a new clutch is to be fitted.
3 Unscrew, in a diagonal and progressive manner, the six bolts and spring washers that secure the clutch cover to the flywheel. This will prevent distortion of the cover and also prevent the cover from suddenly flying off due to binding on the dowels.
4 With all the bolts removed lift the clutch assembly from the locating dowels. Note which way round the friction plate is fitted and lift it from the clutch cover (photo).

5 Clutch – inspection

1 Examine the surfaces of the pressure plate and flywheel for scoring. If this is only light, the parts may be re-used. But, if scoring is excessive the clutch cover must be renewed and the flywheel friction face reground provided the amount of metal being removed is minimal. If any doubt exists renew the flywheel.

4.4 Removing the clutch cover and friction disc

6.3 Removing the release bearing

6.4 Release arm showing fulcrum pin (arrowed)

6.5 Clutch release bearing

2   Renew the friction plate (disc) if the linings are worn down to or near the rivets. If the linings appear oil stained, the cause of the oil leak must be found and rectified. This is most likely to be a failed gearbox input shaft oil seal or crankshaft rear oil seal. Check the friction plate hub and centre splines for wear.

3   Examine the clutch cover and diaphragm spring for wear which will be indicated by loose components. If the diaphragm spring has any blue discoloured areas, the clutch has probably been overheated at some time and the clutch cover should be renewed.

4   Spin the release bearing in the clutch housing and check it for roughness. Hold the outer race and attempt to move it laterally against the inner race. If any excessive movement or roughness is evident, renew the release bearing as described in Section 6.

6   Clutch release bearing and arm – removal and refitting

1   With the gearbox and engine separated to provide access to the clutch, attention can be given to the release bearing located in the clutch housing, over the input shaft.

2   If the gearbox is still in the car, remove the rubber boot and disconnect the clutch cable from the release arm with reference to Section 3.

3   Free the release bearing from the release arm and withdraw it from the guide sleeve (photo).

4   Pull the release arm from the fulcrum pin, then withdraw the arm over to the input shaft (photo).

5   Check the release bearing as described in Section 5. If there are any signs of grease leakage, renew the bearing (photo).

6   Refitting is a reversal of removal.

7   Clutch – refitting

1   It is important that no oil or grease gets on the clutch plate friction linings, or the pressure plate and flywheel faces. It is advisable to refit the clutch with clean hands and to wipe down the pressure plate and flywheel faces with a clean rag before assembly begins.

2   Place the clutch plate against the flywheel, ensuring that it is the corrrect way round. The projecting torsion spring hub should be furthest from the flywheel, and the 'flywheel side' mark towards the flywheel (photo).

3   Fit the clutch cover assembly loosely on the dowels with the previously made marks aligned where applicable. Insert the six bolts and spring washers and tighten them finger tight so that the clutch plate is gripped but can still be moved.

4   The clutch plate must now be centralised so that when the engine and gearbox are mated, the gearbox input shaft splines will pass through the splines in the centre of the clutch plate. Ideally a universal clutch centralising tool should be used or if available an old gearbox

7.2 'Flywheel side' mark on the clutch plate (disc)

7.5a Tightening the clutch cover bolts

7.5b Clutch fitted to flywheel ready for fitting of the gearbox

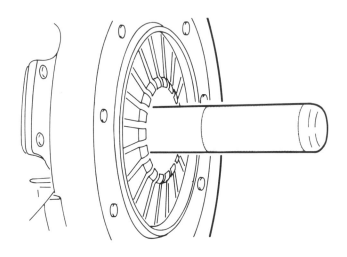

Fig. 5.7 Centralising the clutch friction disc (Sec 7)

input shaft. Alternatively a wooden mandrel can be made.

5   Make sure that the centralising tool is located correctly in the crankshaft spigot bearing then tighten the cover bolts progressively in a diagonal sequence to the specified torque. Remove the tool (photos).

6   Refit the gearbox (Chapter 6) or engine (Chapter 1) as applicable.

8   Fault diagnosis – clutch

Symptom	Reason(s)
Judder when taking up drive	Worn clutch plate friction surfaces or contamination with oil Worn splines on clutch plate or gearbox input shaft Loose engine or gearbox mountings
Clutch drag (failure to disengage)	Clutch plate sticking on input shaft splines Gearbox input shaft seized in crankshaft spigot bearing Faulty automatic cable adjuster
Clutch slip	Worn clutch plate friction surfaces or contamination with oil Weak diaphragm spring due to over-heating
Noise evident on depressing clutch pedal	Dry or worn release bearing

Chapter 6
Manual gearbox and automatic transmission

For modifications, and information applicable to later models, see Supplement at end of manual

Contents

Automatic transmission – fluid level checking 14
Automatic transmission – general description 13
Automatic transmission – removal and refitting 15
Automatic transmission downshift cable – removal, refitting and adjustment 18
Automatic transmission front brake band – adjustment 16
Automatic transmission selector rod – removal, refitting and adjustment 19
Automatic transmission starter inhibitor switch – removal and refitting 17
Automatic transmission vacuum diaphragm unit – removal and refitting 20
Fault diagnosis – manual gearbox and automatic transmission 21
Manual gearbox – general description 1
Manual gearbox – removal and refitting 2

Manual gearbox input shaft (type N) – dismantling and reassembly 10
Manual gearbox input shaft (types A, B and C) – dismantling and reassembly 5
Manual gearbox mainshaft (type N) – dismantling and reassembly 11
Manual gearbox mainshaft (types A, B and C) – dismantling and reassembly 6
Manual gearbox (type N) – dismantling into major assemblies 8
Manual gearbox (type N) – inspection 9
Manual gearbox (type N) – reassembly 12
Manual gearbox (types A, B and C) – dismantling into major assemblies 3
Manual gearbox (types A, B and C) – inspection 4
Manual gearbox (types A, B and C) – reassembly 7

Specifications

Manual gearbox

Type .... Four forward speeds (standard) or five forward speeds (optional on all models except 1.3 litre) and reverse, synchromesh on all forward speeds

Application
1.3 litre .... Types A1 and C
1.6 litre (VV) .... Types A2, B, C and N1
1.6 litre (Economy) .... Types C and N1
2.0 litre .... Types B and N1

Ratios

	A1	A2	B	C	N1
1st	3.66:1	3.34:1	3.65:1	3.58:1	3.65:1
2nd	2.18:1	1.99:1	1.97:1	2.01:1	1.97:1
3rd	1.43:1	1.42:1	1.37:1	1.40:1	1.37:1
4th	1.00:1	1.00:1	1.00:1	1.00:1	1.00:1
5th	–	–	–	–	0.82:1
Reverse	4.24:1	3.87:1	3.66:1	3.32:1	3.66:1

Oil type/specification
4-speed gearbox .... Gear oil, viscosity SAE 80 EP, to Ford spec SQM-2C 9008-A (Duckhams Hypoid 80)
5-speed gearbox .... Gear oil, viscosity SAE 80 EP, to Ford spec ESD-M2C 175-A (Duckhams Hypoid 75W/90S)

Oil capacity - pints (litres) 1.7 (0.98)   1.7 (0.98)   2.6 (1.46)   2.2 (1.25)   3.3 (1.9)

Torque wrench settings

	lbf ft	Nm
Clutch housing to gearbox casing	52 to 66	70 to 90
Clutch housing to engine	30 to 38	40 to 51
Clutch guide sleeve - except C type	7 to 8	9 to 11
C type	15 to 18	21 to 25
Extension housing	33 to 36	45 to 49
Gearbox cover - except C type	6 to 8	9 to 11
C type	15 to 18	21 to 25
Crossmember	14 to 18	20 to 25
Insulator to crossmember	12 to 15	16 to 20
Insulator to gearbox	37 to 42	50 to 57
Reversing light switch	0.7 to 1.5	1 to 2
Selector interlock	13 to 14	17 to 19
Filler plug	24 to 30	33 to 41
5th gear collar nut	89 to 111	120 to 150
5th gear lock plate	15 to 19	21 to 26
Selector lever to extension housing	15 to 19	21 to 26

Automatic transmission

Type	Ford (Bordeaux) C3 three forward speeds and one reverse, epicyclic gear train with hydraulic control and torque converter, automatic transmission optional on 1.6 and 2.0 litre models except 1.6E

Ratios

1st	2.47:1
2nd	1.47:1
3rd	1.00:1
Reverse	2.11:1
Torque converter maximum torque multiplication:	
1.6 litre	2.05:1
2.0 litre	2.35:1

Fluid type/specification	ATF to Ford spec SQM-2C 9010-A (Duckhams D-Matic)
Fluid capacity	11.08 pint (6.3 litre)

Torque wrench settings

	lbf ft	Nm
Driveplate to converter	26 to 28	35 to 40
Sump	12 to 17	16 to 23
Detent cable bracket	12 to 17	16 to 23
Starter inhibitor switch	7 to 10	10 to 14
Brake band adjusting screw locknut	34 to 44	46 to 60
Oil cooler pipe to connector	16 to 18	22 to 24
Oil pipe connector to transmission	18 to 23	24 to 31
Transmission to engine	22 to 27	30 to 37
Drain plug	20 to 29	27 to 39

1   Manual gearbox – general description

All models are fitted with a four-speed gearbox as standard, but a five-speed gearbox is optional on all models except 1.3 litre models.

The A and B type four-speed gearboxes are similar and the overhaul procedures are included in the same Section. Type A gearboxes are only available with an integral clutch housing whereas B type gearboxes may have an integral or bolt-on clutch housing. Overhaul procedures for the C type four-speed gearbox and N type five-speed gearbox are covered separately.

When overhauling the gearbox, due consideration should be given to the costs involved, since it is often more economical to obtain a service exchange or good secondhand gearbox rather than fit new parts to the existing gearbox.

2   Manual gearbox – removal and refitting

The gearbox can be removed in unit with the engine as described in Chapter 1, then separated from the engine on the bench. However, if work is only necessary on the gearbox or clutch it is better to remove the gearbox from under the car. The latter method is described in this Section.

1   Position the car over an inspection pit or alternatively on car ramps and/or axle stands so that there is sufficient working room beneath the car.

2   Disconnect the battery negative lead.

3   Remove the centre console as described in Chapter 12 and withdraw the rubber gaiter. Where a full length console is fitted it is only necessary to remove the front tray (photos).

4   Remove the screws and retaining frame and withdraw the inner rubber gaiter from the gear lever (photos).

5   Using a special splined key remove the screws securing the gear lever to the gearbox and withdraw the gear lever. Note how the gear lever locates over the selector shaft (photos).

6   Remove the propeller shaft as described in Chapter 7.

7   Bend back the lock tabs, then unscrew and remove the bolts from the anti-roll bar rear mounting clamps and lower the anti-roll bar as far as possible.

8   Unhook the exhaust system rubber mounting rings, then lower the exhaust system as far as possible and support it on axle stands. Alternatively suspend it from the underbody with wire.

9   Extract the circlip and withdraw the speedometer cable from the extension housing.

10   Disconnect the wiring from the reversing light switch (photo).

11   Support the gearbox with a trolley jack.

12   Unscrew the central mounting bolt from the crossmember and remove the cup (photos).

13   Unscrew the bolts and remove the mounting crossmember from the underbody. Note the location of the heat shield for the protection of the speedometer cable.

14   Remove the starter motor as described in Chapter 10.

15   Disconnect the clutch cable from the release arm with reference to Chapter 5.

16   Unscrew the bolts securing the gearbox bellhousing to the engine. Note the location of the engine earth cable and the engine-to-gearbox brace (photo).

17   Lower the trolley jack, then with the help of an assistant lift the gearbox direct from the engine and withdraw it from under the car (photos). Do not allow the weight of the gearbox to hang on the input shaft, and make sure that the car is adequately supported since a little rocking may be necessary to free the gearbox from the dowels.

18   Refitting is a reversal of removal, however check that the clutch release arm and bearing are correctly fitted and lightly grease the input shaft splines. Adjust the clutch cable with reference to Chapter 5, refit the starter motor with reference to Chapter 10, and refit the propeller shaft with reference to Chapter 7. Note that the clutch friction disc must be centralised in order for the gearbox input shaft to enter the crankshaft spigot bearing. Also check that the rear engine plate is correctly located on the dowels. Check and if necessary top up the gearbox oil level to within 5.0 mm (0.2 in) of the lower edge of the filler plug hole, then insert and tighten the plug.

2.3a Remove the gear lever knob ...

2.3b ... console front tray ...

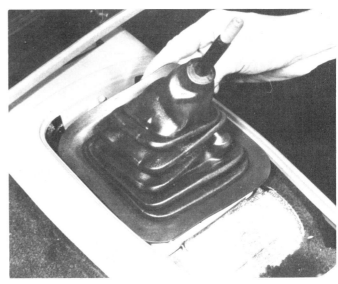

2.3c ... and rubber gaiter

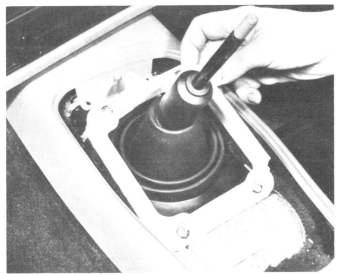

2.4a Remove the retaining frame ...

2.4b ... and inner rubber gaiter

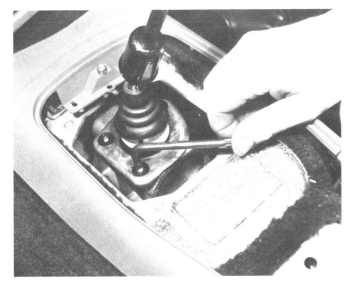

2.5a Remove the screws ...

2.5b ... and lift out the gear lever

2.10 Disconnecting the reversing light switch wiring

2.12a Gearbox mounting crossmember

2.12b Removing the gearbox mounting cup

2.16 Showing engine-to-gearbox brace and bolt

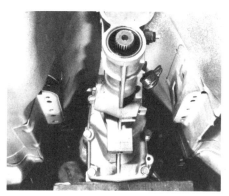

2.17a Removing the gearbox

2.17b Showing the gearbox separated from the engine

3   Manual gearbox (types A, B and C) – dismantling into major assemblies

1   Clean the exterior of the gearbox with paraffin and wipe dry.
2   Remove the clutch release bearing and arm with reference to Chapter 5.
3   Where applicable unbolt the clutch bellhousing from the front of the gearbox.
4   Working through the gear lever aperture, use a screwdriver or small drift to tap out the extension housing rear cover (photo).

Types A and B
5   Unscrew the bolts and remove the top cover and gasket.
6   Invert the gearbox and allow the oil to drain, then turn it upright again.
7   Using a screwdriver, unscrew the selector locking mechanism plug then extract the spring and locking pin if necessary using a pen magnet (photo).

8   Extract the blanking plug from the rear of the gearbox casing and using a suitable drift through the hole, drive out the selector locking plate roll pin (photo).
9   Drive the roll pin from the selector boss then withdraw the selector shaft through the selector forks and out of the rear extension housing (photos).
10   Note the location of the components then withdraw the selector forks, selector locking plate and selector boss (photos).

Type C
11   Unscrew the bolts and remove the top cover and gasket, taking care not to lose the selector locking spring located in the front of the cover.
12   Extract the selector locking ball with a pen magnet or greased screwdriver.
13   Invert the gearbox and allow the oil to drain, then turn it upright again.
14   Using a suitable drift drive the roll pin from the selector boss, but first move the selector shaft forward to prevent damage to 1st gear.

3.4 Removing the extension housing rear cover

3.7 Removing the selector locking pin and spring

3.8 Removing the blanking plug

3.9a Removing the selector boss roll pin

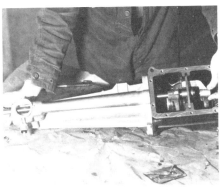

3.9b Withdrawing the selector shaft

3.10a Removing the selector locking plate and selector boss ...

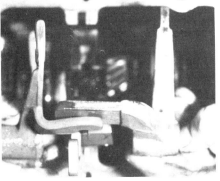

3.10b ... and the selector forks

3.21 Removing the countershaft

3.23 Withdrawing the extension housing and mainshaft

15 Withdraw the selector shaft from the rear extension housing, and remove the selector boss and locking plate.
16 Engage 2nd gear and press the reverse gear relay lever to the rear.
17 Note the location of the selector forks then remove them together with the connecting shaft.
18 Drive out the roll pin and remove the forks from the connecting shaft.

All types
19 Unscrew the bolts securing the extension housing to the main gearbox casing.
20 Release the extension housing complete with mainshaft from the main casing, then turn the extension housing so that the cut-away reveals the countershaft.
21 Invert the gearbox and use a soft metal drift to tap the countershaft rearwards until it can be removed from the rear of the main casing (photo).
22 Turn the gearbox upright and allow the countershaft gear cluster

to move to the bottom of the main casing.
23 Withdraw the extension housing complete with mainshaft from the main casing (photo).
24 Remove the input shaft needle roller bearing from the end of the mainshaft or from the centre of the input shaft.
25 Unscrew the bolts and withdraw the clutch release bearing guide sleeve from the front of the main casing. Note that the cut-out on the sleeve faces to the bottom of the casing. Remove the O-ring (types A and B) or gasket (type C) (photos).
26 Using a soft metal drift drive the input shaft and bearing from the casing. On A and B types, drive the shaft forwards using the drift inside the casing. On the C types, extract the large circlip then drive the assembly rearwards using the drift on the bearing outer race.
27 Remove the countershaft gear cluster together with the thrust washers keeping them identified for location (photo). Take care not to lose the needle roller bearings and spacers from inside the gear cluster.
28 Insert a suitable bolt into the reverse gear idler shaft, and using a nut, washer and socket pull out the idler shaft (photo). Note the fitted position of the reverse idler gear then remove it.

3.25a Unscrew the bolts ...

3.25b ... and remove the clutch release bearing guide sleeve ...

3.25c ... and O-ring

3.27 Removing the countershaft gear cluster

3.28 Removing the reverse idler shaft

3.31 Withdrawing the mainshaft from the extension housing

29 Extract the circlip, where applicable, and withdraw the reverse relay lever from the pivot pin. On the B type also disengage the return spring.

30 Prise out the speedometer drivegear cover from the extension housing and withdraw the drive pinion.

31 Squeeze the ends of the mainshaft bearing circlip together and extract it from the extension housing. Then using a soft-faced mallet drive the mainshaft from the extension housing (photo).

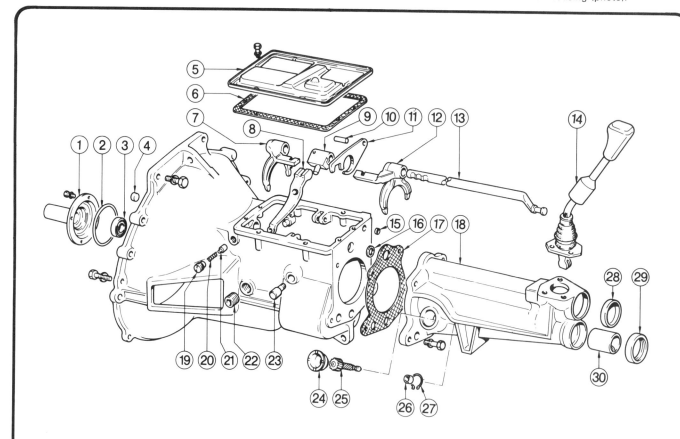

Fig. 6.1 Exploded view of type A and B gearbox housings and selector mechanism (Sec 3)

1 Guide sleeve	11 Selector locking plate	21 Locking pin
2 O-ring	12 1st/2nd gear selector	22 Oil filler plug
3 Oil seal	fork	23 Plug
4 Plug	13 Selector shaft	24 Cap
5 Cover	14 Gear lever assembly	25 Speedometer drive
6 Gasket	15 Plug	pinion
7 3rd/4th gear selector	16 Oil seal	26 Gasket
fork	17 Gasket	27 Retainer
8 Rev. gear relay lever	18 Extension housing	28 Cover
9 Selector boss	19 Threaded plug	29 Oil seal
10 Roll pin	20 Spring	30 Bush

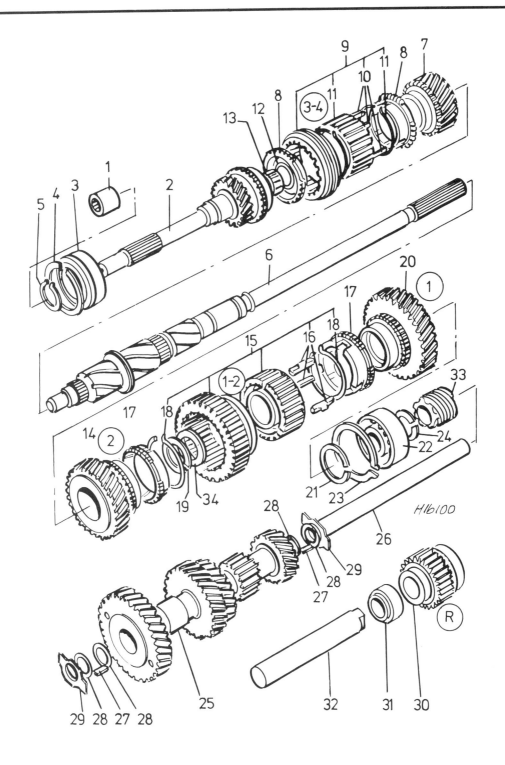

Fig. 6.2 Exploded view of type A gearbox gears (Sec 3)

1	Spigot bearing
2	Input shaft
3	Bearing
4	Large circlip
5	Small circlip
6	Mainshaft
7	3rd gear
8	3rd and 4th gear synchroniser rings
9	3rd/4th synchroniser unit
10	Blocker bars
11	Springs
12	Circlip
13	Needle roller bearing
14	2nd gear
15	1st/2nd synchroniser unit
16	Blocker bars
17	1st and 2nd gear synchroniser ring
18	Springs
19	Circlip
20	1st gear
21	Circlip
22	Mainshaft bearing
23	Circlip
24	Circlip
25	Countershaft gear cluster
26	Countershaft
27	Needle rollers
28	Spacers
29	Thrust plates
30	Reverse idler gear
31	Spacer
32	Reverse idler shaft
33	Speedometer drivegear
34	Thrust washer

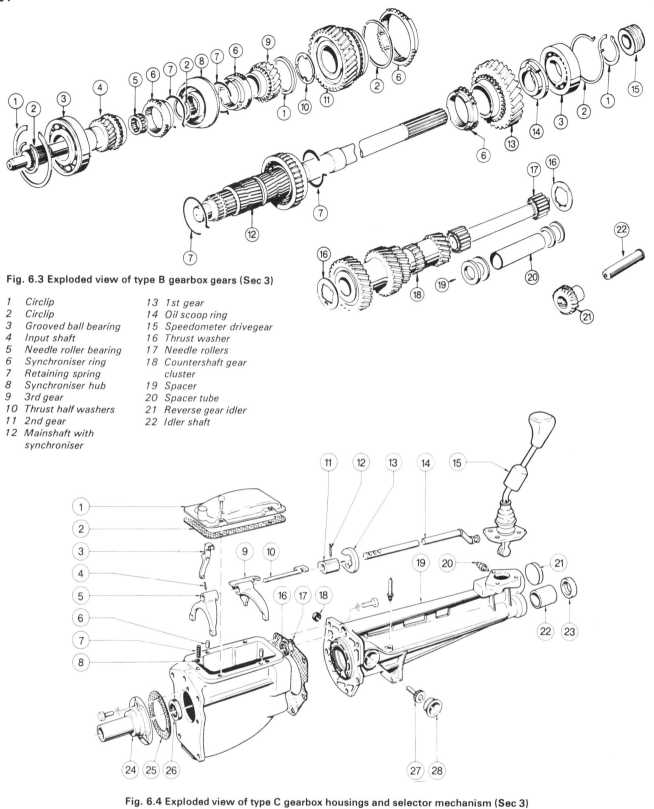

Fig. 6.3 Exploded view of type B gearbox gears (Sec 3)

1 Circlip
2 Circlip
3 Grooved ball bearing
4 Input shaft
5 Needle roller bearing
6 Synchroniser ring
7 Retaining spring
8 Synchroniser hub
9 3rd gear
10 Thrust half washers
11 2nd gear
12 Mainshaft with
   synchroniser
13 1st gear
14 Oil scoop ring
15 Speedometer drivegear
16 Thrust washer
17 Needle rollers
18 Countershaft gear
   cluster
19 Spacer
20 Spacer tube
21 Reverse gear idler
22 Idler shaft

Fig. 6.4 Exploded view of type C gearbox housings and selector mechanism (Sec 3)

1 Cover
2 Gasket
3 Reverse gear relay
   lever
4 Roll pin
5 3rd/4th gear selector
   fork
6 Centring pin
7 Compression spring
8 Locking ball
9 1st/2nd gear selector
   fork
10 Selector fork connecting
   shaft
11 Selector boss
12 Roll pin
13 Selector locking plate
14 Selector shaft
15 Gear lever assembly
16 Oil seal
17 Gasket
18 Oil seal
19 Extension housing
20 Reversing light switch
21 Cover
22 Bush
23 Oil seal
24 Guide sleeve
25 Gasket
26 Oil seal
27 Speedometer drive pinion
28 Cap

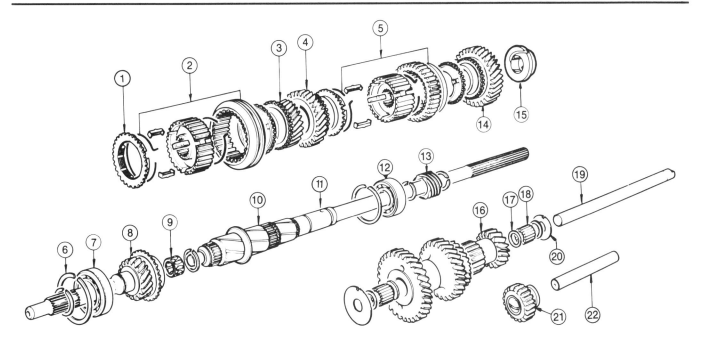

Fig. 6.5 Exploded view of type C gearbox gears (Sec 3)

1	Synchroniser ring	6	Circlip
2	3rd/4th gear synchroniser unit	7	Ball bearing
3	3rd gear	8	Input shaft
4	2nd gear	9	Needle roller bearing
5	1st/2nd synchroniser unit	10	Mainshaft
		11	Locking ball

1   Synchroniser ring
2   3rd/4th gear synchroniser unit
3   3rd gear
4   2nd gear
5   1st/2nd synchroniser unit

6   Circlip
7   Ball bearing
8   Input shaft
9   Needle roller bearing
10 Mainshaft
11 Locking ball

12 Ball bearing
13 Speedometer drivegear
14 1st gear
15 Oil scoop ring
16 Countershaft gear cluster

17 Spacer shim
18 Needle rollers
19 Countershaft
20 Thrust washer
21 Rev. gear idler
22 Idler shaft

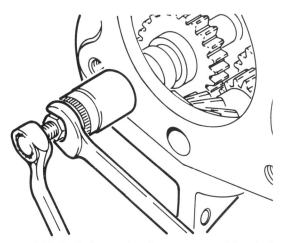

Fig. 6.6 Method of removing the reverse gear idler shaft (Sec 3)

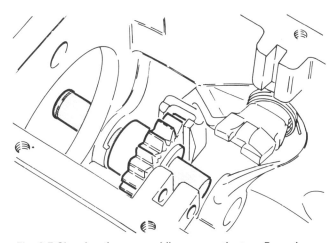

Fig. 6.7 Showing the reverse idler gear on the type B gearbox (Sec 3)

4   Manual gearbox (types A, B and C) – inspection

1   Thoroughly clean the interior of the gearbox, and check for dropped needle rollers and roll pins.
2   Carefully clean and then examine all the component parts for general wear, distortion, slackness of fit, and damage to machined faces and threads.
3   Examine the gears for excessive wear and chipping of the teeth. Renew them as necessary.
4   Examine the countershaft for signs of wear, where the needle rollers bear. If a small ridge can be felt at either end of the shaft it will be necessary to renew it. Renew the thrust washers at each end.
5   The four synchroniser rings should be renewed as a matter of course.

6   The needle roller bearing and cage, located between the nose of the mainshaft and the annulus in the rear of the input shaft, is also liable to wear, and should be renewed as a matter of course.
7   Examine the condition of the two ball bearing assemblies, one on the input shaft and one on the mainshaft. Check them for noisy operation, looseness between the inner and outer races, and for general wear. Normally they should be renewed on a gearbox that is being rebuilt.
8   If either of the synchroniser units is worn it will be necessary to buy a complete assembly as the parts are not sold individually. Also check the blocker bars for wear.
9   Examine the ends of the selector forks where they rub against the channels in the periphery of the synchroniser units. If possible compare the selector forks with new units to help determine the wear that has occurred. Renew them if worn.

10 If the bearing bush in the extension is badly worn it is best to take the extension to your local Ford garage to have the bearing pulled out and a new one fitted.

Note: *This can be done with the mainshaft assembly still located in the extension housing.*

11 The oil seals in the extension housing and clutch release bearing guide sleeve should be renewed as a matter of course. Drive out the old seal with the aid of a drift or screwdriver. It will be found that the seal comes out quite easily. With a piece of wood or suitably sized tube to spread the load evenly, carefully tap a new seal into place ensuring that it enters the bore squarely.

5 Manual gearbox input shaft (types A, B and C) – dismantling and reassembly

1 Extract the small circlip from the input shaft (photo).
2 Locate the bearing outer track on top of an open vice, then using a soft-faced mallet, drive the input shaft down through the bearing.
3 Remove the bearing from the input shaft noting that the groove in the outer track is towards the front splined end of the shaft.
4 Place the input shaft on a block of wood and lightly grease the bearing location shoulder.
5 Locate the new bearing on the input shaft with the circlip groove facing the correct way. Then using a metal tube on the inner track drive the bearing fully home.
6 Refit the small circlip.

5.1 Removing the input shaft bearing retaining circlip

6 Manual gearbox mainshaft (types A, B and C) – dismantling and reassembly

1 Remove the 4th gear synchroniser ring from the 3rd/4th synchroniser unit.
2 Extract the circlip and slide the 3rd/4th synchroniser unit together with the 3rd gear from the front of the mainshaft, using a two-legged puller where necessary. Remove the 3rd gear synchroniser ring (photos).

Type A
3 Extract the circlip retaining the mainshaft bearing then using a suitable puller remove the 1st gear complete with the mainshaft bearing and speedometer drivegear. Alternatively support the 1st gear and press the mainshaft downwards.
4 Remove the 1st gear synchroniser ring from the 1st/2nd synchroniser unit.
5 Extract the circlip and pull off the 1st/2nd synchroniser unit together with 2nd gear using a suitable puller.
6 Separate the 2nd gear from the 1st/2nd synchroniser unit and remove the 2nd gear synchroniser ring.
7 If necessary the synchroniser units may be dismantled, but first mark the hub and sleeve in relation to each other. Slide the sleeve from the hub and remove the blocker bars and springs.

6.2a Remove the circlip ...

Type B
8 Remove the outer ring from the 2nd gear then extract the thrust washer halves.
9 Slide the 2nd gear from the front of the mainshaft and remove the 2nd gear synchroniser ring and thrust ring where applicable (photo).
10 Mark the 1st/2nd synchroniser unit hub and sleeve in relation to each other and note the location of the selector fork groove. Then slide the sleeve forward from the hub and remove the blocker bars and springs.
11 Extract the circlip retaining the mainshaft bearing. Then using a suitable puller remove 1st gear complete with the oil scoop ring, mainshaft bearing and speedometer drivegear (photo). Alternatively, support the 1st gear and press the mainshaft downwards.
12 Remove the 1st gear synchroniser ring.
13 If necessary the 3rd/4th synchroniser unit may be dismantled, but first mark the hub and sleeve in relation to each other. Slide the sleeve from the hub and remove the blocker bars and springs. Note that the 1st/2nd synchroniser hub cannot be removed from the mainshaft.

Type C
14 Extract the circlip and remove the speedometer drivegear and locking ball from the rear of the mainshaft.

6.2b ... and withdraw the 3rd/4th synchroniser unit, 3rd gear synchroniser ring, and 3rd gear

6.9 Removing 2nd gear and synchroniser ring

6.11 Removing the mainshaft bearing retaining circlip

6.21 Assembling the 1st/2nd synchroniser unit (type B)

15 Extract the circlip retaining the mainshaft bearing. Then using a suitable puller remove the 1st gear complete with the oil scoop ring and mainshaft bearing. Alternatively, support the 1st gear and press the mainshaft downwards.

16 Remove the 1st gear synchroniser ring from the 1st/2nd synchroniser unit.

17 Extract the circlip and pull off the 1st/2nd synchroniser unit together with 2nd gear using a suitable puller.

18 Separate the 2nd gear from the 1st/2nd synchroniser unit and remove the 2nd gear synchroniser ring.

19 If necessary the synchroniser units may be dismantled, but first mark the hub and sleeve in relation to each other. Slide the sleeve from the hub and remove the blocker bars and springs.

All types

20 Clean all the components in paraffin, wipe dry and examine them for wear and damage. Obtain new components as necessary. During reassembly lubricate the components with gearbox oil and where new parts are being fitted lightly grease contact surfaces.

21 Commence reassembly by assembling the synchroniser units. Slide the sleeves on the hubs in their previously noted positions then insert the blocker bars and fit the springs as shown in Fig. 6.11 (photo).

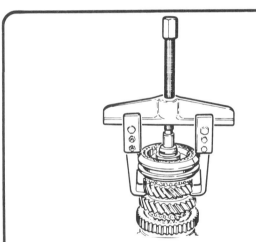

Fig. 6.8 Removing the 3rd gear and 3rd/4th synchroniser unit from the front of the mainshaft (Sec 6)

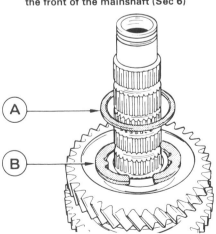

Fig. 6.10 Location of 2nd gear thrust washer retaining ring (A) and thrust washer halves (B) on the type B gearbox (Sec 6)

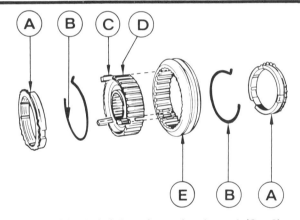

Fig. 6.9 Exploded view of a synchroniser unit (Sec 6)

A	Synchroniser ring	D	Hub
B	Springs	E	Sleeve
C	Blocker bars		

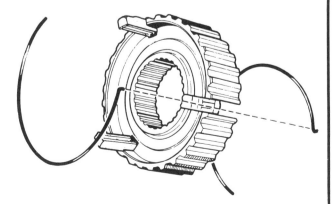

Fig. 6.11 Showing correct assembly of the synchroniser springs (Sec 6)

Type A

22 Slide the 2nd gear onto the rear of the mainshaft and locate the synchroniser ring on the gear cone. Fit the circlip and thrust washer if applicable.

23 Locate the 1st/2nd synchroniser unit on the mainshaft splines with the selector fork groove to the rear. Tap the unit fully home using a metal tube then fit the circlip if applicable.

24 Fit the 1st gear synchroniser ring to the 1st/2nd synchroniser unit with the blocker bars located in the slots.

25 Slide the 1st gear onto the mainshaft.

26 If a new mainshaft bearing or extension housing is being fitted, the thickness of the retaining circlip in the extension housing must be determined at this stage. Using vernier calipers measure the width of the bearing outer track (B) then measure the total width of the bearing location in the extension housing (A) – the difference (ie A minus B) represents the thickness of the retaining circlip.

27 Fit the small circlip if applicable, then loosely locate the bearing retaining circlip as determined from paragraph 26 on the mainshaft.

28 Smear a little grease on the mainshaft then fit the bearing and drive it fully home using a metal tube on the inner track. Fit the circlip.

29 Locate the speedometer drivegear on the mainshaft and use a metal tube to tap it into the position shown in Fig. 6.12.

Type B

30 Fit the 1st gear synchroniser ring to the 1st/2nd synchroniser unit with the blocker bars located in the slots.

31 Slide the 1st gear and oil scoop ring (with the oil groove towards 1st gear) onto the mainshaft.

32 If a new mainshaft bearing or extension housing is being fitted determine the thickness of the retaining circlip as described in paragraph 26, then locate it loosely on the mainshaft.

33 Smear a little grease on the mainshaft, then fit the bearing and drive it fully home using a metal tube on the inner track. Fit the circlip.

34 Locate the speedometer drivegear on the mainshaft and use a metal tube to tap it into the position shown in Fig. 6.12.

35 Fit the 2nd gear synchroniser ring to the 1st/2nd synchroniser unit with the blocker bars located in the slots. Fit the thrust ring where applicable.

36 Slide the 2nd gear onto the front of the mainshaft and retain with the thrust washer halves and outer ring.

Type C

37 Slide the 2nd gear onto the rear of the mainshaft and locate the synchroniser ring on the gear cone.

38 Locate the 1st/2nd synchroniser unit on the mainshaft splines with the selector fork groove to the rear. Tap the unit fully home using a metal tube then fit the circlip.

39 Fit the 1st gear synchroniser ring to the 1st/2nd synchroniser unit with the blocker bars located in the slots.

40 Slide the 1st gear and oil scoop ring (with the oil groove towards 1st gear) onto the mainshaft.

41 If a new mainshaft bearing or extension housing is being fitted determine the thickness of the retaining circlip as described in paragraph 26 then locate it loosely on the mainshaft.

42 Smear a little grease on the mainshaft then fit the bearing and drive it fully home using a metal tube on the inner track. Fit the circlip.

43 Insert the locking ball in the mainshaft detent, then slide on the speedometer drivegear and secure with the circlip.

All types

44 Slide the 3rd gear onto the front of the mainshaft then locate the synchroniser ring on the gear cone.

45 Locate the 3rd/4th synchroniser unit on the mainshaft splines with the long side of the hub facing the front. Tap the unit fully home using a metal tube then fit the circlip. Make sure that the slots in the 3rd gear synchroniser ring are aligned with the blocker bars as the synchroniser unit is being fitted.

46 Fit the 4th gear synchroniser ring to the 3rd/4th synchroniser unit with the blocker bars located in the slots.

---

7   Manual gearbox (types A, B and C) – reassembly

---

1   Immerse the extension housing in hot water for several minutes. Then remove it and quickly insert the mainshaft and push the bearing fully home. If necessary place the extension housing on the edge of the bench and use a soft-faced mallet to drive the mainshaft home (photo).

2   Using long nose pliers and a screwdriver refit the bearing circlip (photo).

3   Apply a little grease to the extension housing mating face and fit a new gasket (photo).

4   Insert the speedometer drive pinion in the extension housing, smear a little sealer on the cover then tap the cover into the housing.

5   Fit the reverse relay lever (and return spring on the B type) onto the pivot pin in the main casing, and fit the circlip.

6   Position the reverse idler gear in the main casing with the long shoulder facing the rear and engaged with the relay lever. Slide in the idler shaft and tap fully home with a soft-faced mallet.

7   Smear grease inside the ends of the countershaft gear cluster, then fit the spacers and needle roller bearings (photo). On the type A there are 21 needle rollers at each end with identical spacers either side of the rollers. On the type B there is a central spacer tube with thin spacers either side followed by 19 needle rollers and thick spacers on each side. Note that the long needle rollers must be fitted to the rear of the gear cluster. On the type C there are 20 needle rollers at each end with identical spacers either side of the rollers. Make sure that there is sufficient grease to hold the needle rollers in position during the subsequent operation, and if available fit a dummy shaft of a length slightly less than the gear cluster.

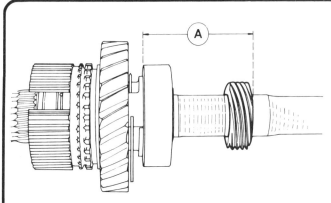

Fig. 6.12 Speedometer drivegear fitting dimension (A) (Sec 6)

Type A gearbox 51.20 mm (2.016 in)
Type B gearbox 49.25 mm (1.939 in)

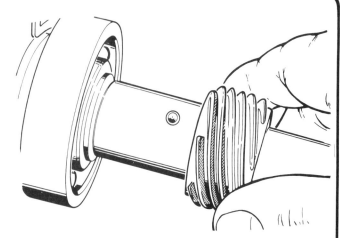

Fig. 6.13 Fitting the speedometer drivegear on the mainshaft on the type C gearbox (Sec 6)

7.1 Fitting the mainshaft to the extension housing

7.2 Fitting the mainshaft bearing circlip to the extension housing

7.3 Locating a new gasket on the extension housing

7.7 Fitting the outer spacer to the countershaft gear cluster needle rollers

8   Stick the thrust washers on the inner faces of the main casing with the location tabs correctly positioned.

9   Lower the gear cluster to the bottom of the main casing keeping the thrust washers in position.

10 Insert the input shaft fully into the main casing using a soft metal drift if necessary. On the C type refit the large circlip.

11 Fit the clutch release bearing guide sleeve together with a new O-ring (types A and B) or gasket (type C). Check that the cut-out on the sleeve faces the bottom of the casing then apply sealer to the bolt threads. Insert them, and tighten to the specified torque in diagonal sequence.

12 Oil the needle roller bearing and locate it in the centre of the input shaft.

13 Insert the mainshaft together with the extension housing into the main casing so that the front of the mainshaft enters the needle roller bearing in the centre of the input shaft. Turn the extension housing so that the cut-away reveals the countershaft bore.

14 While keeping the thrust washers in place, invert the gearbox so that the countershaft gear cluster meshes with the mainshaft and input shaft.

15 Line up the thrust washers and insert the countershaft from the rear of the main casing. Using a soft metal drift drive the countershaft into the main casing until flush. The flat on the rear end of the countershaft must be horizontal (Figs. 6.14 and 6.15).

16 Fully insert the extension housing and make sure that the 4th gear

synchroniser ring is correctly aligned with the synchroniser unit.

17 Apply sealer to the bolt threads then insert them and tighten to the specified torque in diagonal sequence.

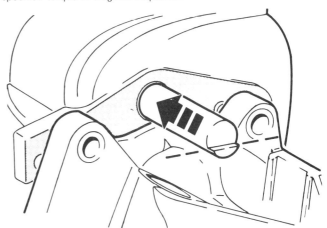

Fig. 6.14 Countershaft flat alignment on type A and B gearboxes (Sec 7)

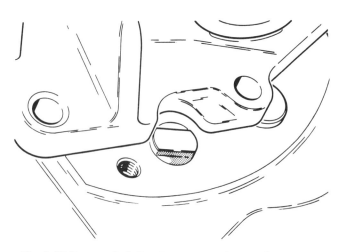

Fig. 6.15 Countershaft flat alignment on the type C gearbox (Sec 7)

Types A and B

18 Locate the selector locking plate in the main casing and retain with the roll pin.

19 Coat the new blanking plug with sealer and tap it into the rear of the casing.

20 Fit the selector forks and selector boss, then insert the selector shaft from the rear and guide it through the selector components.

21 Align the holes then drive the roll pin into the selector boss and selector shaft.

22 Insert the selector locking pin and spring, apply sealer to the plug threads, then insert and tighten the plug.

23 Fit the gearbox top cover together with a new gasket and tighten the bolts to the specified torque in diagonal sequence.

Type C

24 Assemble the selector forks to the connecting shaft, then align the holes and drive the roll pin into the 3rd/4th selector fork and shaft.

25 Engage 2nd gear and press the reverse gear relay lever to the rear.

26 Fit the selector forks together to their respective synchroniser units.

27 Lightly grease the selector shaft then insert it into the rear extension housing. Hold the selector boss and locking plate in position, and guide the selector shaft through the selector components. Note that the roll pin hole in the selector boss must face the rear.

28 Align the holes then drive the roll pin into the selector boss and

selector shaft until it is about 1.0 mm (0.04 in) below the surface.

29 Insert the selector locking ball in the main casing.

30 Grease the selector locking spring and locate it in the top cover.

31 Fit the gearbox top cover together with a new gasket and tighten the bolts to the specified torque in diagonal sequence.

All types

32 Fit the extension housing rear cover using a little sealer, and stake it in several places to secure.

33 Where applicable fit the clutch bellhousing to the front of the gearbox, apply sealer to the bolt threads, then insert the bolts and tighten them to the specified torque in diagonal sequence.

34 Fit the clutch release bearing and arm with reference to Chapter 5.

---

8   Manual gearbox (type N) – dismantling into major assemblies

1 Clean the exterior of the gearbox with paraffin and wipe dry.

2 Remove the clutch release bearing and arm with reference to Chapter 5.

3 Unscrew and remove the reversing light switch (photo).

4 Unbolt the clutch bellhousing from the front of the gearbox. Remove the gasket (photos).

5 Unscrew the bolts and withdraw the clutch release bearing guide sleeve and gasket from the front of the gearbox (photos).

6 Unscrew the bolts and remove the top cover and gasket (photos).

7 Invert the gearbox and allow the oil to drain, then turn it upright again.

8 Unscrew the bolts and lift the 5th gear locking plate from the extension housing (photo).

9 Extract the 5th gear locking spring and pin from the extension housing (photos). Use a screw to remove the pin.

10 Working through the gear lever aperture, use a screwdriver or small drift to tap out the extension housing rear cover (photo).

11 Select reverse gear and pull the selector shaft fully to the rear. Support the shaft with a piece of wood then drive out the roll pin and withdraw the connector from the rear of the selector rod (photos).

12 Unbolt and remove the extension housing from the rear of the gearbox. If necessary tap the housing with a soft-faced mallet to release it from the dowels. Remove the gasket (photos).

13 Prise the cover from the extension housing and withdraw the speedometer drivegear (photo).

14 Select neutral then using an Allen key, unscrew the selector locking mechanism plug from the side of the main casing then extract the spring and locking pin if necessary using a pen magnet (photos).

15 Drive the roll pin from the selector boss and selector shaft.

16 If necessary the selector shaft centralising spring and 5th gear locking control may be removed. Using a small screwdriver push out the pin and plug and slide the control from the selector shaft (photos).

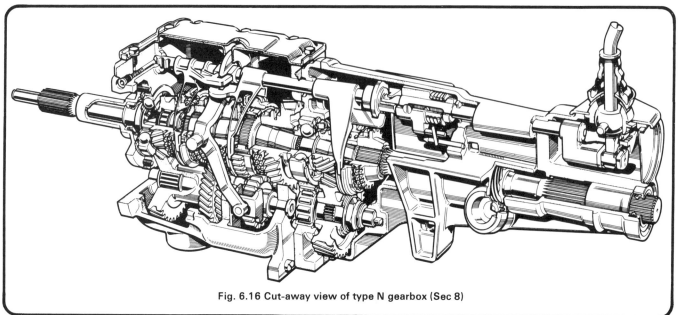

Fig. 6.16 Cut-away view of type N gearbox (Sec 8)

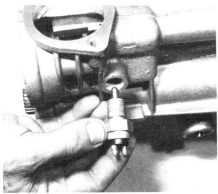

8.3 Removing the reversing light switch

8.4a Clutch bellhousing bolts (arrowed)

8.4b Removing the clutch bellhousing

8.5a Removing the clutch release bearing guide sleeve ...

8.5b ... and gasket

8.6a Remove the bolts ...

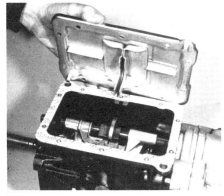

8.6b ... top cover ...

8.6c ... and gasket

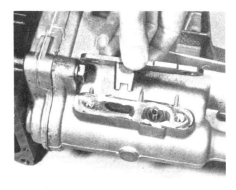

8.8 Removing the 5th gear locking plate

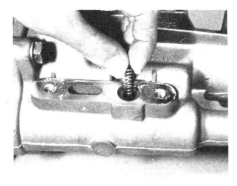

8.9a Extracting the 5th gear locking spring ...

8.9b ... and pin

8.10 Removing the extension housing rear cover

8.11a Drive out the roll pin ...

8.11b ... and remove the selector rod connector

8.11c Selector rod connector

8.12a Removing the extension housing ...

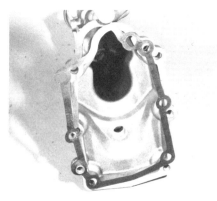

8.12b ... and gasket

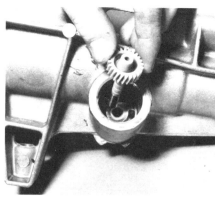

8.13 Removing the speedometer drivegear

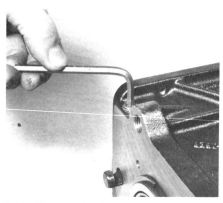

8.14a Unscrew the plug ...

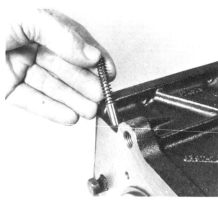

8.14b ... and remove the selector locking spring and pin

8.16a Insert a small screwdriver ...

8.16b ... and push out the plug ...

8.16c ... and pin from the selector shaft centralising spring and 5th gear locking control

8.17a Removing the selector boss and locking plate ...

17 Note the location of the selector components then withdraw the selector shaft from the rear of the gearbox and remove the selector boss and locking plate, 1st/2nd and 3rd/4th selector forks, and 5th gear selector fork and sleeve. Note that the roll pin hole in the selector boss is towards the front (photos).

18 Extract the circlip and pull the 5th gear synchroniser unit from the main casing leaving it loose on the mainshaft (photos).

19 Slide the 5th driven gear from the synchroniser unit hub (photo).

20 Select 3rd gear and either 1st or 2nd gear by pushing the respective synchroniser sleeves – this will lock the mainshaft and countershaft gear cluster.

21 Unscrew and remove the 5th driving gear retaining nut while an assistant holds the gearbox stationary (photo). The nut is tightened to a high torque setting and an additional extension bar may be required.

22 Remove the washer and pull the 5th driving gear from the countershaft gear cluster using a two-legged puller and socket in contact with the cluster. Remove the spacer ring (photos). Select neutral.

23 Extract the circlip retaining the countershaft gear cluster bearing in the intermediate housing (photo).

24 Using a soft-faced mallet tap the intermediate housing free of the main casing and pull the intermediate housing rearwards as far as possible. Using a screwdriver inserted between the intermediate housing and main casing prise the bearing from the shoulder on the countershaft gear cluster and remove it from the intermediate housing (photo).

25 Using a soft metal drift from the front of the main casing, drive the countershaft rearwards sufficient to allow the gear cluster to be lowered to the bottom of the casing.

26 Ease the input shaft from the front of the casing, if necessary using a small drift inside the gearbox to move the bearing slightly forwards, then using levers beneath the bearing circlip (photo).

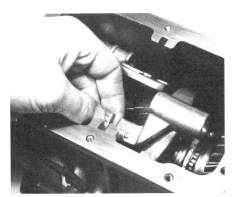

8.17b ... 1st/2nd selector fork ...

8.17c ... 3rd/4th selector fork ...

8.17d ... 5th gear interlock sleeve ...

8.17e ... and 5th gear selector fork

8.18a Extract the circlip ...

8.18b ... and remove the 5th gear synchroniser dog hub ...

8.18c ... and 5th gear synchroniser unit

8.19 Showing the 5th driven gear

8.21 Removing the 5th driving gear retaining nut

8.22a Removing the washer from the 5th driving gear

8.22b Pull the 5th driving gear from the splines with a puller ...

8.22c ... and remove the 5th driving gear from the countershaft gear cluster

8.22d Removing the spacer ring

8.23 Removing the countershaft gear cluster bearing retaining circlip

8.24 Using a screwdriver to remove the countershaft gear cluster bearing from the intermediate housing

8.26 Removing the input shaft

8.27a Removing the 4th gear synchroniser ring

8.27b Removing the input shaft needle roller bearing

8.28a Removing the mainshaft and intermediate housing ...

8.28b ... and gasket

8.29a Removing the countershaft and gear cluster

8.29b View of the countershaft and gear cluster

8.30a Method of removing the reverse gear idler shaft

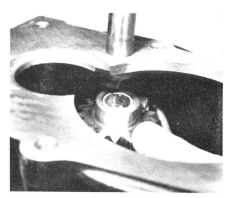

8.30b Removing the reverse idler gear

8.31a Showing location for reverse idler gear guide in the relay lever

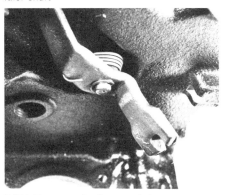

8.31b Reverse relay lever and pivot

8.32 Magnetic disc location in the bottom of the main casing

27 Remove the 4th gear synchroniser ring. Remove the input shaft needle roller bearing from the end of the mainshaft or from the centre of the input shaft (photos).
28 Remove the mainshaft and intermediate housing from the main casing. Remove the gasket (photos).
29 Withdraw the countershaft and gear cluster from the main casing (photos).
30 Insert a suitable bolt into the reverse gear idler shaft, and using a nut, washer and socket pull out the idler shaft. Note the fitted position of the reverse idler gear then remove it (photos).
31 Remove the guide from the reverse relay lever then extract the circlip and remove the relay lever from the pivot (photos).
32 Remove the magnetic disc from the bottom of the main casing. Also remove any needle rollers which may have been displaced from the countershaft gear cluster (photo).

9 Manual gearbox (type N) – inspection

The procedure is basically as given in Section 4, however there are five synchroniser rings, no countershaft gear cluster thrust washers, two ball bearings and one roller bearing (photos).

10 Manual gearbox input shaft (type N) – dismantling and reassembly

The procedure is identical to that described in Section 5 (photos).

9.1a Prising out the oil seal from the clutch release bearing sleeve

9.1b Fitting a new oil seal to the clutch release bearing sleeve

9.1c Location of the speedometer drivegear oil seal in the extension housing

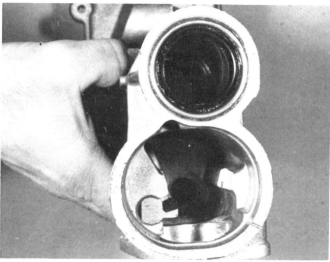

9.1d Rear view of the extension housing showing the mainshaft oil seal and bush

10.1a Extract the circlip from the input shaft ...

10.1b ... and remove the bearing

10.1c Using a metal tube to fit the bearing to the input shaft

11 Manual gearbox mainshaft (type N) – dismantling and reassembly

1   Extract the circlip and slide the 3rd/4th synchroniser unit together with the 3rd gear from the front of the mainshaft, using a two-legged puller where necessary. Separate the gear and unit, then remove the 3rd gear synchroniser ring (photos).

2   Remove the outer ring from the 2nd gear then extract the thrust washer halves (photos).

3   Slide the 2nd gear from the front of the mainshaft and remove the 2nd gear synchroniser ring (photos).

4   Mark the 1st/2nd synchroniser unit hub and sleeve in relation to each other and note the location of the selector fork groove, then slide the sleeve forward from the hub and remove the blocker bars and springs. Note that the synchroniser hub cannot be removed from the mainshaft (photos).

5   Using a suitable puller pull the speedometer drivegear off the rear of the mainshaft (photo).

6   Remove the 5th gear synchroniser unit and 5th driven gear from the mainshaft.

7   Extract the circlip retaining the mainshaft bearing then support the intermediate housing on blocks of wood and drive the mainshaft through the bearing with a soft-faced mallet (photos).

8   Remove the oil scoop ring, 1st gear, and 1st gear synchroniser ring (photos).

11.1a Extract the circlip ...

11.1b ... and remove the 3rd/4th synchroniser and ring ...

11.1c ... and 3rd gear

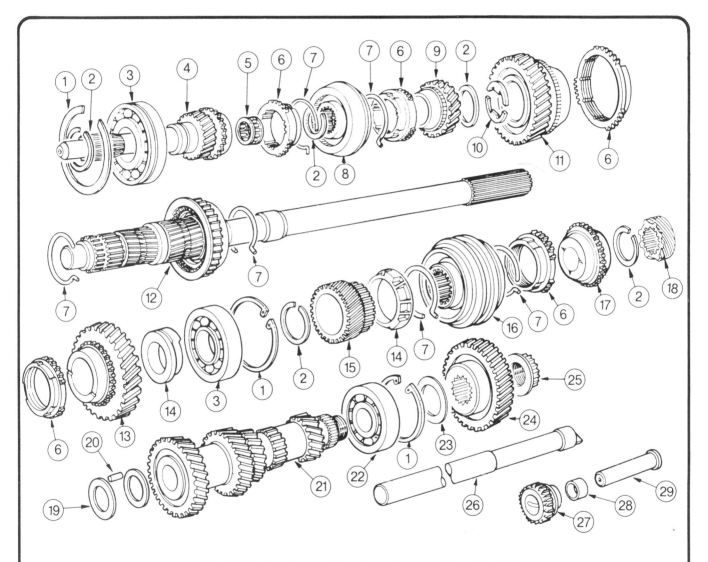

Fig. 6.17 Exploded view of type N gearbox gears (Secs 10 and 11)

1	Circlip	9	3rd gear	16	5th gear synchroniser
2	Circlip	10	Thrust half washer	17	5th gear synchroniser
3	Ball bearing	11	2nd gear		hub
4	Input shaft	12	Mainshaft with	18	Speedometer drivegear
5	Needle roller bearing		synchroniser	19	Spacer
6	Synchroniser ring	13	1st gear	20	Needle rollers
7	Retaining spring	14	Oil scoop ring	21	Countershaft gear
8	3rd/4th gear synchroniser	15	5th gear		cluster

22	Roller bearing
23	Washer
24	4th gear countershaft
25	12 sided nut
26	Countershaft
27	Reverse idler gear
28	Bush
29	Idler shaft

11.2a 2nd gear thrust washers and retaining ring location

11.2b Removing the outer retaining ring

11.2c Removing the thrust washer halves

11.3a Removing the 2nd gear ...

11.3b ... and synchroniser ring

11.4a Removing the 1st/2nd synchroniser sleeve ...

11.4b ... and blocker bars

11.5 Removing the speedometer drivegear with a puller

11.7a Extracting the mainshaft bearing circlip

11.7b Method of driving the mainshaft through the intermediate housing and bearing

11.8a Removing the oil scoop ring and 1st gear

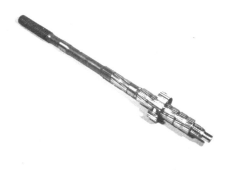

11.8b The dismantled mainshaft

9 If necessary extract the circlip and drive the ball bearing form the intermediate housing using a metal tube (photo). Also the synchroniser units may be dismantled, but first mark the hub and sleeve in relation to each other. Slide the sleeve from the hub and remove the blocker bars and springs.

10 Clean all the components in paraffin, wipe dry and examine them for wear and damage. Obtain new components as necessary. During reassembly lubricate the components with gearbox oil and where new parts are being fitted lightly grease contact surfaces.

11 Commence reassembly by assembling the synchroniser units. Slide the sleeves on the hubs in their previously noted positions, then insert the blocker bars and fit the springs as shown in Fig. 6.11.

12 Support the intermediate housing then, using a metal tube on the outer track, drive in the new bearing and fit the circlip (photo).

13 Fit the blocker bar spring to the rear of the 1st/2nd synchroniser hub followed by the 1st gear synchroniser ring (photo).

14 Slide the 1st gear and oil scoop ring (with the oil groove towards 1st gear) onto the mainshaft.

15 Using a metal tube on the mainshaft bearing inner track, drive the intermediate housing onto the mainshaft and fit the circlip (photo). Make sure that the large circlip is towards the rear of the mainshaft.

16 Locate the 5th driven gear and 5th gear synchroniser with circlip, loose on the mainshaft. Tap the speedometer drivegear lightly onto its shoulder – its final position will be determined later (photo).

11.9 Extracting the bearing retaining circlip from the intermediate housing

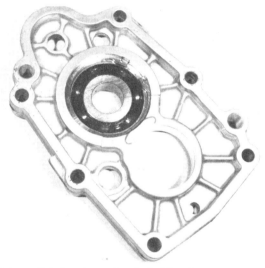

11.12 Intermediate housing and mainshaft bearing

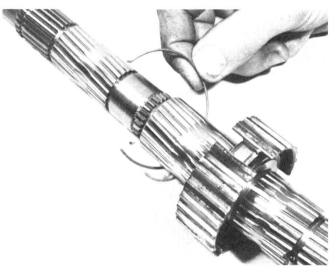

11.13 Fitting the blocker bar spring to the rear of the 1st/2nd synchroniser hub

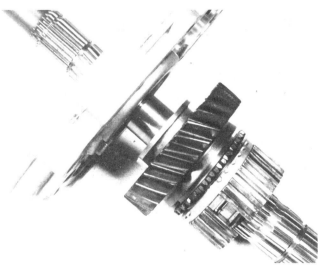

11.15 Fitting the intermediate housing and bearing

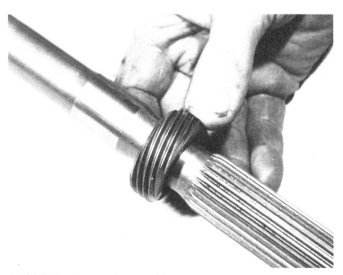

11.16 Fitting the speedometer drivegear

11.19 Showing location hole for 2nd gear thrust washer halves

11.21 Fitting the 3rd/4th synchroniser unit

17 Fit the 1st/2nd synchroniser sleeve to the hub in its previously noted position with the selector groove facing forward then insert the blocker bars and fit the springs as shown in Fig. 6.11.

18 Fit the 2nd gear synchroniser ring to the 1st/2nd synchroniser unit with the blocker bars located in the slots.

19 Slide the 2nd gear onto the front of the mainshaft and retain with the thrust washer halves and outer ring (photo).

20 Slide the 3rd gear onto the front of the mainshaft then locate the synchroniser ring on the gear cone.

21 Locate the 3rd/4th synchroniser unit on the mainshaft splines with the long side of the hub facing the front (photo). Tap the unit fully home using a metal tube then fit the circlip. Make sure that the slots in the 3rd gear synchroniser ring are aligned with the blocker bars as the synchroniser unit is being fitted.

12 Manual gearbox (type N) – reassembly

1 Locate the magnetic disc in the bottom of the main casing.

2 Fit the reverse relay lever onto the pivot and retain with the circlip. Fit the guide to the lever.

3 Position the reverse idler gear in the main casing with the long shoulder facing the rear and engaged with the relay lever. Slide in the idler shaft and tap fully home with a soft-faced mallet.

4 Smear grease inside the end of the countershaft gear cluster then fit the spacers and needle roller bearings – there are 21 needle rollers. Make sure that there is sufficient grease to hold the needle rollers in position during the subsequent operation (photos).

5 Insert the countershaft in the gear cluster until the front end is flush with the front gear on the cluster (photo).

6 Locate the countershaft and gear cluster in the bottom of the main casing.

7 Position a new gasket on the main casing then fit the mainshaft and intermediate housing, and temporarily secure with two bolts.

8 Fit the input shaft needle roller bearing to the end of the mainshaft or in the centre of the input shaft (photo).

9 Fit the 4th gear synchroniser ring to the 3rd/4th synchroniser unit with the cut-outs over the blocker bars, then fit the input shaft assembly and tap the bearing fully into the casing up to the retaining circlip (photo).

10 Invert the gearbox so that the countershaft gear cluster meshes with the input shaft and mainshaft gears.

11 Using a soft metal drift drive the countershaft into the main casing until flush at the front face – the flat on the rear end of the countershaft must be horizontal (photo).

12 Using a metal tube tap the countershaft gear cluster bearing into the intermediate housing and secure with the circlip (photo).

13 Fit the spacer ring then, using a metal tube, tap the 5th driving gear onto the splines of the countershaft gear cluster.

14 Fit the thrust washer and retaining nut. Select 3rd gear and either 1st or 2nd gear by pushing the respective synchroniser sleeves. While an assistant holds the gearbox stationary tighten the nut to the specified torque, then lock it by peening the collar on the nut into the slot in the gear cluster (photos).

15 Select neutral then slide the 5th driven gear into mesh with the driving gear.

16 Slide the 5th gear synchroniser unit complete with spacer onto the 5th driven gear. Then using a metal tube, drive the dog hub and 5th synchroniser ring onto the mainshaft splines while guiding the synchroniser ring onto the blocker bars. Fit the circlip (photos).

17 Tap the speedometer drivegear into its correct position on the mainshaft – the distance between the gear and the 5th gear dog hub circlip should be 123.0 to 124.0 mm (4.843 to 4.882 in) (photo).

18 Locate the 5th gear selector fork in its synchroniser sleeve and

12.4a Inserting the spacers in the countershaft gear cluster ...

12.4b ... followed by the needle rollers ...

12.4c ... and outer spacers

12.5 Showing the countershaft inserted in the gear cluster

12.8 Fitting the input shaft needle roller bearing on the mainshaft

12.9 Fitting the input shaft

12.11 Correct position of countershaft before driving into the main casing

12.12 Fitting the countershaft gear cluster bearing

12.14a Tightening the 5th driving gear nut

12.14b Using a chisel to peen the nut collar

12.14c 5th driving gear nut locked to the countershaft gear cluster

12.16a Fitting the spacer to the 5th gear synchroniser unit

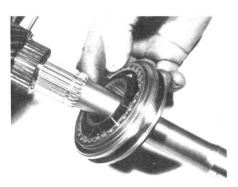

12.16b Fitting the 5th gear synchroniser unit to 5th driven gear

12.16c Fitting the 5th gear synchroniser ring and dog hub to the mainshaft

12.16d Fitting the circlip to the dog hub

12.17 Checking the distance between the circlip and speedometer drivegear

locate the interlock sleeve in the groove (short shoulder to front), then insert the selector shaft through the sleeve and selector fork into the main casing (photo).

19 Locate the 1st/2nd and 3rd/4th selector forks in their respective synchroniser sleeves, position the selector boss and locking plate, and insert the selector shaft through the components into the front of the main casing. The roll pin hole in the selector boss must be towards the front.

20 If removed refit the selector shaft centralising spring and 5th gear locking control by inserting the pin and plug.

21 Align the holes then drive the roll pin into the selector boss and selector shaft (photo).

22 Insert the selector locking pin and spring, apply sealer to the plug threads, then insert and tighten the plug using an Allen key.

23 Fit the speedometer drivegear to the rear extension housing. Apply a little sealer to the cover then press it into the housing (photo).

24 Remove the temporarily fitted bolts from the intermediate housing then select 4th gear.

25 Stick a new gasket to the extension housing with grease, and fit the housing to the intermediate housing. Take care not to damage the rear oil seal, and make sure that the selector shaft centralising spring locates on the pin (photo).

26 Insert the bolts and tighten them to the specified torque in diagonal sequence (photo). Before inserting the three bolts which go right through the main casing, apply sealer to their threads.

27 Select reverse gear and locate the connector on the rear of the selector rod. Support the rod with a piece of wood then drive in the roll pin. Select neutral.

28 Press the rear cover into the extension housing.

29 Check that the 5th gear interlock sleeve is correctly aligned, then insert the 5th gear locking pin and spring.

30 Apply some sealer to the 5th gear locking plate, locate it on the extension housing, and insert and tighten the bolts to the specified torque (photo).

31 Fit the gearbox top cover together with a new gasket and tighten the bolts to the specified torque in diagonal sequence.

32 Fit the clutch release bearing guide sleeve (oil slot downwards) together with a new gasket and tighten the bolts to the specified torque in diagonal sequence. Where necessary apply sealer to the bolt threads.

33 Fit the clutch bellhousing to the front of the gearbox together with a new gasket. Apply sealer to the bolt threads, then insert the bolts and tighten them to the specified torque in diagonal sequence.

34 Insert and tighten the reversing light switch in the extension housing.

35 Fit the clutch release bearing and arm with reference to Chapter 5.

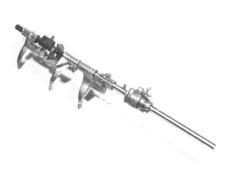

12.18 Selector shaft and components assembled on the bench

12.21 Driving the roll pin into the selector boss

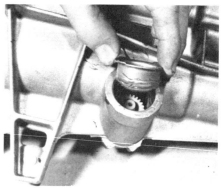

12.23 Fitting the speedometer drivegear cover

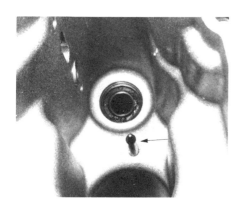

12.25 Location of the selector shaft centralising spring pin

12.26 Tightening the extension housing bolts

12.30 Applying sealer to the 5th gear locking plate location

13 Automatic transmission – general description

The automatic transmission takes the place of the clutch and gearbox, which are, of course, mounted behind the engine.

The unit has a large aluminium content which helps to reduce its overall weight and it is of compact dimensions. A transmission oil cooler is fitted as standard and ensures cooler operation of the transmission under trailer towing conditions. A vacuum connection to the inlet manifold provides smoother and more consistent downshifts under load than is the case with units not incorporating this facility.

The system consists of two main components:

(a) A three element hydrokinetic torque converter coupling, capable of torque multiplication.

(b) A torque/speed responsive and hydraulically operated epicyclic gearbox comprising planetary gearsets providing three forward ratios and one reverse ratio. Due to the complexity of the automatic transmission unit, if performance is not up to standard, or overhaul is necessary, it is imperative that this be left to the local main agents who will have the special equipment for fault diagnosis and rectification.

The content of the following sections is therefore confined to supplying general information and any service information and instruction that can be used by the owner.

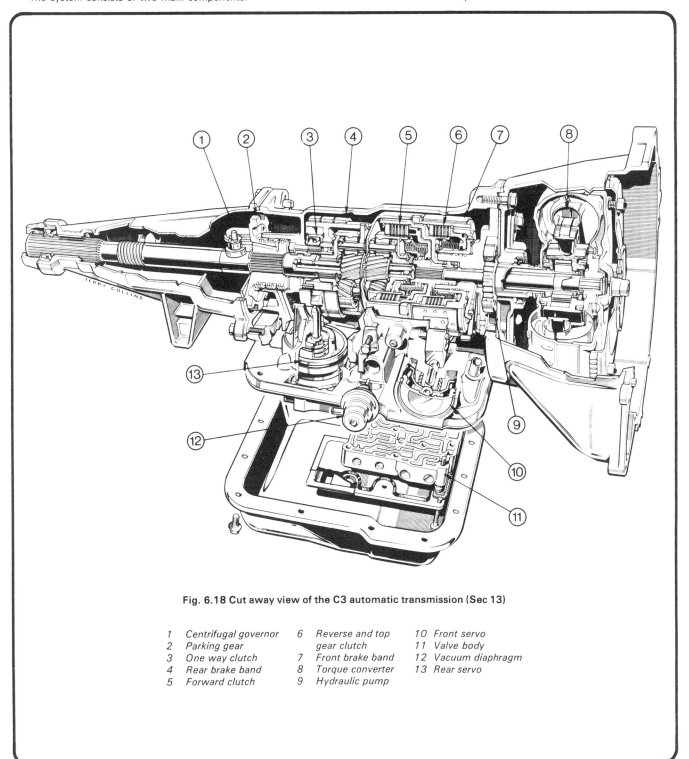

Fig. 6.18 Cut away view of the C3 automatic transmission (Sec 13)

1	Centrifugal governor	6	Reverse and top
2	Parking gear		gear clutch
3	One way clutch	7	Front brake band
4	Rear brake band	8	Torque converter
5	Forward clutch	9	Hydraulic pump

10	Front servo
11	Valve body
12	Vacuum diaphragm
13	Rear servo

14 Automatic transmission – fluid level checking

1   Every 12 000 miles (20 000 km) the automatic transmission fluid level should be checked. First locate the car on level ground and apply the handbrake.
2   Start the engine and let it idle, then apply the footbrake pedal and move the selector lever through all positions three times ending at position P.
3   Wait for approximately one minute then with the engine still idling withdraw the transmission dipstick, wipe it clean with non fluffy rag, re-insert it and withdraw it again. The fluid level should be between the MIN and MAX marks. If necessary top up the level with the correct specified fluid through the dipstick tube.
4   Refit the dipstick and switch off the engine.

15 Automatic transmission – removal and refitting

Any suspected faults must be referred to the main agent before unit removal, as with this type of transmission the fault must be confirmed, using specialist equipment, before it has been removed from the car.
1   Disconnect the battery negative lead.
2   Working in the engine compartment unscrew the four upper transmission-to-engine bolts, noting the location of the earth lead, vacuum line bracket, and dipstick tube bracket.
3   Jack up the car and support on axle stands. Make sure that there is sufficient working room beneath the car.
4   Unhook the exhaust system rubber mounting rings, then lower the exhaust system as far as possible and support it on axle stands. Alternatively suspend it from the underbody with wire.
5   Remove the propeller shaft as described in Chapter 7.
6   Bend back the lock tabs then unscrew and remove the bolts from the anti-roll bar rear mounting clamps and lower the anti-roll bar as far as possible.
7   Remove the oil filler tube and plug the aperture.
8   Unscrew the unions and disconnect the oil cooler pipes from the transmission. Remove the bracket from the engine mounting if necessary.
9   Remove the starter motor as described in Chapter 10.
10 Unclip and remove the selector rod.
11 Unscrew the locknut and disconnect the downshift cable from the transmission.
12 Disconnect the wiring plug from the starter inhibitor switch.
13 Unscrew the bolt and remove the speedometer cable from the extension housing.
14 Support the transmission with a trolley jack.
15 Unscrew the central mounting bolt from the crossmember and remove the cup.
16 Unscrew the bolts and remove the mounting crossmember from the underbody.
17 Lower the transmission three or four inches.
18 Disconnect and unclip the vacuum line.
19 Working through the starter motor aperture, unscrew the driveplate nuts. There are four nuts and it is necessary to turn the crankshaft to locate each one in turn in the aperture.
20 Unscrew the remaining transmission-to-engine bolts and also unbolt the brace.
21 With the help of an assistant lift the transmission from the engine using the trolley jack to take most of the weight. Make sure that the torque converter is held firmly in contact with the transmission oil pump otherwise it could fall out and fluid would be spilled. The car must be adequately supported since it will be necessary to rock the transmission a little to release it.
22 Refitting is a reversal of removal, but first make sure that the torque converter is fully engaged with the oil pump by checking the distance shown in Fig. 6.20. The torque converter drain plug must be aligned with the cut-out in the driveplate. Adjust the downshift cable as described in Section 18, and the selector rod as described in Section 19.

16 Automatic transmission front brake band – adjustment

1   The front brake band should be adjusted every 24 000 miles

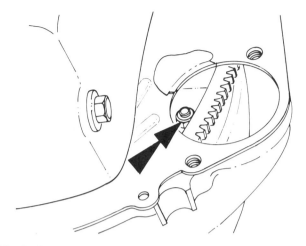

Fig. 6.19 Driveplate nut positioned in the starter motor aperture (Sec 15)

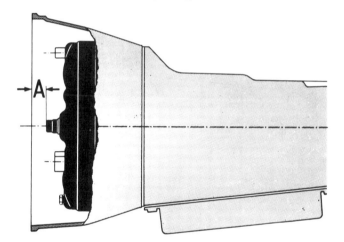

Fig. 6.20 With torque converter correctly fitted dimension A should be 0.4 in (10.0 mm) minimum (Sec 15)

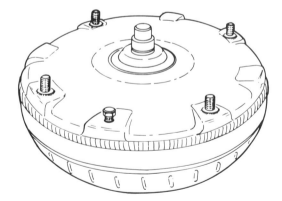

Fig. 6.21 Torque converter studs and drain plug (Sec 15)

(40 000 km). First disconnect the downshift cable from the transmission.
2   Loosen the adjustment screw locknut and back off the screw several turns.
3   Using a suitable torque wrench tighten the screw to 10 lbf ft (14 Nm), then back off two complete turns and tighten the locknut.
4   Reconnect the downshift cable..

17 Automatic transmission starter inhibitor switch – removal and refitting

1   Jack up the front of the car and support on axle stands. Apply the handbrake.
2   Disconnect the wiring plug from the switch.
3   Unscrew the switch and remove the O-ring.
4   Refitting is a reversal of removal. Taking the necessary safety precautions check that the engine will only start with the selector lever in positions P and N, and that the reversing light only glows in position R.

18 Automatic transmission downshift cable – removal, refitting and adjustment

1   Disconnect the downshift inner cable from the carburettor by removing the clip and pin.
2   Unscrew the locknut and release the cable from the carburettor bracket.
3   Jack up the front of the car and support on axle stands. Apply the handbrake.

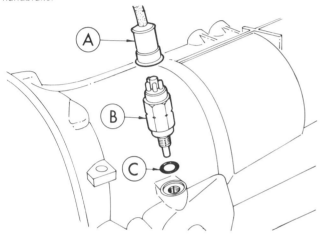

Fig. 6.22 Starter inhibitor switch components (Sec 17)

A   Wiring plug   B   Switch   C   O-ring

4   Unscrew the locknut and disconnect the cable from the transmission bracket and lever.
5   Withdraw the downshift cable from the car.
6   Refitting is a reversal of removal.

7   To adjust the cable first check that the carburettor throttle fully opens when the accelerator pedal is depressed. While an assistant depresses the accelerator pedal turn the lever on the transmission to the kickdown position and lock it in this position. Adjust the cable locknuts to give the dimension shown in Fig. 6.23 then tighten the locknuts.

19 Automatic transmission selector rod – removal, refitting and adjustment

1   Jack up the front of the car and support on axle stands. Apply the handbrake.
2   Unclip and remove the selector rod.
3   Move the selector lever to position D and move the transmission lever two notches from the front stop. Fit the selector rod to the transmission lever then adjust the rod so that it locates directly on the selector lever. Tighten the locknut.

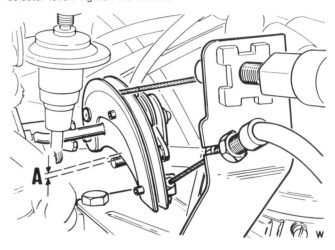

Fig. 6.23 Downshift cable adjustment dimension (Sec 18)

A   =   0.8 to 1.0 mm (0.03 to 0.04 in)

20 Automatic transmission vacuum diaphragm unit – removal and refitting

Refer to Chapter 13, Section 12. The procedures for the C3 and A4LD transmissions are the same.

21 Fault diagnosis – manual gearbox and automatic transmission

Symptom	Reason(s)
Manual gearbox	
Ineffective synchromesh	Worn synchroniser rings
Jumps out of gear	Worn gears or synchronisers Worn selector forks, locking pins and springs
Noisy operation	Worn bearings or gears
Difficulty in engaging gears	Clutch fault Worn selector components Seized input shaft spigot bearing

Automatic transmission
Faults in these units are nearly always the result of low fluid level or incorrect adjustment of the selector linkage or downshift cable. Internal faults should be diagnosed by your main Ford dealer who has the necessary equipment to carry out the work.

Chapter 7 Propeller shaft

Contents

Fault diagnosis – propeller shaft 5
General description 1
Propeller shaft – removal and refitting 2

Propeller shaft centre bearing – renewal 3
Universal joints and centre bearing – testing for wear 4

Specifications

Type .... Two-piece with centre bearing, centre and rear universal joints, front joint either standard universal or rubber coupling according to model

Torque wrench settings

	lbf ft	Nm
Propeller shaft to final drive flange	42 to 49	57 to 67
Centre mounting bracket to floor	13 to 17	18 to 23

1 General description

Drive is transmitted from the gearbox to the final drive unit by means of a two-piece propeller shaft incorporating standard universal joints at the centre and rear. Either a standard universal or rubber coupling is used at the front according to model (photo). A propeller shaft using a rubber coupling may also be fitted in place of an original three universal joint type shaft as a service installation in order to obviate transmission 'whine' and 'growl' symptoms. Due to the location of the final drive unit on the underbody the working angles of the universal joints do not exceed one degree, and therefore wear in the joints is likely to be minimal unless very high mileages have been completed. The universal joints are of the sealed type and cannot be serviced, however it is possible to renew the centre bearing.

2 Propeller shaft – removal and refitting

1   Jack up the rear of the car and support it on axle stands. Chock both front wheels.
2   For better access the rear section of the exhaust system (ie from

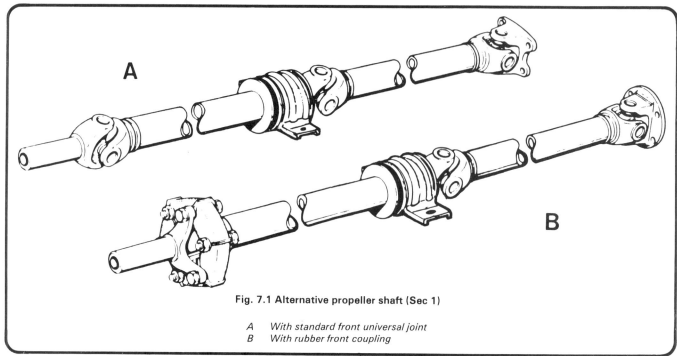

Fig. 7.1 Alternative propeller shaft (Sec 1)

A   With standard front universal joint
B   With rubber front coupling

1.1 Rubber coupling fitted to the front of the propeller shaft on some models

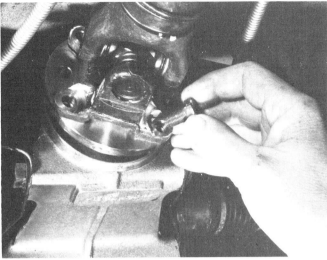

2.4 Removing the bolts securing the propeller shaft to the final drive pinion flange

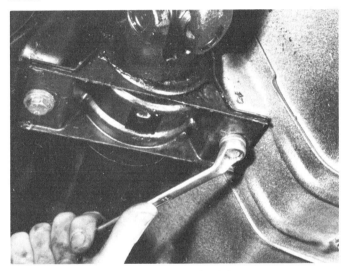

2.5a Removing the centre bearing mounting bolts

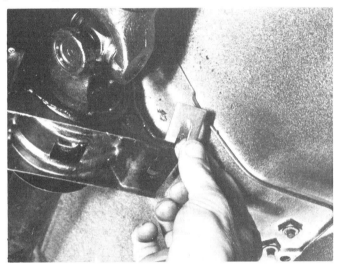

2.5b Removing a slotted shim from the centre bearing

the joint) can be removed as described in Chapter 3, but this is not essential.

3   Mark the rear universal joint and final drive flanges in relation to each other.

4   Unscrew and remove the bolts securing the propeller shaft to the final drive unit while holding the shaft stationary with a long screwdriver inserted between the joint spider (photo). If necessary apply the handbrake as an additional means of holding the shaft stationary.

5   Unscrew the two bolts securing the centre bearing to the underbody and lower the bearing noting the location and number of slotted shims on top of the mounting bracket (photos).

6   Detach the propeller shaft from the final drive unit then pull it from the rear of the gearbox. To prevent any loss of oil/fluid from the gearbox a chamfered plastic cap can be inserted into the oil seal. Alternatively a plastic bag can be positioned on the gearbox and retained with an elastic band.

7   Withdraw the propeller shaft from under the car.

8   Select top gear. Remove the plastic cap or bag and wipe clean the gearbox rear oil seal and the propeller shaft splined spigot.

9   Insert the propeller shaft splined spigot into the gearbox rear extension being careful to avoid damage to the oil seal.

10   Locate the rear of the propeller shaft on the final drive unit, then loosely attach the centre mounting bracket to the underbody with the two bolts.

11   Insert the slotted shims over the top of the bracket.

12   Align the previously made marks if applicable. Then insert the rear flange bolts together with new spring washers and tighten them in diagonal sequence to the specified torque.

13   Tighten the centre mounting bracket bolts to the specified torque.

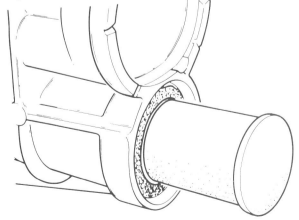

Fig. 7.2 Using a chamfered plastic cap to prevent loss of oil from the gearbox (Sec 2)

14 Using a length of board check that the front and rear sections of the propeller shaft are accurately aligned and if necessary adjust the shim thickness accordingly.

15 Refit the exhaust system if removed, with reference to Chapter 3, then lower the car to the ground.

16 With the car level, check out and if necessary top up the level of oil/fluid in the gearbox. Refer to Chapter 6 on models fitted with automatic transmission for the correct procedure.

3 Propeller shaft centre bearing – renewal

1   Remove the propeller shaft as described in Section 2.

2   Mark the front and rear sections of the propeller shaft in relation to each other. Mark also the exact position of the U-shaped washer beneath the bolt located in the central universal joint.

3   Bend back the locking plate and loosen the bolt in the central universal joint so that the U-shaped washer can be removed (photo).

4   With the U-shaped washer removed, slide the rear section from the front section.

5   Pull the centre bearing bracket together with the insulator rubber from the centre bearing.

6   Remove the outer protective dust cap then, using a suitable puller, pull the centre bearing and inner dust cap from the front propeller shaft section.

7   Wipe clean the centre bearing components. Fit the inner protective dust cap to the new bearing and pack the cavity between the cap and bearing with grease.

8   Using a suitable metal tube on the inner race, push the centre bearing and inner cap onto the front propeller shaft section. Note that the red double seal end of the bearing must face forward.

9   Fit the outer dust cap and pack the cavity between the cap and bearing with grease.

3.3 Propeller shaft centre bearing showing location of bolt (arrowed)

10 If necessary, a new insulator rubber may be fitted to the mounting bracket by bending open the metal tongues. Make sure that the insulator flange is located in the top of the bracket before bending the tongues back.

11 Ease the bracket together with the insulator rubber over the centre bearing.

12 Screw the bolt and locking plate into the end of the front propeller

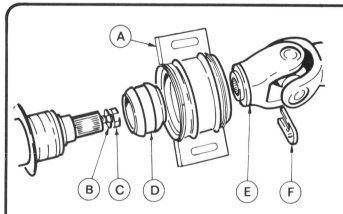

Fig. 7.3 Exploded view of the centre bearing (Sec 3)

A   Mounting bracket with   caps
     rubber insulator   E   Splined universal joint
B   Locking plate   yoke
C   Bolt   F   U-shaped washer
D   Ball bearing and dust

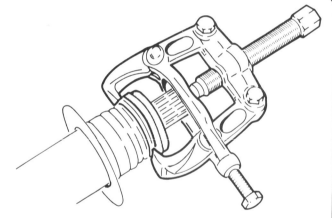

Fig. 7.4 Removing the centre bearing (Sec 3)

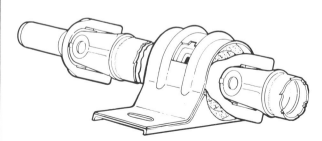

Fig. 7.5 Correct alignment of the front and rear propeller shaft sections – standard front universal joint type (Sec 3)

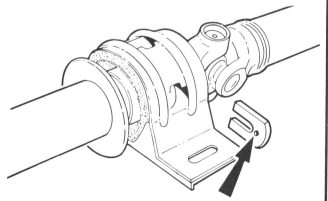

Fig. 7.6 Correct position of peg (arrowed) when refitting the U-shaped washer (Sec 3)

shaft section leaving a sufficient gap for the U-shaped washer to be inserted.

13 Slide the rear section onto the front section making sure that the previously made marks are aligned (refer to Figs. 7.5 and 7.1).

14 Refit the U-shaped washer in its previously noted position with the small peg towards the splines.

15 Tighten the bolts and bend over the locking plate to secure.

---

4 Universal joints and centre bearing – testing for wear

1 Wear in the universal joints is characterised by vibration in the transmission or a knocking noise on taking up the drive.

2 To test a universal joint, jack up the car and support it on axle stands. Then attempt to turn the propeller shaft either side of the joint in alternate opposite directions. Also attempt to lift each side of the joint. Any movement within the universal joint is indicative of considerable wear, and if evident the complete propeller shaft must be renewed.

3 Wear in the centre bearing is characterised by noise in the transmission.

4 The centre bearing is a little more difficult to test for wear. If bearing movement (as distinct from universal joint or rubber insulator movement) can be felt when lifting the propeller shaft front section next to the mounting bracket, the bearing should be removed as described in Section 3 and checked for roughness while spinning the outer race by hand. If excessive wear is evident, renew the bearing.

---

5 Fault diagnosis – propeller shaft

Symptom	Reason(s)
Vibration	Worn universal joints or centre bearing
	Propeller shaft out of balance
	Deteriorated rubber insulator on centre bearing
Knock or 'clunk' when taking up drive	Worn universal joints
	Loose rivet flange bolts
Excessive 'rumble' increasing with road speed	Worn centre bearing

Chapter 8 Final drive and driveshafts

For modifications, and information applicable to later models, see Supplement at end of manual

Contents

Driveshaft – overhaul 7
Driveshaft – removal and refitting 6
Fault diagnosis – final drive and driveshafts 8
Final drive unit – removal and refitting 3

Final drive unit differential bearing oil seals – renewal 5
Final drive unit pinion oil seal – renewal 4
General description 1
Routine maintenance 2

Specifications

Final drive type .... Unsprung, attached to rear underbody and axle crossmember, light alloy housing

Driveshaft type .... Maintenance-free double tripod joint

Final drive lubricant type/specification .... Hypoid gear oil, viscosity SAE 90 EP to Ford spec SQM-2C 9002-AA or 9003-AA (Duckhams Hypoid 90S)

Final drive ratio

1.3 litre	3.77:1
1.6 litre Economy – 4 speed	3.13:1
5 speed	3.38:1
1.6 litre (except Economy) – Hatchback (standard)	3.62:1
Hatchback (trailer package)	3.77:1
Estate	3.92:1
2.0 litre – standard	3.38:1
5 speed gearbox with trailer package	3.62:1

Number of gear teeth:

Crownwheel

3.13:1	47
3.38:1	44
3.62:1	47
3.77:1	49
3.92:1	51

Drive pinion

3.13:1	15
3.38:1	13
3.62:1	13
3.77:1	13
3.92:1	13

Final drive unit

Crownwheel and pinion backlash	0.10 to 0.17 mm (0.004 to 0.007 in)
Crownwheel diameter – 1.3 and 1.6 litre Hatchback	6.5 in
All Estates and 2.0 litre Hatchback	7.0 in
Differential preload – 6.5 in crownwheel	0.11 to 0.15 mm (0.0043 to 0.0059 in)
7.0 in crownwheel	0.13 to 0.17 mm (0.0051 to 0.0067 in)
Oil capacity – 6.5 in crownwheel	0.8 litre; 1.4 pt
7.0 in crownwheel	0.9 litre; 1.6 pt
Driveshaft grease capacity 1.3 and 1.6 litre Hatchback	70 to 90 gr
All Estates and 2.0 litre Hatchback	90 to 110 gr

Torque wrench settings

	lbf ft	Nm
Final drive unit cover	33 to 44	45 to 60
Oil filler plug	25 to 33	35 to 45
Crownwheel to differential bolts	55 to 66	75 to 90
Drive pinion bearing nut (maximum):		
6.5 in crownwheel	88	120
7.0 in crownwheel	103	140
Pinion flange nut	74 to 89	100 to 120
Driveshaft nut	185 to 214	250 to 290
Final drive to crossmember	51 to 66	70 to 90

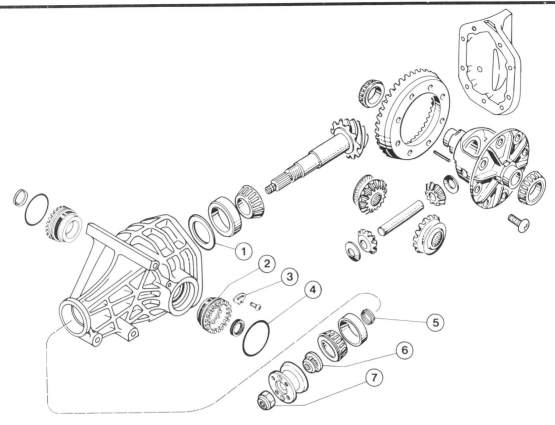

Fig. 8.1 Exploded view of the final drive unit (Sec 1)

1   Compensating washer   5   Collapsible spacer
2   Bearing carrier   6   Pinion bearing nut
3   Locking plate   7   Drive flange nut
4   O-ring

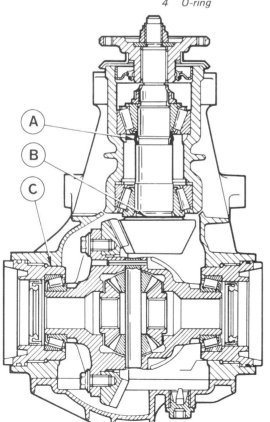

Fig. 8.2 Cross section diagram of the final drive unit (Sec 1)

A   Collapsible spacer
B   Shim
C   Bearing carrier

1 General description

The final drive is of the unsprung type with the final drive unit attached to the rear underbody and axle crossmember. Two driveshafts transmit drive from the final drive unit to the rear wheels which are attached to the fully independent rear suspension. The final drive housing is of light alloy construction.

The pinion runs in two taper roller bearings which are pre-loaded by a collapsible spacer. The differential unit incorporates two planet gears on a single shaft.

The driveshafts are of maintenance-free double tripod joint type.

Overhaul of the final drive unit is not covered in this Chapter owing to the need to use special tools and fixtures not normally available to the home mechanic.

2 Routine maintenance

1   Every 12 000 miles (20 000 km) the final drive unit oil level should be checked and if necessary topped up. To do this either position the car over an inspection pit or jack up the front and rear of the car and support it on axle stands. The car must be level.

2   Using a hexagon key unscrew and remove the filler plug.

3   Using a piece of bent wire check that the oil level is no more than 10 mm (0.4 in) below the filler plug aperture. If necessary top up the level with the recommended oil. Do not overfill.

4   Refit the filler plug and tighten to the specified torque. Do not use any sealing compound on the threads.

5   At the same time examine the driveshaft rubber gaiters for damage and security. The gaiters should be flexed by hand to check inside the folds. Also check that the clips are secure and that there is no leakage of grease.

3 Final drive unit – removal and refitting

1   Loosen the rear roadwheel nuts, then jack up the rear of the car

and support it on axle stands. Chock the front wheels and remove the rear wheels.

2   Remove the rear brake drums with reference to Chapter 9.

3   Unclip the driveshaft outer joint plastic covers from the upper brake backplate bolts (photos).

4   Using a socket through the holes in the hub flanges unscrew the bolts securing the rear hubs to the lower suspension arms (photo).

5   Place a container beneath the final drive unit to catch any spilled oil.

6   Working on one side at a time pull the hub and brake assembly from the suspension arm sufficient to withdraw the driveshaft from the final drive unit (photo).

7   Refit the hub and brake assemblies and secure them with two bolts on each side. Tie the driveshafts to one side making sure that the deflection of each tripod joint does not exceed 13°.

8   Lower the rear section of the exhaust system (ie from the joint) as described in Chapter 3.

9   Mark the rear universal joint and final drive flanges in relation to each other.

10 Unscrew and remove the bolts securing the propeller shaft to the final drive unit while holding the shaft stationary with a long screwdriver inserted between the joint spider.

11 Unscrew the two bolts securing the centre bearing to the underbody and lower the bearing noting the location and number of slotted shims on top of the mounting bracket.

12 Detach the propeller shaft from the final drive unit and tie it to one side.

13 Support the final drive unit with a trolley jack.

14 Unbolt the final drive rear mounting from the underbody, and remove the vent pipe from the hole in the underbody (photos).

15 Unscrew the two short bolts securing the front of the final drive unit to the rear suspension crossmember.

16 Lower the final drive unit slightly then unscrew the nuts and remove the final drive unit mounting through bolts (photo).

17 Lower the final drive unit and withdraw it from under the car (photos).

18 Refitting is a reversal of removal, but do not tighten the mounting nuts and bolts until the final drive unit has been raised so that the rear

3.3a Removing a driveshaft outer joint plastic cover

3.3b A driveshaft outer joint plastic cover and plastic retainers

3.4 Removing the rear hub retaining bolts

3.6 Removing the hub and brake assembly from the rear suspension arm

3.14a Removing the final drive rear mounting bolts

3.14b Removing the final drive vent pipe

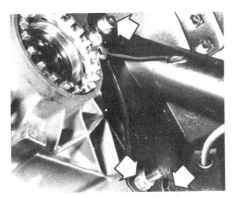

3.16 Final drive mounting bolt locations (arrowed)

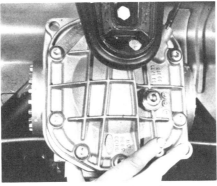

3.17a Removing the final drive unit

3.17b Final drive rear mounting

3.17c Final drive mounting on rear suspension crossmember

4.3 Removing the final drive pinion flange nut

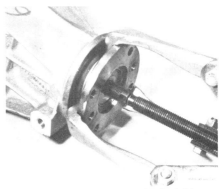

4.4a Using a puller to remove the final drive pinion flange

4.4b Showing splines on the drive flange and pinion

4.5 Pinion oil seal location in the final drive unit

4.9 Tightening the final drive pinion flange nut

mounting is touching the underbody. Refer to Chapters 7 and 3 if necessary when refitting the propeller shaft and exhaust system. Top up the final drive unit oil level with reference to Section 2.

4 Final drive unit pinion oil seal – renewal

1 Remove the propeller shaft as described in Chapter 7.
2 Hold the final drive flange stationary by bolting a long bar to it or by fitting two long bolts to it and inserting a long bar between them.
3 Unscrew the self-locking pinion flange nut (photo).
4 Using a suitable puller pull the drive flange from the pinion (photos). As there may be some loss of oil, place a suitable container beneath the final drive unit.
5 Using a screwdriver, lever the oil seal from the final drive unit (photo).
6 Clean the oil seal seating within the housing, the drive flange, and the end of the pinion.

7 Fill the space between the lips of the new oil seal with grease. Then using a suitable metal tube or block of wood with a hole in it, drive the seal squarely into the final drive housing until flush.
8 Slide the drive flange onto the pinion splines taking care not to damage the oil seal.
9 Fit the self-locking nut and tighten it to the specified torque while holding the drive flange stationary using the method described in paragraph 2 (photo). Ideally a new self-locking nut should be used, and it should not be unscrewed and tightened more than three times otherwise it will lose its self-locking characteristic.
10 Refit the propeller shaft as described in Chapter 7.
11 Top-up the final drive unit oil level with reference to Section 2.

5 Final drive unit differential bearing oil seals – renewal

1 Remove the driveshafts as described in Section 6.
2 Using vernier calipers measure the fitted depth of the oil seals in

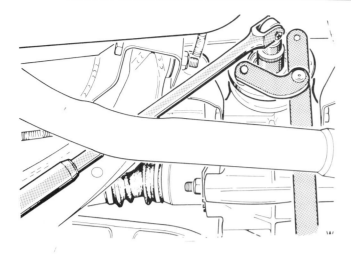

Fig. 8.3 Using a special tool to hold the final drive flange stationary while unscrewing the nut (Sec 4)

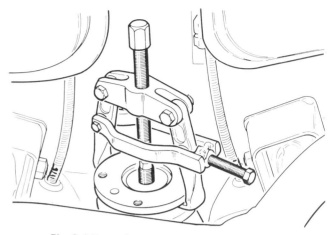

Fig. 8.4 Removing the final drive flange (Sec 4)

Fig. 8.5 Installing the final drive unit pinion oil seal (Sec 4)

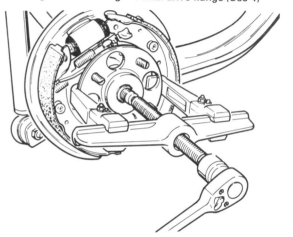

Fig. 8.6 Removing a rear wheel drive flange (Sec 6)

the differential bearing housings. This should be approximately 0.442 in (11.23 mm) measured from the outer face of the retaining ring.

3   Using a screwdriver or hooked instrument, lever the oil seals from the differential bearing housings (photo). If available, Ford tool 15 048 may be used. This tool has internally expanding legs which grip the oil seal.

4   Clean the oil seal seatings in the housings.

5   Smear the lips of both oil seals with a little grease. Then using a suitable metal tube press each seal squarely into its differential bearing

5.3 Differential bearing oil seal location in the final drive unit

housing to the previously noted depth. Alternatively use Ford tool 15 076 noting that the tool can be used in two different positions according to the size of crownwheel fitted.

6   Refit the driveshafts as described in Section 6.

6   Driveshaft – removal and refitting

1   Remove the wheel cap as applicable and loosen the wheel nuts.

2   Loosen the driveshaft nut at the centre of the hub.

3   Jack up the rear of the car and support it on axle stands. Chock the front wheels and release the handbrake.

4   Remove the wheel and the driveshaft nut.

5   Remove the brake drum, with reference to Chapter 9 if necessary.

6   Using a suitable puller, pull the drive flange from the hub and off the driveshaft.

7   Unclip the driveshaft outer joint plastic cover from the upper brake backplate bolts.

8   Unscrew the four bolts securing the hub and brake backplate to the lower suspension arm.

9   Place a container beneath the final drive unit to catch any spilled oil.

10 Pull the hub and brake assembly from the suspension arm sufficient to withdraw the driveshaft from the final drive unit, then withdraw the driveshaft from the hub (photos). Note that the deflection of each tripod joint should not exceed 13°.

11 In order to prevent possible damage to the hydraulic brake pipe, attach the hub and brake assembly loosely to the suspension arm with two bolts.

12 Refitting is a reversal of removal. Tighten the driveshaft nut to the specified torque after lowering the car to the ground. Then lock the nut by staking its outer ring into the groove in the driveshaft. Top up the final drive unit oil level with reference to Section 2.

6.10a Removing a driveshaft from the final drive unit

6.10b Driveshaft inner joint

7 Driveshaft – overhaul

1   Remove the clips from the rubber gaiter.
2   Using a hacksaw, cut the joint cover in line with the driveshaft then use a pair of pliers to peel the cover from the joint until the swaged end is released.
3   Pull the driveshaft stub from the tripod joint.
4   Mark the tripod joint in relation to the driveshaft centre section, then extract the retaining circlip.

5   Push the rubber gaiter and the remains of the joint cover along the driveshaft away from the joint.
6   Using a suitable three-legged puller pull the tripod joint off the splined driveshaft centre section.
7   Remove the plastic washer, joint cover and rubber gaiter from the driveshaft.
8   Remove the rubber O-ring from the groove in the driveshaft stub.
9   Wash all the components in paraffin and wipe dry then examine them for wear and damage. In particular check the tripod joint bearings for rough operation and excessive wear. Renew the compo-

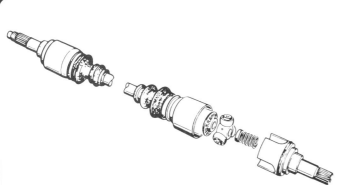

Fig. 8.7 Exploded view of a driveshaft (Sec 7)

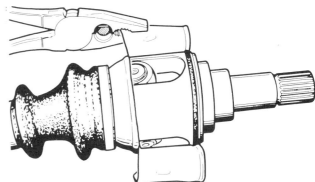

Fig. 8.8 Removing the driveshaft joint cover (Sec 7)

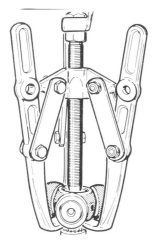

Fig. 8.9 Removing a tripod joint from the driveshaft (Sec 7)

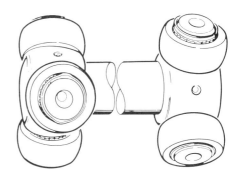

Fig. 8.10 Showing the correct offset position of the driveshaft tripod joints (Sec 7)

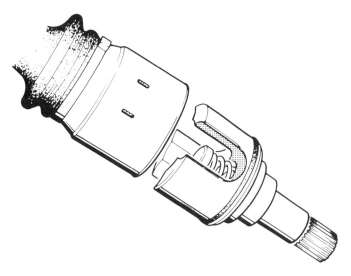

Fig. 8.11 The notches on the joint cover must engage the cut-outs in the driveshaft stub (Sec 7)

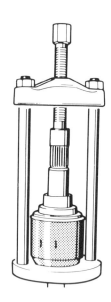

Fig. 8.12 Using a puller to fit the joint cover (Sec 7)

nents as necessary and obtain a new joint cover and rubber O-ring.

10 Locate the rubber gaiter followed by the joint cover and plastic washer (convex side first) onto the driveshaft centre section.

11 Locate the tripod joint on the driveshaft with the previously made marks aligned, and drive it on the splines using a suitable metal tube. Note that the joints on each end of the driveshaft must be offset as shown in Fig. 8.10.

12 Fit the retaining circlip to the end of the driveshaft.

13 Fit the rubber O-ring into the groove in the driveshaft stub, and also locate the spring and pressure pad in the hole inside the stub.

14 Mount the driveshaft centre section in a vice and fit the stub over the tripod joint. Pack the joint with approximately 15 grams of the recommended grease, and smear a little grease onto the rubber O-ring.

15 Push the stub onto the driveshaft so that the internal spring is compressed then, using a suitable puller, pull the joint cover over the stub making sure that the six notches engage with the cut-outs in the stub.

16 Swage the joint cover onto the stub at three equally spaced points

then remove the puller.

17 Swage the remainder of the joint cover onto the stub.

18 From the inner end of the joint cover, pack the joint with 65 to 85 grams of the recommended grease.

19 Locate the rubber gaiter on the joint cover and driveshaft making sure that it is not twisted or stretched. Then fit and tighten the clips.

20 Repeat the procedure given in paragraphs 1 to 19 on the remaining joint.

8 Fault diagnosis – final drive and driveshafts

Symptom	Reason(s)
Noise from final drive unit	Lack of lubricant Worn bearings, crownwheel and pinion Loose or deteriorated final drive unit mountings
Oil leakage from final drive unit	Pinion oil seal or differential bearing oil seals worn
Metallic grating noise from driveshafts	Worn driveshaft joints

Chapter 9 Braking system

For modifications, and information applicable to later models, see Supplement at end of manual

Contents

Brake disc, examination, removal and refitting 6
Brake drum – inspection and renovation 8
Deceleration control valve – removal and refitting 11
Disc caliper – removal, overhaul and refitting 5
Disc pads – inspection and renewal 3
Fault diagnosis – braking system 19
Footbrake pedal – removal and refitting 17
General description 1
Handbrake cable – removal, refitting and adjusting 15
Handbrake lever – removal and refitting 14

Hydraulic brake lines and hoses – removal and refitting 12
Hydraulic system – bleeding 13
Master cylinder – removal, overhaul and refitting 10
Rear brake backplate – removal and refitting 9
Rear brake shoes – inspection and renewal 4
Rear wheel cylinder – removal, overhaul and refitting 7
Routine maintenance 2
Stoplamp switch – removal, refitting and adjusting 18
Vacuum servo unit – description, removal and refitting 16

Specifications

System type	Front discs and rear drums with vacuum servo assistance, dual hydraulic circuit split front/rear, and deceleration sensitive pressure relief valve in rear brake hydraulic line. Cable operated handbrake on rear wheels
Brake fluid type/specification	Brake fluid to Ford spec Amber SAM-6C 9103-A (Duckhams Universal Brake and Clutch Fluid)

Discs

Type – 1.3 and 1.6 litre models	Solid
– 2.0 litre models	Ventilated
Diameter	240.0 mm (9.45 in)
Thickness – 1.3 and 1.6 litre models	12.6 mm (0.5 in)
– 2.0 litre models	24.0 mm (0.95 in)
Maximum run-out (including hub)	0.055 mm (0.002 in)
Minimum pad lining thickness	1.5 mm (0.06 in)

Drums

Internal diameter – 1.3 and 1.6 litre Hatchback and Saloon models ...	203.2 mm (8.0 in)
– 1.8 and 2.0 litre Hatchback and Saloon, and all Estate models	228.6 mm (9.0 in)
Minimum lining thickness	1.0 mm (0.04 in)
Servo unit type	Suspended vacuum

Torque wrench settings

	lbf ft	Nm
Caliper	38 to 45	52 to 61
Rear brake backplate	38 to 48	52 to 64
Hydraulic unions	5 to 7	6.8 to 9.5
Bleed valves (maximum)	8	10.2
Servo to bulkhead	33	45

1 General description

The braking system is of dual hydraulic circuit type with discs at the front and self-adjusting drum brakes at the rear. The front and rear hydraulic circuits are operated independently so that in the event of a failure in one circuit the remaining circuit still functions.

The front calipers are of single piston type with a sliding housing which ensures equal effort to each disc pad. The calipers are self-adjusting by means of a wedged type piston seal which is deformed when the brakes are applied but regains its original shape when the brakes are released.

The rear brakes incorporate leading and trailing shoes operated by double-acting wheel cylinders. The self-adjusting mechanism consists of a toothed quadrant which is kept in contact with a toothed pin attached to the shoe strut by means of a spring. The quadrant incorporates an arm which locates in a slot in the leading shoe. As the linings wear the quadrant is pulled from the pin when the footbrake is operated, and automatically repositioned to effectively lengthen the strut.

The deceleration sensitive valve in the rear brake hydraulic circuit ensures that the rear brakes do not lock before the front brakes during high deceleration.

Fig. 9.1 Braking components fitted to the bulkhead (Sec 1)

A Bracket	D Pushrod
B Master cylinder	E Pedal
C Servo unit	F Stoplamp switch

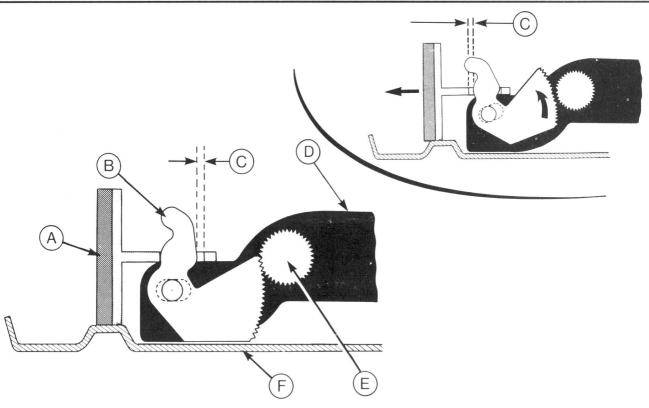

Fig. 9.2 Diagram showing operation of the rear brake self-adjusting mechanism (Sec 1)

A	Leading brake shoe	C	Shoe return gap
B	Quadrant lever	D	Strut

E	Pin	*Inset shows brake applied*
F	Backplate	

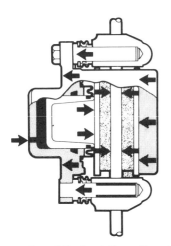

Fig. 9.3 Cross section of the front disc caliper showing force direction when depressing the footbrake pedal (Sec 1)

The handbrake operates on the rear wheels and the handbrake lever operates a switch which illuminates a warning light on the instrument panel. The same light is used as a warning for low fluid level in the master cylinder reservoir. A brake pad wear warning light is also included on the instrument panel.

2   Routine maintenance

1   Every 6000 miles (10 000 km) check and if necessary top up the brake fluid level in the translucent reservoir. Note that the level will drop slightly as the front brake pads wear and topping up to correct this is not necessary. If the level is near the minimum mark the hydraulic circuit should be thoroughly checked for leaks.
2   At the same time check the condition of the hydraulic hoses and

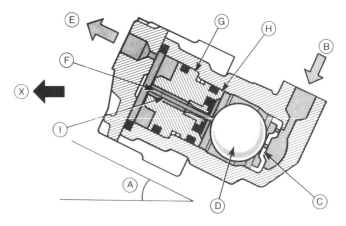

Fig. 9.4 Cross section of the deceleration valve in the rear brake hydraulic circuit (Sec 1)

A	Installation angle	G	Large piston
B	Inlet port	H	Small piston
C	Diffuser	I	Hollow pin
E	Outlet port		
F	Piston bore	*Arrow X indicates front of car*

rigid brake lines, in particular the condition of the plastic coating on the brake lines.
3   Check the disc pads and rear brake shoes for wear and renew them if necessary.
4   Every 12 000 miles (20 000 km) check the operation of the hydraulic fluid level warning system by unscrewing the filler cap from the master cylinder reservoir and holding the switch with the float downwards. With the ignition switched on the warning light should be illuminated (photo).
5   Every 36 000 miles (60 000 km) or three years whichever occurs first, the hydraulic brake fluid should be renewed and the visible rubber dust seals checked for condition and any signs of leakage.

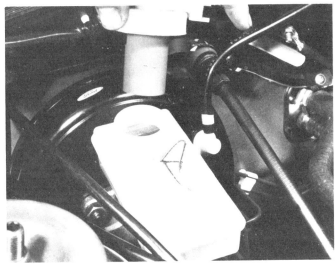

2.4 Checking the hydraulic fluid level warning system

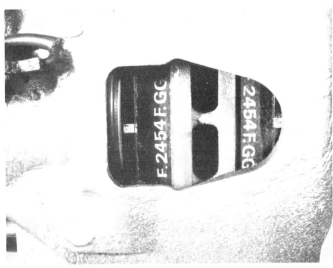

3.1 View of the disc pads through the caliper inspection hole

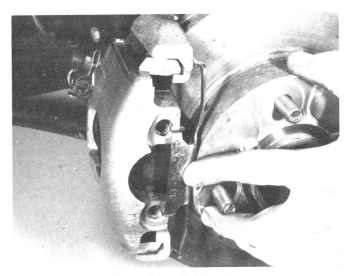

3.6 Removing the caliper retaining clip (Teves)

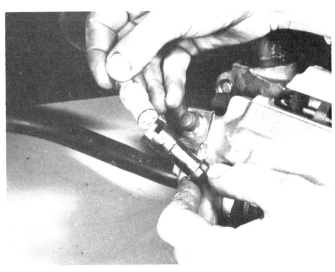

3.7 Disconnecting the disc pad wear sensor plug (Teves)

3 Disc pads – inspection and renewal

1   The disc pad linings can be checked for wear without removing the front wheels. First jack up the front of the car and support on axle stands, and apply the handbrake. Working beneath the car insert a mirror between the caliper and wheel and check that the pad linings are not less than the minimum thickness given in the Specifications (photo).

2   To renew the disc pads remove the wheel.

Girling caliper (1.3 and 1.6 litre models)
3   Where applicable disconnect the wiring to the disc pad wear sensor.

4   Unscrew and remove the upper guide bolt while holding the sleeve stationary with a spanner.

5   Swing the caliper down and lift out the disc pads.

Teves caliper (2.0 litre models)
6   Prise the retaining clip from the piston housing and carrier. Hold it with a pair of pliers to avoid its causing personal injury (photo).

7   Unscrew the nut securing the wear sensor and disconnect the wiring plug (photo).

8   Using a 7 mm hexagon key unscrew and remove the special guide bolts securing the piston housing to the carrier and withdraw the housing (photo). Support the housing on an axle stand to avoid damage to the hydraulic hose.

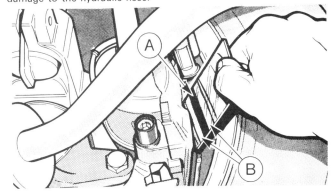

Fig. 9.5 Using a mirror to check the disc pad linings for wear (Sec 3)

A   Brake disc   *B   Disc pad linings*

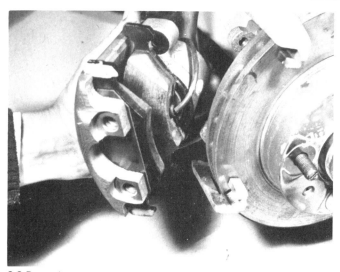

3.8 Removing the caliper (Teves)

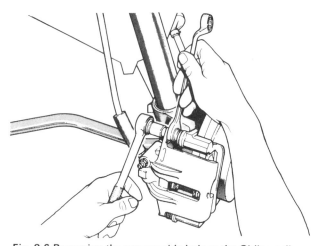

Fig. 9.6 Removing the upper guide bolt on the Girling caliper
(Sec 3)

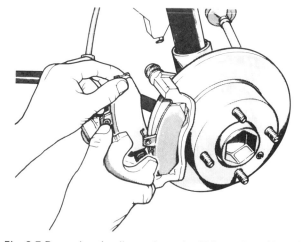

Fig. 9.7 Removing the disc pads on the Girling caliper (Sec 3)

9   Withdraw the disc pads from the housing (photo). It may be
necessary to prise the outer pad with a screwdriver to release it from
the anti-rattle compound.

All calipers
10   Brush the dust and dirt from the housing, piston, carrier, pads and
disc *but do not inhale it as it is injurious to health.* Scrape any scale or
rust from the disc.

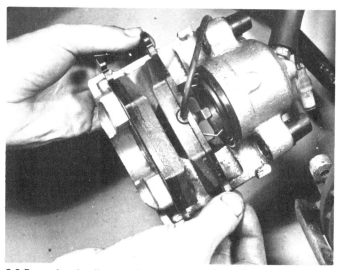

3.9 Removing the disc pads from the caliper (Teves)

11   Push the piston into the housing in order to accommodate the
extra thickness of the new disc pads.
12   Refitting is a reversal of removal, but tighten the bolt(s) to the
specified torque, and on Girling calipers check that the anti-rattle clips
are correctly located in the piston housing. On completion depress the
footbrake pedal several times in order to set the disc pads in their
normal positions.

4   Rear brake shoes – inspection and renewal

For 1.3 and 1.6 Saloon and Hatchback models, see Chapter 13
1   The rear brake shoe linings can be checked for wear without
removing the rear wheels. First jack up the rear of the car and support
on axle stands. Chock the front wheels and release the handbrake.
2   Prise the plug from the brake backplate and using an inspection
lamp or torch check that the brake shoe lining thickness is not less
than the amount given in the Specifications (photo). If necessary
scrape the paint from the edge of the lining and shoe. Refit the plug.
3   To renew the brake shoes remove the wheel, then remove the clip
and pull off the brake drum (photo).
4   Remove the hold down spring from the leading shoe by depressing
the cup with pliers and turning it through 90° (photo).
5   Note the fitted position of the return springs then release the
leading shoe from the wheel cylinder and anchor using a screwdriver
or adjustable spanner (photos). Note the forward rotation arrows on
the brake shoes.
6   Unhook the return springs and remove the leading shoe.
7   Remove the hold down spring from the trailing shoe by depressing
the cup with pliers and turning it through 90°.
8   Withdraw the trailing shoe and disengage the handbrake lever
from the cable.
9   Unhook the springs from the trailing shoe and remove the self-
adjusting strut.
10   Brush the dust from the backplate, wheel cylinder, shoes, strut and
brake drum *but do not inhale it as it is injurious to health.* Scrape any
scale or rust from the drum.
11   Apply a little brake grease to the six shoe contact points on the
backplate.
12   Lubricate the handbrake lever retaining/pivot rivet with one or two
drops of oil then wipe away any excess oil.
13   Check the wheel cylinder for signs of hydraulic fluid leakage and,
if evident, repair or renew the wheel cylinder.
14   Fit the springs to the trailing shoe and attach the self-adjusting
strut.
15   Attach the handbrake cable to the lever and position the trailing
shoe on the wheel cylinder and anchor. Make sure that the upper
return spring is located on the strut.
16   Refit the hold down spring to the trailing shoe.
17   Connect the return springs to the leading shoe then locate the
lower end in the anchor and lever the upper end onto the toothed

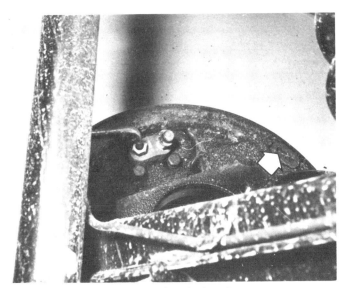
4.2 Rear brake shoe lining inspection plug location

4.3 Removing the rear brake drum retaining clip

4.4 A rear brake shoe hold down spring and cup

4.5a Rear brake components

4.5b Showing rear brake self-adjusting strut and springs

4.5c Rear brake shoe lower anchor and return spring

quadrant lever and wheel cylinder. Take care to avoid damage to the wheel cylinder dust seal.

18   Refit the hold down spring to the leading shoe.

19   Using a screwdriver push the self-adjusting toothed quadrant fully towards the backplate to its initial setting.

20   Refit the brake drum and clip, followed by the wheel. Lower the car to the ground.

21   Depress the footbrake pedal several times in order to set the brake shoes in their normal positions.

5   Disc caliper – removal, overhaul and refitting

1   Jack up the front of the car and support on axle stands. Apply the handbrake and remove the wheel.

2   Remove the brake fluid reservoir filler cap and secure a piece of polythene sheeting over the filler neck with a rubber band. This will reduce the loss of hydraulic fluid in the following procedure.

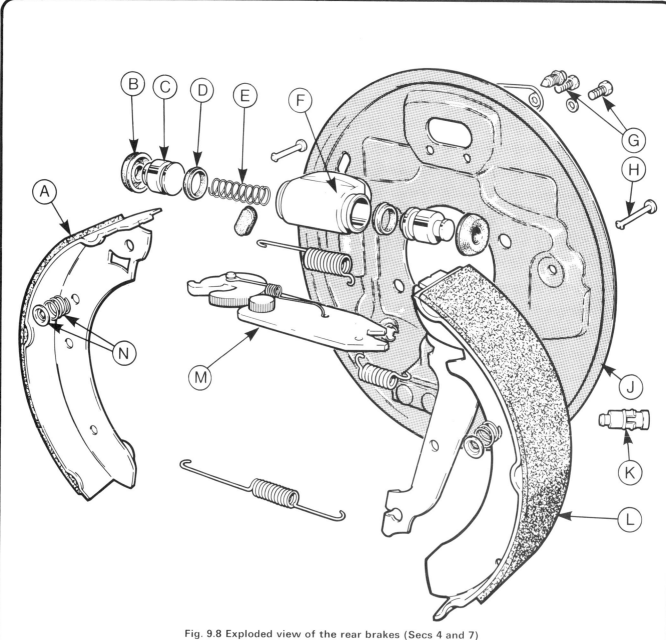

Fig. 9.8 Exploded view of the rear brakes (Secs 4 and 7)
(1.8 and 2.0 litre models)

A	Leading shoe	F	Wheel cylinder housing	K	Adjustment plunger
B	Dust cover	G	Bolts	L	Trailing shoe
C	Piston	H	Hold down pin	M	Self-adjusting strut
D	Piston seal	J	Backplate	N	Hold down spring and cup
E	Spring				

For 1.3 and 1.6 Saloon and Hatchback models, see Chapter 13.

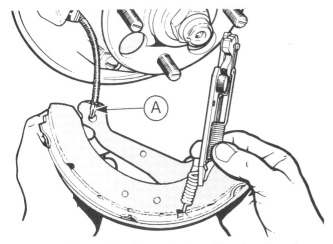

Fig. 9.9 Removing the rear brake trailing shoe (Sec 4)

A   Handbrake cable and slot

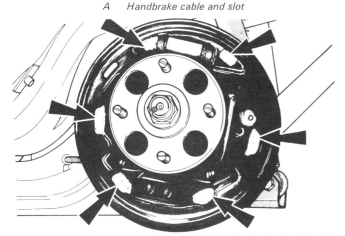

Fig. 9.10 Brake grease application points on the backplate (Sec 4)

3   Release the flexible hose from the rigid brake pipe. Plug or cap the open ends to keep fluid in and dirt out. Unscrew the flexible hose from the caliper.
4   Remove the disc pads as described in Section 3.
5   On the Girling caliper (1.3 and 1.6 litre models) unscrew and remove the lower guide bolt while holding the sleeve stationary with a spanner, then remove the caliper.
6   On the Teves caliper (2.0 litre models) remove the caliper from the car.
7   If necessary unbolt the caliper carrier from the spindle carrier (photos).
8   Position a piece of wood inside the caliper then use low air pressure (ie from a foot pump) to force the piston from the housing.
9   Using a non-metallic instrument remove the piston seal and dust cover.
10   Clean the piston and housing with methylated spirit and allow to dry. Examine the surfaces of the piston and housing for wear, damage and corrosion. If the piston surface alone is unserviceable obtain a repair kit which includes a new piston, but if the piston housing is unserviceable renew the complete caliper. If both surfaces are serviceable obtain a repair kit of seals.
11   Coat the piston and seals with hydraulic fluid then refit them to the housing.
12   Refit the caliper carrier if removed and tighten the bolts to the specified torque.
13   Refit the Girling caliper lower guide bolt and tighten to the specified torque.
14   Refit the disc pads with reference to Section 3.
15   Refit the flexible hose to the caliper and tighten it, then connect the hose to the rigid pipe. Make sure the hose is not kinked or twisted.
16   Remove the polythene sheeting then bleed the hydraulic system as described in Section 13.

5.7a Unscrew the bolts ...

5.7b ... and remove the caliper carrier (circlip shown attached to the carrier)

17   Refit the wheel and lower the car to the ground, then apply the footbrake pedal several times to set the disc pads in their normal positions.

---

6   Brake disc – examination, removal and refitting

1   Jack up the front of the car and support on axle stands. Apply the handbrake.
2   Remove the disc caliper and carrier with reference to Section 5 but do not disconnect the hydraulic pipe. Support the caliper on an axle stand to prevent straining the flexible hose.
3   Rotate the disc and examine it for deep scoring or grooving. Light scoring is normal, but if excessive, the disc should be removed and either renewed or ground by a suitable engineering works.
4   Using a dial gauge or metal block and feeler gauges check that the disc run-out does not exceed the amount given in Specifications.
5   To remove the disc unscrew the cross-head screw and tap the disc from the hub.
6   Refitting is a reversal of removal, but make sure that the mating faces of the disc and hub are clean, and refer to Section 5 when refitting the caliper.

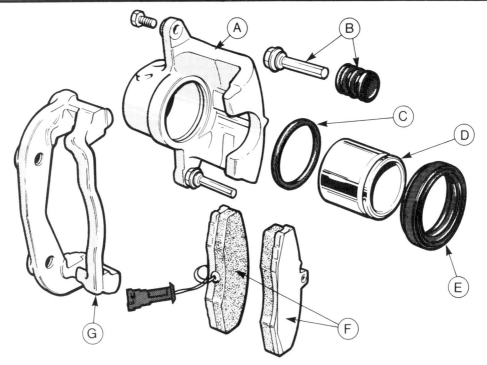

Fig. 9.11 Exploded view of the Girling disc caliper (Sec 5)

A   Housing
B   Guide pin and dust cover
C   Piston seal
D   Piston
E   Dust cover
F   Disc pads
G   Carrier

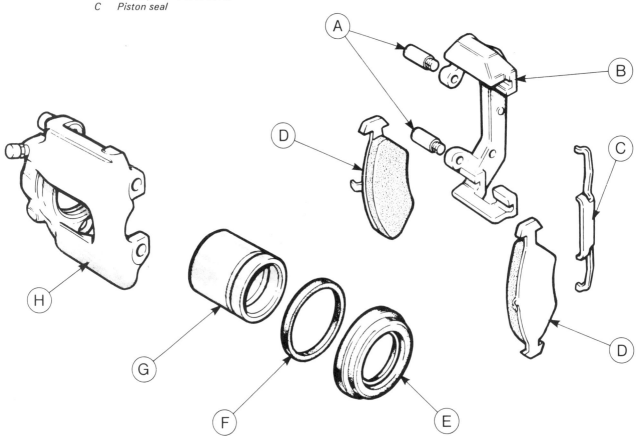

Fig. 9.12 Exploded view of the Teves disc caliper (Sec 5)

A   Guide bolts
B   Carrier
C   Circlip
D   Disc pads
E   Dust cover
F   Piston seal
G   Piston
H   Housing

7   Rear wheel cylinder – removal, overhaul and refitting

1   Jack up the rear of the car and support on axle stands. Chock the front wheels and release the handbrake.
2   Remove the wheel then remove the clip and pull off the brake drum.
3   Fit a brake hose clamp to the flexible brake hose. Alternatively remove the brake fluid reservoir filler cap and secure a piece of polythene sheeting over the filler neck with a rubber band. This will reduce the loss of hydraulic fluid in the following procedure.
4   Unscrew the union nut and disconnect the hydraulic pipe from the wheel cylinder (photo). Plug the pipe to prevent the ingress of foreign matter.
5   Pull the tops of the brake shoes apart so that the self-adjusting strut holds them clear of the wheel cylinder.
6   Unscrew the bolts and withdraw the wheel cylinder and sealing ring.
7   Prise off the rubber dust covers and withdraw the pistons and central spring keeping the pistons identified for position.
8   Prise the seals from the pistons.
9   Clean all the components in methylated spirit and allow to dry. Examine the surfaces of the pistons and cylinder bore for wear, scoring and corrosion. If evident, renew the complete wheel cylinder, but if they are in good condition discard the seals and obtain a repair kit.
10   Dip the inner seals in clean brake fluid and fit them to the piston grooves, using the fingers only to manipulate them. Make sure that the seal lips face into the cylinder as shown in Fig. 9.8.
11   Carefully insert the pistons and central spring then fit the dust covers.
12   Wipe clean the backplate, then fit the wheel cylinder together with a new sealing ring and tighten the bolts.
13   Reconnect the hydraulic pipe and tighten the union nut.
14   Using a screwdriver push the self-adjusting toothed quadrant fully towards the backplate to its initial setting.
15   Refit the brake drum clip and wheel.
16   Remove the brake hose clamp or polythene sheeting as applicable, then bleed the hydraulic system as described in Section 13. If a brake hose clamp has been used it will only be necessary to bleed the one wheel cylinder, otherwise bleed both wheel cylinders.
17   Lower the car to the ground and apply the footbrake pedal several times in order to set the brake shoes in their normal positions.

8   Brake drum – inspection and renovation

1   Whenever the brake drums are removed they should be checked for wear and damage. Light scoring of the friction surface is normal, but if excessive or if the surface has worn oval it may be possible to grind it true. This work should be carried out by a qualified engineer, although it is preferable to renew both rear drums.

9   Rear brake backplate – removal and refitting

1   Remove the rear brake shoes as described in Section 4.
2   Disconnect the handbrake cable from the backplate by extracting the U-clip.
3   Remove the wheel cylinder as described in Section 7.
4   Unclip the driveshaft outer joint plastic cover from the upper brake backplate bolts.
5   Using a socket through the holes in the hub flange unscrew the bolts securing the hub and backplate to the lower suspension arm.
6   Place a container beneath the final drive unit to catch any spilled oil, then withdraw the hub and driveshaft from the final drive unit and remove it from the lower suspension arm.
7   Remove the rear brake backplate.
8   If necessary prise out the handbrake stop button.
9   Refitting is a reversal of removal, but make sure that the mating faces of the hub, backplate and lower suspension arm are clean. Tighten the bolts to the specified torque and refer to Sections 7 and 4 when refitting the wheel cylinder and rear brake shoes. If necessary top up the final drive unit oil level with reference to Chapter 8.

10   Master cylinder – removal, overhaul and refitting

1   Depress the footbrake pedal several times to dissipate the vacuum in the servo unit.
2   Disconnect the wiring from the low level switch on the hydraulic fluid reservoir filler cap (photo).
3   Place a suitable container beneath the master cylinder then unscrew the union nuts and disconnect the hydraulic pipes. Plug the pipes or cover them with masking tape to prevent the ingress of foreign matter.
4   Unscrew the mounting nuts and withdraw the master cylinder from the servo unit. Cover the master cylinder with rag to prevent spilling hydraulic fluid on the paintwork. If accidentally spilt, swill off immediately with copious amounts of cold water.
5   Drain the remaining fluid from the master cylinder, and clean the exterior surfaces with methylated spirit.
6   Pull out the reservoir and prise out the sealing rubbers.
7   Mount the master cylinder in a vice then depress the primary piston slightly and extract the circlip and washer. Withdraw the primary piston assembly.
8   Depress the secondary piston and remove the stop pin from the fluid aperture.
9   Remove the master cylinder from the vice and tap it on the bench to remove the secondary piston assembly.
10   Prise the seals from the secondary piston. Do not attempt to dismantle the primary piston.
11   Clean all the components in methylated spirit and examine them for wear and damage. In particular check the surfaces of the pistons

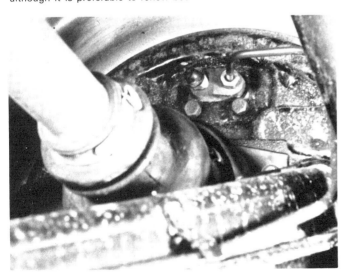

7.4 Rear wheel cylinder hydraulic union nut and retaining bolts

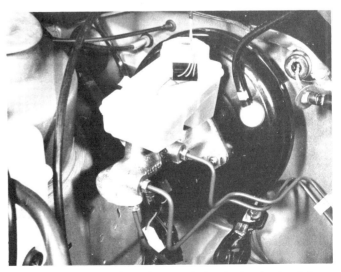

10.2 Brake master cylinder and servo unit showing low level switch wiring plug

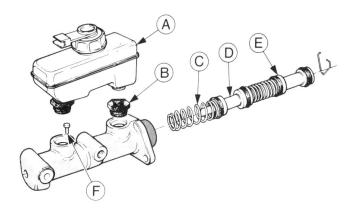

Fig. 9.13 Exploded view of the master cylinder (Sec 10)

A   Reservoir   D   Secondary piston
B   Seal   E   Primary piston
C   Spring   F   Stop pin

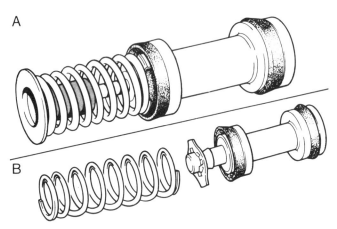

Fig. 9.14 Master cylinder primary piston (A) and secondary piston (B) (Sec 10)

and cylinder bore for scoring and corrosion. If the cylinder bore is worn renew the complete master cylinder otherwise obtain a repair kit including pistons and seals.
12 Check that the inlet and outlet parts are free and unobstructed. Dip the pistons and seals in clean brake fluid.
13 Fit the seals to the secondary piston using the fingers only to manipulate them into the grooves. Note that the sealing lips must face away from each other.
14 Insert the secondary piston and spring into the cylinder. Turn the piston slowly as the first seal enters to avoid trapping the sealing lip. Similarly insert the primary piston and spring then fit the washer and circlip.
15 Depress the primary and secondary pistons and refit the secondary piston stop pin.
16 Fit the sealing rubbers and press the reservoir into them.
17 Refitting is a reversal of removal, but tighten the mounting nuts and pipe union nuts to the specified torque, and finally bleed the hydraulic system as described in Section 13.

11 Deceleration control valve – removal and refitting

1 The deceleration control valve is located on the left-hand side of the engine compartment (photo). Place a suitable container or rags beneath the valve to catch spilled fluid then unscrew the unions, disconnect the hydraulic pipes, and plug them to prevent the ingress of foreign matter.
2 Unbolt the valve from the side panel and remove it from the car.
3 To refit the valve locate it on the bracket and tighten the bolt. Note that the valve can only be fitted with the cover bolts facing forwards.

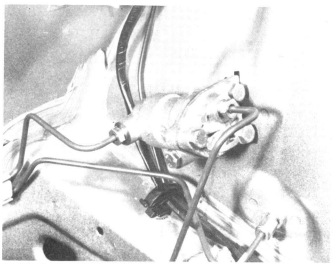

11.1 Brake deceleration control valve

4 Refit and tighten the unions noting that the hydraulic pipe from the master cylinder must be connected to the rear of the valve.
5 Bleed the rear hydraulic system as described in Section 13.

12 Hydraulic brake lines and hoses – removal and refitting

1 To remove a rigid brake line unscrew the unions at each end and where necessary release it from the clips (photos).
2 To remove a flexible brake hose first unscrew the union nuts and disconnect the rigid brake lines from each end. Unscrew the locknuts and remove the flexible hose from the brackets (photos).
3 Refitting is a reversal of removal, but bleed the hydraulic system as described in Section 13.

13 Hydraulic system – bleeding

1 If any of the hydraulic components in the braking system have been removed or disconnected, or if the fluid level in the master cylinder has been allowed to fall appreciably, it is inevitable that air will have been introduced into the system. The removal of all this air from the hydraulic system is essential if the brakes are to function correctly, and the process of removing it is known as bleeding.
2 There are a number of one-man, do-it-yourself, brake bleeding kits currently available from motor accessory shops. It is recommended that one of these kits should be used wherever possible as they greatly simplify the bleeding operation and also reduce the risk of expelled air and fluid being drawn back into the system.
3 If one of these kits is not available then it will be necessary to gather together a clean jar and a suitable length of clear plastic tubing which is a tight fit over the bleed screw, and also to engage the help of an assistant.
4 Before commencing the bleeding operation, check that all rigid pipes and flexible hoses are in good condition and that all hydraulic unions are tight. Take great care not to allow hydraulic fluid to come into contact with the vehicle paintwork, otherwise the finish will be seriously damaged. Wash off any spilled fluid immediately with cold water.
5 If hydraulic fluid has been lost from the master cylinder, due to a leak in the system, ensure that the cause is traced and rectified before proceeding further or a serious malfunction of the braking system may occur.
6 To bleed the system, clean the area around the bleed screw at the caliper or wheel cylinder to be bled (photo). If the hydraulic system has only been partially disconnected and suitable precautions were taken to prevent further loss of fluid, it should only be necessary to bleed that part of the system. However, if the entire system is to be bled start at the front left-hand side wheel.
7 Remove the master cylinder filler cap and top up the reservoir. Periodically check the fluid level during the bleeding operation and top up as necessary.

12.1a Rigid hydraulic brake line connection to a flexible brake hose

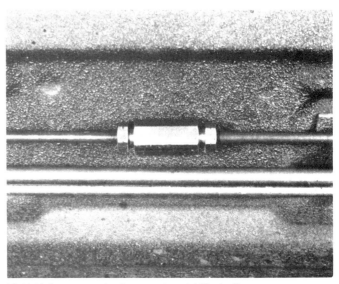

12.1b Union connection between two rigid brake lines

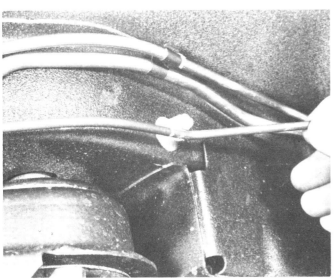

12.1c Removing a rigid brake line from a retaining clip

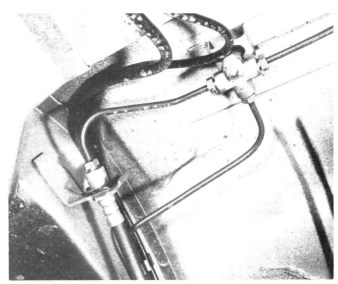

12.2a Rear brake hydraulic lines

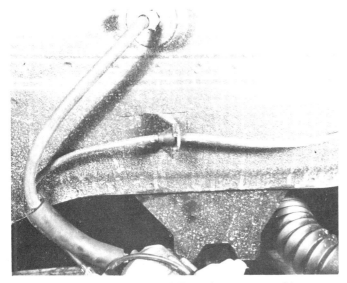

12.2b Front brake flexible hose and disc pad wear sensor wiring

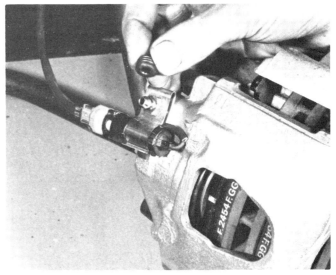

13.6 Removing the dust cover from the bleed screw

8   If a one-man brake bleeding kit is being used, connect the outlet tube to the bleed screw and then open the screw half a turn. If possible position the unit so that it can be viewed from the car, then depress the brake pedal to the floor and slowly release it. The one-way valve in the kit will prevent dispelled air from returning to the system at the end of each stroke. Repeat this operation until clean hydraulic fluid, free from air bubbles, can be seen coming through the tube. Now tighten the bleed screw and remove the outlet tube.

9   If a one-man brake bleeding kit is not available, connect one end of the plastic tubing to the bleed screw and immerse the other end in the jar containing sufficient clean hydraulic fluid to keep the end of the tube submerged. Open the bleed screw half a turn and have your assistant depress the brake pedal to the floor and then slowly release it. Tighten the bleed screw at the end of each downstroke to prevent expelled air and fluid from being drawn back into the system. Repeat this operation until clean hydraulic fluid, free from air bubbles, can be seen coming through the tube. Now tighten the bleed screw and remove the plastic tube.

10 If the entire system is being bled the procedures described above should now be repeated at the front right-hand side wheel followed by the rear right-hand side and rear left-hand side wheels. Do not forget to recheck the fluid level in the master cylinder at regular intervals and top up as necessary.

11 When completed, recheck the fluid level in the master cylinder, top up if necessary and refit the cap. Check the 'feel' of the brake pedal which should be firm and free from any 'sponginess' which would indicate air still present in the system.

12 Discard any expelled hydraulic fluid as it is likely to be contaminated with moisture, air and dirt which makes it unsuitable for further use.

13 When the hydraulic fluid is being renewed at the 36 000 mile (60 000 km) interval it will be necessary to depress the pistons into the calipers in order to remove all the old fluid. To do this remove the disc pads as described in Section 3 then press the pistons fully into the calipers and retain with blocks of wood. Refit the disc pads after bleeding the system dry then fill and bleed as previously described.

14 Handbrake lever – removal and refitting

1   Jack up the rear of the car and support on axle stands. Chock the front wheels and release the handbrake.

2   Extract the clip and clevis pin from the equaliser and disconnect the equaliser from the actuating rod (photo).

3   Working inside the car remove the centre console or rubber gaiter with reference to Chapter 12.

4   Disconnect the wiring from the warning switch then unscrew the mounting bolts and withdraw the handbrake lever. If necessary unbolt the warning switch (photo).

5   Refitting is a reversal of removal, but finally adjust the handbrake cable as described in Section 15.

15 Handbrake cable – removal, refitting and adjusting

1   Jack up the rear of the car and support on axle stands. Chock the front wheels and release the handbrake.

2   Extract the clip and clevis pin from the equaliser and disconnect the equaliser from the actuating rod.

3   Remove the rear brake shoes as described in Section 4.

4   Extract the U-clips securing the handbrake cables to the rear brake backplates, then release the clips from the suspension arms (photo).

5   Pull both outer cables through the crossmember and withdraw the complete cable from the car.

6   Refitting is a reversal of removal. With reference to Section 4, however, before lowering the car to the ground adjust the cable as follows.

7   Make sure that the handbrake lever is fully released then depress the footbrake pedal several times to set the automatic rear brake adjusters.

8   Unscrew the locknut from the adjuster located on the left-hand side outer cable and turn the adjuster until the plastic plungers located in the backplates can just be rotated and the plunger total movement is 0.5 to 1.0 mm (0.02 to 0.04 in) (photos).

9   Tighten the cable adjuster locknut onto the adjuster sleeve, using a suitable spanner or pliers, by between two and four 'clicks'.

10 Lower the car to the ground.

16 Vacuum servo unit – description, removal and refitting

1   The vacuum servo unit is fitted between the footbrake pedal and the master cylinder and provides assistance to the driver when the

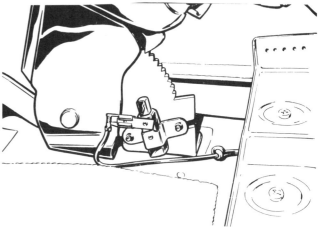

Fig. 9.15 Handbrake warning light switch location (Sec 14)

14.2 View of the handbrake lever and equaliser from below

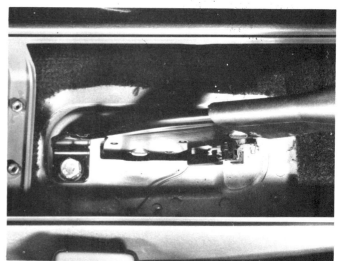

14.4 Handbrake lever and warning switch

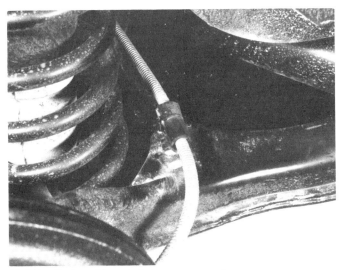

15.4 Handbrake cable and clip to rear suspension arm

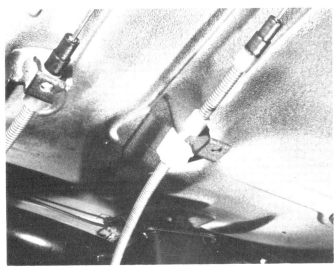

15.8a Handbrake cable adjuster and mounting brackets

15.8b Plastic plunger location for checking handbrake cable adjustment

pedal is depressed. The unit operates by vacuum from the inlet manifold. With the footpedal released vacuum is channelled to both sides of the internal diaphragm, however when the pedal is depressed one side is opened to the atmosphere resulting in assistance to the pedal effort. Should the vacuum servo develop a fault the hydraulic system is not affected, however greater effort will be required at the pedal.

2   To remove the servo unit first remove the master cylinder as described in Section 10.
3   Prise the vacuum hose connection from the servo unit.
4   Working inside the car remove the lower facia panel and disconnect the servo push rod from the pedal.
5   Unscrew the mounting nuts and withdraw the servo unit from the bulkhead.
6   If necessary remove the hose incorporating the check valve and check that it is only possible to blow through it in one direction.
7   Refitting is a reversal of removal, but when fitting the unit to the bulkhead make sure that the pushrod is correctly located in the pedal. Refit the master cylinder with reference to Section 10.

17 Footbrake pedal – removal and refitting

This procedure applies to LHD vehicles. For RHD vehicles the procedure is similar to that described for the Sapphire (Chapter 13, Sections 10 and 14).

1   Disconnect the battery negative lead.
2   Remove the facia lower panels.
3   Using a suitable hooked instrument extract the pivot shaft retaining spring clip located next to the pedal.
4   Extract the clip securing the servo pushrod to the pedal.
5   Slide the pivot shaft to the clutch pedal sufficient to withdraw the footbrake pedal. Note the location of the washers and spacer.
6   If necessary prise the rubber from the pedal.
7   Refitting is a reversal of removal, but if necessary adjust the stoplamp switch as described in Section 18.

18 Stoplamp switch – removal, refitting and adjusting

1   Disconnect the battery negative lead.
2   Remove the facia lower panels.
3   Disconnect the multi-plug then twist the switch anticlockwise and withdraw it from the bracket (photo).
4   To refit the switch insert it into the lockring and, with the pedal against its stop, push in the switch until the outer barrel touches the pedal.
5   Twist the switch clockwise to lock it then fit the multi-plug.
6   Refit the facia lower panels and reconnect the battery negative lead.

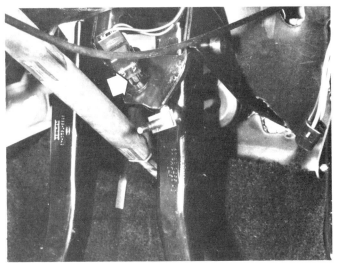

18.3 Stoplamp switch location

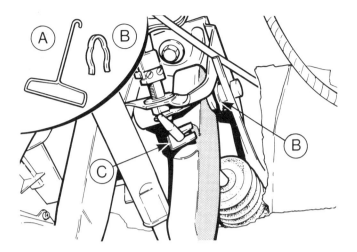

Fig. 9.16 Footbrake pedal removal (Sec 17)

A   Hooked instrument   C   Servo push rod clip
B   Spring clip and location

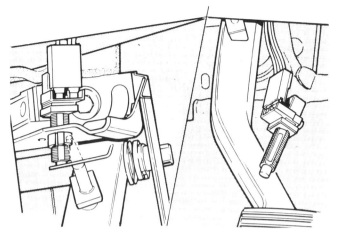

Fig. 9.17 Stoplamp switch fitted (left) and removed (right)
(Sec 18)

19 Fault diagnosis – braking system

Symptom	Reason(s)
Excessive pedal travel	Air in hydraulic system
Uneven braking and pulling to one side	Contaminated linings Seized wheel cylinder or caliper Incorrect tyre pressures
Brake judder	Worn drums and/or discs Excessively worn brake linings Worn front suspension lower balljoint
Brake pedal feels 'spongy'	Air in hydraulic system Worn master cylinder seals
Excessive effort to stop car	Servo unit faulty Excessively worn brake linings Seized wheel cylinder or caliper Contaminated brake linings Failure of front or rear hydraulic circuit

Chapter 10 Electrical system

For modifications, and information applicable to later models, see Supplement at end of manual

Contents

Alternator – fault finding and testing 8
Alternator – maintenance and special precautions 6
Alternator – removal and refitting 7
Alternator brushes – removal, inspection and refitting 9
Battery – charging 5
Battery – electrolyte replenishment 4
Battery – maintenance 3
Battery – removal and refitting 2
Cigarette lighter – removal and refitting 31
Clock – removal and refitting 29
Courtesy light switch – removal and refitting 19
Direction indicator switch – removal and refitting 14
Electric window switch – removal and refitting 21
Fault diagnosis – electrical system 47
Fuses and relays – general 13
General description 1
Graphic information module – removal and refitting 28
Headlamps – alignment 32
Headlamps and headlamp bulbs – removal and refitting 33
Heater motor switch – removal and refitting 22
Horn – removal and refitting 40
Ice warning sender unit – removal and refitting 30
Ignition switch and lock barrel – removal and refitting 15
Instrument panel – removal and refitting 25

Instrument panel gauges – removal and refitting 27
Instrument panel illumination switch – removal and refitting 18
Lamp bulbs – renewal 34
Lighting switch – removal and refitting 16
Low coolant warning switch – removal and refitting 23
Luggage compartment light switch – removal and refitting 20
Radios and tape players (general) – installation 45
Radios and tape players (general) – suppression of interference . 46
Radio (standard) – removal and refitting 44
Rear screen wiper motor – removal and refitting 37
Reversing light switch – removal and refitting 17
Speedometer cable – removal and refitting 26
Starter motor – overhaul 12
Starter motor – removal and refitting 10
Starter motor – testing in the car 11
Trip computer fuel flow sensor – removal and refitting 43
Trip computer module – removal and refitting 41
Trip computer speed sender unit – removal and refitting 42
Warning light control – removal and refitting 24
Windscreen wiper linkage – removal and refitting 36
Windscreen wiper motor – removal and refitting 35
Wiper arms – removal and refitting 39
Wiper blades – renewal 38

Specifications

System type .... 12 volt, negative earth

Battery
Rating:
    8 plates per cell type 270A/50RC
    10 plates per cell type 360A/60RC
    13 plates per cell type 500A/75RC
    15 plates per cell type 610A/110RC
    17 plates per cell type 700A/150RC
Charge condition:
    Poor .... 12.5 volt
    Normal .... 12.6 volt
    Good .... 12.7 volt

Alternator
Type .... Bosch, Lucas or Motorola

Bosch	35 amp	45 amp	55 amp	70 amp
Stator winding resistance	0.13 to 0.143 ohm	0.09 to 0.099 ohm	0.07 to 0.077 ohm	0.05 to 0.055 ohm
Rotor winding resistance	3.4 to 3.74 ohm	3.4 to 3.74 ohm	3.4 to 3.74 ohm	2.8 to 3.08 ohm
Miniumum brush length	5 mm (0.197 in)	5 mm (0.197 in)	5 mm (0.197 in)	5 mm (0.197 in)
Regulated voltage at 4000 rpm and 3 to 7 amp load	13.7 to 14.6 volt	13.7 to 14.6 volt	13.7 to 14.6 volt	13.7 to 14.6 volt

Lucas				
Stator winding resistance	0.128 to 0.138 ohm	Delta type 0.285 to 0.305 ohm Star type 0.088 to 0.108 ohm	0.193 to 0.213 ohm	0.134 ohm
Rotor winding resistance	3.04 to 3.36 ohm	3.04 to 3.36 ohm	3.04 to 3.36 ohm	3.04 to 3.36 ohm
Minimum brush length	5 mm (0.197 in)	5 mm (0.197 in)	5 mm (0.197 in)	5 mm (0.197 in)
Regulated voltage at 4000 rpm and 3 to 7 amp load	13.7 to 14.6 volt	13.7 to 14.6 volt	13.7 to 14.6 volt	13.7 to 14.6 volt

Motorola

Stator winding resistance	0.333 to 0.368 ohm	0.266 to 0.294 ohm	0.228 to 0.252 ohm	0.138 to 0.152 ohm
Rotor winding resistance	3.8 to 4.2 ohm	3.8 to 4.2 ohm	3.8 to 4.2 ohm	3.8 to 4.2 ohm
Minimum brush length	4 mm (0.16 in)	4 mm (0.16 in)	4 mm (0.16 in)	4 mm (0.16 in)
Regulated voltage at 4000 rpm and 3 to 7 amp load	13.7 to 14.6 volt	13.7 to 14.6 volt	13.7 to 14.6 volt	13.7 to 14.6 volt

Starter motor

Type .... Pre-engaged; Lucas, Bosch, Cajavec or Nippondenso

	Minimum brush length	Minimum commutator diameter	Minimum commutator thickness	Armature endfloat
Lucas	8.0 mm (0.32 in)	–	2.05 mm (0.08 in)	0.25 mm (0.010 in)
Bosch	10.0 mm (0.39 in) for 1.1 kW model 8.0 mm (0.32 in) for other models	32.8 mm (1.29 in)	–	0.3 mm (0.012 in)
Cajavec	10.0 mm (0.39 in)	32.8 mm (1.29 in)	–	0.3 mm (0.012 in)
Nippondenso	10.0 mm (0.39 in)	28.0 mm (1.10 in)	–	0.6 mm (0.024 in)

Fuses .... 9 x 10 amp, 4 x 15 amp, 3 x 20 amp, 4 x 30 amp, 1 x 1 amp (optional)

Bulbs

	Wattage
Headlamp (standard)	40/45
Headlamp (halogen)	55/60
Driving lamp	55
Front foglamp	55
Park/side lamps	5
Direction indicators	21
Stop/tail lamps	21/5
Number plate	5
Reverse lamp	21
Rear foglamp	21

Torque wrench settings

	lbf ft	Nm
Alternator adjusting link	15.1 to 18.8	20.5 to 25.5

1 General description

The electrical system is of 12 volt negative earth type. The battery is charged by a belt-driven alternator which incorporates a voltage regulator. The starter motor is of pre-engaged type where a solenoid moves the drive pinion into engagement with the ring gear before the starter motor is energised.

Although repair procedures are given in this Chapter, it may well be more economical to renew worn components as complete units.

2 Battery – removal and refitting

1 The battery is located in the engine compartment on the left-hand side of the bulkhead (photo).
2 Note the location of the leads then unscrew the bolt and disconnect the negative lead.
3 Lift the plastic cover then unscrew the bolt and disconnect the positive lead.
4 Unscrew the clamp bolt and lift the battery from the platform, taking care not to spill any electrolyte on the bodywork (photo).
5 Refitting is a reversal of removal, however do not over-tighten the clamp and terminal bolts.

3 Battery – maintenance

1 Every 12 000 miles (20 000 km) disconnect the leads from the battery and clean the terminals and lead ends. After refitting the leads smear the exposed metal with petroleum jelly.
2 The battery fitted as standard equipment is of the low mainten-ance type and only requires checking at 4 year (or 60 000 mile/100 000 km) intervals. However if a non-standard battery is fitted the following checks should be made on a monthly basis.
3 Check that the plate separators inside the battery are covered with electrolyte. To do this remove the battery covers and inspect through the top of the battery. On batteries with a translucent case it may be possible to carry out the check without removing the covers. If necessary top up the cells with distilled or de-ionized water.

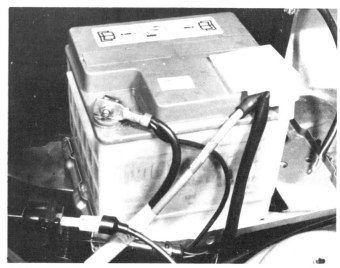

2.1 Battery location

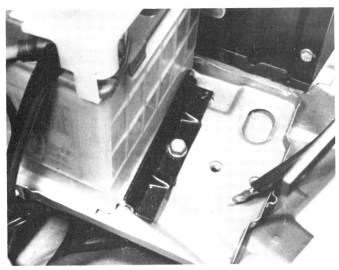

2.4 Battery clamp

4 At the same time wipe clean the top of the battery with a dry cloth to prevent the accumulation of dust and dampness which may cause the battery to become partially discharged over a period.

5 Also check the battery clamp and platform for corrosion. If evident remove the battery and clean the deposits away. Then treat the affected metal with a proprietary anti-rust liquid and paint with the original colour.

6 Whenever the battery is removed it is worthwhile checking it for cracks and leakage. Cracks can be caused by topping up the cells with distilled water in winter *after* instead of *before* a run. This gives the water no chance to mix with the electrolyte, so the former freezes and splits the battery case. If the case is fractured, it may be possible to repair it with a proprietary compound, but this depends on the material used for the case. If electrolyte has been lost from a cell refer to Section 4 for details of adding a fresh solution.

7 If topping up the battery becomes excessive and the case is not fractured, the battery is being over-charged and the voltage regulator may be faulty.

8 If the car covers a small annual mileage it is worthwhile checking the specific gravity of the electrolyte every three months to determine the state of charge of the battery. Use a hydrometer to make the check and compare the results with the following table:

	Ambient temperature above 25°C (77°F)	Ambient temperature below 25°C (77°F)
Fully charged	1.210 to 1.230	1.270 to 1.290
70% charged	1.170 to 1.190	1.230 to 1.250
Fully discharged	1.050 to 1.070	1.110 to 1.130

Note that the specific gravity readings assume an electrolyte temperature of 15°C (60°F); for every 10°C (18°F) below 15°C (60°F) subtract 0.007. For every 10°C (18°F) above 15°C (60°F) add 0.007.

9 If the battery condition is suspect first check the specific gravity of electrolyte in each cell. A variation of 0.040 or more between any cells indicates loss of electrolyte or deterioration of the internal plates.

10 A further test can be made using a voltmeter. Connect the voltmeter across the battery and compare the result with those given in the Specifications under 'charge condition'. The test is only accurate if the battery has not been subject to any kind of charge for the previous six hours. If this is not the case switch on the headlights for 30 seconds then wait four to five minutes before testing the battery.

---

4 Battery – electrolyte replenishment

1 If the battery is in a fully charged state and one of the cells maintains a specific gravity reading which is 0.040 or more lower than the others, then it is likely that electrolyte has been lost from the cell at some time.

2 Top-up the cell with a solution of 1 part sulphuric acid to 2.5 parts of distilled water. If the cell is already fully topped-up draw some

electrolyte out of it with a pipette.

3 It is preferable to obtain ready mixed electrolyte, however if the solution is to be mixed note that **the water must never be added to the sulphuric acid otherwise it will explode.** Always pour the acid slowly onto the water in a glass or plastic container.

---

5 Battery – charging

1 In winter time when heavy demand is placed upon the battery, such as when starting from cold and much electrical equipment is continually in use, it is a good idea to occasionally have the battery fully charged from an external source at the rate of 3.5 to 4 amps.

2 Continue to charge the battery at this rate until no further rise in specific gravity is noted over a four hour period.

3 Alternatively, a trickle charger charging at the rate of 1.5 amps can be safely used overnight.

4 Specially rapid 'boost' charges which are claimed to restore the power of the battery in 1 to 2 hours are not recommended as they can cause serious damage to the battery plates through overheating.

5 While charging the battery note that the temperature of the electrolyte should never exceed 100°F (37.8°C).

---

6 Alternator – maintenance and special precautions

1 Periodically wipe away any dirt which has accumulated on the outside of the unit, and also check that the plug is pushed firmly on the terminals. At the same time check the tension of the drivebelt and adjust it if necessary as described in Chapter 2.

2 Take extreme care when making electrical circuit connections on the car, otherwise damage may occur to the alternator or other electrical components employing semi-conductors. Always make sure that the battery leads are connected to the correct terminals. Before using electric-arc welding equipment to repair any part of the car, disconnect the battery leads and the alternator multi-plug. Disconnect the battery leads before using a mains charger. Never run the alternator with the multi-plug or a battery lead disconnected.

---

7 Alternator – removal and refitting

1 Disconnect the battery negative lead.

2 Loosen the alternator mounting and adjustment nuts and bolts, then swivel the alternator in towards the cylinder block.

3 Slip the drivebelt(s) from the alternator pulley(s).

4 Pull the multi-plug from the rear of the alternator (photo).

5 Remove the mounting and adjustment nuts and bolts, and withdraw the alternator from the engine (photos).

6 Refitting is a reversal of removal, but tension the drivebelt(s) as described in Chapter 2. Where applicable the front mounting bolt should be tightened before the rear mounting bolt, as the rear mounting incorporates a sliding bush.

7.4 Removing the alternator multi-plug (Bosch)

7.5a Removing the alternator

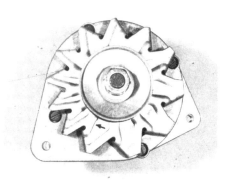

7.5b Front view of the alternator (Bosch)

7.5c Rear view of the alternator (Bosch)

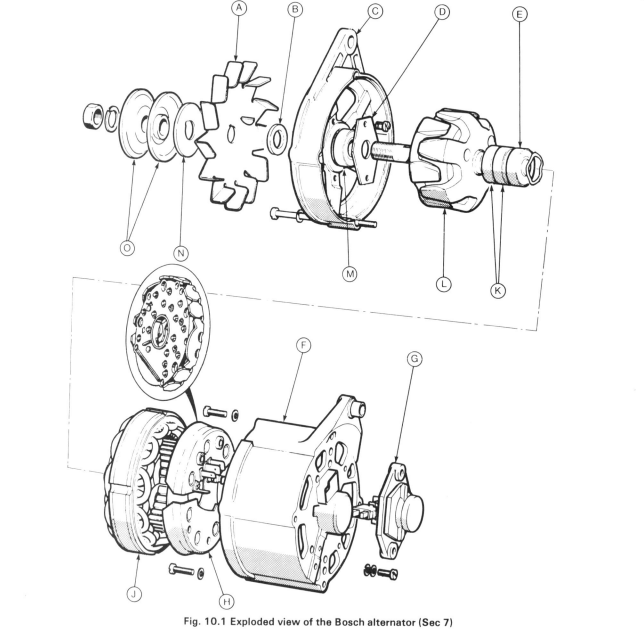

Fig. 10.1 Exploded view of the Bosch alternator (Sec 7)

A   Fan
B   Spacer
C   Drive end housing
D   Drive end bearing retaining
    plate
E   Slip ring end bearing
F   Slip ring end housing
G   Brush box and regulator
H   Rectifier (diode) pack (Inset
    shows N1-70A diode pack)
J   Stator
K   Slip rings
L   Rotor
M   Drive end bearing
N   Spacer
O   Pulley

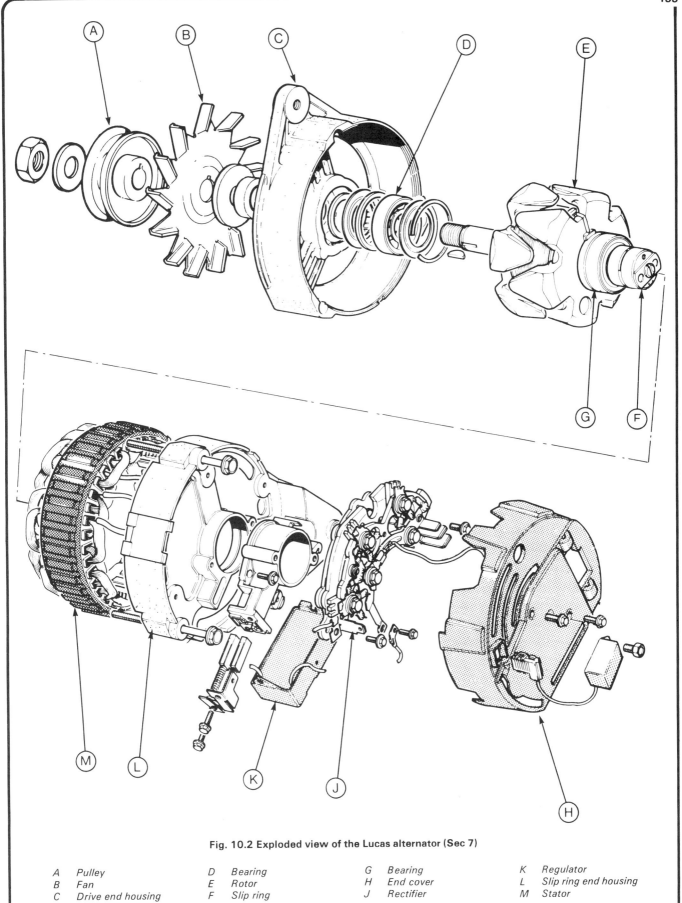

Fig. 10.2 Exploded view of the Lucas alternator (Sec 7)

A	Pulley	D	Bearing
B	Fan	E	Rotor
C	Drive end housing	F	Slip ring

G	Bearing	K	Regulator
H	End cover	L	Slip ring end housing
J	Rectifier	M	Stator

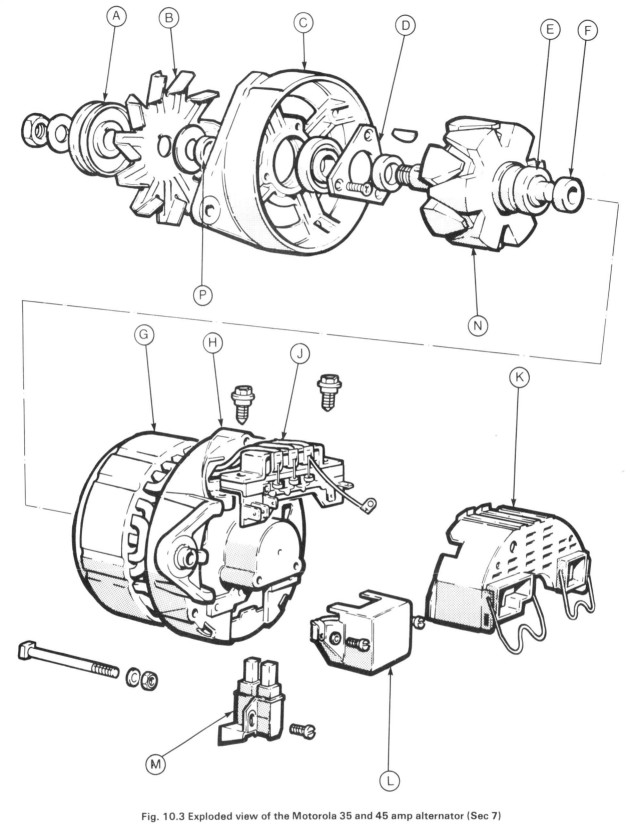

Fig. 10.3 Exploded view of the Motorola 35 and 45 amp alternator (Sec 7)

A	Pulley	E	Slip ring	K	End cover
B	Fan	F	Slip ring end bearing	L	Regulator
C	Drive end housing	G	Stator	M	Brush box
D	Drive end bearing retaining plate	H	Slip ring end housing	N	Rotor
		J	Diode bridge	P	Spacer

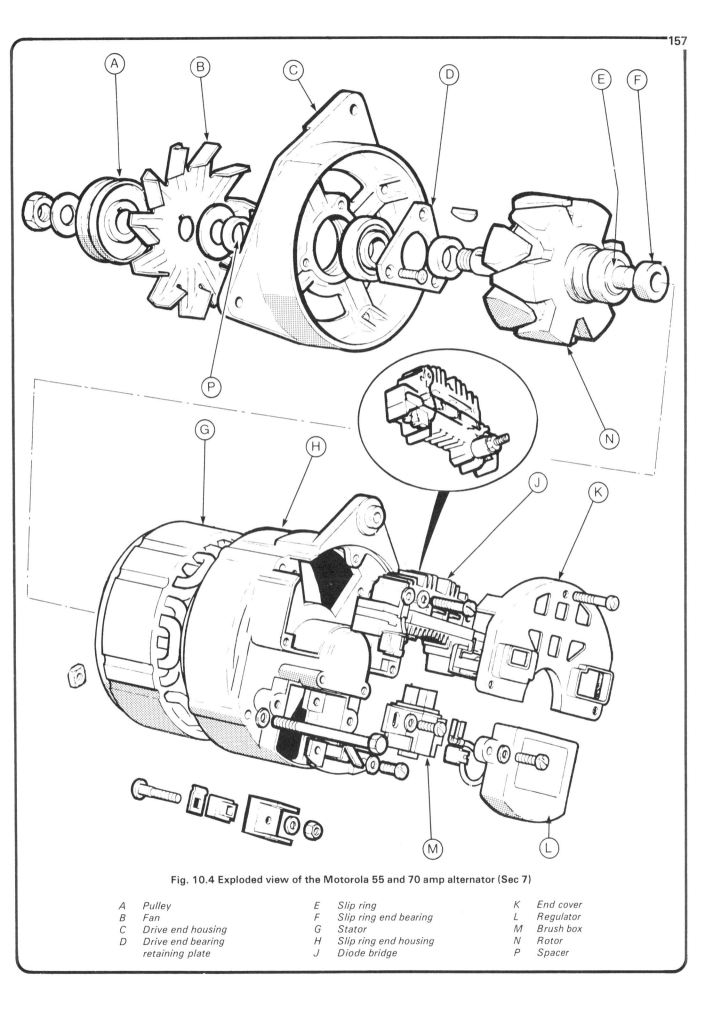

Fig. 10.4 Exploded view of the Motorola 55 and 70 amp alternator (Sec 7)

A	Pulley	E	Slip ring	K	End cover
B	Fan	F	Slip ring end bearing	L	Regulator
C	Drive end housing	G	Stator	M	Brush box
D	Drive end bearing	H	Slip ring end housing	N	Rotor
	retaining plate	J	Diode bridge	P	Spacer

8   Alternator – fault finding and testing

Note: *To carry out the complete test procedure use only the following test equipment – a 0 to 20 volt moving coil voltmeter, a 0 to 100 amp moving coil ammeter, and a 0 to 30 amp rheostat.*

1   Check that the battery is at least 70% charged by using a hydrometer as described in Section 3.
2   Check the drivebelt tension with reference to Chapter 2.
3   Check the security of the battery leads, alternator multi-plug, and interconnecting wire.
4   *To check the cable continuity* pull the multi-plug from the alternator and switch on the ignition being careful not to crank the engine. Connect the voltmeter between a good earth and each of the terminals in the multi-plug in turn. If battery voltage is not indicated, there is an open circuit in the wiring which may be due to a blown ignition warning light bulb if on the small terminal.
5   *To check the alternator output* connect the voltmeter, ammeter and rheostat as shown in Fig. 10.5. Run the engine at 3000 rpm and switch on the headlamps, heater blower and, where fitted, the heated rear window. Vary the resistance to increase the current and check that the alternator rated output is reached without the voltage dropping below 13 volts.

6   *To check the positive side of the charging circuit* connect the voltmeter as shown in Fig. 10.6. Start the engine and switch on the headlamps. Run the engine at 3000 rpm and check that the indicated voltage drop does not exceed 0.5 volt. A higher reading indicates a high resistance such as a dirty connection on the positive side of the charging circuit.
7   *To check the negative side of the charging circuit* connect the voltmeter as shown in Fig. 10.7. Start the engine and switch on the headlamps. Run the engine at 3000 rpm and check that the indicated voltage drop does not exceed 0.25 volt. A higher reading indicates a high resistance such as a dirty connection on the negative side of the charging circuit.
8   *To check the alternator voltage regulator* connect the voltmeter and ammeter as shown in Fig. 10.8. Run the engine at 3000 rpm and when the ammeter records a current of 3 to 5 amps check that the voltmeter records 13.7 to 14.5 volts. If the result is outside the limits the regulator is faulty.

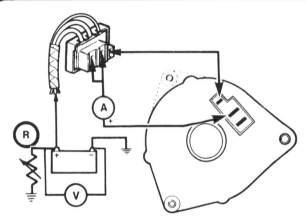

Fig. 10.5 Alternator output test circuit (Sec 8)

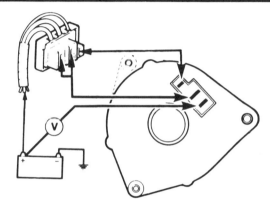

Fig. 10.6 Alternator positive check circuit (Sec 8)

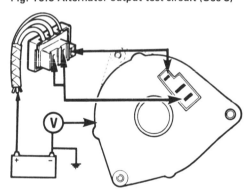

Fig. 10.7 Alternator negative check circuit (Sec 8)

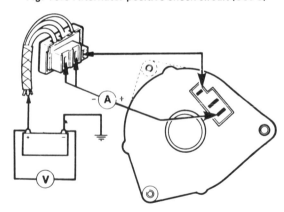

Fig. 10.8 Alternator voltage regulator test circuit (Sec 8)

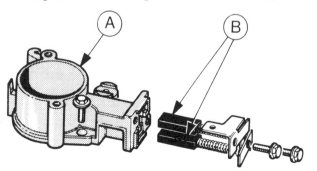

Fig. 10.9 Brush box (A) and brushes (B) fitted to the Lucas alternator (Sec 8)

Fig. 10.10 Brush box and brushes (A) fitted to the Motorola 55 and 70 amp alternator (Sec 8)

9 Alternator brushes – removal, inspection and refitting

1 Disconnect the battery negative lead.

Bosch type

2 Remove the screws and withdraw the regulator and brush box from the rear of the alternator (photos).
3 If the length of either brush is less than the minimum given in the Specifications, unsolder the wiring and remove the brushes and springs (photo).

Lucas type

4 Pull the multi-plug from the rear of the alternator then remove the screws and withdraw the rear cover.
5 Remove the screws and lift the brushes from the brush box.
6 If necessary remove the screws and withdraw the brush box.
7 Renew the brushes if either is less than the minimum length given in the Specifications.

Motorola type

8 Pull the multi-plug from the rear of the alternator.
9 Remove the screws and withdraw the regulator. Note the location of the wires then disconnect them and remove the regulator.
10 Remove the single screw (35 and 45 amp types) or two screws (55 and 70 amp types) and carefully withdraw the brush box.
11 If the length of either brush is less than the minimum given in the Specifications, obtain a new brush box.

All types

12 Wipe clean the slip rings with a fuel-moistened cloth – if they are very dirty use fine glasspaper to clean them then wipe with the cloth (photo).
13 Refitting is a reversal of removal, but make sure that the brushes move freely in their holders.

10 Starter motor – removal and refitting

1 Jack up the front of the car and support on axle stands. Apply the handbrake.
2 Disconnect the battery negative lead.
3 Working beneath the car unscrew the nut and disconnect the main cable from the solenoid (photo).
4 Disconnect the ignition switch wire from the solenoid (photo).
5 Unscrew the mounting bolts and withdraw the starter motor from the gearbox (photos).
6 Refitting is a reversal of removal, but tighten the mounting bolts securely.

11 Starter motor – testing in the car

1 If the starter motor fails to operate first check the condition of the battery as described in Section 3.
2 Check the security and condition of all relevant cables.

Solenoid check

3 Disconnect the battery negative lead and all leads from the solenoid.
4 Connect a 3 watt testlamp between the starter terminal on the solenoid and the solenoid body (Fig. 10.11). The testlamp should light. If not, there is an open circuit in the solenoid windings.
5 Now connect an 18 watt testlamp between both solenoid terminals (Fig. 10.12) then energise the solenoid with a further lead to the spade terminal. The solenoid should be heard to operate and the testlamp should light. Reconnect the solenoid wires.

On load voltage check

6 Connect a voltmeter across the battery terminals then disconnect the low tension lead from the coil positive terminal and operate the starter by turning the ignition switch. Note the reading on the voltmeter which should not be less than 10.5 volts.

9.2a Removing the alternator regulator and brushbox (Bosch)

9.2b Alternator regulator and brushbox (Bosch)

9.3 Checking the length of the alternator brushes (Bosch)

9.12 Alternator slip rings (arrowed) (Bosch)

10.3 Showing starter motor main cable location

10.4 Showing starter motor solenoid ignition switch lead location

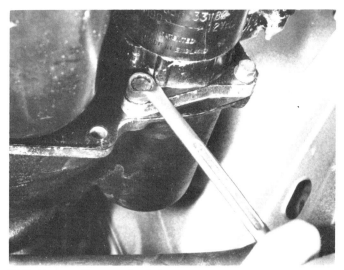

10.5a Unscrew the mounting bolts ...

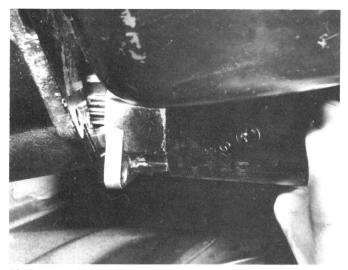

10.5b ... and withdraw the starter motor

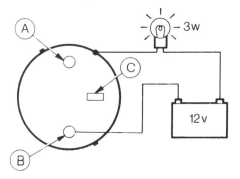

Fig. 10.11 Starter solenoid winding test circuit (Sec 11)

A	Battery terminal	C	Spade terminal
B	Motor terminal		

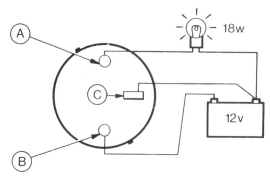

Fig. 10.12 Starter solenoid continuity test circuit (Sec 11)

A	Battery terminal	C	Spade terminal
B	Motor terminal		

7   Now connect the voltmeter between the starter motor terminal on the solenoid and the starter motor body. With the coil low tension lead still disconnected operate the starter and check that the recorded voltage is not more than 1 volt lower than that noted in paragraph 6. If the voltage drop is more than 1 volt a fault exists in the wiring from the battery to the starter.

8   Connect the voltmeter between the battery positive terminal and the terminal on the starter motor. With the coil low tension lead disconnected operate the starter for two or three seconds. Battery voltage should be indicated initially, then dropping to less than 1 volt. If the reading is more than 1 volt there is a high resistance in the wiring from the battery to the starter and the check in paragraph 9 should be made. If the reading is less than 1 volt proceed to paragraph 10.

9   Connect the voltmeter between the two main solenoid terminals and operate the starter for two or three seconds. Battery voltage should be indicated initially then dropping to less than 0.5 volt. If the reading is more than 0.5 volt the ignition switch and connections may be faulty.

10 Connect the voltmeter between the battery negative terminal and the starter motor body, and operate the starter for two or three seconds. A reading of less than 0.5 volt should be recorded; however, if the reading is more, the earth circuit is faulty and the earth connections to the battery and body should be checked.

---

12 Starter motor – overhaul

Note: *Overhaul of the Lucas 5M90 starter is described in this Section; however, overhaul of the Bosch, Cajavec, Nippondenso and Lucas 8M90 starters is similar with reference to Figs. 10.13 to 10.18.*

1   Unscrew the nut and remove the connecting wire from the solenoid (photo).

2   Unscrew the nuts and remove the solenoid from the end bracket (photos).

3   Unhook and remove the solenoid armature and sppring from the engagement lever (photos).

4   Prise the plastic cap from the commutator endplate and ease off the star clip with a screwdriver (photos).

5   Unscrew the two screws from the drive end bracket and withdraw the yoke. Note the location of the washers on the armature, and the yoke location cut-out (photos).

6   Using a suitable metal drift drive the engagement lever pivot from

12.1 Removing the starter motor connecting wire

12.2a Unscrew the nuts ...

12.2b ... and withdraw the solenoid

12.3a Remove the solenoid spring ...

12.3b ... and unhook the armature

12.4a Remove the plastic cap ...

12.4b ... and star clip from the commutator end plate

12.5a Removing the starter drive end bracket screws

12.5b Starter yoke location cut-out (arrowed)

12.6 Removing the starter motor engagement lever pivot

the end bracket. The retaining clip will distort as the pin is removed and must be renewed (photo).

7 Withdraw the armature together with the engagement lever from the end bracket then separate the two components. Remove the rubber block and seal (photos).

8 Remove the screws and withdraw the end plate from the yoke sufficient to slide the two field brushes from their holders. Note the endplate cut-out and take care not to damage the gasket (photos).

9 Mount the armature in a vice then using a suitable metal tube drive the collar from the C-clip. Extract the C-clip and withdraw the collar followed by the drive pinion assembly.

10 Unscrew the nut from the terminal on the endplate, remove the spring washer, plain washer and insulator, then push the stud and second insulator through the endplate and unhook the brushes.

11 If necessary drill out the rivets and remove the brush box and gasket from the endplate.

12 Clean all the components in paraffin and wipe dry.

13 Check the length of the brushes. If either is worn to less than the minimum length given in the Specifications renew them. To do this cut the brush lead and then solder on the new lead. **Note:** *on Bosch short frame starters solder the new lead to the connector.*

14 Clean the commutator with fine glasspaper then wipe clean with a fuel moistened cloth. If it is excessively worn it may be skimmed in a lathe and then polished provided that it is not reduced to under the minimum diameter given in the Specifications. Clean any burrs from the insulation slots, but do not increase the width of the slots.

15 Check the armature windings for good insulation by connecting a testlamp and leads between each commutator segment in turn and the armature shaft; if the bulb glows the insulation is faulty.

16 Check the field windings in the yoke for security and for the condition of soldered joints. Check the continuity and insulation of the windings using a testlamp and leads.

17 Check the bearing bushes for wear and if necessary renew them using a soft metal drift. The bushes should be immersed in clean SAE

12.7a Remove the rubber block (arrowed) ...

12.7b ... and withdraw the armature from the end bracket

12.8a Remove the screws ...

12.8b ... and withdraw the yoke end plate

12.8c Yoke and plate location cut-out (arrowed)

12.18 Using a socket to fit a new star clip to the starter armature shaft

30/40 grade oil for a minimum of 20 minutes before being fitted. The bushes are made of self-lubricating porous bronze and must not be reamed otherwise the self-lubricating quality will be impaired.

18 Reassembly is a reversal of dismantling, but fit a new brush box gasket if necessary. Use a two legged puller to pull the collar onto the C-clip on the armature shaft. Fit a new star clip to the engagement lever pivot pin and to the end of the armature shaft making sure that all endfloat is eliminated from the shaft (photo).

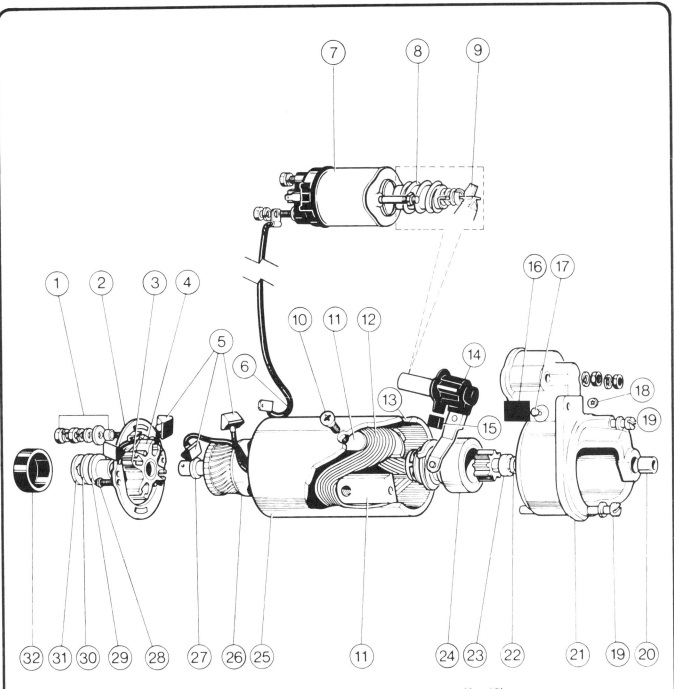

Fig. 10.13 Exploded view of the Lucas 5M90 starter motor (Sec 12)

1	Terminal nuts and washers	9	Engagement lever	18	Retaining clip
2	Commutator end plate	10	Pole screw	19	Housing retaining screws (2)
3	Brush housing	11	Pole shoe	20	Bearing bush
4	Brush springs	12	Field coils	21	Drive end housing
5	Brushes	13	Field to earth connection	22	C clip
6	Connector link, solenoid to starter	14	Rubber seal	23	Thrust collar
7	Solenoid unit	15	Rubber dust pad	24	Drive assembly
8	Return spring	16	Rubber dust cover	25	Main casing (yoke)
		17	Pivot pin		

26	Armature
27	Thrust washer
28	Commutator end plate retaining screws (2)
29	Bearing bush
30	Thrust plate
31	Star clip
32	Dust cover

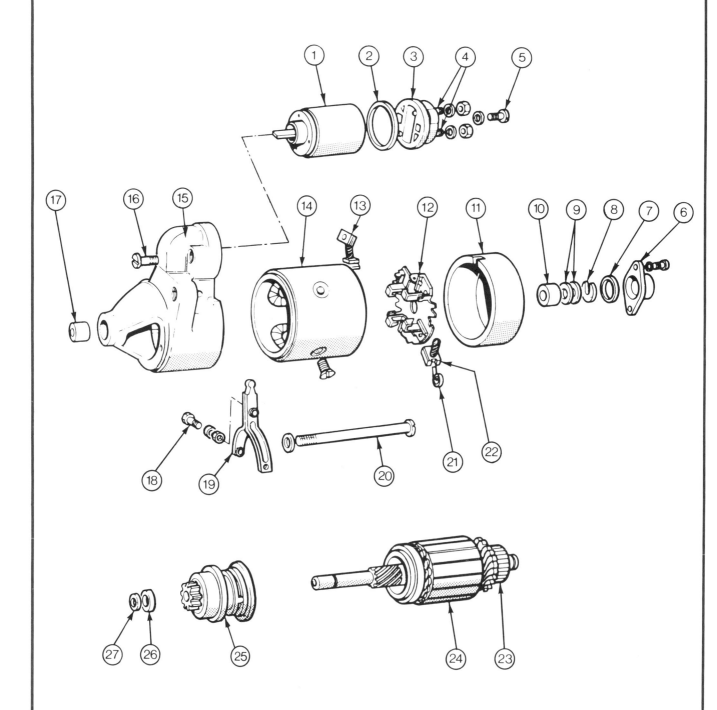

Fig. 10.14 Exploded view of the Bosch long frame starter motor (Sec 12)

1	Solenoid body	8	C clip	15	Drive end housing	22	Brush
2	Gasket	9	Shim washer	16	Solenoid retaining screw	23	Commutator
3	Switch contacts and cover	10	Bearing bush	17	Bearing bush	24	Armature
4	Terminals (main)	11	Commutator end housing	18	Pivot screw	25	Drive pinion and roller
5	Retaining screw	12	Brushbox assembly	19	Actuating lever		clutch assembly
6	End cover	13	Connector link	20	Through bolt	26	Thrust collar
7	Seal	14	Main casing (yoke)	21	Brush spring	27	C-clip

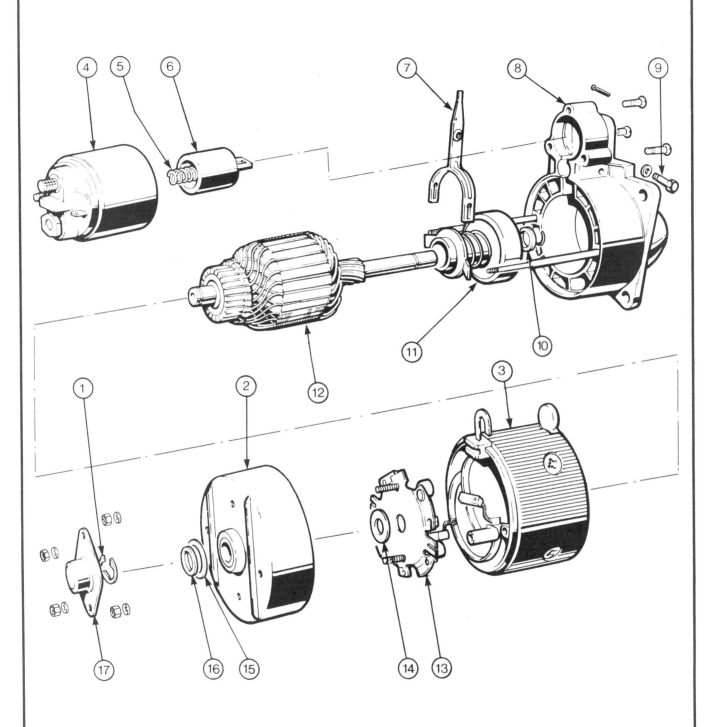

Fig. 10.15 Exploded view of the Cajavec starter motor (Sec 12)

1	E-clip	6	Solenoid armature	11	Drive pinion and roller clutch assembly	14	Brake ring
2	Commutator end cover	7	Actuating lever			15	Sealing ring
3	Main casing (Yoke)	8	Drive end housing	12	Armature	16	Spacer
4	Solenoid body	9	Pivot pin	13	Brushplate	17	End cap
5	Solenoid return spring	10	Thrust collar				

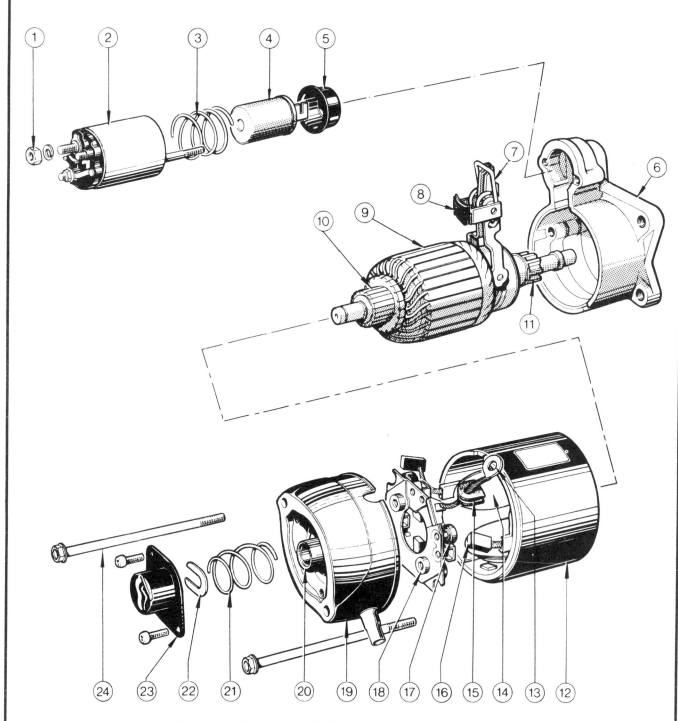

Fig. 10.16 Exploded view of the Nippondenso starter motor (Sec 12)

1 Solenoid terminal nut
2 Solenoid body
3 Solenoid return spring
4 Solenoid armature
5 Seal
6 Drive end housing

7 Actuating lever
8 Pivot assembly
9 Armature
10 Commutator
11 Drive pinion and roller clutch assembly

12 Main casing
13 Connecting link – solenoid to starter
14 Pole shoe
15 Seal
16 Brush
17 Brush spring

18 Brush box assembly
19 Commutator end housing
20 Bush
21 Spring
22 C-clip
23 End cover
24 Through bolt

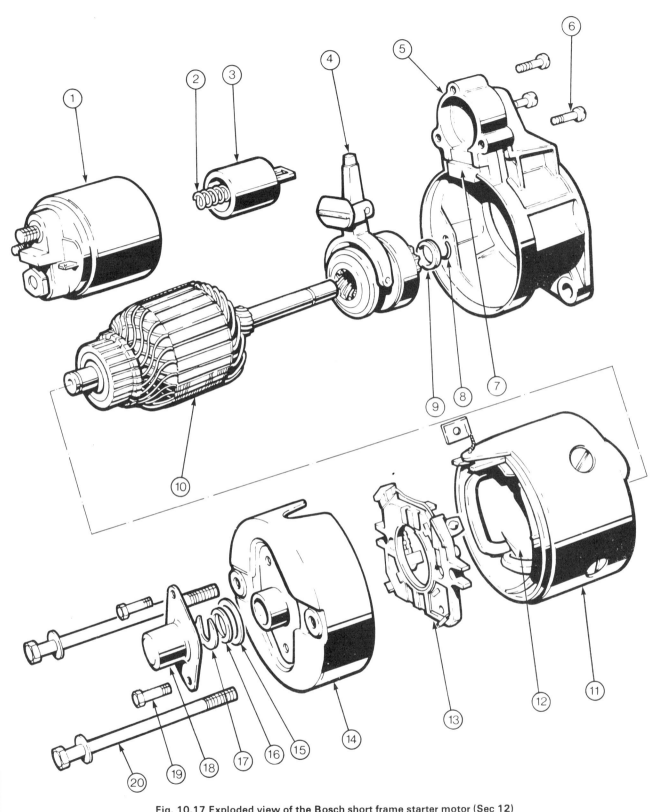

Fig. 10.17 Exploded view of the Bosch short frame starter motor (Sec 12)

1	Solenoid	6	Solenoid bolts (3)	11	Main casing (Yoke)	16	Spacer
2	Solenoid spring	7	Rubber block	12	Pole shoe	17	C-clip
3	Solenoid yoke	8	C-clip	13	Brushplate	18	End cover
4	Actuating lever	9	Thrust collar	14	Commutator end housing	19	Securing bolt
5	Drive end housing	10	Armature	15	Sealing ring	20	Through bolt (2)

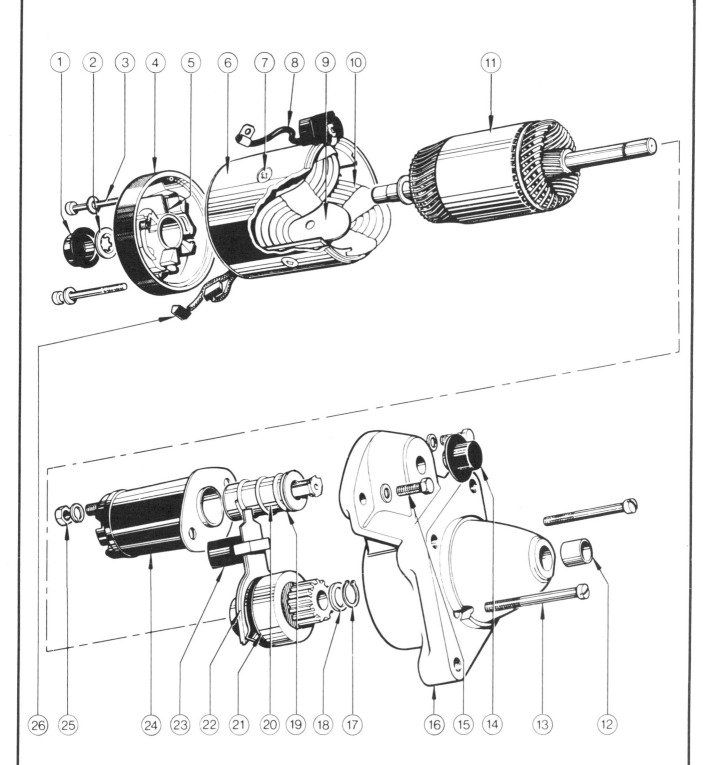

Fig. 10.18 Exploded view of the Lucas 8M90 starter motor (Sec 12)

1	Dust cover	7	Pole screw	14	Dust cover	21	Drive assembly
2	Star clip	8	Connector link	15	Solenoid retaining bolt (2)	22	Engagement lever
3	Commutator end plate retaining bolt	9	Pole shoe	16	Drive end housing	23	Pivot
4	Commutator end plate	10	Field coils	17	C-clip	24	Solenoid body
5	Brush housing	11	Armature	18	Thrust collar	25	Terminal nut and washer
6	Main casing (yoke)	12	Bearing bush	19	Return spring	26	Brushes
		13	Housing retaining screws (2)	20	Solenoid armature		

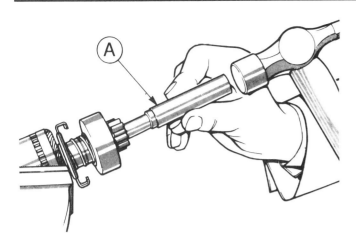

Fig. 10.19 Using a tube (A) to release the collar on the starter armature shaft (Sec 12)

13 Fuses and relays – general

1 The fuses and relays are located in the engine compartment on the right-hand side of the bulkhead and on certain models some additional relays are located beneath the facia panel and on the steering column bracket.

2 Always renew a fuse with one of identical rating and never renew it more than once without finding the source of the trouble (usually a short circuit). Always switch off the ignition before renewing a fuse or relay, and when renewing the wiper motor fuse keep the hands clear of the wiper linkage as it may return to the parked position.

3 Access to the fuses and relays in the fusebox is gained by removing the loose cover and spring clip (if fitted), pulling the plastic clip and removing the cover. All fuses and relays are a push fit (photos).

4 Fuse and relay locations are shown on the fusebox cover and are numbered as follows.

Fuse	Rating (amps)	Circuit (early models)
1	20	Electric windows
2	30	Heated rear screen, heated door mirror
3	10	Clock, intermittent wiper control, econo-warning lights, door locks, defective exterior light bulb warning light
4	30	Heater motor, rear screen wiper, windscreen washer pump
5	30	Headlamp wash/wipe, reversing light
6	15	Horn
7	15	Auxiliary driving lamps
8	15	Wiper motor
9	15	Indicators, brake lights
10	15	Foglamps
11	30	Tailgate, central locking
12	20	Floor area lights, heated seats, delayed action courtesy light, load floor light, digital clock, cigar lighter, trip computer, vanity mirror
13	10	Hazard flasher warning light
14	10	Main beam left
15	10	Main beam right
16	10	Dipped beam left
17	10	Dipped beam right
18	10	Side and tail lights right, glove compartment light, switch illumination, instrument panel illumination
19	10	Switch illumination for front/rear foglamps, side and tail lights left, number plate light, engine compartment light
20	–	–

Relays	Circuit (early models)
1	Automatic transmission inhibitor switch
2	Horn
3	
4	Auxiliary driving lamps
5	Front foglamps
6	Electrically operated tailgate lock
7	Intermittent wiper motor - front
8	Headlamp wash/wipe
9	Seat belt warning light
10	Ignition switch lock
11	Intermittent wiper motor - rear
12	Delayed action courtesy light
13	Heated rear screen and heated door mirror with automatic 'cut-out'

Fuse	Rating (amps)	Circuit (later models)
1	30	Power windows
2	30	Heated rear screen, heated door mirror
3	15	Wiper motor
4	30	Heater blower motor, rear screen wipers, windscreen washer pump
5	30	Headlamp wash, reversing light
6	15	Horn (steering wheel mounted)
7	15	Auxiliary driving lamps
8	10	Clock, intermittent wiper control, econo-warning lights, warning lights for door ajar and defective exterior light bulbs
9	15	Indicators, brake lights
10	15	Foglamps
11	30	Remote tailgate release, central locking
12	25	Floor area lights, heated seats, delayed action courtesy light, load floor light, digital clock, cigar lighter, trip computer, vanity mirror
13	10	Hazard flasher warning light, horn (on multi-function switch)
14	10	Main beam left
15	10	Main beam right
16	10	Dipped beam left
17	10	Dipped beam right
18	10	Switch illumination for front/rear foglamps, side and tail lights left, number plate light, engine compartment light
19	10	Side and tail lights right, glove compartment light, switch illumination, instrument panel illumination
20	25	Fuel system cooling fan

Relays	
I	Driving lamps
II	Foglamps
III	Remote Control Tailgate Release
IV	Start Inhibitor - Automatic Transmission
V	Horn
VI	Daytime Running Lights (Sweden)
VII	Ignition Switch
VIII	Headlamp Washers
IX	Warning Lamp - Seat Belts
X	Intermittent wipe - front wiper
Grey	Heated rear screen/mirrors
Orange	Rear Wiper - Intermittent Operation
Yellow	Courtesy Light Delay

Additional fuses are located under the facia paanel for the Trip computer (1 amp) and Radio (rating according to type). Relays located under the facia are for bulb test control, warning lights, and central door locking. Relays located on the steering column bracket are for hazard warning lights, heated front seats, electrically operated windows and electrically operated aerial.

The fuses are colour coded as follows:

Red	10 amp
Blue	15 amp
Yellow	20 amp
Clear	25 amp
Green	30 amp

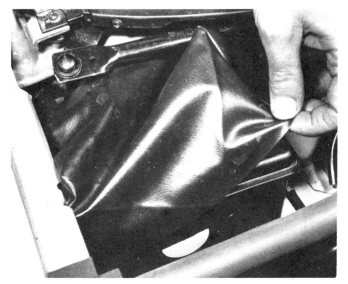

13.3a Removing the fusebox loose cover ...

13.3b ... spring clip ...

13.3c ... and cover

13.3d View of the fuses and relays

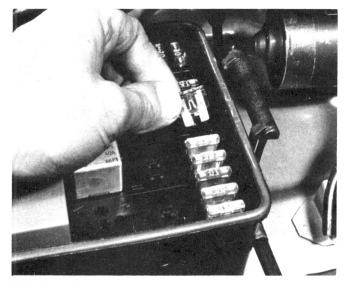

13.3e Removing a fuse

13.3f Removing a relay

14 Direction indicator switch – removal and refitting

1   Disconnect the battery negative lead.
2   Remove the screws and withdraw the upper and lower shrouds from the steering column (photo).
3   Remove the two crosshead screws and withdraw the switch from the steering column, also disconnect the two multi-plugs.
4   Refitting is a reversal of removal.

15 Ignition switch and lock barrel – removal and refitting

1   Disconnect the battery negative lead.
2   Remove the screws and withdraw the upper and lower shrouds from the steering column.
3   Insert the ignition key and turn to position 'I' then depress the spring clip with a suitable instrument and withdraw the steering lock barrel. Slight movement of the key will be necessary in order to align the cam.
4   With the key fully inserted extract the spring clip taking care not to damage its location, then withdraw the key approximately 5 mm (0.2 in) and remove the barrel from the cylinder.
5   Disconnect the wiring multi-plug then remove the two grub screws and withdraw the ignition switch.
6   Refitting is a reversal of removal, but check the operation of the steering lock in all switch positions.

16 Lighting switch – removal and refitting

The procedure is identical to that for the direction indicator switch in Section 14 except for the additional removal and refitting of an earth lead.

17 Reversing light switch – removal and refitting

1   Jack up the front of the car and support on axle stands. Apply the handbrake.
2   Working beneath the car disconnect the wiring and unscrew the switch from the gearbox extension.
3   Refitting is a reversal of removal, but make sure that the wiring is secured clear of the exhaust system.

18 Instrument panel illumination switch – removal and refitting

1   Disconnect the battery negative lead.
2   Using a thin screwdriver prise the switch from the facia.
3   Disconnect the wiring multi-plug and remove the switch (photo).
4   Refitting is a reversal of removal.

14.2 Direction indicator switch (left) and lighting switch (right)

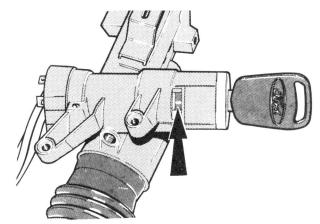

Fig. 10.20 Ignition key lock barrel spring clip location (Sec 15)

19 Courtesy light switch – removal and refitting

1   Open the door and unscrew the cross-head screw.
2   Remove the switch from the door pillar and pull the wire out sufficiently to prevent it from springing back into the pillar (photo).
3   Disconnect the wire and remove the switch.
4   Refitting is a reversal of removal.

18.3 Removing the instrument panel illumination switch

19.2 Removing a courtesy light switch

20 Luggage compartment light switch – removal and refitting

1   A level-sensitive switch is incorporated into the luggage compartment light circuit and is located in the tailgate.
2   Prise the trim panel from inside the tailgate.
3   Disconnect the wiring then remove the screw and withdraw the switch. Note the fitted position of the switch to ensure correct refitting (photo).
4   Refitting is a reversal of removal.

21 Electric window switch – removal and refitting

1   Disconnect the battery negative lead.
2   Using a thin screwdriver and pad prise the front or rear switch assembly (as applicable) from the console or rear door armrests.
3   Disconnect the wiring and remove the switch.
4   Refitting is a reversal of removal.

22 Heater motor switch – removal and refitting

1   Pull off the switch knob using pliers with padded jaws if necessary.
2   Prise out the switch front plate.
3   Squeeze the tabs and withdraw the switch sufficiently to disconnect the multi-plug (photo).
4   Refitting is a reversal of removal.

23 Low coolant warning switch – removal and refitting

1   Turn the expansion tank filler cap 90° in an anticlockwise direction until the first stop is reached, then wait until all the pressure has been released.
2   Remove the filler cap then place a container beneath the tank, disconnect the hose, and drain the coolant.
3   Disconnect the multi-plug then unscrew the collar and pull the switch from the rubber grommet (photo).
4   Refitting is a reversal of removal.

24 Warning light control – removal and refitting

1   Remove the lower facia cover from behind the glove compartment.
2   Pull off the cylindrical clips and lower the control bracket (photo).
3   Disconnect the multi-plug then remove the screws and withdraw the control unit. Where two units are fitted note that the multi-plugs are colour coded to ensure correct fitting.
4   Refitting is a reversal of removal.

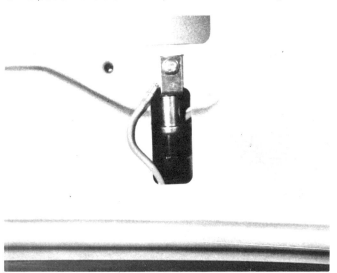

20.3 Luggage compartment light switch location in the tailgate

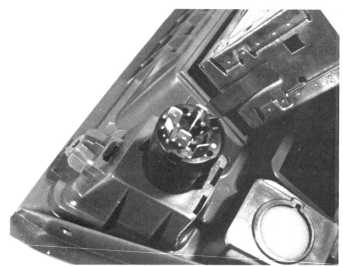

22.3 Rear view of the heater motor switch

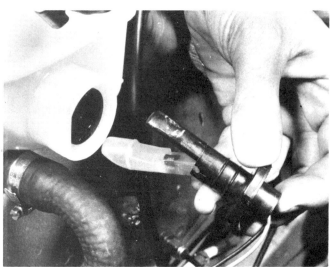

23.3 Removing the low coolant warning switch

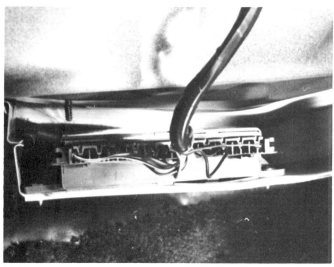

24.2 Warning light control location

25 Instrument panel – removal and refitting

1   Disconnect the battery negative lead.
2   Remove the screw and withdraw the steering column upper and lower shrouds.
3   Where fitted remove the rheostat and intermittent wiper control.
4   Remove the screws and withdraw the panel surround. Note that the right-hand side screw is covered with a plastic cap. Disconnect the plug from the illumination switch (photos).
5   Remove the screws and withdraw the instrument panel sufficiently to disconnect the speedometer cable and multi-plugs (photos).
6   Refitting is a reversal of removal.

26 Speedometer cable – removal and refitting

1   On models fitted with a Trip Computer remove the speed sender as described in Section 42.

2   Remove the instrument panel as described in Section 25.
3   Jack up the front of the car and support on axle stands. Apply the handbrake.
4   On manual gearbox models extract the circlip and remove the speedometer cable from the extension housing (photos).
5   On automatic transmission models unscrew the bolt and remove the clamp and speedometer cable from the transmission housing.
6   Pull the cable through the bulkhead into the engine compartment then bend open the retaining clips and remove the cable.
7   Refitting is a reversal of removal, but make sure that the bulkhead grommet is correctly located. Position the cable according to the colour band locations. The first band must coincide with the grommet, the second band with the first side member clip, and the third band with the side member bracket.

27 Instrument panel gauges – removal and refitting

1   Remove the instrument panel as described in Section 25.

25.4a Remove the cap ...

25.4b ... unscrew the instrument panel surround lower screws ...

25.4c ... upper screws ...

25.4d ... and disconnect the plug from the illumination switch

25.5a Remove the screws ...

25.5b ... withdraw the instrument panel ...

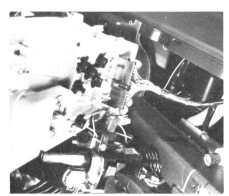

25.5c ... and disconnect the multi-plugs

25.5d Instrument panel

25.5e View of the instrument panel aperture showing the speedometer cable (arrowed)

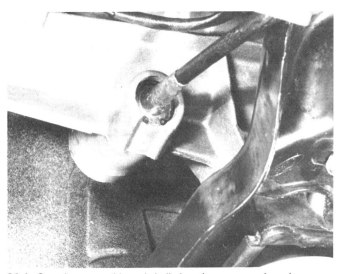

26.4a Speedometer cable and circlip location on manual gearbox models

26.4b Removing the speedometer cable on manual gearbox models

Speedometer head

2   Remove the crosshead screws and withdraw the lens from the upper pegs and lower cut-outs.
3   Remove the two screws and spacers and withdraw the speedometer head from the panel.
4   Refitting is a reversal of removal.

Tachometer

5   Remove the crosshead screws and withdraw the lens from the upper pegs and lower cut-outs.
6   Remove the nuts and washers and withdraw the tachometer.
7   Refitting is a reversal of removal.

Fuel and temperature gauges

8   Remove the crosshead screws and withdraw the lens.
9   Remove the nuts and washers and withdraw the gauge assembly.
10   Refitting is a reversal of removal.

28 Graphic information module – removal and refitting

1   Disconnect the battery negative lead.
2   Remove the screw from the centre facia and withdraw the warning lamp assembly.
3   Remove the screw and retainer, then pull the module from the facia.
4   Prise off the retainer and disconnect the multi-plug. Remove the module.
5   Refitting is a reversal of removal.

29 Clock – removal and refitting

1   Disconnect the battery negative lead.

Standard model

2   Prise the clock from the facia using a thin screwdriver then disconnect the multi-plug.
3   Refitting is a reversal of removal.

Mutli-function digital analogue model

4   Remove the screw from the centre facia and withdraw the warning lamp assembly.
5   Remove the screws and withdraw the clock sufficient to disconnect the multi-plug.

30 Ice warning sender unit – removal and refitting

1   Remove the horn as described in Section 40.

31.2 Rear view of the cigarette lighter

2   Depress the two tangs, disconnect the multi-plug and withdraw the sender unit from the slot on the front panel.
3   Refitting is a reversal of removal.

31 Cigarette lighter – removal and refitting

1   Disconnect the battery negative lead.
2   Reach up behind the lower centre console and push out the lighter after disconnecting the wiring (photo).
3   Remove the bulbholder and ring assembly.
4   Refitting is a reversal of removal.

32 Headlamps – alignment

1   It is recommended that the headlamp alignment is carried out by a Ford garage using modern beam setting equipment. However in an emergency the following procedure will provide an acceptable light pattern.
2   Position the car on a level surface with tyres correctly inflated approximately 10 metres (33 feet) in front of, and at right-angles to, a wall or garage door.
3   Draw a vertical line on the wall corresponding to the centre line of the car. The position of the line can be ascertained by marking the

centre of the front and rear screens with crayon then viewing the wall from the rear of the car.
4   Complete the lines shown in Fig. 10.21.
5   Switch the headlamps on dipped beam and adjust them as necessary using the knobs located behind the headlamps (photo). Cover the headlamp not being checked with cloth.

33 Headlamps and headlamp bulbs – removal and refitting

1   To remove a headlamp bulb open the bonnet then remove the cover by turning it anticlockwise (photo).
2   Pull off the connector then release the spring clip and withdraw the bulb (photos). Do not touch the bulb glass; however, if it is touched, clean it with methylated spirit.
3   To remove the headlamp unit first remove the front grille panel by unscrewing the upper screws.
4   Disconnect the multi-plug from the rear of the unit (photo). When applicable disconnect the headlamp washers
5   Unscrew the mounting bolts and the lower sliding clamp bracket

bolt on the rear of the unit, then withdraw the unit from the car (photos).
6   If required, the headlamp lens can now be removed by releasing the spring clips around its edge.
7   Refitting is a reversal of removal, but do not tighten the headlamp mounting bolts until it is aligned with the front grille panel. When refitting the bulb make sure that the lugs locate in the slots in the holder. Finally check the headlamp alignment as described in Section 32.

34 Lamp bulbs – renewal

Sidelamps
1   Open the bonnet and remove the headlamp rear cover by turning it anticlockwise.
2   Pull and turn the sidelamp bulbholder from the reflector leaving the rubber sleeve in position (photo). On High Series models it is necessary to depress a tab to remove the bulbholder.
3   Pull the wedge type bulb from the bulbholder.

32.5 Adjusting the headlamp alignment

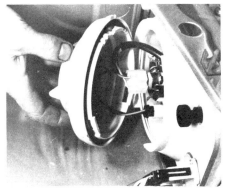

33.1 Removing the headlamp rear cover

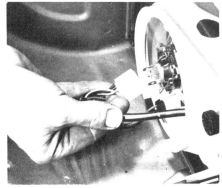

33.2a Pull off the connector ...

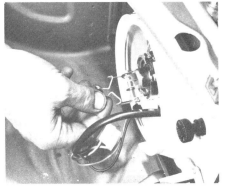

33.2b ... release the clip ...

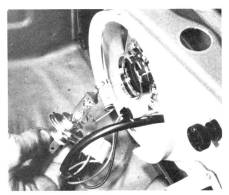

33.2c ... and withdraw the headlamp bulb

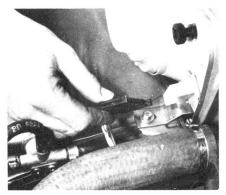

33.4 Disconnecting the headlamp multi-plug

33.5a Unscrew the mounting bolts ...

33.5b ... and withdraw the headlamp unit

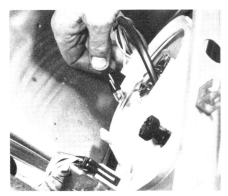

34.2 Removing a sidelamp bulb

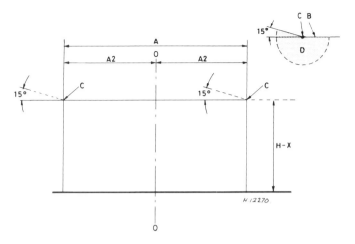

Fig. 10.21 Headlamp alignment chart (Sec 32)

A   Distance between headlamp   H   Height from ground to
    centres   centre of headlamps
B   Light-dark boundary   x   All variants – 16.0 cm
C   Beam centre dipped   (6.3 in or 1.0°)
D   Dipped beam pattern

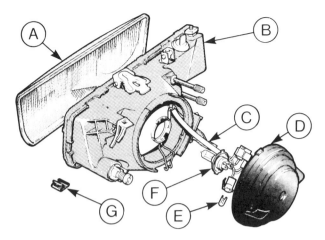

Fig. 10.22 Exploded view of the High Series headlamp (Sec 33)

A   Lens   E   Sidelamp bulb
B   Body   F   Headlamp bulb
C   Loom   G   Retaining clip
D   Cover

Auxiliary driving lamps
4   Twist the cover on top of the headlamp anticlockwise and remove it.
5   Remove the clip and withdraw the bulb.
6   Disconnect the wiring and remove the bulb.

Front direction indicator lamps
7   On Low Series models push the lamp rearward into its aperture until the plastic tang is locked then extract the lamp (photo).
8   On High Series (Ghia) models push the release lever up into the bumper recess and extract the lamp.
9   Twist the bulbholder anticlockwise and remove it from the lamp then push and twist the bulb to remove it (photo).
10 On Low Series models release the plastic tang before refitting the lamp.

Front foglamps
11 Remove the front direction indicator lamp as described in paragraphs 7 to 10.
12 Unhook the clip, withdraw the lamp so that the plug can be disconnected, then remove the lamp.

Side direction (repeater) indicator lamps
13 Turn the steering full lock to the side being worked on.
14 Remove the screws securing the splash shield to the inner body panel, noting the location of the screw covers in the engine compartment (photo).
15 Squeeze the retainers and withdraw the lamp.
16 Twist the bulbholder anticlockwise and remove it from the lamp then pull out the wedge type bulb (photo).

Rear lamp cluster (Hatchback)
17 Working in the luggage compartment press the plastic tab inwards and withdraw the bulbholder (photos).
18 Press and twist the bulbs to remove them (photo).

Rear lamp cluster (Estate)
19 Working in the luggage compartment turn the tabs a quarter turn and remove the rear side trim panel cover.
20 Push out the retaining tabs and withdraw the bulbholder.
21 Press and twist the bulbs to remove them.

Rear number plate lamp
22 Prise the lamp from the rear bumper using a small screwdriver to depress the two spring clips (photos).
23 Twist the bulbholder anticlockwise and remove it from the lamp then pull out the wedge type bulb (photos).

Interior lamp and luggage compartment lamp
24 With the lamp switched off prise out the lamp with a screwdriver (photo).

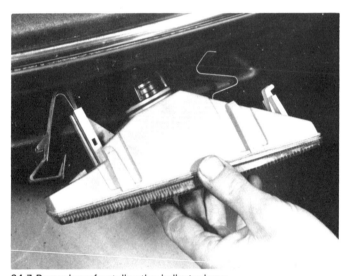

34.7 Removing a front direction indicator lamp

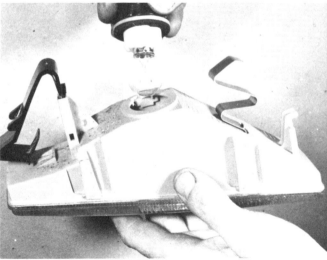

34.9 Removing a front direction indicator bulbholder

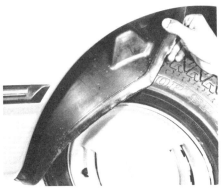

34.14 Removing the splash shield for access to the side direction indicator lamp

34.16 Removing the side direction indicator lamp

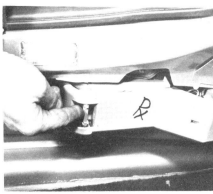

34.17a Press in the plastic tab ...

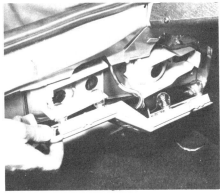

34.17b ... and withdraw the rear lamp cluster (Hatchback)

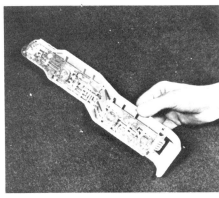

34.17c Rear lamp cluster (Hatchback)

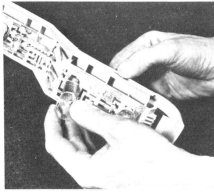

34.18 Removing a rear lamp cluster bulb

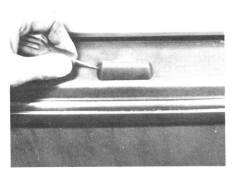

34.22a Depress the spring clips ...

34.22b ... and remove the rear number plate lamp

34.23a Rear number plate bulbholder

34.23b Removing a rear number plate bulb

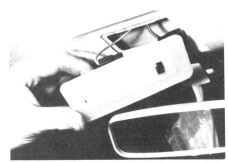

34.24a Removing the interior lamp

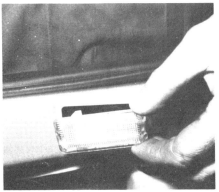

34.24b Removing the luggage compartment lamp

25 Press and twist the bulb to remove it (photo).

Glove compartment lamp
26 Open the glove compartment lid and pull the wedge type bulb from the bulbholder.

Ashtray lamp
27 Remove the ashtray drawer, pull out the bulbholder, and pull out the wedge type bulb.

Heater motor switch lamp
28 Pull off the switch knob using padded pliers if necessary.
29 Press and twist the bulb to remove it.

Map reading lamp
30 Remove the interior lamp as described in paragraphs 24 to 26.
31 Insert a finger in the interior lamp aperture and push out the map reading lamp.
32 Pull out the bulbholder then pull out the wedge type bulb.

Heater control lamp
33 Remove the instrument panel as described in Section 25.
34 Prise off the bezel and pull out the wedge type bulb.

Vanity mirror lamp
35 Pull down the sun visor then prise off the mirror and lens.
36 Extract the festoon type bulbs from the spring contacts.

Facia warning lamp
37 Remove the centre facia screw and withdraw the warning lamp assembly at the same time disconnect the multi-plug.
38 Twist the bulbholder through 90° and remove it. The bulb cannot be removed from the bulbholder.

Hazard warning lamp
39 Remove the upper steering column shroud (1 screw).
40 With the switch off, pull off the cover then pull out the wedge type bulb using small pliers if necessary.

Instrument panel lamp
41 Remove the instrument panel as described in Section 25.
42 Twist the bulbholder through 90° and remove it (photos).
43 On the small black bulbholders the bulb can be removed but on the large white bulbholders this is not possible (photos).

Econolight warning lamp
44 Remove the instrument panel as described in Section 25.
45 Pull off the multi-plug then remove the screw and withdraw the econolight assembly. If a bulb is faulty the complete assembly must be renewed.

---

35 Windscreen wiper motor – removal and refitting

This procedure is only possible on LHD cars. For RHD follow Section 36.
1   Open the bonnet then operate the wiper motor and switch off the ignition when the spindle nut is accessible (photo).
2   Unscrew the spindle nut and remove the linkage arm.
3   Unscrew the mounting bolts, disconnect the multi-plug and remove the wiper motor.
4   Refitting is a reversal of removal, but tighten the mounting bolts to the specified torque. Note that the linkage can only be fitted to the spindle in one position.

---

36 Windscreen wiper linkage – removal and refitting

1   Remove the wiper arms as described in Section 39.
2   Open the bonnet and disconnect the washer tube.
3   Unscrew the front screws from the ribbed cowl panel, then close the bonnet and unscrew the rear screws having first removed the screw covers. Remove the cowl panel.
4   Disconnect the multi-plug to the wiper motor.
5   Unbolt the mounting bracket and remove it together with the linkage and motor.
6   Unscrew the spindle nut and the mounting bolts and separate the

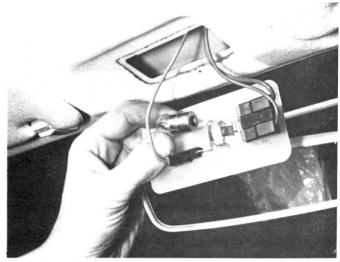

34.25a Removing the interior lamp bulb

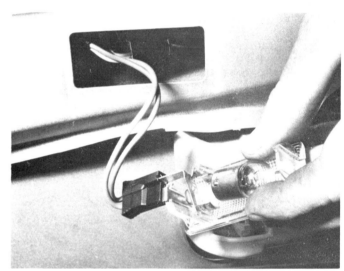

34.25b Removing the luggage compartment lamp bulb

34.42a Removing a small bulbholder from the instrument panel

34.42b Removing a large bulbholder from the instrument panel

34.43a The bulb can be separated from the small bulbholder ...

34.43b ... but the large bulb and bulbholder cannot be separated

35.1 Windscreen wiper motor location

motor from the linkage and bracket.

7   Refitting is a reversal of removal, but tighten the nuts and bolts to the specified torque.

37 Rear screen wiper motor – removal and refitting

1   Remove the wiper arm as described in Section 39.
2   Open the tailgate and carefully prise off the trim panel using a wide blade screwdriver.
3   Unscrew the mounting bolts and the earth lead and disconnect the multi-plug.
4   Withdraw the wiper motor and bracket and disconnect the washer hose. If necessary unbolt the wiper motor from the bracket.
5   Refitting is a reversal of removal, but tighten the bolts to the specified torque.

38 Wiper blades – renewal

1   The wiper blades should be renewed when they no longer clean the windscreen or tailgate window effectively.
2   Lift the wiper arm away from the windscreen or tailgate window.
3   With the blade at 90° to the arm depress the spring clip and slide the blade clear of the hook then slide it up off the arm (photo).

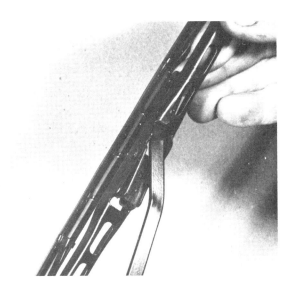

38.3 Removing a wiper blade

4   If necessary extract the two metal inserts and unhook the wiper rubber.
5   Fit the new rubber and blade in reverse order making sure where necessary that the cut-outs in the metal inserts face each other.

39 Wiper arms – removal and refitting

1   Remove the wiper blades as described in Section 38.
2   Lift the hinged covers and remove the nuts and washers securing the arms to the spindles (photo).
3   Mark the arms and spindles in relation to each other then prise off the arms using a screwdriver. Take care not to damage the paintwork.
4   Refitting is a reversal of removal.

40 Horn – removal and refitting

1   The horn(s) is located in front of the radiator beneath the front panel (photo).
2   Disconnect the battery negative lead.
3   Disconnect the wiring from the horn then unbolt the bracket from the underbody.
4   Refitting is a reversal of removal.

41 Trip computer module – removal and refitting

1   Disconnect the battery negative lead.
2   Remove the screw and withdraw the surround.
3   Remove the crosshead screws and withdraw the module sufficient to disconnect the multi-plug.
4   Unscrew the nuts and remove the brackets from the module.
5   Refitting is a reversal of removal.

42 Trip computer speed sender unit – removal and refitting

1   The speed sender unit is located in the engine compartment on the right-hand side of the bulkhead.
2   Disconnect the multi-plug from the sender unit.
3   Unscrew the two nuts then remove the crosshead screws and withdraw the bracket and sender.
4   Unscrew the nut and separate the sender from the bracket.
5   Refitting is a reversal of removal.

43 Trip computer fuel flow sensor – removal and refitting

1   The fuel flow sensor is located on the left-hand side of the engine compartment.
2   Note the location of the fuel pipes then disconnect them from the sensor.
3   Disconnect the multi-plug.
4   Remove the screws and withdraw the sensor and bracket.
5   Unscrew the nuts and separate the sensor from the bracket.
6   Refitting is a reversal of removal, however note the arrows which indicate the direction of fuel flow and the top of the unit.

44 Radio (standard) – removal and refitting

1   Disconnect the battery negative lead.
2   Pull off the control knobs.
3   Unscrew the two nuts and plain washers and remove the trim panel.
4   Using a hooked instrument pull the mounting tangs towards the centre of the radio and extract the radio from the aperture (photo).
5   Disconnect the aerial, speaker plugs, earth lead and feed wire.
6   Unscrew the nuts and remove the washers and mounting plate. Remove the plastic bracket and plate from the rear of the radio.
7   Refitting is a reversal of removal.

45 Radios and tape players (general) – installation

A radio or tape player is an expensive item to buy, and will only

39.2 Wiper arm retaining nut location

40.1 Horn location

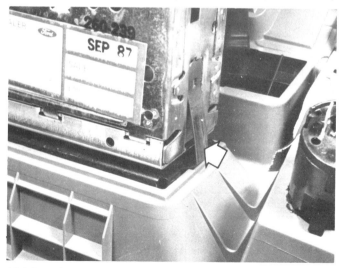

44.4 Rear view of the radio retaining clips (arrowed)

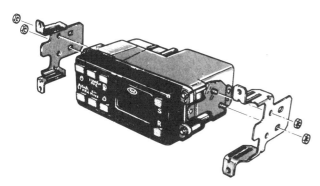

Fig. 10.23 Trip computer module (Sec 41)

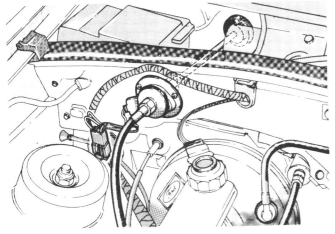

Fig. 10.24 Trip computer speed sender unit location in the bulkhead (Sec 42)

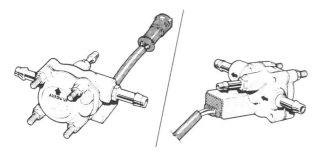

Fig. 10.25 Showing trip computer fuel flow sensor flow and mounting arrows (Sec 43)

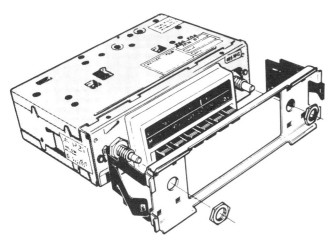

Fig. 10.26 Radio and mounting plate (Sec 44)

give its best performance if fitted properly. It is useless to expect concert hall performance from a unit that is suspended from the dashpanel by string with its speaker resting on the back seat or parcel shelf! If you do not wish to do the installation yourself, there are many in-car entertainment specialists who can do the fitting for you.

Make sure the unit purchased is of the same polarity as the vehicle. Ensure that units with adjustable polarity are correctly set before commencing installation.

It is difficult to give specific information with regard to fitting, as final positioning of the radio/tape player, speakers and aerial is entirely a matter of personal preference. However, the following paragraphs give guidelines to follow which are relevant to all installations.

Radios

Most radios are a standardised size of 7 inches wide, by 2 inches deep – this ensures that they will fit into the radio aperture provided in most cars. If your car does not have such an aperture, then the radio must be fitted in a suitable position either in, or beneath, the dashboard. Alternatively, a special console can be purchased which will fit between the dashpanel and the floor, or on the transmission tunnel. These consoles can also be used for additional switches and instrumentation if required. Where no radio aperture is provided, the following points should be borne in mind before deciding exactly where to fit the unit.

(a)   The unit must be within easy reach of the driver wearing a seatbelt.

(b)   The unit must not be mounted in close proximity to an electronic tachometer, the ignition switch and its wiring, or the flasher unit and associated wiring.

(c)   The unit must be mounted within reach of the aerial lead, and in such a place that the aerial lead will not have to be routed near the components detailed in the preceding paragraph 'b'.

(d)   The unit should not be positioned in a place where it might cause injury to the car occupants in an accident; for instance under the dashpanel above the driver's or passenger's legs.

(e)   The unit must be fitted really securely.

Some radios will have mounting brackets provided together with instructions; others will need to be fitted using drilled and slotted metal strips, bent to form mounting brackets – these strips are available from most accessory stores. The unit must be properly earthed, by fitting a separate earth lead between the casing of the radio and the vehicle frame.

Use the radio manufacturer's instructions when wiring the radio into the vehicle's electrical system. If no instructions are available, refer to the relevant wiring diagram to find the location of the radio 'feed' connection in the vehicle's wiring circuit. A 1-2 amp 'in-line' fuse must be fitted in the radio's feed wire – a choke may also be necessary (see next Section).

The type of aerial used, and its fitted position is a matter of personal preference. In general the taller the aerial, the better the reception. It is best to fit a fully retractable aerial – especially, if a mechanical car-wash is used or if you live in an area where cars tend to be vandalised. In this respect electric aerials which are raised and lowered automatically when switching the radio on or off, are convenient, but are more likely to give trouble than the manual type.

When choosing a site for the aerial, the following points should be considered:

(a)   The aerial lead should be as short as possible; this means that the aerial should be mounted at the front of the vehicle.

(b)   The aerial must be mounted as far away from the distributor and HT leads as possible.

(c)   The part of the aerial which protrudes beneath the mounting point must not foul the roadwheels, or anything else.

(d)   If possible, the aerial should be positioned so that the coaxial lead does not have to be routed through the engine compartment.

(e)   The plane of the panel on which the aerial is mounted should not be so steeply angled that the aerial cannot be mounted vertically (in relation to the 'end-on' aspect of the vehicle). Most aerials have a small amount of adjustment available.

Having decided on a mounting position, a relatively large hole will have to be made in the panel. The exact size of the hole will depend upon the specific aerial being fitted, although, generally, the hole required is of $\frac{3}{4}$ inch diameter. On metal bodied cars, a 'tank-cutter' of the relevant diameter is the best tool to use for making the hole. This tool needs a small diameter pilot hole drilled through the panel, through which the tool clamping bolt is inserted. On GRP bodied cars, a 'hole saw' is the best tool to use. Again, this tool will require the drilling of a small pilot hole. When the hole has been made the raw edges should be de-burred with a file and then painted, to prevent corrosion.

Fit the aerial according to the manufacturer's instructions. If the aerial is very tall, or if it protrudes beneath the mounting panel for a considerable distance it is a good idea to fit a stay between the aerial and the vehicle frame. This stay can be manufactured from the slotted and drilled metal strips previously mentioned. The stay should be securely screwed or bolted in place. For best reception, it is advisable to fit an earth lead between the aerial and the vehicle frame – this is essential on fibreglass bodied vehicles.

It will probably be necessary to drill one, or two holes through bodywork panels in order to feed the aerial lead into the interior of the car. Where this is the case ensure that the holes are fitted with rubber grommets to protect the cable, and to stop possible entry of water.

Positioning and fitting of the speaker depends mainly on its type. Generally, the speaker is designed to fit directly into the aperture already provided in the car (usually on the shelf behind the rear seats, or in the top of the dashpanel). Where this is the case, fitting the speaker is just a matter of removing the protective grille from the aperture and screwing or bolting the speaker in place. Take great care not to damage the speaker diaphragm whilst doing this. It is a good idea to fit a 'gasket' between the speaker frame and the mounting panel in order to prevent vibration – some speakers will already have such a gasket fitted.

If a 'pod' type speaker was supplied with the radio, the best acoustic results will normally be obtained by mounting it on the shelf behind the rear seat. The pod can be secured to the mounting panel with self-tapping screws.

When connecting a rear mounted speaker to the radio, the wires should be routed through the vehicle beneath the carpets or floor mats preferably through the middle, or along the side of the floorpan, where they will not be trodden on by passengers. Make the relevant connections as directed by the radio manufacturer.

By now you will have several yards of additional wiring in the car; use PVC tape to secure this wiring out of harm's way. Do not leave electrical leads dangling. Ensure that all new electrical connections are properly made (wires twisted together will not do) and completely secure.

The radio should now be working, but before you pack away your tools it will be necessary to 'trim' the radio to the aerial. Follow the radio manufacturer's instructions regarding this adjustment.

Tape players

Fitting instructions for both cartridge and cassette stereo tape players are the same and in general the same rules apply as when fitting a radio. Tape players are not usually prone to electrical interference like radios – although it can occur – so positioning is not so critical. If possible, the player should be mounted on an even keel. Also, it must be possible for a driver wearing a seatbelt to reach the unit in order to change, or turn over, tapes.

For the best results from speakers designed to be recessed into a panel, mount them so that the back of the speaker protrudes into an enclosed chamber within the vehicle (eg; door interiors or the boot cavity).

To fit recessed type speakers in the front doors first check that there is sufficient room to mount the speaker in each door without it fouling the latch or window winding mechanism. Hold the speaker against the skin of the door, and draw a line, around the periphery of the speaker. With the speaker removed draw a second 'cutting' line within the first, to allow enough room for the entry of the speaker back but at the same time providing a broad seat for the speaker flange. When you are sure that the 'cutting-line' is correct, drill a series of holes around its periphery. Pass a hacksaw blade through one of the holes and then cut through the metal between the holes until the centre section of the panel falls out.

De-burr the edges of the hole and then paint the raw metal to prevent corrosion. Cut a corresponding hole in the door trim panel – ensuring that it will be completely covered by the speaker grille. Now drill a hole in the door edge and a corresponding hole in the door surround. These holes are to feed the speaker leads through – so fit

grommets. Pass the speaker leads through the door trim, door skin and out through the holes in the side of the door and door surround. Refit the door trim panel and then secure the speaker to the door using self-tapping screws. **Note**: If the speaker is fitted with a shield to prevent water dripping on it, ensure that this shield is at the top.

'Pod' type speakers can be fastened to the shelf behind the rear seat, or anywhere else offering a corresponding mounting point on each side of the car. If the 'pod' speakers are mounted on each side of the shelf behind the seat, it is a good idea to drill several large diameter holes through to the trunk cavity, beneath each speaker – this will improve the sound reproduction. 'Pod' speakers sometimes offer a better reproduction quality if they face the rear window – which then acts as a reflector – so it is worthwhile experimenting before finally fixing the speakers.

46 Radios and tape players (general) – suppression of interference

To eliminate buzzes and other unwanted noises, costs very little and is not as difficult as sometimes thought. With a modicum of common sense and patience and following the instructions in the following paragraphs, interference can be virtually eliminated.

The first cause for concern is the generator. The noise this makes over the radio is like an electric mixer and the noise speeds up when you rev the engine (if you wish to prove the point, you can remove the fanbelt and try it). The remedy for this is simple; connect a 1.0 mf to 3.0 mf capacitor between earth, probably the bolt that holds down the generator base, and the *output* terminal on the alternator. This is most important, for if you connect it to the other terminal you will probably damage the generator permanently (see Fig. 10.27).

A second common cause of electrical interference is the ignition system. Here a 1.0 mf capacitor must be connected between earth and the SW or + terminal on the coil (see Fig. 10.28). This may stop the tick-tick sound that comes over the speaker. Next comes the spark itself.

There are several ways of curing interference from the ignition HT system. One is the use of carbon-cored HT leads as original equipment. Where copper cable is substituted then you must use resistive spark plug caps (see Fig. 10.29) of about 10 000 ohm to 15 000 ohm resistance. If, due to lack of room, these cannot be used, an alternative is to use 'in-line' suppressors – if the interference is not too bad, you may get away with only one suppressor in the coil to distributor line. If the interference does continue (a 'clacking' noise) then modify all HT leads.

At this stage it is advisable to check that the radio is well earthed, also the aerial and to see that the aerial plug is pushed well into the set and that the radio is properly trimmed (see preceding Section). In addition, check that the wire which supplies the power to the set is as short as possible. At this stage it is a good idea to check that the fuse is of the correct rating. For most sets this will be about 1 to 2 amps.

At this point, the more usual causes of interference have been suppressed. If the problem still exists, a look at the cause of interference may help to pinpoint the component generating the stray electrical discharges.

The radio picks up electromagnetic waves in the air; now some are made by regular broadcasters, and some, which we do not want, are made by the car itself. The home made signals are produced by stray electrical discharges floating around in the car. Common producers of these signals are electrical motors, ie, the windscreen wipers, electric screen washers, electric window winders, heater fan or an electric aerial if fitted. Other sources of interference are flashing turn signals and instruments. The remedy for these cases is shown in Fig. 10.30 for an electric motor whose interference is not too bad and Fig. 10.31 for instrument suppression. Turn signals are not normally suppressed. In recent years, radio manufacturers have included in the line (live) of the radio, in addition to the fuse, an 'in-line' choke. If your circuit lacks one of these, put one in as shown in Fig. 10.32.

All the foregoing components are available from radio stores or accessory stores. If you have an electric clock fitted, this should be suppressed by connecting a 0.5 mf capacitor directly across it as shown for a motor in Fig. 10.30.

If after all this, you are still experiencing radio interference, first assess how bad it is, for the human ear can filter out unobtrusive unwanted noises quite easily. But if you are still adamant about eradicating the noise, then continue.

As a first step, a few 'experts' seem to favour a screen between

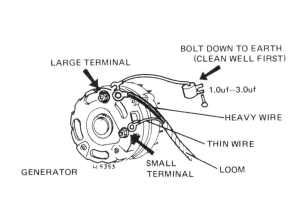

Fig. 10.27 The correct way to connect a capacitor to the alternator (Sec 46)

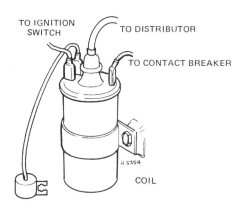

Fig. 10.28 The capacitor must be connected to the ignition switch side of the coil (Sec 46)

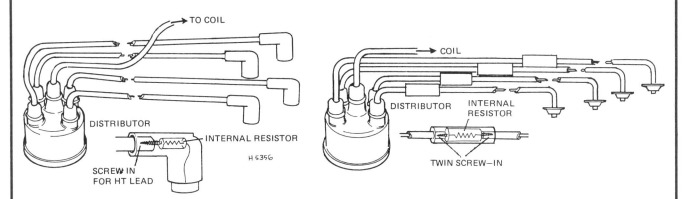

Fig. 10.29 Ignition HT lead suppressors (Sec 46)

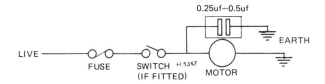

Fig. 10.30 Correct method of suppressing electric motors (Sec 46)

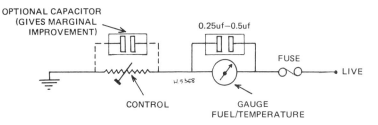

Fig. 10.31 Method of suppressing gauges and their control units (Sec 46)

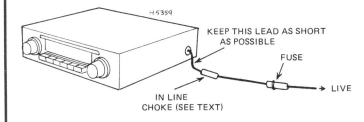

Fig. 10.32 An 'in-line' choke should be fitted into the live supply lead as close to the unit as possible (Sec 46)

the radio and the engine. This is OK as far as it goes – literally! – for the whole set is screened anyway and if interference can get past that then a small piece of aluminium is not going to stop it.

A more sensible way of screening is to discover if interference is coming down the wires. First, take the live lead; interference can get between the set and the choke (hence the reason for keeping the wires short). One remedy here is to screen the wire and this is done by buying screened wire and fitting that. The loudspeaker lead could be screened also to prevent 'pick-up' getting back to the radio although this is unlikely.

Without doubt, the worst source of radio interference comes from the ignition HT leads, even if they have been suppressed. The ideal way of suppressing these is to slide screening tubes over the leads themselves. As this is impractical, we can place an aluminium shield over the majority of the lead areas. In a vee- or twin-cam engine this is relatively easy but for a straight engine, the results are not particularly good.

Now for the really impossible cases, here are a few tips to try out. Where metal comes into contact with metal, an electrical disturbance is caused which is why good clean connections are essential. To remove interference due to overlapping or butting panels, you must bridge the join with a wide braided earth strap (like that from the frame to the engine/transmission). The most common moving parts that could create noise and should be strapped are, in order of importance:

(a) Silencer to frame
(b) Exhaust pipe to engine block and frame
(c) Air cleaner to frame
(d) Front and rear bumpers to frame
(e) Steering column to frame
(f) Bonnet and boot lids to frame
(g) Hood frame to bodyframe on soft tops

These faults are most pronounced when (1) the engine is idling, (2) labouring under load. Although the moving parts are already connected with nuts, bolts, etc, these do tend to rust and corrode, thus creating a high resistance interference source.

If you have a 'ragged' sounding pulse when mobile, this could be wheel or tyre static. This can be cured by buying some anti-static powder and sprinkling inside the tyres.

If the interference takes the shape of a high pitched screeching noise that changes its note when the car is in motion and only comes now and then, this could be related to the aerial, especially if it is of the telescopic or whip type. This source can be cured quite simply by pushing a small rubber ball on top of the aerial as this breaks the electric field before it can form; but it would be much better to buy yourself a new aerial of a reputable brand. If, on the other hand, you are getting a loud rushing sound every time you brake, then this is brake static. This effect is most prominent on hot dry days and is cured only by fitting a special kit, which is quite expensive.

In conclusion, it is pointed out that it is relatively easy, and therefore, cheap, to eliminate 95 per cent of all noise, but to eliminate the final 5 per cent is time and money consuming. It is up to the individual to decide if it is worth it. Please remember also, that you cannot get a concert hall performance out of a cheap radio.

Finally, players and eight track players are not usually affected by car noise, but in a very bad case, the best remedies are the first three suggestions plus using a 3 – 5 amp choke in the 'live' line and in difficult cases screen the live and speaker wires.

Note: *If your car is fitted with electronic ignition, then it is not recommended that either the spark plug resistors or the ignition coil capacitor be fitted as these may damage the system. Most electronic ignition units have built-in suppression and should, therefore, not cause interference.*

47 Fault diagnosis – electrical system

Symptom	Reason(s)
Starter fails to turn engine	Battery discharged or defective
	Battery terminal and/or earth leads loose
	Starter motor connections loose
	Starter solenoid faulty
	Starter solenoid faulty
	Starter brushes worn or sticking
	Starter commutator dirty or worn
Starter turns engine very slowly	Battery discharged
	Starter motor connections loose
	Starter brushes worn or sticking
Starter noisy	Pinion or flywheel ring gear teeth badly worn
	Mounting bolts loose
Battery will not hold charge for more than a few days	Battery defective internally
	Electrolyte level too low
	Battery terminals loose
	Alternator drivebelt(s) slipping
	Alternator or regulator faulty
	Short circuit
Ignition light stays on	Alternator faulty
	Alternator drivebelt(s) broken
Ignition light fails to come on	Warning bulb blown or open circuit
	Alternator faulty
Instrument readings increase with engine speed	Voltage stabilizer faulty
Fuel or temperature gauge gives no reading	Wiring open circuit
	Sender unit faulty
	Gauge faulty
Fuel or temperature gauge gives maximum reading all the time	Wiring short circuit
	Gauge faulty
Lights inoperative	Bulb blown
	Fuse blown
	Battery discharged
	Switch faulty
	Wiring open circuit
	Bad connection due to corrosion
Failure of component motor	Commutator dirty or burnt
	Armature faulty
	Brushes sticking or worn
	Armature bearings seized
	Fuse blown
	Wiring loose or broken
	Field coils faulty

Wiring diagrams commence overleaf

Colour code

BL	Blue	RS Pink
BR	Brown	RT Red
GE	Yellow	SW Black
GR	Grey	VI Violet
GN	Green	WS White

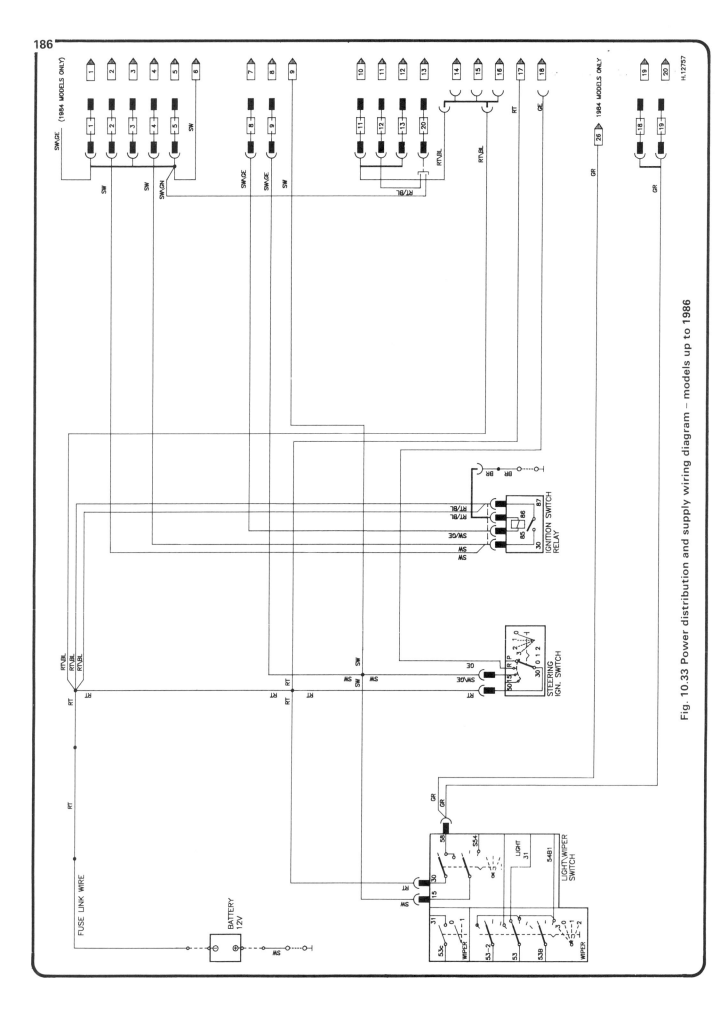

Fig. 10.33 Power distribution and supply wiring diagram – models up to 1986

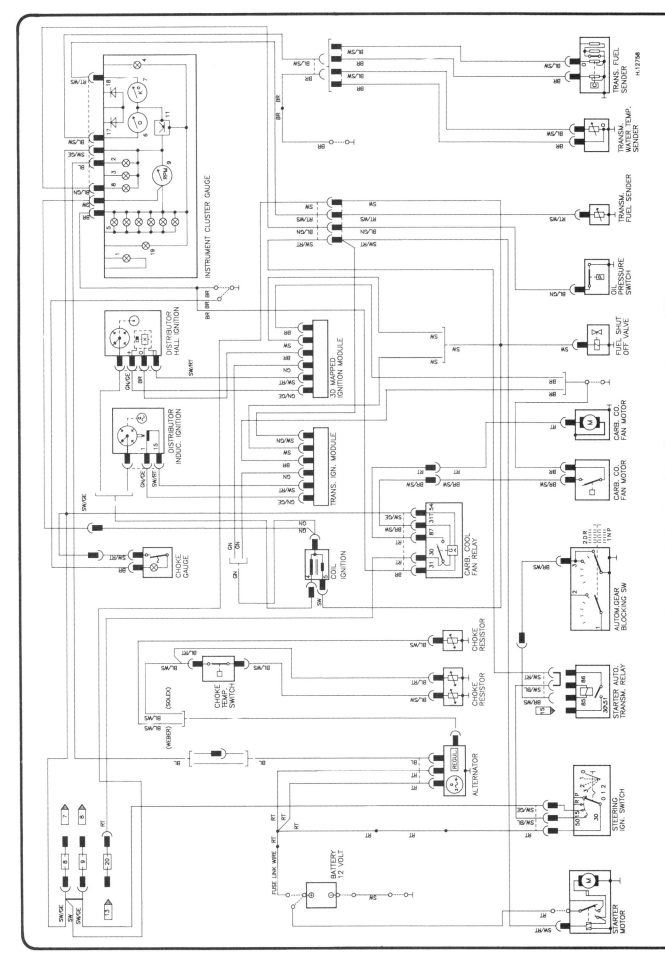

Fig. 10.34 Starting and charging wiring diagram – models up to 1984

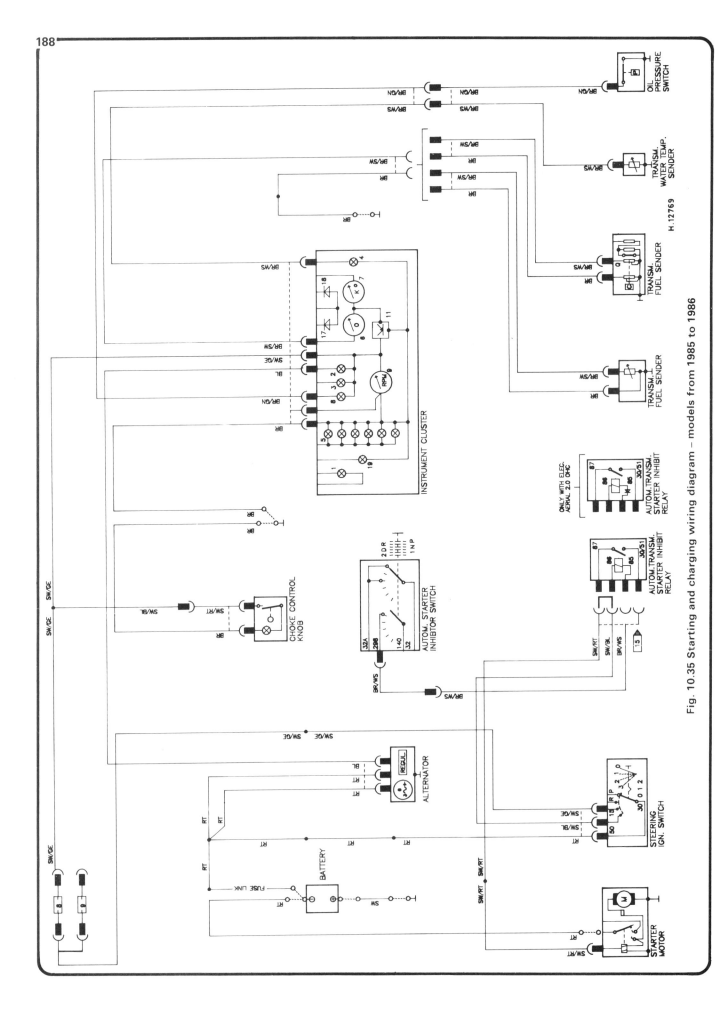

Fig. 10.35 Starting and charging wiring diagram – models from 1985 to 1986

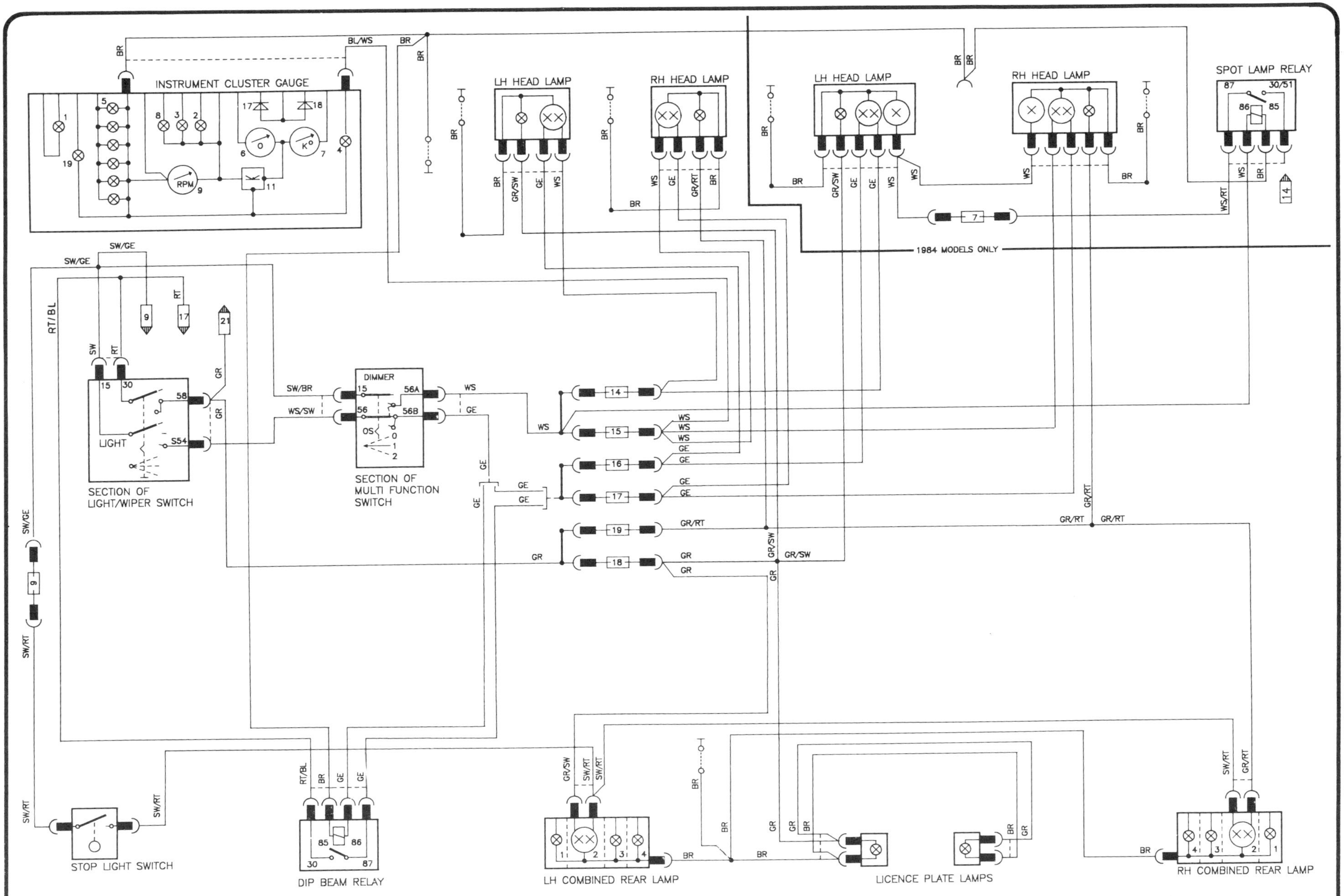

Fig. 10.36 Exterior lights wiring diagram – models up to 1986

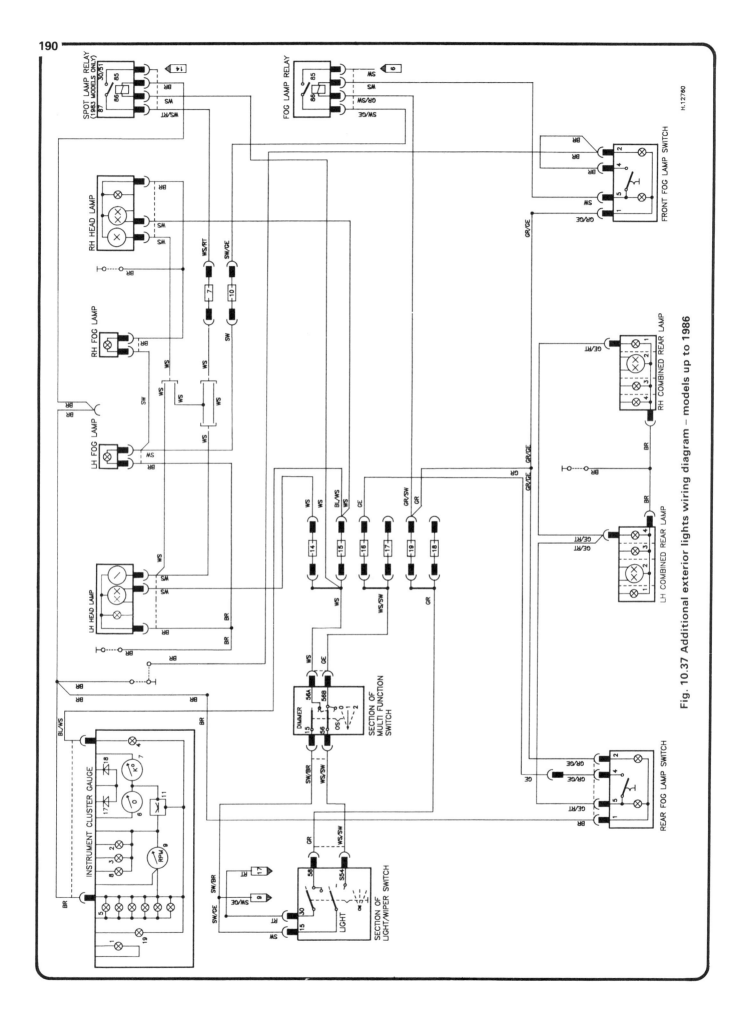

Fig. 10.37 Additional exterior lights wiring diagram – models up to 1986

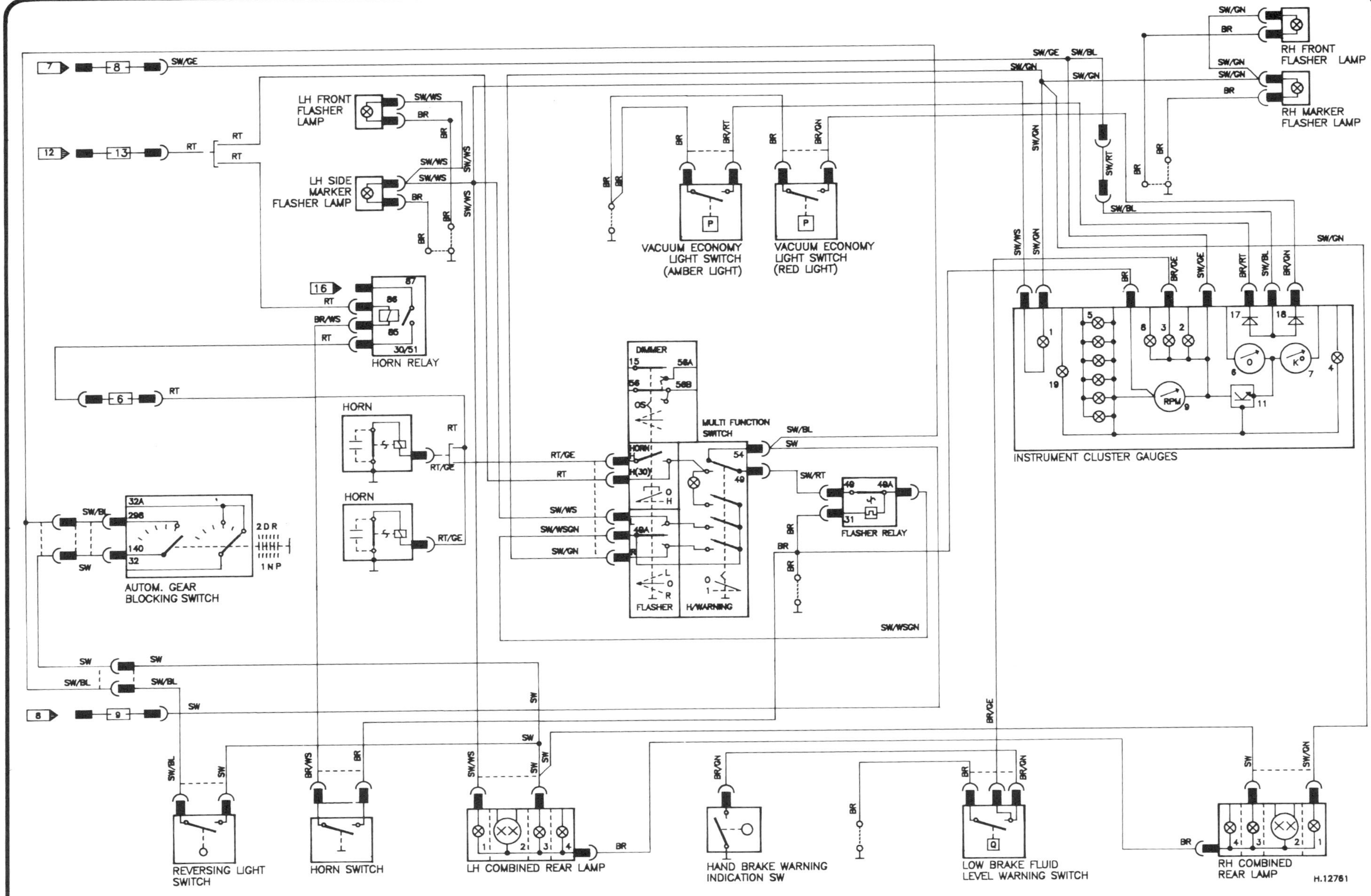

Fig. 10.38 Indicating and hazard warning wiring diagram – models up to 1986

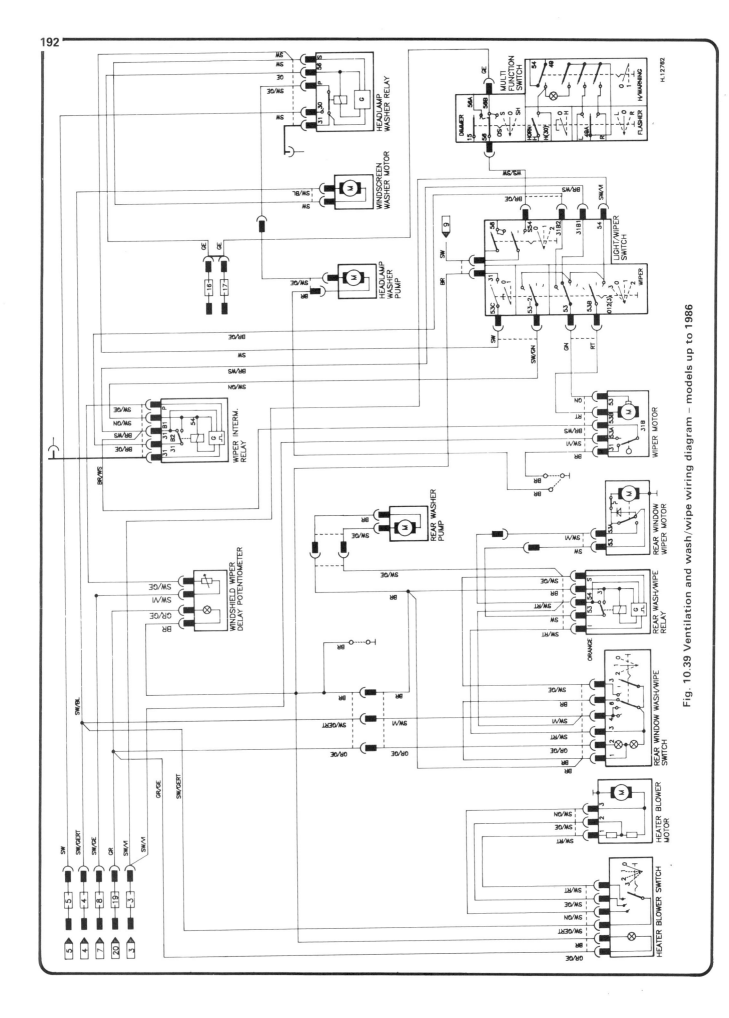

Fig. 10.39 Ventilation and wash/wipe wiring diagram – models up to 1986

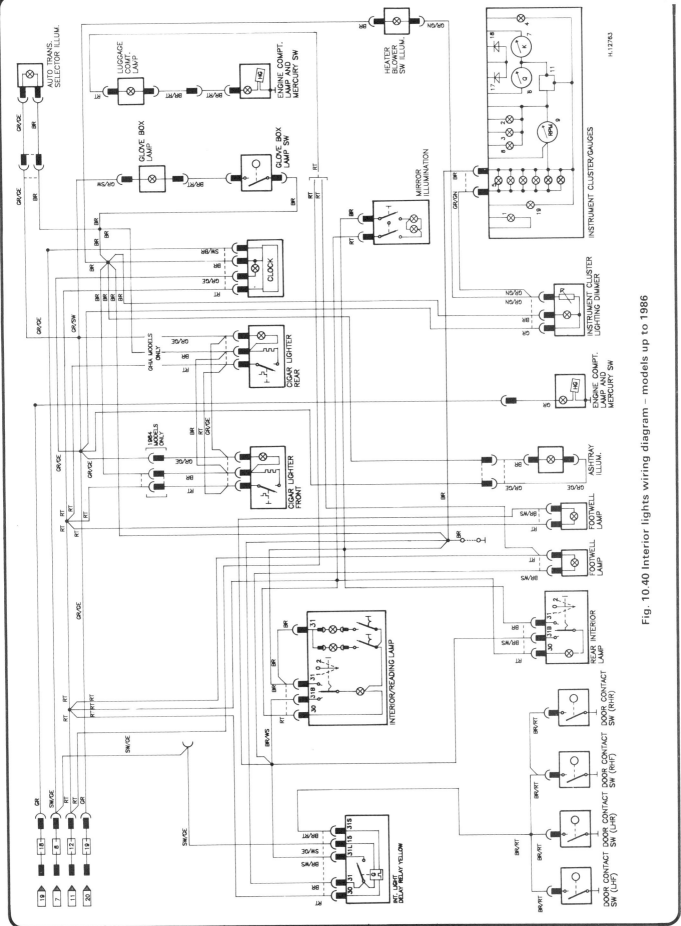

Fig. 10.40 Interior lights wiring diagram – models up to 1986

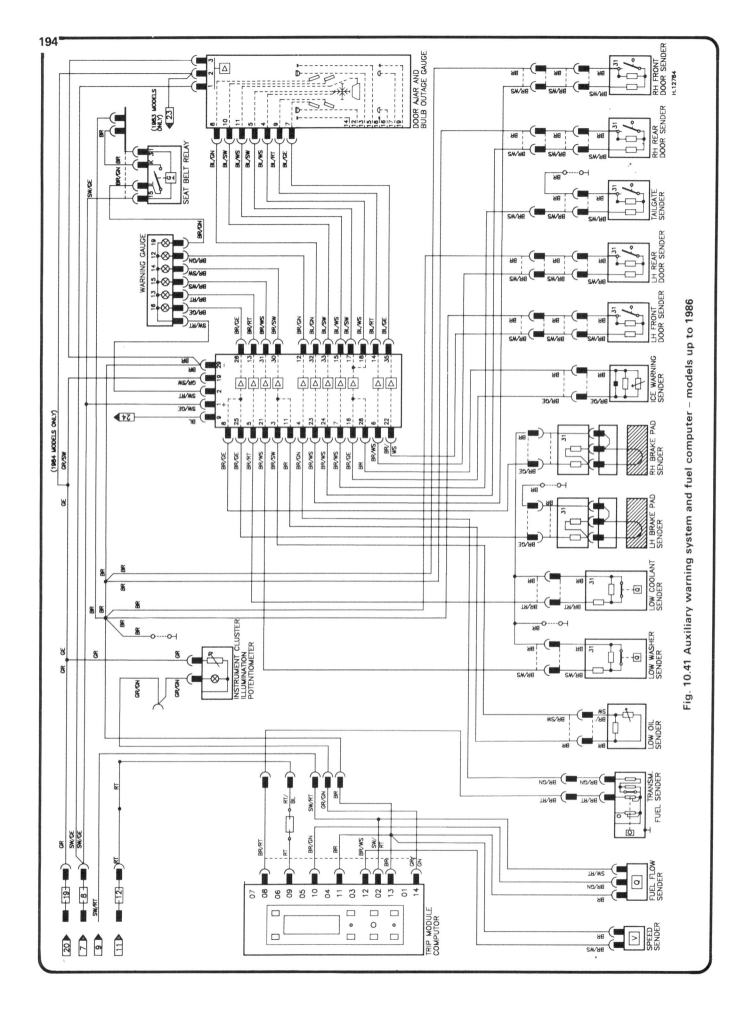

Fig. 10.41 Auxiliary warning system and fuel computer – models up to 1986

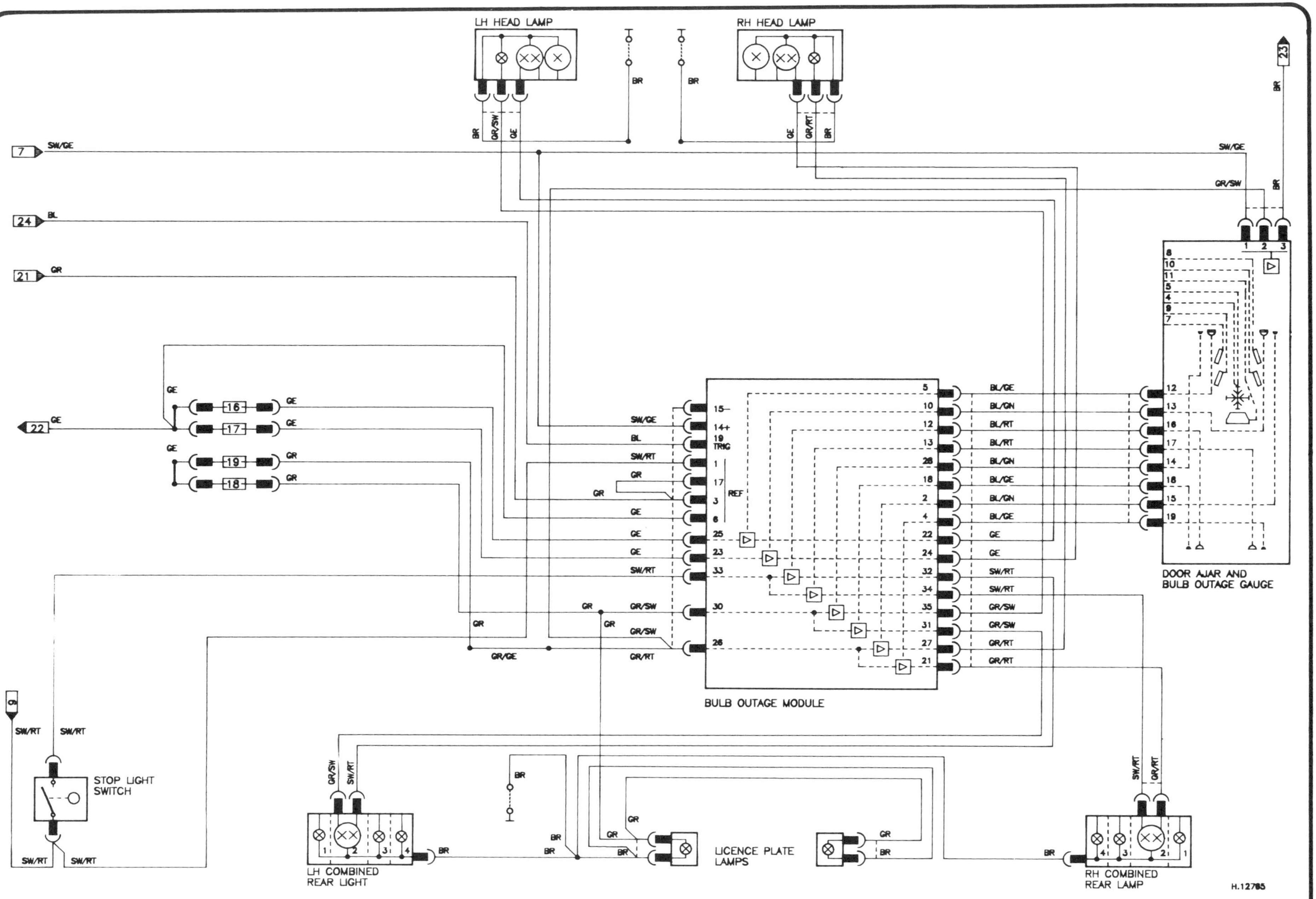

Fig. 10.42 Bulb failure warning wiring diagram – models up to 1984

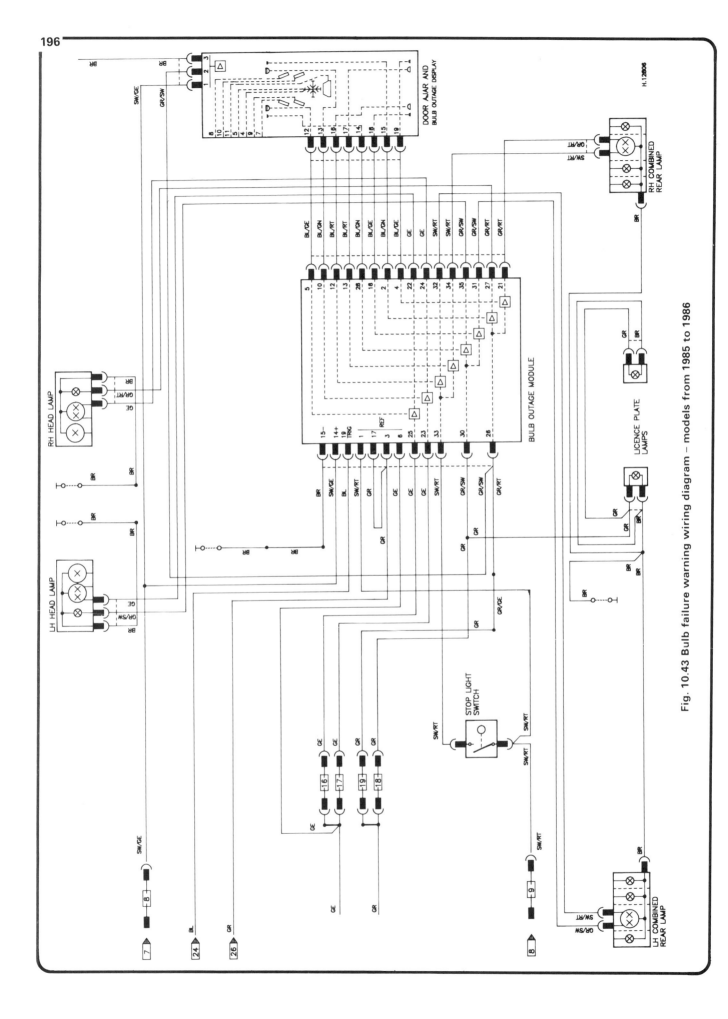

Fig. 10.43 Bulb failure warning wiring diagram – models from 1985 to 1986

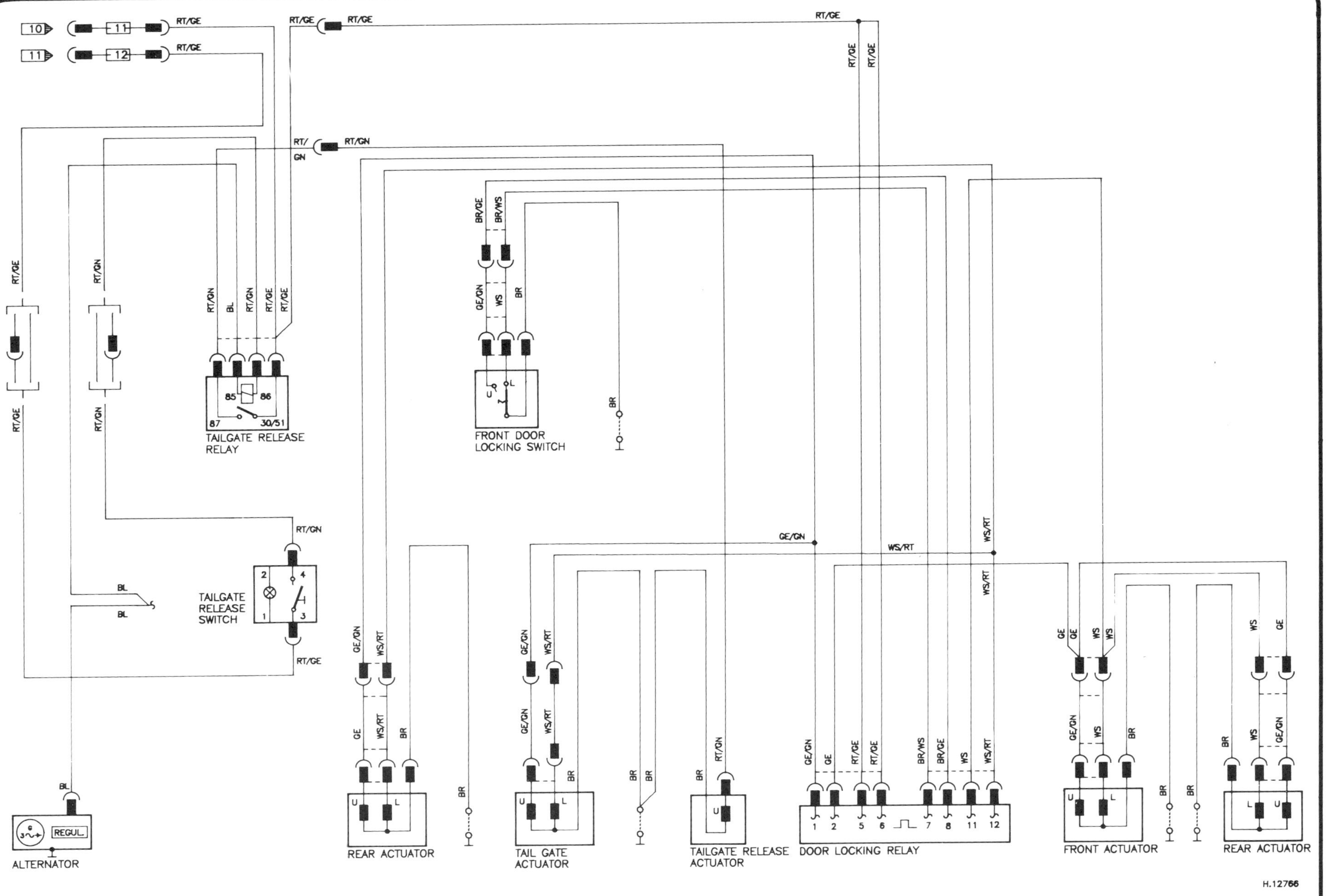

Fig. 10.44 Central locking wiring diagram – models up to 1986

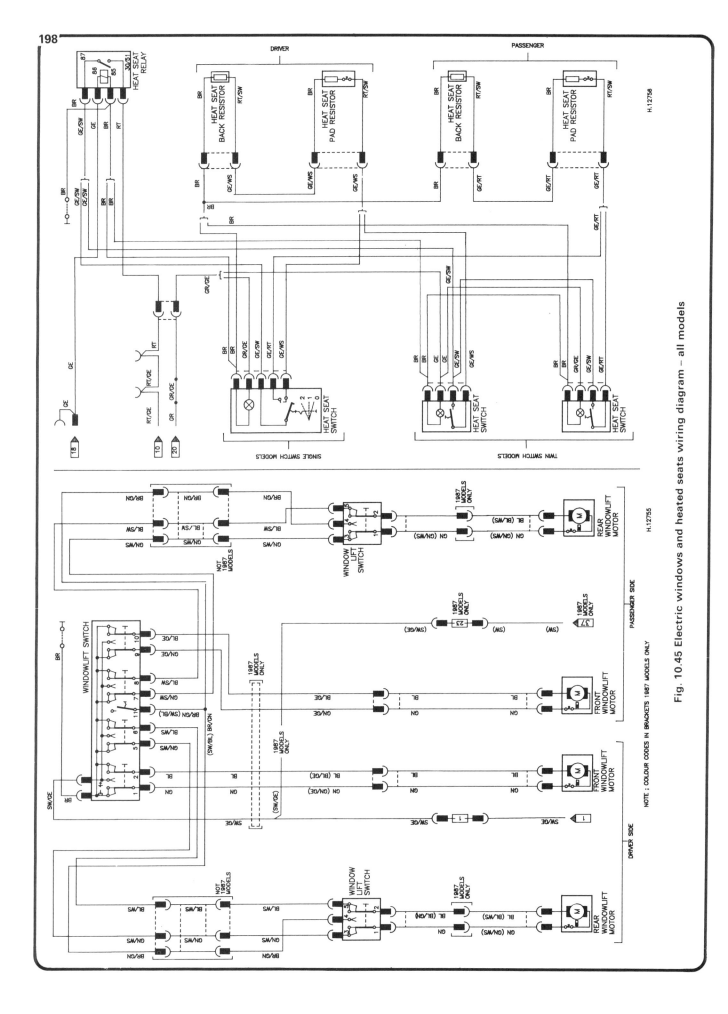

Fig. 10.45 Electric windows and heated seats wiring diagram – all models

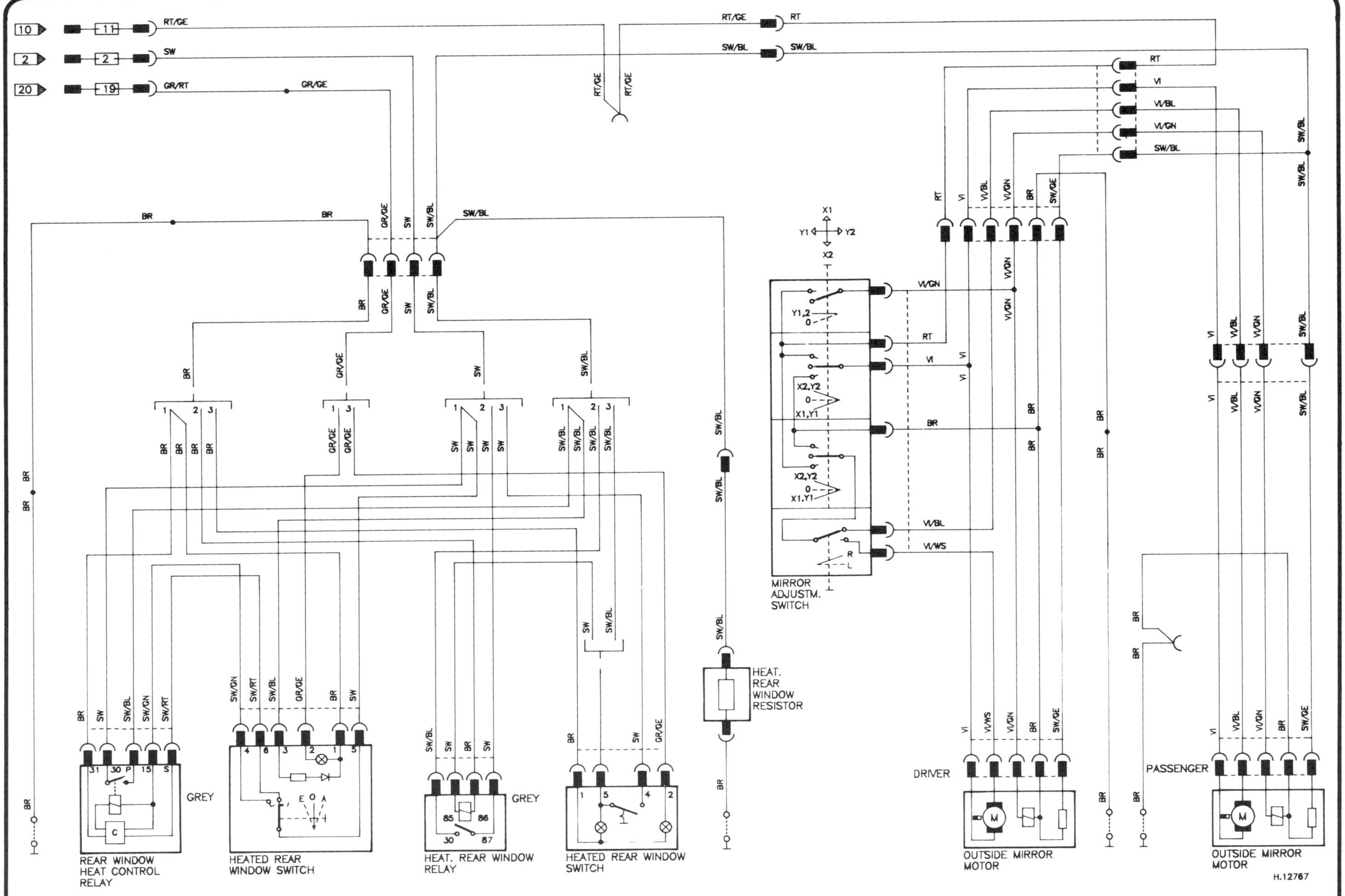

Fig. 10.46 Electric mirror and heated rear window wiring diagram – models up to 1986

1.3/1.6 OHC

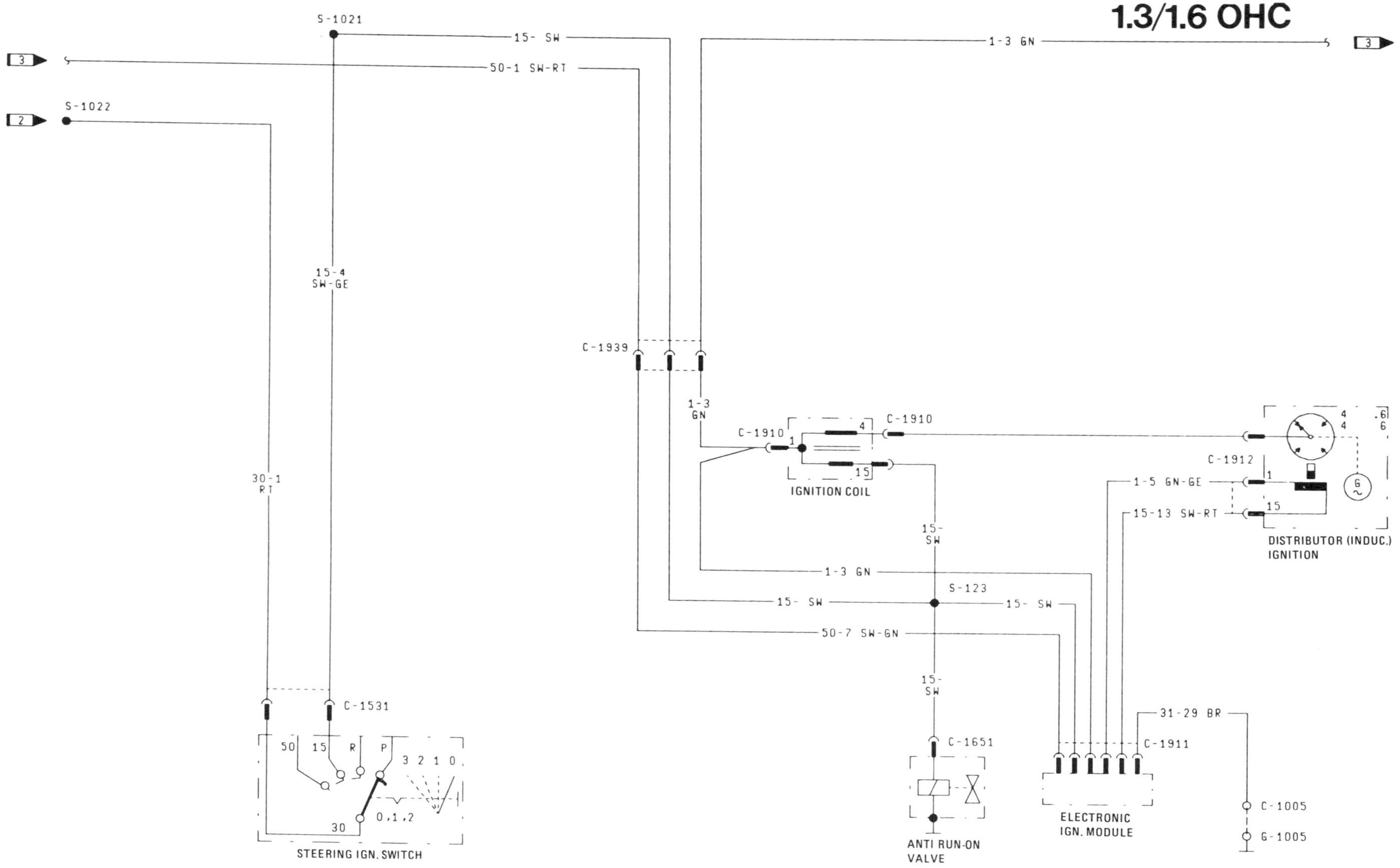

DISTRIBUTOR (INDUC.) IGNITION

C-1912

1-5 GN-GE

15-13 SW-RT

31-29 BR

C-1911

C-1005

G-1005

ELECTRONIC IGN. MODULE

1-3 GN

C-1910

IGNITION COIL

15-SW

S-123

15-SW

C-1651

ANTI RUN-ON VALVE

15-SW

1-3 GN

15-SW

50-7 SW-GN

1-3 GN

C-1910

C-1939

15-SW

50-1 SW-RT

S-1021

15-4 SW-GE

C-1531

STEERING IGN. SWITCH

30-1 RT

S-1022

Fig. 10.47 1.3 and 1.6 engine management wiring diagram – models from 1985 to 1986

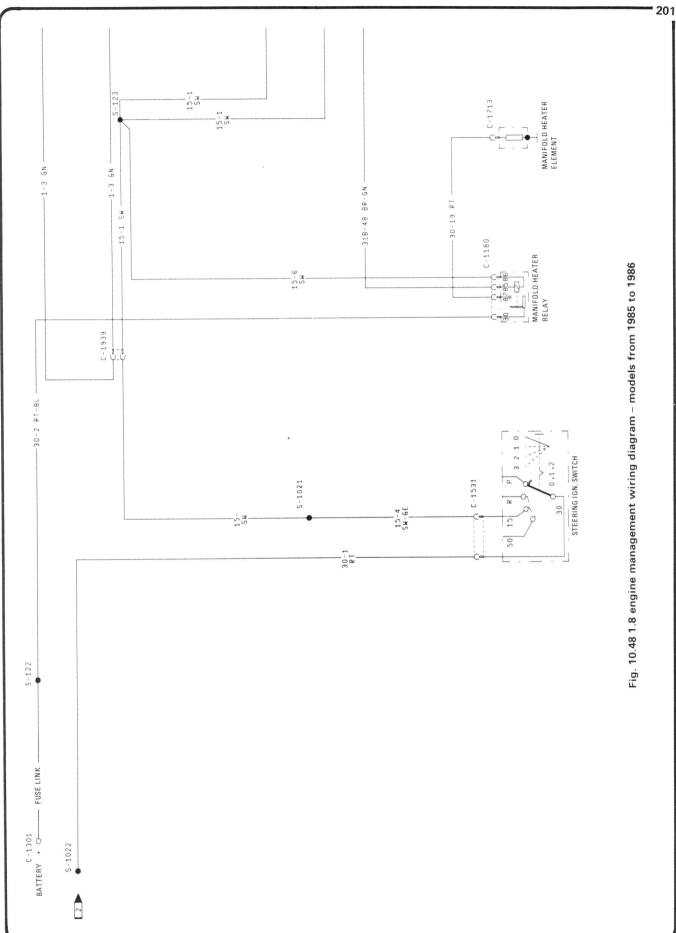

Fig. 10.48 1.8 engine management wiring diagram – models from 1985 to 1986

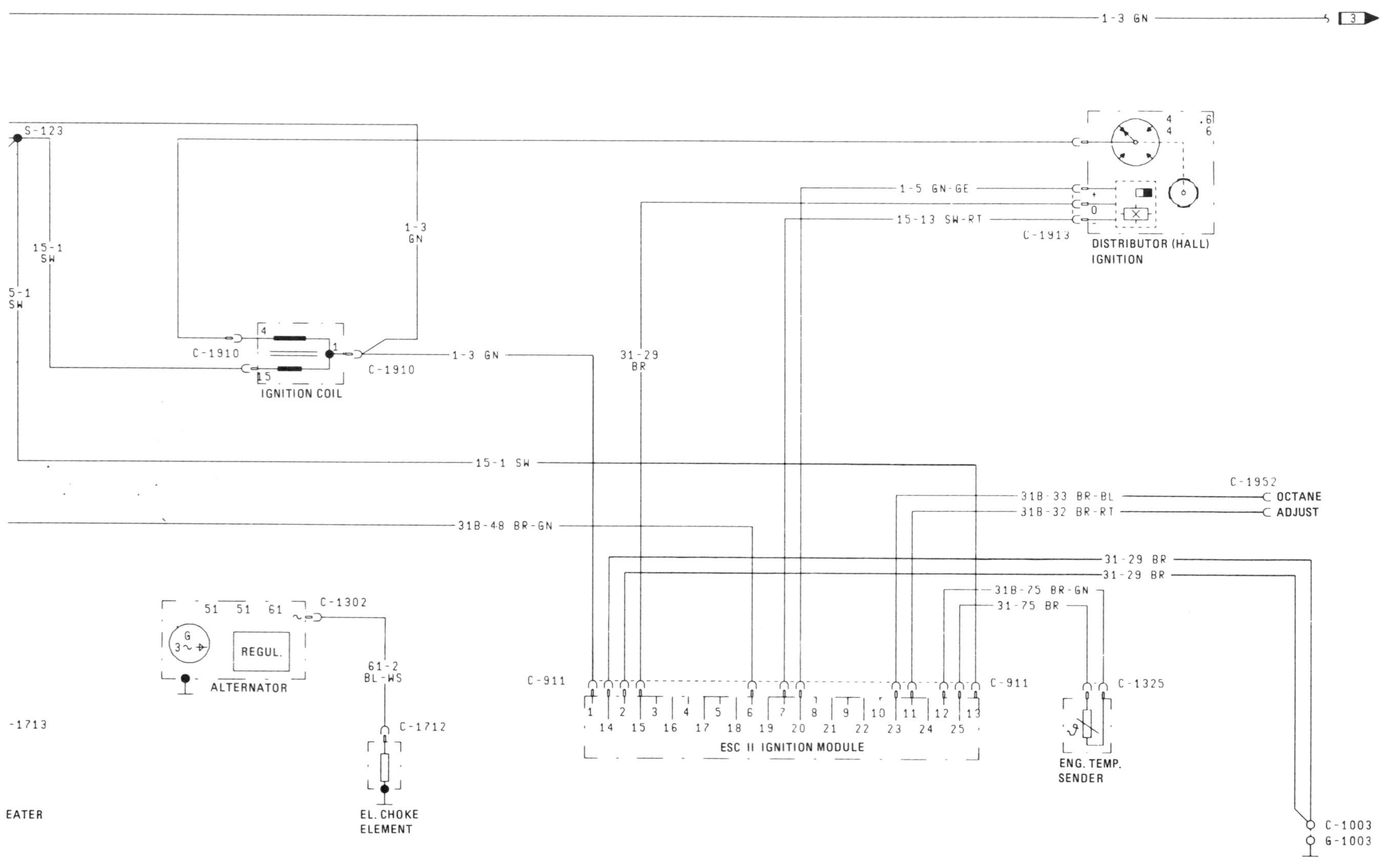

Fig. 10.48 (continued) 1.8 engine management wiring diagram – models from 1985 to 1986

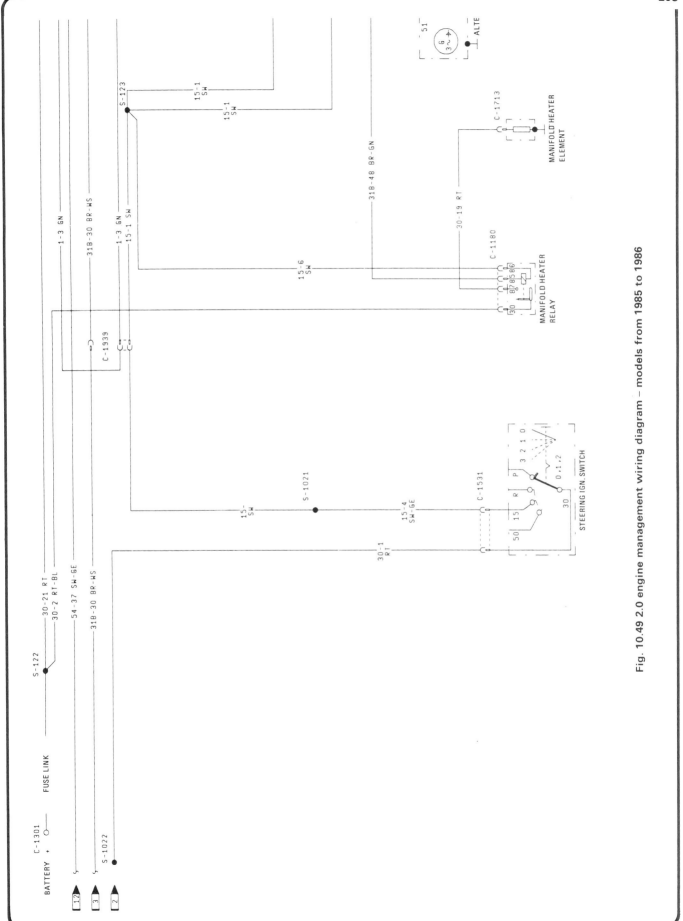

Fig. 10.49 2.0 engine management wiring diagram – models from 1985 to 1986

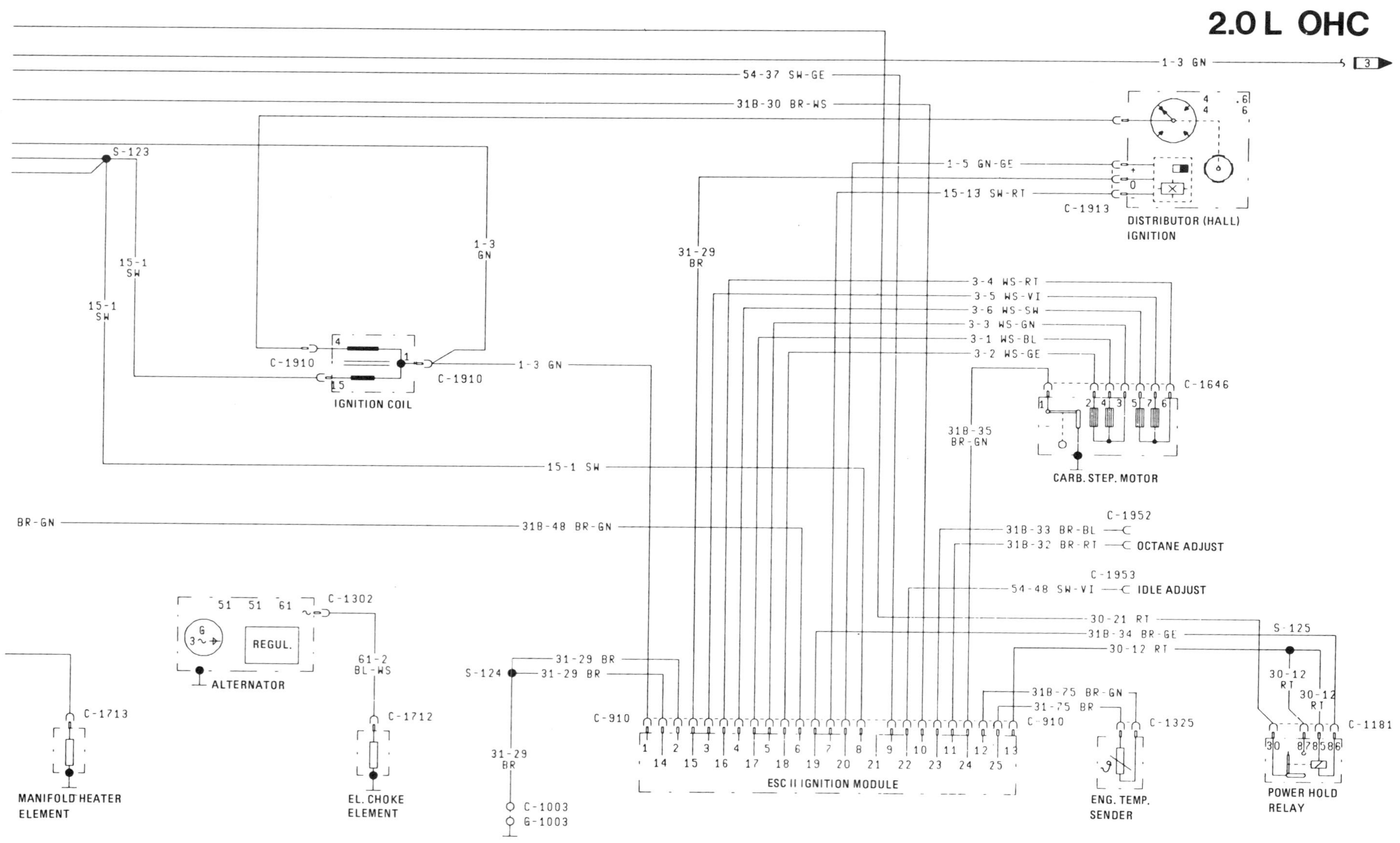

2.0 L OHC

DISTRIBUTOR (HALL)
IGNITION

C-1913

C-1646

CARB.STEP.MOTOR

POWER HOLD
RELAY

C-1181

S-125

30-12
RT

30-12
RT

OCTANE ADJUST

IDLE ADJUST

C-1952

C-1953

ENG. TEMP.
SENDER

C-1325

1-3 GN

1-5 GN-GE

15-13 SW-RT

3-4 WS-RT
3-5 WS-VI
3-6 WS-SW
3-3 WS-GN
3-1 WS-BL
3-2 WS-GE

31B-35
BR-GN

31B-33 BR-BL
31B-32 BR-RT

54-48 SW-VI

30-21 RT
31B-34 BR-GE
30-12 RT

31B-75 BR-GN
31-75 BR
C-910

13
25

12
24

11
23

10
22

9
21

8
20

7
19

6
18

5
17

4
16

3
15

2
14

1

ESC II IGNITION MODULE

54-37 SW-GE

31B-30 BR-WS

31-29
BR

15-1 SW

31B-48 BR-GN

31-29 BR
31-29 BR

S-124

31-29
BR

C-1003
G-1003

C-910

IGNITION COIL

1-3
GN

C-1910

C-1910

1-3 GN

15-1
SW

C-1712

EL. CHOKE
ELEMENT

61-2
BL-WS

C-1302

REGUL.

ALTERNATOR

51 51 61

G
3

S-123

15-1
SW

15-1
SW

C-1713

MANIFOLD HEATER
ELEMENT

BR-GN

Fig. 10.49 (continued) 2.0 engine management wiring diagram – models from 1985 to 1986

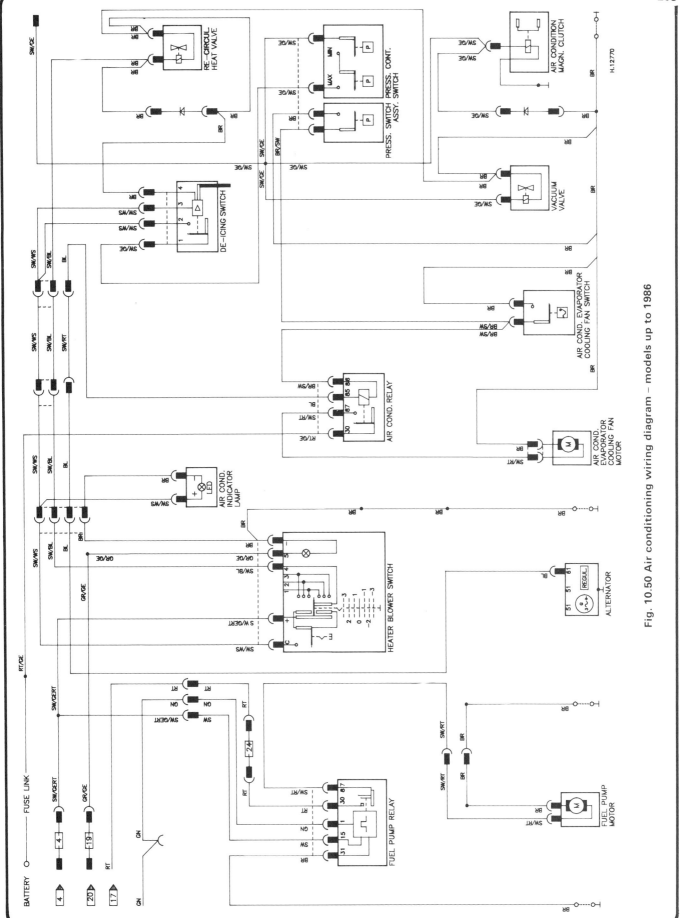

Fig. 10.50 Air conditioning wiring diagram – models up to 1986

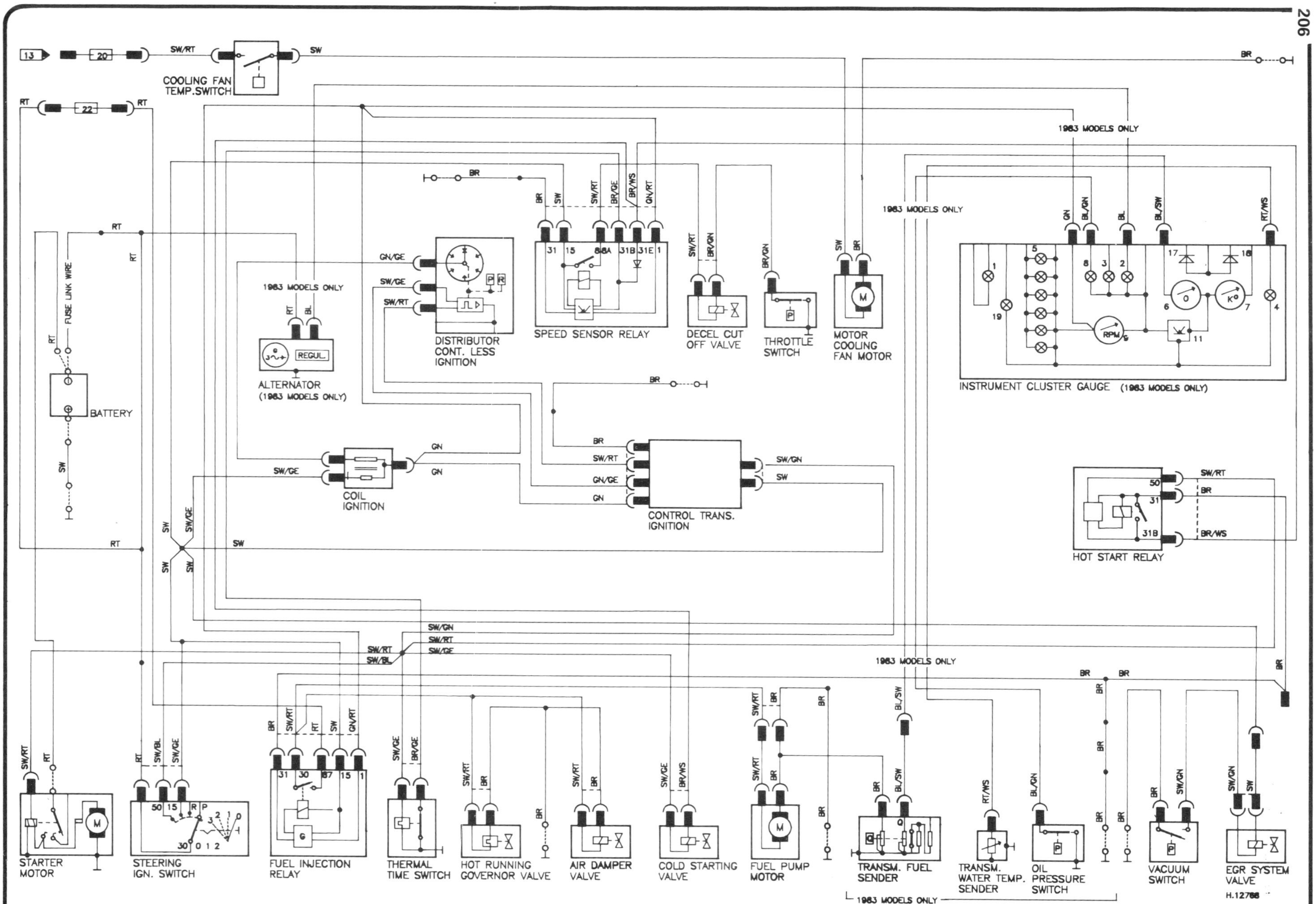

Fig. 10.51 Fuel injection and EGR wiring diagram – models from 1985 to 1986

Chapter 11 Suspension and steering

For modifications, and information applicable to later models, see Supplement at end of manual

Contents

Fault diagnosis – suspension and steering 28
Front anti-roll bar – removal and refitting 7
Front suspension crossmember – removal and refitting 3
Front suspension lower arm – removal, overhaul and refitting 6
Front suspension spindle carrier – removal and refitting 4
Front suspension strut – removal and refitting 8
Front wheel bearings – renewal 5
General description 1
Power-steering gear – removal and refitting 21
Power-steering pump – removal and refitting 23
Power-steering system – bleeding 22
Rear coil spring – removal and refitting 12
Rear shock absorber – removal and refitting 11
Rear suspension and final drive assembly – removal and
reftting 9

Rear suspension/final drive unit rear mounting – renewal 14
Rear suspension front mounting – renewal 13
Rear suspension lower arm – removal and refitting 15
Rear wheel bearings – renewal 10
Roadwheels and tyres – general 27
Routine maintenance 2
Steering column – removal, overhaul and refitting 17
Steering gear rubber bellows – renewal 24
Steering gear (standard) – overhaul 20
Steering gear (standard) – removal and refitting 19
Steering intermediate shaft and coupling – removal and
refitting 18
Steering wheel – removal and refitting 16
Track rod end – removal and refitting 25
Wheel alignment – checking and adjusting 26

Specifications

Front suspension
Type .... Independent MacPherson struts, coil springs and anti-roll bar, double-acting telescopic shock absorbers incorporated in struts

Rear suspension
Type .... Independent, semi-trailing arms and coil springs, double-acting shock absorbers mounted behind the coil springs on Saloon models, but concentric with the coil springs on Estate models, self-levelling shock absorbers on Ghia Estate models

Steering
Type .... Rack-and-pinion steering gear linked to collapsible type steering column by flexible coupling and universal joint. power-assisted steering optional on 2.0 litre models

Number of turns lock-to-lock:
  – manual steering 4.15
  – power-assisted steering 3.58
Power-steering pump drivebelt tension .... 10.0 mm (0.4 in) deflection midway between water pump and power-steering pump under firm thumb pressure
Steering gear lubricant .... Semi-fluid grease
Power steering fluid .... ATF to Ford specification SQM-2C 9010-A (Duckhams D-Matic)

Front wheel alignment
Toe – checking .... 0.5 mm (0.02 in) toe-out to 4.5 mm (0.18 in) toe-in
  – setting .... 1.0 to 3.0 mm (0.04 to 0.12 in) toe-in
Nominal caster angle (non adjustable):
  Hatchback (Standard) .... +1°57'
  Hatchback (Heavy Duty) .... +2°1'
  Estate (Standard) .... +1°56'
  Estate (Standard Business) .... +1°52'
  Estate (Standard Business Nivomat) .... +1°36'
  Estate (Heavy Duty Standard) .... +2°11'
  Estate (Heavy Duty Nivomat) .... +1°55'
  Note: *Maximum difference side to side* .... 1°0'
Nominal camber angle (non adjustable):
  Hatchback (Standard) .... -0°16'
  Hatchback (Heavy Duty) .... +0°7'
  Estate (Standard) .... -0°16'
  Estate (Standard Business) .... -0°21'
  Estate (Standard Business Nivomat) .... -0°21'
  Estate (Heavy Duty Standard) .... +0° 5'
  Estate (Heavy Duty Nivomat) .... +0°5'
  Note: *Maximum difference side to side* .... 1°15'

Wheels

Type	Pressed steel disc with vents
Size – Standard	13 x 4.50 in
– Heavy Duty	13 x 5.50 in

Tyres

Sizes – Hatchback/Saloon	165 SR/TR 13, 165 HR 13, 185/70 SR/TR 13, 185/70 HR 13, 195/60 HR 14 or 195/60 VR 14
Sizes – Estate	175 SR/TR 13, 175 HR 13, 195/70 HR 13, 195/65 HR 14 or 195/60 HR 14

Pressures (cold) in lbf/in² (bar):

	Front	Rear
All models, normal load*	26 (1.8)	26 (1.8)
Hatchback/Saloon, full load	29 (2.0)	36 (2.5)
Estate, full load:		
175 SR/TR 13 and 175 HR 13	29 (2.0)	40 (2.8)
195/70 HR 13	29 (2.0)	48 (3.3)
195/60 HR 14	29 (2.0)	36 (2.5)

*Normal load is defined as up to three passengers (or equivalent). For sustained high speeds add 1.5 lbf/in² (0.1 bar) for every 6 mph (10 km/h) over 100 mph (160 km/h).

Torque wrench settings

	lbf ft	Nm
Front suspension		
Hub retaining nut	229 to 258	310 to 350
Lower arm balljoint	48 to 63	65 to 85
Strut upper mounting nut	29 to 38	40 to 52
Strut to spindle	59 to 66	80 to 90
Anti-roll bar clamp	33 to 41	45 to 56
Anti-roll bar to lower arm	51 to 66	70 to 90
Crossmember	51 to 66	70 to 90
Lower arm pivot nut	See Chapter 13	
Rear suspension		
Suspension arm to crossmember	59 to 70	80 to 95
Guide plate to floor	30 to 37	41 to 51
Guide plate to crossmember	51 to 64	69 to 88
Steering (manual)		
Track rod end to steering arm	18.5 to 22	25 to 30
Track rod end locknut	42 to 50	57 to 68
Track rod inner balljoint	55 to 63	75 to 85
Pinion cover nut	51 to 74	70 to 100
Slipper plug	3 to 4	4 to 5
Coupling shaft to steering shaft	14.5 to 18.5	20 to 25
Coupling to pinion	14.5 to 22	20 to 30
Column mounting pinch-bolt	33.5 to 40	45 to 55
Steering wheel nut	33.5 to 40	45 to 55
Steering gear to crossmember	See Chapter 13	
Steering (power)		
Coupling clamp bolts	12 to 15	16.3 to 20.4
Coupling pinch-bolts	12 to 15	16.3 to 20.4
Rack yoke cover plate	16 to 17	22 to 24
Coupling nuts	15 to 20	20 to 27
Pressure hose to pump	19 to 22	26 to 31
Return hose to pump	12 to 15	16.4 to 20.5
Pump pulley bolt	7 to 8	10 to 12
Track rod end locknut	42 to 50	57 to 68
Track rod end to steering arm	18 to 22	25 to 30
Track rod inner balljoint	52 to 56	70 to 77
Column clamp and nuts	13 to 17	17 to 24
Steering gear to crossmember	See Chapter 13	
Wheels		
Wheel nuts	74	100

1 General description

The front suspension is of independent MacPherson strut type incorporating coil springs and double-action telescopic shock absorbers. An anti-roll bar is mounted to the rear of the suspension arms and controls the fore-and-aft movement of the struts as well as stabilising any roll tendency of the front suspension. All suspension mounting points are of rubber. The lower end of the strut is attached to the suspension arm by a sealed balljoint. The front wheel bearings are of matched self-setting taper roller design and no adjustment is required or possible.

The rear suspension is of independent type incorporating semi-trailing arms, coil springs and double-acting shock absorbers. On Hatchback and Saloon models the shock absorbers are mounted behind the coil springs, but on Estate models they are concentric with the coil springs. Additionally on Ghia Estate models the shock absorbers are of the self-levelling type. All suspension mounting points are of rubber. The rear wheel bearings are of double taper-roller design and similar to the front wheel bearings.

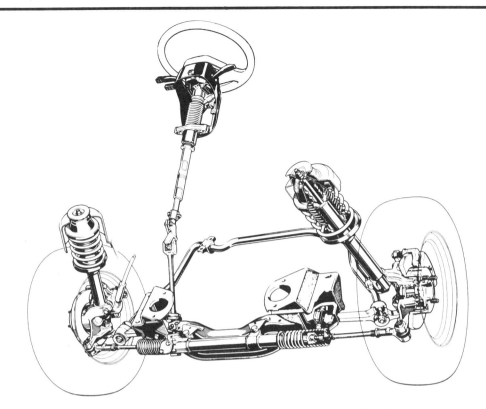

Fig. 11.1 Front suspension and steering components (Sec 1)

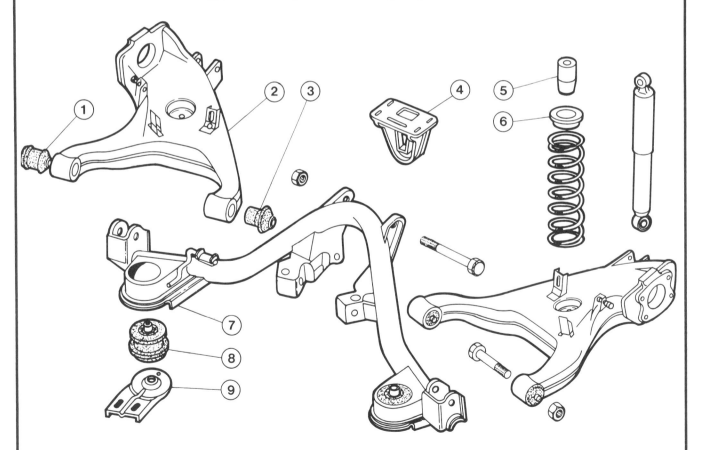

Fig. 11.2 Rear suspension components (Sec 1)

1 Outer rubber bush	4 Rear rubber mounting	6 Spring seat pad	8 Mounting rubber
2 Lower suspension arm	5 Bump rubber	7 Rear axle crossmember	9 Guide plate
3 Inner rubber bush			

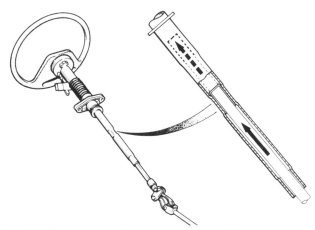

Fig. 11.3 Cross section diagram of the collapsible safety steering column (Sec 1)

The steering is of rack-and-pinion type incorporating a safety steering column. Power-assisted steering is optional on 2.0 litre models.

2   Routine maintenance

1   Every 6000 miles (10 000 km) examine the tyre walls and tread for wear and damage, in particular splits and bulges which if evident will require renewal of the tyre. If abnormal tyre wear is evident a thorough check of the suspension should be made.
2   At the same interval check and adjust the tyre pressures and check the tightness of the wheel nuts.
3   Every 12 000 miles (20 000 km) examine all steering and suspension linkages for wear and damage. Make sure that all dust covers are intact and secure. Check the front suspension lower balljoints by levering up the suspension arms (see Fig. 11.4) – the total free movement must not exceed 0.5 mm (0.020 in). The track rod end balljoints can be checked in a similar manner or by observation while an assistant 'rocks' the steering wheel.

Fig. 11.4 Checking the front suspension lower balljoints for wear (Sec 2)

3   Front suspension crossmember – removal and refitting

1   Remove the steering gear as described in Section 19 or 21.
2   Unscrew and remove the bolts securing the engine mountings to the crossmember.
3   Slightly raise the engine with a trolley jack and support it with an axle stand and block of wood. Alternatively support the engine with a

bar resting on wooden blocks on the front suspension struts as described in Chapter 1 for removing the sump.
4   Unscrew and remove the self-locking nuts, washers and pivot bolts securing the lower suspension arms to the crossmember, and pull out the arms. Note that the pivot bolt heads face to the rear.
5   Support the crossmember with a trolley jack, then unscrew and remove the four mounting bolts.
6   Lower the crossmember and withdraw it from under the car.
7   Refitting is a reversal of removal, but do not tighten the lower suspension pivot bolt nuts until the weight of the car is on the front suspension. Refer to Section 19 and 21 when refitting the steering gear.

4   Front suspension spindle carrier – removal and refitting

1   Remove the front brake caliper with reference to Chapter 9, however do not disconnect the hydraulic hose. Suspend the caliper with wire from the coil spring.
2   Remove the cross-head screw and withdraw the brake disc from the hub.
3   Disconnect the track rod end from the spindle carrier with reference to Section 25.
4   Extract the split pin and unscrew the nut securing the lower suspension arm to the spindle carrier (photo).
5   Using a balljoint separator tool, disconnect the lower suspension arm from the spindle carrier.
6   Unscrew and remove the pinch-bolt and withdraw the spindle carrier from the suspension strut. If difficulty is experienced wedge the clamp legs apart using a suitable cold chisel.
7   Refitting is a reversal of removal, but tighten all nuts and bolts to the specified torque and fit new split pins.

4.4 Front suspension lower balljoint and nut

5   Front wheel bearings – renewal

1   Remove the front suspension spindle carrier as described in Section 4.
2   Screw the wheel nuts fully into the studs with their flat faces towards the flange, then mount the assembly in a vice as shown in Fig. 11.6.
3   Prise the cap from the spindle carrier and unscrew the hub nut with a socket (photo). Note that the nut has a right-hand thread on all models manufactured before late December 1982, but as from this date left-hand thread assemblies were progressively fitted to the right-hand spindle carrier. The modified right-hand hub is identified by the letter 'R' stamped on its outer face (Fig. 11.7) or by the colour of the nylon insert of the nut; blue indicates normal (RH) thread, yellow indicates LH thread.
4   Remove the splined washer and tap the spindle carrier from the hub. Remove the bearing inner races and rollers from the carrier and hub.
5   Prise the oil seal from the carrier.

5.3 Removing the inner cap from the spindle carrier

6   Using a soft metal drift, drive the bearing outer races from the carrier taking care not to damage the inner surface of the carrier.
7   Clean the carrier and hub with paraffin, wipe dry, and examine them for damage and wear. Note that the components are machined to close tolerances. The bearings are supplied in matched pairs therefore extra care is necessary to ensure that all foreign matter is removed.

8   Using a suitable metal tube drive the bearing outer races fully into the carrier.
9   Pack the inner bearing races and taper rollers with high melting point lithium based grease, and locate the outer bearing in the carrier.
10 Fill the cavities between the sealing lips of the oil seal with grease then drive it fully into the carrier using a block of wood or suitable metal tube.
11 Tap the spindle carrier and outer bearing onto the hub, and fit the inner bearing and splined washer.
12 With the hub mounted in the vice refit the hub nut and tighten it to the specified torque.
13 Tap the cap into the spindle carrier.
14 Refit the spindle carrier with reference to Section 4.

6   Front suspension lower arm – removal, overhaul and refitting

1   Jack up the front of the car and support on axle stands. Apply the handbrake.
2   Unscrew and remove the self-locking nut, washer and pivot bolt securing the lower suspension arm to the crossmember, and pull the arm out (photo). Note that the pivot bolt head faces to the rear.
3   Extract the split pin and unscrew the nut securing the lower suspension arm to the spindle carrier. Using a balljoint separator tool, disconnect the arm from the carrier.
4   Unscrew the nut from the end of the anti-roll bar, remove the dished washer and rubber bush, and remove the lower suspension arm.
5   If necessary the inner bush may be removed by using a long bolt with nut, washers and metal tube. Dip the new bush in soapy water before fitting it using a single continuous action to avoid deformation

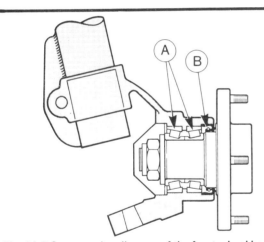

Fig. 11.5 Cross section diagram of the front wheel bearings (Sec 5)

A   Matched taper bearings   B   Oil seal

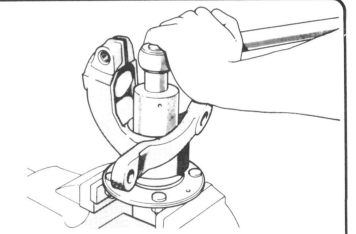

Fig. 11.6 Unscrewing the front hub nut (Sec 5)

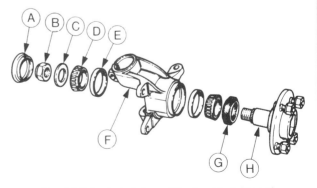

Fig. 11.8 Exploded view of the front hub (Sec 5)

A   Cap   E   Outer race
B   Locknut   F   Spindle carrier
C   Splined washer   G   Oil seal
D   Taper bearing   H   Hub

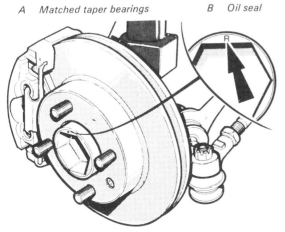

Fig. 11.7 Identification of the modified right-hand side front hub incorporating a left-hand thread (Sec 5)

6.2 Front suspension lower arm inner pivot bolt

7.2a Bend back the locktabs ...

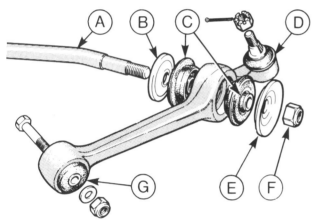

Fig. 11.9 Front suspension lower arm components (Sec 6)

A	Anti-roll bar	E	Front dished washer
B	Rear dished washer	F	Locknut
C	Bush	G	Pivot bush
D	Balljoint		

of the bush. If the balljoint is worn, renew the complete arm, however it is possible to renew the dust seal separately.
6   Refitting is a reversal of removal, but do not tighten the pivot bolt until the weight of the car is on the front suspension. Tighten all nuts to the specified torque and fit a new split pin to the balljoint nut.

7.2b ... unscrew the bolts and remove the anti-roll bar rear mounting clamps

7   Front anti-roll bar – removal and refitting

1   Jack up the front of the car and support on axle stands. Apply the handbrake.
2   Bend back the locktabs and unscrew the four bolts from the rear mounting clamps (photos).
3   Unscrew the nuts from the front ends of the anti-roll bar and remove the front dished washers and front rubber bushes (photo).
4   Unscrew and remove the self-locking nut, washer and pivot bolt from the inner end of one of the lower suspension arms and pull the arm from the crossmember. Note that the pivot bolt head faces to the rear.
5   Withdraw the anti-roll bar from the lower suspension arms.
6   Remove the rear rubber bushes and dished washers and also the rear clamp rubber bushes.
7   Examine the rubber bushes for damage and deterioration and renew them if necessary.
8   Refitting is a reversal of removal. Note that the front and rear dished washers are not interchangeable – see Chapter 13, Section 16.

7.3 Anti-roll bar front mounting

Make sure that the convex sides of the dished washers face the rubber bushes. Do not tighten the anti-roll bar mounting bolts or the lower suspension arm pivot bolt until the weight of the car is on the front suspension. After tightening the rear mounting clamp bolts, lock them by bending the locktabs onto the flats.

8 Front suspension strut – removal and refitting

1   Remove the front brake caliper with reference to Chapter 9, however do not disconnect the hydraulic hose. Support the caliper on an axle stand.

2   Unscrew and remove the strut pinch-bolt from the spindle carrier and wedge the clamp legs slightly apart using a suitable cold chisel (photo).

3   Lever the lower suspension arm downwards to separate the spindle carrier from the strut.

4   Working in the engine compartment unscrew the strut upper mounting nut at the same time supporting the strut from below (photo). If the strut piston rod rotates hold it stationary with a 6 mm hexagon key.

5   Withdraw the suspension strut from under the wing (photo).

6   Using spring compressor clamps, compress the coil spring. Do not attempt to compress the coil spring without using purpose-made clamps otherwise personal injury may occur.

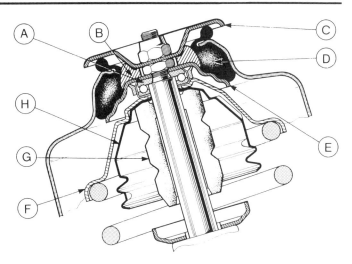

Fig. 11.10 Cross section of the front suspension strut upper mounting (Sec 8)

A Bearing	E Lower cap
B Nylon spacer	F Spring seat
C Cup	G Bump stop
D Insulator	H Gaiter

8.2 Removing the front suspension strut pinch-bolt

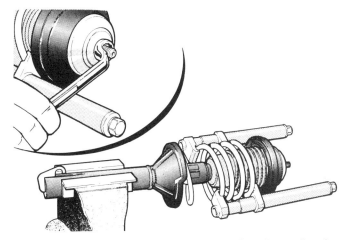

Fig. 11.11 Using spring compressor clamps when dismantling the front suspension strut (Sec 8)

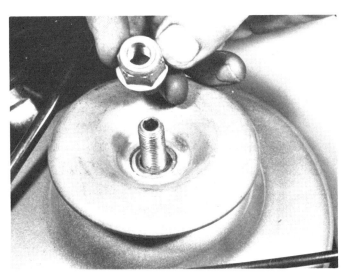

8.4 Removing the front suspension strut upper mounting nut

8.5 Front suspension strut

8.7 Showing the front suspension strut spring retaining nut

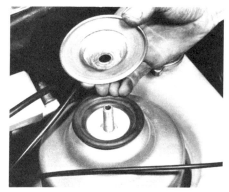

8.8a Removing the front suspension strut upper mounting cap

8.8b View of the front suspension strut upper mounting from below

9.7 A rear suspension guide plate

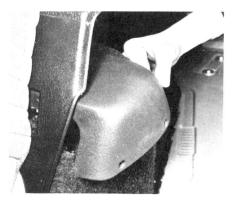

9.9a Remove the trim cover ...

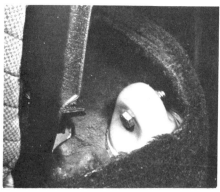

9.9b ... for access to the rear shock absorber upper mountings on Saloon/Hatchback models

7   Unscrew the nut from the piston rod and withdraw the cup, bearing, seat, gaiter, coil spring and bump stop (photo).

8   Working in the engine compartment remove the upper cup and nylon spacer and if necessary prise out the rubber insulator (photos).

9   Clean all the components and examine them for wear and deterioration. Check the action of the strut shock absorber by mounting the strut vertically in a vice and operating the piston rod several times through its full stroke. If any uneven resistance is evident the strut must be renewed.

10 Refitting is a reversal of removal, however the nylon centralizing spacer should be located over the piston rod before fitting the strut to the top mounting. Make sure that the spring ends are correctly located in the shaped seats. Tighten the nuts and bolt to the specified torque and refit the front brake caliper with reference to Chapter 9.

9   Rear suspension and final drive assembly – removal and refitting

1   Remove the propeller shaft as described in Chapter 7. The rear of the car should be supported under the longitudinal underbody members.

2   Disconnect the handbrake cable from the handbrake lever by removing the circlip and pin.

3   Unclip the handbrake outer cables from the underbody.

4   Disconnect the hydraulic brake pipes from the brackets on the underbody with reference to Chapter 9.

5   Place suitable blocks beneath the rear wheels then lower the car so that the rear coil springs are lightly loaded and reposition the axle stands under the underbody members.

6   Support the final drive unit with a trolley jack.

7   Unscrew and remove the bolts securing the guide plates to the underbody and rear suspension crossmember (photo). Remove the guide plates.

8   Unscrew and remove the bolts securing the final drive rear mounting to the underbody.

9   Working inside the rear of the car unscrew and remove the rear

shock absorber upper mounting bolts/nuts. On Saloon/Hatchback models access is gained by removing the trim cover behind the side cushions (photo). On Estate models pull back the floor covering and remove the self-tapping screws from the covers.

10 Using a trolley jack and wooden beam positioned beneath the longitudinal underbody members raise the rear of the car until the rear suspension and final drive assembly can be withdrawn from under the car.

11 If necessary the assembly may be dismantled with reference to the relevant Section of this Chapter and Chapter 8.

12 Refitting is a reversal of removal, but make sure that the rear coil springs are correctly located. Tighten all nuts and bolts to the specified torque. After completion bleed the brakes and adjust the handbrake as described in Chapter 9, and check the final drive unit oil level as described in Chapter 8. Refer to Chapter 7 when refitting the propeller shaft.

10 Rear wheel bearings – renewal

1   Remove the relevant wheel cap as necessary, then apply the handbrake and loosen the hub retaining nut. The nut is tightened to a high torque requiring a long socket extension bar. Loosen the wheel nuts.

2   Jack up the rear of the car and support on axle stands. Chock the front wheels and release the handbrake. Remove the wheel.

3   Remove the clip and withdraw the brake drum.

4   Unscrew the hub retaining nut and using a suitable puller, withdraw the drive flange from the driveshaft.

5   Prise off the plastic clips and remove the cover from the rear of the backplate.

6   Mark the rear wheel bearing housing in relation to the backplate then unscrew the four bolts from the rear suspension lower arm and withdraw the housing. Temporarily refit the brake backplate with two bolts to avoid straining the brake hydraulic pipe.

7   Prise out the inner and outer oil seals and withdraw the taper roller bearings.

8 Using a soft metal drift, drive the bearing outer races from the housing taking care not to damage the inner surface of the housing.
9 Clean the bearing housing and drive flange with paraffin, wipe dry, and examine them for damage and wear. Renew them as necessary.
10 Using a suitable metal tube drive the bearing outer races fully into the housing.
11 Pack the inner bearing races and taper rollers with high melting-point lithium based grease and locate them in the housing.
12 Fill the cavities between the sealing lips of the oil seals with grease then using a block of wood or suitable metal tube drive in the oil seals until flush with the outer edges of the bearing housing.
13 Remove the two bolts, fit the bearing housing, then insert and tighten the bolts to the specified torque.
14 Fit the cover to the rear of the backplate and press on the plastic clips.
15 Tap the drive flange onto the driveshaft splines and into the wheel bearings, and fit a new hub retaining nut and washer loosely.
16 Fit the brake drum and retaining clip.
17 Refit the wheel and tighten the nuts.
18 Lower the car to the ground, apply the handbrake, and tighten the hub retaining nut to the specified torque. Lock the nut by peening into the slot (photo).
19 Refit the wheel cap as necessary.

11 Rear shock absorber – removal and refitting

Note: *On Estate models fitted with heavy duty Nivomat shock absorbers follow the procedure given in Section 12 as the coil spring is an integral part of the shock absorber.*

Saloon/Hatchback models
1 With the weight of the car on the rear suspension work under the car to unscrew and remove the shock absorber lower mounting bolt (photo).
2 Working in the rear compartment, remove the crosshead screws and withdraw the trim cover behind the side cushion.
3 While an assistant supports the shock absorber unscrew and remove the upper mounting bolt.
4 Withdraw the shock absorber from under the car.
5 Refitting is a reversal of removal, but tighten the bolts securely.

Estate models
6 Jack up the rear of the car and support on axle stands. Chock the front wheels.
7 Support the rear suspension lower arm with a trolley jack.

10.18 Method of locking the rear hub retaining nut

11.1 Rear shock absorber lower mounting (Saloon/Hatchback models)

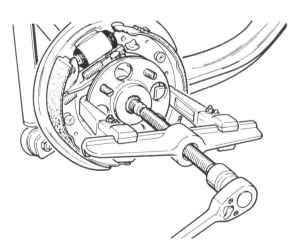

Fig. 11.12 Using a puller to withdraw the rear wheel drive flange (Sec 10)

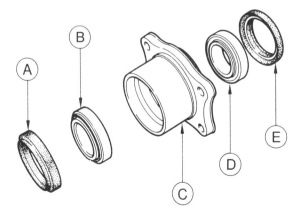

Fig. 11.13 Exploded view of the rear wheel hub (Sec 10)

A	Outer oil seal	D	Inner bearing
B	Outer bearing	E	Inner oil seal
C	Hub		

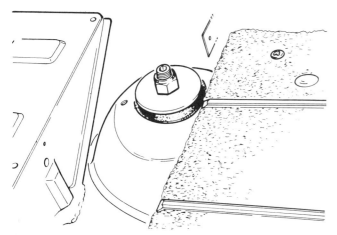

Fig. 11.14 Rear shock absorber upper mounting nut location on Estate models (Sec 11)

12.12 Rear coil spring and rubber seat (Saloon/Hatchback models)

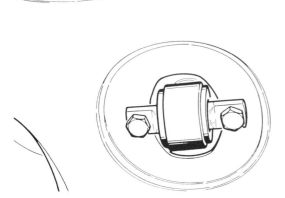

Fig. 11.15 Rear shock absorber lower mounting bolts on Estate models (Sec 11)

8   Working in the rear compartment fold the rear seat backrest forwards, remove the screws and lift off the wheel arch trim cover.
9   Unscrew and remove the shock absorber upper mounting nut.
10 Unscrew the lower mounting bolts from the bottom of the rear suspension lower arm and withdraw the shock absorber downwards.
11 Refitting is a reversal of removal, but tighten the nut and bolts securely.

12 Rear coil spring – removal and refitting

1   Jack up the rear of the car and support on axle stands. Chock the front wheels.
2   Remove the wheel. Release the handbrake then remove the clip and withdraw the brake drum.
3   Unclip the driveshaft outer joint plastic cover from the upper brake backplate bolts.
4   Using a socket through the holes in the drive flange, unscrew and remove the four bolts securing the wheel bearing housing and brake backplate to the suspension lower arm.
5   Withdraw the driveshaft complete with hub from the lower arm and final drive unit. Place a container beneath the final drive unit to catch any spilled oil.
6   Temporarily refit the brake backplate with two bolts to avoid straining the brake hydraulic pipe.
7   Unclip the brake hydraulic hose from the underbody mounting bracket. Do not disconnect the hydraulic line.
8   Support the lower suspension arm with a trolley jack.
9   On Saloon/Hatchback models unscrew and remove the shock absorber lower mounting bolt.
10 On Estate models fitted with standard shock absorbers remove the shock absorber as described in Section 11. On Estate models fitted

with heavy duty Nivomat shock absorbers disconnect the top and bottom mountings.
11 Unbolt and remove the rear suspension crossmember guide plate from the underbody on the side being worked on.
12 Lower the suspension arm and withdraw the coil spring/heavy duty shock absorber and the rubber spring seat (photo).
13 Refitting is a reversal of removal, but tighten all nuts and bolts to the specified torque. Check and if necessary top up the final drive unit oil level as described in Chapter 8.

13 Rear suspension front mounting – renewal

1   Jack up the rear of the car and support on axle stands. Chock the front wheels.
2   Remove the two bolts securing the guide plate to the underbody.
3   Flatten the locktab and unscrew the mounting bolt. Withdraw the guide plate and spacer.
4   Using a length of wood lever the suspension crossmember a few inches from the underbody and insert the wood to retain.
5   Using Ford tool 15-014 (Fig. 11.6) or locally made tool, pull the mounting from the crossmember.
6   Dip the new mounting in soapy water and use the tool to press the mounting fully into the crossmember.
7   Remove the length of wood and insert the guide plate bolts loosely, together with the locktab and spacer.
8   Tighten the mounting bolt then the two remaining bolts to the specified torque and lock the mounting bolt by bending the locktab.
9   Lower the car to the ground.

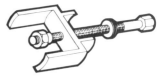

Fig. 11.16 Ford tool 15-014 for removing the rear suspension front mounting (Sec 13)

14 Rear suspension/final drive unit rear mounting – renewal

1   Jack up the rear of the car and support on axle stands. Chock the front wheels.
2   Support the final drive unit with a trolley jack.
3   Unscrew and remove the four mounting bolts.
4   Lower the final drive unit sufficient to unbolt the mounting.
5   Fit the new mounting using a reversal of the removal procedure, but tighten the bolts to the specified torque.

15 Rear suspension lower arm – removal and refitting

1   Remove the rear coil spring as described in Section 12.
2   Unclip the handbrake cable and brake hydraulic line from the suspension arm. Do not disconnect the hydraulic line.
3   Remove the brake backplate from the suspension arm and tie it to one side.
4   Note the fitted position of the pivot bolts then unscrew and remove them and withdraw the suspension arm from under the car (photo).
5   If necessary the pivot bushes may be renewed using a long bolt, nut, washers and suitable metal drift. Dip the new bushes in soapy water to facilitate their fitting.
6   Refitting is a reversal of removal, but delay tightening the pivot bolts to the specified torque until the weight of the car is on the rear suspension. Refer to Section 12 when refitting the coil spring.

16 Steering wheel – removal and refitting

1   Set the front wheels in the straight-ahead position.
2   Prise the insert from the centre of the steering wheel and disconnect the horn supply wire (photos).
3   With the ignition key inserted check that the steering lock is disengaged.
4   Unscrew the retaining nut and withdraw the steering wheel from the hexagon shaped inner column (photo).
5   Refitting is a reversal of removal, but first check that the lug on the indicator cam is aligned with the cut-out in the steering wheel. Tighten the retaining nut to the specified torque.

15.4 Rear suspension lower arm pivot bolt

16.2a Prise off the centre insert ...

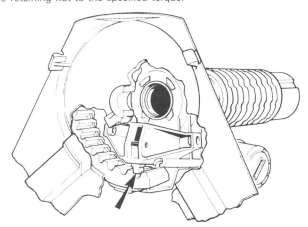

Fig. 11.17 Cut-away view of the steering lock (Secs 16 and 17)

16.2b ... and disconnect the horn supply wire

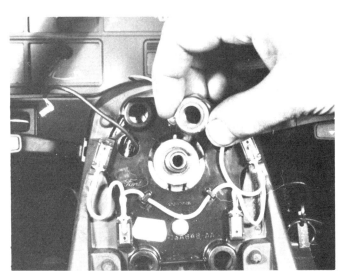

16.4 Removing the steering wheel retaining nut

17 Steering column – removal, overhaul and refitting

1   Set the front wheels in the straight-ahead position.
2   Remove the trim panels below the facia (photos).
3   Remove the screws and withdraw the steering column upper and lower shrouds (photos).
4   Disconnect the battery negative lead.
5   Remove the crosshead screws and withdraw the two combination switches from the column.
6   Remove the screw and withdraw the bonnet release lever.
7   Working in the engine compartment unscrew the bolt securing the intermediate shaft to the inner column, swivel the clamp plate to one side, and disconnect the intermediate shaft (photos).
8   Unscrew the nuts securing the outer column to the facia.
9   Disconnect the multi-plugs and withdraw the column assembly upwards.
10 Mount the outer column in a soft jawed vice.
11 Remove the steering wheel as described in Section 16.
12 Remove the indicator arm and the bearing thrust washer.
13 Slide the inner column from the outer column, and remove the thrust washer and spring from the inner column.
14 Lever the upper and lower bearings from the outer column.
15 Clamp the bottom of the inner column in a vice and pull off the

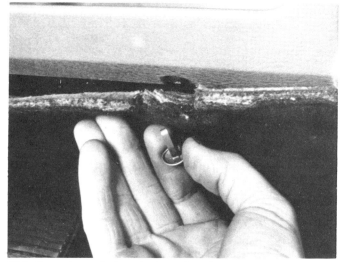

17.2a Removing a clip from the lower facia trim

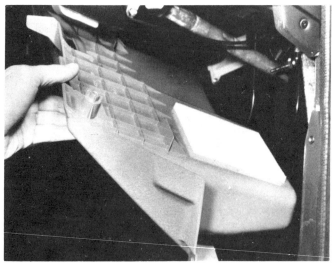

17.2b Removing the lower facia panel

17.2c Removing the side trim

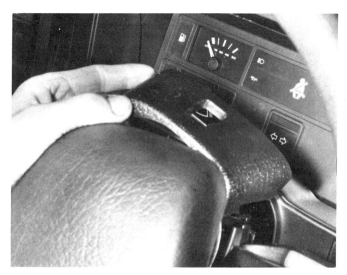

17.3a Removing the steering column upper shroud ...

17.3b ... and lower shroud

17.7a Intermediate shaft to steering column universal joint

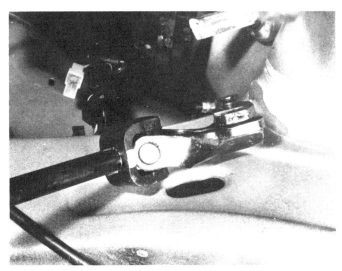

17.7b Intermediate shaft disconnected from the steering column

lower nylon bush. Take care not to collapse the inner column sections otherwise it must be renewed.

16 If necessary insert the ignition key and turn to position '1', depress the spring clip with a suitable instrument and withdraw the steering lock barrel. Remove the two grub screws and withdraw the ignition switch.

17 Clean all the components and examine them for wear and damage. Renew them as necessary.

18 Refit the ignition switch and steering lock barrel.

19 With the triangular section of the inner column mounted in a vice, push on the nylon bush to the position shown in Fig. 11.20.

20 Lubricate the upper and lower bearings with grease then push them into the outer column.

21 Locate the spring and thrust washer on the inner column then slide the inner column into the outer column.

22 Fit the upper bearing thrust washer and the indicator cam.

23 Clean the hexagon section of the inner column and refit the steering wheel with reference to Section 16.

24 Check that the distance between the lower bearing in the outer column and the welded washer on the inner column is between 11.0 and 13.0 mm (0.43 and 0.51 in). If not, the column has been damaged and should be renewed.

25 Check that the bulkhead bush is serviceable and correctly fitted and renew if necessary. An incorrectly fitted bush can result in the ingress of water.

26 Refit the column assembly in the car and tighten the upper mounting nuts lightly. Loosen the mounting pinch-bolt.

27 Temporarily fit the upper column shroud and adjust the position of

the steering column until there is a gap of 5.0 mm (0.2 in) between the shroud and the facia.

28 Tighten the pinch-bolt and the mounting nuts and remove the upper column shroud.

29 With the steering wheel in the straight-ahead position reconnect the intermediate shaft and tighten the clamp plate bolt to the specified torque.

30 Refit the bonnet release lever and combination switches and reconnect the multi-plugs.

31 Refit the steering column shrouds and trim panels.

32 Reconnect the battery negative lead.

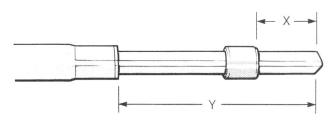

Fig. 11.18 Exploded view of the steering column (Sec 17)

A	Indicator cam	D	Outer column
B	Thrust washers	E	Spring
C	Bearings	F	Inner column

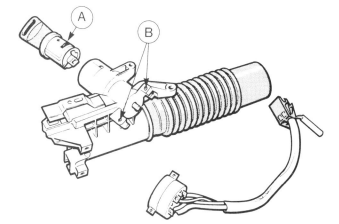

Fig. 11.19 Steering lock barrel securing clip (A) and ignition switch grab screw locations (B) (Sec 17)

Fig. 11.20 Inner column nylon bush location (Sec 17)

X = 52.0 mm (2.05 in)
Y = 186.0 to 192.0 mm (7.32 to 7.56 in)

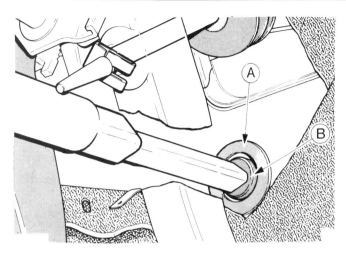

Fig. 11.21 Bulkhead bush (A) and inner column bush (B) (Sec 17)

Fig. 11.22 Master spline location on the steering gear pinion and intermediate shaft clamp (Sec 18)

18 Steering intermediate shaft and coupling – removal and refitting

1   Jack up the front of the car and support on axle stands. Apply the handbrake.
2   Working in the engine compartment unscrew the bolt securing the intermediate shaft to the inner column, swivel the clamp plate to one side, and disconnect the intermediate shaft.
3   Unscrew and remove the clamp bolt securing the flexible coupling to the steering gear (photo).
4   Mark the coupling in relation to the pinion then pull off the intermediate shaft and remove it from the car. The pinion has a master spline but marking it will facilitate refitting it.
5   Refitting is a reversal of removal, but tighten the bolts to the specified torque.

19 Steering gear (standard) – removal and refitting

1   Jack up the front of the car and support on axle stands. Apply the handbrake.
2   Set the front wheels in the straight-ahead position.
3   Unscrew and remove the clamp bolt securing the intermediate shaft to the steering gear (photo).
4   Extract the split pins and unscrew the track rod end nuts.
5   Using a balljoint separator tool disconnect the track rod ends from the steering arms.
6   Unscrew the mounting bolts and withdraw the steering gear from the front suspension crossmember.
7   Remove the track rod ends with reference to Section 25.
8   Refitting is a reversal of removal, but before reconnecting the intermediate shaft, set the steering wheel and front wheels in the straight-ahead position. If a new steering gear is being fitted the pinion position can be ascertained by halving the number of turns necessary to move the rack from lock-to-lock. Tighten the nuts and bolts to the specified torque and fit a new split pin. Finally check and if necessary adjust the front wheel alignment as described in Section 26.

20 Steering gear (standard) – overhaul

1   Clean the exterior of the steering gear with paraffin and wipe dry.
2   Mount the steering gear in a vice then remove and discard the clips and slide the rubber bellows off the track rods.
3   Move the rack fully to the left and grip the rack in a soft jawed vice (Fig. 11.23).
4   If the original track rods are fitted use a pipe wrench to unscrew the balljoint from the rack and remove the track rod. If service replacement track rods are fitted use a spanner on the machined flats.
5   Remove the right-hand track rod in the same way.
6   Using a hexagon key unscrew and remove the slipper plug and remove the spring and slipper.

18.3 Intermediate shaft to steering gear lower flexible coupling

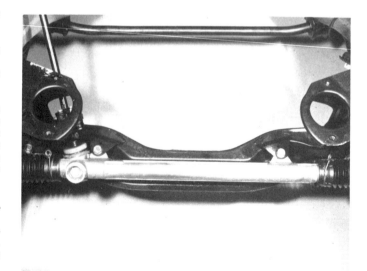

19.3 Steering gear location on the front suspension crossmember (engine removed)

7   Prise out the pinion dust cover, then using Ford tool 13-009 or locally made four segment tool, unscrew the pinion retaining nut and withdraw the pinion and bearing using a twisting action.
8   Withdraw the rack from the steering gear housing.

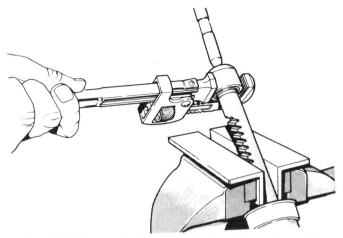

Fig. 11.23 Unscrewing the track rods from the steering rack (Sec 20)

Fig. 11.25 Ford tool 13-009 for removing the steering gear pinion retaining nut (Sec 20)

9   Clean all the components in paraffin and wipe dry. Examine them for wear and damage and renew them as necessary. If necessary the rack support bush in the housing can be renewed.
10   Lightly coat the rack with the specified semi-fluid grease and insert it into the housing.
11   Coat the pinion and bearing with grease and locate it in the housing at the same time meshing it with the rack.
12   Fit the retaining nut and tighten to the specified torque. Lock the nut by peening the housing in four places.
13   Move the rack to its central position then fit the slipper, spring and plug, and tighten the plug to the specified torque. Loosen the plug 60° to 70°.
14   Using a piece of string and a spring balance check that the turning torque of the pinion is between 0.8 and 1.4 Nm (0.6 and 1.0 lbf ft). To do this accurately turn the pinion anticlockwise half a turn from its central position and measure the torque while turning the pinion clockwise through one complete turn.
15   If necessary tighten or loosen the slipper plug until the torque is correct. Then lock by peening the housing in three positions around the circumference of the top of the plug.
16   Refit the track rods and tighten the balljoints to the specified torque. Lock the balljoints by staking.

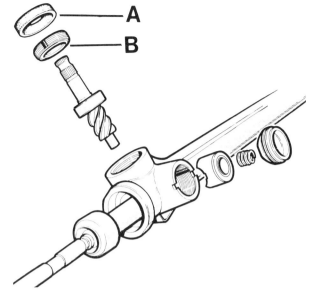

Fig. 11.24 Exploded view of the pinion end of the steering gear (Sec 20)

A   Pinion dust cover   B   Pinion retaining nut

17   Refit the rubber bellows to the rack tube. Fit and tighten new screw type clips.
18   Refit the pinion dust cover ('A' in Fig. 11.24) after filling with semi-fluid grease.

21 Power-steering gear – removal and refitting

1   Jack up the front of the car and support on axle stands. Apply the handbrake.
2   Set the front wheels in the straight-ahead position.
3   Unscrew and remove the clamp bolt securing the intermediate shaft to the steering gear.
4   Extract the split pins and unscrew the track rod end nuts.
5   Using a balljoint separator tool disconnect the track rod ends from the steering arms.
6   Place a suitable container beneath the steering gear then unscrew the pressure and return pipe unions and drain the power steering fluid. Cover the pipe ends and steering gear apertures with masking tape to prevent the ingress of foreign matter.
7   Unscrew the mounting bolts and withdraw the steering gear from the front suspension crossmember.
8   Remove the track rod ends with reference to Section 25.

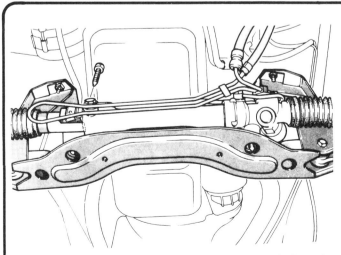

Fig. 11.26 Removing the power-steering gear – note the looped cooling pipe (Sec 21)

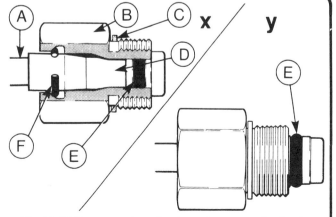

Fig. 11.27 Cut-away view of a pipe union connection for the power-steering gear (Sec 21)

X	Installed	B	Coupling nut	E	O-ring
Y	O-ring exposed	C	PTFE seal	F	Snap ring
A	Pipe	D	Pre-formed end		

9   Refitting is a reversal of removal, but before reconnecting the intermediate shaft, set the steering wheel and front wheels in the straight-ahead position. If a new steering gear is being fitted the pinion position can be ascertained by halving the number of turns necessary to move the rack from lock-to-lock. Tighten the nuts and bolts to the specified torque and fit new split pins. Take care not to overtighten the unions and note that with the unions fully tightened it is still possible to rotate and move the pipes. Refill and bleed the power steering as described in Section 22, and finally check and if necessary adjust the front wheel alignment as described in Section 26.

22 Power-steering system – bleeding

1   Unscrew the filler cap from the power-steering pump and top up the fluid level to the maximum mark using the specified fluid.
2   Disconnect the low tension negative lead from the ignition coil and crank the engine several times for two second periods while slowly turning the steering wheel from lock-to-lock. Top up the fluid level if necessary and continue cranking the engine until the fluid is free of air bubbles.
3   Reconnect the coil lead and start the engine. Check the system for leaks.
4   Switch off the engine and refit the filler cap.

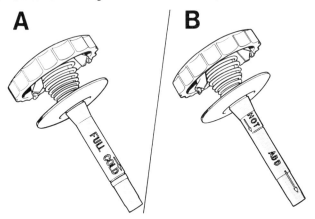

Fig. 11.28 Power-steering filler cap and dipstick (Sec 22)

A   Cold level marking   *B   Hot level marking*

23 Power-steering pump – removal and refitting

1   Place a suitable container under the power-steering pump, disconnect the fluid pipes, and drain the fluid.
2   Remove the drivebelts as described in Chapter 2. Unbolt the pulley if necessary to ease removal.
3   Unscrew the nuts and bolts and remove the pump.
4   Refitting is a reversal of removal, but tighten the nuts and bolts to the specified torque. Tension the drivebelts as described in Chapter 2. Refill the power-steering system with fluid and bleed it as described in Section 22.

24 Steering gear rubber bellows – renewal

1   Remove the track rod end as described in Section 25.
2   Remove the clips and slide the bellows from the track rod and steering gear.
3   Slide the new bellows over the track rod and onto the steering gear. Where applicable make sure that the bellows seats in the cut-outs provided in the track rod and housing (support end only).
4   Fit and tighten the clips.
5   Refit the track rod ends as described in Section 25.

25 Track rod end – removal and refitting

1   Jack up the front of the car and support on axle stands. Apply the handbrake and remove the relevant wheel.

25.3 Removing the split pin from the track rod end

25.4a Using a balljoint separator tool to release the track rod end from the steering arm

25.4b Track rod end

2   Mark the track rod and track rod end in relation to each other then loosen the locknut a quarter of a turn.

3   Extract the split pin and unscrew the balljoint nut (photo).

4   Using a balljoint separator tool release the track rod end from the steering arm (photos).

5   Unscrew the track rod end from the track rod noting the number of turns necessary to remove it.

6   Refitting is a reversal of removal, but tighten the nuts to the specified torque and fit a new split pin. On completion check and if necessary adjust the front wheel alignment as described in Section 26.

26 Wheel alignment – checking and adjusting

1   Accurate wheel alignment is essential for good steering and slow tyre wear. Before checking it, make sure that the car is only loaded to kerbside weight and that the tyre pressures are correct.

2   Place the car on level ground with the wheels in the straight-ahead position, then roll the car backwards 12 ft (4 metres) and forwards again.

3   Using a wheel alignment gauge check that the front wheels are aligned as given in the Specifications.

4   If adjustment is necessary loosen the track rod end locknuts and the outer bellows clips, then rotate each track rod by equal amounts until the setting is correct. Hold the track rod ends in their horizontal position with a spanner while making the adjustment. For example, to increase toe-in, both track rods need to be in effect shortened by turning them so that less thread is visible at the track rod ends.

5   Tighten the locknuts and outer bellows clips.

6   Provided the track rods have been adjusted by equal amounts the steering wheel should be central when moving straight-ahead. However if centralising is necessary first ascertain the correction angle in degrees, then rotate both track rods in the same direction approximately 19° for every 1° of correction required. To turn the steering wheel clockwise the track rods must be turned clockwise as viewed from the left-hand side of the car.

7   Camber and castor angles are preset and cannot be adjusted; however, if their accuracy is suspect they can be checked by a suitably equipped garage.

27 Roadwheels and tyres – general

1   Clean the insides of the roadwheels whenever they are removed and where applicable remove any rust and repaint them.

2   At the same time remove any flints or stones which may have become embedded in the tyres and also examine the tyres for damage and splits. Check the tread depth and renew the tyres if this is approaching the legal minimum.

3   The wheels should be rebalanced half way through the life of the tyres to compensate for loss of rubber.

4   Check and adjust the tyre pressures regularly and make sure that the dust caps are correctly fitted. Do not forget to check the spare tyre.

28 Fault diagnosis – suspension and steering

Symptom	Reason(s)
Excessive play in steering	Worn rack-and-pinion or steering gear bushes Worn track rod end balljoints Worn lower suspension arm balljoints
Wanders or pulls to one side	Incorrect wheel alignment Worn track rod end balljoints Worn lower suspension arm balljoints Uneven tyre pressures Faulty shock absorber
Heavy or stiff steering	Seized track rod end or suspension balljoint Incorrect wheel alignment Low tyre pressures Lack of lubricant in steering gear Faulty power-steering system (where applicable)
Wheel wobble and vibration	Roadwheels out of balance or damaged Faulty shock absorbers Worn wheel bearings Worn track rod ends or suspension arm balljoints
Excessive tyre wear	Incorrect wheel alignment Faulty shock absorbers Incorrect tyre pressures Roadwheels out of balance

Chapter 12 Bodywork and fittings

For modifications, and information applicable to later models, see Supplement at end of manual

Contents

Bonnet – removal and refitting	7
Bonnet lock – removal and refitting	10
Bonnet lock cable – removal and refitting	9
Bumpers – removal and refitting	25
Centre console – removal and refitting	28
Door – removal and refitting	14
Door check arm – removal and refitting	17
Door inner trim panel – removal and refitting	15
Door interior handle remote control – removal and refitting	16
Door lock – removal and refitting	19
Door mirror – removal and refitting	24
Door private lock – removal, inspection and refitting	18
Facia panel – removal and refitting	27
Front door window – removal and refitting	21
General description	1
Headlining – removal and refitting	26
Heater assembly – overhaul	35
Heater assembly – removal and refitting	34
Heater controls – removal and refitting	33
Heater motor – removal and refitting	36
Maintenance – bodywork and fittings	6
Maintenance – bodywork and underframe	2
Maintenance – upholstery and carpets	3
Major body damage – repair	5
Minor body damage – repair	4
Radiator grille panel – removal and refitting	11
Rear door window – removal and refitting	22
Rear parcel shelf side-member – removal and refitting	31
Rear seat catch – removal and refitting	30
Seats – removal and refitting	29
Sliding roof – removal, refitting and adjustment	32
Tailgate – removal and refitting	8
Tailgate lock – removal and refitting	12
Tailgate strut – removal and refitting	13
Window regulator – removal and refitting	23
Windscreen, tailgate and fixed rear quarter windows – removal and refitting	20

1 General description

The bodyshell is of all-steel welded construction and is of computer based design which includes nearly 12 000 separate elements. The aeroback body style incorporates one-piece side panels and doors, and the bumpers are made of impact-resistant polycarbonate. The complete body undergoes a twenty stage paint and body protection process including comprehensive wax injection into closed cavities.

2 Maintenance – bodywork and underframe

1   The general condition of a vehicle's bodywork is the one thing that significantly affects its value. Maintenance is easy but needs to be regular. Neglect, particularly after minor damage, can lead quickly to further deterioration and costly repair bills. It is important also to keep watch on those parts of the vehicle not immediately visible, for instance the underside, inside all the wheel arches and the lower part of the engine compartment.

2   The basic maintenance routine for the bodywork is washing – preferably with a lot of water, from a hose. This will remove all the loose solids which may have stuck to the vehicle. It is important to flush these off in such a way as to prevent grit from scratching the finish. The wheel arches and underframe need washing in the same way to remove any accumulated mud which will retain moisture and tend to encourage rust. Paradoxically enough, the best time to clean the underframe and wheel arches is in wet weather when the mud is thoroughly wet and soft. In very wet weather the underframe is usually cleaned of large accumulations automatically and this is a good time for inspection.

3   Periodically, it is a good idea to have the whole of the underframe of the vehicle steam cleaned, engine compartment included, so that a thorough inspection can be carried out to see what minor repairs and renovations are necessary. Steam cleaning is available at many garages and is necessary for removal of the accumulation of oily grime which sometimes is allowed to become thick in certain areas. If steam cleaning facilities are not available, there are one or two excellent grease solvents available which can be brush applied. The dirt can then be simply hosed off.

4   After washing paintwork, wipe off with a chamois leather to give an unspotted clear finish. A coat of clear protective wax polish will give added protection against chemical pollutants in the air. If the paintwork sheen has dulled or oxidised, use a cleaner/polisher combination to restore the brilliance of the shine. This requires a little effort, but such dulling is usually caused because regular washing has been neglected. Always check that the door and sill drain holes are completely clear so that water can drain out (photos). Bright work should be treated in the same way as paintwork. Windscreens and windows can be kept clear of the smeary film which often appears, by adding a little ammonia to the water. If they are scratched, a good rub with a proprietary metal polish will often clear them. Never use any form of wax or other body or chromium polish on glass.

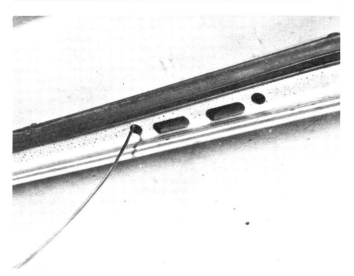

2.4a Clearing a door drain hole

2.4b Clearing a sill drain hole

3 Maintenance – upholstery and carpets

1   Mats and carpets should be brushed or vacuum cleaned regularly to keep them free of grit. If they are badly stained remove them from the vehicle for scrubbing or sponging and make quite sure they are dry before refitting. Seats and interior trim panels can be kept clean by wiping with a damp cloth. If they do become stained (which can be more apparent on light coloured upholstery) use a little liquid detergent and a soft nail brush to scour the grime out of the grain of the material. Do not forget to keep the headlining clean in the same way as the upholstery. When using liquid cleaners inside the vehicle do not over-wet the surfaces being cleaned. Excessive damp could get into the seams and padded interior causing stains, offensive odours or even rot. If the inside of the vehicle gets wet accidentally it is worthwhile taking some trouble to dry it out properly, particularly where carpets are involved. *Do not leave oil or electric heaters inside the vehicle for this purpose.*

4 Minor body damage – repair

The photographic sequences on pages 246 and 247 illustrate the operations detailed in the following sub-sections.

Repair of minor scratches in bodywork

If the scratch is very superficial, and does not penetrate to the metal of the bodywork, repair is very simple. Lightly rub the area of the scratch with a paintwork renovator, or a very fine cutting paste, to remove loose paint from the scratch and to clear the surrounding bodywork of wax polish. Rinse the area with clean water.

Apply touch-up paint to the scratch using a fine paint brush; continue to apply fine layers of paint until the surface of the paint in the scratch is level with the surrounding paintwork. Allow the new paint at least two weeks to harden: then blend it into the surrounding paintwork by rubbing the scratch area with a paintwork renovator or a very fine cutting paste. Finally, apply wax polish.

Where the scratch has penetrated right through to the metal of the bodywork, causing the metal to rust, a different repair technique is required. Remove any loose rust from the bottom of the scratch with a penknife, then apply rust inhibiting paint to prevent the formation of rust in the future. Using a rubber or nylon applicator fill the scratch with bodystopper paste. If required, this paste can be mixed with cellulose thinners to provide a very thin paste which is ideal for filling narrow scratches. Before the stopper-paste in the scratch hardens, wrap a piece of smooth cotton rag around the top of a finger. Dip the finger in cellulose thinners and then quickly sweep it across the surface of the stopper-paste in the scratch; this will ensure that the surface of the stopper-paste is slightly hollowed. The scratch can now be painted over as described earlier in this Section.

Repair of dents in bodywork

When deep denting of the vehicle's bodywork has taken place, the first task is to pull the dent out, until the affected bodywork almost attains its original shape. There is little point in trying to restore the original shape completely, as the metal in the damaged area will have stretched on impact and cannot be reshaped fully to its original contour. It is better to bring the level of the dent up to a point which is about $\frac{1}{8}$ in (3 mm) below the level of the surrounding bodywork. In cases where the dent is very shallow anyway, it is not worth trying to pull it out at all. If the underside of the dent is accessible, it can be hammered out gently from behind, using a mallet with a wooden or plastic head. Whilst doing this, hold a suitable block of wood firmly against the outside of the panel to absorb the impact from the hammer blows and thus prevent a large area of the bodywork from being 'belled-out'.

Should the dent be in a section of the bodywork which has a double skin or some other factor making it inaccessible from behind, a different technique is called for. Drill several small holes through the metal inside the area – particularly in the deeper section. Then screw long self-tapping screws into the holes just sufficiently for them to gain a good purchase in the metal. Now the dent can be pulled out by pulling on the protruding heads of the screws with a pair of pliers.

The next stage of the repair is the removal of the paint from the damaged area, and from an inch or so of the surrounding 'sound' bodywork. This is accomplished most easily by using a wire brush or abrasive pad on a power drill, although it can be done just as effectively by hand using sheets of abrasive paper. To complete the preparation for filling, score the surface of the bare metal with a screwdriver or the tang of a file, or alternatively, drill small holes in the affected area. This will provide a really good 'key' for the filler paste.

To complete the repair see the Section on filling and re-spraying.

Repair of rust holes or gashes in bodywork

Remove all paint from the affected area and from an inch or so of the surrounding 'sound' bodywork, using an abrasive pad or a wire brush on a power drill. If these are not available a few sheets of abrasive paper will do the job just as effectively. With the paint removed you will be able to gauge the severity of the corrosion and therefore decide whether to renew the whole panel (if this is possible) or to repair the affected area. New body panels are not as expensive as most people think and it is often quicker and more satisfactory to fit a new panel than to attempt to repair large areas of corrosion.

Remove all fittings from the affected area except those which will act as a guide to the original shape of the damaged bodywork (eg headlamp shells etc). Then, using tin snips or a hacksaw blade, remove all loose metal and any other metal badly affected by corrosion. Hammer the edges of the hole inwards in order to create a slight depression for the filler paste.

Wire brush the affected area to remove the powdery rust from the surface of the remaining metal. Paint the affected area with rust inhibiting paint; if the back of the rusted area is accessible treat this also.

Before filling can take place it will be necessary to block the hole in some way. This can be achieved by the use of zinc gauze or aluminium tape.

This sequence of photographs deals with the repair of the dent and paintwork damage shown in this photo. The procedure will be similar for the repair of a hole. It should be noted that the procedures given here are simplified — more explicit instructions will be found in the text

In the case of a dent the first job — after removing surrounding trim — is to hammer out the dent where access is possible. This will minimise filling. Here, the large dent having been hammered out, the damaged area is being made slightly concave

Now all paint must be removed from the damaged area, by rubbing with coarse abrasive paper. Alternatively, a wire brush or abrasive pad can be used in a power drill. Where the repair area meets good paintwork, the edge of the paintwork should be 'feathered', using a finer grade of abrasive paper

In the case of a hole caused by rusting, all damaged sheet-metal should be cut away before proceeding to this stage. Here, the damaged area is being treated with rust remover and inhibitor before being filled

Mix the body filler according to its manufacturer's instructions. In the case of corrosion damage, it will be necessary to block off any large holes before filling — this can be done with aluminium or plastic mesh, or aluminium tape. Make sure the area is absolutely clean before ...

... applying the filler. Filler should be applied with a flexible applicator, as shown, for best results; the wooden spatula being used for confined areas. Apply thin layers of filler at 20-minute intervals, until the surface of the filler is slightly proud of the surrounding bodywork

Initial shaping can be done with a Surform plane or Dreadnought file. Then, using progressively finer grades of wet-and-dry paper, wrapped around a sanding block, and copious amounts of clean water, rub down the filler until really smooth and flat. Again, feather the edges of adjoining paintwork

The whole repair area can now be sprayed or brush-painted with primer. If spraying, ensure adjoining areas are protected from over-spray. Note that at least one inch of the surrounding sound paintwork should be coated with primer. Primer has a 'thick' consistency, so will find small imperfections

Again, using plenty of water, rub down the primer with a fine grade wet-and-dry paper (400 grade is probably best) until it is really smooth and well blended into the surrounding paintwork. Any remaining imperfections can now be filled by carefully applied knifing stopper paste

When the stopper has hardened, rub down the repair area again before applying the final coat of primer. Before rubbing down this last coat of primer, ensure the repair area is blemish-free – use more stopper if necessary. To ensure that the surface of the primer is really smooth use some finishing compound

The top coat can now be applied. When working out of doors, pick a dry, warm and wind-free day. Ensure surrounding areas are protected from over-spray. Agitate the aerosol thoroughly, then spray the centre of the repair area, working outwards with a circular motion. Apply the paint as several thin coats

After a period of about two weeks, which the paint needs to harden fully, the surface of the repaired area can be 'cut' with a mild cutting compound prior to wax polishing. When carrying out bodywork repairs, remember that the quality of the finished job is proportional to the time and effort expended

Zinc gauze is probably the best material to use for a large hole. Cut a piece to the approximate size and shape of the hole to be filled, then position it in the hole so that its edges are below the level of the surrounding bodywork. It can be retained in position by several blobs of filler paste around its periphery.

Aluminium tape should be used for small or very narrow holes. Pull a piece off the roll and trim it to the approximate size and shape required, then pull off the backing paper (if used) and stick the tape over the hole; it can be overlapped if the thickness of one piece is insufficient. Burnish down the edges of the tape with the handle of a screwdriver or similar, to ensure that the tape is securely attached to the metal underneath.

Bodywork repairs – filling and re-spraying

Before using this Section, see the Sections on dent, deep scratch, rust holes and gash repairs.

Many types of bodyfiller are available, but generally speaking those proprietary kits which contain a tin of filler paste and a tube of resin hardener are best for this type of repair. A wide, flexible plastic or nylon applicator will be found invaluable for imparting a smooth and well contoured finish to the surface of the filler.

Mix up a little filler on a clean piece of card or board – measure the hardener carefully (follow the maker's instructions on the pack) otherwise the filler will set too rapidly or too slowly.

Using the applicator apply the filler paste to the prepared area; draw the applicator across the surface of the filler to achieve the correct contour and to level the filler surface. As soon as a contour that approximates to the correct one is achieved, stop working the paste – if you carry on too long the paste will become sticky and begin to 'pick up' on the applicator. Continue to add thin layers of filler paste at twenty-minute intervals until the level of the filler is just proud of the surrounding bodywork.

Once the filler has hardened, excess can be removed using a metal plane or file. From then on, progressively finer grades of abrasive paper should be used, starting with a 40 grade production paper and finishing with 400 grade wet-and-dry paper. Always wrap the abrasive paper around a flat rubber, cork, or wooden block – otherwise the surface of the filler will not be completely flat. During the smoothing of the filler surface the wet-and-dry paper should be periodically rinsed in water. This will ensure that a very smooth finish is imparted to the filler at the final stage.

At this stage the 'dent' should be surrounded by a ring of bare metal, which in turn should be encircled by the finely 'feathered' edge of the good paintwork. Rinse the repair area with clean water, until all of the dust produced by the rubbing-down operation has gone.

Spray the whole repair area with a light coat of primer – this will show up any imperfections in the surface of the filler. Repair these imperfections with fresh filler paste or bodystopper, and once more smooth the surface with abrasive paper. If bodystopper is used, it can be mixed with cellulose thinners to form a really thin paste which is ideal for filling small holes. Repeat this spray and repair procedure until you are satisfied that the surface of the filler, and the feathered edge of the paintwork are perfect. Clean the repair area with clean water and allow to dry fully.

The repair area is now ready for final spraying. Paint spraying must be carried out in a warm, dry, windless and dust free atmosphere. This condition can be created artificially if you have access to a large indoor working area, but if you are forced to work in the open, you will have to pick your day very carefully. If you are working indoors, dousing the floor in the work area with water will help to settle the dust which would otherwise be in the atmosphere. If the repair area is confined to one body panel, mask off the surrounding panels; this will help to minimise the effects of a slight mis-match in paint colours. Bodywork fittings (eg chrome strips, door handles etc) will also need to be masked off. Use genuine masking tape and several thicknesses of newspaper for the masking operations.

Before commencing to spray, agitate the aerosol can thoroughly, then spray a test area (an old tin, or similar) until the technique is mastered. Cover the repair area with a thick coat of primer; the thickness should be built up using several thin layers of paint rather than one thick one. Using 400 grade wet-and-dry paper, rub down the surface of the primer until it is really smooth. While doing this, the work area should be thoroughly doused with water, and the wet-and-dry paper periodically rinsed in water. Allow to dry before spraying on more paint.

Spray on the top coat, again building up the thickness by using several thin layers of paint. Start spraying in the centre of the repair area and then, using a circular motion, work outwards until the whole repair area and about 2 inches of the surrounding original paintwork is covered. Remove all masking material 10 to 15 minutes after spraying on the final coat of paint.

Allow the new paint at least two weeks to harden, then, using a paintwork renovator or a very fine cutting paste, blend the edges of the paint into the existing paintwork. Finally, apply wax polish.

5　Major body damage – repair

Where serious damage has occurred or large areas need renewal due to neglect, it means certainly that completely new sections or panels will need welding in and this is best left to professionals. If the damage is due to impact, it will also be necessary to completely check the alignment of the bodyshell structure. Due to the principle of construction, the strength and shape of the whole car can be affected by damage to one part. In such instances the services of a Ford agent with specialist checking jigs are essential. If a body is left misaligned, it is first of all dangerous as the car will not handle properly, and secondly uneven stresses will be imposed on the steering, engine and transmission, causing abnormal wear or complete failure. Tyre wear may also be excessive.

6　Maintenance – bodywork and fittings

1　Every 12 000 miles (20 000 km) check the operation of the door locks and check straps and lubricate the hinges with a little oil. Also lubricate the hinges of the bonnet and tailgate, and the bonnet release mechanism.
2　Do not attempt to lubricate the steering lock.
3　At the same time check the underbody for damage and corrosion, in particular the condition of the underseal. Apply new underseal and carry out repairs as necessary.

7　Bonnet – removal and refitting

1　Support the bonnet in its open position and place some cardboard or rags beneath the corners.
2　Unscrew the cross-head screw and remove the earth cable from the rear edge of the bonnet (photos).
3　Mark the location of the hinges with a pencil, then loosen the four bolts (photo).
4　With the help of an assistant remove the bolts and lift the bonnet from the car.
5　Refitting is a reversal of removal, but adjust the hinges to their original positions before tightening the bolts. Check that the bonnet is central within its aperture and aligned with the surrounding bodywork.

7.2 Removing the bonnet earth cable

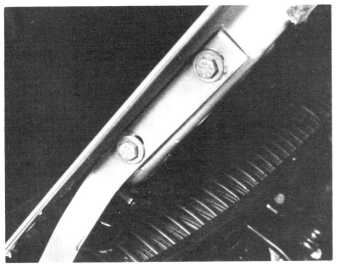

7.3 Bonnet hinge

If necessary adjust the front bump stops and make any necessary adjustment to the striker to ensure that it fully engages the lock (photo). To adjust the striker loosen the locknut and turn the striker head with a screwdriver.

8 Tailgate – removal and refitting

1   Disconnect the battery negative lead.
2   Open the tailgate and prise out the trim panel using a wide blade screwdriver.
3   Disconnect the wiring from the heated rear window, lock solenoid and remote release, interior light switch, rear wash/wipe and door ajar sensor. Before pulling the wiring from the tailgate tie string to each wire so that the wire can be repositioned correctly.
4   While an assistant supports the tailgate, disconnect the struts by prising out the retaining clips (photos). Do not remove the clips completely, just raise them by 4 mm (0.16 in) maximum and then pull the strut off its mounting.
5   Remove the plugs from the headlining, unscrew the hinge nuts, and withdraw the tailgate from the car (photo).
6   Refitting is a reversal of removal, but do not fully tighten the hinge nuts until the tailgate is positioned centrally in its aperture. If necessary adjust the striker so that the tailgate shuts correctly (photo).

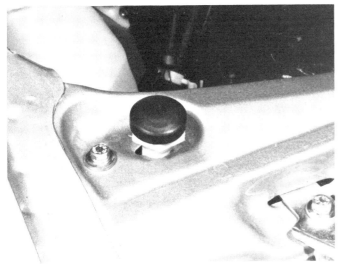

7.5a Bonnet adjustable bump stop

7.5b Bonnet striker and safety catch

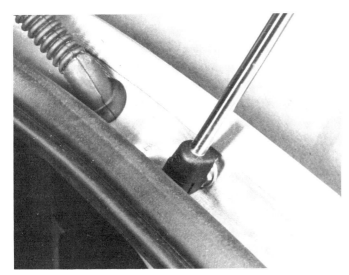

8.4a Tailgate strut location

8.4b Releasing a tailgate strut spring clip

8.5 Tailgate hinge

8.6 Tailgate striker

9.3 Bonnet lock cable end fittings

11.1 Removing the radiator grille panel upper screws

11.2 Radiator grille panel location insert

12.4 Tailgate lock

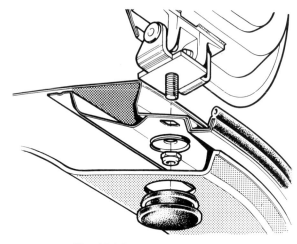

Fig. 12.1 Tailgate hinge (Sec 8)

9 Bonnet lock cable – removal and refitting

1   Remove the screws and withdraw the lower steering column shroud.
2   Remove the single screw and withdraw the lock cable bracket from the steering column.
3   Working in the engine compartment, pull the outer cable end fitting from the bracket and release the inner cable end fitting from the lock lever (photo).
4   Release the cable from the clips in the engine compartment.
5   Pull the cable through the bulkhead into the passenger compartment.
6   Refitting is a reversal of removal, but make sure that the rubber grommet is correctly located in the bulkhead.

10 Bonnet lock – removal and refitting

1   Working in the engine compartment disconnect the cable from the bonnet lock.
2   Remove the three cross-head screws and withdraw the lock from the front panel.
3   Refitting is a reversal of removal.

11 Radiator grille panel – removal and refitting

1   Remove the cross-head screws from the top of the panel (photo).
2   Lift the panel from the rubber inserts and withdraw from the car (photo).
3   Refitting is a reversal of removal.

12 Tailgate lock – removal and refitting

1   Open the tailgate and prise out the trim panel using a wide blade screwdriver.
2   Prise out the clip and withdraw the lock barrel.
3   Unbolt the support bracket.
4   Remove the special screws (if necessary using a suitable key) and withdraw the lock assembly (photo).
5   Refitting is a reversal of removal.

13 Tailgate strut – removal and refitting

1   Support the tailgate in its open position with a suitable prop.
2   Prise off the spring clips at each end of the strut and withdraw the strut from the pivot studs.
3   Refitting is a reversal of removal, but make sure that the piston rod end of the strut is fitted to the main body.

14 Door – removal and refitting

1 On models equipped with an electric mirror, electric windows, door-mounted speakers, or door ajar sensors, remove the trim panel as described in Section 15 and disconnect the wiring inside the door.

2 Unscrew and remove the bolt securing the check arm to the pillar (photo).

3 On front doors, remove the side trim panel, and on rear doors remove pillar trim.

4 On the front driver's door remove the lower facia panels and disconnect the face level vent hose.

5 On the front passenger's door remove the face level vent cover.

6 Support the door on blocks of wood.

7 Unscrew the hinge nuts and remove the support plates from the door pillars (photo).

8 Withdraw the door from the car.

9 Refitting is a reversal of removal, but do not tighten the hinge nuts until the door is positioned centrally in the body aperture and aligned with the surrounding bodywork. If necessary remove the lock striker before adjusting the door, then refit it and adjust it so that the lock operates correctly (photo).

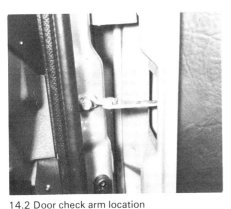

14.2 Door check arm location

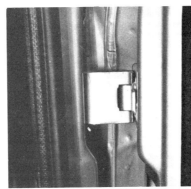

14.7 Door hinge

14.9 Door striker

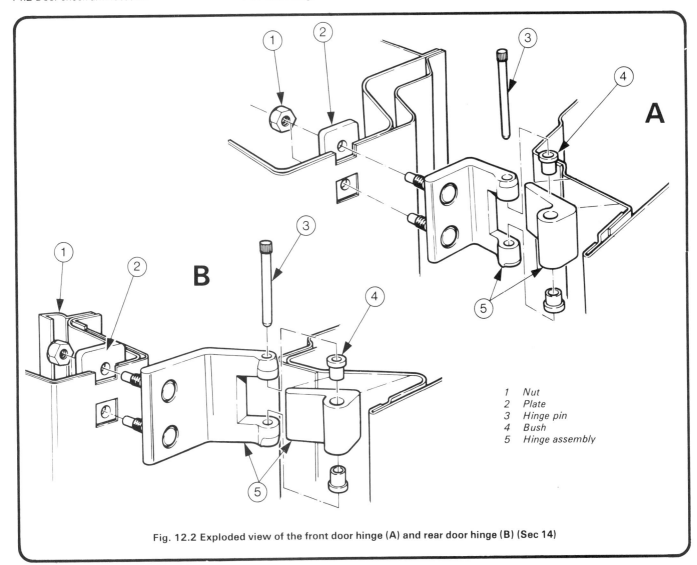

1 Nut
2 Plate
3 Hinge pin
4 Bush
5 Hinge assembly

Fig. 12.2 Exploded view of the front door hinge (A) and rear door hinge (B) (Sec 14)

15 Door inner trim panel – removal and refitting

1   Prise the cover from the window regulator handle (photo).
2   Note the position of the handle with the window shut, then remove the cross-head screw and withdraw the handle and bezel (photo).
3   Remove the screw and withdraw the trim panel from behind the door grip (photo).
4   Remove the screws, lift the interior door handle, and withdraw the surround and grip (photos).
5   Remove the screws and release the door pocket from the trim panel (photo). On models with electric mirrors it will also be necessary to disconnect the multi-plug on the driver's side.
6   Using a wide-blade screwdriver prise the trim panel away from the door. To prevent damage to the panel only prise under the clips (photo).
7   If necessary peel the polythene sheet from the door. Note the location of the air release flap and window regulator spacer (photo).
8   Refitting is a reversal of removal, but make sure that all the retaining clips are correctly aligned before pressing them into the door, and make sure that the upper lip of the panel locates under the exterior mirror control panel.

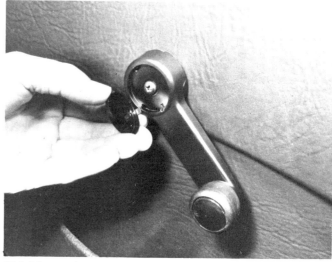

15.1 Prise out the cover ...

15.2a ... remove the screw ...

15.2b ... and withdraw the window regulator handle ...

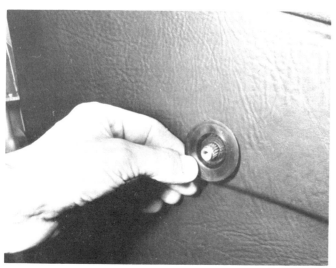

15.2c ... and bezel

15.3 Removing door grip inner trim panel

15.4a Remove the screws ...

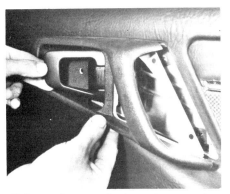

15.4b ... and remove the door grip surround

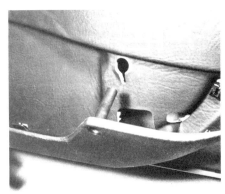

15.5 Removing the door pocket

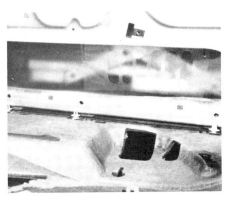

15.6 Showing door inner trim panel and clips

15.7 Air release flap on the door trim panel polythene sheet

16.2a Remove the screws ...

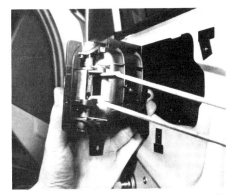

16.2b ... and withdraw the door interior handle remote control

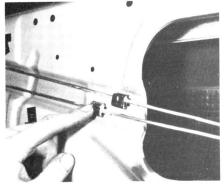

16.4 Door interior handle remote control rod guide locations

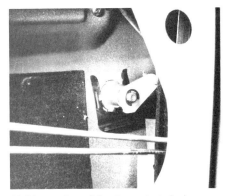

18.2 Inner view of the door private lock

16 Door interior handle remote control – removal and refitting

1   Remove the inner trim panel as described in Section 15.
2   Remove the cross-head screws and slide the control downwards from the door aperture (photos).
3   Disconnect the two rods and withdraw the control.
4   Refitting is a reversal of removal, but check that the two rods are correctly located in the guides (photo).

17 Door check arm – removal and refitting

1   Remove the inner trim panel as described in Section 15.
2   Remove the single bolt securing the arm to the body.
3   Unbolt the check arm and withdraw it from inside the door.
4   Refitting is a reversal of removal.

18 Door private lock – removal, inspection and refitting

1   Remove the inner trim panel as described in Section 15.
2   Pull out the retaining clip using pliers, then unhook the lock from the rod and withdraw it from outside the door (photo).
3   To dismantle the lock first extract the circlip and remove the endplate and nylon lever.
4   Remove the return spring.
5   Prise the cap from the key end of the lock and discard it.
6   Insert the key and pull out the lock barrel.
7   Hold the tumblers in position with the finger and thumb then remove the key and shutter plate.
8   Remove the tumblers *keeping them in strict order*. Remove the springs.
9   Clean all the components in paraffin and wipe dry, then examine them for wear and damage. Renew any components as necessary.

10 Reassembly and refitting is a reversal of dismantling and removal, but lightly lubricate the lock barrel with a little oil and apply a little grease inside the shutter plate. Fit a new cap over the shutter plate and bend it back over the lock housing. Fit a new gasket between the lock and the door panel.

19 Door lock – removal and refitting

1 Remove the inner trim panel as described in Section 15.
2 Fully close the window.
3 Remove the cross-head screws then reach inside the door and turn the lock to disconnect it from the control rods (photo).
4 Where applicable, disconnect the door ajar switch wiring.
5 Withdraw the lock from inside the door.
6 Refitting is a reversal of removal.

19.3 Door lock retaining screw locations

20 Windscreen, tailgate and fixed rear quarter windows – removal and refitting

The windscreen, tailgate and fixed quarter windows are direct glazed to the body using special adhesive. Purpose made tools are required to remove the old glass and fit the new glass, therefore this work is best entrusted to a specialist.

21 Front door window – removal and refitting

1 Remove the inner trim panel as described in Section 15.
2 Unscrew the bezel from the exterior mirror remote control knob and withdraw the trim panel (manually operated mirrors only).
3 From the rear of the door remove the single screw securing the rear window channel. With the window raised, unclip the rear channel.
4 Lower the window until the lower support channel is visible through the aperture at the bottom of the door. Prise the regulator arms from the sockets in the channel, then lower the window to the bottom of the door.
5 Pull the channel from the rear of the window aperture, then tilt the window forwards and lift it out through the aperture.
6 Refitting is a reversal of removal, but position the rear window channel screw to give the window at least 5.0 mm (0.2 in) fore and aft clearance.

22 Rear door window – removal and refitting

1 Remove the inner trim panel as described in Section 15.
2 Prise off the quarter trim panel from inside the door, then remove the screw and withdraw the outer trim panel.
3 Remove the three screws and withdraw the rear window channel.
4 Lower the window until the lower support channel is visible

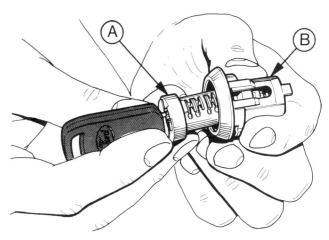

Fig. 12.3 Removing the door private lock barrel (A) from the housing (B) (Sec 18)

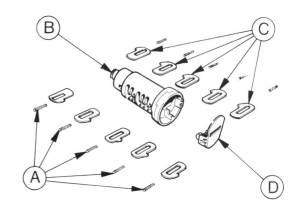

Fig. 12.4 Exploded view of the front door private lock barrel (Sec 18)

A   Springs   C   Tumblers
B   Lock barrel   D   Shutter plate

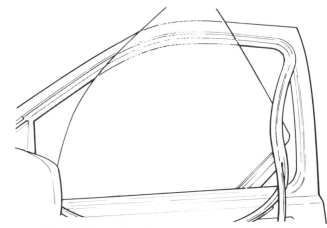

Fig. 12.5 Removing the front door window (Sec 21)

through the aperture at the bottom of the door. Prise the regulator arm from the socket in the channel, then lower the window to the bottom of the door.
5 Pull the channel from the front of the window aperture, then tilt the window rearwards and lift it out through the aperture.
6 Refitting is a reversal of removal, but position the rear window channel screws to give the window at least 5.0 mm (0.2 in) fore and aft clearance.

23 Window regulator – removal and refitting

1 Remove the inner trim panel as described in Section 15.
2 Lower the window until the lower support channel is visible through the aperture at the bottom of the door (photo). Prise the regulator arm(s) from the socket(s) in the channel, then lower the window to the bottom of the door.
3 Drill out the rivets retaining the window regulator. On front doors also drill out the rivets retaining the guide channel (photo).
4 Withdraw the regulator and where applicable the guide channel through the door aperture.
5 Refitting is a reversal of removal, but fit new rivets using a hand riveter.

24 Door mirror – removal and refitting

1 On electric mirrors first remove the inner trim panel as described in Section 15 and disconnect the wiring multi-plug.
2 On manually operated mirrors unscrew the bezel from the control knob (photo).
3 On all models prise off the trim panel from the front (photo).
4 Remove the screws and withdraw the mirror from the door (photo). On electric mirrors also disconnect the multi-plug.

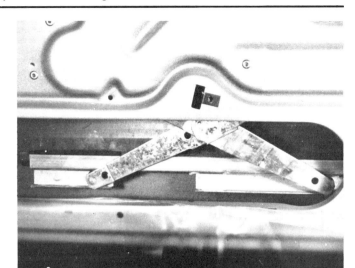

23.2 Front door window lower support channel and regulator arms

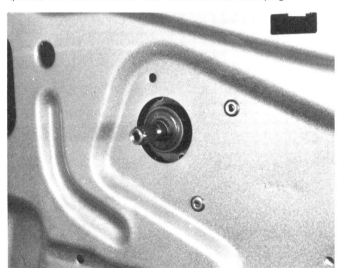

23.3 Window regulator retaining rivet locations

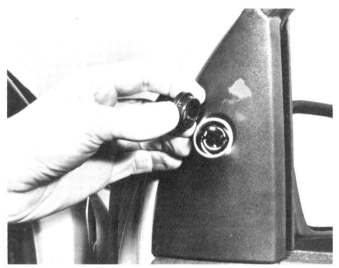

24.2 Unscrew the bezel ...

24.3 ... and remove the door mirror trim panel

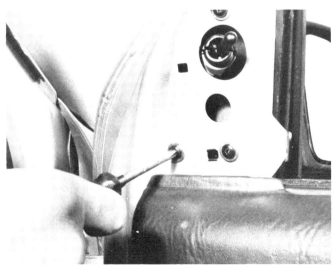

24.4 Removing the door mirror

5   Where applicable unclip the cover from the rear of the mirror.
6   To remove the glass on fixed type mirrors either lower the glass
from the balljoint (High Series models) or remove the screw (Low
Series models). On manual and electric mirrors insert a small screwdriver through the small hole in the bottom of the mirror and turn the
locking ring.
7   Refitting is a reversal of removal.

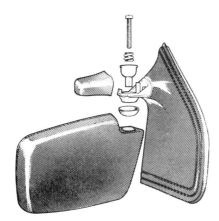

Fig. 12.6 Exploded view of fixed type mirror (Sec 24)

25 Bumpers – removal and refitting

1   On the front bumper remove the radiator grille panel as described
in Section 11 and also disconnect the direction indicator and fog
lamps as necessary with reference to Chapter 10.
2   On the rear bumper disconnect the number plate lamps with
reference to Chapter 10.
3   On front and rear bumpers reach behind the wings at each end of

the bumper and turn the fastener through 90° to remove it. On Ghia
models also unclip the support straps.
4   Unscrew the mounting bolt(s) and pull the bumper direct from the
car (photo). Resistance may be felt during the initial movement until
the side pegs are released from the clips.
5   Refitting is a reversal of removal.

26 Headlining – removal and refitting

1   The headlining is of moulded type and can be removed in one
piece through the tailgate aperture. First loosen the upper screws of
the trim panels touching the headlining.
2   Prise off the covers and remove the headlining and handgrip
screws. Remove the handgrips.
3   Where applicable remove the sliding roof as described in Section
32.
4   Support the headlining then remove the screws and withdraw the
sun visors and clips.
5   Unscrew the special fasteners, lower the headlining, and withdraw
it through the tailgate aperture.
6   Refitting is a reversal of removal.

27 Facia panel – removal and refitting

1   Disconnect the battery negative lead.
2   Remove the screws and withdraw the upper and lower shrouds
from the steering column.
3   Remove the screws and withdraw the driver's side facia and lower
the side trim panels. Where applicable disconnect the radio speaker
wiring.
4   Pull out the ashtray, remove the screws and withdraw the pocket
or cassette compartment as applicable (photos).
5   Unscrew the knob from the gearstick then remove the screws and
withdraw the rubber gaiter and surround.
6   Remove the screws and push the console rearwards.

25.4a Front bumper mounting bolt

25.4b Rear bumper mounting bolts

27.4a Removing the ashtray

27.4b Removing the facia pocket

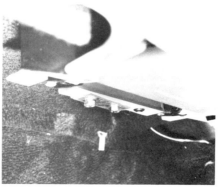

27.7a Passenger side lower facia mounting
bolts

27.7b Rear view of the passenger side lower
facia

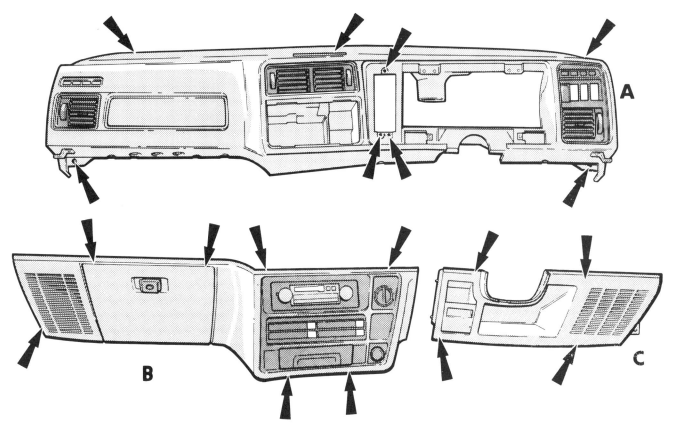

Fig. 12.7 Facia panel screw locations (Sec 27)

A   Upper facia panel

B   Lower facia panel
    (passenger side)

C   Lower facia panel (drivers
    side)

7   Open the glovebox then remove the screws and withdraw the passenger side lower facia panel. Disconnect the wiring from the speaker, glovebox lamp, ashtray lamp, heater switch, cigarette lighter, and radio (photos).
8   Remove the instrument panel as described in Chapter 10.
9   Remove the trip computer and door ajar monitor as applicable, with reference to Chapter 10.
10 Remove the foglamp and heated rear window switches with reference to Chapter 10.
11 Remove the heater switch controls with reference to Section 33.
12 Disconnect the auxiliary warning multi-plug.
13 Remove the retaining screws and withdraw the main facia panel through the passenger door, at the same time disconnect the heater vent hoses.
14 Refitting is a reversal of removal.

28 Centre console – removal and refitting

Full length console
1   Remove the screws from the front console and lift it over the gearstick at the same time releasing the rubber gaiter (photo).
2   Remove the screws and where applicable disconnect the clip, then lift away the rear console (photos).
3   Remove the screws and withdraw the lower console panel (photos).

Short console
4   Prise out the cover and remove the rear screw.
5   Prise out the tray mat (automatic transmission models) or centre screw covers (manual gearbox models).
6   Remove the centre screws and withdraw the console.

Full length and short consoles
7   Refitting is a reversal of removal.

29 Seats – removal and refitting

Front seats
1   Adjust the seat fully forwards, and on seats with height adjustment unhook the spring from the rear cross tube.
2   Unscrew and remove the rear mounting bolts (photo).
3   Adjust the seat fully to the rear then unscrew and remove the front mounting bolts.
4   Withdraw the seat from the car.

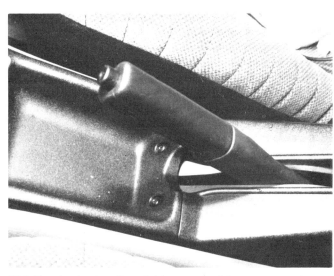

28.1 Showing front section retaining screws of the centre console

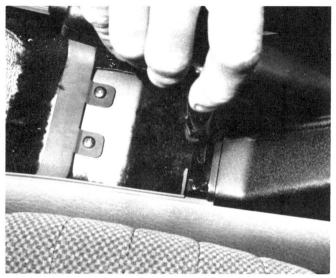

28.2a Showing centre console rear section front screws ...

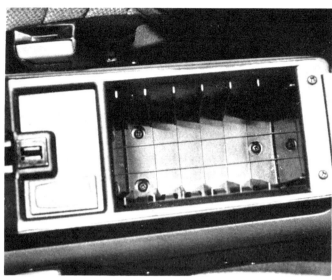

28.2b ... and rear screws

28.3a Removing lower console panel front screws ...

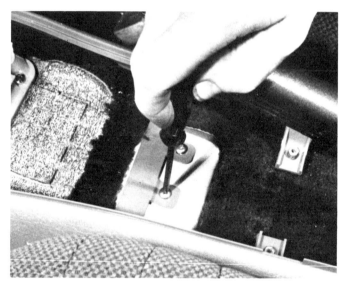

28.3b ... centre screws ...

28.3c ... and rear screws

29.2 Front seat rear mounting bolts

5   Refitting is a reversal of removal, but tighten the inner mounting bolts first. On seats with height adjustment locate the spring between the weld pipes on the cross tube.

Rear seat cushion
6   Remove the mounting screws below the front of the cushion. On split seat versions the centre screws secure the hinge.
7   Lift out the cushion.
8   Refitting is a reversal of removal.

Rear seat backrest
9   Fold the rear seat backrest forwards.
10 Remove the screws securing the hinges to the backrest, and withdraw the backrest.
11 If necessary the hinge and pivot assemblies can be removed after removing the screws.
12 Refitting is a reversal of removal.

---

30 Rear seat catch – removal and refitting

1   Fold the rear seat backrest forwards.

Base and L models
2   Unscrew the catch knob from the top of the seat.
3   Pull the cushion and cover aside, then unbolt and remove the catch from the backrest. If necessary remove the screws and withdraw the strikers.
4   Refitting is a reversal of removal, but make sure that the catch operating rod is located correctly in the guide.

GL and Ghia models
5   With the parcel shelf removed, remove the screws and withdraw the cover for access to the catch.
6   Unbolt the catch from the mounting bracket (photo).
7   Using a small screwdriver push out the pin securing the catch to the link.
8   Withdraw the catch from under the parcel shelf side-member.
9   If necessary lift the catch lever, push out the pin, and remove the link. The lever can be removed by drilling out the rivets.
10 Refitting is a reversal of removal.

---

31 Rear parcel shelf side-member – removal and refitting

1   Remove the centre parcel shelf.
2   Unhook and remove the rear seat side cushion (photo).
3   With the rear seat backrest folded forwards, lift the catch lever and push out the pin to disconnect it from the link (photo).
4   Remove the screws and withdraw the rear parcel shelf side-member. If necessary for access to the aerial, prise the trim from the inner panel (photo).
5   Refitting is a reversal of removal.

30.6 Showing the rear seat catch mechanism

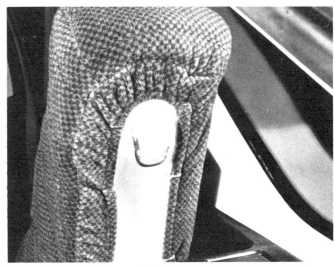
31.2 Removing the rear seat side cushion

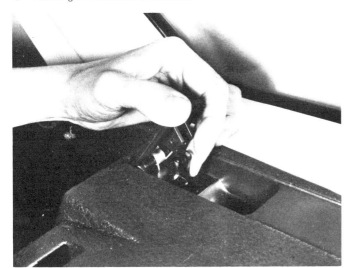
31.3 Disconnecting the rear seat catch link from the lever

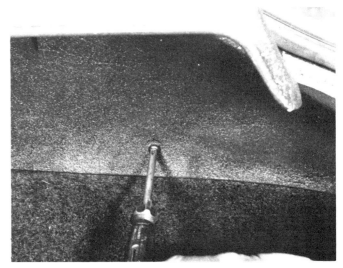
31.4a Removing the rear parcel shelf side-member retaining screws

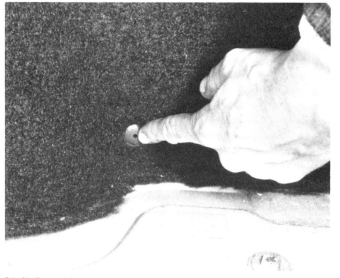

31.4b Rear side trim clip

31.4c View of aerial with rear side trim removed

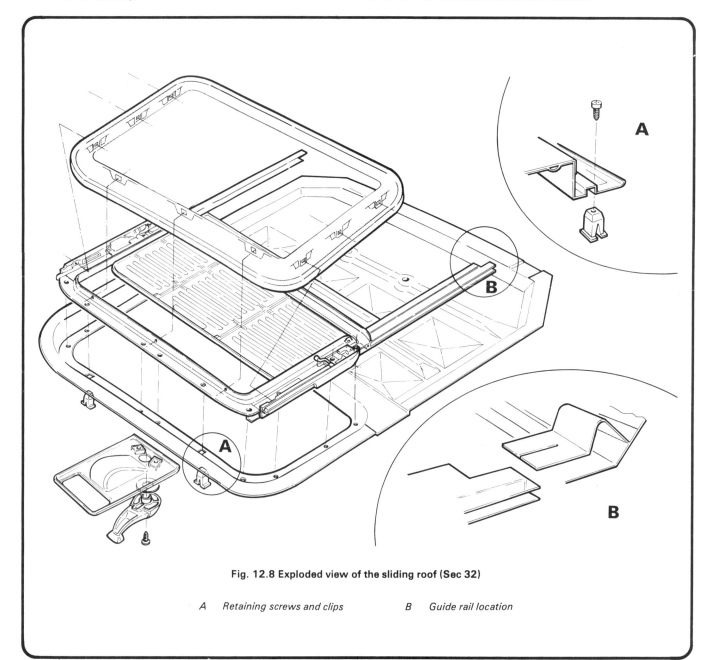

Fig. 12.8 Exploded view of the sliding roof (Sec 32)

A   Retaining screws and clips   B   Guide rail location

32 Sliding roof – removal, refitting and adjustment

1 Fully open the sliding roof then remove the control screw and remove the handle.
2 Working on top of the sliding roof, remove the screws from the perimeter.
3 Lift the front rail and withdraw the assembly forward from the aperture. Do not damage the paintwork.
4 Refitting is a reversal of removal, but make sure that the guide rails are correctly located. Finally adjust the sliding roof as follows.

Adjustment

5 Fully open and close the sliding roof then check that the front edge is flush with or a maximum of 2.0 mm (0.079 in) *below* the adjacent roof panel. The rear edge should be flush with or a maximum of 2.0 mm (0.079 in) *above* the adjacent roof panel.
6 If adjustment is necessary, remove the three screws securing the lower frame to the glass and slide the lower frame back into the roof. Loosen the centre screws and either the front or rear screws located on the sides of the glass. Reposition the glass as necessary then tighten the screws.
7 After making the adjustment slide the lower frame forward and fit the three screws.

34.2a Heater hose locations

33 Heater controls – removal and refitting

1 Disconnect the battery negative lead.
2 Remove the steering column shrouds and instrument panel surround as described in Chapter 10.
3 Detach the centre console as described in Section 28 and move it to the rear.
4 Remove the passenger side trim panel.
5 Remove the heater switch and bezel with reference to Chapter 10.
6 Disconnect the wiring from the glove compartment light and cigar lighter.
7 Remove the lower facia panel from the passenger side.
8 Remove the two screws and disconnect the control cables from the heater.
9 Remove the screws securing the controls to the facia, slide the controls through and withdraw the assembly downwards. Remove the bulb and holder.
10 Refitting is a reversal of removal, but adjust the cables by moving the levers fully to the top and bottom stops. Note that resistance will be felt as the cables are repositioned.

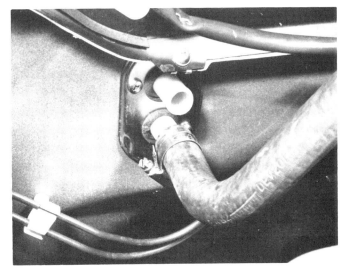

34.2b Removing a heater hose

34 Heater assembly – removal and refitting

1 Disconnect the battery negative lead.
2 Note the location of the heater hoses on the bulkhead then disconnect and plug them. Alternatively secure them high enough to prevent the coolant from draining (photos). If the coolant is still hot release the pressure in the cooling system with reference to Chapter 2.
3 To prevent unnecessary spillage when the heater is removed, blow into the upper heater pipe until all the coolant is removed.
4 Remove the screws and withdraw the heater pipe cover from the bulkhead (photo).
5 Detach the centre console as described in Section 28 and move it to the rear.
6 Remove the passenger side trim panel.
7 Remove the heater switch and bezel with reference to Chapter 10.
8 Disconnect the wiring from the glove compartment light and cigar lighter (photo).
9 Remove the lower facia panel from the passenger side.
10 Remove the two screws and disconnect the control cables from the heater (photo).
11 Disconnect the air hoses.
12 Unscrew the mounting bolts then move the heater to the rear until the pipes are clear of the bulkhead. Withdraw the heater assembly to the left (photos). If necessary remove the lower facia bracket.
13 Refitting is a reversal of removal, but adjust the cables by moving the levers fully to the top and bottom stops. Note that resistance will be felt as the cables are repositioned. Finally fill the cooling system as described in Chapter 2.

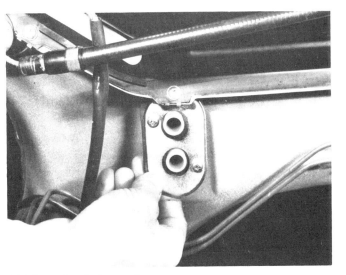

34.4 Removing the heater pipe cover

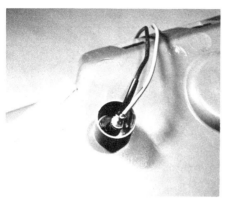

34.8 Rear view of the glove compartment light wiring

34.10 Heater control cable location

34.12a Heater mounting bolt

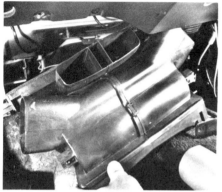

34.12b Removing the heater assembly

34.12c Side view of the heater assembly

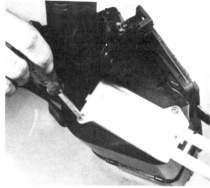

35.1a Remove the screws ...

35.1b ... and withdraw the heater matrix

35.3 Showing the heater air valve

36.2a Remove the bolts ...

36.2b ... and withdraw the heater motor cover

36.3 Heater motor and wiring

35 Heater assembly – overhaul

1   With the heater assembly removed, remove the screws and slide the matrix from the casing (photos).
2   Cut the gasket in line with the casing joint, then use screwdrivers to prise off the clips and separate the casing halves.
3   Remove the air valves, then align the levers as necessary and press them from the casing (photo).
4   Clean all the components and hose the matrix to ensure that any debris is removed. If necessary use a chemical cleaner to clear the inner tubes of the matrix. Renew the components as necessary.
5   Reassembly is a reversal of the dismantling procedure.

36 Heater motor – removal and refitting

1   Disconnect the battery negative lead.
2   Unclip the brake servo vacuum pipe then remove the bolts, pull off the rubber moulding and withdraw the heater motor cover (photos).
3   Disconnect the wiring from the motor and detach the earth lead from the bracket (photo).
4   Unscrew the mounting nuts and withdraw the motor from the bulkhead.
5   Unclip and remove the casing halves.
6   Disconnect the wiring, then prise open the clamp and withdraw the heater motor and fans.
7   Refitting is a reversal of removal.

1985 model Ford Sierra L

1987 model Ford Sierra Sapphire GLS

Chapter 13 Supplement:
Revisions and information on later models

Contents

Introduction 1
Specifications 2
Routine maintenance 3
Engine 4
  Introduction
  Valve cover fastenings – later models
  Cylinder head bolts – later models
  Timing belt tension (later models) – checking and adjustment
Cooling system 5
  Draining and refilling (later models)
  Radiator (Sapphire) – removal and refitting
Fuel system (carburettor models) 6
  Air cleaner (1.8 and later 2.0 models) – removal and refitting
  Fuel pump – models with air conditioning
  Accelerator cable – removal and refitting (later models)
  Fuel vapour separator – description
  Fuel vapour separator – removal and refitting
  Carburettor adjustments – warning
  VV carburettor – diaphragm renewal
  VV carburettor – accelerator pump repair
  VV carburettor – correction of unstable idle
  Carburettor speed control system – description and maintenance
  Weber 2V carburettor (1.6 Economy) – description
  Weber 2V carburettor (1.6 Economy) – idle adjustments
  Weber 2V carburettor (1.6 Economy) – overhaul
  Weber 2V carburettor (1.6 Economy) – automatic choke adjustment
  Weber 2V carburettor (later 2.0 models) – description
  Weber 2V carburettor (later 2.0 models) – idle adjustments
  Weber 2V carburettor (later 2.0 models) – removal and refitting
  Weber 2V carburettor (later 2.0 models) – overhaul
  Weber 2V carburettor (later 2.0 models) – automatic choke adjustment
  Weber 2V carburettor (later 2.0 models) – stepper motor adjustment
  Weber 2V carburettor – choke vacuum pull-down
  Pierburg 2V carburettor – description
  Pierburg 2V carburettor – idle adjustments
  Pierburg 2V carburettor – removal and refitting
  Pierburg 2V carburettor – dismantling (carburettor removed)
  Pierburg 2V carburettor – reassembly
  Pierburg 2V carburettor – fast idle adjustment
  Fuel cooling blower – 2.0 litre OHC engine (pre-1985)
  Engine conditions required for operation on unleaded fuel

Fuel injection system 7
  Description
  Air cleaner element – removal and refitting
  Idle adjustment
  Throttle position sensor – removal and refitting
  Idle speed control valve – removal and refitting
  Airflow meter – removal and refitting
  Fuel injectors – removal and refitting
  Fuel pump – removal and refitting
  Fuel filter – renewal
  Fuel pressure regulator – removal and refitting
  Inlet manifold – removal and refitting
  Engine conditions required for operation on unleaded fuel
  Fuel pump inertia switch (July 1986 on)
  Fault diagnosis – fuel injection system
Engine management systems 8
  Introduction
  ESC II module – caution
  ESC II module – removal and refitting
  EEC IV module – removal and refitting
  Carburettor stepper motor (2.0) – removal and refitting
  Coolant temperature sensor – removal and refitting
  Engine management module (1.8, 1987 on)
  Manifold heater (carburettor models) – removal and refitting
  Relay locations
  Fuel pump inertia switch – models with EEC IV (July 1986 on)
  Fault diagnosis – engine management systems
Ignition system 9
  Description (later models)
  Ignition timing marks – all models
  Ignition module (2.0 fuel injection models) – removal and refitting
  Distributor cap and rotor (2.0 fuel injection models) – removal and refitting
  Distributor (2.0 fuel injection models) – removal and refitting
  Distributor cap securing clips – early Bosch type
  Ignition timing – adjustments for running on unleaded fuel
Clutch 10
  Adjustment (all models) – checking and correcting
  Clutch pedal (Sapphire) – removal and refitting
Manual gearbox 11
  Countershaft bearing modification (type N)
  Lubricant type (type N)
  Refitting (all models)

Manual gearbox oil level (all types)
Gear selector modifications (type N)
Gearchange lever gaiter – modification
Automatic transmission (type A4LD) 12
Description
Selector lever positions – modification
Fluid level checking
Brake band adjustment
Removal and refitting
Starter inhibitor switch renewal
Downshift cable – adjustment
Downshift cable (solenoid-operated) – adjustment
Selector rod – removal, refitting and adjustment
Vacuum diaphragm unit – removal and refitting
Final drive and driveshafts 13
Driveshaft nuts – later models
Driveshaft (models with ABS) – removal and refitting
Driveshaft (models with ABS) – overhaul
Final drive unit (all models) – removal and refitting
Final drive output flange oil seals (models with ABS) – renewal
Rear axle rubber mounting-to-body bolts (1986 on)
Braking system 14
Brake pad renewal – Girling calipers (all 1.3 and 1.6)
Brake disc – removal and refitting (later models)
Brake disc renewal – all models
Brake shoes – removal and refitting (all 1.3 and 1.6
Hatchback/Saloon models)
Brake pedal height – adjustment
Anti-lock braking system (ABS) – description
Rear disc pads (ABS) – inspection and renewal
Rear caliper (ABS) – removal and refitting
Rear caliper (ABS) – overhaul
Rear disc shield (ABS) – removal and refitting
Fluid reservoir (ABS) – removal and refitting
Hydraulic unit (ABS) – removal and refitting
Hydraulic unit accumulator (ABS) – removal and refitting
Hydraulic unit pump and motor (ABS) – removal and refitting
Hydraulic unit pressure switch (ABS) – removal and refitting
Valve block (ABS) – removal and refitting
Computer module (ABS) – removal and refitting
Wheel sensors (ABS) – removal and refitting
Hydraulic system (ABS) – bleeding
Handbrake cable – adjustment
Handbrake cable – removal and refitting
Brake pedal (Sapphire) – removal and refitting
Front disc brakes (Sapphire)
Electrical system 15
Alternator mounting bracket – refitting
Alternator (Mitsubishi) – brush renewal
Alternator (Lucas A127) – general
Starter motors (1987 on) – general
Fuses and relays
Flasher unit (all models) – removal and refitting
Rear screen wiper motor (all models) – parking diode renewal
Windscreen washer pump (all models) – removal and refitting
Windscreen washer jets – removal and refitting
Rear screen washer pump – removal and refitting
Headlamp wash/wipe system – general
Headlamp wiper blade – renewal
Headlamp washer pump – removal and refitting
Headlamp washer jets – removal, refitting and adjustment
Headlamp wiper motor – removal and refitting
Headlamp unit (1987 on) – removal and refitting

Front direction indicator (1987 on) – bulb renewal
Auxiliary driving lamp (1987 on) – bulb renewal
Front foglamp (1987 on) – bulb renewal
Horn switch (steering wheel mounted) – removal and refitting
Auxiliary warning system – description
Auxiliary warning system – testing and fault finding
Auxiliary warning system – component renewal
Standard clock – removal and refitting (alternative housing)
Digital clock (later models) – bulb renewal
Heater/air conditioning blower switch – bulb renewal
Trip computer (1985 on) – module removal and refitting
Trip computer (1985 on) – bulb renewal
Instruments (1987 on)
Seat heating pad – removal and refitting
Central door locking
Electric window motor – removal and refitting
Dim-dip lighting system
Radio (DIN fixing) – removal and refitting
Radio with power amplifier – removal and refitting
Radio aerial – removal and refitting
In-car entertainment – 1987 on
Rear screen aerial amplifier – removal and refitting
Aerial – location and access
Suspension and steering 16
Front anti-roll bar mountings – all models
Rear anti-roll bar – removal and refitting
Rear wheel bearings (later models) – renewal
Rear wheel hub-to-suspension arm bolts
Steering track rod balljoints
Rear coil spring (models with ABS) – removal and refitting
Rear suspension lower arm (models with ABS) – removal
and refitting
Wheel stud (all models) – renewal
Wheels and tyres – general care and maintenance
Bodywork and fittings 17
Bumper decorative mouldings (all models) – fitting
Bumpers – removal and refitting
Radiator grille (1987 on) – removal and refitting
Bonnet release with cable broken (all models)
Wing protective liners (later models)
Door lock striker adjustment – 1985 on
Door inner trim removal – all models (except Sapphire)
Rear quarter window spoilers – general
Opening rear quarter window – removal and refitting
Front seats
Front seat air cushion – removal and refitting
Front seat air adjust ball – removal and refitting
Seat belts – general
Front seat belts (1987 on)
Rear seat
Roofrack – fitting to Sapphire Saloon
Rear spoiler (Sapphire Saloon)
Heating and ventilation equipment – (1987 on)
Plastic components
Air conditioning system – description
Air conditioning system – precautions
Air conditioning system – maintenance
Air conditioning system – component renewal
Air conditioning/heavy duty heater vacuum solenoid –
new design (October 1986 on)
Door trim panel – Sapphire Saloon – removal and refitting
Luggage boot lid (Sapphire) – removal and refitting

1 Introduction

This Supplement contains information which is additional to, or a revision of, material in the first twelve Chapters. Most of the material concerns additions or changes to the fuel, ignition and engine management systems on later models, but some items apply to all models from the start of production.

The Sections in the Supplement follow the same order as the Chapters to which they relate (although there may be more than one

Section per Chapter). The Specifications are grouped together for convenience, but they follow Chapter order.

It is recommended that before any particular operation is undertaken, reference be made to the appropriate Section(s) of the Supplement. In this way changes to procedures or components can be noted before referring to the main Chapters.

It should be noted that in much Ford literature the Hatchback version is referred to as a 5-door Saloon. In this Manual, the Saloon (Sapphire) is of four-door notchback type.

2 Specifications

The specifications below are revisions of, or supplementary to, those at the beginning of the preceding Chapters.

Engine – later models
General

	1.6 HC E and E-max	1.8 HC E	2.0 HC i
Engine code	LSD/LSE	REB/RED	NRB/N4A
Bore	81.32 mm	86.20 mm	90.82 mm
	(3.202 in)	(3.394 in)	(3.576 in)
Stroke	76.95 mm	76.95 mm	76.95 mm
	(3.030 in)	(3.030 in)	(3.030 in)
Cubic capacity	1597 cc	1796 cc	1993 cc
	(97.4 cu in)	(109.6 cu in)	(121.6 cu in)
Compression ratio	9.5 : 1	9.5 : 1	9.2 : 1
Maximum rpm – continuous	5950	5850	6050
Maximum rpm – intermittent	6175	6075	6275
Maximum power (DIN, kW @ rpm)	55 @ 4900	66 @ 5400	85 @ 5500
Maximum torque (DIN, Nm @ rpm)	123 @ 2900	140 @ 3500	160 @ 4000

Cylinder block
Bore diameter in mm (in):

	1.6 (LSD/LSE)	1.8 (REB/RED)
Standard 1	81.300 to 81.310	86.180 to 86.190
	(3.2008 to 3.2012)	(3.3929 to 3.3933)
Standard 2	81.310 to 81.320	86.190 to 86.200
	(3.2012 to 3.2016)	(3.3933 to 3.3937)
Standard 3	81.320 to 81.330	86.200 to 86.210
	(3.2016 to 3.2020)	(3.3937 to 3.3941)
Standard 4	81.330 to 81.340	86.210 to 86.220
	(3.2020 to 3.2024)	(3.3941 to 3.3945)
Oversize A	81.810 to 81.820	86.690 to 86.700
	(3.2209 to 3.2213)	(3.4130 to 3.4134)
Oversize B	81.820 to 81.830	86.700 to 86.710
	(3.2213 to 3.2217)	(3.4134 to 3.4138)
Oversize C	81.830 to 81.840	86.710 to 86.720
	(3.2217 to 3.2220)	(3.4138 to 3.4142)
Standard service	As standard 4	As Standard 4
Oversize 0.5	As Oversize C	As Oversize C
Oversize 1.0	82.330 to 82.340	87.210 to 87.220
	(3.2413 to 3.2417)	(3.4335 to 3.4339)

Camshaft
Endfloat (1.6 LSD only) in mm (in) .... 0.090 to 0.170 (0.0035 to 0.0067)

Pistons – 1.6 and 1.8
Diameter in mm (in):

	1.6 (LSD/LSE)	1.8 (REB/RED)
Standard 1	81.265 to 81.275	86.145 to 86.155
	(3.1994 to 3.1998)	(3.3915 to 3.3919)
Standard 2	81.275 to 81.285	86.155 to 86.165
	(3.1998 to 3.2002)	(3.3919 to 3.3923)
Standard 3	81.285 to 81.295	86.165 to 86.175
	(3.2002 to 3.2006)	(3.3923 to 3.3927)
Standard 4	81.295 to 81.305	86.175 to 86.185
	(3.2006 to 3.2010)	(3.3927 to 3.3931)
Standard service size	81.290 to 81.315	86.170 to 86.195
	(3.2004 to 3.2014)	(3.3925 to 3.3935)
Oversize 0.5	81.790 to 81.815	86.670 to 86.695
	(3.2201 to 3.2211)	(3.4122 to 3.4132)
Oversize 1.0	82.290 to 82.315	87.170 to 87.195
	(3.2398 to 3.2407)	(3.4319 to 3.4329)
Clearance in bore (new) in mm (in)	0.015 to 0.050	0.015 to 0.050
	(0.0006 to 0.0020)	(0.0006 to 0.0020)
Ring gap (fitted) in mm (in):		
Top and centre	0.30 to 0.50	0.30 to 0.50
	(0.012 to 0.020)	(0.012 to 0.020)
Bottom	0.40 to 1.40	0.40 to 1.40
	(0.016 to 0.055)	(0.016 to 0.055)

Pistons – 2.0 (1985 on)
Diameter in mm (in):

Standard service size	90.790 to 90.815 (3.5744 to 3.5754)
Oversize 0.5	91.290 to 91.315 (3.5941 to 3.5951)
Oversize 1.0	91.790 to 91.815 (3.6138 to 3.6148)
Clearance in bore (new) in mm (in)	0.015 to 0.050 (0.0006 to 0.0020)

Ring gap (fitted) in mm (in):
    Top and centre .... 0.40 to 0.60 (0.016 to 0.024)
    Bottom .... 0.40 to 1.40 (0.016 to 0.055)

Gudgeon pin
Length in mm (in):
    1.6 (LSD/LSE), 1.8 (REB/RED) and 2.0 (1985 on) .... 68.0 to 68.8 (2.6772 to 2.7087)

Cylinder head
Cast marking:
    1.6 (LSD/LSE) 62/64
    1.8 (REB/RED) 20/85
    2.0 (NRB/N4A) 20/0

Valve timing
    1.6 (LSD/LSE) .... As earlier 1.6 (Chapter 1)
    1.8 (REB/RED) .... As 2.0 (Chapter 1)

Inlet valves

	1.6 (LSD)	1.6 (LSE)	1.8 (REB/RED)
Length in mm (in)	112.55 (4.4311)	112.65 to 113.65 (4.4350 to 4.4744)	111.75 to 112.75 (4.3996 to 4.4390)
Head diameter in mm (in)	41.80 to 42.20 (1.6457 to 1.6614)	41.80 to 42.20 (1.6457 to 1.6614)	41.80 to 42.20 (1.6457 to 1.6614)

Exhaust valves

	1.6 (LSD)	1.6 (LSE)	1.8 (REB/RED)
Length in mm (in)	112.55 (4.4311)	112.05 to 113.75 (4.4114 to 4.4783)	111.15 to 112.15 (4.3760 to 4.4154)
Head diameter in mm (in)	34.00 to 34.40 (1.3386 to 1.3543)	34.00 to 34.40 (1.3386 to 1.3543)	34.00 to 34.40 (1.3386 to 1.3543)

Torque wrench settings

	lbf ft	Nm
Cylinder head bolts:		
'Star' socket head (thread length 38 mm)	As Chapter 1	As Chapter 1
'Torx' socket head (thread length 70 mm):		
Stage 1	26 to 30	35 to 40
Stage 2	52 to 55	70 to 75
Stage 3 (after 5 minutes)	Tighten a further 90°	Tighten a further 90°
Crankshaft pulley bolt (class 10.9 or 11.0)	74 to 85	100 to 115

Fuel system – carburettor models
Fuel pump (electric type)
Application .... All models with air conditioning
Delivery .... 0.4 litre (0.7 pint) minimum in 30 seconds

Carburettor application and type
1.6 (LCS and LSD) .... Weber twin venturi (2V) with vacuum-controlled secondary throttle opening

1.8 (REB) .... Pierburg twin venturi (2V) with vacuum-controlled secondary throttle opening

2.0 (1985 on) .... Weber twin venturi (2V) with idle speed control (ISC)

Carburettor calibration
Weber 2V – 1.6 models:
    Idle speed .... 800 ± 25 rpm
    Idle CO .... 0.75 to 1.25%
    Fast idle speed (engine warm) .... 1600 to 1800 rpm (middle step of cam)
    Float height .... 5.5 to 6.5 mm (0.217 to 0.256 in)
    Choke vacuum pull-down (max) .... 6.0 to 6.5 mm (0.236 to 0.256 in)
    Throttle barrel diameter .... 28/30 mm
    Venturi diameter .... 21/23 mm
    Main jet 97/110
    Air correction jet 185/90
    Emulsion tube F59/F22
    Idle jet 50/40
Weber 2V – 2.0 models (Carburettor Nos 83HF 9510 AA/BA, 85HF 9510 CA/DA):
    Idle speed .... 800 rpm (electrically-controlled)
    Idle CO .... 0.75 to 1.25%
    Float height .... 7.5 to 8.5 mm (0.295 to 0.335 in)
    Choke vacuum pull-down (max):
        Manual transmission .... 9.0 mm (0.354 in)
        Automatic transmission .... 8.0 mm (0.315 in)
    Throttle barrel diameter .... 30/34 mm
    Venturi diameter .... 25/27 mm
    Main jet:
        Manual transmission 112/135
        Automatic transmission 110/135

Air correction jet:
    Manual transmission 165/150
    Automatic transmission 160/150
Emulsion tube F22/F22
    Idle jet 45/45
Automatic choke setting .... Centre index

Weber 2V – 2.0 models (Carburettor Nos 85HF 9510 CB/DB):
Idle speed .... 875 rpm (electronically-controlled)
Idle CO .... 1.0 ± 0.25%
Float height .... 8.0 ± 0.5 mm (0.32 ± 0.02 in)
Choke vacuum pull-down (max) .... 6.0 mm (0.24 in)
Throttle barrel diameter .... 30/34 mm
Venturi diameter .... 25/27 mm
Main jet 110/130
Air correction jet:
    Manual transmission 160/160
    Automatic transmission 170/160
Emulsion tube F22/F22
Idle jet 42/45
Automatic choke setting .... Centre index

Pierburg 2V:
Idle speed .... 800 ± 20 rpm
Idle CO 1.3%
Fast idle speed (engine warm) .... 830 ± 30 rpm (on lowest step of cam)
Venturi diameter .... 23/26 mm
Main jet 107.5/130
Idle fuel jet 45
Idle air bleed 115
Choke pull-down adjustment .... 3.0 mm (0.118 in)
Automatic choke setting .... Centre index
Float level .... Not adjustable

Fuel system – fuel injection models
System type
System type .... Bosch L-Jetronic

Fuel pump
Type .... Electric, roller cell
Output pressure .... Greater than 5 bar (72.5 lbf/in²) at 12 volts, no flow
Regulated pressure .... 2.5 bar (36.3 lbs/in²)

Idle data
Idle speed (non-adjustable)
    Automatic transmission .... 800 rpm
    Manual transmission .... 875 rpm
Idle CO .... 0.5 to 1.0%

Torque wrench setting	lbf ft	Nm
Idle speed control valve	6 to 8	8.5 to 10.5

Ignition system – later models
System type
1.8 and 1985 on 2.0 .... Breakerless, Hall effect, with electronically-controlled advance

Ignition timing
Static or idle (vacuum pipe disconnected):
    1.8 and 1985 on 2.0 (except injection) .... 10° BTDC
    2.0 injection .... 12° BTDC

Ignition timing – unleaded fuel
Static or idle (vacuum pipe disconnected):
    1.3 (VV carburettor) .... 8° BTDC
    1.6 (VV carburettor) .... 8° BTDC
    1.6 (2V carburettor) .... 6° BTDC
    1.8 (2V carburettor) .... 6° BTDC
    2.0 (2V carburettor):
        June 1982 to November 1984 .... 4° BTDC
        November 1984 on .... 6° BTDC
    2.0 (fuel injection) .... 8° BTDC

Spark plugs
Type – pre-November 1985:
    1.8 .... Motorcraft BRF 22X or Champion F7YC
Electrode gap – pre-November 1985 .... 0.75 mm (0.030 in)

Type – November 1985-on:

1.3 (VV carburettor)	Motorcraft BRF 22 or Champion F7YC
1.6E (VV carburettor)	Motorcraft BRF 32 or Champion F7YC
1.6E Max (2V carburettor)	Motorcraft BRF 22 or Champion F7YC
1.6 (VV carburettor)	Motorcraft BRF 22 or Champion F7YC
1.8 (2V carburettor)	Motorcraft BRF 22 or Champion F7YC
2.0 low compression (2V carburettor)	Motorcraft BRF 42 or Champion F7YC
2.0 high compression (2V carburettor)	Motorcraft BRF 32 or Champion F7YC
2.0 (fuel injection)	Motorcraft BRF 22C or 32X, or Champion F7YC
Electrode gap – November 1985 on	0.6 mm (0.024 in)

Clutch (later models)
Clutch plate diameter

1.6 litre (4-speed)	190.5 mm (7.5 in)
1.6 litre (5-speed), 1.8 and 2.0 litre	215.9 mm (8.5 in)

Automatic transmission (later models)
General

Maker's designation	A4LD
Type	Four forward speeds and one reverse; automatic torque converter lock-up in higher gears
Application	1.8 and later 2.0

Ratios

1st	2.47 : 1
2nd	1.47 : 1
3rd	1.00 : 1
4th	0.75 : 1
Reverse	2.11 : 1
Torque converter (maximum multiplication):	
1.8	2.05 : 1
2.0	2.35 : 1

Transmission fluid

Type	ATF to Ford spec SQM-2C 9010-A (Duckhams D-Matic)
Capacity (including converter and oil cooler)	8.5 litres (15 pints) approx

Torque wrench settings

	lbf ft	Nm
Converter housing to transmission case	30 to 35	40 to 48
Rear extension to transmission case	30 to 35	40 to 48
Driveplate to torque converter	24 to 28	32 to 38
Sump bolts:		
Plastic gasket	6 to 8	8 to 11
Cork gasket	11 to 13	15 to 18
Downshift cable bracket	13 to 16	18 to 22
Starter inhibitor switch	7 to 10	10 to 14
Brake band adjuster locknut	37 to 43	50 to 58
Oil cooler pipes	16 to 18	22 to 24
Converter housing to engine	22 to 27	30 to 36
Kickdown solenoid bolts	21 to 30	29 to 41

Final drive and driveshafts
Lubricant type – limited slip differential

Initial fill	SAE 90 oil to Ford spec ESWM2C 104 A (Duckhams Hypoid 90DL)
Top up only (0.2 litre/0.35 pint max)	SAE 90 oil to Ford spec 5QM2C 9002 AA (Duckhams Hypoid 90S)

Final drive ratios (1984 on)
1.6:

Hatchback	3.62 : 1
Saloon	3.62 : 1
Estate:	
4-speed	3.92 : 1
5-speed	3.62 : 1

1.8:

4-speed	3.62 : 1
5-speed	3.92 : 1
Automatic	3.62 : 1

2.0 litre (carburettor):

Manual	3.62 : 1
Automatic	3.38 : 1

2.0 litre (fuel injection):
    Manual .... 3.92 : 1
    Automatic .... 3.62 : 1

Driveshaft lubrication (all models)
Grease type .... Lithium base molybdenum disulphide grease/Ford part No A775X IC9004 AA (Duckhams LBM 10)

Torque wrench settings

	lbf ft	Nm
Rear axle rubber mounting-to-body securing bolts – later type	44	60
Driveshaft flange screws (with ABS)	28 to 32	38 to 43

Braking system (1987 on)
Brake disc wear limits
Minimum thickness:
    Front, solid .... Not known
    Front, ventilated .... 22.8 mm (0.898 in)
    Rear (ABS) .... 8.9 mm (0.350 in)
Thickness variation .... 0.01 mm (0.0004 in)

Torque wrench settings

	lbf ft	Nm
All models with ventilated discs:		
Caliper slide pin bolts	15 to 18	20 to 25
Models with ABS:		
Caliper anchor bracket bolts (front and rear)	45	61
Rear caliper slide bolts	26	35
Rear hub flange nut	214	290
Hydraulic actuator to bulkhead	37	51
Accumulator to pump housing	34	46
Pump mounting bolt	7	9
Wheel sensor bolt	8	11
High pressure pipe union	9	12

Electrical system
Alternator
Type .... Mitsubishi AST
Rating 55A
Startor winding resistance .... 0.8 ohms
Rotor winding resistance .... 2.7 to 3.1 ohms
Brush wear limit .... 5.0 mm (0.197 in)
Regulating voltage at 4000 rpm and 3 to 7 amp load .... 13.7 to 14.6 volts

Torque wrench settings

	lbf ft	Nm
Alternator mounting bolts (with coloured patch on threads)	30 to 38	41 to 51
Alternator mounting bolts (without coloured patch)	14.7 to 18.4	20 to 25

Suspension and steering
Front wheel alignment (1987 on)
Toe:
    Checking .... 0.5 mm (0.020 in) toe-out to 4.5 mm (0.177 in) toe-in
    Setting .... 1.0 to 3.0 mm (0.039 to 0.118 in) toe-in

Castor (non-adjustable)
Saloon and Hatchback:
    Standard .... 1°52' positive
    Heavy duty .... 1°53' positive
Estate:
    Standard and business pack .... 1°50' positive
    Heavy duty .... 2°07' positive
Maximum side-to-side variation .... 1°0'

Camber (non-adjustable)
Saloon and Hatchback:
    Standard .... 0°21' negative
    Heavy duty .... 0°04' positive
Estate:
    Standard and business pack .... 0°19' negative
    Heavy duty .... 0°05' positive

Torque wrench settings

	lbf ft	Nm
Steering pump mounting bolts (blue finish)	38 to 47	52 to 64
Rear anti-roll bar retaining clips	15 to 18	20 to 25
Front suspension arm inner pivot nut:		
Stage 1	33	45
Back off, then Stage 2	11	15
Stage 3	Tighten through further 90°	
Steering gear-to-crossmember bolts:		
Stage 1	33	45
Back off, then Stage 2	11	15
Stage 3	Tighten through further 90°	
Rear hub-to-suspension arm bolts (see Section 16):		
Type 'A'	38 to 47	52 to 64
Type 'B'	60 to 74	80 to 100

Bodywork and fittings

Torque wrench settings – air conditioning

	lbf ft	Nm
Fan to condenser	6 to 8	8 to 11
Compressor bracket to engine:		
M10	63 to 68	85 to 92
M12	81 to 89	110 to 120
Compressor to bracket and strap	48 to 55	65 to 75

Dimensions and weights – 1985/86

Overall dimensions

	Hatchback	Estate
Length	173.5 in (4.407 m)	177.4 in (4.506 m)
Width (including mirrors):		
Base	71.7 in (1.821 m)	71.7 in (1.821 m)
L	73.5 in (1.867 m)	73.5 in (1.867 m)
GL	75.6 in (1.920 m)	73.5 in (1.867 m)
Ghia	75.6 in (1.920 m)	75.6 in (1.920 m)
Height:		
All except Ghia	55.9 in (1.420 m)	56.8 in (1.443 m)
Ghia	55.9 in (1.420 m)	59.3 in (1.506 m)

Kerb weights

	Hatchback	Estate
1.3 L, 4-speed manual	1020 kg (2249 lb)	–
1.6 L, 4-speed manual	1025 kg (2260 lb)	1075 kg (2370 lb)
1.6 L, 5-speed manual	1035 kg (2282 lb)	1085 kg (2392 lb)
1.8 L, 5-speed manual	1060 kg (2337 lb)	1100 kg (2426 lb)
1.8 L, 4-speed automatic	1060 kg (2337 lb)	1100 kg (2426 lb)
2.0 GL, 5-speed manual	1080 kg (2381 lb)	1120 kg (2470 lb)
2.0 GL, 4-speed automatic	1080 kg (2381 lb)	1120 kg (2470 lb)
For Base deduct from L	10 kg (22 lb) approx	
For GL add to L	15 kg (33 lb) approx	
For Ghia add to L	70 kg (154 lb) approx	

Dimensions and weights – 1987 on

Overall length

Saloon	175.9 in (4468 mm)
Hatchback	174.2 in (4425 mm)
Estate	177.6 in (4511 mm)

Overall width

	75.6 in (1920 mm)

Height (unladen)

Saloon and Hatchback	53.5 in (1358 mm)
Estate	54.6 in (1387 mm)

Weights (kerb)

1.6 Hatchback and Saloon:	
Base 4-speed	2260 lb (1025 kg)
L 4-speed	2271 lb (1030 kg)
L 5-speed and auto	2293 lb (1040 kg)
LX 4-speed	2337 lb (1060 kg)
GL 5-speed and auto	2337 lb (1060 kg)
Ghia 5-speed and auto	2426 lb (1100 kg)
1.8 Hatchback and Saloon:	
L 4-speed	2304 lb (1045 kg)
L 5-speed and auto	2326 lb (1055 kg)
LX 4-speed	2370 lb (1075 kg)
LX 5-speed and auto	2370 lb (1075 kg)
GL 5-speed and auto	2370 lb (1075 kg)
Ghia 5-speed and auto	2459 lb (1115 kg)
2.0 Hatchback and Saloon (carburettor):	
L 5-speed and auto	2326 lb (1055 kg)
LX 5-speed and auto	2370 lb (1075 kg)
GL 5-speed and auto	2392 lb (1085 kg)
Ghia 5-speed and auto	2481 lb (1125 kg)

Under-bonnet view of Sierra 2.0iS

1 Battery	7 Airflow meter	13 Windscreen washer reservoir	18 Brake fluid reservoir
2 Brake servo non-return valve	8 Fuel pressure regulator	14 Coolant expansion tank	19 Fuse box
3 Ignition coil	9 Air intake hose	15 Oil filler cap	20 Windscreen wiper motor
4 Suspension strut top	10 Throttle housing	16 Idle speed control valve	21 Engine oil dipstick
5 Fuel filter	11 Alternator	17 Plenum chamber/intake	
6 Air cleaner	12 VIN plate	manifold	

2.0 Hatchback and Saloon (fuel injection):
    GL5 5-speed and auto .... 2414 lb (1095 kg)
    Ghia 5-speed and auto .... 2503 lb (1135 kg)
1.6 Estate:
    Base 4-speed .... 2381 lb (1080 kg)
    L 4-speed .... 2403 lb (1090 kg)
    L 5-speed and auto .... 2426 lb (1100 kg)
1.8 Estate:
    L 4-speed .... 2426 lb (1100 kg)
    L 5-speed and auto .... 2446 lb (1110 kg)
    GL 5-speed and auto .... 2470 lb (1120 kg)
Ghia 5-speed and auto .... 2558 lb (1160 kg)
2.0 Estate (carburettor):
    L 5-speed and auto .... 2459 lb (1115 kg)
    GL 5-speed and auto .... 2503 lb (1135 kg)
    Ghia 5-speed and auto .... 2591 lb (1175 kg)
2.0 Estate (fuel injection):
    Ghia 5-speed auto .... 2613 lb (1185 kg)

3 Routine maintenance

1   On all models, the 6000 mile service should be carried out at least every 6 months, even if the specified mileage has not been covered. This is because some systems and fluids deteriorate with time as well as with use.
2   Vehicles used under adverse conditions (mainly short trips, extremes of temperature, or full-time towing) may benefit from more frequent engine oil changes than specified.
3   On 1985 2.0 models there is no longer any need to check the idle speed: the management system keeps it correct.
4   On vehicles with air conditioning, follow the maintenance instructions given in Section 17.
5   On fuel injection models, renew the fuel filter every 24 000 miles (Section 7).

4 Engine

Introduction
1   Few changes have been made to the engines fitted to later models. Unless otherwise stated, the procedures in Chapter 1 still apply and also cover the 1.8 version introduced in 1984.
2   When carrying out major work on the 2.0 fuel injection engine, it will be necessary to remove or disconnect fuel injection components instead of the carburettor. Refer to Section 7 for details.
3   On vehicles with air conditioning, any work in the engine bay which entails disconnection of refrigerant pipes must not be undertaken until the air conditioning system has been professionally discharged. Refer to Section 17.

Valve cover fastenings – later models
4   From late 1983, the valve cover is secured by bolts and special reinforcing plates. This change coincides with modifications to the timing cover, valve cover gasket and the valve cover itself. Old and new pattern components are interchangeable only in complete sets.
5   When refitting a new pattern valve cover, arrange the reinforcing plates as detailed in Fig. 13.1 and tighten the bolts in the following stages.

    Stage 1 – Bolts 1 to 6
    Stage 2 – Bolts 7 and 8
    Stage 3 – Bolts 9 and 10
    Stage 4 – Bolts 7 and 8 (again)

Cylinder head bolts – later models
6   From early 1984, the 'star' socket head cylinder head bolts have been replaced by 'T55 Torx' socket head bolts. The two types of bolt head are shown in Fig. 13.2.
7   The appropriate 'Torx' tool will be required for removing and refitting the new type bolts.
8   Revised torque wrench settings apply to the new bolts – see Specifications. There is no need to retighten the bolts after running the engine.
9   'Torx' cylinder head bolts must be renewed every time after slackening.

10   Old and new type bolts are interchangeable, but only in complete sets – the two types must not be mixed on the same engine.

Timing belt tension (later models) – checking and adjustment
11   The timing belt tensioner on later models is not spring-loaded. A different adjustment procedure is used, preferably employing Ford tension gauge 21-113.
12   The engine must be cold when checking belt tension.
13   Gain access to the belt (Chapter 1, Section 11).
14   Turn the crankshaft clockwise, using the crankshaft pulley bolt,

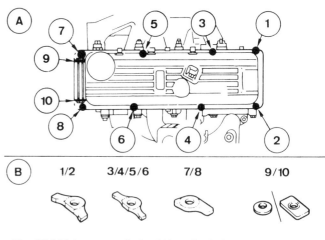

**Fig. 13.1 Valve cover bolts (A) and reinforcing plates (B).
For tightening sequence see text (Sec 4)**

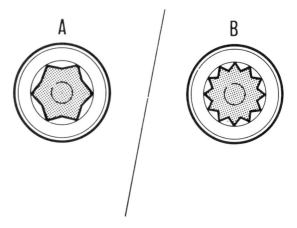

Fig. 13.2 Alternative types of cylinder head bolt (Sec 4)

A   T55 Torx   B   Star

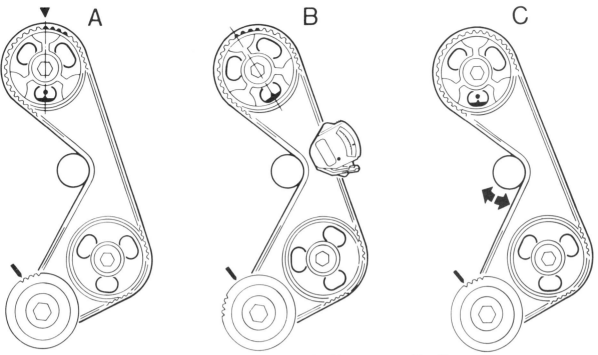

Fig. 13.3 Timing belt tension checking sequence (Sec 4)

A   No 1 at TDC   B   60° BTDC for checking   C   Return to TDC for adjustment

through at least two complete revolutions. Finish with No 1 piston at TDC firing.

15 From this position, turn the crankshaft 60° anti-clockwise. This distance corresponds to three teeth on the camshaft sprocket.

16 The belt tension should now ideally be checked by applying Ford tension gauge 21-113 to the longest run. Desired gauge readings are:

Used belt – 4 to 5
New belt – 10 to 11

17 If the tension gauge is not available, a rough guide is that belt tension is correct when the belt can be twisted 90° in the middle of the longest run with the fingers (photo).

18 If adjustment is necessary, turn the crankshaft clockwise to bring No 1 cylinder to TDC firing.

19 Slacken the belt tensioner fastenings and move the tensioner to increase or decrease the tension as required. Tighten the fastening.

20 Turn the crankshaft 90° clockwise, then turn it anti-clockwise to the position previously used when checking the tension (60° BTDC).

21 Repeat the procedure as necessary until the tension is correct, then refit the belt cover and other disturbed components.

5   Cooling system

Draining and refilling (later models)

1 Some later models are fitted with a radiator drain plug. When present, this should be used in preference to disturbing the bottom hose (photo).

2 1985 model year vehicles are fitted with a bleed spigot on the thermostat housing. In use this spigot is covered with a rubber cap. The cap should be removed when commencing draining, and not refitted until coolant flows from the spigot when refilling (photo).

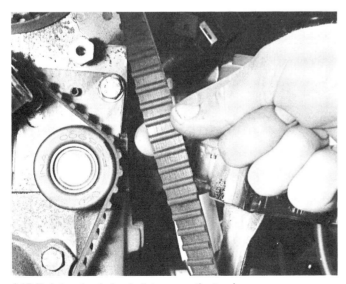

4.17 Twisting the timing belt to assess the tension

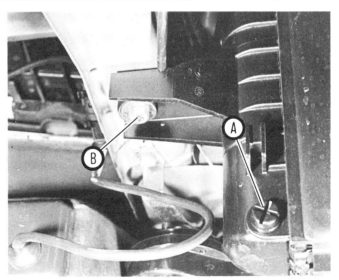

5.1 Radiator drain plug (A) and mounting bolt (B)

5.2 Removing clip from bleed spigot cap

5.4 Radiator upper mounting clip centre plug

Radiator (Sapphire) – removal and refitting
3   The operations are essentially as described in Chapter 2, Section 6, except that the upper fixings are of plastic clip type.
4   Pull out the centre plug and then squeeze the clip retaining tabs together, at the same time lowering the radiator (photo).
5   Removal of the upper and lower sections of the fan shroud will make operations easier. The sections are held together with plastic clips which can be removed after pushing out their centre pins.

6   Fuel system (carburettor models)

Air cleaner (1.8 and later 2.0 models) – removal and refitting
1   Proceed as described in Chapter 3, Section 2, but note that there is an additional retaining screw on top of the valve cover.

Fuel pump – models with air conditioning
2   On models with air conditioning, an electric fuel pump is fitted instead of a mechanical one. Removal and refitting procedures are as follows.
3   Disconnect the battery earth terminal.
4   Raise the vehicle and support it securely on axle stands.
5   Clean the area around the pump mounting just forward of the fuel tank.
6   Using a hose clamping tool, or self-locking pliers, clamp the fuel inlet hose to the pump to prevent loss of fuel then disconnect the hose from the pump.
7   Disconnect the fuel outlet hose from the pump and allow the fuel to drain into a container.
8   Disconnect the multi-pin plug from the pump.
9   Release the pump mounting bracket clamp and slide the pump out of the mounting.
10   Refitting is a reversal of removal, but make sure that the rubber insulator is correctly located around the pump body.

Accelerator cable – removal and refitting (later models)
11   On later models the cable outer is retained by a plastic clip which is withdrawn forwards to release the cable (photo). The tool shown in Chapter 3, Fig. 3.2, is therefore not required.

Fuel vapour separator – description
12   All later carburettor models are fitted with a fuel vapour separator; on all but 2.0 models the separator incorporates a pressure regulator as well (photo).

13   The function of the separator is to purge fuel vapour from the fuel line, so avoiding hot start difficulties.

Fuel vapour separator – removal and refitting
14   Identify the fuel supply, fuel return and carburettor supply lines. Remove the hose clips, then disconnect and plug the lines. Be prepared for fuel spillage.
15   Remove the two securing screws and remove the separator complete with bracket.
16   Refit in the reverse order of removal, using new hose clips if necessary.

Carburettor adjustments – warning
17   Certain adjusting screws are 'tamperproofed' at the factory by means of seals, caps or similar devices. The object is to discourage, and detect, adjustment by unqualified persons.
18   In some European countries (though not yet in the UK) it is an offence to have on the road a vehicle with missing tamperproof seals.
19   Before removing any tamperproof devices, satisfy yourself that you are not in breach of local or national anti-pollution laws by so doing. Do not remove any such device from a vehicle which is still under warranty.
20   On completion of adjustments, fit new tamperproof devices where these are required by law.

VV carburettor – diaphragm renewal
21   When overhauling a VV carburettor, note that the latest type of diaphragm is coloured blue. The old type was coloured black. A blue diaphragm should be used for renewal of both old and new types.
22   The colour of the diaphragm fitted to a particular carburettor can be ascertained without dismantling (Fig. 13.7).

VV carburettor – accelerator pump repair
23   If malfunction of the accelerator pump is suspected, obtain a repair kit from a Ford dealer.
24   Remove and drain the carburettor, remove the pump cover and extract the pump components. Discard everything except the spring. Discard the pump cover also, but keep the screws.
25   Fit the new components as shown in Fig. 13.8, being careful not to obscure the vacuum passage in the mating flange (the hole in the diaphragm goes over the passage). When fitting the coloured spacer, in the absence of instructions to the contrary in the kit, fit the black spacer to 1.3 models and the blue spacer to 1.6 models.
26   Secure the pump cover and refit the carburettor.

VV carburettor – correction of unstable idle
27   Should the idle speed and/or mixture prove impossible to set due to apparent instability, proceed as follows.

6.11 Accelerator cable securing clip partly withdrawn

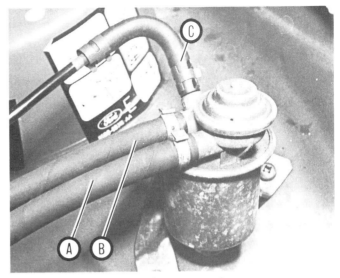

6.12 Fuel vapour separator and pressure regulator
A   Fuel supply hose   C   Fuel return hose
B   Carburettor fuel feed hose

Fig. 13.4 Air cleaner retaining screws (arrowed) (Sec 6)

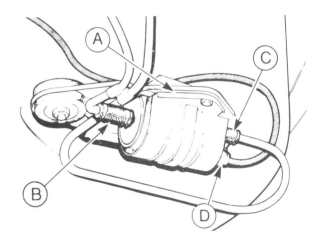

Fig. 13.5 Electric fuel pump (Sec 6)

A   Bracket   C   Fuel outlet
B   Fuel inlet   D   Wiring connector

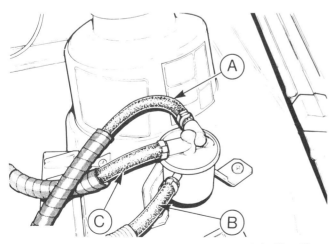

Fig. 13.6 Fuel vapour separator – 2.0 models (Sec 6)

A   Fuel return   C   Carburettor supply
B   Fuel supply

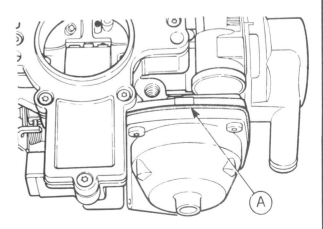

Fig. 13.7 VV Carburettor diaphragm exposed edge (Sec 6)

28 Remove the air cleaner and disconnect the battery earth lead.
29 Remove the choke cover, making alignment marks for reassembly if none are present. Remove the gasket.
30 Find the three screws which secure the choke housing to the carburettor body. Slacken each screw slightly, then tighten it to 2 Nm (1.5 lbf ft).
31 Refit the gasket and choke cover, making sure that the gasket is correctly located and observing the choke cover alignment marks. Adjust the idle speed and mixture (Chapter 3, Section 11).

Carburettor speed control system – description and maintenance

32 Fitted to later 1.3 and 1.6 models with a VV carburettor, the carburettor speed control system aims to improve driveability during the warm-up phase in cold ambient conditions.
33 The main component of the system is the carburettor speed control valve (CSCV). Under the influence of manifold vacuum the CSCV admits extra air to the inlet manifold, so weakening what would otherwise be an excessively rich mixture.
34 Vacuum is applied to the CSCV via a delay valve, a ported vacuum switch (PVS) and a thermal vacuum switch (TVS). The delay valve prevents premature operation of the CSCV during start-up, and damps out the effect of sudden changes in throttle position. The PVS responds to coolant temperature, only allowing vacuum to pass to the CSCV when coolant temperature is below 35°C (95°F). The TVS responds to air temperature, only allowing vacuum to pass when air temperature is below 10°C (50°F). Thus the CSCV is only activated when both coolant and ambient air temperatures are low.

35 Maintenance of the system is confined to checking the security and condition of the various hoses. Repair of individual components is not possible.
36 Vacuum switches may be tested by feeling for the presence or absence of vacuum under the appropriate conditions with the engine running. Testing of other components is by substitution of known good units.

Weber 2V carburettor (1.6 Economy) – description

37 The twin venturi (2V) Weber carburettor fitted to 1.6 Economy models is very similar to that fitted to 2.0 models and described in Chapter 3.
38 The main difference is in the method used to open the secondary throttle valve: on 1.6 Economy models this is achieved by vacuum developed in the primary venturi. Thus the secondary throttle valve will not open until engine speed and load warrant it, even if the driver floors the throttle.
39 Other differences from the earlier Weber carburettor are of a minor nature.

Weber 2V carburettor (1.6 Economy) – idle adjustments

40 Refer to Chapter 3, Section 11 for the procedure, and to Fig. 13.14 for the location of the adjustment screws.

Weber 2V carburettor (1.6 Economy) – overhaul

41 Refer to Chapter 3, Section 15. Note that this carburettor has no low vacuum enrichment device, and refer to Fig. 13.15 for the details of the secondary throttle vacuum unit. For float level adjustment see Fig. 13.19.

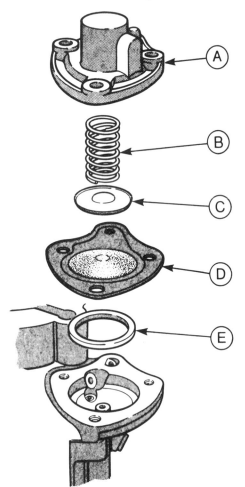

Fig. 13.8 VV carburettor accelerator pump components (Sec 6)

A Cover   D Diaphragm
B Spring   E Coloured spacer
C Plate

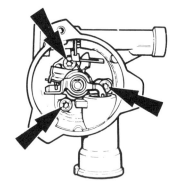

Fig. 13.9 VV carburettor choke housing fixing screws (arrowed) (Sec 6)

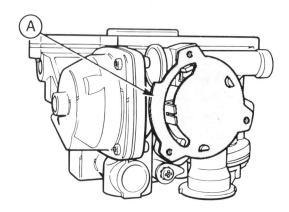

Fig. 13.10 VV carburettor choke cover gasket (A) correctly aligned (Sec 6)

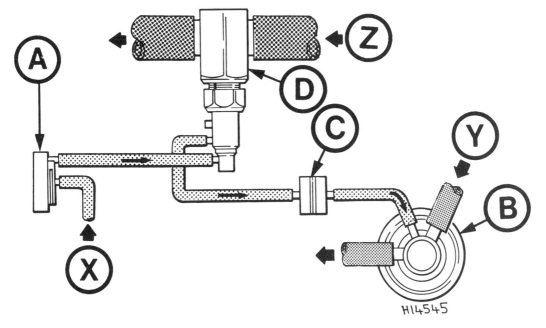

Fig. 13.11 Schematic view of the CSC system (Sec 6)

A TVS
B CSCV
C Delay valve
D PVS
X Manifold vacuum
Y From air cleaner
Z Coolant

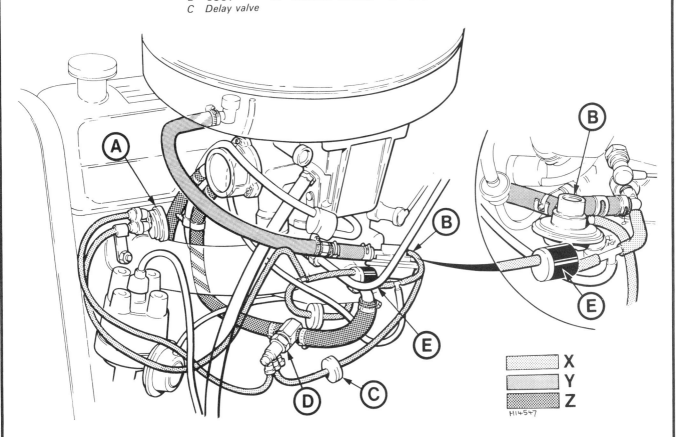

Fig. 13.12 Location of CSC system components (Sec 6)

A TVS
B CSCV
C Delay valve
D PVS
E Fuel trap (1.6 only)
X Manifold vacuum
Y From air cleaner
Z Coolant

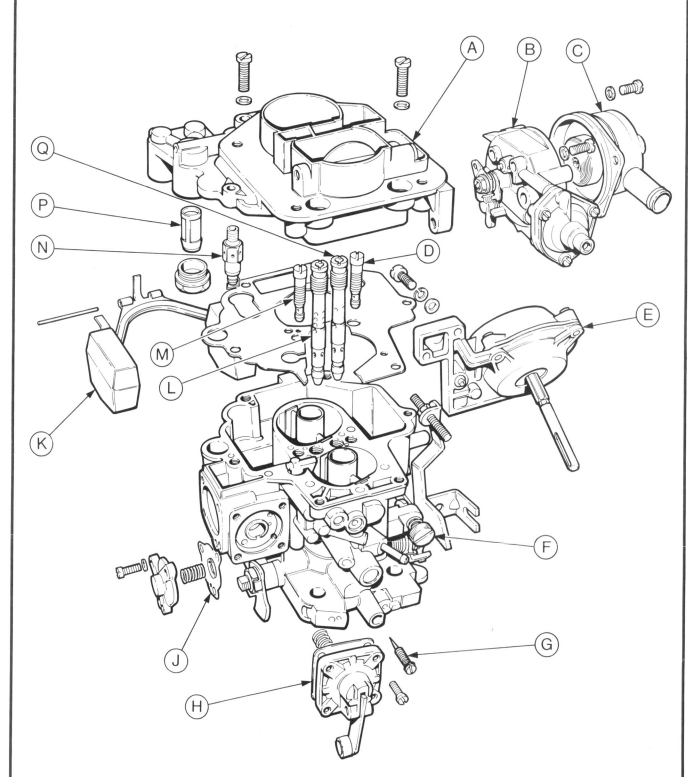

Fig. 13.13 Exploded view of Weber 2V carburettor fitted to 1.6 Economy models (Sec 6)

A   Cover
B   Choke lever housing
C   Choke bimetal housing
D   Secondary idle jet

E   Secondary throttle vacuum
    unit
F   Idle speed adjustment screw
G   Idle mixture adjustment
    screw

H   Accelerator pump diaphragm
J   Power valve diaphragm
K   Float
L   Primary emulsion tube

N   Needle valve
P   Fuel inlet filter
Q   Secondary emulsion tube

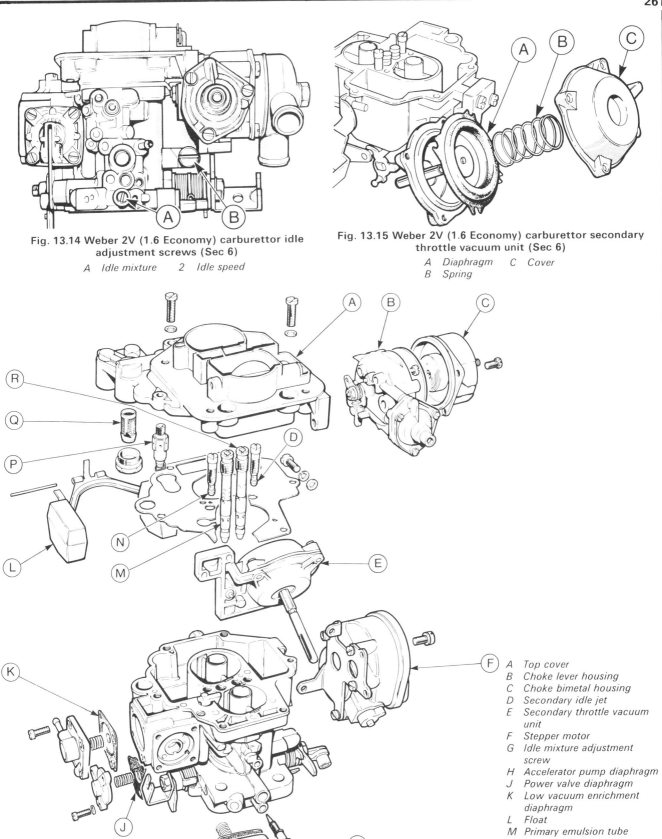

Fig. 13.14 Weber 2V (1.6 Economy) carburettor idle
adjustment screws (Sec 6)

A   Idle mixture   2   Idle speed

Fig. 13.15 Weber 2V (1.6 Economy) carburettor secondary
throttle vacuum unit (Sec 6)

A   Diaphragm   C   Cover
B   Spring

A   Top cover
B   Choke lever housing
C   Choke bimetal housing
D   Secondary idle jet
E   Secondary throttle vacuum
    unit
F   Stepper motor
G   Idle mixture adjustment
    screw
H   Accelerator pump diaphragm
J   Power valve diaphragm
K   Low vacuum enrichment
    diaphragm
L   Float
M   Primary emulsion tube
N   Primary idle jet
P   Needle valve
Q   Fuel inlet filter
R   Secondary emulsion tube

Fig. 13.16 Exploded view of Weber carburettor fitted to
later 2.0 models (Sec 6)

Weber 2V carburettor (1.6 Economy) – automatic choke adjustment

42 Refer to Chapter 3, Section 16, and to the Specifications at the beginning of this Chapter. Note that fast idle speed is adjusted with the screw on the third (middle) step of the fast idle cam. The choke phasing adjustment is not required.

Weber 2V carburettor (later 2.0 models) – description

43 The twin venturi (2V) Weber carburettor fitted to 1985 model year vehicles with the 2 litre engine is similar to earlier Webers. Like the version fitted to 1.6 Economy models, opening of the secondary throttle valve is controlled by vacuum developed in the primary venturi.
44 A unique feature of this carburettor is the stepper motor attached to the throttle linkage. This motor, under the control of the ESC II module, maintains a steady idle speed; it also controls the throttle position during deceleration, start-up and immediately after shut-off. Optimum fuel economy and good emission levels are thereby achieved.
45 The automatic choke on this carburettor is heated electrically and not by coolant.

Weber 2V carburettor (later 2.0 models) – idle adjustments

46 The idle speed should not be adjusted at the carburettor, since it is controlled by the ESC II module. The idle speed can be adjusted to a limited extent using the yellow wire described in Section 9, paragraphs 28 to 36.
47 Idle mixture can be adjusted as described in Chapter 3, Section 11. Refer to Fig. 13.17.

Weber 2V carburettor (later 2.0 models) – removal and refitting

48 Disconnect the battery earth lead.
49 Remove the air cleaner.
50 Disconnect the choke and stepper motor wiring. The stepper motor multi-plug locking device must be depressed to release the plug. Pull on the plug, not on the wires.
51 Unclip the throttle arm from the throttle lever and remove the throttle cable bracket.
52 Disconnect and plug the fuel line from the carburettor. If a crimped hose clip is fitted, cut it off and obtain a new clip for refitting.
53 Disconnect the vacuum pipe(s) from the carburettor, noting their connecting points if there is any possibility of confusion.
54 Remove the four securing nuts and lift off the carburettor. Recover the gasket.
55 Refit in the reverse order of removal.

Weber 2V carburettor (later 2.0 models) – overhaul

56 Refer to Chapter 3, Section 15. After removal of the stepper motor, which is secured by four screws, the procedure is identical. For float level adjustment see Figs. 13.19 and 13.20.

Weber 2V carburettor (later 2.0 models) – automatic choke adjustment

57 Refer to Chapter 3, Section 16 and to the Specifications at the beginning of this Chapter. Note that this choke is heated electrically rather than by coolant, and that the choke phasing and fast idle adjustments are not required.

Fig. 13.17 Idle mixture adjusting screw (arrowed) – Weber 2V carburettor (later 2.0 models) (Sec 6)

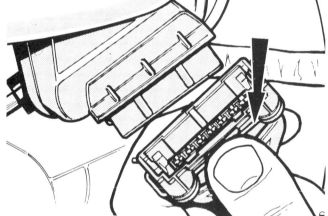

Fig. 13.18 Depressing locking clip (arrowed) when disconnecting stepper motor multi-pin plug (Sec 6)

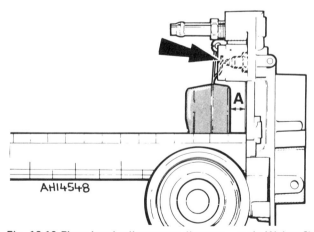

Fig. 13.19 Float level adjustment diagram – early Weber 2V carburettor (Sec 6)

Adjusting tang arrowed   A   Float height (see Specifications)

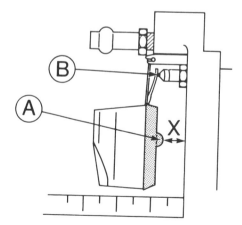

Fig. 13.20 Float level adjustment diagram – later Weber 2V carburettor (Sec 6)

A   Raised portion of float   X   Float height (see
B   Adjustment tang   Specifications)

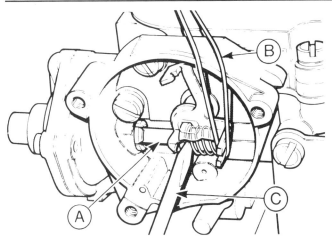

Fig. 13.21 Choke pull-down check – Weber 2V carburettor (Sec 6)

A   *Pull-down diaphragm rod*   C   *Small screwdriver*
B   *Rubber band*

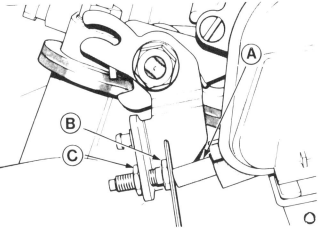

Fig. 13.22 Stepper motor adjustment – Weber 2V carburettor (Sec 6)

A   *Plunger*   C   *Locknut*
B   *Adjustment screw*

Weber 2V carburettor (later 2.0 models) – stepper motor adjustment
58 After overhaul, or if the setting has been disturbed, an initial adjustment should be made to the stepper motor as follows.
59 With the carburettor refitted, run the engine until it reaches operating temperature. Connect a tachometer to the engine. The air cleaner must be fitted and all electrical loads (lights, heater blower etc) switched off.
60 Accelerate the engine to a speed greater than 2500 rpm, allow it to return to idle, then repeat. Insert a 1.0 mm (0.04 in) feeler blade between the stepper motor plunger and the adjusting screw.
61 With the feeler blade in place, engine speed should be 875 ± 25 rpm. Release the locknut and turn the plunger adjusting screw if necessary to achieve this, then tighten the locknut.
62 Again accelerate the engine to more than 2500 rpm twice, re-insert the feeler blade and check that the engine speed is still as specified.
63 Remove the feeler blade. Stop and restart the engine, watching the stepper motor plunger to see that it goes through its cycle (Section 8).
64 Check the idle mixture (CO) adjustment and correct if necessary.
Note: *Where fitted, the yellow idle speed adjusting lead should be disconnected from under the coil securing screw before adjustments commence, and refitted on completion.*

Weber 2V carburettor – choke vacuum pull-down
65 On all vehicles fitted with a Weber 2V carburettor, should cold starting prove hesitant or difficult, the vacuum pull-down adjustment may be increased to 8.0 mm (0.31 in).
66 The adjustment procedure is described in Chapter 3, Section 16.

Pierburg 2V carburettor – description
67 The Pierburg twin venturi (2V) carburettor fitted to 1.8 models is similar to the Weber 2V fitted to 1.6 Economy models. The opening of the throttle valves is sequential, the secondary throttle valve opening being controlled by vacuum developed in the primary venturi.
68 The automatic choke is heated both electrically and by coolant; electrical heating is via a manifold-mounted thermoswitch, which opens when the coolant temperature reaches a certain value. An external vacuum pull-down unit opens the choke valve under the influence of manifold vacuum.
69 An accelerator pump delivers extra fuel when the throttle is opened suddenly. A power valve enriches the mixture under the full throttle conditions.
70 An unusual feature of this carburettor is that the float level cannot be adjusted, neither can the needle valve be renewed.

Pierburg 2V carburettor – idle adjustments
71 Refer to Chapter 3, Section 11, and to Fig. 13.24.

Pierburg 2V carburettor – removal and refitting
72 Disconnect the battery earth lead.
73 Remove the air cleaner.

74 Disconnect the automatic choke electrical lead from the manifold thermoswitch.
75 Unclip the throttle arm from the throttle lever (photo).
76 Disconnect and plug the fuel line from the carburettor. If a crimped hose clip is fitted, cut it off and obtain a worm drive clip for refitting (photo).
77 Depressurize the cooling system by removing the expansion tank cap, then disconnect and plug the automatic choke coolant hoses (photo).
78 Remove the three Torx screws which secure the carburettor to the manifold and remove the carburettor (photo).
79 Refit in the reverse order of removal. Check the idle speed and mixture on completion.

Pierburg 2V carburettor – dismantling (carburettor removed)
Top cover
80 Remove the five screws (four on later models) which secure the top cover (photo).
81 Lift the cover off the carburettor body, noting the relationship between the fast idle cam and the throttle linkage (photo).
82 With the cover removed, the main jets are accessible (photo). Apart from these jets and the idle jet (on top of the cover), no other jets, tubes or valves should be removed. Do not attempt to remove the float or the needle valve.
83 The fuel inlet pipe may be removed by unscrewing it. It incorporates a filter which cannot be renewed separately (photo).

Secondary throttle vacuum unit
84 Remove the two securing screws and prise free the balljoint to remove the vacuum unit (photo).
85 Do not attempt to dismantle the vacuum unit. No spares for it are available.
Accelerator pump
86 Remove the four retaining screws from the pump cover (photo).
87 Remove the cover, diaphragm, spring, seal retainer and seal. Note the orientation of the seal retainer (photos).
Power valve
88 Remove the two securing screws and remove the valve complete (photo).
89 Carefully release the nylon clips with a small screwdriver and separate the valve into its component parts (photo).
Automatic choke
90 Remove the central bolt from the water jacket and take off the jacket. Note the O-rings under the head of the bolt and round the rim of the jacket (photo).
91 Look for alignment marks on the bimetal housing and the choke lever carrier. If none are present, make some. Remove the three screws which secure the clamp ring and take off the clamp ring and bimetal housing (photos).

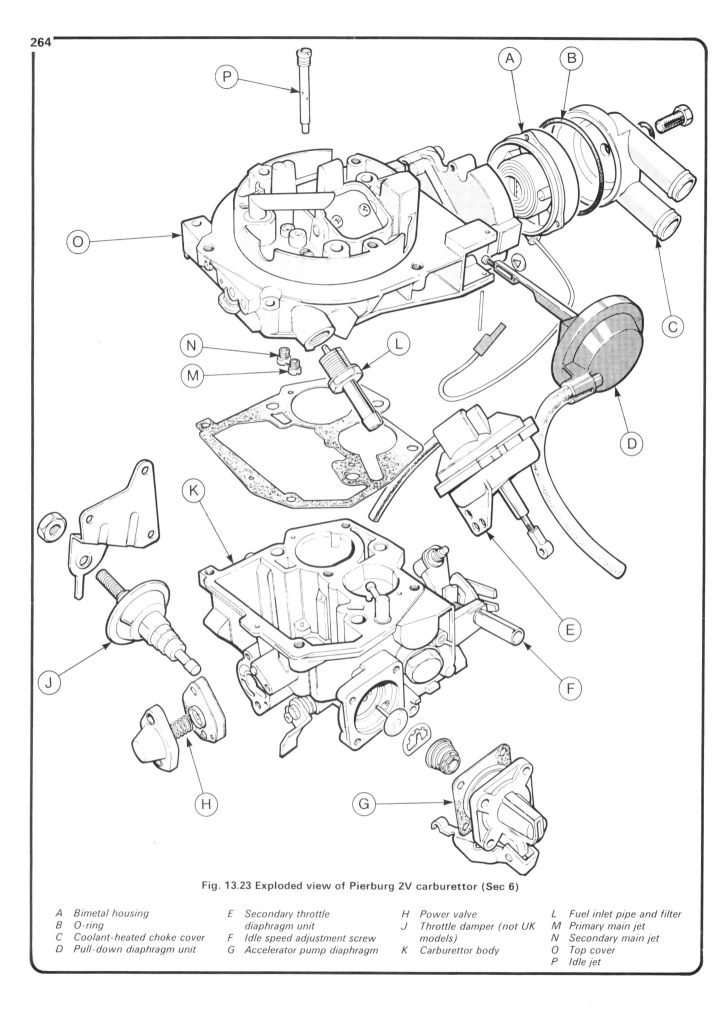

Fig. 13.23 Exploded view of Pierburg 2V carburettor (Sec 6)

A Bimetal housing
B O-ring
C Coolant-heated choke cover
D Pull-down diaphragm unit

E Secondary throttle
   diaphragm unit
F Idle speed adjustment screw
G Accelerator pump diaphragm

H Power valve
J Throttle damper (not UK
   models)
K Carburettor body

L Fuel inlet pipe and filter
M Primary main jet
N Secondary main jet
O Top cover
P Idle jet

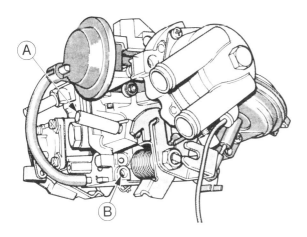

Fig. 13.24 Pierburg 2V carburettor adjustment screws
(Sec 6)

A Idle speed screw   *B Idle mixture screw*

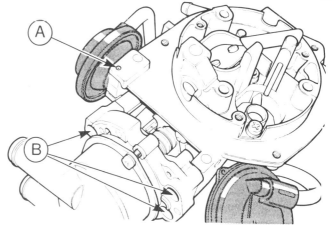

Fig. 13.25 Choke pull-down diaphragm unit removal –
Pierburg 2V carburettor (Sec 6)

A Roll pin   *B Choke lever housing screws*

6.75 Throttle arm-to-lever clip (arrowed)

6.76 Crimped type (production) hose clip (arrowed)

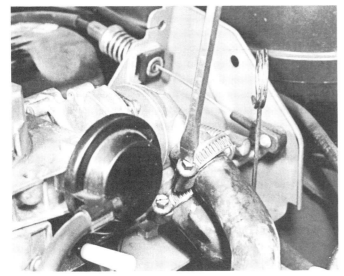

6.77 Disconnecting coolant hose from automatic choke

6.78 Removing caburettor fixing screws (arrowed)

6.80 Carburettor top cover fixing screws.
Later models have four screws, not five

6.81 Removing top cover (Pierburg 2V
carburettor)

6.82 Primary (A) and secondary (B) main
jets (Pierburg 2V carburettor)

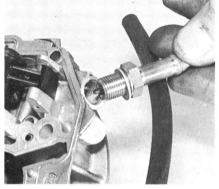

6.83 Fuel inlet pipe with integral filter

6.84 Removing secondary throttle vacuum
unit (Pierburg 2V carburettor)

6.86 Removing accelerator pump cover
(Pierburg 2V carburettor)

6.87A Accelerator pump diaphragm
(Pierburg 2V carburettor)

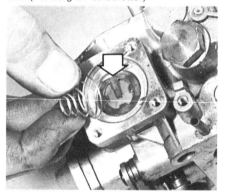

6.87B Accelerator pump spring – retainer
flat (arrowed)

6.87C Accelerator pump seal

92 The choke lever carrier can be removed from the carburettor body, either with or without the bimetal housing and water jacket, after removing its securing screws (photo).
93 The choke pull-down diaphragm assembly can be removed after removal of the choke lever carrier by driving out its roll pin and prising off the star clip.

Pierburg 2V carburettor – reassembly
94 Use new gaskets, O-rings, etc during reassembly and (where applicable) new diaphragm and other components contained in repair kits.
95 Reassemble in the reverse order of dismantling. When fitting the top cover, make sure that the gasket is the right way round and that the fuel riser aligns with its pick-up channel (Fig. 13.27).
96 When refitting the choke lever carrier, make sure that the linkage is correctly engaged. Observe the alignment marks when securing the bimetal housing. Any three of the six clamp ring screw holes can be used.

97 Accelerator pump delivery is determined by the position of the lever operating cam (photo). This should not be adjusted, not least because the desired delivery quantity is not known.
98 To check the choke pull-down, position the fast idle screw on the highest step of the cam. Press the pull-down adjusting screw towards the pull-down diaphragm and measure the choke valve opening with a twist drill or gauge rod of the specified diameter. Adjust if necessary using a 2 mm Allen key (photo).
99 Adjust the idle speed and mixture, and the fast idle speed, after refitting.

Pierburg 2V carburettor – fast idle adjustment
100 The carburettor must be installed, the engine warmed up, and the idle speed and mixture correctly adjusted.
101 Remove the air cleaner.
102 With the engine running, position the fast idle screw on the lowest (6th) step of the fast idle cam. Measure the engine speed and compare it with that given in the Specifications.

6.88 Removing the power valve

6.89 Power valve components

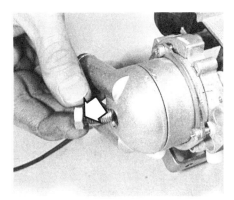

6.90 Choke cover retaining bolt – O-ring seal (arrowed)

6.91A Choke housing-to-carrier alignment marks (arrowed)

6.91B Removing clamp ring and bimetal housing

6.92 Removing choke lever carrier

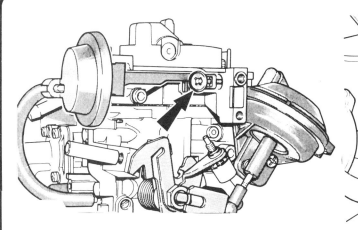

Fig. 13.26 Choke pull-down diaphragm unit removal – Pierburg 2V carbruettor (Sec 6)

Star clip (arrowed) must be prised off

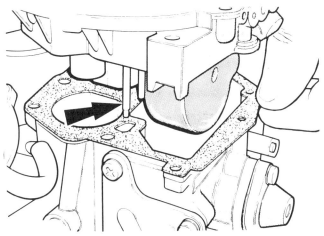

Fig. 13.27 Fuel riser (arrowed) must enter its pick-up channel when reassembling Pierburg 2V carburettor (Sec 6)

103 If adjustment is necessary, remove the tamperproof plug from the fast idle screw by crushing it with pliers. Stop the engine and open the throttle to gain access to the screw with a small screwdriver. Turn the screw a small amount clockwise to increase the speed, anti-clockwise to reduce it, then reseat the screw on the lowest step of the cam and recheck the engine speed. Repeat as necessary.
104 Fit a tamperproof cap where this is required by law, then refit the air cleaner.

Fuel cooling blower – 2.0 litre OHC engine (pre-1985)
105 During extremely hot weather (32°C/90°F or above), problems of hesitation may be experienced on restarting after a long journey or period of idling.
106 This is due to high under bonnet temperatures causing fuel vapourisation, and can be overcome by fitting a fuel cooling blower motor and ducting system available from your Ford dealer.

6.97 Accelerator pump operating cam (arrowed)

6.98 Choke pull-down adjustment

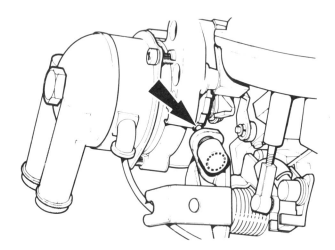

**Fig. 13.28 Fast idle screw on lowest (6th) step of cam –
Pierburg 2V carburettor (Sec 6)**

107 It is emphasised that this is not a common problem and will only occur under the severest of the aforementioned conditions.
108 Your Ford dealer should be consulted if it is felt that this problem is evident.

Engine conditions required for operation on unleaded fuel
109 To run an engine on unleaded fuel, certain criteria must be met, and it may be helpful to first describe the various terms used for the different types of fuel.
110 **Normal fuel:** In addition to the natural lead content found in crude oil, lead content of 0.4 g/litre is added during manufacture.
111 **Low lead fuel:** Fuel which has a low amount of lead added during manufacture (0.15 g/litre), in addition to the natural lead found in crude oil.
112 **Unleaded fuel:** Has no lead added during manufacture, but still has the natural lead content of crude oil.
113 **Lead free fuel:** Contains no lead. It has no lead added during manufacture, and the natural lead content is refined out. This type of fuel is **not** available for general use and should not be confused with unleaded fuel.
114 To run an engine continuously on unleaded fuel, suitable hardened valve seat inserts must be fitted to the engine.
115 The 'B' series OHC engines fitted to the Sierra range which have suitable valve seats fitted at manufacture can be identified by letters stamped on the cylinder head next to No 4 spark plug as follows:

1.6 litre A–K–M–MM–N
1.8 litre S
2.0 litre A–L–P–PP–R

Note: *Some earlier engines (those stamped with a letter A) were designed to run on Liquid Petroleum Gas, and these engines may also be run on unleaded fuel.*
116 Vehicles which have no identification letter stamped on the cylinder head as above, and are not fitted with suitable valve seats, may still be run on unleaded fuel (although continuous use is not recommended), provided that every fourth tank filling is of normal fuel, ie – three tanks of unleaded fuel followed by one tank of normal fuel.
117 When running a vehicle on unleaded fuel, the ignition timing **must** be retarded as described in Section 9.

7   Fuel injection system

Description
1   The fuel injection system is of the Bosch L-Jetronic type. The system is under the overall control of the EEC IV (electronic engine control) module, which also regulates ignition timing.
2   Fuel is supplied by an electric pump via a pressure regulator. The four fuel injectors receive an electrical pulse once per crankshaft revolution. The length of the pulse determines the amount of fuel injected; pulse length is computed by the EEC IV module on the basis of information received from the various sensors.
3   Inducted air passes through a vane airflow meter (VAF). A flap in the meter is deflected in proportion to the airflow; this deflection is converted into an electrical signal for the EEC IV module. An adjustable bypass channel provides the means of idle mixture adjustment.
4   A throttle position sensor (TPS) enables the EEC IV module to read not only throttle position but also its rate of change. Extra fuel can thus be provided for acceleration when the throttle is opened suddenly. Information from the TPS is also used in applying fuel cut-off on the overrun.
5   Idle speed is controlled by a variable orifice solenoid valve which regulates the passage of air bypassing the throttle valve. The valve is under the control of the EEC IV module; there is no provision for direct adjustment of the idle speed.
6   Other sensors inform the EEC module of coolant and air temperature; on automatic transmission models another sensor registers the change from P or N to a drive range, and causes the idle speed to be adjusted accordingly.
7   When air conditioning is fitted, a signal from the compressor clutch to the EEC IV module enables idle speed to be maintained despite the load imposed by the compressor.

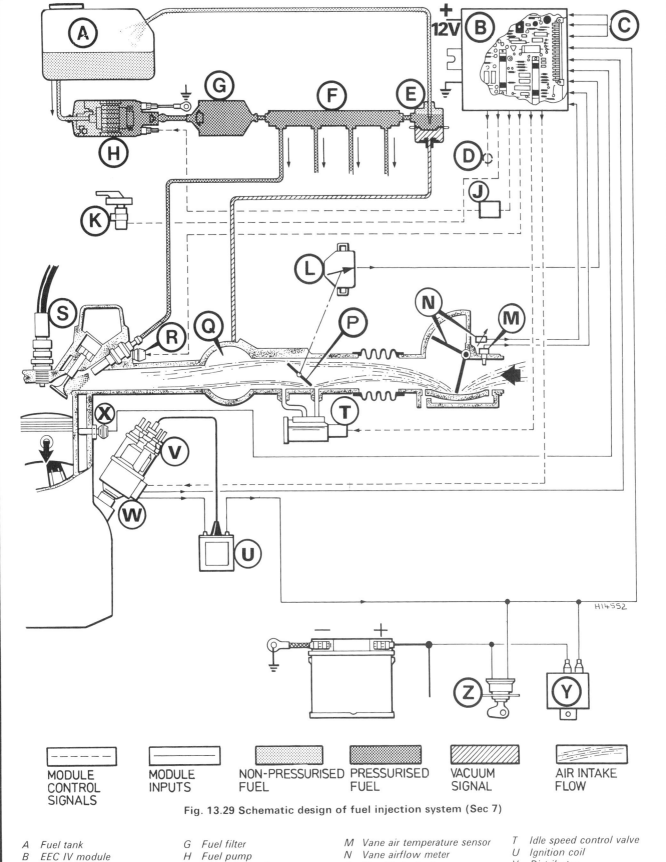

H14552

MODULE CONTROL SIGNALS	MODULE INPUTS	NON-PRESSURISED FUEL	PRESSURISED FUEL	VACUUM SIGNAL	AIR INTAKE FLOW

Fig. 13.29 Schematic design of fuel injection system (Sec 7)

A   Fuel tank
B   EEC IV module
C   Module inputs
D   Self-test output
E   Fuel pressure regulator
F   Fuel rail

G   Fuel filter
H   Fuel pump
J   Fuel pump relay
K   CVT transducer (not UK models)
L   Throttle position sensor

M   Vane air temperature sensor
N   Vane airflow meter
P   Throttle butterfly
Q   Intake manifold
R   Fuel injector
S   Spark plug

T   Idle speed control valve
U   Ignition coil
V   Distributor
W   Ignition module
X   Coolant temperature sensor
Y   Power relay
Z   Ignition switch

Air cleaner element – removal and refitting

8   Release the four retaining clips and lift off the air cleaner lid. The airflow meter is attached to it: be careful not to strain the wiring or displace the air intake hose.

9   Lift out the old element, noting which way up it is fitted.

10 Wipe clean inside the air cleaner housing, then fit the new element, sealing lip uppermost (photo).

11 Refit the air cleaner lid and secure with the spring clips (photo).

Idle adjustment

12 Idle speed is controlled by the EEC IV module and the only means of adjustment is by using the yellow wire described in Section 9, paragraphs 28 to 36. If a CO meter (exhaust gas analyser) is available, the idle mixture can be checked and adjusted as follows. Refer to Section 6, paragraphs 17 to 20.

13 Have the engine at normal operating temperature and connect a CO meter and tachometer to it.

14 Run the engine at 3000 rpm for 15 seconds, then allow it to idle. Read the CO level and compare it with the value specified.

15 If adjustment is necessary, remove the tamperproof plug from the base of the airflow meter. Turn the mixture adjusting screw until the CO level is correct (photo).

16 If the above procedure takes more than 30 seconds, run the engine at 3000 rpm for 15 seconds before proceeding further. Repeat this every 30 seconds until adjustment is complete.

17 On completion, fit a new tamperproof cap where required by law.

Throttle position sensor – removal and refitting

18 Disconnect the battery earth lead.

19 Free the sensor multi-plug from its clip below the idle speed control valve. Disconnect the multi-plug, pulling on the plug halves, not on the wiring.

20 Relieve the locktabs, make alignment marks and remove the throttle position sensor retaining bolts (photo). Pull the sensor off the shaft.

21 Do not rotate the centre of the sensor past its normal limits of travel.

22 Refit in the reverse order to removal, making sure that the sensor is fitted the right way round and that the flat on the centre of the sensor goes over the flat on the shaft. Observing the previously made alignment marks, fit and tighten the bolts and secure with the locktabs.

23 Reconnect the battery earth lead and check for correct operation.

Idle speed control valve – removal and refitting

24 Disconnect the battery earth lead.

25 Disconnect the multi-plug from the idle speed control valve by releasing the retaining clip and pulling on the plug, not on the wiring (photo).

26 Remove the two retaining nuts and take the valve off the inlet manifold (photo). Recover the gasket.

27 Clean the valve and manifold mating surface before refitting. Take care not to introduce dirt into the manifold.

28 Refit in the reverse order of removal, using a new gasket.

29 Reconnect the battery earth lead on completion. Start the engine and check that the idle is steady: if not, check for air leaks around the valve.

Airflow meter – removal and refitting

30 Disconnect the battery earth lead.

31 Release the locking clip and disconnect the multi-plug from the airflow meter, pulling on the plug, not on the wiring (photo).

7.10 Air cleaner element

7.11 Air cleaner lid toggle clip

7.15 Airflow meter removed and inverted to show mixture adjusting screw tamperproof plug (arrowed)

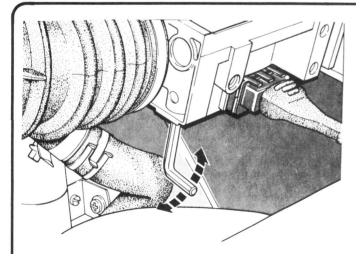

Fig. 13.30 Adjusting the idle mixture (Sec 7)

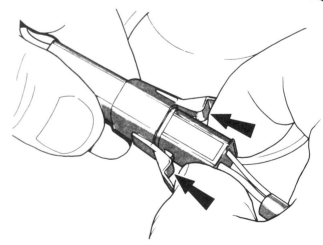

Fig. 13.31 Raising locktabs to disconnect throttle position sensor multi-pin plug (Sec 7)

32 Remove the air intake hose from the airflow meter.

33 Release the four clips which secure the top of the air cleaner. Remove the air cleaner top and the airflow meter together.

34 Remove the four bolts to separate the air cleaner from the airflow meter (photo).

35 Refit in the reverse order of removal. Make sure that the seal in the air cleaner top is correctly located, and that the intake hose clip is correctly aligned.

36 Check the exhaust CO level on completion and adjust if necessary.

Fuel injectors – removal and refitting

37 Disconnect the battery earth lead.

38 Unclip and remove the air intake hose, disconnecting the crankcase ventilation pipe from it.

39 Disconnect the HT leads from the distributor cap and move them aside. Remove the screening can and the distributor cap.

40 Disconnect the multi-plugs from the idle speed control valve, the throttle position sensor and the coolant temperature sensor.

41 Disconnect the vacuum and fuel return pipes from the fuel pressure regulator, and the fuel feed pipe from the fuel rail. Be prepared for some fuel spillage.

42 Disconnect the multi-plugs from the injectors (photo).

43 Remove the three bolts which secure the fuel rail (photo). Remove the rail complete with injectors and fuel pressure regulator.

44 To remove an injector from the rail, extract its retaining clip.

45 Fit new seals to the tops and bottoms of *all* injectors, even if only one was disturbed. Coat the seals with silicone grease to Ford specification ESEM-1C171A and fit new clips.

46 Refit in the reverse order to removal. Make sure that all multi-plugs are securely fastened.

47 Check the exhaust CO level on completion and adjust if necessary.

7.20 Throttle position sensor retaining bolts (arrowed)

7.25 Disconnecting the idle speed control valve multi-plug. Do not disconnect by pulling on the wire

7.26 Unscrewing an idle speed control valve retaining nut

7.31 Disconnecting airflow meter multi-pin plug

7.34 Air cleaner-to-airflow meter bolts

7.42 Fuel injector multi-pin plug disconnected. Fuel rail front fixing bolt (arrowed)

7.43 Fuel rail rear fixing bolts (arrowed)

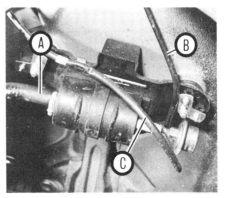

7.48 Fuel pump and pressure regulator
A Inlet hose   C Electrical feed
B Outlet hose

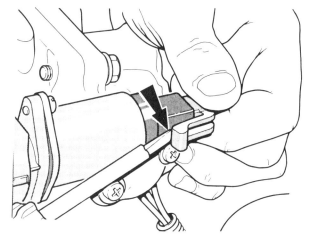

Fig. 13.32 Prising up retaining clip (arrowed) to release idle speed control valve multi-pin plug (Sec 7)

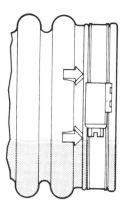

Fig. 13.33 Air intake hose clip correctly aligned (Sec 7)

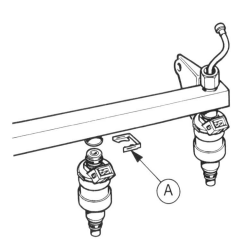

Fig. 13.34 Injector-to-rail retaining clip (A) (Sec 7)

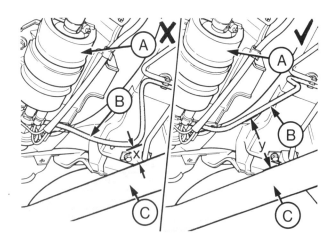

Fig. 13.35 Correct and incorrect method of fitting fuel pressure line to pump and damper (Sec 7)

A　Pump　　　　　X = 30 mm (1.2 in) approx
B　Pressure line　Y = 100 mm (3.9 in) approx
C　Exhaust pipe

Fuel pump – removal and refitting
48 The fuel pump is located underneath the car, next to the fuel tank (photo).
49 Disconnect the battery earth lead.
50 Raise and securely support the rear of the car.
51 Clamp the pump inlet hose to minimise fuel loss. Use a clamp with protected jaws to avoid damage to the hose.
52 Position a drain pan beneath the pump and disconnect the inlet and outlet hoses, be prepared for fuel spillage, and possibly some spray from the outlet side if the system is still under pressure. Plug the hoses to prevent leakage and dirt entry.
53 Disconnect the wiring multi-plug, slacken the clamp bolt and remove the pump from its clamp.
54 A flow damper is fitted to the fuel pump output side. Should the damper fail, the pump will become noisy.
55 When refitting the damper of the pump, be careful to route the fuel pressure line correctly. It is possible accidentally to reverse the banjo connection, so bringing the fuel pressure line too close to the exhaust pipe (Fig. 13.35).
56 After refitting and securing the pump, but before lowering the car, reconnect the battery and have an assistant switch the ignition on and off several times to pressurize the system. Check for leaks around the pump; if all is satisfactory, switch off the ignition and lower the car.

Fuel filter – renewal
57 The fuel filter is located under the bonnet, on the left-hand inner wing (photo).
58 Disconnect the battery earth lead.
59 Position a drain pan underneath the filter. Disconnect the inlet and outlet hoses, being prepared for fuel spray and spillage.
60 Release the filter clamp retaining screws or bolts and remove the filter.
61 Dispose of the old filter carefully, since it contains fuel.
62 Fit the new filter, making sure that the arrows point in the direction of fuel flow.
63 Secure the filter clamp and attach the inlet and outlet hoses.
64 Reconnect the battery and switch the ignition on and off several times whilst an assistant checks for leaks.

Fuel pressure regulator – removal and refitting
65 Disconnect the battery earth lead.
66 Position a drain pan below the fuel pressure regulator. Disconnect the fuel feed and return pipes from the regulator. Be prepared for some fuel spray and spillage.
67 Disconnect the vacuum line from the regulator.
68 Undo the large retaining nut at the base of the regulator and remove the regulator (photo).
69 Refit in the reverse order of removal. Check for leaks on completion, pressurizing the system by switching the ignition on and off several times.

7.57 Fuel filter, outer union (arrowed)

7.68 Unscrewing fuel pressure regulator base nut

Inlet manifold – removal and refitting

70 Disconnect the battery earth lead.

71 Drain the cooling system.

72 Disconnect and move aside the HT leads.

73 Disconnect the throttle cable from the throttle valve housing and from its bracket.

74 Remove the air intake hose from the airflow meter and the throttle valve housing.

75 Disconnect the multi-plugs from the fuel injectors, the throttle position sensor, the idle speed control valve and the coolant temperature sensor.

76 Disconnect the fuel and vacuum hoses from the fuel pressure regulator; be prepared for some fuel spillage.

77 Disconnect the manifold coolant connection and the brake servo vacuum line.

78 Unbolt the manifold and remove it, complete with throttle valve housing, fuel injectors etc – these can be removed later if required. Recover the gasket.

79 Refit in the reverse order of removal. Use a new manifold gasket, and new injector seals if they have been disturbed.

Engine conditions required for operation on unleaded fuel

80 Refer to Section 6, paragraphs 109 to 117, and Section 9, paragraphs 28 to 36.

Fuel pump inertia switch (July 1986 on)

81 Refer to Section 8, paragraphs 42 to 46.

Fault diagnosis – fuel injection system

82 Fault diagnosis for the home mechanic is confined to checking the security and good condition of electrical, fuel and vacuum connections. Haphazard tinkering is more likely to do harm than good.

83 Testing of a suspect component by substitution is possible, but potentially expensive unless spares are available on a 'sale or return' basis.

84 The EEC IV module incorporates a self-test facility which can be used by a Ford dealer, or other competent specialist, to diagnose various possible faults.

8 Engine management systems

Introduction

1 The 1.8 and 2.0 engines fitted to later Sierra models are under the control of 'black boxes' which regulate both the fuel and the ignition systems to optimise power, economy and emission levels.

2 The 'black box' fitted to carburettor models is known as the ESC II (Electronic Spark Control Mk II) module. On fuel injection models the more powerful EEC IV (Electronic Engine Control Mk IV) module is used.

3 Both types of module receive inputs from sensors monitoring coolant temperature, distributor rotor position and (on carburettor models) manifold vacuum. Outputs from the module control ignition timing, inlet manifold heating and (except on 1.8 models) idle speed. The EEC IV module also has overall control of the fuel injection system, from which it receives information.

4 Provision is made for the ignition timing to be retarded to allow the use of unleaded fuel if necessary. On 2.0 models there is also a facility for increasing the idle speed. For details, refer to Section 6, paragraphs 109 to 117, and Section 9, paragraphs 28 to 36.

5 The EEC IV module contains self-test circuitry which enables a technician with the appropriate test equipment to diagnose faults in a very short time. A 'limited operation strategy' (LOS) means that the car is still driveable, albeit at reduced power and efficiency, in the event of a failure in the module or its sensors.

6 Due to the complexity and expense of the test equipment dedicated to the engine management system, suspected faults should be investigated by a Ford dealer or other competent specialist. This Section deals with component removal and refitting, and with some simple checks and adjustments.

ESC II module – caution

7 Although it will tolerate all normal under-bonnet conditions, the ESC II module may be adversely affected by water entry during steam cleaning or pressure washing of the engine bay.

8 If cleaning the engine bay, therefore, take care not to direct jets of water or steam at the ESC II module. If this cannot be avoided, remove the module completely, and protect its multi-plug with a plastic bag.

ESC II module – removal and refitting

9 Disconnect the battery earth lead.

10 Disconnect the vacuum pipe from the module (photo).

11 Release the locking catch and disconnect the multi-plug (photo).

12 Remove the three securing screws and detach the module and bracket.

13 Although there are only four screws securing the back cover to the module, at least one of them is sealed in production to detect tampering. Do not attempt to open the module unless it is of no further use. In any case parts are not available.

14 Refit in the reverse order of removal. Make sure that the multi-plug is securely fitted and the locking catch engaged.

EEC IV module – removal and refitting

15 Disconnect the battery earth lead.

16 Remove the trim from below the glovebox on the passenger side (pre-1987 models), or the crash pad from above the glovebox (1987 on).

OCTANE ADJUST 1	OCTANE ADJUST 2	IDLE SPEED ADJUST	NEUTRAL /DRIVE SWITCH

DISTRIBUTOR HALL EFFECT SWITCH	INLET MANIFOLD VACUUM TRANSDUCER	ENGINE COOLANT TEMPERATURE SENSOR	AIR CONDITIONING CLUTCH	IDLE SWITCH

ESC II

IGNITION COIL	INTAKE HEATER ASSEMBLY RELAY	CARBURETTOR STEPPER MOTOR	POWER HOLD RELAY

H14550

NOT APPLICABLE TO 1.8 LITRE VARIANTS

Fig. 13.36 Schematic diagram of ESC II module operation (Sec 8)

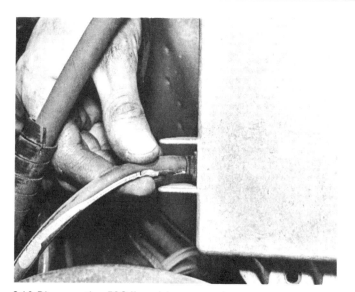

8.10 Disconnecting ESC II module vacuum pipe

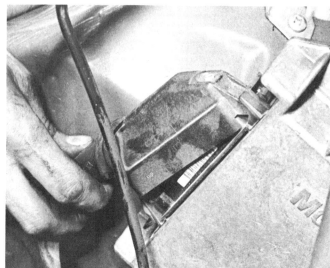

8.11 Disconnecting ESC II module multi-pin plug

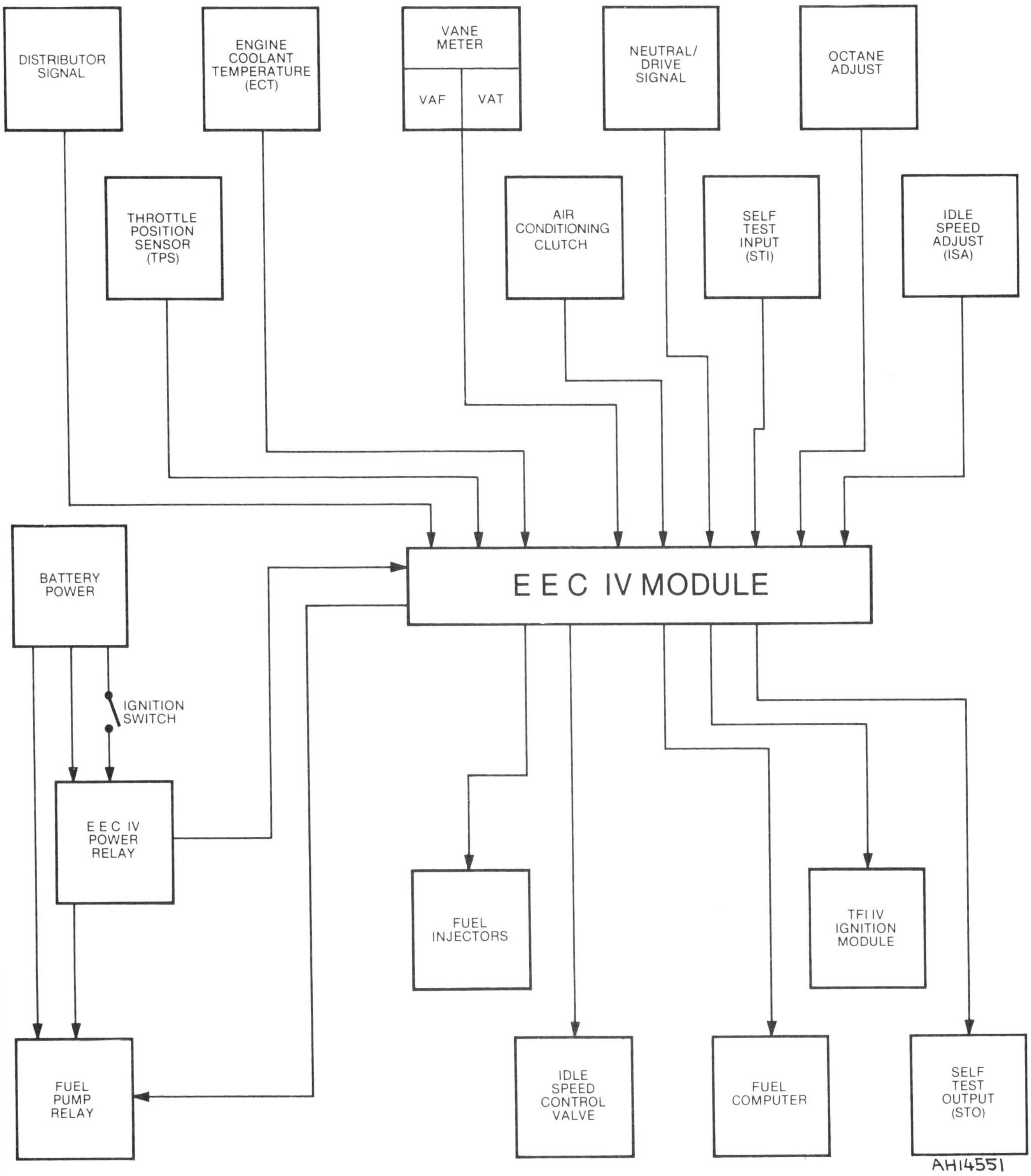

Fig. 13.37 Schematic diagram of EEC IV module operation (Sec 8)

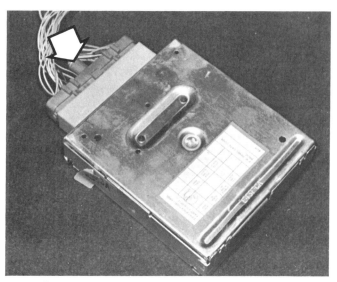

8.17 EEC IV module unclipped – multi-pin plug fixing bolt arrowed

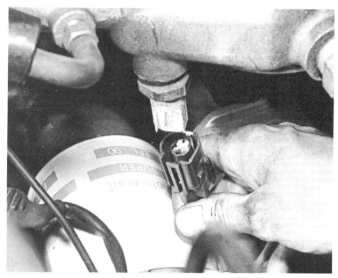

8.26 Coolant temperature sensor multi-pin plug

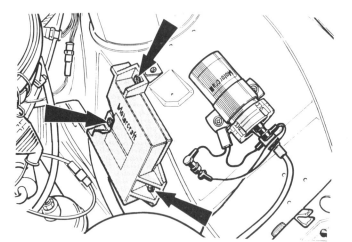

Fig. 13.38 ESC II module retaining screws (arrowed) (Sec 8)

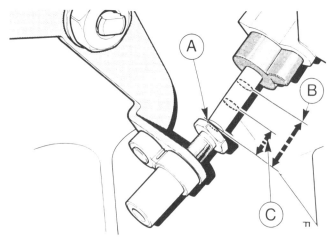

Fig. 13.39 Stepper motor plunger positions (Sec 8)

A   Vent manifold/start   C   Normal idle
B   Anti-diesel (anti-run on)

17 Unclip and lower the module. Disconnect the multi-plug after removing its central retaining bolt (photo).
18 Refit in the reverse order of removal. The multi-plug will only fit in one way.

Carburettor stepper motor (2.0) – removal and refitting
19 Disconnect the battery earth lead.
20 Remove the air cleaner.
21 Disconnect the stepper motor multi-plug by releasing its locking clip and pulling on the plug, not on the wires.
22 Remove the four screws which secure the stepper motor bracket to the carburettor. Remove the motor and bracket and separate them.
23 Refit in the reverse order of removal, then check and adjust the idle mixture and carry out the initial adjustment of the stepper motor, both as described in Section 6.
24 Observe the stepper motor plunger while the engine is stopped and restarted. Immediately after switching off, the plunger should move to the 'anti-dieseling' position; after a few seconds it should extend to the 'vent manifold/start' position.

Coolant temperature sensor – removal and refitting
25 With the engine cold, drain the cooling system. Save the coolant if it is fit for re-use.
26 Disconnect the temperature sensor multi-plug by pulling the plug downwards. Do not pull on the wiring (photo).
27 Unscrew the sensor from the inlet manifold and remove it.
28 Refit in the reverse order of removal. After refilling the cooling system, run the engine to normal operating temperature, then allow it to cool down and check the coolant level.

Engine management module (1.8, 1987 on)
29 This ESC hybrid module is smaller than the ESC II it supersedes. It is mounted on the left-hand inner wing within the engine compartment.
30 The module uses the following inputs to calculate optimum spark advance.

Engine speed and crankshaft position (from the distributor)
Inlet manifold vacuum
Coolant temperature

31 As before, the module controls an intake manifold heater.
32 Refer to Specifications section for ignition settings.
33 The colour of the octane adjuster wires is given in Section 9.

Manifold heater (carburettor models) – removal and refitting
34 Do not attempt to remove the manifold heater while it is hot.
35 Disconnect the battery earth lead.
36 Remove the air cleaner to improve access.

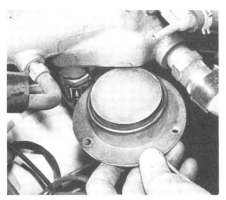

8.37 Removing the manifold heater

8.39 Removing manifold heater relay

8.41 Fuel pump and power relays unclipped. Fuel pump relay (arrowed)

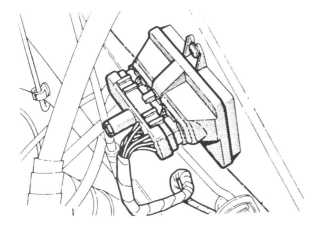

Fig. 13.40 ESC hybrid module (Sec 8)

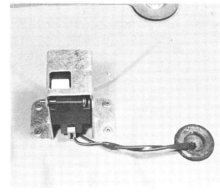

8.44 Fuel cut-off inertia switch (Sapphire)

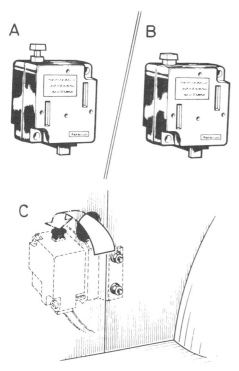

Fig. 13.41 Fuel pump inertia switch (Sec 8)

A   Activated mode (fuel   C   Trim panel access hole
    cut-off)   (arrowed)
B   Normal mode (fuel flowing)

37 Remove the three bolts which secure the heater to the underside of the manifold. Disconnect the electrical feed and remove the heater; recover the gasket and O-ring (photo).
38 Refit in the reverse order of removal. Use a new O-ring and gasket, and be careful to tighten the securing bolts evenly, otherwise the heater may tilt and jam in its recess.

Relay locations
39 On carburettor models, the manifold heater and (when applicable) the power hold relays are in a box on the left-hand bulkhead (photo).
40 On fuel injection models, the fuel pump relay and the EEC IV power supply relay are located behind the glovebox. They are accessible after removing the lower trim panel and freeing the EEC IV module from its mountings.
41 The fuel pump relay also carries the fuel pump fuse; they share a common multi-plug (photo).

Fuel pump inertia switch – models with EEC IV (July 1986 on)
42 From the above date all models with the EEC IV engine management system are fitted with a fuel pump cut-off inertia switch.
43 In the event of an accident, the switch will automatically break the electrical circuit to the fuel pump, shutting off the fuel supply to the engine.
44 The inertia switch is located behind the passenger compartment left-hand trim panel (Hatchback or Estate) or in the spare wheel well (Sapphire Saloon) (photo).

45 The switch incorporates a reset button, which should normally be in the depressed position.

46 Should the engine fail to start, before beginning any diagnostic procedures, check that the reset button is in the depressed position.

Fault diagnosis – engine management systems

47 If a fault is suspected in an engine management system, do not immediately blame the 'black box'. Check first that all wiring is in good condition and that all multi-plugs are securely fitted.

48 Unless components are freely available for testing by substitution, further investigation of faults should be left to a Ford dealer or other competent specialist.

---

9   Ignition system

Description (later models)

1 The ignition system fitted to 1.8 and 2.0 carburettor models closely resembles that found on earlier 1.6 Economy models and described in Chapter 4. The system is under the control of the car's ESC module.

2 On 2.0 fuel injection models the system is similar, but there is also a coil switching module which provides a 'limp home' facility should the EEC IV module lose control of the system.

Ignition timing marks – all models

3 One of two types of crankshaft pulley may be fitted, according to the pulley type. The timing marks will vary as shown (Fig. 13.42).

Ignition module (2.0) fuel injection models – removal and refitting

4 Disconnect the battery earth lead.

5 Disconnect the multi-plug from the module, which is located on the distributor (pre-1987 models) or on the inner wing (1987 on). Press the locking lugs inwards to release the plug and pull on the plug, not on the cable (photo).

6 Remove the two screws which secure the module. On the distributor-mounted module these screws are deeply recessed: a thin socket or box spanner will be needed. Pull the module downwards to remove it from the distributor, or lift it from the wing, as appropriate.

7 When refitting the distributor-mounted module, coat the rear face of the module with heat sink compound to Ford specification 81SF-12103-AA.

8 Do not force the module up into the distributor or the contacts may be damaged.

9 Secure the module with its screws, reconnect the multi-plug and the battery earth lead and run the engine to check for correct operation.

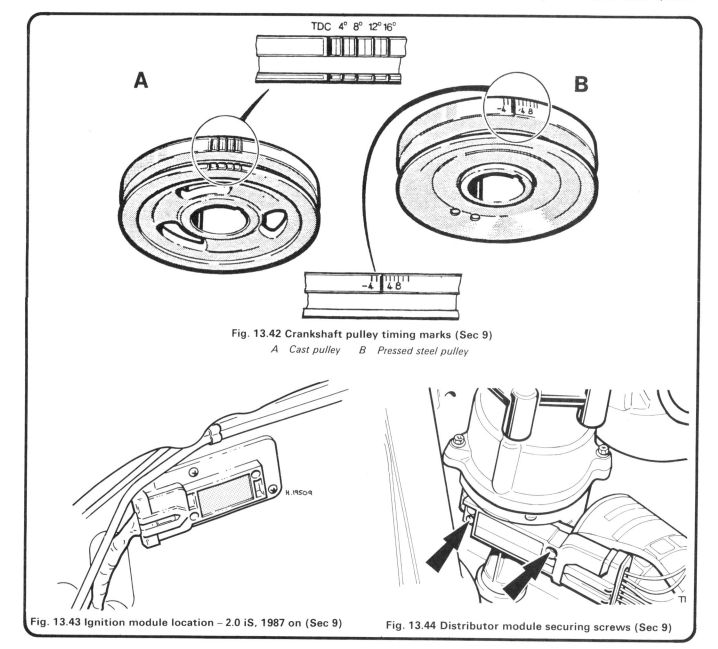

Fig. 13.42 Crankshaft pulley timing marks (Sec 9)

A   Cast pulley   B   Pressed steel pulley

Fig. 13.43 Ignition module location – 2.0 iS, 1987 on (Sec 9)   **Fig. 13.44 Distributor module securing screws (Sec 9)**

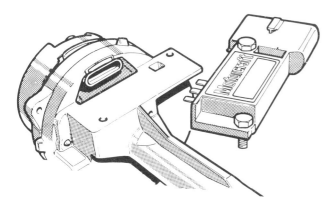

Fig. 13.45 Distributor module removed (Sec 9)

Distributor cap and rotor (2.0 fuel injection models) – removal and refitting

10 Disconnect the HT leads from the distributor cap.
11 Unclip the screening can from the distributor cap and disconnect its earth strap (photo).
12 Remove the two crosshead screws which secure the distributor cap and lift off the cap (photo).
13 To remove the rotor, remove the securing screws and lift it off. Notice the square and round locating holes which prevent incorrect fitting (photos).
14 The rotor tip may be coated with silicone grease. Originally this grease was believed to assist in suppressing radio interference, but later information suggests that it may have the opposite effect. Do not attempt to clean the grease off if it is present; if radio interference is a problem, consult a Ford dealer or car electrical specialist.
15 Refit the rotor and cap in the reverse order of removal.

Distributor (2.0 fuel injection models) – removal and refitting

16 Do not remove the distributor unnecessarily, since the initial accuracy of ignition timing is difficult to regain. Sealing compound is applied to the distributor clamp bolt in production to detect tampering.
17 Disconnect the battery earth lead.
18 Remove the distributor cap and screening can.
19 Turn the crankshaft to bring No 1 piston to its firing point. Note the position of the rotor tip in relation to the alignment notch on distributor rim. Mark the appropriate notch if there is more than one.
20 Release its locking clip and disconnect the distributor or ignition module multi-plug. Pull on the plug, not on the wiring.
21 Remove the distributor clamp bolt and lift out the distributor.
22 Refit in the reverse order of removal. As a rough guide to timing, at the firing point the leading edge of one of the vanes should be in line with the rib on the Hall Effect sensor (photo).
23 Check the ignition timing as described in Chapter 4, but disregard the reference to vacuum advance.

Distributor cap securing clips – early Bosch type

24 On early Bosch type distributors it is possible that, with the cap removed, if the engine is cranked, the securing clips may fall inward and jam the trigger rotor arm, knocking it out of alignment.
25 If this happens, then the distributor will have to be renewed as the trigger rotor cannot be repositioned.
26 Care should therefore be taken not to crank the engine with the distributor cap removed.
27 Later distributors have redesigned clips which obviate the problem.

Ignition timing – adjustment for running on unleaded fuel

28 To run an engine on unleaded fuel the ignition timing must be retarded to prevent detonation and/or pre-ignition. **Note:** This detonation or pre-ignition cannot always be detected (by ear) and it should not be assumed that because the engine appears to be running normally the ignition does not need to be retarded. Failure to retard the ignition can result in serious damage to the engine.

9.5 Disconnecting the distributor multi-pin plug

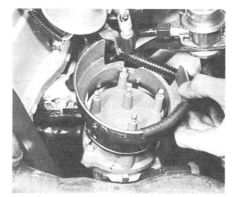

9.11 Removing the distributor screening can

9.12 Extracting a distributor cap screw

9.13A Extracting a rotor fixing screw

9.13B Different shaped rotor locating holes (arrowed)

9.22 Alignment of vane leading edge and sensor rib for basic timing

29 If any doubt exists as to engine identification (see Section 6, paragraph 109) consult your Ford dealer. If the engine is suitable for use with unleaded fuel, proceed as follows.

30 On vehicles equipped with conventional mechanical distributors and with no electronic engine management system, the ignition timing is retarded in the normal fashion by turning the distributor. Refer to Chapter 4.

31 On vehicles equipped with either ESC or EEC IV management systems, obtain an ignition retarding 'service lead' from your Ford dealer.

32 On vehicles fitted with an octane/idle adjustment three-pin multi-plug located near to the coil, fit the service lead to the multi-plug, then cut the appropriate wire(s) at the position shown in Fig. 13.46 according to the table in paragraph 35. Refer to the note in paragraph 34 before cutting any wires.

33 Fit the service lead terminal under one of the coil securing screws.

34 On vehicles fitted with the Lucar type connectors shown in Fig. 13.47 located near the coil, make up a short loom or looms to connect between the appropriate connectors and one of the coil securing screws. Cut the appropriate wire(s) according to paragraph 35.

Note: *On some vehicles you will find a single yellow lead which is fitted during production. This lead should be removed before fitting the service lead. It is important that the yellow wire on the service lead is not cut if the vehicle had the yellow production lead fitted.*

35 Degrees of retardation:

Model	Wire earthed	Retardation
ESC II	Blue	2 degrees
	Red	4 degrees
	Red and blue	6 degrees
EEC IV	Red	2 degrees
and ESC	Blue	4 degrees
(1987 on)	Red and blue	6 degrees

For ignition settings required to enable unleaded fuel to be used, see Specifications.

Note: *Wires are earthed by leaving them connected in the service lead, ie,* **do not** *cut wire(s) to be earthed.*

36 On completion of ignition adjustment, the engine idle speed and CO content should be checked and adjusted as necessary. On all 2.0 litre models, the idle speed can be raised by 75 rpm by earthing the yellow wire. If the yellow wire is already earthed, then disconnecting it and insulating it should result in the idle speed dropping by 75 rpm.

10 Clutch

Adjustment (all models) – checking and correcting

1 It is possible for the self-adjusting mechanism on the clutch pedal to malfunction, because of incorrect setting previously, so that the clutch cable is over-tensioned. Clutch slip and rapid wear will result. The adjustment may be checked as follows.

2 Have an assistant lift the clutch pedal to the top of its travel. With the pedal held in this position, grasp the cable outer where it meets the bulkhead and check that it can be pulled away from the bulkhead by hand. If so, adjustment is correct.

3 If the cable tension is excessive, try to free the adjuster pawl by jerking the inner cable sharply away from the bulkhead. If this does not work, a new cable will be required.

4 Free the old cable by cutting through the inner at the release arm. **Wear safety glasses during this procedure.** Remove the cable from the release arm and pedal.

5 Fit the new cable, and have the assistant hold the clutch pedal up against its stop until the inner has been connected, both to the pedal and to the release arm.

6 Operate the pedal a few times, then check the adjustment as just described.

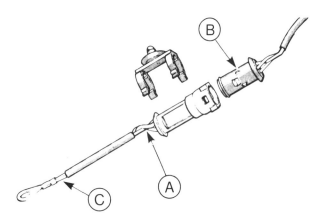

Fig. 13.46 Ignition retarding service lead and plug (Sec 9)

A   Red, blue, yellow   C   Wire cutting point
B   Multi-pin plug

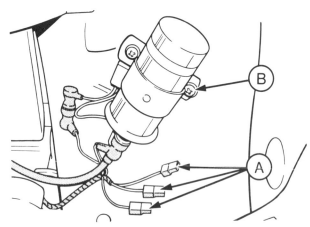

Fig. 13.47 Lucar type connections at ignition coil (Sec 9)

A   Red, blue, yellow   B   Coil fixing screw

10.11A Pedal bracket right-hand fixing nut

10.11B Pedal bracket top fixing bolt

10.13A Cross-shaft end circlip

10.13B Pedal bracket sub-assembly nuts

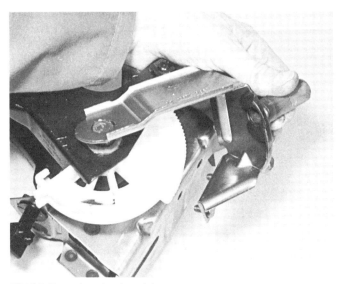
10.13C Removing clutch pedal

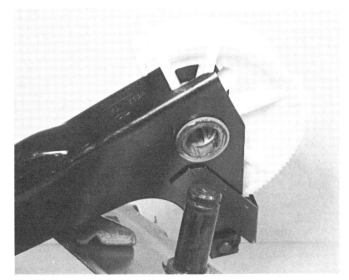
10.14A Clutch pedal with self-adjuster quadrant

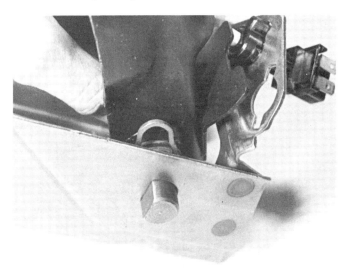
10.14B Cross-shaft inboard circlip at brake pedal

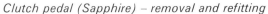

Clutch pedal (Sapphire) – removal and refitting

7 Remove the facia lower panel (driver's side). Disconnect the battery negative lead.

8 Disconnect the clutch cable from the pedal.

9 Disconnect the leads from the stop-lamp switch.

10 Remove the clip from the end of the brake pedal pushrod.

11 Unscrew the two nuts (servo securing) and single bolt which hold the pedal bracket to the bulkhead (photos).

12 Carefully withdraw the pedal box from around the steering column.

13 With the assembly on the bench, extract the shaft end circlip, unscrew the two small self-locking nuts and separate the clutch pedal assembly from the complete bracket assembly (photos).

14 By extracting the remaining circlips, the shafts can be knocked out of the brackets and the pedals removed (photos).

15 Reassembly is a reversal of dismantling. Apply grease to the shaft and bushes and operate the clutch pedal two or three times to set the clutch pedal.

---

11 Manual gearbox

Countershaft bearing modification (type N)

1 On early models the countershaft bearing bore was 33 mm long; on later models it is 27.75 mm long, and the needle rollers are correspondingly shorter.

2 When rebuilding an old pattern gearbox, use the new shorter rollers and insert two extra spacers behind them (Fig. 13.48).

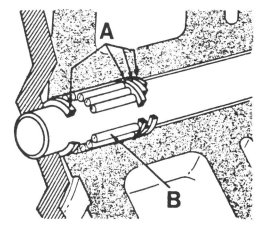

Fig. 13.48 Roller spacer arrangement when reassembling early type gearbox (Sec 11)

A   Spacer   B   Rollers

Lubricant type (type N)
3   If persistent difficulty is experienced in engaging 1st or 2nd gear, the use of a semi-synthetic oil may improve matters. Such an oil (see *Recommended lubricants and fluids*) is used in production from 1987 model year.
4   To change the oil on an earlier gearbox, syphon out the old oil via the filler/level plug. Measure the volume of oil removed to be certain that it has all been recovered.
5   Take care not to overfill the gearbox with oil, as this may itself cause gearshift problems.

Refitting (all models)
6   When refitting the gearbox, secure the clutch release arm fully rearwards with wire or string. This will avoid problems due to the release bearing falling forwards.

Manual gearbox oil level (all types)
7   Overfilling of the gearbox can cause overheating leading to leakage and difficult gear changing.
8   The table below gives the correct distance below the oil filler plug to which the gearbox should be filled.

Gearbox type	Oil level
All four-speed gearboxes	0 to 5 mm (0.197 in) below lower edge of filler hole
All five-speed gearboxes up to April 1984 (build code EG)	Level with bottom edge of oil filler hole
All five-speed gearboxes built from May 1984 (build code EC) to end of April 1985 (build code FP) and all vehicles built prior to April 1984 and subsequently fitted with a modified transmission extension housing	20 to 25 mm (0.788 to 0.985 in) below lower edge of filler hole
All five-speed gearboxes built from May 1985 onwards (build code FB)	0 to 5 mm (0.197 in) below lower edge of filler hole

Gear selector modifications (type N)
9   During 1987, internal modifications were made to the interlock and biasing (loading) functions of the gear selector mechanism.
10 Old and new pattern components are not interchangeable.
11 When refitting the 5th gear locking plate on the modified transmission, only tighten the bolts finger tight at first. Check the engagement of all gears, changing the position of the plate slightly if necessary. Fully tighten the bolts when satisfied.

Gearchange lever gaiter – modification
12 The plate which retains the gearchange lever gaiter has been modified on later models and is secured by four plastic clips.

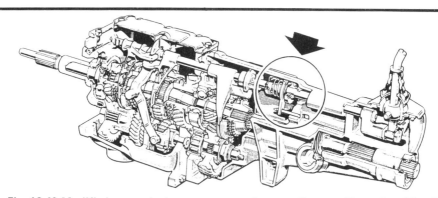

Fig. 13.49 Modified gear selector components (arrowed) – type N gearbox (Sec 11)

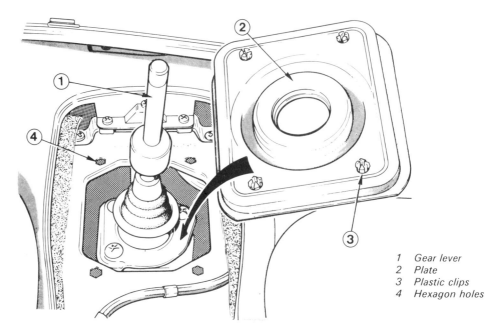

1   Gear lever
2   Plate
3   Plastic clips
4   Hexagon holes

Fig. 13.50 Later type gearchange lever gaiter retaining plate (Sec 11)

12 Automatic transmission (Type A4LD)

Description

1 The A4LD transmission, fitted to 1984 and later models, has four forward speeds and one reverse. The fourth speed ratio makes it effectively an overdrive, maximum speed being obtained in third. The transmission will only change into fourth when DE is selected. When D is selected, only the first three gears are used (see next sub-section).
2 A lock-up clutch in the torque converter is engaged in third and fourth gears, so eliminating losses due to converter slip.
3 Apart from the points just mentioned, the A4LD transmission is very similar to the C3 transmission described in Chapter 6.

Selector lever positions – modification

4 On 1987 models, the DE (drive economy 4th gear lock-up) index mark has been changed to D, while the D index mark has been changed to 3.
5 The freewheel facility is only applied when D is selected.

Fluid level checking

6 Proceed as described in Chapter 6, Section 14.

Brake band adjustment

7 Proceed as in Chapter 6, Section 6, but note that there are now two brake bands to adjust (Fig. 13.51).

Removal and refitting

8 Proceed as described in Chapter 6, Section 15. When refitting, note that distance A in Fig. 6.20 should be 8 mm (0.32 in) minimum for the A4LD transmission.
9 Refer to the relevant paragraphs in this Section when adjusting the selector rod and downshift cable after refitting.

Starter inhibitor switch renewal

10 Proceed as described in Chapter 6, Section 17.

Downshift cable – adjustment

11 Make up a setting gauge to the dimensions shown in Fig. 13.52.
12 Release the downshift cable adjusting nut and locknut and unscrew them to the end of their thread.
13 Have an assistant depress the throttle pedal as far as it will go. Make sure that the pedal travel is not restricted by mats or carpets.
14 Turn the throttle cable adjusting nut to achieve a dimension X (Fig. 13.53) of 10 mm (0.39 in). Use the 10 mm end of the setting gauge to check this gap. Make sure that the spring and the spring cup do not turn when turning the adjusting nut.
15 Remove the setting gauge and re-insert it with the 8 mm end in gap X. Have the assistant release the throttle pedal: the gauge will be clamped in position.
16 Pull the downshift cable outer sleeve in the direction arrowed (Fig. 13.53) to take up any slack. Hold the sleeve in this position and secure it with the downshift cable adjusting nut and locknut. Tighten the nuts.
17 Remove the setting gauge. Adjustment is now complete.

Downshift cable (solenoid-operated) – adjustment

18 From May 1986 the A4LD automatic transmission downshift cable has been replaced by a solenoid unit.
19 The solenoid is bolted to the transmission housing and connected to the kickdown lever by a cable.
20 To adjust the cable, loosen the solenoid bracket securing screws.
21 With the selector lever in any position switch on the ignition.
22 **Under no circumstances start the engine.**
23 Depress the accelerator pedal as far as it will go, actuating the kickdown.
24 Hold the pedal in this position.
25 Turn the kickdown lever anti-clockwise against its stop, then slide the solenoid and bracket forwards to put the cable under slight tension.
26 Tighten the lower bolt, then the upper to the specified torque.
27 Release the accelerator pedal, when the kickdown cable should return to its normal position.
Note: If the tension in the cable is set too high the kickdown lever may return to its normal position inadvertently during operation. Ideally there should be approximately 0.2 mm (0.007 in) play between the

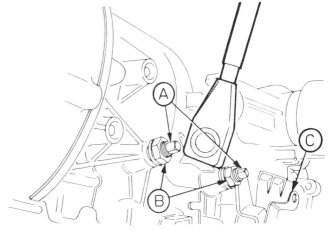

Fig. 13.51 Brake band adjustment (A4LD transmission) (Sec 12)

A Adjustment screws   C Downshift lever
B Locknuts

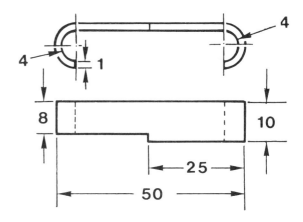

Fig. 13.52 Downshift setting gauge – dimensions in mm (Sec 12)

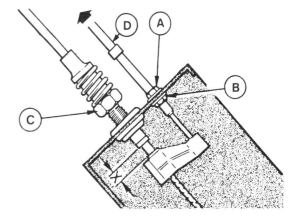

Fig. 13.53 Downshift cable adjustment (Sec 12)

A Adjusting nut   D Downshift cable
B Locknut   X See text
C Throttle cable adjusting nut

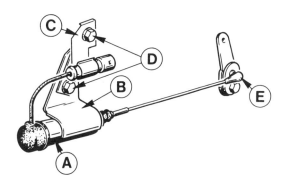

Fig. 13.54 Solenoid-operated downshift assembly (Sec 12)

A Solenoid	D Securing bolts
B Bracket	E Ball socket connector
C Multi-pin plug holder	

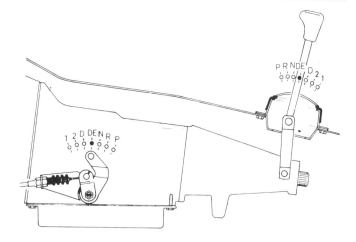

Fig. 13.55 Selector rod positions – pre-1987 (Sec 12)

kickdown lever and its stop when the accelerator pedal is fully depressed.

Selector rod – removal, refitting and adjustment
28 Refer to Chapter 6, Section 19, and note the following points.

(a) *The weight of the vehicle must be on its wheels when adjustment is carried out*
(b) *Adjustment is made in position DE (Fig. 13.5) or D (1987 on)*

Vacuum diaphragm unit – removal and refitting
29 It should be noted that failure of this unit can cause fluid loss due to fluid being drawn into the inlet manifold, and under some circumstances 'pinking' (pre-ignition).
30 Raise the vehicle or place it over an inspection pit.
31 Unbolt the driveshaft centre bearing from the floor.
32 Support the transmission with a jack and remove the rear mounting crossmember.
33 Lower the transmission as necessary to gain access to the vacuum diaphragm unit.
34 Disconnect the vacuum hose at the vacuum diaphragm.
35 Remove the diaphragm bracket bolt and then the bracket.
36 Lift out the diaphragm and actuating pin.
37 Refit in the reverse order, but first check that the throttle valve is free to move and use a new O-ring seal.
38 Check the transmission fluid level on completion.

13 Final drive and driveshafts

Driveshaft nuts – later models
1 From September 1983 (build code DJ) the staked driveshaft nuts have been superseded by self-locking nuts with nylon inserts. The left-hand nut has a **left-hand thread**, ie it is undone in a clockwise direction.
2 New nuts should be used each time after slackening. The tightening torque is unchanged (see Chapter 8 Specifications).
3 Staked type nuts are still available for earlier models.

Driveshaft (models with ABS) – removal and refitting
4 Chock the front wheels. Raise and support the rear of the vehicle.
5 Remove the six 'Torx' screws which secure the inboard flange to the final drive unit. Recover the three double lockwashers. Support the driveshaft.
6 Similarly remove the six screws which secure the outboard flange to the rear hub. Remove the driveshaft.
7 At all times, avoid bending the CV joints to excessive angles, and do not allow the shaft to hang down from one end.
8 Refit by reversing the removal operations. Tighten the flange screws to the specified torque.

Driveshaft (models with ABS) – overhaul
9 The CV joints cannot be overhauled, but they can be renewed separately, as can the rubber gaiters. Check when purchasing gaiters

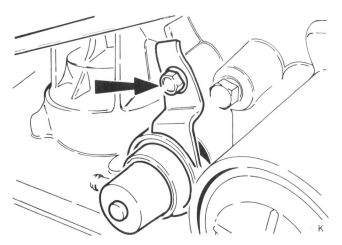

Fig. 13.56 Vacuum diaphragm unit securing bolt – C3 automatic transmission (Sec 12)

whether the grease required for the CV joints is included.
10 Remove the driveshaft as described in the previous sub-section.
11 Undo or cut the clips which secure the rubber gaiters. Pull the gaiters back from the CV joints.
12 Release the CV joints by removing the outer circlips (one per joint) which secure them to the shaft. Pull off the joints and remove the inner circlips.
13 The gaiters can now be removed from the shaft.
14 Renew components as necessary. The gaiter clips must be renewed in any case.
15 Pack the CV joints with the specified type and quantity of grease (see Fig. 13.57).
16 Fit the gaiters and the CV joint inner covers to the shaft. Fit the inner circlips. Apply sealant (Ford part No. A87SX X014834 AR) to the protective cover face where it will meet the CV joint (inset in Fig. 13.58). Clean any grease off the corresponding face of the joint.
17 Fit the CV joints, grooves outermost, and secure them with the outer circlips.
18 Secure the gaiters with the new clips.
19 Refit the driveshaft.

Final drive unit (all models) – removal and refitting
20 When removing the final drive unit, note the location and number of any shims fitted behind the top rear securing bolts. Refit the shims in their original positions.
21 When fitting a new final drive unit, tighten the front and the bottom rear securing nuts and bolts, then measure gap A (Fig. 13.60) if present and fit shims to fill the gap. If no gap is present, no shims are needed. Tighten the top rear nut and bolt on completion.
22 Shims are available in thicknesses of 0.5, 1.0 and 1.5 mm (0.02, 0.04 and 0.06 in).

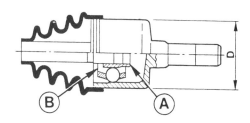

Fig. 13.57 Driveshaft joint identification and grease quantity – models with ABS (Sec 13)

Diameter D	Grease at A	Grease at B
100 mm	60 g	10 g
108 mm	80 g	15 g

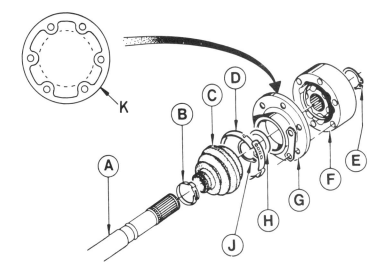

Fig. 13.58 Driveshaft CV joint assembly (models with ABS) (Sec 13)

A	Shaft	F	Constant velocity joint
B	Wire clip	G	Protective cover
C	Gaiter	H	Dished washer (if fitted)
D	Clip	J	Inner circlip
E	Outer circlip	K	Sealant application

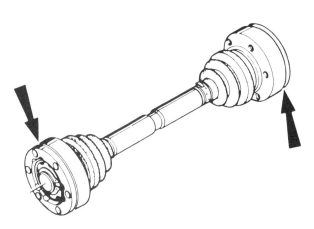

Fig. 13.59 Correct fitting of CV joints with grooves (arrowed) outermost (models with ABS) (Sec 13)

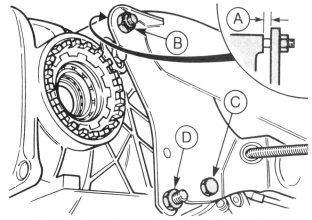

Fig. 13.60 Final drive fitting details (Sec 13)

A	Gap to be shimmed	C	Front bolt
B	Top rear nut	D	Bottom rear nut

Final drive unit (models with ABS) – removal and refitting
23 The procedure is similar to that described in Chapter 8, Section 3, but the driveshaft inner CV joints can simply be unbolted from the output flanges. Tie the driveshafts up so that the joints are not strained.
24 When refitting, tighten the driveshaft flange screws to the specified torque.

Final drive output flange oil seals (models with ABS) – renewal
25 Remove the final drive unit as described earlier.
26 Remove the rear cover from the final drive unit. This is secured by nine 'Torx' screws. Any oil left inside the unit will be released when the cover is removed.
27 Clean old sealant from the cover mating faces, taking care to keep it out of the interior of the unit.
28 Remove the circlips which secure the output flanges inside the differential. *Do not get the circlips mixed up,* as their thickness is selected and may differ from left to right.
29 Withdraw the output flanges and stubs. Clean the seal rubbing faces.
30 Measure the fitted depths of the old oil seals, then prise them from

their locations. Clean the seal seats.
31 Pack the lips of the new seals with grease (if they are not supplied ready-greased). Fit the seals, lips inwards, and drive them in to the depth previously noted, using a piece of tube.
32 Refit the output flanges and stubs, being careful not to damage the seal lips. Secure them with the same circlips.
33 Apply liquid sealant (to Ford spec SQM 4G 9523 A) to the mating faces of the final drive unit and the rear cover.
34 Fit the rear cover. Insert the cover screws and tighten them evenly to the specified torque (Chapter 8 Specifications).
35 Refit the final drive unit.

Rear axle rubber mounting-to-body bolts (1986 on)
36 Since May 1986 (build code GJ) new rear axle rubber mounting-to-body securing bolts and washer assemblies have been used.
37 If the mounting bolts are removed during service for repair to the rear axle, the old type bolts and washers should be discarded and the new type fitted.
38 The earlier type bolts were coloured blue, the later type are gold coloured.
39 Note the new tightening torque given in the Specifications.

14 Braking system

Brake pad renewal – Girling calipers (all 1.3 and 1.6)

1   To avoid bending the caliper slide pins when renewing the brake pads, observe the following precautions:

    (a) *Do not lever between the piston and disc to depress the piston. Ideally a spreader tool, applying equal force to both sides of the caliper, should be used.*

    (b) *Do not pull or push on the caliper to alter the steering position*

    (c) *When freeing a stuck pad, only do so with the caliper securing bolts fitted and as shown in Fig. 13.61. Do not use a screwdriver on the piston side in case the seals are damaged*

2   Should the slide pins be bent despite the above, they are available separately.

Brake disc – removal and refitting (later models)

3   Proceed as in Chapter 8, Section 6, but note that on later models the disc is secured by a spring clip on one of the wheel studs and not by a screw (photo).

4   Mark the disc-to-hub relationship before removing the disc, since otherwise it may be refitted in any of four positions. However, if disc run-out is excessive, the disc may be deliberately refitted in a different position in an attempt to improve matters. Try the disc in all four positions before condemning it. Earlier type discs may be refitted without the securing screw provided that a wheel stud clip is fitted instead.

Brake disc renewal – all models

5   1987 model brake discs are thicker in the area where the wheel studs pass through, and the studs are correspondingly longer. The later type discs can be fitted to earlier models, but if the old wheel studs are 36.5 mm (1.44 in) long they will have to be replaced with 38 or 40 mm (1.50 or 1.58 in) long studs. Seek advice when buying the new disc.

Brake shoes – removal and refitting (all 1.3 and 1.6 Hatchback/Saloon models)

6   Slacken the rear wheel nuts, then raise and securely support the rear of the car. Remove the rear wheel on the side being worked on.

7   Prise off the spring clip which secures the brake drum. Release the handbrake and pull off the drum. If the drum will not pass over the shoes, it is possible to release the automatic adjusting mechanism by inserting a screwdriver through the small hole in the drum and pressing down on the ratchet (photos). Some trial and error will be necessary until the technique is mastered.

8   Remove the top and bottom shoe return springs, using a wire hook or a pair of long-nosed pliers. Note the fitted positions of the springs for reference when refitting (photos).

9   Remove the hold-down cups, springs and pins by depressing the cups and turning them through 90° (photo).

10 Pull the bottom of the leading (front) shoe towards the front of the car so that the self-adjusting ratchets separate, then disengage the shoe from the strut by twisting it. Remove the shoe and adjuster mechanism.

11 Pull the trailing (rear) shoe away from the backplate far enough to gain access to the handbrake cable. Disconnect the handbrake cable

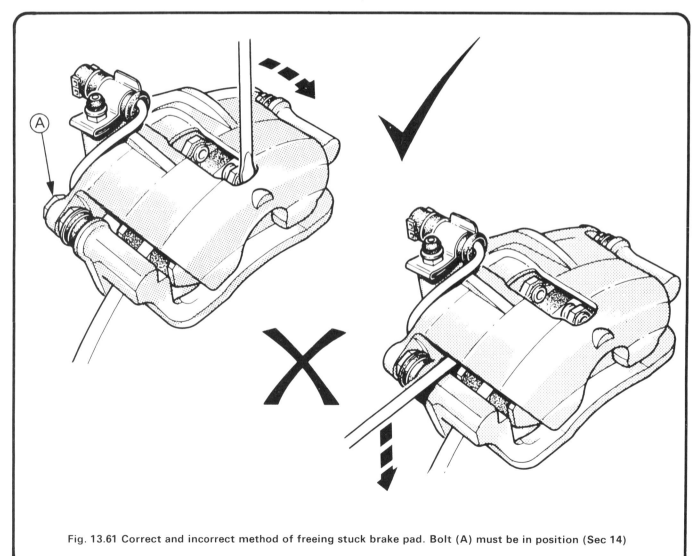

Fig. 13.61 Correct and incorrect method of freeing stuck brake pad. Bolt (A) must be in position (Sec 14)

14.3 Brake disc securing clip

14.7A Releasing brake shoe self-adjuster

14.7B Screwdriver located to release shoe self-adjuster. Drum removed for clarity

14.8A Brake shoe upper return spring (arrowed)

14.8B Brake shoe lower return spring

14.9 Removing a shoe hold-down spring cup

14.11 Disconnecting handbrake cable from trailing shoe lever

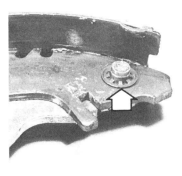

14.13 Handbrake (shoe) lever pivot pin retaining clip (arrowed)

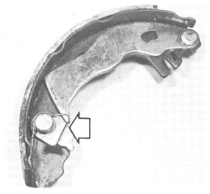

14.15 Self-adjuster ratchets fully retracted ready for shoe refitting (arrowed)

from the lever and remove the shoe with strut and lever (photo).

12 Clean and inspect all components, and lubricate the shoe contact points on the backplate – see Chapter 9, Section 4, paragraphs 10 and 11.

13 Remove the strut from the trailing shoe by unhooking it from its spring. If a handbrake lever is not attached to the new shoe, remove the old lever by prising off the clip and driving out the pin. Use a new clip on reassembly (photo).

14 Similarly transfer the self-adjusting components to the new leading shoe. Note that a small clearance (0.2 mm/0.008 in) must exist between the underside of the smaller ratchet segment and the brake shoe web. Insert feeler blades of this thickness beneath the ratchet when fitting the spring clip, then withdraw the blades. The larger segment should be fitted without any clearance.

15 Commence reassembly by engaging the self-adjusting ratchet teeth as shown (photo).

16 Offer the trailing shoe to the backplate, fitting the handbrake cable

to the handbrake lever and (if not already done) the strut and spring to the top of the shoe (photo).

17 Fit the leading shoe and adjuster mechanism, engaging the hole in the adjuster with the hook on the strut (photo).

18 Fit the top and bottom return springs: this is most easily done by allowing the ends of the shoes to pass in front of the wheel cylinder and the bottom pivot point, then engaging the shoes in their correct positions after the springs have been fitted. Be careful not to damage the wheel cylinder rubber boots.

19 Fit and secure the hold-down pins, springs and cups.

20 Back off the self-adjusting mechanism, by depressing the lower (small) ratchet segment, to enable the brake drum to pass over the shoes. Centre the shoes relative to the backplate.

21 Refit the drum, making sure that the small hole is in line with one of the two large holes in the hub. Secure the drum with its spring clip over one of the wheel studs.

22 Have an assistant operate the footbrake several times: a series of

14.16 Spring and strut fitted to trailing shoe

14.17 Engaging the adjuster hole (arrowed) with the hook on the strut

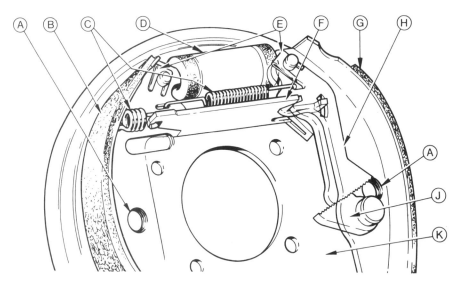

Fig. 13.62 Bendix type self-adjusting rear brake (RH side) (Sec 14)

A	Hold-down components	D	Wheel cylinder	G	Leading shoe	J	Small ratchet
B	Trailing shoe	E	Spring clips	H	Large ratchet	K	Backplate
C	Strut and top return springs	F	Strut				

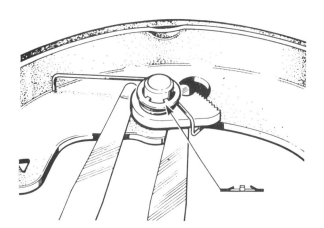

Fig. 13.63 Using feeler blades under small ratchet to give clearance. Retaining clip (arrowed) (Sec 14)

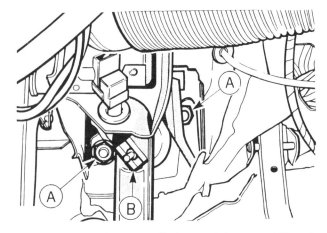

Fig. 13.64 Servo/master cylinder retaining nuts (A) and push-rod clip (B) (Sec 14)

clicks should be heard from the drum as the self-adjusting mechanism operates. When the clicking no longer occurs, adjustment is complete.
23 Renew the brake shoes on the other side of the car, then check the handbrake adjustment (Chapter 9, Section 15).
24 Refit the roadwheels, lower the car and tighten the wheel nuts.
25 Avoid harsh braking if possible until the new linings have bedded in.

Brake pedal height – adjustment
26 On 2.0 fuel injection models without ABS, poor braking performance coupled with low pedal height can be rectified in the following way.
27 Remove the driver's side underdash trim panel.
28 Remove and discard the pushrod-to-pedal retaining clip (B in Fig. 13.64).
29 Unscrew the servo/master cylinder mounting nuts (A).
30 Carefully withdraw the servo/master cylinder away from the engine compartment rear bulkhead and have an assistant lift the brake pedal until the pushrod can be released from the pedal arm.
31 Remove and discard the white spacer from the pushrod.
32 Fit a new longer red-coloured spacer (Part no 81AB 24390 CA) to the pushrod.
33 Engage the pushrod with the pedal arm and remount the servo/master cylinder.
34 Tighten the nuts to 35 lbf ft (48 Nm).
35 Fit a new pushrod clip (Part no 1584819).
36 Adjust the stop-lamp switch as described in Chapter 9, Section 18.

Anti-lock braking system (ABS) – description
37 This system is available as a factory-fitted option on all models. The system comprises a computer, roadwheel sensors, hydraulic actuator with electrically-driven hydraulic pump, and the necessary valves and switches.
38 The purpose of the system is to prevent wheel(s) locking during heavy brake applications. This is achieved by automatic release of the brake on the locked roadwheel and then reapplying the brake. This procedure is carried out four times per second by the control valves in the valve block. The valves are controlled by the computer which in turn receives information from the sensors which monitor the locked or unlocked state of the roadwheels.
39 When ABS is specified on Sierra models, rear disc brakes are fitted instead of drum brakes. The driveshafts and associated components are also different. The front disc brake components are very similar to those described in Chapter 9, to which reference should be made for procedures not given in this Section.

Note: *The photographs of ABS components were taken using a Ford Granada. The system fitted to the Sierra differs slightly in having the valve block mounted remotely from the hydraulic unit.*

Rear disc pads (ABS) – inspection and renewal
40 It is necessary to remove the rear wheels in order to inspect the rear pads. The pads can be viewed through the top of the caliper after removing the spring clip. If any one pad is worn down to the minimum specified, all four pads (on both rear wheels) must be renewed.

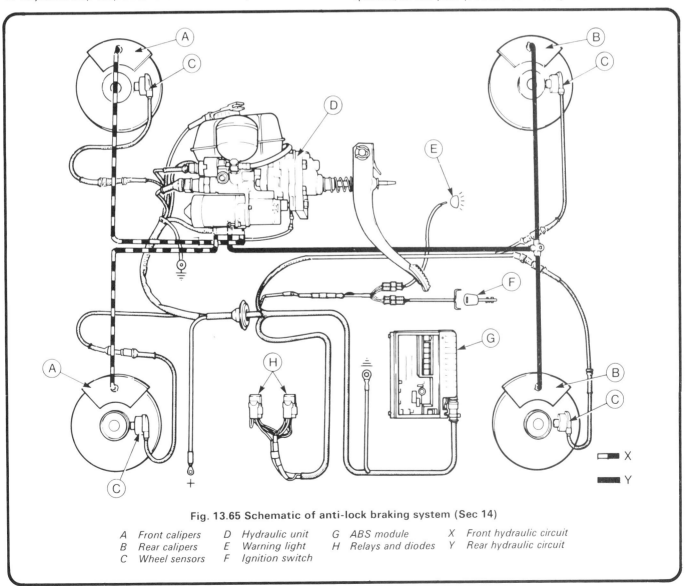

Fig. 13.65 Schematic of anti-lock braking system (Sec 14)

A	Front calipers	D	Hydraulic unit	G	ABS module	X	Front hydraulic circuit
B	Rear calipers	E	Warning light	H	Relays and diodes	Y	Rear hydraulic circuit
C	Wheel sensors	F	Ignition switch				

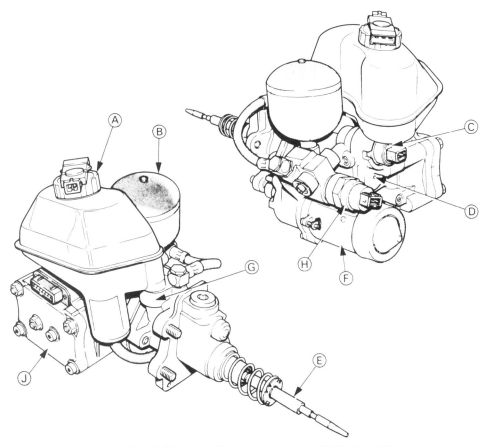

Fig. 13.66 Hydraulic actuation unit (ABS) (Sec 14)

A	Fluid reservoir	D	Master cylinder	F Electric motor and hydraulic
B	Accumulator	E	Push-rod	pressure pump
C	Main valve			G Pressure switch

A   Fluid reservoir   D   Master cylinder   F   Electric motor and hydraulic   H   Booster
B   Accumulator   E   Push-rod   pressure pump   J   Valve block
C   Main valve   G   Pressure switch

41 Free the handbrake cable from its clip on the suspension lower arm.
Release the handbrake.
42 Remove the caliper slide bolt nearest the front, counterholding the
slide pin with another spanner (photo).
43 Disconnect the pad wear warning wires, when fitted (photo).
44 Swing the caliper rearwards and remove the pads (photo). *Do not
press the brake pedal with the caliper removed.*
45 Clean the caliper and surrounding components, taking the proper
precautions to avoid inhaling the dust (asbestos hazard).
46 Retract the caliper piston, by turning it clockwise, to accommodate
the extra thickness of the new pads. There is a Ford tool (No 12-006)
for this purpose, but a pair of circlip pliers or any similar tool can be
used instead (photo).
47 Remove any backing paper from the new pads, then fit them to the
caliper bracket. Be careful not to contaminate the friction surfaces with
oil or grease.
48 Swing the caliper over the pads. Refit and tighten the slide bolt.
49 Reconnect the pad wear warning wires, when fitted.
50 Repeat the operations on the other rear caliper.
51 Secure the handbrake cable, refit the wheels and lower the vehicle.
Tighten the wheel nuts.
52 Switch on the ignition and pump the brake pedal several times to
bring the pads up to the discs. Switch off the ignition and check the
operation of the handbrake.
53 Avoid harsh braking if possible until the new pads have bedded in.

Rear caliper (ABS) – removal and refitting
54 With the ignition off, pump the brake pedal at least 20 times (or
until it becomes hard) to depressurise the system.
55 Chock the front wheels and release the handbrake. Slacken the rear
wheel nuts, raise and support the vehicle and remove the relevant
wheel.
56 Disconnect the pad wear warning wires, when fitted.

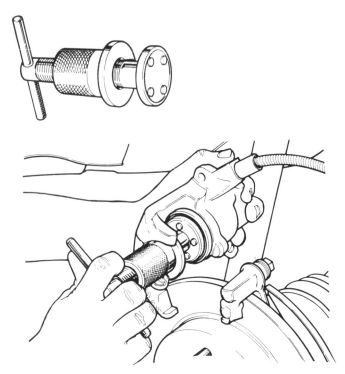

**Fig. 13.67 Ford tool 12-006 for winding back the rear caliper
pistons (Sec 14)**

14.42 Undoing a rear caliper front slide bolt

14.43 Pad wear warning multi-plug (arrowed) on rear caliper

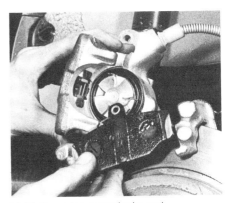

14.44 Removing a rear brake pad

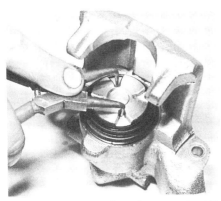

14.46 Rotating the caliper piston to retract it

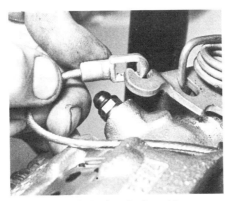

14.58A Unhook the handbrake cable ...

14.58B ... and remove the rear caliper

57 Disconnect the flexible hose from the brake pipe. Plug or cap the open unions to reduce spillage and to keep dirt out. Unscrew the flexible hose from the caliper and remove it.

58 Remove the two slide bolts. Lift the caliper off the pads and bracket, at the same time unhooking the handbrake cable (photos). Alternatively, the two bracket-to-hub bolts can be removed and the caliper and bracket separated on the bench.

59 Refit by reversing the removal operations, but before refitting the wheel, bleed both rear calipers as described later in this Section.

60 When bleeding is complete, pump the brake pedal several times to bring the pads up to the disc, then check the operation of the handbrake.

Rear caliper (ABS) – overhaul

Note: *Complete dismantling of the rear caliper should not be attempted unless Ford spring compressor (tool No 12-007) is available, or unless the problems likely to arise in the absence of the tool are understood. Renewal of the piston seal and dust boot requires no special tools.*

61 Clean the caliper externally and mount it in a soft-jawed vice.

62 Rotate the piston anti-clockwise until it is protruding from the bore by about 20 mm (0.8 in). Free the dust boot from the groove in the piston, then carry on unscrewing the piston and remove it. Remove and discard the dust boot.

63 The piston and bore may now be cleaned and examined, and the piston seal and dust boot renewed, as described for the front caliper.

64 The piston adjuster nut seal should also be renewed. Remove the circlip from the piston, then extract the thrust washers, wave washer and thrust bearing. Note the fitted sequence of these components. Finally remove the nut (photos).

65 Remove the seal from the nut, noting which way round it is fitted. Clean the nut with methylated spirit. Lubricate the new seal with clean hydraulic fluid and fit it to the nut.

66 For further dismantling it is virtually essential to have Ford tool 12-007. This tool appears to be a cut-down adjuster nut with a handle

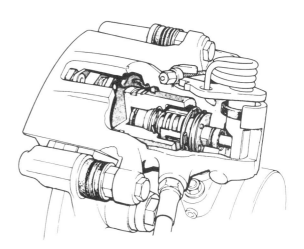

Fig. 13.68 Sectional view of a rear caliper (Sec 14)

for turning it. In the workshop it was found that the actual piston adjuster nut could be used to compress the spring if it were turned with circlip pliers (photo). This works well enough for dismantling, but reassembly proved extremely difficult because of the limited clearance between the skirt of the nut and the caliper bore.

67 Having compressed the adjuster spring just enough to take the load off the circlip, release the circlip inside the caliper bore. Remove the spring compressor, then extract the circlip, spring cover, spring and washer (photos).

68 A long thin pair of circlip pliers will now be needed to release the key plate retaining circlip from the caliper bore (photo). With the circlip removed, the pushrod and key plate can be pulled out.

69 Remove the handbrake strut from the caliper bore.

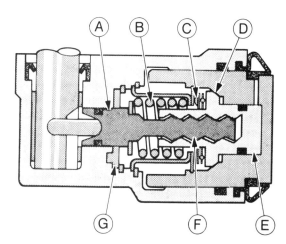

Fig. 13.69 Part section of rear caliper showing
self-adjusting mechanism (brakes released) (Sec 14)

A   Handbrake pushrod   E   Adjuster nut
B   Preload spring   F   Quick thread
C   Preload washer   G   Key plate
D   Clutch face

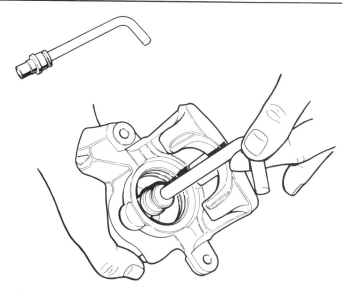

Fig. 13.70 Ford tool 12-007 for compressing the rear caliper
spring (Sec 14)

70 Remove the handbrake lever return spring and stop bolt. Pull the
lever and shaft nut out of the caliper. Prise out the shaft seal.
71 Clean up the handbrake shaft using wire wool; renew the shaft if it
is badly corroded. The shaft bush in the caliper can also be renewed if
necessary. Pull out the old bush with an internal puller or slide hammer,
press in the new bush to 7.5 mm (0.30 in) below the shaft seal lip. The
slot in the side of the bush must line up with the pushrod bore in the
caliper.

72 Having renewed components as necessary, commence reassembly
by smearing a little brake grease or anti-seize compound on the
handbrake shaft and bush.
73 Fit a new handbrake shaft seal to the caliper. Pass the shaft through
the seal and into the caliper, being careful not to damage the seal lips.
74 Refit the handbrake lever stop bolt and return spring.
75 Refit the handbrake strut, lubricating it with brake grease.
76 Fit a new O-ring to the base of the pushrod. Refit the pushrod and

14.64A Removing the circlip from a rear
caliper piston ...

14.64B ... followed by a thrust washer ...

14.64C ... a wave washer and (not shown)
another thrust washer ...

14.64D ... the thrust bearing ...

14.64E ... and the adjuster nut itself. Note
seal (arrowed) on nut

14.66 Using the adjuster nut to compress
the caliper spring

14.67A Extract the circlip ...

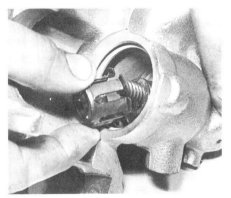

14.67B ... the spring cover ...

14.67C ... the spring itself ...

14.67D ... and the washer

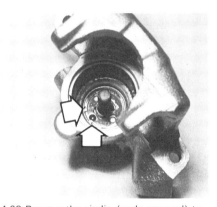

14.68 Remove the circlip (ends arrowed) to release the pushrod and key plate

14.81 Dust boot fitted to caliper and piston

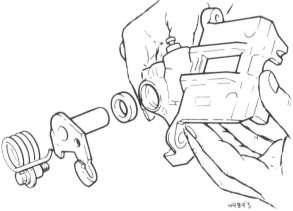

Fig. 13.71 Handbrake lever and associated components (Sec 14)

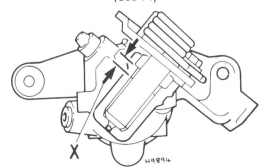

Fig. 13.72 Handbrake shaft bush correctly fitted (Sec 14)

X = 7.5 mm (0.30 in)

the key plate, engaging the pip on the key plate with the recess in the caliper. Secure the key plate with the circlip.

77 Refit the washer, spring and spring cover. Compress the spring and refit the circlip, then release the spring compressor.

78 Lubricate the caliper bore with clean hydraulic fluid and fit a new piston seal.

79 Reassemble the piston components. Lubricate the contact face of the adjuster nut with a little brake grease, then fit the adjuster nut (with new seal), thrust bearing, thrust washer, wave washer and the second thrust washer. Secure with the circlip.

80 Fit a new dust boot. The manufacturers recommend that it be fitted to the caliper groove and the piston fitted afterwards; it is also possible to fit the boot to the piston first and engage it in the caliper groove afterwards. Either way it is a fiddly business.

81 Refit the piston and screw it into the caliper, then fit whichever lip of the dust boot was left free (photo).

82 Renew the slide pin gaiters and apply a little anti-seize compound to the slide pins when reassembling the caliper to the bracket.

Rear disc shield (ABS) – removal and refitting

83 Remove the rear wheel trim. Apply the handbrake and chock the front wheels.

84 Slacken the hub flange (driveshaft stub) nut. This nut is very tight. The left-hand nut has a left-hand thread, therefore it is undone clockwise.

85 Slacken the rear wheel nuts, raise and support the vehicle and remove the relevant rear wheel.

86 Free the handbrake cable from its clip in the suspension lower arm.

87 Remove the two bolts which secure the caliper bracket to the hub. Lift the caliper and bracket off the disc and suspend it without straining the flexible hose.

88 Remove the spring clip from the wheel stud. Mark the disc-to-hub relationship and remove the disc.

89 Remove the hub flange nut and the flange itself.

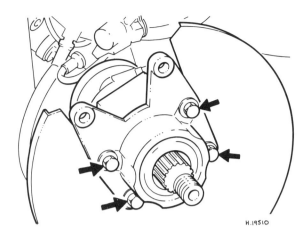

Fig. 13.73 Four bolts (arrowed) securing the rear hub
carrier (Sec 14)

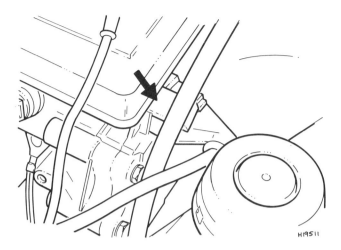

Fig. 13.74 Reservoir securing clip (arrowed) also supports
clutch cable (Sec 14)

90 Unscrew the four bolts which secure the hub carrier. Pull the hub
carrier off the driveshaft stub and remove the disc shield.
91 Refit by reversing the removal operations. Carry out the final
tightening of the hub flange nut with the wheels on the ground.

Fluid reservoir (ABS) – removal and refitting
92 Disconnect the battery negative lead.
93 Depressurise the hydraulic system by pumping the brake pedal at
least 20 times, or until it becomes hard.
94 Disconnect the multi-plugs and remove the reservoir cap.
95 Remove the reservoir securing screw. Also remove the reservoir
securing clip, noting how it supports the clutch cable.
96 Make arrangements to catch spilt fluid, then disconnect the low
pressure hose from its connections to the pump. The hose is secured by
a spring clip (photos). Allow the brake fluid to drain out of the hose.
97 Pull the reservoir out of the seals on the hydraulic unit and remove
it (photo).
98 Note the spigot locating bush on the rear inlet union, which may
stay in the hydraulic unit or may come out with the reservoir (photo).
99 Refit by reversing the removal operations. Use new seals between
the hydraulic unit and the reservoir.
100 Bleed the complete hydraulic system on completion. Check for
leaks around the disturbed components.

Hydraulic unit (ABS) – removal and refitting
101 Disconnect the battery negative lead.
102 Depressurise the hydraulic system by pumping the brake pedal at
least 20 times, or until it becomes hard.
103 Disconnect the six multi-plugs from the hydraulic unit. They are all
different, so there is no need to label them. When a plug has a spring
clip retainer, lift the clip before pulling out the plug. To release the
pump plug, pull back the rubber boot and the plug sleeve (photos).
104 Unbolt the earth strap from the unit.
105 Make arrangements to catch spilt hydraulic fluid. Identify the
hydraulic pipes and disconnect them from the base of the unit. Plug or
cap the open unions to keep fluid in and dirt out.
106 Remove the underdash trim on the driver's side. Disconnect the
spring clip which secures the hydraulic unit pushrod to the brake
pedal.
107 Have an assistant support the hydraulic unit. Remove the four nuts
which hold the unit to the bulkhead (photo). Withdraw the unit from
under the bonnet.
108 Recover the sealing compound from the unit and the bulkhead.
109 Drain the hydraulic fluid from the reservoir. *Do not actuate the
pushrod with the unit removed.*
110 Dismantling of the hydraulic unit should be limited to the
operations described in the following sub-sections. These operations
can all be carried out without removing the unit from the vehicle if
wished.
111 Refit by reversing the removal operations, noting the following
points:

(a) Do not refill the reservoir until the end of refitting
(b) Use new sealing compound between the unit and the
    bulkhead
(c) Make sure that the hydraulic pipes are reconnected to the
    correct unions
(d) Bleed the complete hydraulic system on completion

Hydraulic unit accumulator (ABS) – removal and refitting
112 Disconnect the battery negative lead.
113 Depressurise the hydraulic system by pumping the brake pedal at
least 20 times, or until it becomes hard.
114 Wrap a clean rag round the base of the accumulator to catch any
spilt fluid.
115 Unscrew the accumulator using a hexagon key. Remove the
accumulator, being prepared for fluid spillage (photos).
116 When refitting, fit a new O-ring to the base of the accumulator. Fit
the accumulator and tighten it.
117 Reconnect the battery. Switch on the ignition and check that the
hydraulic unit pump stops within 60 seconds. If not, there may be
something wrong with the accumulator.
118 Bleed the complete hydraulic system.

*Hydraulic unit pump and motor (ABS) – removal and
refitting*
119 Remove the accumulator as described previously.
120 Disconnect the high pressure hose from the pump. Be prepared for
fluid spillage.
121 Disconnect the low pressure hose from the pump. Allow the fluid
to drain out of the reservoir through the hose.
122 Disconnect the multi-plugs from the pressure switch and the
pump motor.
123 Remove the pump mounting bolt (photo).
124 Pull the pump and motor assembly off the mounting spigot and
remove it.
125 Recover the mounting bushes and renew them if necessary.
126 If a new pump is to be fitted, transfer the pressure switch to it,
using a new O-ring.
127 Commence refitting by offering the pump to the spigot, then
reconnecting the low pressure hose.
128 Refit and tighten the pump mounting bolt.
129 Reconnect the high pressure hose, using new sealing washers on
the banjo union.
130 Refit the accumulator, using a new O-ring.
131 Reconnect the multi-plugs and the battery.
132 Refill the reservoir, then switch on the ignition and allow the pump
to prime itself. Do not let the pump run for more than two minutes, then
let it rest for 10 minutes. Check for leaks around the disturbed
components.
133 Bleed the complete hydraulic system.

14.96A Extract the spring clip ...

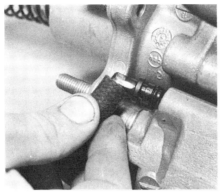

14.96B ... and disconnect the hose

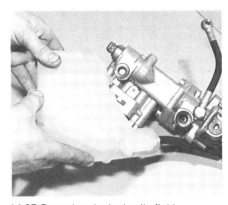

14.97 Removing the hydraulic fluid reservoir

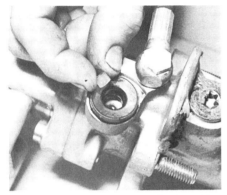

14.98 The spigot locating bush fits into this union

14.103A Disconnecting a fluid level sensor plug

14.103B Disconnecting the main valve plug

14.103C Disconnecting the pressure switch multi-plug

14.107 Four nuts (arrowed) which hold the hydraulic unit to the bulkhead

14.115A Unscrew the accumulator

14.115B Removing the accumulator. Note O-ring (arrowed)

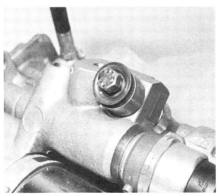

14.123 Hydraulic unit pump mounting bolt

14.136 Unscrewing the pressure switch

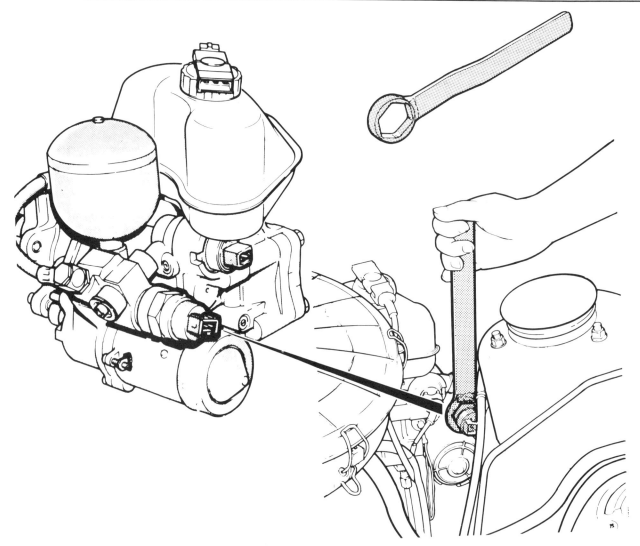

Fig. 13.75 Ford tool No 12-008 for removing the hydraulic unit pressure switch. LHD shown, RHD similar (Sec 14)

Hydraulic unit pressure switch (ABS) – removal and refitting

Note: *To remove the pressure switch from the hydraulic unit in situ, Ford tool No 12-008, or equivalent, will be required. The switch may be removed without special tools after removing the hydraulic unit complete or the pump alone.*

134 Disconnect the battery negative lead.

135 Depressurise the hydraulic system by pumping the brake pedal at least 20 times, or until it becomes hard.

136 Disconnect the multi-plug from the switch, then unscrew and remove it (photo).

137 When refitting, use a new O-ring on the switch. Position the plastic sleeve so that the hole in the sleeve is facing pump motor (photo). Tighten the switch.

138 Reconnect the multi-plug and the battery.

139 Bleed the complete hydraulic system.

Valve block (ABS) – removal and refitting

140 Disconnect the battery negative lead.

141 Depressurise the hydraulic system by pumping the brake pedal at least 20 times, or until it becomes hard.

142 Slacken the left-hand front wheel nuts. Raise and support the front of the vehicle and remove the left-hand front wheel.

143 Remove the protective liner from inside the front wing (Section 17).

144 Clean around the unions on the valve block. Have rags and a drain pan ready to catch spilt hydraulic fluid, then disconnect the unions. Plug or cap open unions.

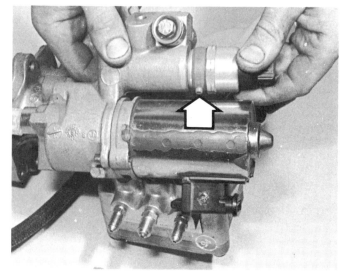

14.137 Refitting the pressure switch. Hole (arrowed) in plastic sleeve must face pump motor

Fig. 13.76 Removing the ABS valve block bracket nuts (arrowed) (Sec 14)

145 Disconnect the multi-plug and the earth strap from the valve block.
146 Working through the wheel arch, remove the three nuts which secure the valve block bracket.
147 Remove the valve block and bracket, being careful not to spill hydraulic fluid on the paintwork.
148 Do not attempt to dismantle the valve block. The pressure control valve in the rear brake line union can be renewed separately, but that is all.
149 Refit by reversing the removal operations. Bleed the complete hydraulic system on completion, and check all disturbed unions for leaks.

Computer module (ABS) – removal and refitting
150 Disconnect the battery.
151 From the passenger side, remove the crash pad trim panel (photo).
152 To remove the now exposed module, push it as necessary to release the retaining catch.
153 Withdraw the module, at the same time disconnecting the multi-pin plug (photo).
154 Refitting is a reversal of removal. Connect the battery and check the operation of the ABS warning lamp as described in your owner's handbook.

Wheel sensors (ABS) – removal and refitting
Front wheel
155 Raise the vehicle and support securely on axle stands.
156 Unclip the wiring loom so that the wheel sensor multi-pin plug can be disconnected.
157 Unscrew the fixing bolt and withdraw the sensor (photos).
158 Before refitting the sensor, clean the bore in the hub carrier and smear the bore and sensor with wheel bearing grease.
159 Use a new O-ring seal.
Rear wheel
160 Raise the rear of the vehicle, support securely on axle stands and remove the roadwheel. Release the handbrake.
161 Lift up the rear seat cushion then remove the side kick panel to gain access to the wheel sensor wiring plug connector.
162 Disconnect the wiring and prise out the floor panel grommet then feed the wiring through the panel.
163 Release the handbrake cable from the clip on the lower suspension arm.
164 Unscrew the front slide bolt and swivel the caliper upwards.
165 Unscrew the wheel sensor fixing bolt and remove the sensor.
166 Before refitting the sensor, clean the bore and apply wheel bearing grease to the bore and the sensor. Use a new O-ring, and fit the sensor flush.
167 Tighten the caliper slide bolt to the specified torque.

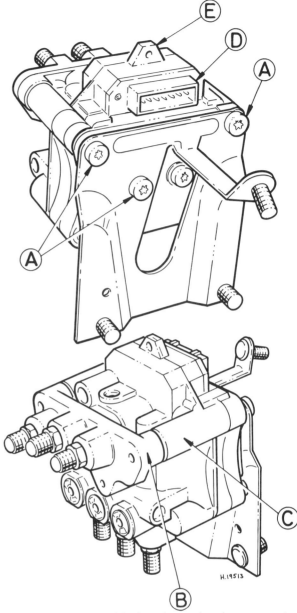

Fig. 13.77 ABS valve block and associated components (Sec 14)

A Bracket screws   D Multi-plug connector
B Adaptor plate   E Earth strap anchor point
C Valve block

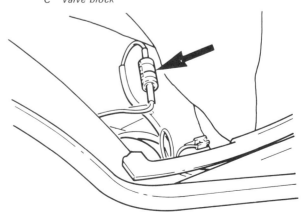

Fig. 13.78 Rear wheel ABS sensor wiring plug connector (arrowed) (Sec 14)

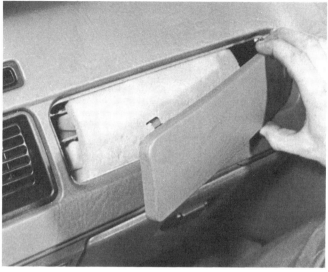

14.151 Remove the trim panel for access to the ABS module

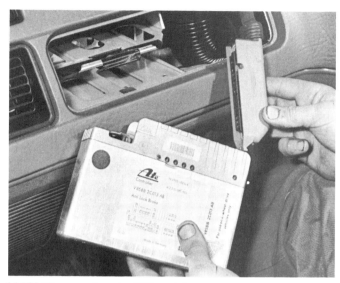

14.153 Disconnecting the ABS module

14.157A Removing a front sensor securing bolt

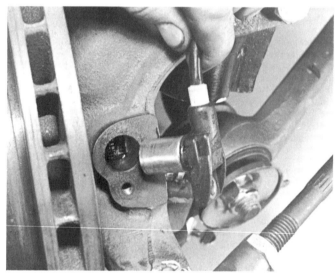

14.157B Removing a front sensor

Hydraulic system (ABS) – bleeding

Caution: *Remember that brake fluid is poisonous and that the rear brake hydraulic system may be under considerable pressure. Take care not to allow hydraulic fluid to spray into the face or eyes.*

168 Keep the fluid reservoir replenished throughout the bleeding operations.

169 Fit a bleed tube to the left-hand front caliper and immerse the end of the tube in a jar containing some hydraulic fluid.

170 Open the bleed valve one full turn and have an assistant depress the brake pedal fully and hold it down.

171 Close the bleed valve and release the brake pedal. Repeat the procedure until fluid ejected from the end of the tube is free from air bubbles.

172 Repeat the operations on the right-hand front caliper.

173 Fit the bleed tube to the left-hand rear caliper and open the bleed valve one full turn.

174 Have an assistant depress the brake pedal fully and hold it down.

175 Switch on the ignition to position II.

176 Allow the fluid to bleed from the tube for at least 15 seconds, when the fluid should be free from air bubbles.

177 Close the bleed valve.

178 Release the brake pedal, wait for the hydraulic pump to stop.

179 Fit the bleed tube to the right-hand rear caliper and open the bleed valve one full turn.

180 Have your assistant depress the brake pedal through half its travel and hold it there. Allow the fluid to bleed from the tube for at least 15 seconds, when the fluid should be free from air bubbles.

181 Close the bleed valve.

182 Release the brake pedal and wait for the hydraulic pump to stop then switch off the ignition.

183 Top up the reservoir with clean fluid.

184 When the hydraulic system is being bled for the purpose of renewing the fluid at the specified service interval, as each caliper is bled, operate the brake pedal continuously until clean fluid is seen to enter the jar.

185 When the hydraulic pump is running its note will be heard to change once fluid has purged through it. Do not allow the pump to run continuously for more than two minutes. If it does run for a longer period, switch off the ignition and allow the motor to cool for ten minutes.

Handbrake cable (ABS) – adjustment

186 The handbrake is normally self-adjusting in use. Adjustment may be required to compensate for cable stretch over a long period, and is also necessary after fitting a new cable.

187 Chock the front wheels, release the handbrake and raise and support the rear of the vehicle.

188 Release the adjuster locknut from the adjuster nut. Back off the adjuster nut, slackening the cable until both handbrake levers on the calipers are resting against their stops (photo).

189 Paint alignment marks between each handbrake lever and the caliper body (photo).

190 Tighten the adjuster nut until one of the handbrake levers just starts to move – as shown by the alignment marks.

191 Apply the handbrake and release it a few times to equalise the cable runs. Check that the handbrake control travel is correct.

192 Tighten the locknut onto the adjuster nut finger tight, then tighten a further two or four 'clicks' using self-locking pliers or a peg spanner.

193 Lower the vehicle.

Handbrake cable (ABS) – removal and refitting

194 Slacken the rear wheel nuts and chock the front wheels. Raise and support the rear of the vehicle and remove both rear wheels. Release the handbrake.

195 Slacken off the handbrake cable adjuster locknut and adjuster nut.

196 Free the cable from the equaliser yoke by removing the circlip and clevis pin.

197 Unhook the cable inner from the handbrake levers on the calipers. Free the cable outer from the caliper brackets (photos).

198 Free the cable from the lower arm and underbody brackets and remove it.

199 Refit by reversing the removal operations, but before refitting the rear wheels, adjust the cable as described previously.

Brake pedal (Sapphire) – removal and refitting

200 The operations are described in Section 10 of this Supplement in conjunction with the clutch pedal.

Front disc brakes (Sapphire)

201 The calipers on these models are similar to the earlier Teves type.

202 The outboard pad has a self-adhesive coating to hold it away from the disc as an aid to fuel economy. Remember to peel off the backing paper when fitting new pads (photo).

14.188 Handbrake cable adjuster. Locknut has already been backed off adjuster nut

14.189 Alignment marks painted on lever and body

14.197A Handbrake cable inner attached to lever on caliper

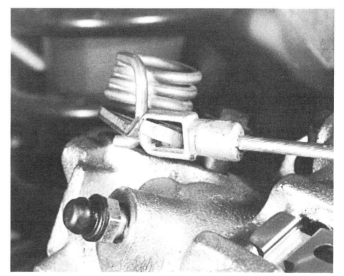

14.197B Handbrake cable outer attached to caliper bracket

14.202 Fitting a new outboard disc pad (Sapphire)

15 Electrical system

Alternator mounting bracket – refitting
1   To avoid breakage of the alternator mounting bracket lugs it is important that the following procedure is adhered to when refitting and tightening the mounting bolts.
2   Always refit the large flat washer (A in Fig. 13.79).
3   Earlier models (pre-1985) also have a small washer (B) which must be fitted between the sliding bush and the mounting bracket.
4   Ensure the bushes and bolts are assembled as shown in Fig. 13.79 and then tighten all bolts to the specified torque (see Specifications) in the following sequence:

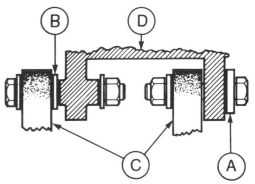

Fig. 13.79 Alternator mounting bracket arrangements (Sec 15)

A   Large washer   C   Mounting bracket (engine)
B   Small washer (pre 1985 D   Mounting lugs (alternator)
    only)

(a)   Tighten the adjustment strap bolt
(b)   Tighten the front mounting
(c)   Tighten the rear (sliding bush) mounting

Alternator (Mitsubishi) – brush renewal
5   Remove the alternator from the vehicle.
6   Unscrew the pulley nut. To prevent the shaft rotating, insert an Allen key in the end of the shaft.
7   Remove the spring washer, pulley, fan, spacer and dust shield.
8   Scribe an alignment mark along the length of the alternator to facilitate reassembly of the drive end housing, stator and rear housing.
9   Unscrew the through-bolts and withdraw the drive end housing from the rotor shaft.
10 Take off the seal and spacer from the rotor shaft.
11 Remove the rotor from the rear housing and the stator, This may

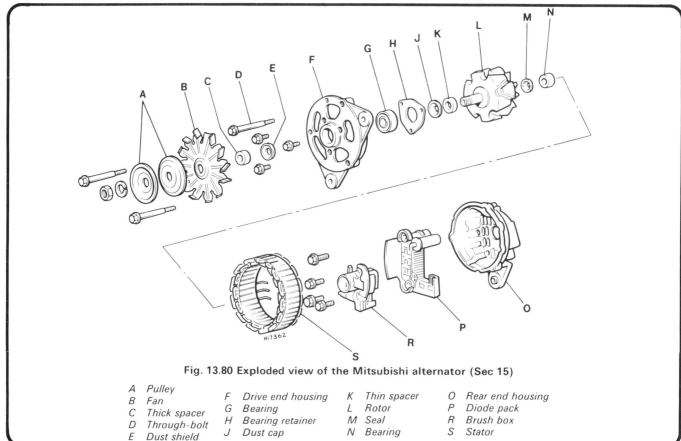

Fig. 13.80 Exploded view of the Mitsubishi alternator (Sec 15)

A   Pulley   F   Drive end housing   K   Thin spacer   O   Rear end housing
B   Fan   G   Bearing   L   Rotor   P   Diode pack
C   Thick spacer   H   Bearing retainer   M   Seal   R   Brush box
D   Through-bolt   J   Dust cap   N   Bearing   S   Stator
E   Dust shield

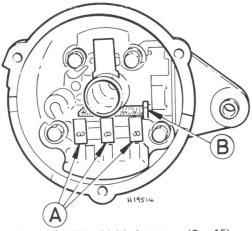

Fig. 13.81 Mitsubishi alternator (Sec 15)

A *Stator connections*   B *Brush box to rectifier terminal*

require the application of local heat to the rear housing by a large soldering iron.

12 Unscrew the four bolts and withdraw the rectifier/stator assembly from the rear housing.

13 Unsolder the stator leads from the rectifier pack terminals. Also unsolder the connection between the rectifier pack and the brush box. Use a pair of pliers when unsoldering to act as a heat sink, otherwise the diodes may be damaged.

14 Examine the surfaces of the slip rings. Clean them with a petrol-soaked cloth or, if necessary, fine glass paper.

15 Solder the new brush box connection to the rectifier pack, again using pliers as a heat sink. Solder the stator leads to the rectifier.

16 Bolt the stator and rectifier to the rear housing.

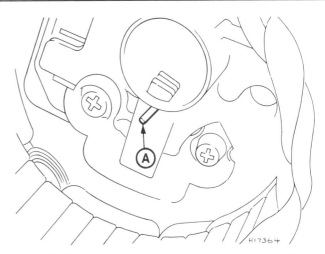

Fig. 13.82 Alternator brushes held in retracted position (Sec 15)

A *Thin rod*

17 Insert a thin rod (an Allen key is ideal) through the hole in the rear housing to hold the brushes in the retracted position.

18 Fit the rotor to the rear housing and then remove the temporary rod to release the brushes.

19 Reassemble the remaining components by reversing the dismantling operations. Make sure that the scribed lines are in alignment.

Alternator (Lucas A127) – general

20 The alternator may be fitted to 1987 and later models. As will be seen from Fig. 13.83, there are some differences from the earlier Lucas type (Chapter 10, Fig. 10.2).

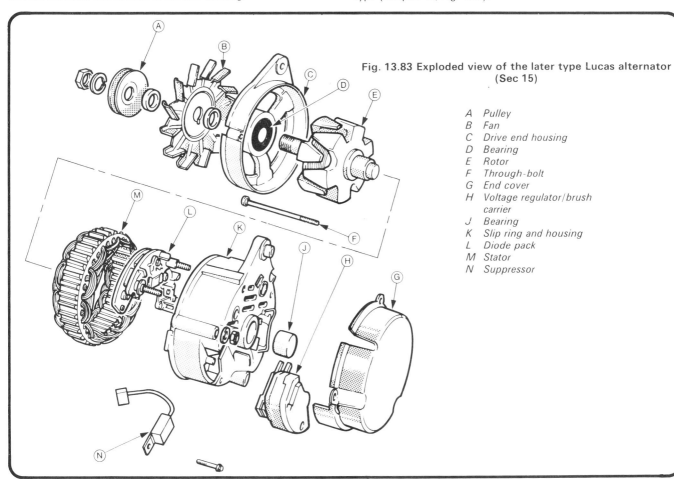

Fig. 13.83 Exploded view of the later type Lucas alternator (Sec 15)

A *Pulley*
B *Fan*
C *Drive end housing*
D *Bearing*
E *Rotor*
F *Through-bolt*
G *End cover*
H *Voltage regulator/brush carrier*
J *Bearing*
K *Slip ring and housing*
L *Diode pack*
M *Stator*
N *Suppressor*

21 Brush renewal is as described in Chapter 10, Section 9, but it is necessary to renew the complete voltage regulator/brush carrier assembly.

Starter motors (1987 on) – general
22 Exploded views of three new types of starter motor are given in Figs. 13.84 to 13.86.

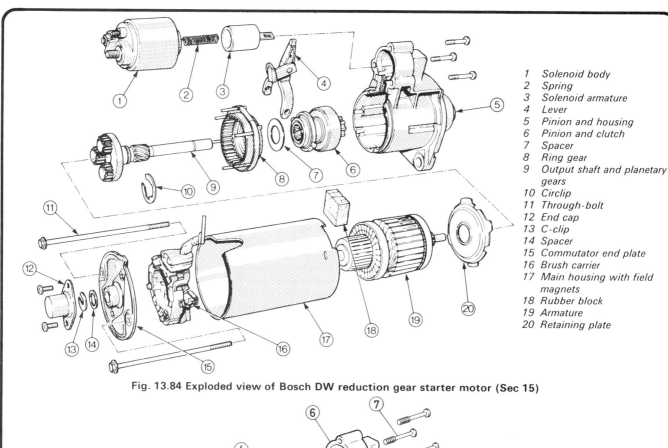

1   Solenoid body
2   Spring
3   Solenoid armature
4   Lever
5   Pinion and housing
6   Pinion and clutch
7   Spacer
8   Ring gear
9   Output shaft and planetary gears
10 Circlip
11 Through-bolt
12 End cap
13 C-clip
14 Spacer
15 Commutator end plate
16 Brush carrier
17 Main housing with field magnets
18 Rubber block
19 Armature
20 Retaining plate

Fig. 13.84 Exploded view of Bosch DW reduction gear starter motor (Sec 15)

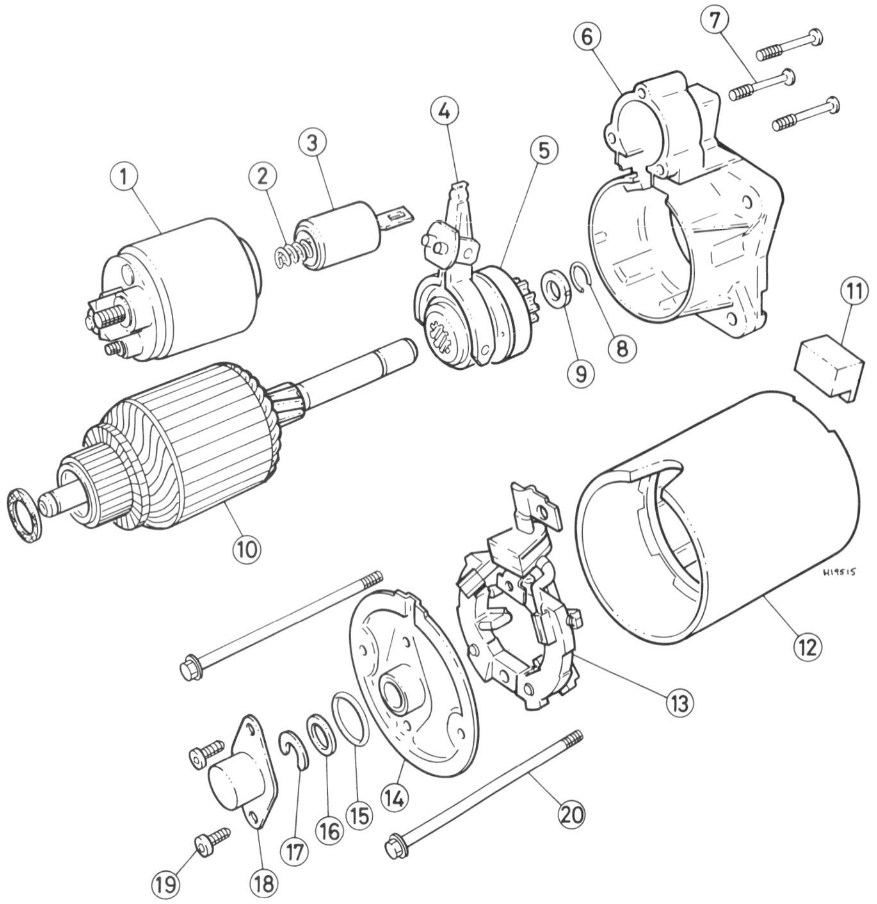

1   Solenoid body
2   Spring
3   Solenoid armature
4   Lever
5   Pinion and clutch
6   Pinion end housing
7   Solenoid screws
8   Circlip
9   Collar
10 Armature
11 Rubber block
12 Main housing with field magnets
13 Brush carrier
14 Commutator end plate
15 Sealing ring
16 Spacer
17 C-clip
18 End cap
19 Screw
20 Through-bolt

Fig. 13.85 Exploded view of Bosch DM starter motor (Sec 15)

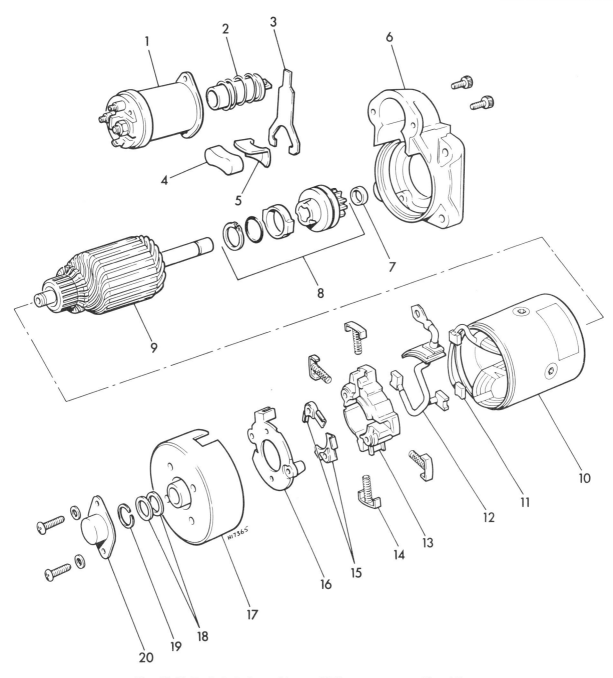

Fig. 13.86 Exploded view of Lucas M79 starter motor (Sec 15)

1 Solenoid body	7 Thrust washer	11 Field brushes	16 Brush carrier insulator
2 Solenoid armature	8 Pinion and clutch	12 Brush link	17 Commutator end cover
3 Lever	9 Armature	13 Brush carrier	18 Spacers
4 Rubber block	10 Main housing and field	14 Brush spring and retainer	19 C-clip
5 Support bracket	windings	15 Insulators	20 End cap
6 Pinion end housing			

23 Overhaul procedures are similar to those in Chapter 10, Section 12. Also note the following points:

(a) *Bosch DW and DM motors have permanent magnets instead of field coils. Be careful not to damage the magnets – they are brittle*

(b) *When reassembling the reduction gear motor (Bosch DW), apply a little silicone grease to the reduction gears*

Fuses and relays

24 The arrangement of the fuses and relays for 1987 models is as follows.

Central fusebox

Engine compartment, right-hand side of scuttle

Fuse	Circuit protected	Rating (A)
1	LH headlamp main beam and auxiliary lamp	20
2	RH headlamp main beam and auxiliary lamp	20
3	LH dipped headlamp	10
4	RH dipped headlamp	10
5	LH parking lamps	10
6	RH parking lamps	10
7	Instrument panel illumination, rear number plate	15
8	Spare	–

9	Headlamp wash/wipe. Auto trans kickdown	30
10	Central locking, courtesy lamps, clock, mirrors	20
11	Fuel pump – air conditioner (carburettor)	20
12	Hazard warning system	10
13	Cigar lighter	30
14	Horn	30
15	Wipers/washers	30
16	Heated rear screen and mirrors	30
17	Front foglamps, dim-dip lighting	20
18	Heater blower motor	30
19	Spare	–
20	Direction indicators, reversing lamps	15
21	Stop-lamps	15
22	Instrument and control circuits	10
23	Fuel pump (4x4 variants)	20
24	Power windows	30

Relays

1	Ignition switch
2	Dim-dip lighting
3	Headlamp wash/wipe
4	Spare
5	Windscreen wiper (intermittent)
6	Interior lighting (timer delay)
7	Anti-lock braking system (ABS)
8	Electronic kickdown (auto transmission)
9	Fuel pump air conditioning (carburettor versions)
10	Headlamps – main beam
11	Engine management system
12	Inhibitor switch (auto transmission)
A	Spare
B	Rear foglamps
C	Horn
D	Engine management system
E	Electrically-operated and heated mirror
F	Headlamps – dipped beam
G	Spare
H	Front foglamps

Facia panel fusebox
Under right-hand side of facia, adjacent to heater

Fuse	Circuit protected	Rating (A)
30	Anti-lock braking system (ABS)	20
31	ABS pump	30
33	Fuel pump (fuel injection)	15
35	Engine management	1

Instrument panel bracket (driver's side)
L1 Flasher relay

Below instrument panel (passenger's side)
Relays

M3	Air conditioner
M4	Cooling fan – air conditioner
M6	Hydraulic pump (ABS)

Modules (various locations)

P1	ABS
P2	Fuel injection system
P3	Control-auxiliary warning system
L2	Heated windscreen (timer)
L3	Windscreen heater element

Flasher unit (all models) – removal and refitting

25 The direction indicator/hazard warning flasher unit is clipped to a bracket above the steering column. Gain access by removing the lower facia panel on the driver's side (Chapter 12, Setion 27). Alternatively, remove the instrument panel (Chapter 10, Section 25).
26 Unclip the flasher unit and disconnect its multi-plug (photo).
27 Fit and secure the new flasher unit, check for correct operation, then refit the lower facia panel.

Rear screen wiper motor – parking diode renewal

28 If the rear screen wiper fails to park, it may be that the parking diode is defective. Proceed as follows.

15.26 Flasher unit unclipped (arrowed)

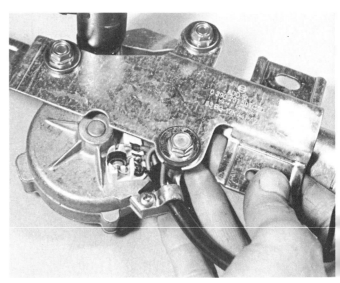

15.29 Rear screen wiper motor

29 Remove the rear screen wiper motor (Chapter 10, Section 37). The diode is located on the rear face of the motor (photo).
30 Carefully unsolder the diode, using long-nosed pliers as a heat sink. Note which way round it is fitted.
31 Test the diode with a multi-meter or battery and bulb. It should pass current one way (bulb lights, or zero resistance) but not the other (bulb does not light, or very high resistance). If it conducts in both directions or in neither direction, renew it.
32 Make sure the new diode is fitted the right way round and solder it into position, again using pliers as a heat sink.

Windscreen washer pump (all models) – removal and refitting

33 On pre-1987 models, the combined windscreen/headlamp washer fluid reservoir is located on the right-hand side of the engine compartment. On 1987 models the reservoir is mounted under the right-hand front wing but it has a filler within the engine compartment (photos).
34 The pump is a push fit in the base of the reservoir (photos).
35 Syphon out the contents of the reservoir, then wriggle the pump out of its grommet.

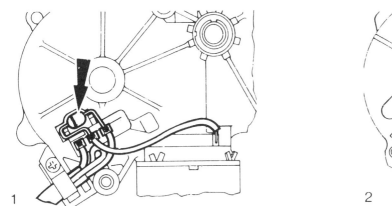
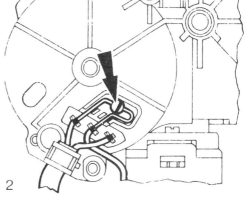

Fig. 13.87 Rear screen wiper motor parking diode (arrowed). Orientation of diode is important (Sec 15)

1 Bosch type   2 SWF type

15.33A Fluid reservoir upper fixing bolt

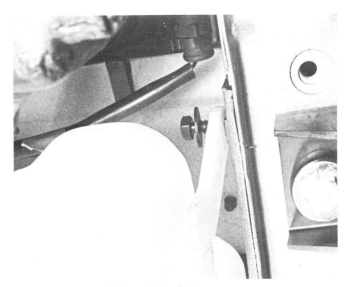

15.33B Fluid reservoir lower fixing bolt

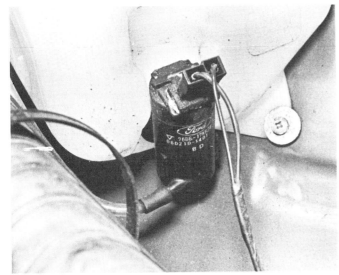

15.34A Windscreen washer pump (pre 1987)

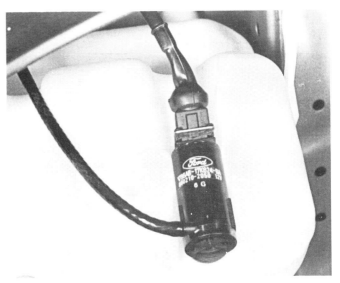

15.34B Windscreen washer pump (1987)

15.34C Washer pump removed

Fig. 13.88 Removing a windscreen washer jet (Sec 15)

36 Disconnect the wiring connectors and the pipe.
37 Refit in the reverse order of removal, using a new grommet if necessary. Use a little liquid detergent as a lubricant.
38 Refill the reservoir and check for correct operation.

Windscreen washer jets – removal and refitting
39 Pull or carefully prise the jet and its carrier forwards to release it from the cowl panel. Disconnect the hose and remove the jet and carrier.
40 Refit in the reverse order of removal. Check the aim of the jet and adjust if necessary by means of a pin.

Rear screen washer pump – removal and refitting
41 The procedure is similar to that described for the windscreen washer pump, but on pre-1987 models it is necessary to remove the rear left-hand side trim panel to gain access to the reservoir.

Headlamp wash/wipe system – general
42 This system operates only when dipped headlamps are on.

Headlamp wiper blade – renewal
43 Swivel the wiper arm clear of the lamp lens.
44 Hold the wiper arm stationary and prise the blade from its retainer.
45 Fit the new blade by reversing the removal operations.

Headlamp washer pump – removal and refitting
46 Syphon the fluid from the reservoir, disconnect the multi-pin plug and the hose.
47 Lever the pump from the reservoir using a screwdriver as a lever.
48 Refitting is a reversal of removal.

Headlamp washer jets – removal, refitting and adjustment
49 Remove the radiator grille (Chapter 12, Section 11).
50 Disconnect the washer pipes from the jets.
51 Separate the upper and lower halves of the jet by carefully prising with a screwdriver. Remove the jet halves.
52 Refit in the reverse order of removal, then adjust the aim of the jets as follows.
53 Refer to Fig. 13.91 to determine the jet aiming areas. Mark the areas on the headlamp glass with a wax crayon or similar.
54 Insert Ford tool 32 004 into the jet so that the slots are engaged. Manipulate the tool so that its end touches the desired aiming area, then repeat on the other jet.
55 Check for correct operation, then clean the crayon marks from the glass.

Headlamp wiper motor – removal and refitting
56 Swivel the plastic cover from the wiper arm mounting nut. Pull the washer hose from the jet on the blade.

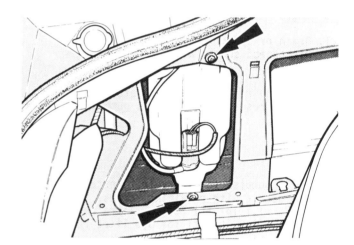

Fig. 13.89 Rear screen washer pump and reservoir on pre-1987 Hatchback. Fixing bolts arrowed (Sec 15)

Fig. 13.90 Prising up headlamp washer jet

(A) to expose nozzle (B) (Sec 15)

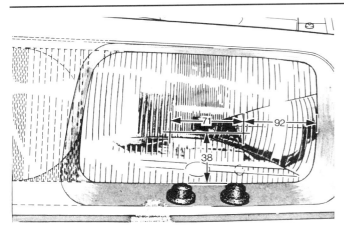

Fig. 13.91 Headlamp washer jet aiming areas (Sec 15)

Dimensions in mm. Left-hand side shown.
Right-hand side is mirror image.

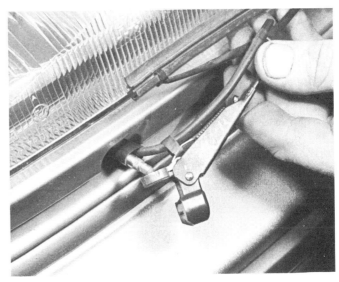

15.57 Removing a headlamp wiper arm

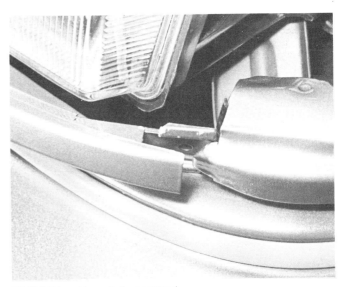

15.63A Trim strip end disconnected

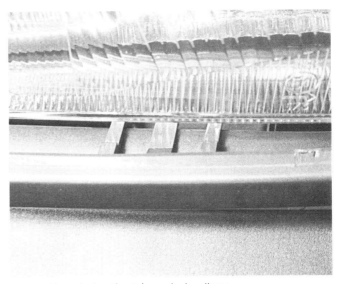

Fig. 13.92 Adjusting headlamp washer jet with Ford Tool
32004 (Sec 15)

57 Unscrew the wiper arm fixing nut and remove the arm (photo).
58 Remove the radiator grille as described in Section 17.
59 Unscrew the wiper motor bracket from the headlamp housing. Access is obtained from under the wheel arch.
60 If the vehicle is equipped with foglamps, then the headlamp unit must be removed when the right-hand headlamp wiper motor is to be removed. Disconnect the wiper motor multi-plug.
61 Refitting is a reversal of removal.

Headlamp unit (1987 on) – removal and refitting
62 If headlamp wiper arms are fitted, refer to paragraph 57 and remove them.
63 Extract the top two radiator grille screws and ease the grille forward until the lugs can be released from the headlamp housings and the wing guides. Remove the trim strip by pulling its centre point towards you (photos).
64 If headlamp wipers are fitted, unscrew the wiper motor bracket and slide the motor rearwards out of the guide.
65 Remove the wiring plug from the rear of the headlamp then unscrew the two headlamp retaining screws and nut. Release the spring and withdraw the direction indicator lamp (photos).
66 Pull the headlamp forwards, swivel it and remove it sideways.
67 Refitting is a reversal of removal.

Front direction indicator (1987 on) – bulb renewal
68 Working within the engine compartment, unhook the direction lamp retaining spring from its anchorage next to the headlamp. Withdraw the lamp unit (photos).
69 The bulb holder can be removed by turning it in an anti-clockwise direction (photo).

Auxiliary driving lamp (1987 on) – bulb renewal
70 Working within the engine compartmentt, prise the retaining bar back and remove the cover from the rear of the lamp (photo).

15.63B Trim strip locating tabs under headlamp

15.65A Headlamp main multi-pin plug

15.65B Headlamp lower fixing bracket screw

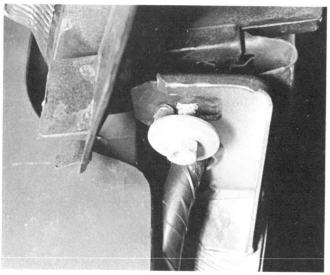

15.65C Headlamp side fixing screw

15.65D Headlamp top bracket

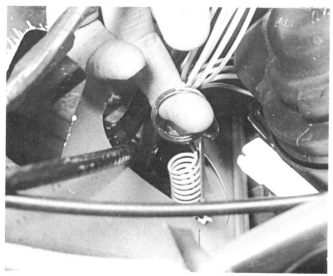

15.68A Releasing front indicator lamp anchor spring

15.68B Withdrawing front direction indicator lamp

71 Compress the legs of the bulb holder clip and swivel the clip from the bulb holder (photo).
72 Withdraw the bulb and disconnect the wiring plug (photo). Do not touch the bulb glass with the fingers.
73 Fit the new bulb by reversing the removal procedure.

Front foglamp (1987 on) – bulb renewal
74 Unscrew the two securing screws and withdraw the lamp until the leads can be disconnected (photo).
75 Release the spring clip and withdraw the bulb holder (photo). Refitting is a reversal of removal, but adjust the beam if necessary by turning the beam adjustment screw.

Horn switch (steering wheel mounted) – removal and refitting
76 Disconnect the battery.
77 Insert the blade of a small screwdriver and prise out the horn button from the centre of the steering wheel (photo).
78 Disconnect the leads from the terminals.
79 Prise out the centre disc to expose the steering wheel retaining nut (photos).
80 Refitting is a reversal of removal.

Auxiliary warning system – description
81 Fitted to GL and Ghia models, the auxiliary warning system (AWS) monitors the levels of fuel, coolant, washer fluid and (at start-up only) engine oil. On pre-1987 models, it also gives warning of brake pad wear. The five warning lights should all illuminate for a few seconds when the ignition is first switched on, then all go out. If a light remains on, the appropriate fluid level or system should be checked as soon as possible. If a light flashes, a circuit fault is indicated and the fluid level should be verified in the traditional way.
82 On Ghia models the AWS also includes a graphic display unit, consisting of an outline of the car and symbols representing its doors and lights. Warning is given to the driver of doors ajar and of running light bulb failure (except main beam). The stop-light circuit is also checked: after switch-on the stop-light symbols will remain lit until the brake pedal is first depressed. If all is well they will then extinguish.
83 The graphic display unit carries a central snowflake symbol, which will show yellow when the outside temperature falls to 4°C (39°F), and red at or below 0°C (32°F).
84 The coolant and washer fluid sensors are reed switches, operated by floating magnets. The fuel level sensor is incorporated in the gauge sender unit. The oil level sensor is built into a special dipstick.
85 Brake pad wear warning is achieved by incorporating a wire loop in the friction material of one pad on each caliper. When the loop is broken, the warning light illuminates.
86 All AWS sensors, including the 'door ajar' switches, incorporate resistors in such an arrangement that the control assembly can read the difference between open sensor contacts and an open-circuit in the wiring.
87 The AWS control unit, and (when fitted) the bulb failure monitor, are located behind the glovebox on pre-1987 models.
88 On 1987 models, the control and bulb failure modules are located behind the driver's side kick panel.

Auxiliary warning system – testing and fault finding
89 Thorough testing and fault finding should be left to a Ford dealer or other competent electrical specialist, having the necessary test equipment. Unskilled or uninformed testing may cause damage.
90 Investigation of malfunctions should begin by checking that all wiring is intact and securely connected. If checking wires or sensors for continuity, always disconnect the control unit and/or bulb failure monitor before so doing, otherwise damage may be caused.
91 Note that false oil level readings can result if the car is parked on a slope. False 'bulb out' warnings may occur if incorrect wattage bulbs are fitted.

Auxiliary warning system – component renewal
Warning lamp bulbs
92 See Chapter 10, Section 34, paragraphs 37 and 38.

Ice warning sender
93 See Chapter 10, Section 30.

Graphic display unit
94 See Chapter 10, Section 28.

15.69 Removing front direction indicator lamp bulb

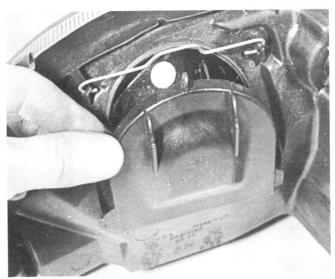
15.70 Auxiliary lamp rear cover

15.71 Auxiliary lamp bulb holder and leads

15.72 Withdrawing auxiliary lamp bulb

15.74 Front foglamp retaining screw

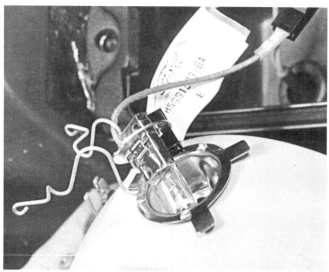

15.75 Front foglamp bulb withdrawn

15.77 Horn button removed

15.79A Removing steering wheel hub centre disc

15.79B Steering wheel hub centre disc removed

Door ajar switch
95 Remove the door inner trim panel (Chapter 12, Section 15).
96 Pull the switch out of its location in the lock, disconnect its wiring plug and remove it.
97 Refit in the reverse order of removal. Check the switch for correct operation before refitting the trim panel.

Low coolant level switch
98 See Chapter 10, Section 23.

Low washer fluid level switch
99 Empty the washer reservoir to below the level of the switch.
100 Disconnect the switch wiring plug and prise the switch out of its grommet.
101 Refit in the reverse order of removal, using a new grommet if necessary. Check for leaks, and for correct operation of the switch, when refilling the reservoir.

Control unit and bulb failure monitor
102 Refer to Chapter 10, Section 24. When a bulb failure monitor is fitted, to avoid confusion its multi-plug is coloured green, the control unit plug is coloured brown.

Standard clock – removal and refitting (alternative housing)
103 Removal of the clock is covered in Chapter 10, Section 29, but on some models an alternative housing is used.
104 To remove the clock from this type of housing, first remove the single screw from under the top edge of the facia panel in which the clock is housed.
105 The complete housing panel may then be tilted forward and the clock securing screws removed.
106 Refit in the reverse order.

Digital clock (later models) – bulb renewal
107 Remove the clock (Chapter 10, Section 29).
108 Extract the appropriate bulb and holder for renewal.
109 Fit the new bulb and refit the clock.

Heater/air conditioning blower switch – bulb renewal
110 Remove the switch knob (Chapter 10, Section 22). The knob illumination bulb is now accessible.
111 Prise out the switch plate for access to the plate illumination bulb.
112 Check for correct operation of the new bulb, then refit the disturbed components.

Trip computer (1985 on) – module removal and refitting
113 Removal is similar to the procedure given in Chapter 10, Section 41, except that the new computer does not have separate mounting brackets.
114 To disconnect the multi-plug, press in the retaining lug and pull on the plug.
115 Refit in the reverse order of removal.

Trip computer (1985 on) – bulb renewal
116 Remove the computer module, then extract the bulb by twisting its base anti-clockwise with pliers.
117 Fit and secure the new bulb. Reconnect the module multi-plug to check for correct operation, then refit the module.

Instruments (1987 on)
118 The printed circuit board, multi-plug and fuel and temperature gauges are different from earlier versions (photo).
119 The fuel gauge indicates the fuel level even after switching off the ignition.
120 The instruments are sealed units, no adjustment or calibration being possible.
121 Removal and refitting of the instrument panel is as described in Chapter 10, Section 25.

Seat heating pad – removal and refitting
122 Disconnect the pad electrical connectors under the seat.
123 Remove the seat (see Chapter 12, Section 29). Remove the seat cushion trim or backrest trim as necessary.

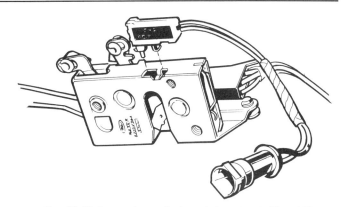

Fig. 13.93 Door ajar switch and door latch (Sec 15)

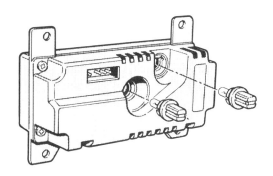

Fig. 13.94 Digital clock bulb holders (Sec 15)

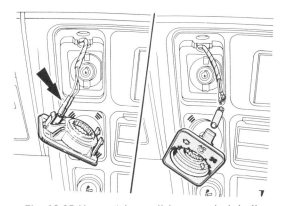

Fig. 13.95 Heater/air conditioner switch bulb.
Connectors arrowed (Sec 15)

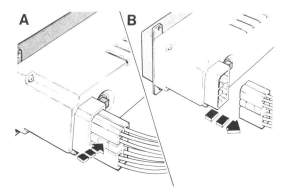

Fig. 13.96 Trip computer multi-pin plug (Sec 15)

A   Depress tab   B   Plug withdrawn

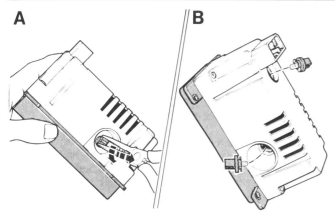

Fig. 13.97 Trip computer bulb renewal (Sec 15)

A   Using pliers to remove bulb   B   Bulb locations

124 Note which way round the pad is fitted, then remove the wire clips and adhesive tape which secure it to the seat. Retrieve the tie-rod and fit it to the new pad.
125 Fit the new pad with the thermostat facing the cushion foam. Secure the pad with wire clips and tape, making sure that it is not too tight – it must be able to flex when sat on.
126 Refit the cushion or backrest trim, being careful not to trap or kink the pad.
127 Refit the seat, reconnect the wiring and check the pads for correct operation.

Central door locking
Front and rear door lock solenoid – removal and refitting
128 The central door locking solenoids are bolted to a bracket which in turn is bolted to the door lock assembly.
129 To remove a solenoid, first remove the door interior trim panel as described in Chapter 12, Section 15.
130 Disconnect the multi-plugs for the solenoid, lock switch and door ajar switch.
131 Disconnect the two interior handle remote control rods.
132 Disconnect the door lock and exterior handle control rods.
133 Remove the screws securing the door lock assembly to the door and lift the assembly out.
134 The solenoid may then be removed from the lock assembly by removing the two securing screws.
135 The lock switch is also secured to the assembly by two screws.
136 Refit in the reverse order and check the operation of the door lock.

15.118 Instrument panel (Sapphire)

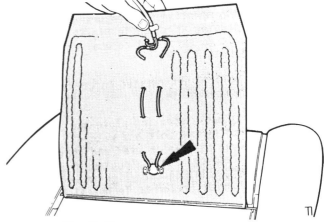

Fig. 13.98 Seat heating pad (Sec 15)
Thermostat (arrowed) faces foam

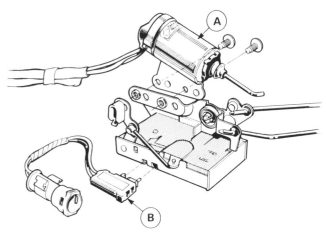

Fig. 13.99 Door lock assembly (Sec 15)

A   Solenoid   B   Door ajar switch

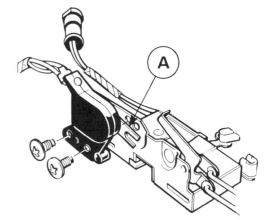

Fig. 13.100 Door lock switch cut-out (A) (Sec 15)

Tailgate lock solenoid – removing and refitting (Hatchback version described, Estate similar)
137 Open the tailgate and remove the interior trim panel (refer to Chapter 12, Section 12).
138 Disconnect the solenoid and lock operation rods, and disconnect the multi-plug and earth tag from the tailgate.
139 Remove the screws securing the solenoid to the lock assembly and lift out the solenoid.
140 Refit in the reverse order and check the operation of the lock.

Fig. 13.101 Removing tailgate lock solenoid (Hatchback)
(Sec 15)

Electric window motor – removal and refitting
141 Remove the door interior trim panel as described in Chapter 12, Section 15.
142 Remove the window regulator assembly as described in Chapter 12, Section 23.
143 Disconnect the multi-plug.
144 Remove the three bolts securing the motor to the regulator assembly, and lift the motor from the assembly.
145 The motor can be separated from the drive gear by removing the screw.
146 Refit in the reverse order, ensuring the drive gear is correctly meshed with the regulator.

Dim-dip lighting system
147 Recent legislation requires that all vehicles registered after the 1st April 1987 should be equipped with a dim-dip lighting system.
148 The system provides the headlamps with a brightness between that of the sidelamps and the headlamps on normal dipped beam.
149 The purpose of the system is to prevent vehicles being driven on sidelamps only.
150 Full information will be given in the driver's handbook, but basically, the dim-dip lamps are in operation whenever the light switch is in the first 'ON' position and the ignition is switched on.
151 All Sierras built after October 1st 1986 (build code GR) are equipped with additional relays to enable the dim-dip system to be fitted.
152 For details of the relays, which are all located in the fusebox, and of the fuses, refer to Fig. 13.125.

Radio (DIN fixing) – removal and refitting
153 An increasing number of radio/cassette units have DIN standard fittings. Two special tools, obtainable from in-car entertainment specialists, are required for removal.
154 Insert the tools into the holes in the front of the radio and push them in until they snap into place. Pull the tools outwards to release the radio (photo).
155 When refitting the radio, just push it into its bracket until the retaining lugs snap into place.

Radio with power amplifier – removal and refitting
156 Several different radio kits are currently being installed in different Sierra models, some of which have a power amplifier.
157 The radio removal and fitting instructions are adequately covered, all installations being basically the same.
158 The power amplifier is housed under the radio in the space formerly used for cassette storage.
159 To remove the amplifier, undo the two screws under the top edge of the amplifier unit.
160 Slide the unit forward, out from the centre console housing until the multi-plugs can be disconnected. Remove the unit.
161 Refit in the reverse order.

Radio aerial – removal and refitting
162 Remove the rear parcel shelf side-member on the side concerned (Chapter 12, Section 31).

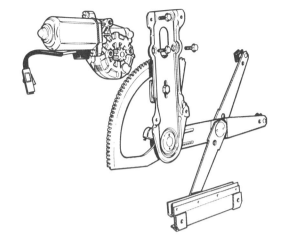

Fig. 13.102 Power-operated window motor and regulator
(Sec 15)

Fig. 13.103 Radio/cassette removal tool (Sec 15)

15.154 Removing radio with special tools (arrowed)

163 Remove the upper retaining nut, spacer and sealing washer from the top of the aerial. Collapse the aerial mast.
164 On power-operated aerials, remove the lower mounting support bracket screw and disconnect the power lead.
165 Pull the aerial into the car and disconnect the aerial lead. Note that the lead may have a screw fitting instead of the usual pull-off type (photo).
166 The aerial leads runs through the roof. If it is wished to renew the lead, it may be considered easier to leave the old lead in place and run a new one under the carpet. Follow existing wire runs where possible.
167 Refit in the reverse order of removal. With non-power aerials, make sure that the foot of the aerial enters its mounting (photo).

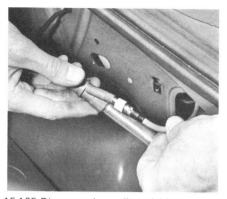

15.165 Disconnecting radio aerial lead

15.167 Base of radio aerial entering mounting

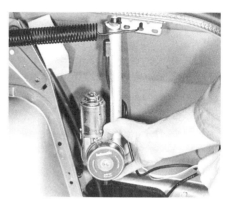

15.178 Fitting electric aerial to Sapphire

Fig. 13.104 Aerial amplifier location (Saloon) (Sec 15)

Retaining screws arrowed

In-car entertainment – 1987 on

168 Various options are available on later vehicles, some types of equipment being factory fitted as standard depending upon model. These include a six speaker sound system, an aerial integral with the rear screen and an isolator module (located below the tailgate glass in Hatchback and Estate models, and behind the rear parcel tray trim panel in Saloons).

169 Interference suppression is comprehensive on later vehicles and is applied to all electric motors as well as the provision of filters and earth bonding to all essential components.

Rear screen aerial amplifier – removal and refitting

170 Disconnect the battery.

Saloon

171 Remove the rear parcel shelf.

172 Disconnect the leads, extract the fixing screws and remove the amplifier.

Hatchback

173 Remove the tailgate trim panel, extract the amplifier bracket fixing screws.

Estate

174 Remove the tailgate trim panel and extract the four speaker bracket screws.

All models

175 Refitting is a reversal of removal.

Aerial – location and access

176 Access to the rear wing-mounted aerial on Hatchback versions is described in Chapter 12, Section 31.

177 On Sapphire Saloon models, access is obtained after opening the luggage boot and removing the right-hand trim panel.

178 If an electrically-operated aerial is being fitted, instead of a manually raised type, connect it in accordance with the manufacturer's instructions which will normally be as follows (photo).

Co-axial lead to radio
Power lead to 'ignition on' side of fusebox (10A circuit) or to any live take-off point using in-line fuse. Power feed usually red
Black wire to earth
Radio sensing wander lead (green or blue) to spade terminal or plug connector at rear of radio

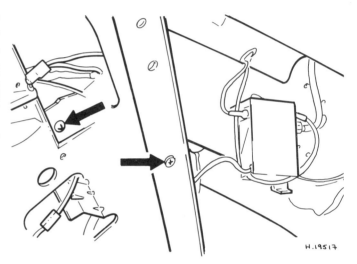

Fig. 13.105 Aerial amplifier bracket screws (arrowed) on Hatchback version (Sec 15)

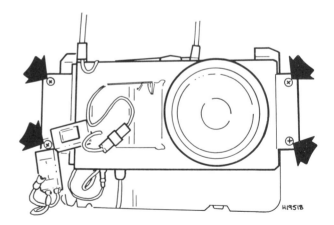

Fig. 13.106 Speaker/aerial amplifier bracket screws (arrowed) on Estate version (Sec 15)

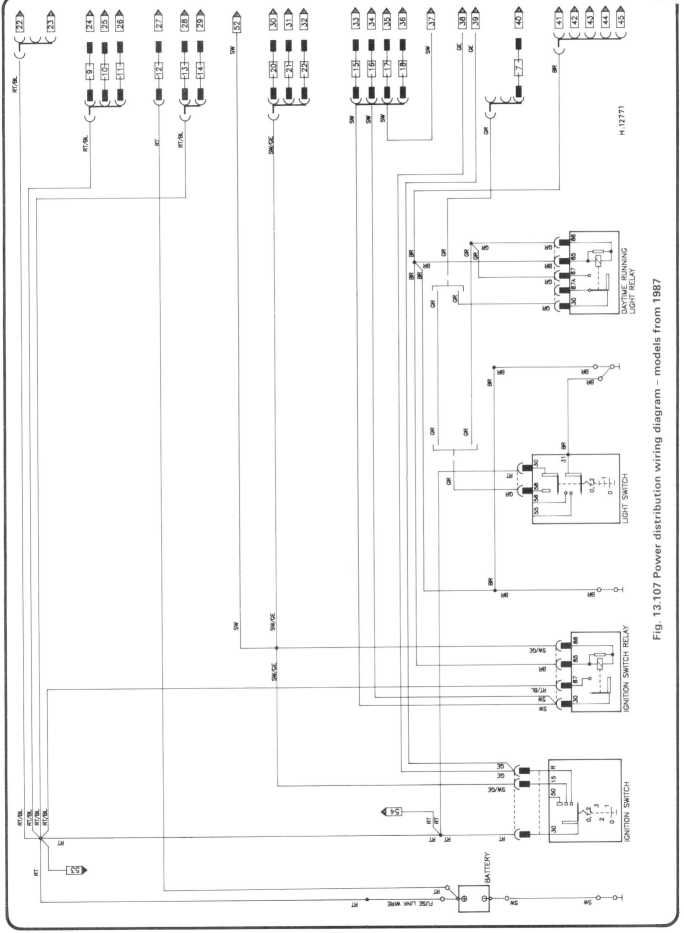

Fig. 13.107 Power distribution wiring diagram – models from 1987

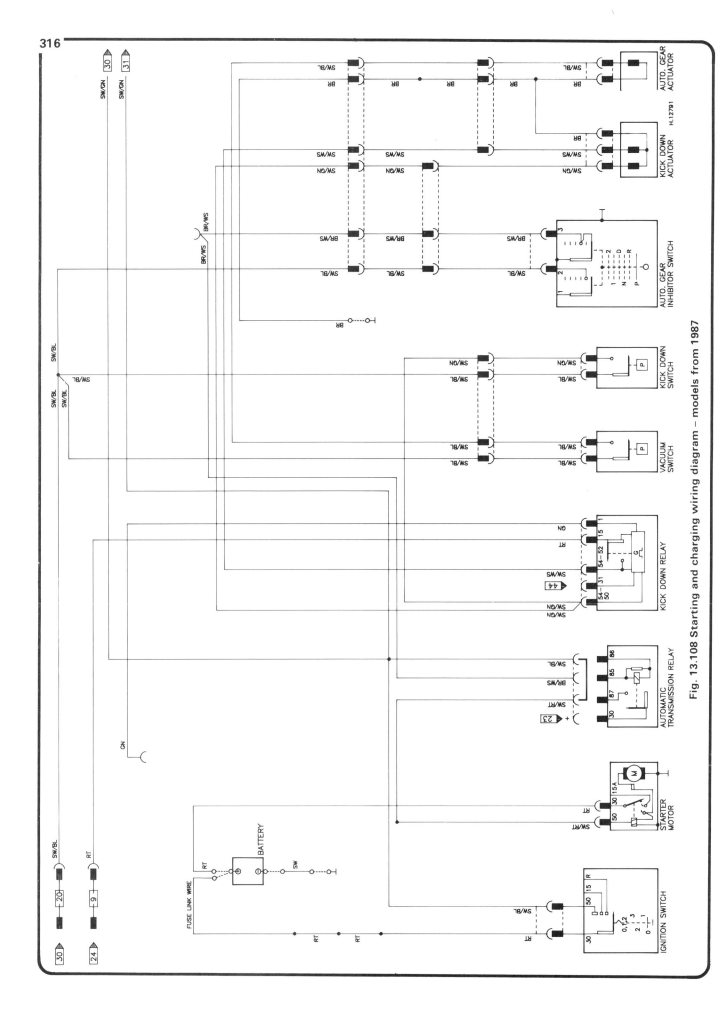

Fig. 13.108 Starting and charging wiring diagram – models from 1987

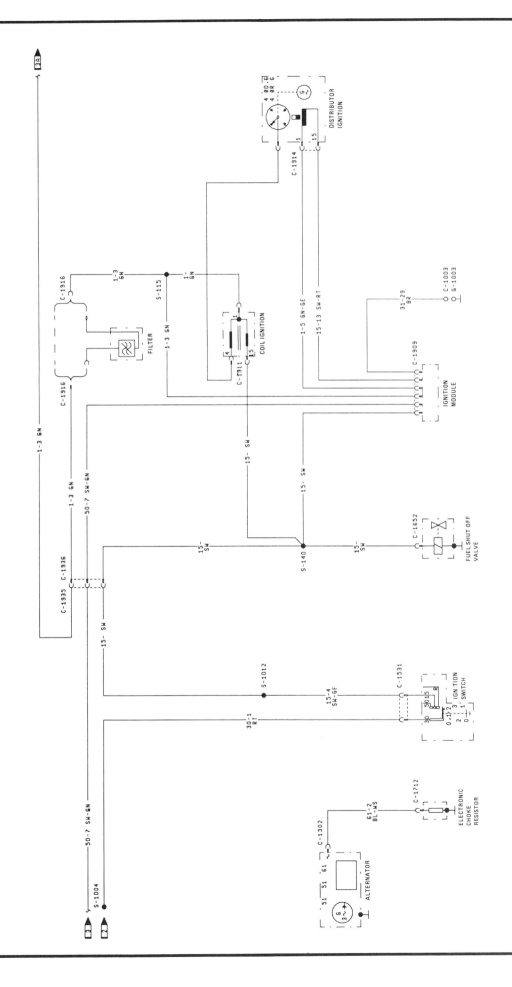

Fig. 13.109 1.6 engine management wiring diagram – models from 1987

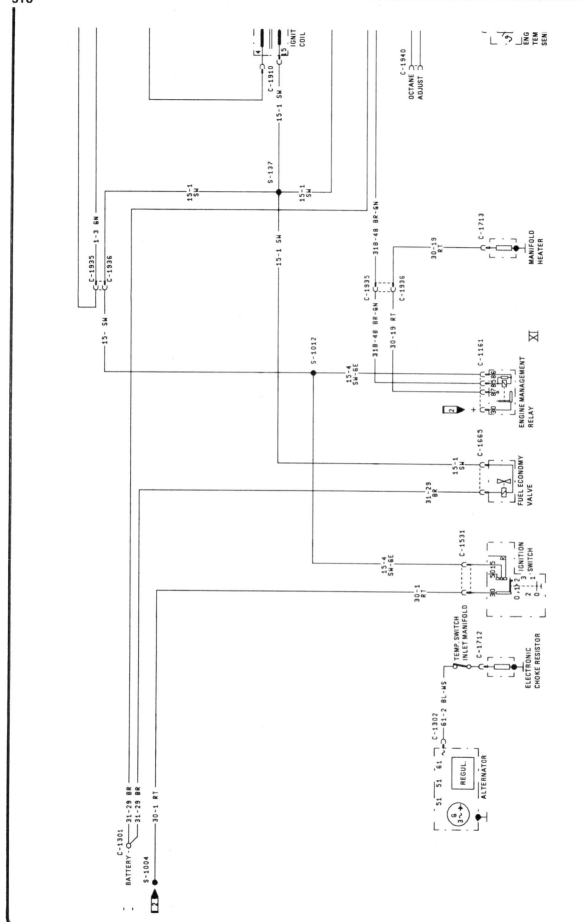

Fig. 13.110 1.8 engine management wiring diagram – models from 1987

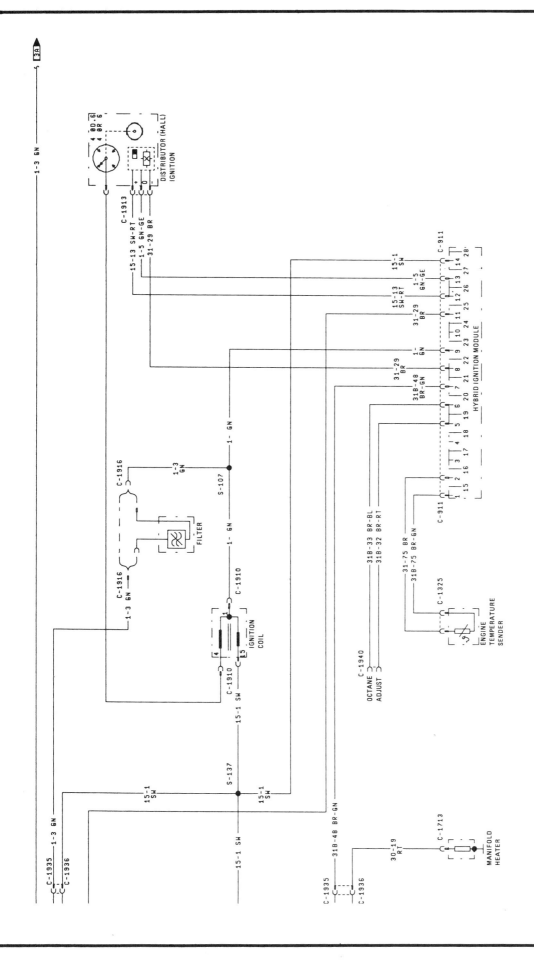

Fig. 13.110 (continued) 1.8 engine management wiring diagram – models from 1987

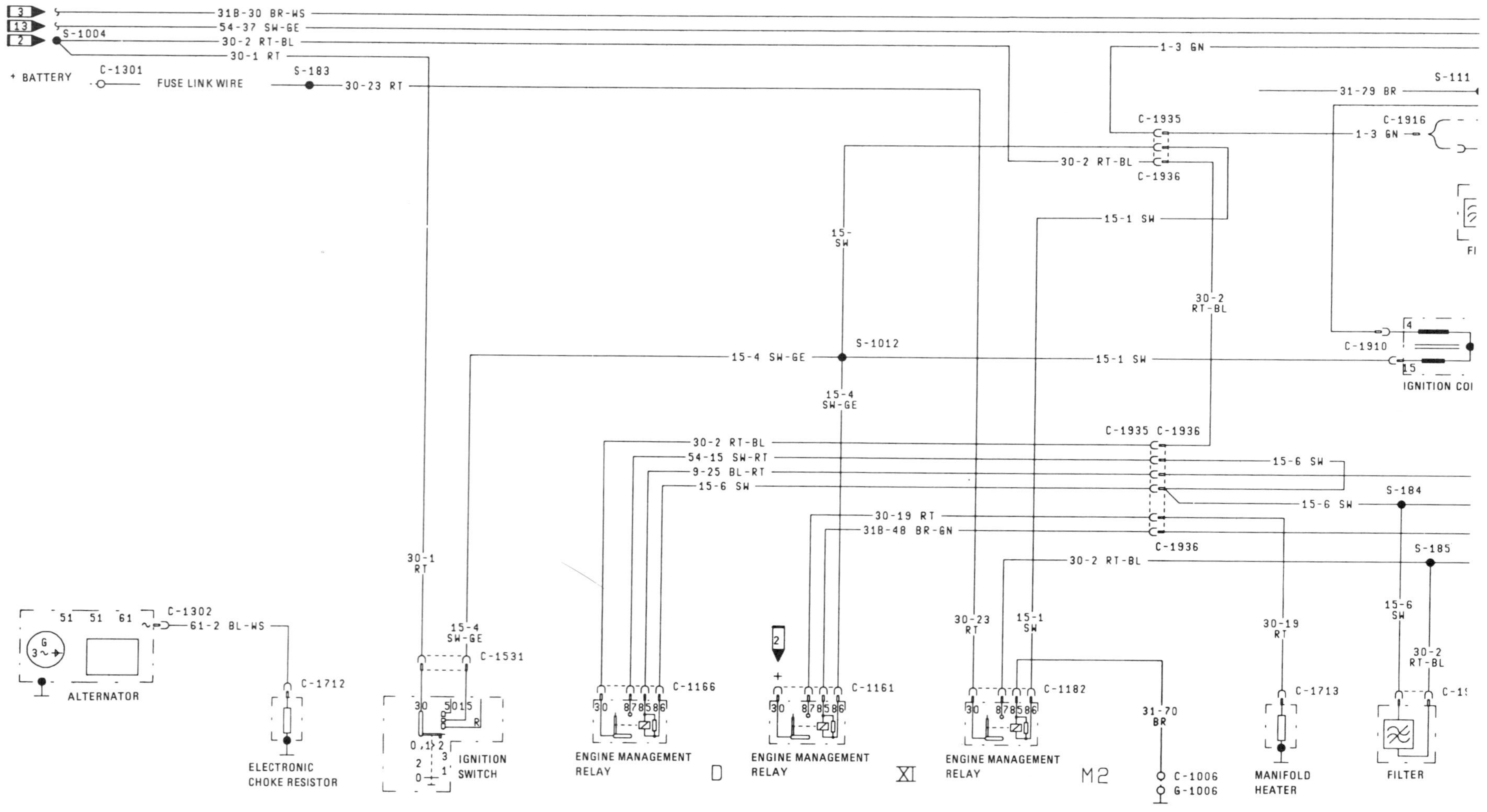

Fig. 13.111 2.0 engine management wiring diagram – models from 1987

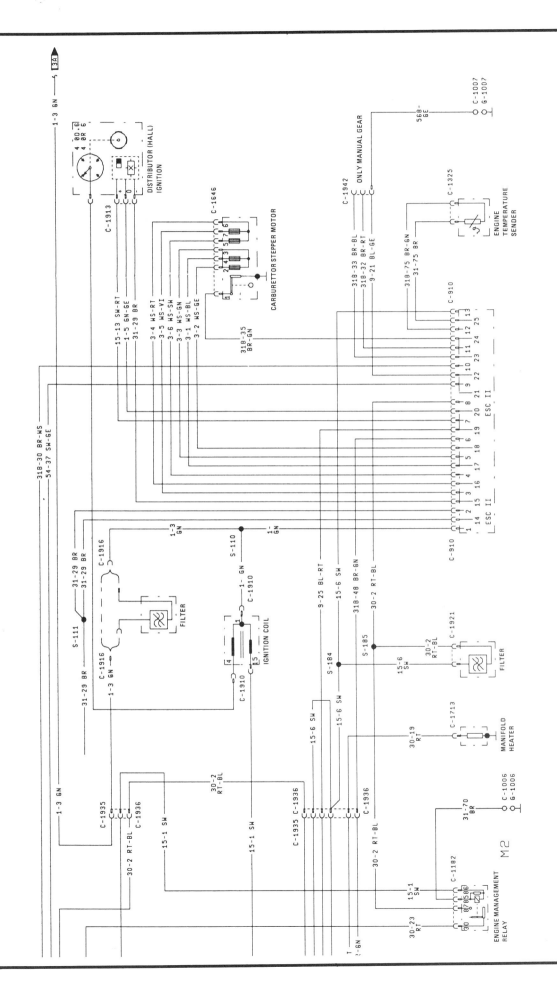

Fig. 13.111 (continued) 2.0 engine management wiring diagram – models from 1987

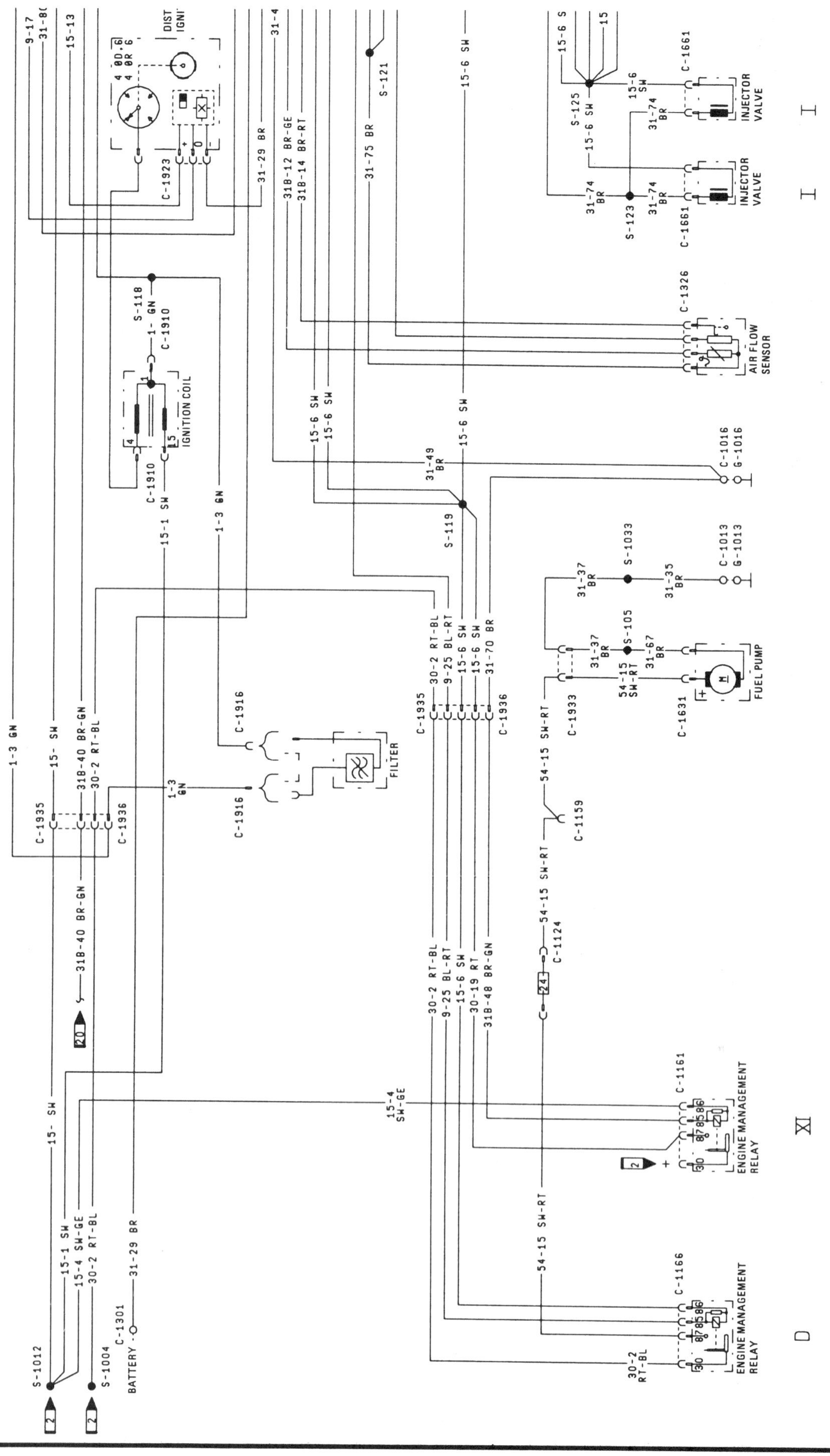

Fig. 13.112 Fuel injection wiring diagram – models from 1987

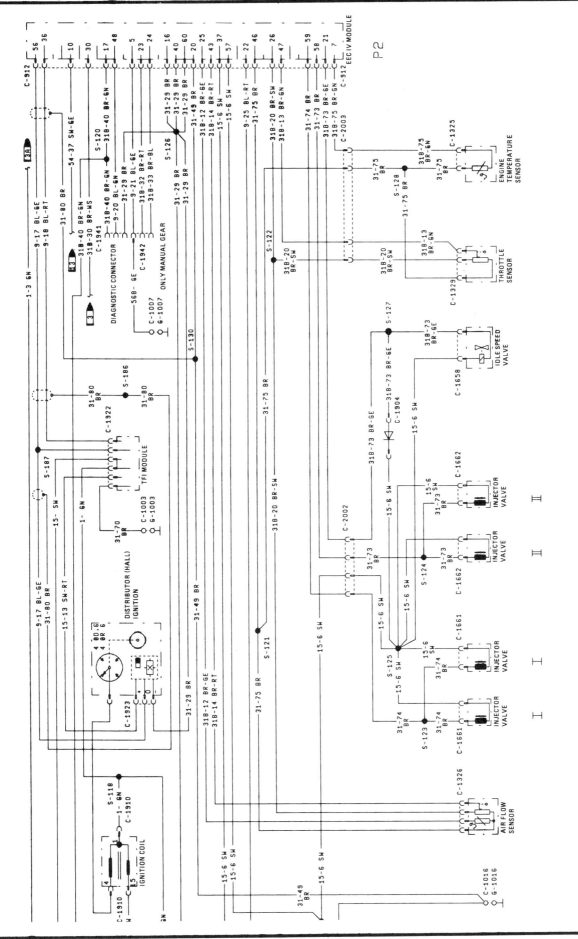

Fig. 13.112 (continued) Fuel injection wiring diagram – models from 1987

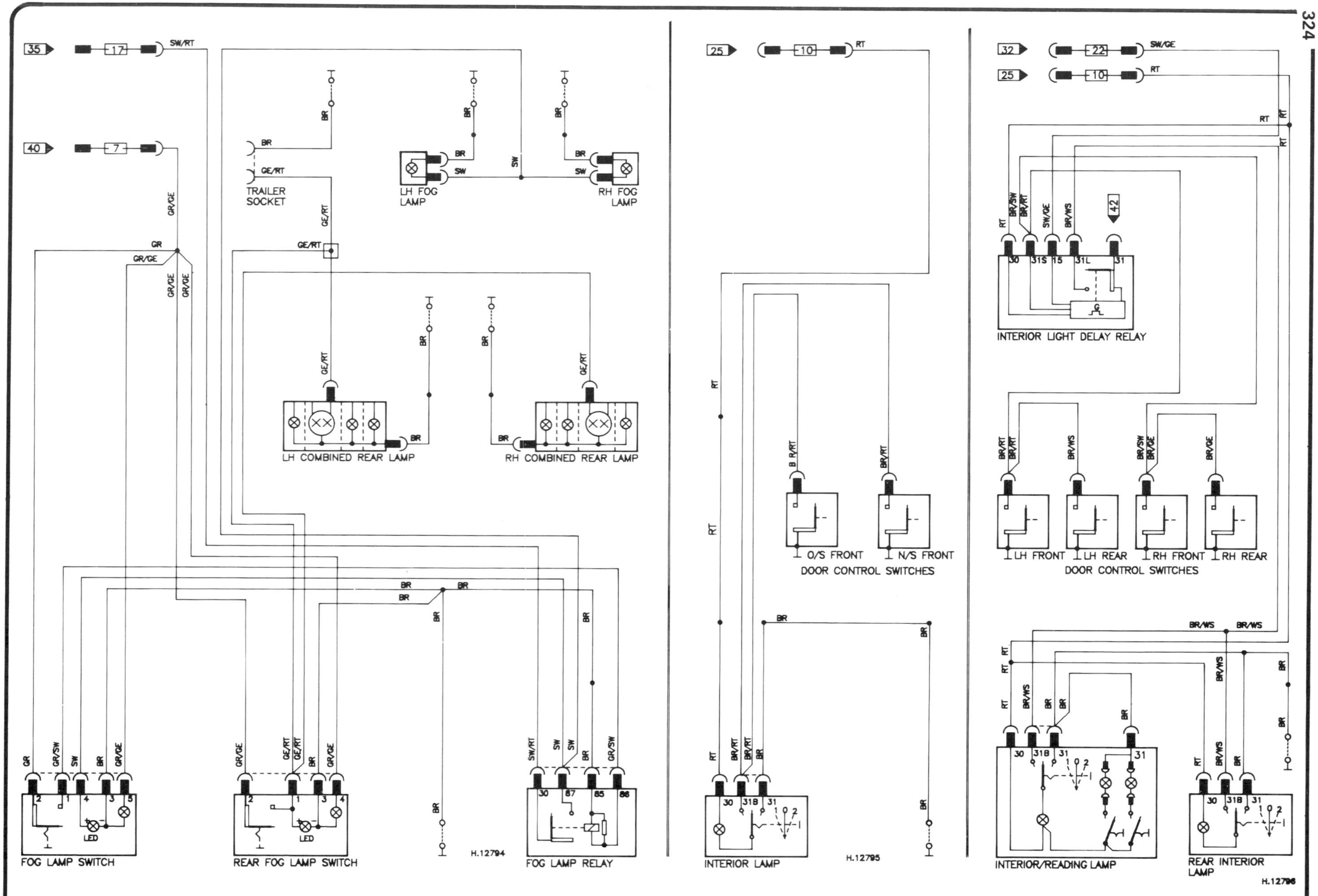

Fig. 13.113 Foglamps and interior lights wiring diagram – models from 1987

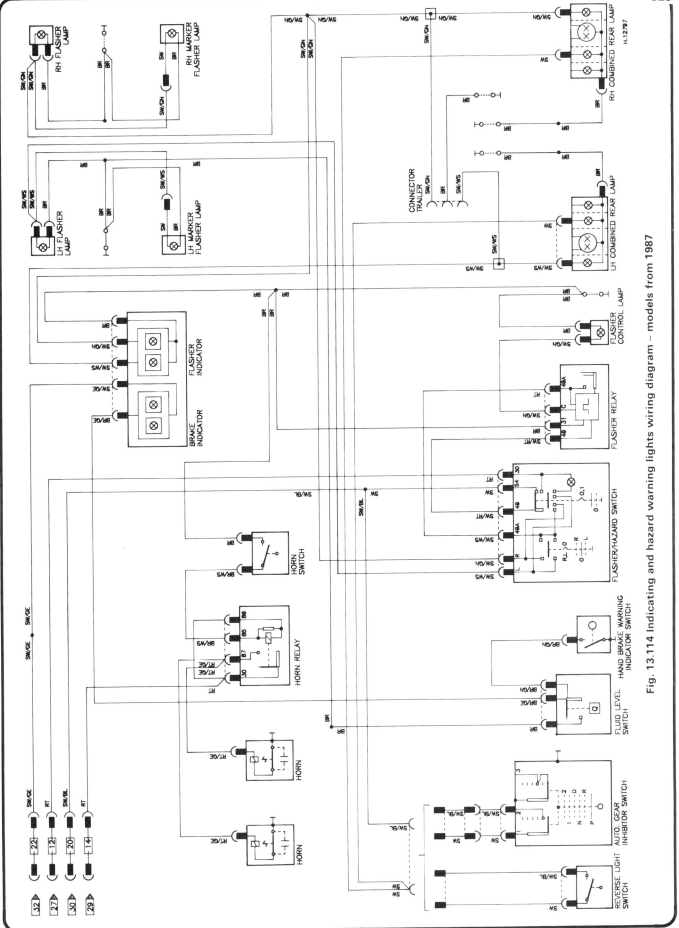

Fig. 13.114 Indicating and hazard warning lights wiring diagram – models from 1987

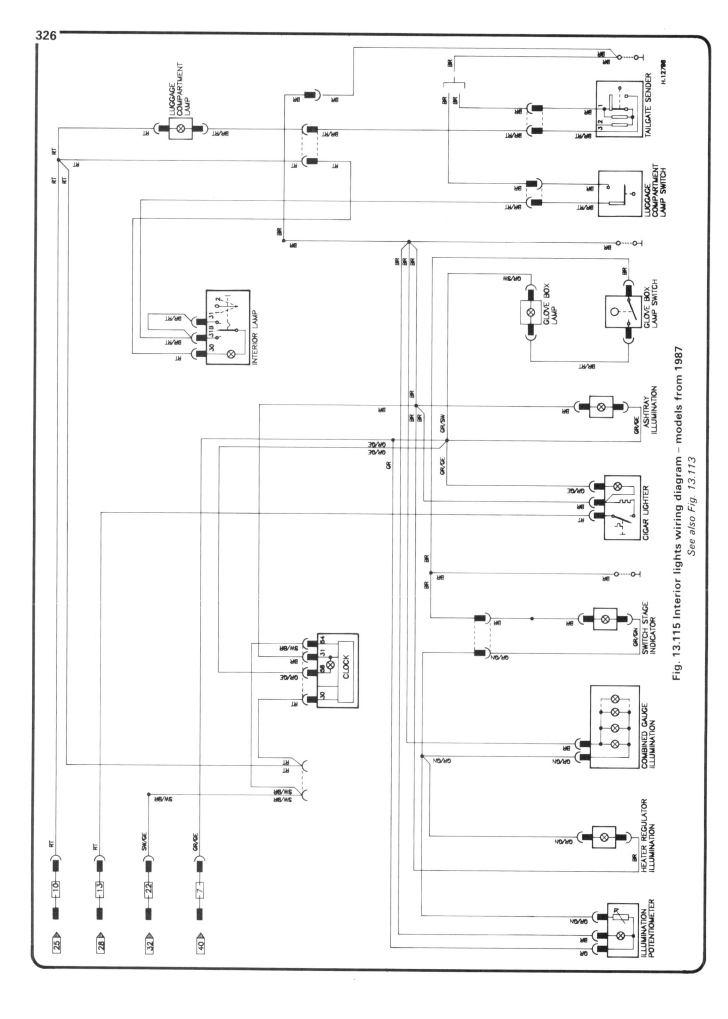

Fig. 13.115 Interior lights wiring diagram – models from 1987

See also Fig. 13.113

H.12798

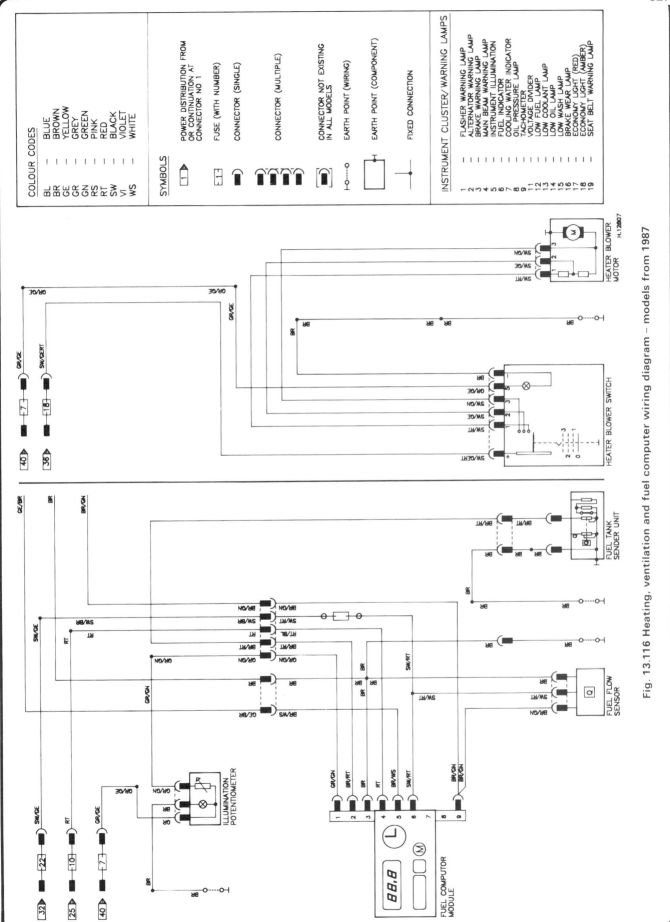

Fig. 13.116 Heating, ventilation and fuel computer wiring diagram – models from 1987

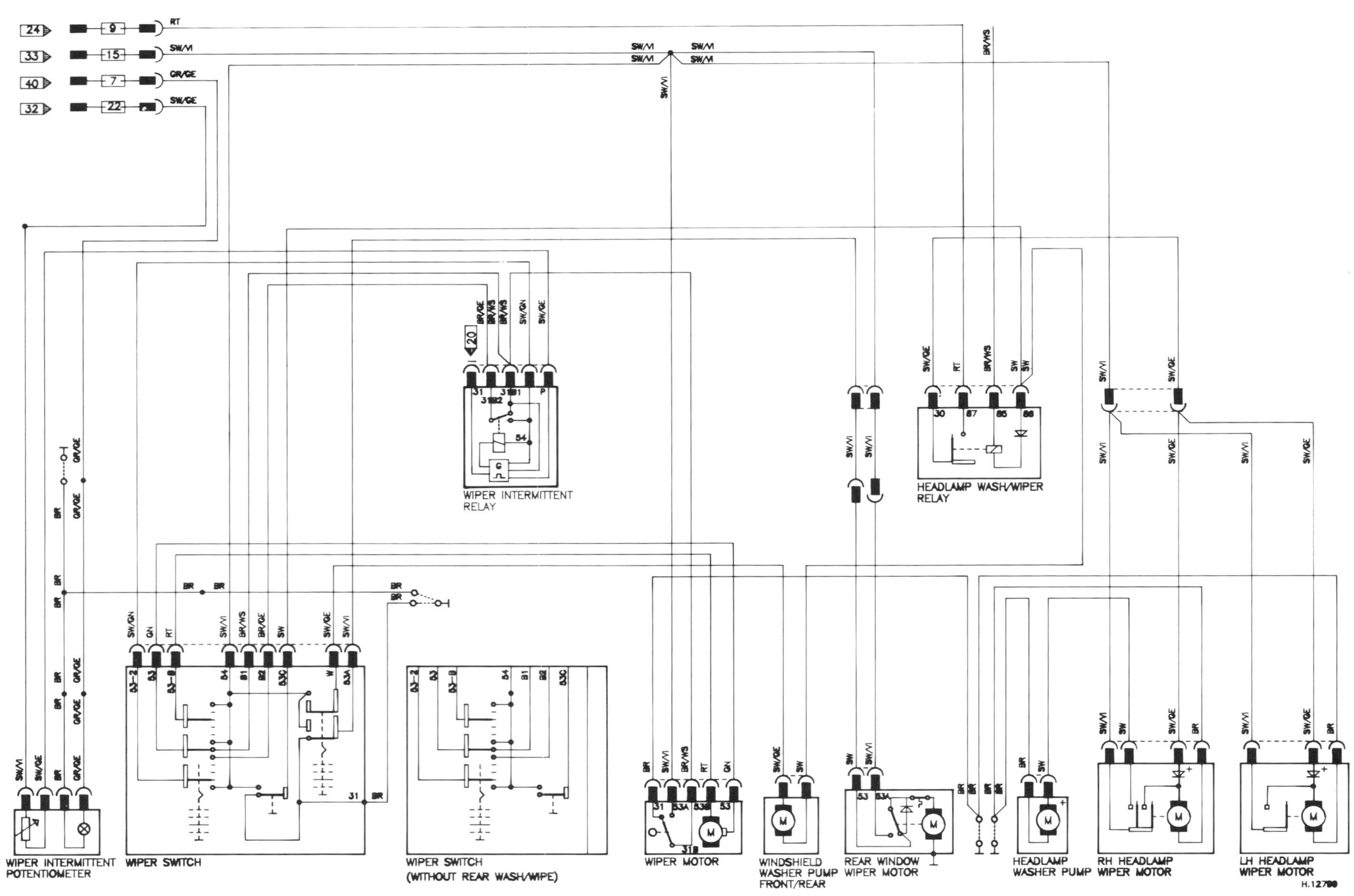

LH HEADLAMP WIPER MOTOR

RH HEADLAMP WIPER MOTOR

HEADLAMP WASHER PUMP

HEADLAMP WASH/WIPER RELAY

REAR WINDOW WIPER MOTOR

WINDSHIELD WASHER PUMP FRONT/REAR

WIPER MOTOR

WIPER INTERMITTENT RELAY

WIPER SWITCH (WITHOUT REAR WASH/WIPE)

WIPER SWITCH

WIPER INTERMITTENT POTENTIOMETER

Fig. 13.117 Wash/wipe wiring diagram – models from 1987

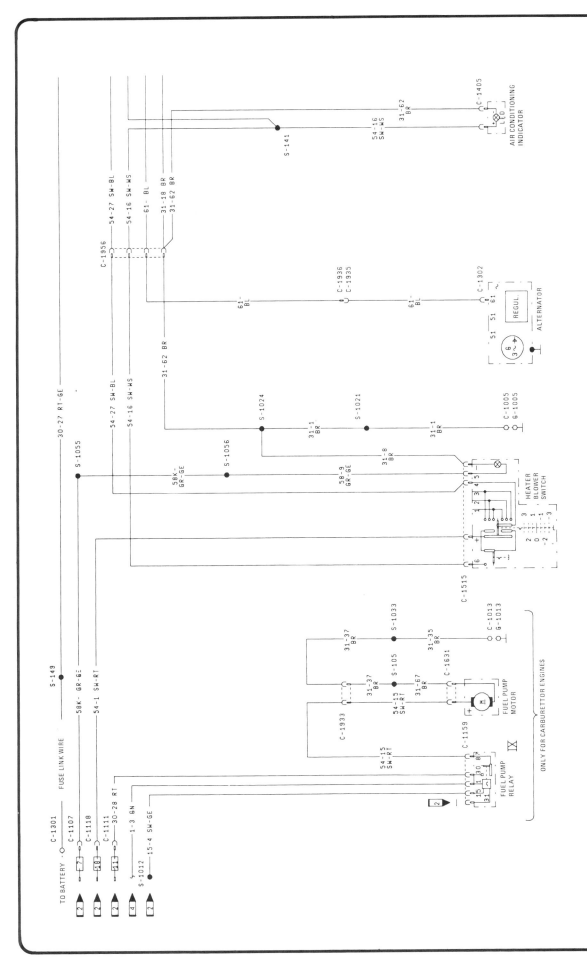

Fig. 13.118 Air conditioning wiring diagram – models from 1987

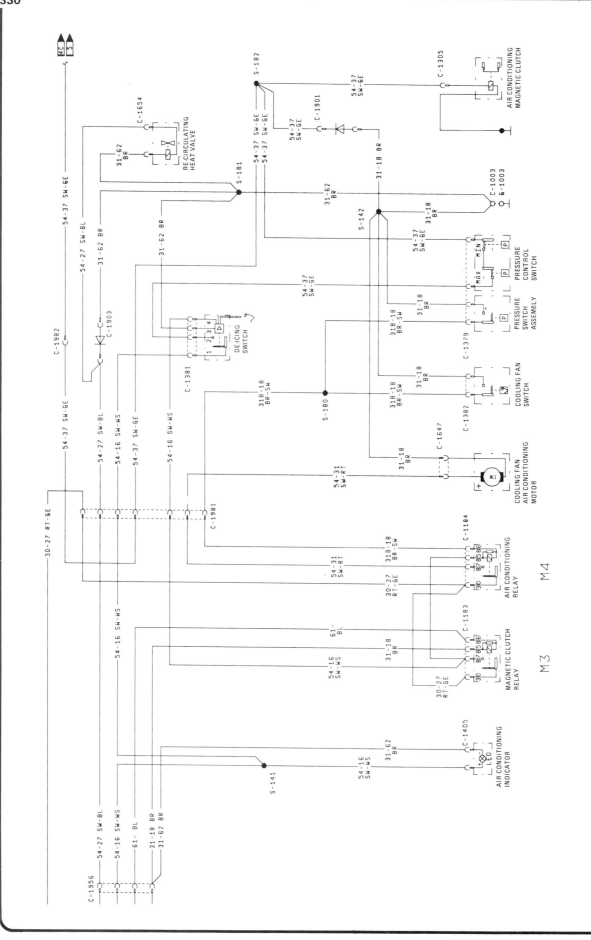

Fig. 13.118 (continued) Air conditioning wiring diagram – models from 1987

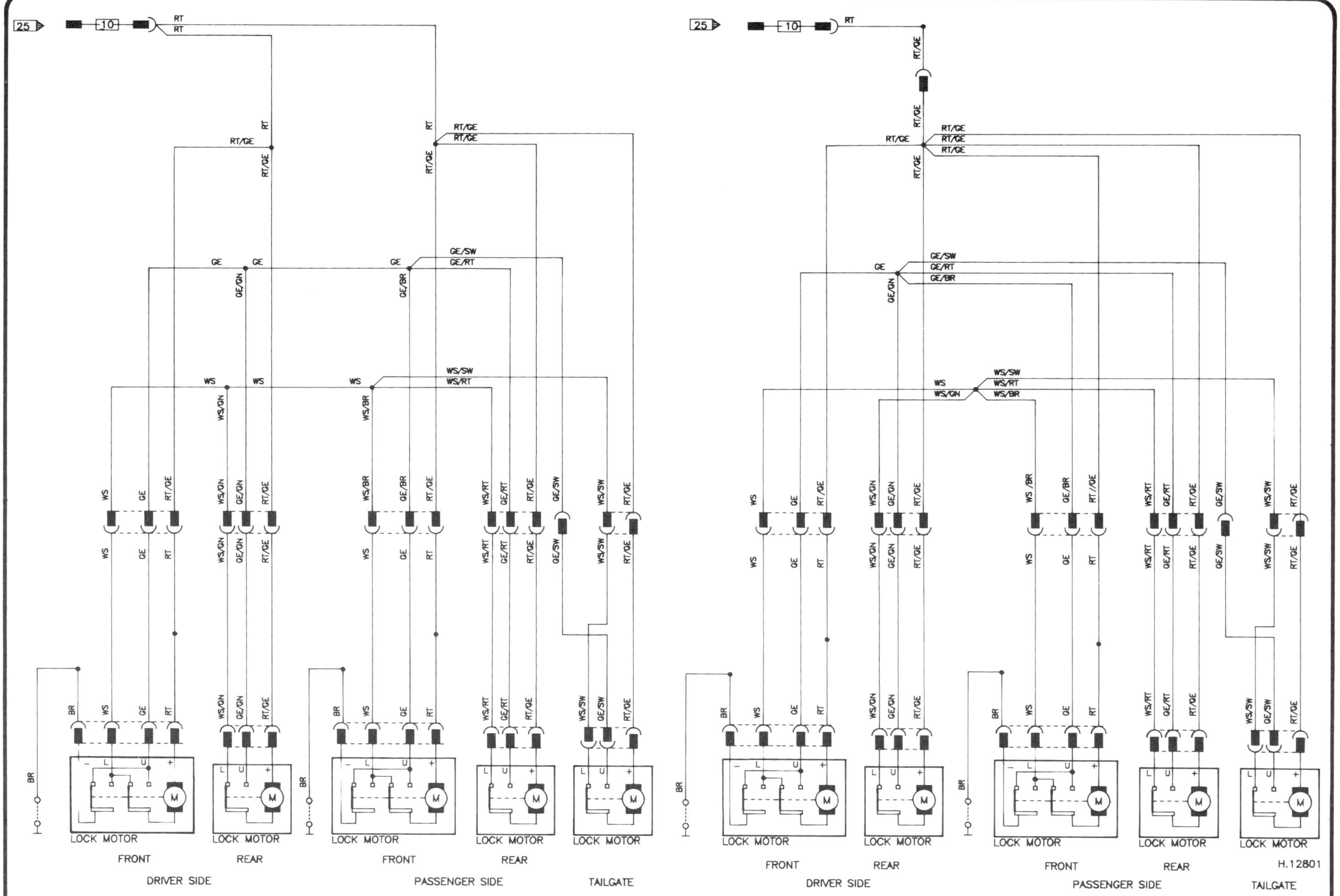

Fig. 13.119 Central door locking – models from 1987

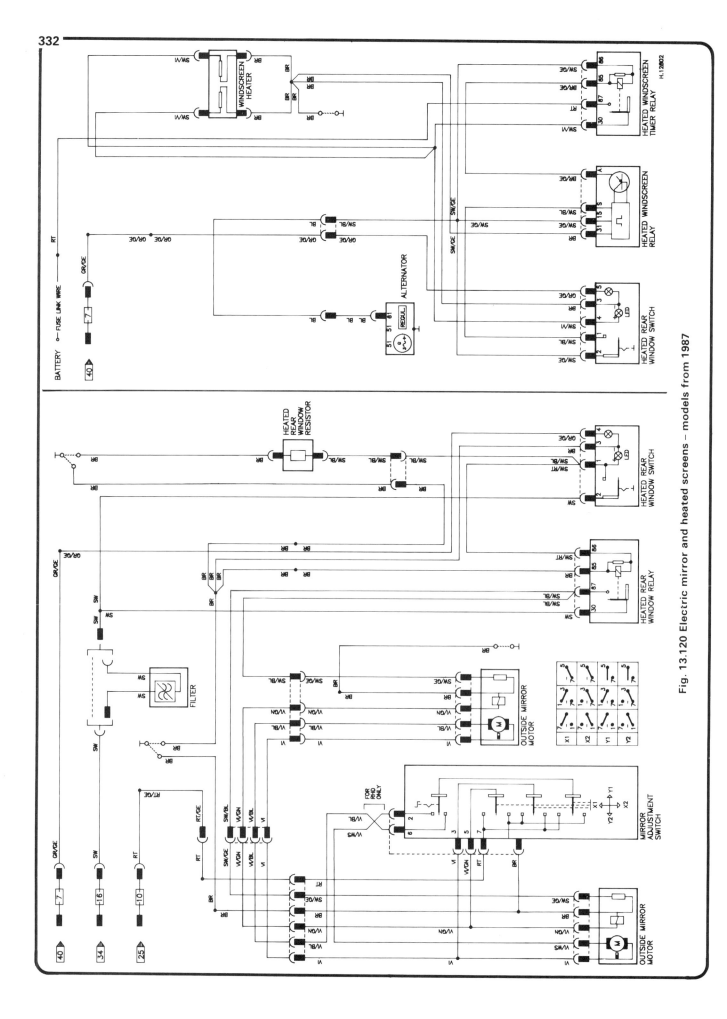

Fig. 13.120 Electric mirror and heated screens – models from 1987

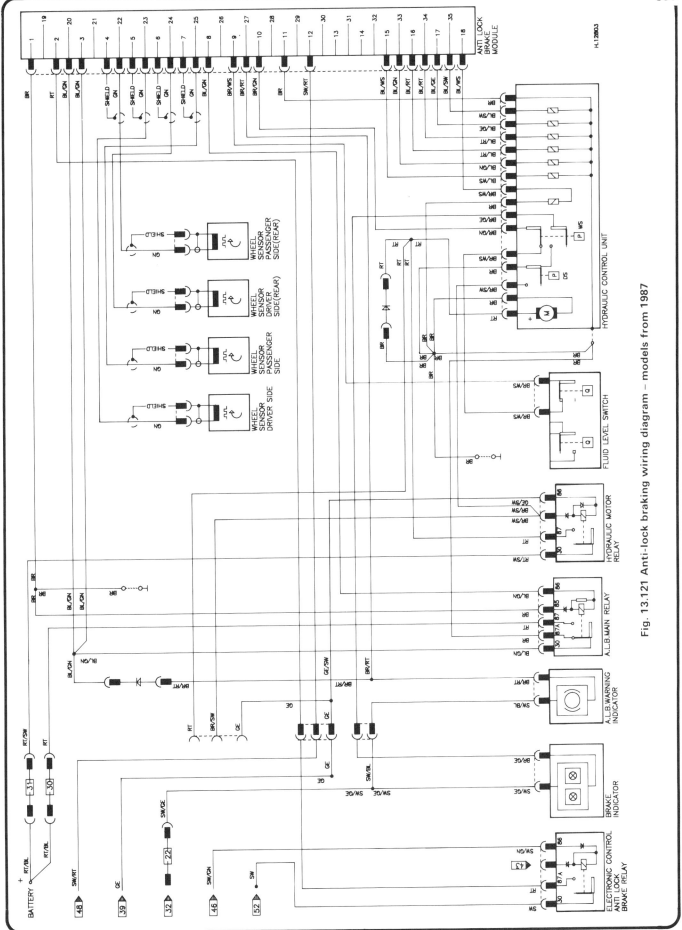

Fig. 13.121 Anti-lock braking wiring diagram – models from 1987

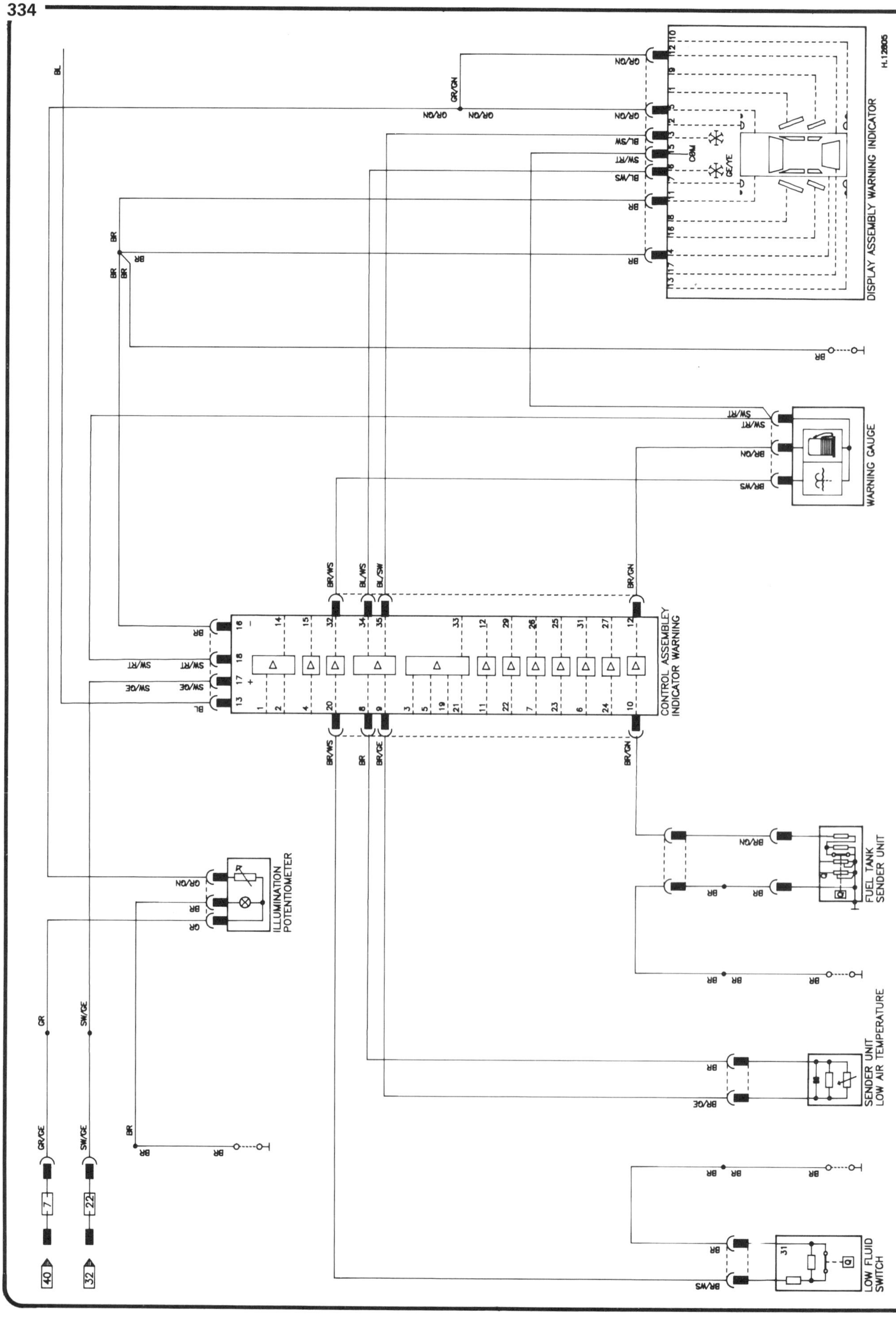

Fig. 13.122 Auxiliary warning lamps wiring diagram – models from 1987

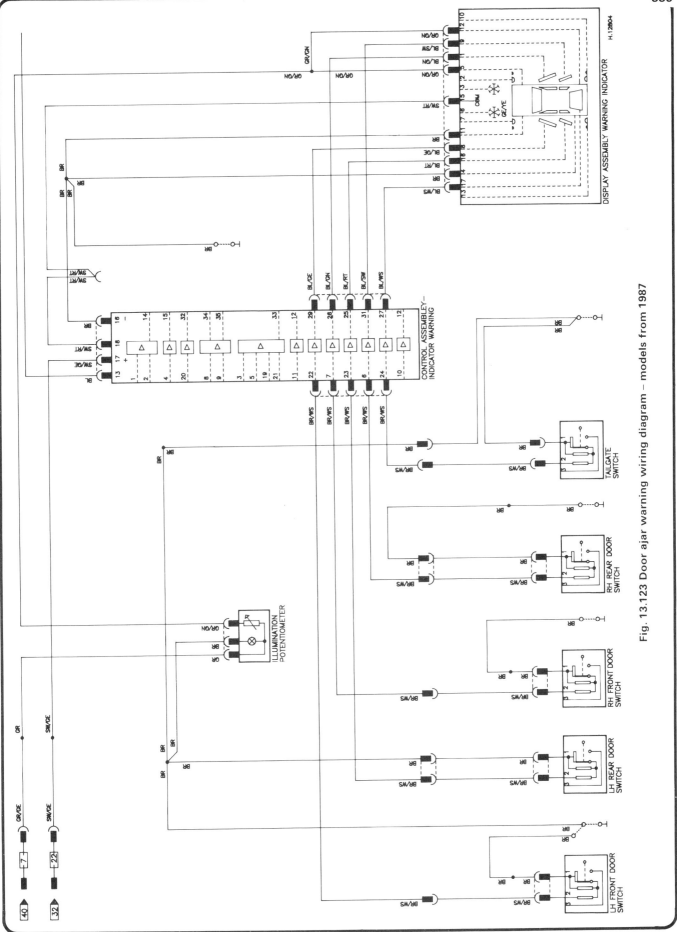

Fig. 13.123 Door ajar warning wiring diagram – models from 1987

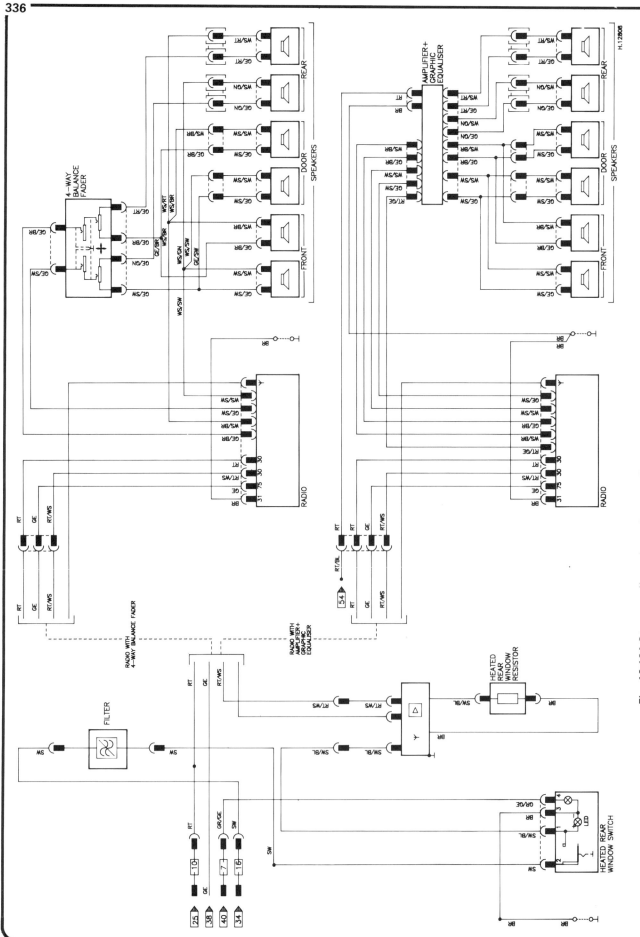

Fig. 13.124 Stereo radio and speaker equaliser wiring diagram – models from 1987

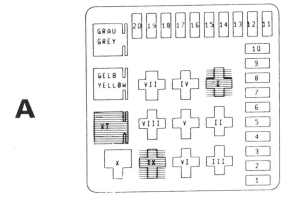

A – Sierra '86	Relay number	Colour
	I	White
	IX	Green
	XI	Blue
B – Sierra '87	B	Blue
	II	Blue
	X	White

	Fuse	Amperage	Circuit
A – Sierra '86	14	20	Left-hand main beam
	15	20	Right-hand main beam
	16	10	Left-hand dipped beam
	17	10	Right-hand dipped beam
	18	10	Left-hand parking light
	19	10	Right-hand parking light
	20	15	Dim-dipped beam
B – Sierra '87	1	20	Left-hand main beam
	2	20	Right-hand main beam
	3	10	Left-hand dipped beam
	4	10	Right-hand dipped beam
	5	10	Left-hand parking light
	6	10	Right-hand parking light

Fig. 13.125 Dim-dip lighting relays and fuses – models from 1986

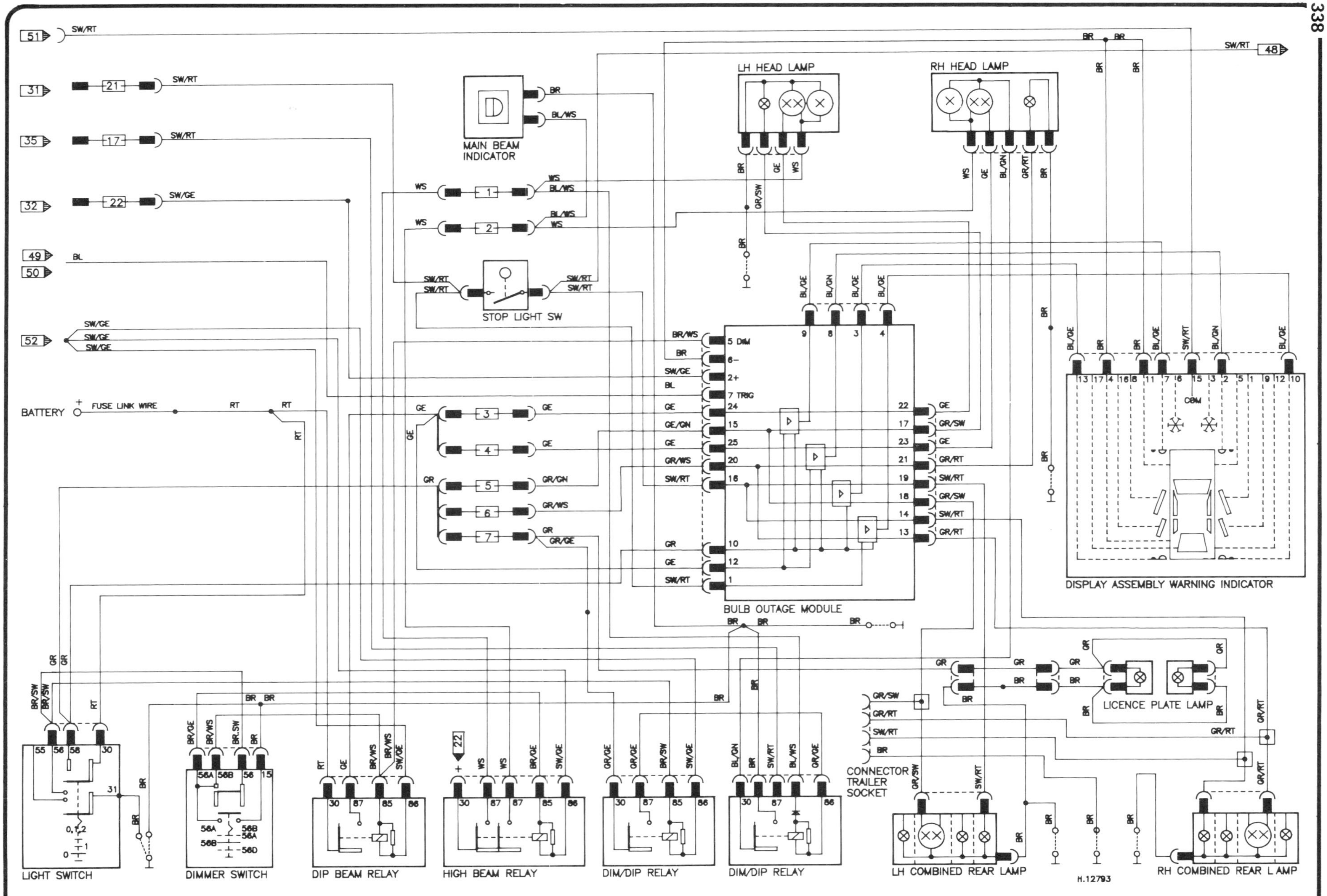

338

Fig. 13.126 Dim-dip lighting and bulb failure warning wiring diagram – models from 1986

DISPLAY ASSEMBLY WARNING INDICATOR

RH COMBINED REAR LAMP

LICENCE PLATE LAMP

LH COMBINED REAR LAMP

H.12793

RH HEAD LAMP

CONNECTOR TRAILER SOCKET

LH HEAD LAMP

BULB OUTAGE MODULE

DIM/DIP RELAY

DIM/DIP RELAY

MAIN BEAM INDICATOR

HIGH BEAM RELAY

STOP LIGHT SW

DIP BEAM RELAY

DIMMER SWITCH

BATTERY   FUSE LINK WIRE

LIGHT SWITCH

16.2 Later type anti-roll bar mountings. Plastic covers (arrowed)

16.6 Prising off a rear anti-roll bar connecting strap

16.7 Rear anti-roll bar retaining clip

16 Suspension and steering

Front anti-roll bar mountings – all models

1   As noted in Chapter 11, Section 7, the front and rear dished washers which retain the anti-roll bar front mounting bushes are not interchangeable. The front washer is yellow, and has a deeper dish than the rear washer, which is black.
2   From November 1983, plastic covers were fitted between the washers and the bushes (photo).
3   From September 1984, the bushes themselves were modified. New bushes can be fitted to earlier models, but both left-hand and right-hand bushes must be renewed together.
4   Do not fully tighten the anti-roll bar end nuts until the weight of the vehicle is on its wheels.

Rear anti-roll bar – removal and refitting

5   Slacken the rear wheel nuts, chock the front wheels and raise and securely support the rear of the car. Remove the rear wheels.
6   Prise off the straps which connect the anti-roll bar to the lower suspension arms (photo).
7   Unbolt the two retaining clips from the floor and remove the anti-roll bar (photo).

8   Remove the rubber mountings and the connecting straps. Use liquid detergent as a lubricant when fitting new mounting components.
9   Refit in the reverse order of removal. Tighten the retaining clip bolts to the specified torque.

Rear wheel bearings (later models) – renewal

10   On later models the hub retaining nut (elsewhere known as driveshaft or axle nut) **on the left-hand side has a left-hand thread.** See Section 13 of this Chapter for details.

Rear wheel hub-to-suspension arm bolts

11   There are two different types of bolt used to secure the rear wheel hub to the lower suspension arm.
12   The differences are shown in Fig. 13.12.
13   The two types of bolt must not be mixed on one vehicle, but may be changed for complete sets of either type. **Note:** A complete set is eight bolts, four each side.
14   Note also that the bolts have different tightening torques (refer to the Specifications).

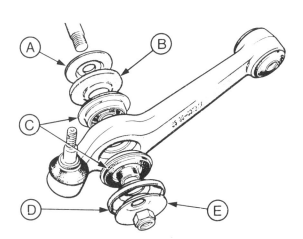

Fig. 13.127 Front anti-roll bar end mountings (1985 on) (Sec 16)

A   Rear (black) washer
B   Plastic cover
C   Bushes
D   Plastic cover
E   Front (yellow) washer

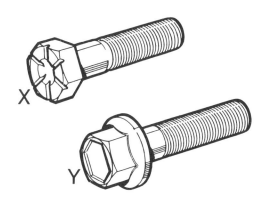

Fig. 13.128 Alternative types of rear hub to suspension arm bolts (Sec 16)

X   Type A   Y   Type B

Steering track rod balljoints
15 The method of securing the track rod inboard balljoints to the steering rack by peening (Chapter 11, Section 20, paragraph 16) can be superseded if preferred by the following alternative method.
16 Coat the threads of the tie-rod with Loctite 270 then tighten the balljoints to a torque wrench setting of 65 lbf ft (88 Nm).

Rear coil spring (models with ABS) – removal and refitting
17 Chock the front wheels. Raise and support the rear of the vehicle.
18 Unbolt the driveshaft flange from the rear hub.
19 Prise off the anti-roll bar strap on the side concerned.
20 Unclip the brake hose union from the bracket, and the brake pipe from the floor, on the side concerned. If working on the left-hand side, also unbolt the brake pipe three-way union from the floor.
21 Support the lower suspension arm with a trolley jack.
22 Remove the shock absorber lower mounting bolt and separate the shock absorber from the lower suspension arm. (On Estate models it may be necessary to remove the shock absorber completely.)
23 Unbolt the suspension crossmember guide plate from the underbody on the side concerned.
24 Lower the jack. Remove the spring and the rubber seat.
25 Refitting is a reversal of removal. Tighten all fastenings to the specified torque, when known.

Rear suspension lower arm (models with ABS) – removal and refitting
26 Remove the rear disc shield as described in Section 14.
27 Unhook the exhaust system from its rear mountings.
28 Disconnect the brake pipes from the flexible hoses. Free the brake pipes from the brackets on the lower arms.
29 Unclip the handbrake cable from the lower arm.
30 Disconnect the ABS wheel sensor and unclip the wiring.
31 Remove the propeller shaft (Chapter 7, Section 2).
32 Prise off the anti-roll bar strap on the side concerned.
33 Remove the rear spring as described earlier in this Section.
34 Remove the suspension arm-to-crossmember pivot bolts. Lower the arm and remove it.
35 Refit by reversing the removal operations, noting the following points:

   (a) Check the gearbox oil level if much was lost during propeller shaft removal
   (b) Carry out final tightening of the arm-to-crossmember pivot bolts (Chapter 11 Specifications) with the weight of the vehicle on its wheels
   (c) Bleed the brake hydraulic system (Section 14)

Wheel stud (all models) – renewal
36 Several different lengths of wheel stud have been fitted in production, sometimes with a corresponding change in brake disc thickness. Make sure that the correct studs are purchased.
37 The following procedure is specified by the manufacturer as applying to the rear wheels, but there is no reason to suppose that it will not work on the front.
38 Remove the wheel and the brake disc or drum.

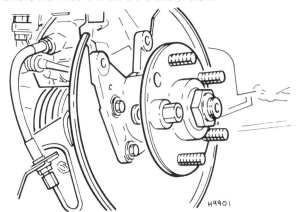

Fig. 13.129 Fitting a wheel stud using a nut and spacer (Sec 16)

39 Drive the wheel stud out of the hub flange.
40 Insert the new stud from the inboard side of the flange. Engage the splines by hand pressure, then draw the stud into place with a wheel nut and progressively thicker spacers.
41 Refit the brake disc or drum and the wheel.

Wheels and tyres – general care and maintenance
42 Wheels and tyres should give no real problems in use provided that a close eye is kept on them with regard to excessive wear or damage. To this end, the following points should be noted.
43 Ensure that tyre pressures are checked regularly and maintained correctly. Checking should be carried out with the tyres cold and not immediately after the vehicle has been in use. If the pressures are checked with the tyres hot, an apparently high reading will be obtained owing to heat expansion. Under no circumstances should an attempt be made to reduce the pressures to the quoted cold reading in this instance, or effective underinflation will result.
44 Underinflation will cause overheating of the tyre owing to excessive flexing of the casing, and the tread will not sit correctly on the road surface. This will cause a consequent loss of adhesion and excessive wear, not to mention the danger of sudden tyre failure due to heat build-up.
45 Overinflation will cause rapid wear of the centre part of the tyre tread coupled with reduced adhesion, harsher ride, and the danger of shock damage occurring in the tyre casing.
46 Regularly check the tyres for damage in the form of cuts or bulges, especially in the sidewalls. Remove any nails or stones embedded in the tread before they penetrate the tyre to cause deflation. If removal of a nail *does* reveal that the tyre has been punctured, refit the nail so that its point of penetration is marked. Then immediately change the wheel and have the tyre repaired by a tyre dealer. Do *not* drive on a tyre in such a condition. In many cases a puncture can be simply repaired by the use of an inner tube of the correct size and type. If in any doubt as to the possible consequences of any damage found, consult your local tyre dealer for advice.
47 Periodically remove the wheels and clean any dirt or mud from the inside and outside surfaces. Examine the wheel rims for signs of rusting, corrosion or other damage. Light alloy wheels are easily damaged by 'kerbing' whilst parking, and similarly steel wheels may become dented or buckled. Renewal of the wheel is very often the only course of remedial action possible.
48 The balance of each wheel and tyre assembly should be maintained to avoid excessive wear, not only to the tyres but also to the steering and suspension components. Wheel imbalance is normally signified by vibration through the vehicle's bodyshell, although in many cases it is particularly noticeable through the steering wheel. Conversely, it should be noted that wear or damage in suspension or steering components may cause excessive tyre wear. Out-of-round or out-of-true tyres, damaged wheels and wheel bearing wear/maladjustment also fall into this category. Balancing will not usually cure vibration caused by such wear.
49 Wheel balancing may be carried out with the wheel either on or off the vehicle. If balanced on the vehicle, ensure that the wheel-to-hub relationship is marked in some way prior to subsequent wheel removal so that it may be refitted in its original position.
50 General tyre wear is influenced to a large degree by driving style – harsh braking and acceleration or fast cornering will all produce more rapid tyre wear. Interchanging of tyres may result in more even wear, but this should only be carried out where there is no mix of tyre types on the vehicle. However, it is worth bearing in mind that if this is completely effective, the added expense of replacing a complete set of tyres simultaneously is incurred, which may prove financially restrictive for many owners.
51 Front tyres may wear unevenly as a result of wheel misalignment. The front wheels should always be correctly aligned according to the settings specified by the vehicle manufacturer.
52 Legal restrictions apply to the mixing of tyre types on a vehicle. Basically this means that a vehicle must not have tyres of differing construction on the same axle. Although it is not recommended to mix tyre types between front axle and rear axle, the only legally permissible combination is crossply at the front and radial at the rear. When mixing radial ply tyres, textile braced radials must always go on the front axle, with steel braced radials at the rear. An obvious disadvantage of such mixing is the necessity to carry two spare tyres to avoid contravening the law in the event of a puncture.

53 In the UK, the Motor Vehicles Construction and Use Regulations apply to many aspects of tyre fitting and usage. It is suggested that a copy of these regulations is obtained from your local police if in doubt as to the current legal requirements with regard to tyre condition, minimum tread depth, etc.

17 Bodywork and fittings

Bumper decorative mouldings (all models) – fitting
1 New bumpers are supplied without the decorative moulding fitted. Special primer and adhesive tape are specified by the makers for retaining the moulding: it is suggested that the DIY mechanic consults a Ford dealer, either to have the job done or to acquire sufficiently small quantities of primer and tape.
2 The moulding and the adhesive tape must both be warmed to 45°C (113°F) immediately before use. The primer must be allowed to dry for three minutes before meeting the tape.

Bumpers – removal and refitting
Front (1985 to 1986)
3 Working under the front of the vehicle, unscrew the two bumper fixing bolts.
4 If fitted, disconnect the foglamp multi-pin plug.
5 Working under the front wings, extract the fixing screws and pull the protective underwing shield away from the ends of the bumper.
6 Grip the bumper and pull it directly from the vehicle.
7 Before fitting the bumper, check that the O-ring and reinforcement plate are located at the right-hand mounting point.
8 The help of an assistant will make installation easier, especially to engage the side pins positively.
9 Tighten the bolts and refix the protective underwing shields.
10 If necessary, the bumper can be adjusted for height using a Torx screwdriver which is at least 150.0 mm in length.
Front (1987)
11 The removal operations are similar to those described earlier except that the bumper is secured only by the end fixing screws. Centre support is provided by square section spigots. Pull the bumper straight out to remove. This later type of bumper is adjustable for height as previously described (photos).
Rear (all years)
12 From inside the luggage compartment, unscrew the two bumper fixing screws then disconnect the leads from the rear number plate lamps (photo).
13 Working under each side of the vehicle, turn each of the quarter turn fixings to release the ends of the bumper (photos).
14 Pull the bumper directly from the vehicle.
15 Refitting is a reversal of removal, but the help of an assistant will facilitate installation.
16 The bumper is adjustable for height in a simiar way to the front bumper (photo).

Radiator grille (1987 on) – removal and refitting
17 Open the bonnet and extract the two screws from the front face of the grille (photo).
18 Remove the grille after releasing its lugs and clips from the headlamp housings and wing guides (photos).
19 Refitting is a reversal of removal, but align the grille carefully before tightening the fixing screws.

Bonnet release with cable broken – all models
20 Should the bonnet release cable break with the bonnet shut, the bonnet may be opened as follows.
21 Raise and securely support the front of the car. Using an inspection light or torch, look up between the radiator and the radiator grille panel and locate the circular hole below the bonnet lock (photo).
22 Insert a screwdriver into the hole so that it passes to the right of the striker. Twist or lever the lock sliding plate to the right until the striker jumps free. The bonnet can now be opened.

Wing protective liners (later models)
23 Both front and rear wings have plastic protective liners secured by screws and reinforcement plates and turn buckles (photos).

Door lock striker adjustment – 1985 on
24 Later door lock strikers are secured by two Torx screws (photo).

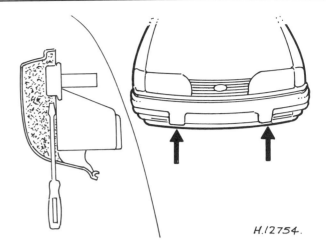

H.12754.

Fig. 13.130 Front bumper height adjustment (Sec 17)

17.11A Front bumper mounting spigot and socket

17.11B Front bumper end fixing screw

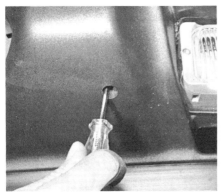

17.11C Adjusting the height of a front bumper

17.11D Front bumper height adjusting screw

17.12 Rear bumper mounting screw

17.13A Rear bumper end quarter turn screw

17.13B Rear bumper end fixing dovetail

17.16 Rear bumper height adjusting screw

17.17 Radiator grille fixing screw

17.18A Radiator grille upper fixing clip

17.18B Radiator grille lower fixing clip

17.21 Access hole (arrowed) below bonnet lock

17.23A Underwing shield fixing screw

17.23B Releasing underwing shield turnbuckle

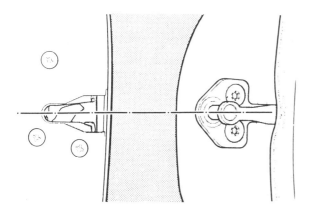

Fig. 13.131 Door lock striker correctly aligned (Sec 17)

17.24 Later type door lock striker

25 When fitting or adjusting such a striker, align the striker with the centre of the lock opening (Fig. 13.13).

Door inner trim removal – all models (except Sapphire)
26 To avoid damaging the door trim, it is recommended that a tool be made similar to that shown in Fig. 13.13 and used to release the securing clips.
27 If a clip will not release even with the aid of the tool, sever it with a chisel or knife and fit a new clip on reassembly.

Rear quarter window spoilers – general
28 Rear quarter window spoilers (popularly known as 'ears') are fitted to vehicles from 1985. The spoilers are believed to improve stability under some driving conditions.
29 Kits are available for fitting these spoilers, and the associated front spoiler, to earlier vehicles. Seek advice from a Ford dealer if contemplating the purchase of such a kit, since tools for inserting blind anchor nuts and blind rivets may be required.
30 Note that where they are not screwed into place, the rear quarter window spoilers are secured by adhesive.

Opening rear quarter window – removal and refitting
31 Remove the trim from around the window. It is secured by five screws.
32 Remove the two screws which secure the locking catch to the body.
33 Remove the screw covers from the hinges. Support the glass and remove the hinge screws; lift out the glass.
34 If a new window is being fitted, transfer the locking catch to it.
35 Refit in the reverse order of removal.

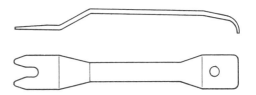

Fig. 13.132 Door trim clip removal tool (Sec 17)

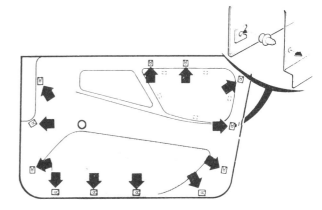

Fig. 13.133 Door trim panel clip locations (arrowed) (Sec 17)

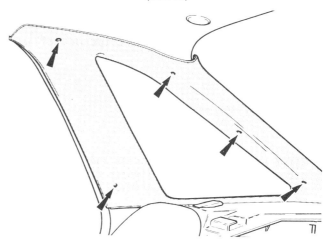

Fig. 1.134 Quarter window trim panel fixing screws (arrowed) (Sec 17)

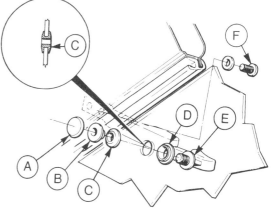

Fig. 13.135 Quarter window locking catch details (Sec 17)

A   Cap   D   Spacer
B   Retainer   E   Catch
C   Grommet   F   Screw (one of two)

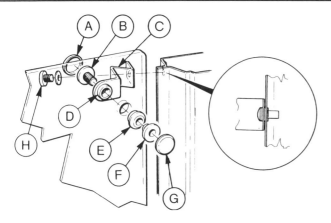

Fig. 13.136 Quarter window hinge details (Sec 17)

A   Cap   E   Grommet
B   Screw   F   Retainer
C   Hinge   G   Cap
D   Spacer   H   Screw

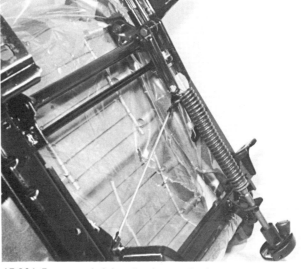

17.36A Front seat height adjusting mechanism

Front seats

36 Certain vehicles are equipped with height adjustable front seats and may have mechanically or pneumatically adjustable lumbar supports. When removing a height-adjustable rear seat, the heavy tension spring must be released from the floor (photos).

Front seat air cushion – removal and refitting

37 Remove the seat as described in Chapter 12, Section 29.
38 Straighten the seat back cover retaining tangs and pull the cover upwards to expose the air cushion.
39 Cut through the securing rings and remove the pipe clamps. Withdraw the air cushion assembly from the seat.
40 Refitting is a reversal of removal, use new securing rings.

Front seat air adjustable ball – removal and refitting

41 Remove the front seat as described in Chapter 12, Section 29.
42 Extract the two screws which hold the metal tube to the seat then cut through the plastic hose as close to the metal tube as possible. Discard the tube and the inflator.
43 When refitting the assembly, fit a new pipe clamp over the plastic hose and then warm the end of the hose in boiling water until it is pliable. Push the metal tube into the plastic hose, ensuring a hose overlap of at least 20.0mm (0.8 in).
44 Crimp a new clamp onto the hose to ensure an airtight seal.
45 Clamp the metal tube to the seat.
46 Refit the seat as described in Chapter 12.

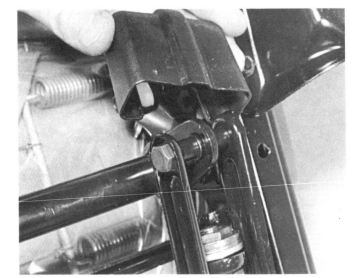

17.36B Seat crank protective cover

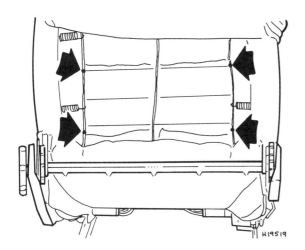

Fig. 13.137 Air cushion securing 'HOG' rings (Sec 17)

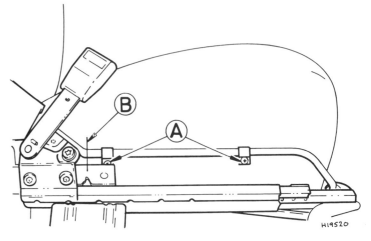

Fig. 13.138 Air cushion tube and inflator (Sec 17)

A   Tube clamps   B   Hose cutting point

Seat belts – general

47 All models are fitted with inertia reel front seat belts. Rear seat belts are available for earlier models and standard on later vehicles.

48 Periodically inspect the belts to check that they are not chafed or cut, and verify the operation of the inertia reel mechanism. Check the mountings for security.

49 Do not use strong detergent, bleach or dye on the belt webbing, as such agents may weaken it.

50 The inertia reel mechanism is not repairable. In the event of malfunction the complete belt must be renewed. Belts which have been subject to impact loads should also be renewed.

51 When renewing a belt or a buckle mounting, note carefully the fitted sequence of washers, spacers, etc, and adhere to this when refitting.

52 If it is wished to fit rear seat belts, purchase belts of a reputable make which are stated to be suitable for the Sierra. Such belts should be fitted according to the maker's instructions.

Front seat belts (1987 on)

53 The front seat belt upper anchor point is vertically adjustable to suit the requirements of the wearer (photo).

Rear seat

54 On certain models, the rear seat is split 60/40 as an aid to carrying

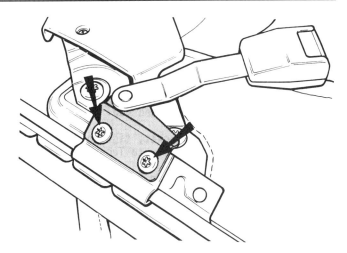

Fig. 13.139 Torx type seat belt stalk bolts (arrowed) (Sec 17)

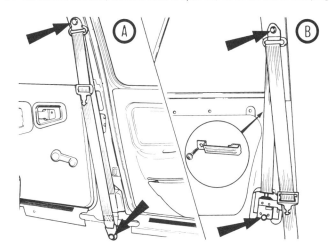

Fig. 13.140 Front seat belt anchor points (Sec 17)

A Five-door   B Three-door

Fig. 13.141 Rear seat belt floor anchorages (arrowed) (Sec 17)

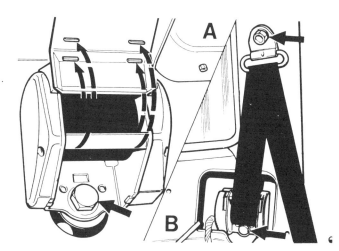

Fig. 13.142 Rear seat belt reel anchor points (Sec 17)

A Hatchback   B Estate

17.53 Seat belt upper anchor release button

17.54A Split rear seat release knob (Sapphire)

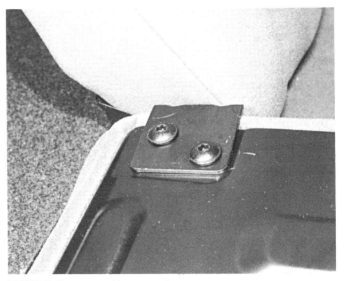

17.54B Split rear seat hinge securing screws

long loads (photos).
55 On Sapphire Saloon models with a fixed rear seat backrest, the backrest is secured by three Torx screws accessible after removing the seat cushion, and by three nuts accessible from inside the boot.

Roofrack – fitting to Sapphire Saloon
56 Due to the fact that exterior type gutters are no longer fitted to this model, the two plastic covers on each side of the roof panel should be

slid aside and the roofrack mounted on the gutters which are now exposed.

Rear spoiler (Sapphire Saloon)
57 When fitting a rear spoiler as an accessory, make sure that the luggage compartment lid bump stops are screwed out so that they project 20.0 mm (0.8 in). This is to prevent the spoiler fixings damaging the paintwork when closing the lid.

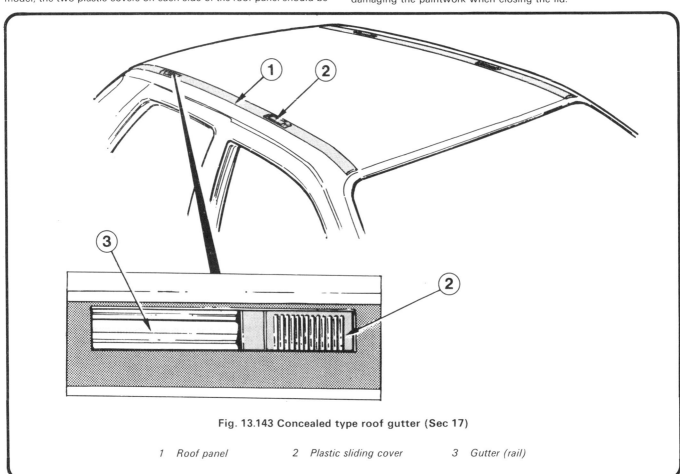

Fig. 13.143 Concealed type roof gutter (Sec 17)

1   Roof panel   2   Plastic sliding cover   3   Gutter (rail)

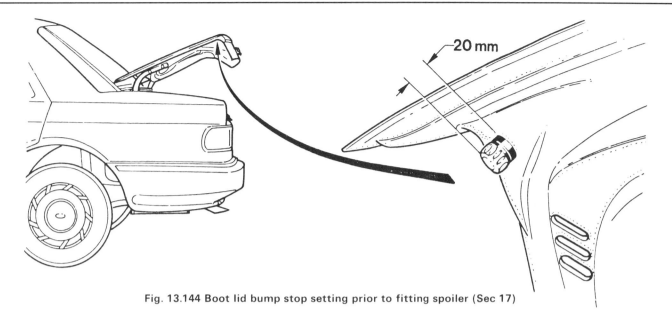

Fig. 13.144 Boot lid bump stop setting prior to fitting spoiler (Sec 17)

Heating and ventilation system (1987 on)

58 A rear footwell heater is available on 1987 and later models as an option. Basically it comprises ducting from the front-mounted heater casing with a facia panel control.

59 Extraction of stale air is carried out on later models by venting it into the luggage compartment side panel grilles and out through flap valves located behind the rear bumpers (photo).

Plastic components

60 With the use of more and more plastic body components by the vehicle manufacturers (eg, bumpers, spoilers, and in some cases major body panels), rectification of more serious damage to such items has become a matter of either entrusting repair work to a specialist in this field, or renewing complete components. Repair of such damage by the DIY owner is not really feasible owing to the cost of the equipment and materials required for effecting such repairs. The basic technique involves making a groove along the line of the crack in the plastic using a rotary burr in a power drill. The damaged part is then welded back together by using a hot air gun to heat up and fuse a plastic filler rod into the groove. Any excess plastic is then removed and the area rubbed down to a smooth finish. It is important that a filler rod of the correct plastic is used, as body components can be made of a variety of different types (eg, polycarbonate, ABS, polypropylene).

61 Damage of a less serious nature (abrasions, minor cracks etc) can be repaired by the DIY owner using a two-part epoxy filler repair material. Once mixed in equal proportions, this is used in similar fashion to the bodywork filler used on metal panels. The filler is usually cured in twenty to thirty minutes, ready for sanding and painting.

62 If the owner is renewing a complete component himself, or if he has repaired it with epoxy filler, he will be left with the problem of finding a suitable paint for finishing which is compatible with the type of plastic used. At one time the use of a universal paint was not possible owing to the complex range of plastics encountered in body component applications. Standard paints, generally speaking, will not bond to plastic or rubber satisfactorily. However, it is now possible to obtain a plastic body parts finishing kit which consists of a pre-primer treatment, a primer and coloured top coat. Full instructions are normally supplied with a kit, but basically the method of use is to first apply the pre-primer to the component concerned and allow it to dry for up to 30 minutes. Then the primer is applied and left to dry for about an hour before finally applying the special coloured top coat. The result is a correctly coloured component where the paint will flex with the plastic or rubber, a property that standard paint does not normally possess.

Air conditioning system – description

63 An air conditioning system is available as an optional extra on certain larger-engined models. In conjunction with the heater, the system enables any reasonable air temperature to be achieved inside

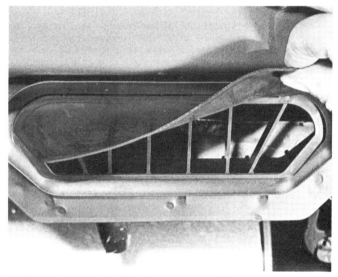

17.59 Stale air extractor flap (bumper removed)

the car; it also reduces the humidity of the incoming air, aiding demisting even when cooling is not required.

64 The refrigeration side of the air conditioning system functions in a similar way to a domestic refrigerator. A compressor, belt-driven from the crankshaft pulley, draws refrigerant in its gaseous phase from an evaporator. The compressed refrigerant passes through a condenser where it loses heat and enters its liquid phase. After dehydration the refrigerant returns to the evaporator where it absorbs heat from air passing over the evaporator fins. The refrigerant becomes a gas again and the cycle is repeated.

65 Various subsidiary controls and sensors protect the system against excessive temperature and pressures. Additionally, engine idle speed is increased when the system is in use to compensate for the additional load imposed by the compressor.

Air conditioning system – precautions

66 Although the refrigerant is not itself toxic, in the presence of a naked flame (or a lighted cigarette) it forms a highly toxic gas. Liquid refrigerant spilled on the skin will cause frostbite. If refrigerant enters the eyes, rinse them with a dilute solution of boric acid and seek medical advice immediately.

67 In view of the above points, and of the need for specialised

Fig. 13.145 Layout of air conditioning system components
(Sec 17)

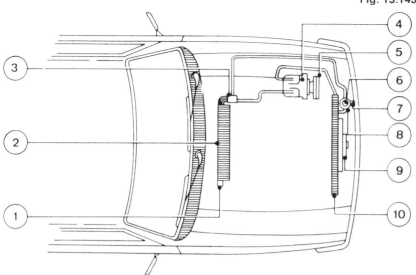

1   De-ice thermostat
2   Evaporator
3   Expansion valve
4   Compressor
5   Compressor clutch
6   Pressure switch
7   Sight glass
8   Dehydrator/collector
9   Cooling fan
10 Condenser

equipment for evacuating and recharging the system, any work which requires the disconnection of a refrigerant line must be left to a specialist.

68 Do not allow refrigerant lines to be exposed to temperatures above 230°F (110°C), eg, during welding or paint drying operations.

69 Do not operate the air conditioning system if it is known to be short of refrigerant, or further damage may result.

Air conditioning system – maintenance

70 Regularly inspect the compressor drivebelt for correct tension and good condition. Tension is adjusted in the same way as for the alternator drivebelt.

71 At the 12 000 mile/12 monthly service, remove the radiator grille and clean any leaves, insects, etc, from the condenser coil and fins. Be very careful not to damage the condenser fins: use a soft brush, or a compressed air jet, along (not across) the fins.

72 Before refitting the grille, check the refrigerant charge as follows. The engine should be cold and the ambient temperature should be between 64 and 77°F (18 and 25°C).

73 Start the engine and allow it to idle. Observe the refrigerant sight glass and have an assistant switch on the air conditioning to fan speed III. A few bubbles should be seen in the sight glass as the system starts up, but all bubbles should disappear within 10 seconds. Persistent bubbles, or no bubbles at all, mean that the refrigerant charge is low. Switch off the system immediately if the charge is low and do not use it again until it has been recharged.

74 Operate the air conditioning system for at least 10 minutes each month, even during cold weather, to keep the seals, etc, in good condition.

75 Regularly inspect the refrigerant pipes, hoses and unions for security and good condition.

76 The air conditioning system will lose a proportion of its charge through normal seepage – typically up to 100 g (4 oz) per year – so it is as well to regard periodic recharging as a maintenance operation.

Air conditioning system – component renewal

77 Only those items which can be renewed without discharging the system are described here. Other items must be dealt with by a Ford dealer or air conditioning specialist.

Compressor drivebelt

78 Disconnect the battery earth lead.

79 Remove the fan (Chapter 2, Section 10).

80 Slacken the compressor strap and pivot bolts, move the compressor towards the engine and remove the old drivebelt.

81 Fit the new drivebelt, position the compressor to achieve the correct belt tension and tighten the strap and pivot bolts.

82 Refit and secure the fan and reconnect the battery.

83 Recheck the belt tension after it has run for at least 10 minutes under load.

Condenser fan and motor

84 Disconnect the battery earth lead and remove the radiator grille. On Ghia models, remove the front bumper completely.

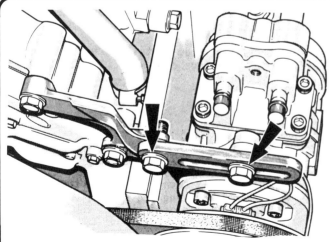

Fig. 13.146 Typical air conditioner compressor drivebelt adjuster bolts (arrowed) (Sec 17)

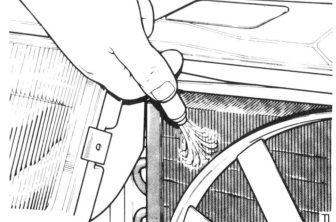

Fig. 13.147 Cleaning condenser fins with compressed air jet (Sec 17)

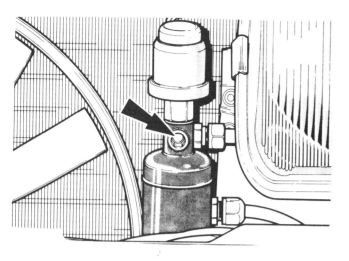

Fig. 13.148 Refrigerant sight glass (arrowed) (Sec 17)

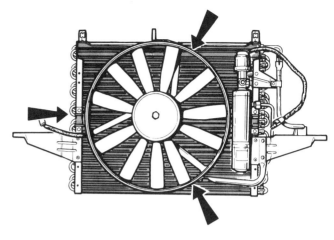

Fig. 13.149 Condenser fan securing bolts (arrowed) (Sec 17)

85 Disconnect the fan wiring connector at the right-hand side of the condenser.
86 Remove the three securing bolts and remove the fan and motor. Turn the frame to position the fan wiring on the dehydrator side to avoid damaging the wiring. Take care also not to damage the condenser fins or tube.
87 To remove the fan blades from the motor, remove the retaining nut and circlip. **The nut has a left-hand thread,** ie, it is undone clockwise.
88 With the blades removed, the motor can be unscrewed from the frame.
89 Reassemble and refit in the reverse order of dismantling and removal.

De-ice thermostat
90 Disconnect the battery and remove it.
91 Remove the plenum chamber right-hand cover plate, disconnecting vacuum hoses and washer hoses as necessary.
92 Disconnect the thermostat from the evaporator casing and remove it. Also remove the thermostat probe.
93 Refit in the reverse order of removal.

Heater/air conditioning controls
94 The procedure is similar to that in Chapter 12, Section 33, but additionally the vacuum hoses must be disconnected from the control unit vacuum valve during removal, and reconnected when refitting.

Air conditioning/heavy duty heater vacuum solenoid – new design (October 1986 on)
95 The recirculation air control flap vacuum solenoid located on the right-hand inner wing, near the bulkhead, has been redesigned from the above date.
96 This is to prevent moisture ingress causing corrosion and subsequent failure of the solenoid, which in turn prevents the recirculation air control flap operating, causing windscreen misting.
97 To fit a new type solenoid, disconnect the electrical leads and vacuum lines and remove the solenoid from the bulkhead.
98 Fit the new type solenoid in the reverse order.

Door trim panel – Sapphire Saloon – removal and refitting
99 The trim panel on these models is of moulded type secured by screws instead of clips.
100 Extract the screw from the door lock interior handle escutcheon plate. Remove the plate (photo).
101 On models with manually-operated windows, prise out the escutcheon plate from the regulator handle, extract the screw and remove the handle.
102 Prise out the door pull handle trim strip then extract the handle screws (photos).
102 Remove the exterior mirror triangular trim plate from inside the door (photos).

104 Extract the door trim panel fixing screws from the edges of the door and tidy bin (photos).
105 Slide the panel upwards, to disengage the turned over lip from the retaining clips and remove it (photos).
106 Refitting is a reversal of removal.

Luggage boot lid (Sapphire) – removal and refitting
107 Open the boot lid and mark the position of the hinges on the underside of the lid using a wax crayon or masking tape (photo).
108 Unscrew the hinge bolts and, with the help of an assistant, lift the lid from the car.
109 If the hinges must be removed, unhook the counterbalance springs (photo).
110 Refitting is a reversal of removal, adjust the lid for alignment if necessary, while the hinge bolts are finger tight.
111 Adjust the striker as necessary to ensure smooth positive closure (photo).
112 The lid lock and solenoid (central locking) are removable after unscrewing the retaining bolts (photo).

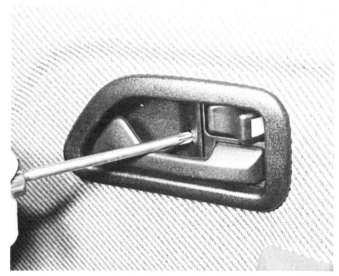

17.100 Extracting interior handle escutcheon plate screw

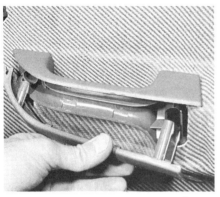

17.102A Removing door pull handle trim strip

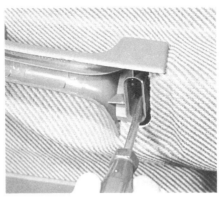

17.102B Extracting door pull handle fixing screws

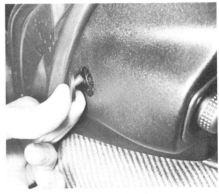

17.103A Exterior mirror trim plate screw cover

17.103B Exterior electrically-operated mirror trim plate withdrawn

17.104A Door interior trim panel fixing screw

17.104B Door interior trim panel fixing screw at tidy bin

17.105A Door trim panel top fixing clip

17.105B Door trim panel top turned over lip

17.107 Luggage boot hinge on lid (Sapphire)

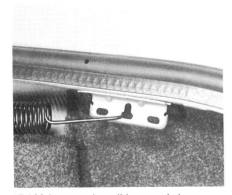

17.109 Luggage boot lid counterbalance spring

17.111 Luggage boot lid lock striker

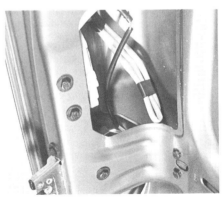

17.112 Luggage boot lid lock details

General repair procedures

Whenever servicing, repair or overhaul work is carried out on the car or its components, it is necessary to observe the following procedures and instructions. This will assist in carrying out the operation efficiently and to a professional standard of workmanship.

Joint mating faces and gaskets

Where a gasket is used between the mating faces of two components, ensure that it is renewed on reassembly, and fit it dry unless otherwise stated in the repair procedure. Make sure that the mating faces are clean and dry with all traces of old gasket removed. When cleaning a joint face, use a tool which is not likely to score or damage the face, and remove any burrs or nicks with an oilstone or fine file.

Make sure that tapped holes are cleaned with a pipe cleaner, and keep them free of jointing compound if this is being used unless specifically instructed otherwise.

Ensure that all orifices, channels or pipes are clear and blow through them, preferably using compressed air.

Oil seals

Whenever an oil seal is removed from its working location, either individually or as part of an assembly, it should be renewed.

The very fine sealing lip of the seal is easily damaged and will not seal if the surface it contacts is not completely clean and free from scratches, nicks or grooves. If the original sealing surface of the component cannot be restored, the component should be renewed.

Protect the lips of the seal from any surface which may damage them in the course of fitting. Use tape or a conical sleeve where possible. Lubricate the seal lips with oil before fitting and, on dual lipped seals, fill the space between the lips with grease.

Unless otherwise stated, oil seals must be fitted with their sealing lips toward the lubricant to be sealed.

Use a tubular drift or block of wood of the appropriate size to install the seal and, if the seal housing is shouldered, drive the seal down to the shoulder. If the seal housing is unshouldered, the seal should be fitted with its face flush with the housing top face.

Screw threads and fastenings

Always ensure that a blind tapped hole is completely free from oil, grease, water or other fluid before installing the bolt or stud. Failure to do this could cause the housing to crack due to the hydraulic action of the bolt or stud as it is screwed in.

When tightening a castellated nut to accept a split pin, tighten the nut to the specified torque, where applicable, and then tighten further to the next split pin hole. Never slacken the nut to align a split pin hole unless stated in the repair procedure.

When checking or retightening a nut or bolt to a specified torque setting, slacken the nut or bolt by a quarter of a turn, and then retighten to the specified setting.

Locknuts, locktabs and washers

Any fastening which will rotate against a component or housing in the course of tightening should always have a washer between it and the relevant component or housing.

Spring or split washers should always be renewed when they are used to lock a critical component such as a big-end bearing retaining nut or bolt.

Locktabs which are folded over to retain a nut or bolt should always be renewed.

Self-locking nuts can be reused in non-critical areas, providing resistance can be felt when the locking portion passes over the bolt or stud thread.

Split pins must always be replaced with new ones of the correct size for the hole.

Special tools

Some repair procedures in this manual entail the use of special tools such as a press, two or three-legged pullers, spring compressors etc. Wherever possible, suitable readily available alternatives to the manufacturer's special tools are described, and are shown in use. In some instances, where no alternative is possible, it has been necessary to resort to the use of a manufacturer's tool and this has been done for reasons of safety as well as the efficient completion of the repair operation. Unless you are highly skilled and have a thorough understanding of the procedure described, never attempt to bypass the use of any special tool when the procedure described specifies its use. Not only is there a very great risk of personal injury, but expensive damage could be caused to the components involved.

Conversion factors

Length (distance)
Inches (in)	X	25.4	= Millimetres (mm)	X	0.0394	= Inches (in)
Feet (ft)	X	0.305	= Metres (m)	X	3.281	= Feet (ft)
Miles	X	1.609	= Kilometres (km)	X	0.621	= Miles

Volume (capacity)
Cubic inches (cu in; in³)	X	16.387	= Cubic centimetres (cc; cm³)	X	0.061	= Cubic inches (cu in; in³)
Imperial pints (Imp pt)	X	0.568	= Litres (l)	X	1.76	= Imperial pints (Imp pt)
Imperial quarts (Imp qt)	X	1.137	= Litres (l)	X	0.88	= Imperial quarts (Imp qt)
Imperial quarts (Imp qt)	X	1.201	= US quarts (US qt)	X	0.833	= Imperial quarts (Imp qt)
US quarts (US qt)	X	0.946	= Litres (l)	X	1.057	= US quarts (US qt)
Imperial gallons (Imp gal)	X	4.546	= Litres (l)	X	0.22	= Imperial gallons (Imp gal)
Imperial gallons (Imp gal)	X	1.201	= US gallons (US gal)	X	0.833	= Imperial gallons (Imp gal)
US gallons (US gal)	X	3.785	= Litres (l)	X	0.264	= US gallons (US gal)

Mass (weight)
Ounces (oz)	X	28.35	= Grams (g)	X	0.035	= Ounces (oz)
Pounds (lb)	X	0.454	= Kilograms (kg)	X	2.205	= Pounds (lb)

Force
Ounces-force (ozf; oz)	X	0.278	= Newtons (N)	X	3.6	= Ounces-force (ozf; oz)
Pounds-force (lbf; lb)	X	4.448	= Newtons (N)	X	0.225	= Pounds-force (lbf; lb)
Newtons (N)	X	0.1	= Kilograms-force (kgf; kg)	X	9.81	= Newtons (N)

Pressure
Pounds-force per square inch (psi; lbf/in²; lb/in²)	X	0.070	= Kilograms-force per square centimetre (kgf/cm²; kg/cm²)	X	14.223	= Pounds-force per square inch (psi; lbf/in²; lb/in²)
Pounds-force per square inch (psi; lbf/in²; lb/in²)	X	0.068	= Atmospheres (atm)	X	14.696	= Pounds-force per square inch (psi; lbf/in²; lb/in²)
Pounds-force per square inch (psi; lbf/in²; lb/in²)	X	0.069	= Bars	X	14.5	= Pounds-force per square inch (psi; lbf/in²; lb/in²)
Pounds-force per square inch (psi; lbf/in²; lb/in²)	X	6.895	= Kilopascals (kPa)	X	0.145	= Pounds-force per square inch (psi; lbf/in²; lb/in²)
Kilopascals (kPa)	X	0.01	= Kilograms-force per square centimetre (kgf/cm²; kg/cm²)	X	98.1	= Kilopascals (kPa)

Torque (moment of force)
Pounds-force inches (lbf in; lb in)	X	1.152	= Kilograms-force centimetre (kgf cm; kg cm)	X	0.868	= Pounds-force inches (lbf in; lb in)
Pounds-force inches (lbf in; lb in)	X	0.113	= Newton metres (Nm)	X	8.85	= Pounds-force inches (lbf in; lb in)
Pounds-force inches (lbf in; lb in)	X	0.083	= Pounds-force feet (lbf ft; lb ft)	X	12	= Pounds-force inches (lbf in; lb in)
Pounds-force feet (lbf ft; lb ft)	X	0.138	= Kilograms-force metres (kgf m; kg m)	X	7.233	= Pounds-force feet (lbf ft; lb ft)
Pounds-force feet (lbf ft; lb ft)	X	1.356	= Newton metres (Nm)	X	0.738	= Pounds-force feet (lbf ft; lb ft)
Newton metres (Nm)	X	0.102	= Kilograms-force metres (kgf m; kg m)	X	9.804	= Newton metres (Nm)

Power
Horsepower (hp)	X	745.7	= Watts (W)	X	0.0013	= Horsepower (hp)

Velocity (speed)
Miles per hour (miles/hr; mph)	X	1.609	= Kilometres per hour (km/hr; kph)	X	0.621	= Miles per hour (miles/hr; mph)

Fuel consumption*
Miles per gallon, Imperial (mpg)	X	0.354	= Kilometres per litre (km/l)	X	2.825	= Miles per gallon, Imperial (mpg)
Miles per gallon, US (mpg)	X	0.425	= Kilometres per litre (km/l)	X	2.352	= Miles per gallon, US (mpg)

Temperature

Degrees Fahrenheit = (°C x 1.8) + 32

Degrees Celsius (Degrees Centigrade; °C) = (°F - 32) x 0.56

*It is common practice to convert from miles per gallon (mpg) to litres/100 kilometres (l/100km), where mpg (Imperial) x l/100 km = 282 and mpg (US) x l/100 km = 235

Index

A

Accelerator
    cable removal, refitting and adjustment – 67, 256
    pedal removal and refitting – 68
Air cleaner and element
    removal and refitting
        carburettor models – 64, 256
        fuel injection models – 270
Air cleaner temperature control
    testing – 65
Air conditioning system
    air conditioning/heavy duty heater vacuum solenoid – 349
    components renewal – 348
    description – 347
    maintenance – 348
    precautions – 347
    torque wrench settings – 252
Alternator
    brushes removal, inspection and refitting – 159, 300
    fault finding and testing – 158
    general – 301
    maintenance and special precautions – 153
    mounting bracket refitting – 300
    removal and refitting – 153
Antifreeze/corrosion inhibitor mixture – 55
Automatic transmission
    description – 123
    downshift cable removal, refitting and adjustment – 125
    fault diagnosis – 125
    fluid level checking – 124
    front brake band adjustment – 124
    removal and refitting – 124
    selector rod removal, refitting and adjustment – 125
    specifications – 98
    starter inhibitor switch removal and refitting – 125
    torque wrench settings – 98
    vacuum diaphragm unit (type C3) removal and refitting – 284
Automatic transmission (type A4LD)
    brake band adjustment – 124, 283
    description – 283
    downshift cable adjustment – 283
    downshift cable adjustment (solenoid operated) – 283
    fluid level checking – 124, 283
    removal and refitting – 124, 283
    selector lever positions, modification – 283
    selector rod removal, refitting and adjustment – 125, 284
    specifications – 250
    starter inhibitor switch renewal – 125, 283
    torque wrench settings – 250
    vacuum diaphragm unit, removal and refitting – 284
Auxiliary shaft
    examination and renovation – 44
    refitting – 47
    removal – 35
Auxiliary warning system
    components renewal – 309 to 311
    description – 309
    testing and fault finding – 309

B

Battery
    charging – 153
    electrolyte replenishmnet – 153
    maintenance – 152
Big-end bearings
    examination and renovation – 43
Bleeding the brakes – 146
Bleeding the power steering – 222
Bodywork and fittings – 222 *et seq*, 341 *et seq*
Bodywork and fittings
    air conditioning system – 347 to 349
    bonnet – 228, 230, 341
    bumpers – 236, 341
    centre console – 237
    description – 224
    doors – 231 to 235, 341
    facia panel – 236
    headlining – 236
    heater – 241, 243
    maintenance
        bodywork and underframe – 224
        general – 228
        upholstery and carpets – 225
    plastic components – 347
    radiator grille panel – 230, 341
    rear parcel shelf side-member – 239
    rear spoiler (Sapphire Saloon) – 346
    repair
        major damage – 228
        minor damage – 225
        sequence (colour) – 226, 227
    roof rack (Sapphire Saloon) – 346
    seat belts – 345
    seats – 237, 239, 344
    sliding roof – 241
    tailgate – 229, 230, 234
    windows – 234, 235
    windscreen – 234
    wing protective liners (later models) – 341
Bonnet
    lock cable removal and refitting – 230
    lock removal and refitting – 230
    release with broken cable – 341
    removal and refitting – 228
Braking system – 137 *et seq*, 286 *et seq*
Braking system
    deceleration control valve – 146
    description – 137
    disc brakes, front – 139, 142, 143, 286, 299
    drum brakes, rear – 140, 145, 286
    fault diagnosis – 150
    footbrake pedal – 149
    handbrake – 148, 299
    hydraulic system
        bleeding – 146, 298
        lines and hoses – 146

maintenance, routine – 138
master cylinder – 145
pad renewal – 286
pedal – 149, 289, 299
specifications – 137, 251
stoplamp switch – 149
torque wrench settings – 137, 251
vacuum servo unit – 148
Braking system (models with ABS)
anti-lock braking system – 289
computer module removal and refitting – 297
fluid reservoir removal and refitting – 294
handbrake cable
adjustment – 299
removal and refitting – 299
hydraulic system, bleeding – 298
hydraulic unit
accumulator removal and refitting – 294
pressure switch removal and refitting – 296
pump and motor removal and refitting – 294
removal and refitting – 294
rear caliper
overhaul – 291
removal and refitting – 290
rear disc pads
inspection and renewal – 289
rear disc shield
removal and refitting – 293
valve block removal and refitting – 296
wheel sensors removal and refitting – 297
Bulbs, lamp – 152, 175, 311
Bumpers
decorative mouldings fitted – 341
removal and refitting – 236, 341

C

Cam followers – 43
Camshaft
examination and renovation – 43
refitting – 49
removal – 32
Capacities, general – 6
Carburettor (Ford Variable Venturi – VV)
accelerator pump repair – 256
correction of unstable idle – 256
description – 69
diaphragm renewal – 256
overhaul – 70
speed control system description and maintenance – 258
Carburettor (Pierburg 2V)
description – 263
dismantling (carburettor removed) – 263
fast idle adjustment – 267
idle adjustments – 263
reassembly – 266
removal and refitting – 263
secondary throttle vacuum unit – 263
Carburettors (general)
adjustments warning – 256
removal and refitting – 68
slow running adjustment – 68
specifications – 63, 248, 249
Carburettor (Weber twin venturi – 2V)
automatic choke overhaul and adjustment – 76
choke vacuum pulldown – 263
description – 73
overhaul – 74
1.6 economy models
automatic choke adjustment – 262
description – 258
idle adjustments – 258
overhaul – 258
later 2.0 models
automatic choke adjustment – 262

description – 262
idle adjustments – 262
overhaul – 262
removal and refitting – 262
stopper motor adjustment – 263
Carpets – 225
Central door locking system – 312
Centre console
removal and refitting – 237
Cigarette lighter
removal and refitting – 174
Clock
removal and refitting – 174, 311
Clock, digital (later models)
bulb renewal – 311
Clutch – 92 *et seq*, 280
Clutch
adjustment, checking and correcting – 280
cable removal and refitting – 93
description – 92
fault diagnosis – 96
inspection – 94
pedal removal, overhaul and refitting – 92, 280
refitting – 95
release bearing and arm removal and refitting – 95
removal – 94
specifications – 92, 250
torque wrench settings – 92
Coil, ignition
description and testing – 87
Connecting rods – 39, 43, 46
Conversion factors – 352
Coolant level sensor – 60
Cooling fan, thermo-viscous
removal and refitting – 60
Cooling system – 53 *et seq*, 255 *et seq*
Cooling system
antifreeze/corrosion inhibitor mixture – 55
description – 54
draining – 55, 255
drivebelt – 59
expansion tank and coolant level sensor – 60
fault diagnosis – 62
filling – 55, 255
flushing – 55
radiator – 56
specifications – 53
temperature gauge transmitter – 61
thermostat – 57
thermo-viscous cooling fan – 60
torque wrench settings – 53
water pump – 58
Courtesy light switch – 171
Crankcase ventilation system
description and maintenance – 41
Crankshaft
examination and renovation – 43
refitting – 45
removal – 39
Crankshaft oil seals
renewal
front – 37
rear – 37
Cylinder block and bores
examination and renovation – 43
Cylinder head
bolts (later models) – 254
decarbonising and renovation – 44
dismantling – 34
reassembly – 49
refitting – 49
removal – 30

D

Decarbonising – 44

Deceleration control valve
  removal and refitting – 46
Digital clock (later models)
  bulb renewal – 311
Dimensions, vehicle – 6, 252, 254
Direction indicator switch – 171
Disc brakes, front
  caliper removal, overhaul and refitting – 142
  disc
    examination, removal and refitting – 143
    removal and refitting (later models) – 286, 299
    renewal (later models) – 286
  pads
    inspection and renewal – 139
    renewal (Girling calipers: all 1.3 and 1.6 models) – 286, 299
Distributor
  cap securing clips (early Bosch type) – 279
  removal, examination and refitting – 85
Distributor (2.0 iS)
  cap and rotor removal and refitting – 279
  removal and refitting – 279
Doors
  central locking – 312
  check arm removal and refitting – 233
  inner trim panel removal and refitting – 232
  inner trim removal (all models except Sapphire) – 343
  interior handle remote control removal and refitting – 233
  lock
    removal and refitting – 234
    striker adjustment (1985 on) – 341
  private lock removal, inspection and refitting – 233
  removal and refitting – 231
  trim panel (Sapphire Saloon) removal and refitting – 349
Drivebelt (water pump/alternator)
  checking, renewal and adjustment – 59
Drum brakes, rear
  backplate removal and refitting – 145
  drum inspection and renovation – 145
  shoes
    inspection and renewal – 140
    removal and refitting
      all 1.3 and 1.6 Hatchback/Saloon models – 286
  wheel cylinder removal, overhaul and refitting – 145

E

Electrical system – 151 et seq, 300 et seq
Electrical system
  aerial
    location and access – 314
    rear screen amplifier – 314
    removal and refitting – 313
  alternator – 153, 158, 159, 300 to 302
  auxiliary warning system – 309
  battery – 152, 153
  central door locking – 312
  cigarette lighter – 174
  clock – 174, 311
  description – 152
  dim-dip lighting system – 313
  electric window motor – 313
  fault diagnosis – 19, 185
  flasher unit – 304
  fuses and relays – 169, 303
  graphic information module – 174
  headlamp
    wash/wipe system – 306
    washer jets – 306
    washer pump – 306
    wiper blade – 306
    wiper motor – 306
  headlamps – 174, 175
  horn – 180
  ice warning sender unit – 174
  in-car entertainment (1987 on) – 314
  instrument panel and gauges – 173
  instruments (1987 on) – 311
  lamp bulbs – 152, 175, 307, 309, 311
  radio – 180, 182, 313
  rear screen washer pump – 306
  rear screen wiper motor – 179, 304
  seat heating pad – 311
  specifications – 151, 251
  speedometer cable – 173
  starter motors – 159, 160, 302
  switches – 171, 172, 309, 311
  torque wrench settings – 152, 251
  trip computer – 180, 311
  warning light control – 172
  windscreen washer – 304, 306
  windscreen wiper – 178
  wiper arms – 180
  wiper blades – 179
  wiring diagrams – 186 to 206, 315 to 338
Electronic module, ignition
  removal and refitting – 90
Engine – 23 et seq, 254 et seq
Engine
  adjustment after overhaul – 51
  ancillary components
    refitting – 51
    removal – 30
  auxiliary shaft – 35, 44, 47
  big-end bearings – 43
  cam followers – 43
  camshaft – 32, 43, 49
  connecting rods – 39, 43, 46
  crankcase ventilation system – 41
  crankshaft – 39, 43, 45
  crankshaft oil seals – 37
  cylinder block and bores – 43
  cylinder head – 30, 34, 44, 49, 254
  decarbonising – 44
  description – 26
  dismantling – 29
  examination and renovation – 41
  fault diagnosis – 20, 52
  firing order – 23
  flywheel/driveplate – 36, 47
  flywheel ring gear – 44
  introduction – 254
  main bearings – 39, 43, 45
  management systems – 273 to 278
  mountings – 41
  oil filter – 39
  oil pump – 38, 41, 47
  operations possible with engine in car – 26
  operations requiring engine removal – 26
  pistons – 39, 43, 46
  reassembly – 44
  refitting – 51
  removal – 28
  removal method – 26
  specifications – 23, 247, 248
  sump – 36, 47
  timing belt and sprockets – 35, 44, 50, 254
  torque wrench settings – 26, 248
  valves – 44, 51, 254
Engine management systems
  carburettor stepper motor (2.0 models)
    removal and refitting – 276
  coolant temperature sensor removal and refitting – 276
  ESC II module
    caution – 273
    removal and refitting – 273
  ESC IV module removal and refitting – 273
  ESC module (1.8 1987 on)
    description – 276
  fault diagnosis – 278
  fuel pump inertia switch – models with EEC IV (July 1986 on) – 277
  introduction – 273

manifold heater (carburettor models)
    removal and refitting – 276
relay locations – 277
Exhaust system
checking, removal and refitting – 80
Expansion tank and coolant level sensor
removal and refitting – 60

F

Facia panel
removal and refitting – 236
Fault diagnosis – 19 *et seq*
Fault diagnosis
braking system – 150
clutch – 96
cooling system – 62
electrical system – 19, 185
engine – 20, 52
engine management systems – 278
final drive and driveshafts – 136
fuel system
    carburettor – 81
    fuel injection – 273
ignition system – 90
manual gearbox and automatic transmission – 125
propeller shaft – 129
suspension and steering – 223
Final drive and driveshafts – 130 *et seq, 284 et seq*
Final drive and driveshafts
description – 132
driveshaft
    nuts (later models) – 284
    overhaul – 135
    removal and refitting – 134
driveshaft (models with ABS)
    overhaul – 284
    removal and refitting – 284
fault diagnosis – 136
final drive
    differential bearing oil seals renewal – 133
    output flange oil seals (models with ABS) renewal – 285
    pinion oil seal renewal – 133
    unit (all models) removal and refitting – 132, 284
    unit (models with ABS) removal and refitting – 285
maintenance, routine – 132
rear axle rubber mounting-to-body bolts (1986 on) – 285
specifications – 130, 250 to 251
torque wrench settings – 251
Firing order – 23
Flasher unit
removal and refitting – 304
Flywheel/driveplate
refitting – 47
removal – 36
Flywheel ring gear
examination and renovation – 44
Footbrake pedal
removal and refitting – 149
Fuel and exhaust systems – 63 *et seq*, 256 *et seq*
Fuel cooling blower (2.0 litre OHC engine pre-1985) – 267
Fuel filter (fuel injection models)
renewal – 272
Fuel gauge sender unit
removal and refitting – 67
Fuel pressure regulator
removal and refitting
    carburettor models – 66
    fuel injection models – 272
Fuel pump
inertia switch (July 1986 on) – 273
models with air conditioning – 256
removal and refitting (fuel injection models) – 272
testing, removal, servicing and refitting (carburettor models) – 65
Fuel system (carburettor)
accelerator cable – 67, 256

accelerator pedal – 68
air cleaner and element – 64, 256
air cleaner temperature control – 65
carburettor – 63, 68 to 76, 248, 249, 256 to 267, 276
description – 64
fault diagnosis – 81
fuel cooling blower – 267
fuel gauge sender unit – 67
fuel pressure regulator – 66
fuel pump – 65, 256
fuel tank – 66
fuel, unleaded – 268, 273
fuel vapour separator – 256
specifications – 63, 248, 249
torque wrench settings – 64
Fuel system (fuel injection)
air cleaner element – 270
airflow meter removal and refitting – 270
description – 268
fault diagnosis – 273
fuel filter – 272
fuel injectors removal and refitting – 271
fuel pressure regulator – 272
fuel pump – 272, 273
fuel, unleaded – 273
idle adjustment – 270
idle speed control valve removal and refitting – 270
specifications – 249
throttle position sensor removal and refitting – 270
Fuel tank
removal, servicing and refitting – 66
Fuel, unleaded
engine conditions required – 268, 273
Fuel vapour separator
description – 256
removal and refitting – 256
Fuses and relays – 169

G

Gearbox, manual
description – 98
fault diagnosis – 125
gear selector modifications (type N) – 282
gearchange lever gaiter modification – 282
oil level – 282
refitting – 98, 282
removal – 98
specifications – 97
torque wrench settings – 97
type N
    countershaft bearing modification – 282
    dismantling into major assemblies – 110
    gear selection modifications – 282
    input shaft dismantling and reassembly – 106, 115
    inspection – 115
    lubricant type – 282
    mainshaft dismantling and reassembly – 116
    reassembly – 120
type A, B, and C
    dismantling into major assemblies – 100
    input shaft dismantling and reassembly – 106
    inspection – 105
    mainshaft dismantling and reassembly – 106
    reassembly – 108
General repair procedures – 351
Graphic information module
removal and refitting – 174

H

Handbrake
cable removal, refitting and adjusting – 148
lever removal and refitting – 148

Headlamps
alignment – 174
bulb renewal – 175
removal and refitting – 175
washer
jets removal, refitting and adjustment – 306
pump removal and refitting – 306
Headlining
removal and refitting – 236
Heater
assembly
overhaul – 243
removal and refitting – 241
controls removal and refitting – 241
motor removal and refitting – 243
Heater/air conditioning blower switch
bulb renewal – 311
Heating and ventilation system (1987 on) – 347
Horn
removal and refitting – 180
HT leads – 88
Hydraulic system, brake
bleeding – 146
lines and hoses removal and refitting – 146

I

Ice warning sender unit
removal and refitting – 174
Ignition module (2.0) fuel injection models
removal and refitting – 278
Ignition switch and lock barrel
removal and refitting – 171
Ignition system – 82 et seq, 278 et seq
Ignition system
coil – 87
description – 83, 278
distributor – 85
distributor (2.0 fuel injection models) – 279
distributor cap and rotor (2.0 fuel injection models) – 279
distributor cap securing clips (early Bosch type) – 279
electronic module – 90
fault diagnosis – 90
maintenance, routine – 84
module (2.0) – 278
spark plugs and HT leads – 88, 89
specifications – 82, 249, 250
timing – 87, 279
vacuum advance system valve and fuel trap – 90
Instrument panel
gauges removal and refitting – 173
removal and refitting – 173

J

Jacking – 10

L

Lamp bulbs
renewal – 175, 307, 309, 311
Lighting switch – 171
Lighting system, dim-dip – 313
Low coolant warning switch – 172
Lubricants and fluids, recommended – 12
Luggage boot lid (Sapphire) – 349
Luggage compartment light switch – 172

M

Main bearings
refitting – 45
removal – 39

Maintenance, routine
automatic transmission
driveshaft cable and shaft lever linkage lubrication – 14
fluid level check/top-up – 14, 124
front brake band adjustment – 14, 124
bodywork and fittings
air conditioning system – 348
bodywork and underframe – 224
general – 228
upholstery and carpets – 225
brakes
disc pads check for wear – 14, 138, 139
hydraulic fluid level check/top up – 14, 138
hydraulic fluid level warning light operation check – 14, 138
hydraulic fluid renewal – 14, 138
hydraulic lines leakage check – 14, 138
rear brake shoes check for wear – 14, 138, 140
vacuum servo hose check – 14
cooling system
antifreeze renewal – 14, 55
coolant leaks check – 14
coolant level check/top up – 14
drivebelt tension and condition check – 14, 59
pressure cap and seal check/renew – 14
driveshaft and final drive
final drive oil check/top up – 14, 132
gaiters check – 14, 132
electrical system
battery – 14, 152
equipment and lights operation check – 14
windscreen washer reservoir fluid level check/top up – 14
engine
crankcase emission vent valve renewal – 14, 41
oil change – 14, 254
oil filler cap cleaning – 14
oil filter renewal – 14, 39
oil leaks check – 14
oil level check/top up – 14
valve clearances check/adjust – 14, 51
exhaust system – 14, 80
fuel system
air filter element renewal – 14, 64
fuel filter renewal (fuel injection models) – 254
fuel leaks check – 14
slow running adjustment check – 14, 68
ignition system
distributor cap, rotor and HT leads check and clean – 14, 84
distributor lubrication – 14
spark plugs renewal – 14, 84, 88
manual gearbox oil level check/top up – 14, 282
safety precautions – 13
service schedules – 14, 254
suspension, steering linkages and balljoints check – 14, 210
tyres
condition check – 14, 210, 223
pressures check/adjust – 14, 208, 210, 223
wheels – 14, 223
Manifold, exhaust
removal and refitting – 79
Manifold, inlet
removal and refitting
carburettor models – 77
fuel injection models – 273
Manual gearbox/automatic transmission – 97 et seq, 282 et seq
Manual gearbox see **Gearbox, manual**
Master cylinder, brake
removal, overhaul and refitting – 145
Mirror, door
removal and refitting – 235
Mountings, engine
renewal – 41

O

Oil filter
renewal – 39

Oil pump
examination and renovation – 41
refitting – 47
removal – 38

P

Pedal
removal and refitting
accelerator – 68
brake – 149, 289, 299
clutch – 92, 280
Pistons and connecting rods
examination and renovation – 43
refitting – 46
removal – 39
Propeller shaft – 126 *et seq*
Propeller shaft
centre bearing renewal – 128
description – 126
fault diagnosis – 129
removal and refitting – 126
torque wrench settings – 126
type – 126
universal joints and centre bearing
testing for wear – 129

R

Radiator
removal, inspection, cleaning and refitting – 56, 256
Radiator grille panel
removal and refitting – 230
Radio aerial
removal and refitting – 313
Radio (DIN fixing)
removal and refitting – 313
Radios and tape players (general)
installation – 180
suppression of interference – 182
Radio (standard)
removal and refitting – 180
Radio with power amplifier – 313
Rear brakes *see* **Drum brakes, rear**
Rear parcel shelf side-member
removal and refitting – 239
Rear screen washer pump
removal and refitting – 306
Rear screen wiper motor
parking diode renewal – 304
removal and refitting – 179
Repair procedures, general – 351
Reversing light switch – 171
Roadwheels *see* **Wheels**
Routine maintenance *see* **Maintenance, routine**

S

Safety precautions – 13
Seat belts – 345
Seat heating pad – 311
Seats
front
removal and refitting – 237, 344
air adjustable ball – 344
air cushion – 344
rear
description – 345
catch removal and refitting – 239
seat backrest – 239
seat cushion – 239
Sliding roof
removal, refitting and adjustment – 241

Spare parts
buying – 7
to carry in car – 20
Spark plugs
condition (colour chart) – 89
general – 88
specifications – 82
torque wrench settings – 83
Speedometer cable
removal and refitting – 173
Starter motor
overhaul – 160
removal and refitting – 159
testing in the car – 159
Steering
column removal, overhaul and refitting – 218
description – 210
fault diagnosis – 223
gear – 220
gear rubber bellows renewal – 222
intermediate shaft and coupling
removal and refitting – 220
roadwheel alignment checking and adjusting – 223
specifications – 207, 251
torque wrench settings – 208, 252
track rod end removal and refitting – 222, 340
Steering gear (power)
bleeding – 221
gear – 221
pump removal and refitting – 222
removal and refitting – 221
specifications – 207
torque wrench settings – 208
Steering gear (standard)
overhaul – 220, 340
removal and refitting – 220
Steering wheel
removal and refitting – 217
Stoplamp switch
removal, refitting and adjusting – 149
Sump
refitting – 47
removal – 36
Supplement: Revisions/information on later models – 245 *et seq*
Supplement: revisions and information on later models
introduction – 246
specifications – 247 to 254
Suspension and steering – 207 et seq, 339 *et seq*
Suspension, front
anti-roll bar
mountings – 339
removal and refitting – 212
crossmember removal and refitting – 210
description – 208
fault diagnosis – 223
front wheel bearings – 210
lower arm removal, overhaul and refitting – 211
specifications – 207, 251
spindle carrier removal and refitting – 210
strut removal and refitting – 213
torque wrench settings – 252
Suspension, rear
and final drive assembly removal and refitting – 214
and final drive unit rear mounting renewal – 216
anti-roll bar removal and refitting – 339
coil spring
removal and refitting – 216
coil spring (models with ABS)
removal and refitting – 340
description – 208
fault diagnosis – 223
front mounting renewal – 216
lower arm removal and refitting – 217
lower arm (models with ABS), removal and refitting – 340
rear wheel bearings – 214, 339
rear wheel hub-to-suspension arm bolts – 339

shock absorber removal and refitting – 215
specifications – 207
torque wrench settings – 208, 252
Switches
removal and refitting
courtesy light – 171
direction indicator – 171
electric window – 172
heater motor – 172
horn switch – 309
ignition switch and lock barrel – 171
instrument panel illumination – 171
lighting – 171
low coolant warning – 172
luggage compartment light – 172
reversing light – 171
stoplamp – 149

T

Tailgate
glass removal and refitting – 234
lock removal – 230
strut removal and refitting – 230
Tape player – 182
Temperature gauge transmitter
removal and refitting – 61
Thermostat
removal, testing and refitting – 57
Thermo-viscous cooling fan – 60
Timing belt
examination and renovation – 44
tension checking and adjustment – 254
Timing belt and sprockets
refitting – 50
removal – 35
Timing, ignition
adjustment – 87, 279
Tools
general – 8
to carry in car – 20
Towing – 10
Trip computer
bulb renewal (1985 on) – 311
fuel flow sensor removal and refitting – 180
module removal and refitting
pre-1985 – 180
1985 on – 311
speed sender unit removal and refitting – 180
Tyres
general – 223
maintenance – 210, 340
pressures – 208
specifications – 208

U

Underframe
maintenance – 224

Upholstery
maintenance – 225
Unleaded fuel – 268, 273, 279

V

Vacuum servo unit, brake
description, removal and refitting – 148
Vacuum advance sustain valve and fuel trap
removal and refitting – 90
Valve cover fastenings (later models) – 254
Valves
clearances adjustment – 51
grinding – 44
Vehicle identification numbers – 7

W

Warning light control
removal and refitting – 172
Water pump
removal and refitting – 58
Water pump/alternator drivebelt – 59
Weights, vehicle – 6, 252
Wheel alignment – 223
Wheel bearings
renewal
front – 210
rear – 214, 339
Wheel studs (all models) renewal – 340
Wheels
general care and maintenance – 223, 340
specifications – 208, 251
Window
electric motor removal and refitting – 313
rear quarter spoilers – 343
regulator removal and refitting – 235
removal and refitting
fixed rear quarter – 234
front door – 234
opening rear quarter – 343
rear door – 234
Windscreen
removal and refitting – 234
Windscreen washer
jets removal and refitting – 306
pump removal and refitting – 304
Windscreen wiper
linkage removal and refitting – 178
motor removal and refitting – 178
Wiper
arms removal and refitting – 180
blades renewal – 179
Wiring diagrams – 186 to 206, 315 to 338
Working facilities – 9

Printed by
J H Haynes & Co Ltd
Sparkford Nr Yeovil
Somerset BA22 7JJ England

TECHNICAL   PERSONAL